QuickTime for Java

A Developer Reference

QuickTime for Java

A Developer Reference

Tom Maremaa and William Stewart
Apple Computer, Inc.

Morgan Kaufmann

ACADEMIC PRESS, a Harcourt Science and Technology Company

San Diego   San Francisco   New York   Boston

London   Sydney   Tokyo

Academic Press
A Harcourt Science and Technology Company
525 B Street, Suite 1900, San Diego, CA 92101-4495 USA
http://www.academicpress.com

Academic Press
24-28 Oval Road, London NW1 7DX United Kingdom
http://www.hbuk.co.uk/ap/

Morgan Kaufmann
340 Pine Street, Sixth Floor, San Francisco, CA 94104-3205 USA
http://www.mkp.com

Library of Congress Catalog Card Number: 99-63308

ISBN: 0-12-305440-0

Printed in the United States of America

99 00 01 02 03 IP 6 5 4 3 2 1

Acknowledgments

Tom Maremaa wishes to thank the following individuals who have contributed to the development of this book:

From the QuickTime engineering team: Peter Hoddie and Chris Flick, both of whom provided insights and ideas for various drafts of the book. From the QuickTime for Java team: Roger Smith and Anant Sonome for their contributions to the book's reference section. Thanks to David Singer for project management.

The book was enhanced by the many thoughtful comments and suggestions from the worldwide Java community of developers that included Patrick Beard, Gavin Bell, Todd Blume, John Burkey, James Dempsey, Bob Gonsalves, Mark Howe, Gary Hughes, Dr. Douglas Lyon, Michael Rose, Michael Schaff, and Ian Wilkinson. All made important contributions to the beta draft of the manuscript.

Thanks to the QuickTime documentation team—George Towner and Steven Gulie—for guidance, review, and encouragement.

This book drew on the expert skills of the Apple Technical Publications department: David Arrigoni, illustrator; Laurel Rezeau, developmental editor; Ruth Anderson, layout and design; and Michael Hinkson, project manager.

Finally, thanks to Bill for bringing both QuickTime for Java and this book to life, and for pushing my understanding of this new technology to another level.

William Stewart wishes to thank the following individuals who have contributed to the development of this book:

The QuickTime team in general for their help and encouragement.

QuickTime for Java has been under a limited seeding for over a year before this release. The developers on the support list have provided us with excellent feedback, requests, sample code, and bug reports. They have shown considerable patience and fortitude in dealing with a developing framework. Three individuals deserve special mention:

Todd Blume, for his hours of conversation and his critical eye. His help in the design of the Spaces and Controllers architecture was considerable and very much appreciated.

Eric Smith, for being one of the first to adopt the technology.

John Burkey, for stretching the bounds of what can be done with it.

Much of the original intention of QuickTime for Java was inspired by the excellent work done by the designers at Kaleida Labs in the development of the ScriptX language. The original engineering team that began this current project were also from Kaleida Labs: Ross Nelson, Robert Lockstone, Suzan Ehdaie, and myself. Karl May, Jim Wagner, Dimitry Nasledov, and Larry Hamel also joined us in the first stage of this endeavor. In its second and current incarnation, Roger Smith, Anant Sonone (Engineering), and David Singer (Project Management), along with Mitchell Weinstock (Product Marketing), Kevin Calhoun (Project Management), David Harrington, Gary Little, and Alan Samuel (Developer Relations) made their appreciated contributions.

A special thanks to Patrick Beard for his thoughtful conversations and contributions.

Apple's Mac OS Runtime for Java team for their hard work.

Finally, thanks to Tom for his efforts above and beyond.

April 1999

Contents

Chapter 3   Integrating QuickTime with Java   73

Chapter 4   QTCanvas, QTDrawable, and QTFactory   97

Part 2   Using QuickTime From Java   109

Chapter 5   Displaying and Streaming Movies   111

Chapter 6   QuickTime Media and Presenters   125

About This Book

This book describes the software architecture and programming model of QuickTime for Java. The QuickTime for Java API, developed by Apple Computer for Macintosh, Windows, and Java^{TM}, lets you build applets and applications that play movies, synthesize music and audio, display virtual reality environments, and animate graphics on a user's computer desktop. QuickTime for Java is a set of libraries that lets you tap into the power of Apple's robust and highly evolved multi-media QuickTime technology. If you are a programmer, the technical parts of this book teach you how to call QuickTime for Java methods and how to integrate its capabilities into your software.

The CD-ROM at the back of this book is designed to run on both Macintosh and Windows computers. The CD-ROM contains the basic QuickTime software, a wealth of sample code, and interface files to help in your development efforts. Although not as complete as Apple's official Software Development Kit (SDK), the CD-ROM provides enough material to get you started with QuickTime for Java programming.

This book is designed to bring you up to speed rapidly, chapter by chapter, with QuickTime for Java's multimedia capabilities. It is divided into four parts:

- Part I, QuickTime for Java Fundamentals

- Part II, Using QuickTime from Java

- Part III, The QuickTime for Java Software Architecture

- Part IV, QuickTime for Java Reference

GETTING MORE INFORMATION

This book and its companion CD-ROM are designed to get you started with QuickTime for Java programming. For further help and information, you can choose among these routes:

- The bibliography lists books and websites that tell you more about QuickTime's various technologies and how to use them.

- The QuickTime website, http://www.apple.com/quicktime, contains links to thousands of pages of current technical and marketing information, including the latest sample code, working demos, and online technical documentation.

- The QuickTime Software Development Kit is your essential resource for developing software that uses QuickTime. In one CD-ROM, it packs all the interfaces, detailed documentation, tools, and sample code you need.

- By accessing http://www.apple.com/developer, you can find out about becoming a registered Apple developer. Several levels of participation are available, depending on your needs. This kind of direct connection can provide you with the ultimate in technical support while you're working with QuickTime.

QuickTime for Java

A Developer Reference

QuickTime for Java Fundamentals

Part I is an introduction to the fundamentals of QuickTime and QuickTime for Java.

It includes the following chapters:

Chapter 1, "Introducing QuickTime and QuickTime for Java"

Chapter 2, "QuickTime Basics"

Chapter 3, "Integrating QuickTime with Java"

Chapter 4, "QTCanvas, QTDrawable, and QTFactory"

1 Introducing QuickTime and QuickTime for Java

When introduced in 1991, QuickTime 1.0 seemed to catch the industry by surprise. Given the state of the technology back then, few expected to see *software* movies running on their computer desktops—movies you could control and play back with synchronized audio and video. Nor did programmers expect to find, when they looked under the hood of the movie engine, an elegantly designed, component-based architecture that allowed them to build on and expand the capabilities of their own applications.

Though it originally ran only on the Macintosh and delivered digital video in a movie player that was about the size of a postage stamp, QuickTime became an instant hit. In a short period of time, it gained widespread popularity and recognition, and it was used in numerous software applications, movies, and games that landed on millions of CD-ROMs. Because it was part of the Mac OS, most users were not even aware that it was on their systems, except when it came time to play a movie or listen to an audio track. With subsequent versions, QuickTime grew larger, more robust, and extensible—and fully cross-platform. With Apple's commitment to developing the software and the inspired efforts of Apple's QuickTime engineering team, the multimedia engine had matured to support a wide variety of media formats and media types. Indeed, it had become the perfect instrument for delivering high-quality digital content over the Internet.

Over time, QuickTime had evolved to include the capabilities of QuickDraw 3D, QuickTime VR, and other emerging Apple technologies, such as streaming and multicasting over the Web. It had become the core multimedia technology used in over 11,500 CD-ROM titles and hundreds of new DVD titles. Entertainment giants like Fox Interactive, Disney, and Pixar were using it to deliver digital video. When Lucas film wanted to release the trailer to its much-anticipated *Star Wars* movie prequel, it chose QuickTime—and QuickTime only—as its platform for delivery. The result was more than 3.5 million downloads of the movie from Apple's website.

By 1999, QuickTime had evolved to become the equivalent of five large multimedia toolkits with more than 2500 APIs, extensively documented and available for programmers and application developers to produce full-length movies, music, animated sprites, virtual reality, and 3D modeling. QuickTime for Java is yet another step in that evolution.

A Brief History

Software developers had been asking Apple Computer to extend QuickTime's reach for years. When Java arrived, it was a natural next step. What developers wanted was another way to get at QuickTime. If they didn't want to use the C programming language, they could use Java instead.

QuickTime for Java was developed to meet these needs. The idea was to integrate the write-once, run-everywhere capabilities of Java with QuickTime's robust media architecture. The initial release would concentrate strongly on the display and presentation of QuickTime media, providing capabilities that had been absent or lacking from the Java language itself. Concurrently, when Apple shut down Kaleida in early 1996, it wanted to salvage some of the excellent design work that had gone into the development of ScriptX, an object-oriented programming language targeted specifically at multimedia title creation. The ScriptX architecture provided some of the scaffolding for the QuickTime for Java libraries and subsequent design and programming models.

An early version of the QuickTime for Java technology was first demonstrated at the JavaOne conference in 1998. The current version is now available free to the Java community and other QuickTime developers at `http://www.apple.com/quicktime/qtjava`.

If you are unfamiliar with QuickTime or need to brush up on fundamentals before exploring the QuickTime for Java API, you may want to start with Chapter 2, "QuickTime Basics." In that chapter, we focus on the key concepts that you need to know in order to begin programming with QuickTime for Java. If you're a C programmer and need to get up to speed with the Java programming language, there are many excellent books available to you. A list is provided in the bibliography section of this book. Although a comprehensive discussion of Java is beyond the scope of this book, we provide a brief introduction to the essentials of the language in Chapter 3, "Integrating QuickTime with Java."

In this introductory chapter, we take a brief look at

- QuickTime for Java as a set of classes that offer equivalent APIs you can use to take advantage of QuickTime's power and functionality on both Mac OS and Windows platforms

- a `QTSimpleApplet` you can create that presents any QuickTime content, including movies, images, sound, MIDI, QuickTime VR, and QuickDraw 3D in a few lines of Java code

- QuickTime itself, focusing on the QuickTime media abstraction layer, the movie file format, and the rich set of media services provided by the API

USING THE QUICKTIME FOR JAVA API

If you're a Java or QuickTime programmer and want to harness the power of QuickTime's multimedia engine, you'll find a number of important advantages to using the QuickTime for Java API. For one thing, the API lets you access QuickTime's native runtime libraries and, additionally, provides you with a feature-rich Application Framework that enables you to integrate QuickTime capabilities into Java software.

Aside from representation in Java, QuickTime for Java also provides a set of packages that forms the basis for the Application Framework found in the `quicktime.app` group. The focus of these packages is on using QuickTime to present different kinds of media. The framework uses the interfaces in the `quicktime.app` packages to abstract and express common functionality that exists between different QuickTime objects.

As such, the services that the QuickTime for Java Application Framework renders to the developer can be viewed as belonging to the following categories:

- creation of objects that present different forms of media, using `QTFactory.makeDrawable()` methods

- various utilities (classes and methods) for dealing with single images as well as groups of related images

- spaces and controllers architecture, which enables you to deal with complex data generation or presentation requirements

- composition services that allow the complex layering and blending of different image sources

- timing services that enable you to schedule and control time-related activities

- video and audio media capture from external sources

- exposure of the QuickTime visual effects architecture

All of these are built on top of the services that QuickTime provides. The provided interfaces and classes in the `quicktime.app` packages can be used as a basis for developers to build on and extend in new ways, not just as a set of utility classes you can use. These services and capabilities are discussed in detail in Chapter 3, "Integrating QuickTime with Java."

USING QUICKTIME IN THE PRODUCTION SPACE

QuickTime provides some powerful constructions that can simplify the production of applications or applets that contain or require multimedia content. Although we do not address directly the often complex production processes that can be involved, a combination of some of the techniques that are illustrated in the example code presented in this book can provide a basis to both simplify and extend the work that is involved in such productions.

For example, a multimedia presentation often includes many different facets: some animation, some video, and a desire for complex presentation and interactive delivery of this content. The spaces and controllers architecture (Chapter 13) and the services that it provides to build animations, which are discussed in some detail in Chapter 15, "Animation and Compositing," provide the ability to deliver presentations that can be both complex in their construction and powerful in the interactive capabilities that are provided to the user.

The media requirements for such presentations can also be complex. They may include the "standard" digital video, animated characters, and customized musical instruments. QuickTime's ability to reference movies that exist on local and remote servers provides a great deal of flexibility in the delivery of digital content.

A movie can also be used to contain the media that is used for animated characters and/or customized musical instruments. Thus, in Chapter 15, a cell-based sprite animation is built where the images that make up the character are retrieved from a movie that is built specifically for this purpose. In Chapter 10, a movie is constructed that contains both custom instruments and a description of the instruments that should be used from QuickTime's built-in Software Synthesizer to play a tune.

In both cases we see a QuickTime movie used to contain media and transport this media around. Your application then uses this media to recreate its presentation. The movie in these cases is not meant to be played but is used solely as a media container. And like the example above, this movie can be stored locally or remotely and retrieved by the application when it is actually viewed. Of course, the same technique can be applied to any of the media types that QuickTime supports. The sprite images and custom instruments are only two possible applications of this technique.

A further interesting use of QuickTime in this production space is the ability of a QuickTime movie to both contain the media data that it presents as well as to hold a reference to external media data. In Chapter 8, "Creating, Editing, and Importing QuickTime Movies," we present several ways that QuickTime movies can both import and export media, including the capability of a movie to reference media data stored in other movies or media file formats. In Chapter 6, "QuickTime Media and Presenters," this data model that QuickTime supports is discussed and forms a basis of the ability for movies to reference data in powerful and complex ways.

For example, this enables both an artist to be working on the images for an animated character and a programmer to be building the animation using these same images. This can save time, as the production house does not need to keep importing the character images, building intermediate data containers, and so on. As the artist enhances the characters, the programmer can immediately see these in his or her animation, because the animation references the same images.

AN OVERVIEW OF QUICKTIME FOR JAVA

QuickTime for Java enables Java and QuickTime programmers alike to take full advantage of QuickTime's multimedia capabilities. At its simplest level, QuickTime for Java lets you write a Java applet and run that applet on a variety of platforms. Java can be used in an applet, for example, to make Web pages more interactive so that users will be able to interact with those pages in ways they haven't before. At an advanced level, using the power and functionality of QuickTime, you can write applications that composite images, capture music and audio, create special effects, and use sprites for animation.

A SET OF JAVA CLASSES WITH TWO LAYERS

The QuickTime API is implemented as a set of Java classes in Quick-Time for Java. These classes offer equivalent APIs for using QuickTime functionality on both Mac OS and Windows platforms.

The QuickTime for Java API consists of two layers. There is a core layer that provides the ability to access the QuickTime native runtime libraries (its API) and an Application Framework layer that makes it easy for Java programmers to integrate QuickTime capabilities into their Java software. The Application Framework layer includes

- the integration of QuickTime with the Java runtime, which includes sharing display space between Java and QuickTime and passing events from Java into QuickTime

- a set of classes that provides a number of services that simplify the authoring of QuickTime content and operation

The QuickTime for Java classes are grouped into a set of packages on the basis of common functionality, common usage, and their organization in the standard QuickTime header files. The packages provide both an object model for the QuickTime API and a logical translation or *binding* of the native function calls into Java method calls. In Chapter 3, "Integrating QuickTime with Java," we discuss in detail the grouping and usage of these packages, as well as how this logical translation works.

SUPPORT FOR DIFFERENT JAVA VIRTUAL MACHINES

The QuickTime for Java API supports all fully compliant Virtual Machines (VMs). On the Macintosh, it supports Apple's Macintosh Runtime for Java (MRJ) 2.1 or later; under Windows, JDK 1.1 or later. The Java VM used must be fully compliant with at least the JDK 1.1 specification and implementation from Sun Microsystems.

QuickTime for Java can also run in an applet, provided that the browser or applet viewer has one of the supported Java VMs chosen. Currently this requires the use of the Java Plug-in on Windows for Netscape Navigator and Internet Explorer browsers because those browsers do not provide a fully compliant Java 1.1 VM. On the Macintosh, you can use the Internet Explorer version 4 browser with an applet tag if MRJ 2.1 is chosen as your default VM. For Netscape Navigator version 4 on the Macintosh, QuickTime for Java applets must be viewed using the MRJ Plug-in.

This requires the HTML page to have different tags (OBJECT, EMBED, or APPLET, for instance), depending on the browser. In the Software Development Kit (SDK) available for download from Apple's QuickTime for Java website (`http://www.apple.com/quicktime/qtjava`) or the CD-ROM at the back of this book, a JavaScript script (`Applet-Tag.JS`) is provided that inserts the appropriate tag when the page is viewed.

VERSION NUMBERING

The minimal version required of QuickTime is expressed in the version number of QuickTime for Java. Thus, the current release is known as QuickTime for Java version 3, which means that it is basically compatible with QuickTime 3. Subsequent releases of QuickTime for Java that have QuickTime 4 APIs in abundance will be renumbered QuickTime for Java version 4.

THE QTSIMPLEAPPLET

On the CD-ROM accompanying this book, you'll find many code samples that demonstrate various techniques you can use to write your own Java programs using QuickTime for Java.

A good starting point is the `QTSimpleApplet` program, a code snippet of which is shown in Example 1.1. This program is useful for taking advantage of QuickTime presentation on the Internet to display multimedia content—and this is accomplished in less than a dozen lines of Java code. Figure 1.1 shows the output of the `QTSimpleApplet`, running locally on the user's computer in an Internet Explorer browser window. The resultant QuickTime movie, which you can control with the standard QuickTime movie controller buttons, uses the media as specified in the applet tag—in this case, sample.mov.

The QTSimpleApplet example uses QTFactory() methods that belong to the quicktime.app package to manufacture QuickTime objects that are able to present any of the wide range of media that QuickTime supports. That media may include video, audio, text, timecode, music/MIDI, sprite animation, tween, MPEG, or even movies that let you use Apple's QuickTime VR and QuickDraw 3D capabilities. The code sample is discussed in detail in Chapter 3, "Integrating QuickTime with Java."

EXAMPLE 1.1 *QTSimpleApplet.java*

```
public class QTSimpleApplet extends Applet {
    private Drawable myQTContent;
    private QTCanvas myQTCanvas;

    public void init () {
        try {
            QTSession.open();
            setLayout (new BorderLayout());
            myQTCanvas = new QTCanvas (QTCanvas.kInitialSize, 0.5F, 0.5F);
            add (myQTCanvas, "Center");

            QTFile file = new QTFile (getCodeBase().getFile() + getParameter("file"));
            myQTContent = QTFactory.makeDrawable (file);
        } catch (Exception qtE) {
                ...
                // handle exception
        }
    }

    public void start () {
        try {
            if (myQTCanvas != null)
                myQTCanvas.setClient (myQTContent, true);
        } catch (QTException e) {
                }
    }
```

```
public void stop () {
    if (myQTCanvas != null)
        myQTCanvas.removeClient();
}

public void destroy () {
    QTSession.close();
}
}
```

FIGURE 1.1   *The QTSimpleApplet running in a browser window*

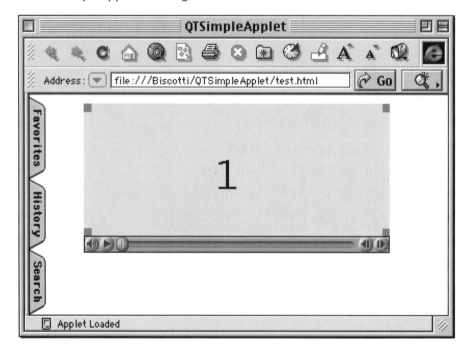

An Overview of QuickTime

QuickTime is composed of three distinct elements—the QuickTime Movie file format, the QuickTime Media Abstraction Layer, and a rich set of built-in QuickTime media services. These three elements enable programmers to realize the full benefits of the QuickTime software architecture.

The *QuickTime Movie file format* specifies a standard means of storing digital media compositions. Using this container format, it is possible to store not only individual media assets, such as video frames or audio samples, but also to store a complete description of the overall media composition. This might include a description of the spatial and auditory relationships between multiple video and audio channels in a more complex composition.

QuickTime also specifies a comprehensive software architecture known as the *QuickTime Media Abstraction Layer*. This abstraction layer defines how software tools and applications can access the robust set of media support services built into QuickTime. It also specifies how hardware can accelerate performance-critical portions of the Quick-Time system. Finally, the QuickTime Media Abstraction Layer outlines the means by which component software developers can extend and enhance the media services accessible through QuickTime.

This powerful and flexible digital media architecture includes a comprehensive set of built-in capabilities that software developers can use as a foundation for their tools. Thus, QuickTime-based applications are able to provide a richer, more extensible range of features to the user than would otherwise be possible.

MOVIE FILE FORMAT

QuickTime specifies its own file format called a QuickTime Movie. This file format is an extremely flexible container format for virtually any type of digital media asset. While QuickTime in no way requires you to store your media in QuickTime Movie files, most programmers find that the QuickTime Movie file format is the most convenient and useful format for storing common digital media types, such as audio and video. QuickTime Movie files are platform-neutral, open, and extensible.

Because of this ability to work with QuickTime Movie files on any computing platform, the QuickTime Movie format continues to grow in popularity. A QuickTime Movie file can be used on any user's computer with most video editing software; users can share these files in collaborative work environments made up of a diverse collection of media editing and capture tools.

QuickTime Movie files have long been the most popular format for delivering video on personal computer CD-ROMs. More recently, the QuickTime Movie format has become the most widely adopted format for publishing digital video on the Internet.

SUPPORT FOR OTHER MEDIA FILE FORMATS

While the QuickTime Movie format has many advantages as a container for digital media, there are many other digital media file formats in common use. QuickTime provides transparent access to the most popular digital media formats. If you use the QuickTime Media Abstraction Layer to access and manipulate digital media, your application will be able to work with a wide variety of digital media formats, including QuickTime Movies, with no additional work.

The QuickTime architecture defines how any developer can extend QuickTime so that it supports additional digital media file formats. This capability means that new file format support can be added to QuickTime at any time and that it will work seamlessly with all existing QuickTime-enabled applications. This extensibility helps to ensure that QuickTime applications are well positioned to take advantage of new trends in the changing world of digital media.

Digital Video File Formats

On the Windows platform, Microsoft has long promoted the AVI (Audio/Video Interleaved) file format for the storage of digital media. As a result, many Windows users have digital video stored in AVI format. QuickTime has the ability to work with these AVI files. This capability means that Windows users can step up to the power and flexibility of the QuickTime architecture without having to leave their existing media content behind.

The MPEG video standard was developed to provide a format for delivering digital media to the consumer market. Because MPEG provides relatively high-quality sound and video and relatively low data rates, it has been successful in some markets. QuickTime provides direct access to MPEG-1 audio and video.

Recently, the first generation of new DV-standard digital video cameras have appeared. (This digital transfer of DV standard files is accomplished using the IEEE-1394 standard based on Apple Computer's FireWire technology.) Manufacturers such as Sony and Panasonic are shipping these high-quality, professional video cameras under the name DVCam or DVCPro. Because these cameras use digital storage, and some use digital transfer technology, there is no generation quality loss when the media is edited or copied. And because of the high-quality images and ease of use features, DV is being rapidly accepted in the professional video market and is expected to succeed in the consumer space in the future. All DV cameras use the same format for storing digital sound and video. QuickTime is able to work directly with the digital media streams from these cameras. This means that QuickTime applications are immediately enabled to work with DV media, including the ability to losslessly edit different DV clips.

Audio File Formats

One of the most common formats for storing digital audio is the AIFF (Audio Interchange File Format) file created by Apple Computer. It provides the ability to store almost any format of digital audio, including multichannel sound and very high-resolution sound.

Because of these abilities, it is a popular format for storing audio in the professional audio market, as well as the consumer and Internet markets. QuickTime provides direct access to digital audio stored in AIFF files.

Microsoft also provides a file format for storing digital audio, called Wave. As a result of Microsoft's support, this format is common on the Windows platform, primarily in the consumer market. It is also a popular format for audio on the Internet. QuickTime provides direct access to most digital audio stored in most Wave audio files.

One of the most common audio files on the Internet is a format developed by Sun called AU. This format has capabilities similar to Microsoft's Wave format and is most commonly used for relatively low quality audio. QuickTime directly supports AU audio files, ensuring that audio files from the Internet can be easily accessed by any application.

Another common audio file format on the Internet is MPEG layer 3 audio. MPEG audio provides significantly better audio quality at the same data size used by Wave and AU files. QuickTime provides direct access to MPEG layer 3 audio streams.

STILL IMAGE FORMATS

While QuickTime is best known as software for working with dynamic media types such as video and sound, QuickTime also provides extensive support for working with still images. This capability is extremely important to applications working with dynamic media because it is very common to combine still images with video. QuickTime provides the same features in its still image support as in its dynamic media support. That means that image files are accessed directly in place with no transcoding or data duplication, that support for a rich set of standard file formats is built into QuickTime, and that developers can easily add support for new image file formats.

One of the most powerful tools for digital image manipulation is Adobe Photoshop. As a result, Adobe Photoshop files are one of the most common containers for still images. QuickTime supports direct access to Adobe Photoshop files, including display of the layers created by earlier versions of Photoshop. QuickTime also provides access to the alpha channel stored in some Photoshop files, making it easy to composite Photoshop files on top of digital video. On the Macintosh platform, QuickDraw pictures have always been a popular image format because of their great power and flexibility and the built-in operating system support. QuickTime provides direct access to Quick-Draw Picture files, ensuring consistent access to this popular format.

On the Windows platform, Bitmap (BMP) files have been popular because of their simplicity and built-in operating system support. QuickTime enables applications to directly access BMP images. On the Internet, GIF and JPEG (JFIF) image files are used on almost every Web page. Because of the incredible pervasiveness of the Internet, there is a vast library of images stored in these formats. By providing direct access to both GIF and JPEG images, QuickTime makes it easy for any application to use these pervasive file formats.

The Silicon Graphics platform has long been popular as an environment for creating and working with extremely high-resolution digital images. Many of the images created on the SGI platform are stored in the Silicon Graphics image format. QuickTime provides direct access to these image files, including the alpha channel compositing information stored in some Silicon Graphics image files. This capability ensures that QuickTime users will be able to work with images created on the Silicon Graphics platform.

QuickTime has been designed to support continuity with other file formats and standards. QuickTime doesn't obsolete existing data formats, so you can continue to use your existing content as you switch over to or start using a QuickTime-based solution. QuickTime does not demand that legacy data be abandoned or that time-consuming and expensive conversions be performed before your non-QuickTime data can be used.

QuickTime Media Abstraction Layer

The key to QuickTime's flexibility and performance is the QuickTime Media Abstraction Layer. This foundation technology is an advanced, component-based software architecture that provides software and hardware developers full access to the built-in QuickTime services and also specifies how to accelerate and extend QuickTime's capabilities through a powerful plug-in framework.

The QuickTime Media Abstraction Layer specifies a comprehensive set of services covering virtually all aspects of digital media creation, editing, and playback. These services include:

- timing and synchronization

- audio and image data compression and decompression

- image blitting, format conversion, scaling, composition, and transcoding

- audio mixing, sample rate conversion, and format conversion

- audio and video effects and transitions

- synchronized storage read and write

- media capture

- media import and export

- standard user interface elements, such as movie controllers, media previewers, and media capture dialogs

One of the most compelling features of the QuickTime Media Abstraction Layer is the broad range of media types supported. QuickTime includes built-in support for 10 different media types (video, audio, text, timecode, music/MIDI, sprite/animation, tween, MPEG, QuickTime VR, and QuickDraw 3D). For each of the built-in media types, QuickTime provides a set of media-specific services appropriate for managing each particular media type. QuickTime supports media types that are appropriate for all types of digital media publishing, whether the intended target is tape, CD-ROM, or the Internet.

The QuickTime Media Abstraction Layer also provides you with a high degree of isolation from underlying media hardware services. The abstraction of low-level hardware services such as clocks and timers, storage devices, video displays and frame buffers, audio mixers, music synthesizers, media capture devices, and graphics chips means that QuickTime-based applications are easier to develop and maintain. In most cases, you don't need to be concerned with the details of how QuickTime media interact with the underlying hardware.

WORKING WITH VIDEO

Working with digital video can be extremely confusing. There are dozens of different compression formats to choose from. There are both hardware-based and software-based playback engines and several different file formats used by different manufacturers.

Many tools for working with video only support one or two file formats and a few different compression formats. Some tools may not be able to take advantage of hardware acceleration. QuickTime's Media Abstraction Layer provides the ability to work with any file format and any compression format. Tools created to work with QuickTime are immediately enabled to work with all these file formats.

Similarly, QuickTime provides the ability to work with nearly any video compression format through its Image Compression Manager. The Image Compression Manager provides a standard way for tools to manipulate any kind of compressed video, ensuring that all QuickTime-based tools can support all compression formats in use today as well as new formats that will emerge. The Image Compression Manager makes it just as easy to work with uncompressed video, ensuring that the highest possible quality of video can be manipulated by QuickTime tools. The Image Compression Manager also provides a hardware abstraction layer that isolates tools from the underlying implementation of each compression format. This means that users can install new video hardware and existing QuickTime-based tools will be able to immediately take advantage of the new hardware.

The QuickTime Movie file format doesn't impose any restrictions on the characteristics of video that may be stored in a QuickTime Movie file. For example, video can be stored at any frame rate, not just those frame rates that are common in the broadcast industry. While this ensures that QuickTime Movies can easily be used to store NTSC, PAL, and film frame rate video, it also means that QuickTime Movies can be used for MPEG, CD-ROM, and Internet video. Furthermore, because there is no upper limit on the frame rate of a QuickTime movie, it is an ideal format for high frame rate animations, and it is ready to support future digital video standards that may enable even higher frame rates.

In addition to providing support for playing back digital video, QuickTime also provides a set of tools for manipulating digital video. Because most professional video work is field based, QuickTime contains a set of services that make it easy for tools to independently access each field in a video stream and easily reorder or duplicate fields to provide effects such as backwards playback or slow motion. QuickTime is also able to combine video images in a variety of ways including cross-fades and alpha channel–based compositions.

Because there are so many different Motion JPEG formats in common use, Apple Computer worked with a group of digital video companies to standardize how Motion JPEG is stored. QuickTime contains support for these standard Motion JPEG formats as well as support for a number of other Motion JPEG formats, such as AVR (Avid Video Resolution). To make it easy to move between different kinds of Motion JPEG, QuickTime contains a number of transcoders that allow video to be converted from one Motion JPEG format to another without introducing any recompression artifacts.

MPEG

The MPEG media format has become an important data type in a variety of established and emerging digital media markets. MPEG-1 content is commonly employed in VideoCD and CD-ROM titles because of its relatively good image quality and is used widely on the Internet due to its comparatively low bit-rate requirements.

Responding to increased interest in this industry-standard media format, Apple added support for MPEG-1 to the QuickTime architecture in 1994. MPEG-1 playback has traditionally required special-purpose hardware to provide high-quality playback performance. Indeed, the original QuickTime implementation relied upon dedicated hardware to decode MPEG-1 streams.

With the advances in processor technologies, however, it has now become feasible to decode these streams in software without the need for dedicated decoder hardware. And using the latest version of the QuickTime MPEG Extension, QuickTime customers are now able to take full advantage of MPEG-1 without any special-purpose hardware. The integration of MPEG-1 into QuickTime provides an excellent case study in how QuickTime adds value to existing industry standards.

For all the benefits of MPEG-1 as an audio and video format (VHS-quality images and high-quality audio at single-speed CD-ROM data rates), MPEG-1 has many characteristics that have made its use in PC-based interactive multimedia applications relatively limited. With QuickTime, many of these limitations can be overcome. The first challenge in making MPEG content easily accessible is to cope with the wide range of encoding conventions utilized in different manufacturers encoders. The Internet contains a great deal of MPEG content that is only partially compliant with the MPEG-1 specification. Likewise, early MPEG encoders often generated MPEG streams that were playable only when using specific hardware decoders. QuickTime's MPEG support is very robust, enabling it to work with a very wide variety of MPEG-1 content.

Due to the complex compression scheme used for MPEG-1 media, basic media transport operations such as frame-accurate positioning, fast forward, and reverse playback have usually not been supported in other MPEG-1 systems. When integrated into QuickTime, however, MPEG-1 inherits these standard capabilities associated with all QuickTime dynamic media.

Basic editing operations, such as copy and paste, on MPEG-1 streams have generally been relegated to high-end MPEG encoding workstations. Again, the complexities of the MPEG format have made this capability all but absent in PC-based decoding solutions. Under QuickTime, MPEG-1 content can be manipulated in largely the same ways that other forms of video and audio streams can be. In fact, it is entirely straightforward to use QuickTime's audio mixing and image compositing features to combine MPEG content with other QuickTime media types such as text titles, sprite animations, or music tracks.

For software developers, QuickTime makes adding support for MPEG streams to their applications an easy task. With QuickTime, MPEG content is accessed and controlled from an application in the same way that other media types are supported. When this ease-of-integration is considered alongside QuickTime's high-quality, high-performance MPEG-1 software decode capabilities, MPEG media becomes a more compelling data type for many uses.

As QuickTime's MPEG support is enhanced further to support more types of MPEG content—such as MPEG layer 3 audio, MPEG-2, and MPEG variants used in DVD-Video—it is expected that QuickTime will be able to support ease-of-use and integration features similar to those that have been provided for MPEG-1.

THE EMERGENCE OF DV

In the last year, most major video camera manufacturers have introduced digital video camcorders based on the DV standard. Examples of these cameras include the Sony DSR-200 and DCR-VX 1000 and the Panasonic AG-EZ1U and PV-DV1000. These DV cameras use a new tape format that stores the video and sound in a purely digital format. The video and sound data can be transferred to another DV camera or deck using a new high-speed connector called FireWire (also known as IEEE 1394). Because the video and sound are transferred through a digital connector, there is no loss of image or sound quality—every copy is identical to the original.

Hardware manufacturers such as Apple, Adaptec, Miro, Radius, and Truevision are creating products that provide FireWire connectors for personal computers. The availability of FireWire connectors on personal computers means that users will be able to digitally transfer the sound and video captured with their DV cameras into their computers.

The video and sound output of these DV clips is of very high quality, in part because of the many advantages of the digital tape format and digital data transfer. Once DV clips are stored on the computer's hard disk, how to work with the video becomes an issue. The manufacturers of the DV cameras created an entirely new compression technology to store the video, and a new file format to go with it. As a result, there are almost no dedicated tools available to work with DV media. QuickTime bridges the differences between the new DV format and existing sound and video tools.

The QuickTime software architecture has the ability to work with a wide range of digital media file formats and video compression formats. QuickTime has built-in support for the DV file format. This means that all currently QuickTime-enabled applications are able to work with DV streams without any changes. DV data can be played back, edited, combined with other digital video standards like Motion JPEG, and even converted into other formats. QuickTime users don't have to learn a whole new set of tools to take advantage of DV.

Because DV data can be used from any QuickTime-enabled application, the DV sound and video can be easily converted to other formats for delivery. The final format might be a QuickTime movie compressed with Cinepak or Indeo for CD-ROM delivery, a QuickTime movie compressed with Sorenson for Internet delivery, or an MPEG bit-stream for delivery on a VideoCD. In all these cases, the highest possible image quality is maintained because all data is digitally transferred, so no noise is ever introduced into the signal.

Edited DV data may also be delivered back to a DV tape. QuickTime contains a DV encoder that enables users to create DV streams directly. If users have been working with DV data, no recompression is necessary so the full image quality is maintained in the final DV stream. But users can also start with more traditional digital video formats, such as Motion JPEG. QuickTime can re-encode the Motion JPEG media into the DV format. Once QuickTime has encoded the digital media into a DV stream, that file can be transferred back to a DV camera or deck using FireWire.

All of QuickTime's support for DV is software based. This means that any computer running QuickTime can access DV data. On high-end machines, QuickTime's software DV decoder will provide the ability to play back DV streams at quarter image size. And for offline processing, QuickTime's software DV decoder can provide full-frame, full-quality images. On other machines, the performance will be lower. Many users require full-screen, full-motion playback in order to accurately edit their DV media. The QuickTime architecture is both scalable and extensible, enabling third-party developers to accelerate QuickTime with DV playback hardware. Many companies have announced support for QuickTime's DV capabilities, including Adaptec, DPS, Miro, Octopos, Promax, and Radius. These DV accelerators allow full-screen, full-motion playback and editing of DV media. And because of QuickTime's Media Abstraction Layer, the DV acceleration hardware will work with all QuickTime-enabled applications, not just those written to work with a particular vendor's hardware.

The built-in capabilities of QuickTime mean that users of DV cameras don't have to worry about the details of the digital media formats they are using. Users can choose from a wide range of QuickTime-enabled tools for their DV editing, instead of having to wait for tools to emerge that support this new video format. Users can easily work with DV media in the same way they work with digital video today. This ease of use, high level of integration, and rapid technology adoption are all possible because the QuickTime architecture was designed to be easily extended to accommodate new technologies, such as DV, as they continue to emerge.

RENDERING VISUAL EFFECTS

One of the most time-consuming aspects of working with digital video on a computer workstation today is rendering visual effects. Video editors often have to limit their use of motion, transitions, and filters because of the lengthy rendering times that these effects can require. Hardware vendors have created plug-in boards that can accelerate the rendering of many of these effects, often performing them in real time. Unfortunately, these hardware solutions have only been available in closed proprietary systems. There have been no open standards for real time visual effects.

QuickTime contains enhancements to the QuickTime software architecture that will enable QuickTime-based applications to work with visual effects in a standard way and take advantage of hardware acceleration when available. QuickTime's support for visual effects comprises these key elements:

■ *Standard effects description container*

QuickTime defines a standard way to describe visual effects. This effects description is built on a flexible and extensible data container format called QuickTime atoms. The use of the QuickTime atom container format ensures that QuickTime will be able to describe any visual effect in use today and any new effects that will be created in the future. By providing a standard container for describing visual effects, QuickTime provides a common means for software applications to communicate with visual effects rendering engines. This enables the same description to be used with either a hardware or a software visual effects renderer, ensuring that the description of the effect is independent of the underlying technology used to render the effect.

■ *Built-in renderers for common effects*

While QuickTime has the ability to work with any kind of visual effect, there is a set of visual effects that are commonly used. To ensure that all users have access to these common effects, QuickTime includes a large set of built-in software-based effects. These effects include cross-fade, chroma keying, SMPTE wipes, and color adjustments. By providing a complete set of standard visual effects, QuickTime helps to establish common ground around which greater industry-wide standardization of effects descriptions can be achieved.

QuickTime provides the foundation for more productive video editing. Users will be able to use hardware-accelerated visual effects in a range of tools. QuickTime provides the common ground that enables software effects, hardware-accelerated effects, and video editing tools to work transparently together. In many cases, users will be able to directly play back the results of their edits without any rendering delays. And as new effects algorithms become available, whether in hardware or software, QuickTime-enabled applications will be able to take immediate advantage of them.

AUDIO SUPPORT

Because audio plays such an important part in almost any digital media project, QuickTime provides an unparalleled level of support for working with all kinds of digital audio. QuickTime's support for audio goes well beyond the ability to simply synchronize one audio channel with video playback. A QuickTime movie file can contain an unlimited number of parallel sound tracks. Each sound track has an independent sample rate, sample size, and audio format.

This flexibility is critical for digital media creators who are working with audio from a variety of different types of devices. For example, digital audio from an audio CD has a sample rate of 44.1 kHz; from a DAT, 48 kHz; and from a DVCam, 32 kHz. The ability to store any combination of audio formats and sample rates in a single file is a powerful feature of the QuickTime movie format as it means that digital media creators can effortlessly combine audio from a variety of sources without having to be concerned about format differences.

Because the QuickTime Movie file format allows for complex digital audio compositions to be created, the QuickTime software architecture must be able to support the playback of these compositions. Built into QuickTime is the ability to mix together an arbitrary number of simultaneous audio channels, with the number limited only by the performance of the computer on which QuickTime is running. The ability to work with an unlimited number of audio channels, each potentially of a different audio format, is made possible by the Sound Manager components.

The Sound Manager provides a rich set of services for playing, mixing, synchronizing, digitizing, decompressing, and compressing digital audio. The Sound Manager contains software services that allow a system with only one or two hardware audio channels to play back any number of digital audio channels. If the digital audio is compressed, the Sound Manager will decompress it in real time as the audio is being played.

While the Sound Manager provides all of its services in software, any of its capabilities can be enhanced by the addition of hardware accelerators. For example, the audio mixing and sample rate conversion can be carried out by a hardware card that might use more sophisticated algorithms than the Sound Manager can provide in real time on the system's main processor. Because of QuickTime's hardware abstraction layer, users can install such hardware, and it becomes transparently available to all QuickTime-enabled applications.

The Sound Manager also provides powerful synchronization services. A sample clock is available for each audio channel that allows applications to know exactly which audio sample is currently being played. This sample clock also provides the basis for synchronizing other digital media with the audio channel—for example, digital video or another channel of audio. Without the availability of a sample clock, applications can never know exactly which audio sample is currently being played, making precise synchronization impossible. Yet many other systems for working with digital media fail to provide this essential capability.

While the services of the Sound Manager for mixing, resampling, and decompressing are most commonly used in real time for playing back one or more channels of digital audio, these same services can be used by tools in an offline mode. This capability is important because it means that tools can leverage the built-in capabilities of QuickTime to provide some, or all, of their audio-processing capabilities. For users, this means that more tools are able to provide a broader range of audio capabilities because QuickTime makes providing fundamental audio capabilities easy.

Because there are so many different file formats for storing digital audio, QuickTime provides the ability to work with most popular audio file formats. In addition to the QuickTime Movie format, which is an extremely flexible means for storing digital audio compositions, QuickTime also supports AIFC, AIFF, AU, AVI, Macintosh sound resources, OMF, Sound Designer II, uLaw, and Wave. Because Quick-Time provides access to so many standard audio file formats, tool developers are able to easily support these audio file formats as well. For users of these tools, that means no need to worry about what format digital audio is stored in because QuickTime makes it possible to work with most popular formats.

QUICKTIME MUSIC ARCHITECTURE/MIDI SUPPORT

While the audio services provided by QuickTime are extremely powerful and flexible, there are applications for which standard audio data is impractical due to size or data rate constraints or which have a need for a more interactive form of audio experience. Especially in the context of the Internet, the challenges of delivering high-quality, interactive audio over the relatively narrow-band data channels most users can access are substantial.

MIDI provides very compact representations of musical performances. The MIDI data format describes a performance in terms of a very compact time-based sequence of discrete musical events such as note events (note on, note off, etc.) rather than as a series of digitized audio samples. Furthermore, since MIDI separates the description of the musical performance from the descriptions of the specific instruments needed to realize the complete composition, a great deal of interactive potential is embodied in a MIDI performance.

QuickTime provides extensive support for MIDI within its interactive music architecture. In fact, the QuickTime Music Architecture (QTMA) exists entirely apart from MIDI. MIDI is not required to take advantage the QuickTime Music Architecture. However, as a practical matter most music applications work with MIDI data today. So for compatibility reasons, QuickTime supports a superset of the functionality implied by the MIDI format. The QuickTime Music Architecture is composed of four major elements:

- music synthesizer architecture
- instrument library component
- note sequencer
- MIDI importer/exporter

QuickTime provides a fully specified architecture for implementing and accessing music synthesizers. These synthesizers can be hardware- or software-based. There is a well-defined architecture to allow different synthesizers to plug in to QuickTime. By default, QuickTime includes a built-in software-based synthesizer that provides a set of capabilities that can be delivered across the full range of computers that support QuickTime.

For composers and title developers there is a huge benefit to providing a ready-to-use synthesizer in the base QuickTime architecture. With standard MIDI data, there has been a long-standing problem of ensuring consistency of the MIDI performance across a wide variety of software and hardware platforms. While General MIDI addresses this problem somewhat, it has its own drawbacks. By delivering music content through QuickTime, the issue of consistency is largely solved since QuickTime is able to ensure a consistent platform for music playback across all the various software and hardware systems.

All music synthesizers need instruments to be able to make sound. To that end, QuickTime augments its built-in synthesizer with a General MIDI-compatible instrument library. This library provides a standard set of instruments in a very compact form. Since the range of expressiveness of a synthesizer is largely defined by the sorts of instruments it can utilize, the QuickTime Music Architecture also includes support for custom instruments that can augment or replace the standard instruments that ship with QuickTime. Within this framework, there is virtually no limit to the range of instrumentation that can be created in QuickTime.

The third key element of the QuickTime Music Architecture is the note sequencer. The note sequencer component serves the purpose of communicating with QuickTime synthesizers to start and stop individual notes. The note sequencer manages an overall performance as described by a list of note events to be performed over time. By including this higher-level service, much of the difficulty of working with music data from within applications can be eliminated. It becomes a simple matter to create, edit, and control the playback of complex compositions.

The last component of the QuickTime Music Architecture is the MIDI file import/export service. By providing data interchange with MIDI files, it becomes a simple matter to work with a wide range of existing music composition and editing software tools. As with support for other media file formats, the MIDI file importer significantly reduces the effort required to integrate standard music data formats with other QuickTime media.

GOALS

It has always been the goal of QuickTime to help simplify the use and integration of digital media of all kinds. As QuickTime has evolved since its introduction in 1991, an ever-expanding set of built-in services has been added to the base architecture. Over the years, support for a much richer set of media types has been added. And at the same time these advancements have been added to QuickTime, the key principles and architectural concepts introduced in QuickTime 1.0 remain intact in version 4.0 and beyond. This stability has enabled software and hardware developers to enjoy excellent overall compatibility and technological continuity while being able to reap the substantial benefits of an evolving QuickTime.

2

QuickTime Basics

QuickTime is centered on two fundamental concepts: the software movie, a data structure that your application code creates, and a component-based architecture that provides an extensible and flexible framework.

In QuickTime, a *movie* is a structure of references—specifically references to chunks of data located elsewhere. You could think of it as a directory that lists and organizes audio and video, as well as animated graphics, virtual reality panoramas, still images, text, and other elements. The data chunks that a QuickTime movie organizes may have many different types and be stored in different formats. When you run a movie, QuickTime fetches and interprets these various chunks and plays them back sequentially at specified intervals of time.

QuickTime's component-based architecture was designed from the beginning to be extensible. QuickTime consists of over 200 different software components. These software components are divided into one of over 20 different categories, with the components in each category providing a specific service. This component-based architecture allows QuickTime to be continuously updated to support new technologies by adding new components or by enhancing existing ones. Developers, too, can add their own software components, allowing their technology to take advantage of all the benefits of QuickTime integration.

QuickTime for Java represents all of the QuickTime structures that are described in this chapter as classes in a set of packages. The translation of these QuickTime structures—for example, movies and sprites—to a QuickTime for Java class is discussed in Chapter 3, "Integrating QuickTime with Java." The reference section in the second half of the book has a complete listing of the classes that are available in this release (version 3) of QuickTime for Java.

This chapter is not a comprehensive discussion of QuickTime. The first book in this series, *Discovering QuickTime*, provides an introduction to QuickTime, with many useful programming examples and other resources. You may also want to read *Inside Macintosh: QuickTime* and *Inside Macintosh: QuickTime Components*. Both volumes are available as Acrobat PDF files on the CD-ROM at the back of this book. You can also find the PDF files at Apple's QuickTime website at www.apple.com/quicktime.

The focus of this chapter is on the following topics that are relevant to working with the QuickTime for Java API:

- the structure of QuickTime movies: tracks, media types, and handlers

- the graphics systems that QuickTime provides

- how sprites and sprite worlds enable animation and compositing

- the QuickTime Music Architecture, which provides a software synthesizer

- tweening

- sequence grabbing, which enables you to capture and record external media for storage and later playback

- importing and exporting different media types

- QuickTime VR

- QuickDraw 3D

INTRODUCTION TO MOVIES

QuickTime allows you to manipulate time-based data such as video and audio sequences. The metaphor of a movie is used to describe time-based data. QuickTime stores its time-based data in objects called *movies*.

Like a motion picture, a single QuickTime movie can contain more than one stream of data. Each data stream is called a *track*. Tracks in QuickTime movies do not actually contain the movie's data but rather each track refers to a single media structure that, in turn, contains references to the actual media data. The media data may be stored on disks, CD-ROM volumes, or other storage devices. It may be local or remote and thus need to be obtained through the use of HTTP or FTP Internet protocols. A movie can mix data that is available locally and data that is stored at a remote location. The data may also be sourced from a live video broadcast using the RSTP protocol.

With all these disparate media types and data source options, the real power and flexibility of QuickTime becomes apparent, as QuickTime's Movie Toolbox handles all of the issues involved in getting this media and synchronizing and presenting the playback of a movie.

THE MOVIE STRUCTURE

Each movie is a standardized data structure stored in memory that you access only through QuickTime calls. The movie structure is like a directory: It holds a few pieces of general information but mainly contains pointers to external data. Each movie has overall timing characteristics—scale, rate, and duration—that determine how it plays in real time. A movie is made up of tracks, each of which plays a particular type of data during a specified part of the movie's overall time line. Each track has a media structure that points to and characterizes all the pieces of data that are presented to the user when the track plays. When QuickTime plays a movie, it fetches and processes data of various types, as specified by the movie's tracks, and presents the data to the user according to the movie's overall time line (see Figure 2.1).

FIGURE 2.1 *Movie composition*

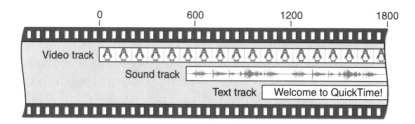

TIME AND THE MOVIE TOOLBOX

The Movie Toolbox allows your application to use the full range of features provided by QuickTime. This toolbox provides functions that allow you to load, play, create, edit, and store objects that contain time-based data. The Movie Toolbox must provide a description of the time basis of that data as well as a definition of the context for evaluating that time basis. In QuickTime, a movie's time basis is referred to as its *time base.* Geometrically, you can think of the time base as a vector that defines the direction and velocity of time for a movie. The context for a time base is called its *time coordinate system.*

Time Coordinate Systems

A movie's time coordinate system provides the context for evaluating the passage of time in the movie. If you think of the time coordinate system as defining an axis for measuring time, it is only natural that this axis would be marked with a scale that defines a basic unit of measurement. In QuickTime, that measurement system is called a *time scale.*

A QuickTime time scale defines the number of time units that pass each second in a given time coordinate system. A time coordinate system that has a time scale of 1 measures time in seconds. Similarly, a time coordinate system that has a time scale of 60 measures sixtieths of a second. In general, each time unit in a time coordinate system is equal to (1/time scale) seconds. Some common time scales are listed in Table 2-1.

TABLE 2-1   *Common movie time scales*

Time scale	Absolute time measured
1	Seconds
60	Sixtieths of a second (Macintosh ticks)
1000	Milliseconds
22050	Sound sampled at 22 kHz (kilohertz)

A particular point in time in a time coordinate system is represented using a *time value.* A time value is expressed in terms of the time scale of its time coordinate system. Without an appropriate time scale, a time value is meaningless. For example, a time value of 180 translates to 3 seconds with a time scale of 60, but it translates to 180 seconds with a time scale of 1. Because all time coordinate systems tie back to absolute time (that is, time as we measure it in seconds), the Movie Toolbox can translate time values from one time coordinate system into another.

Time coordinate systems have a finite maximum *duration* that defines the maximum time value (the minimum time value is always 0). Note that as a QuickTime movie is edited, the duration changes. As the value of the time scale increases (as the time unit for a coordinate system gets smaller in terms of absolute time), the maximum absolute time that can be represented in a time coordinate system decreases.

Figure 2.2 illustrates a movie's time coordinate system. A movie always starts at time 0. The time scale defines the unit of measure for the movie's time values. The duration specifies how long the movie lasts in this time scale.

FIGURE 2.2   *A movie's time coordinate system*

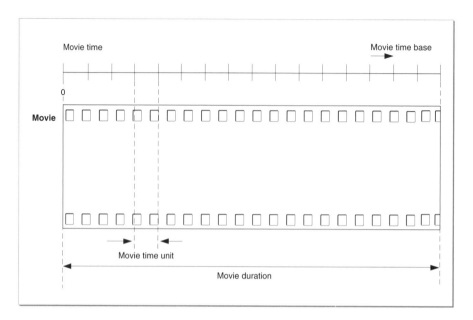

Time Bases

A movie's time base defines its current time value and the *rate* at which time passes for the movie. The rate specifies the speed and direction in which time travels in a movie. Negative rate values indicate backward movement through a movie's data; positive values move forward. The time base also contains a reference to the clock that provides timing for the time base. QuickTime clocks are implemented as components that are managed by the Component Manager.

Time bases exist independently of any specific time coordinate system. However, time values extracted from a time base are meaningless without a time scale. Therefore, whenever you obtain a time value from a time base, you must specify the time scale of the time value result. The Movie Toolbox translates the time base's time value into a value that is sensible in the specified time scale.

Note that a time base differs from a time coordinate system, which provides the foundation for a time base. (A time coordinate system is the field of play that defines the coordinate axis for a time base.) A time base operates in the context of a time coordinate system. It has a rate, which implies a direction as well as a speed through the movie.

Figure 2.3 shows an example of how time relations work in QuickTime movies.

FIGURE 2.3   *An example of time relations in QuickTime movies*

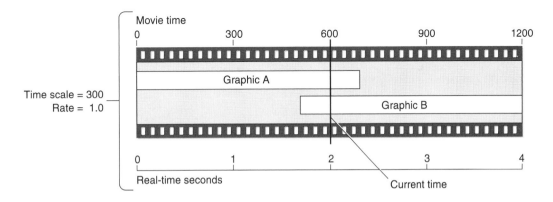

TRACKS

A movie can contain one or more tracks. Each track refers to media data that can be interpreted within the movie's time coordinate system. Each track begins at the beginning of the movie. However, a track can end at any time. In addition, the actual data in the track may be offset from the beginning of the movie. Tracks with data that does not commence at the beginning of a movie contain empty space that precedes the track's media data.

At any given point in time, a particular track may or may not have media data. No single track needs to have media data during the entire movie. As you move through a movie, you gain access to the data that is described by each of the enabled tracks.

Figure 2.4 shows a movie that contains five tracks. The lighter shading in each track represent the time offset between the beginning of the movie and the start of the track's data. When the movie's time value is 6, there are three enabled tracks: Video 1 and Audio 1, and Video 2, which is just being enabled. The Other 1 track does not become enabled until the time value reaches 8. The Audio 2 track becomes enabled at time value 10.

A movie can contain one or more *layers*. Each layer contains one or more tracks that may be related to one another. The Movie Toolbox builds up a movie's visual representation layer by layer. For example, in Figure 2.4, if the images contained in the Video 1 and Video 2 tracks overlap spatially, the user sees the image that is stored in the front layer. You assign individual tracks to movie layers using Movie Toolbox functions.

FIGURE 2.4   *A movie containing several tracks*

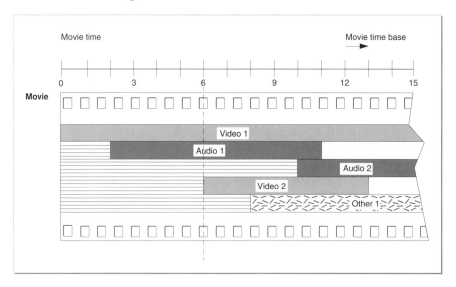

Each track in a movie represents a single stream of data in a movie and is associated with a single media type. All of the tracks in a movie use the movie's time coordinate system. That is, the movie's time scale defines the basic time unit for each of the movie's tracks. Each track begins at the beginning of the movie, but the track's data might not begin until some time value other than 0. This intervening time is represented by blank space—in an audio track the blank space translates to silence; in a video track the blank space generates no visual image. Each track has its own duration. This duration need not correspond to the duration of the movie. Movie duration always equals the duration of the longest track. The duration of a track within a movie is shown in Figure 2.5.

FIGURE 2.5 *The duration of a track in a movie*

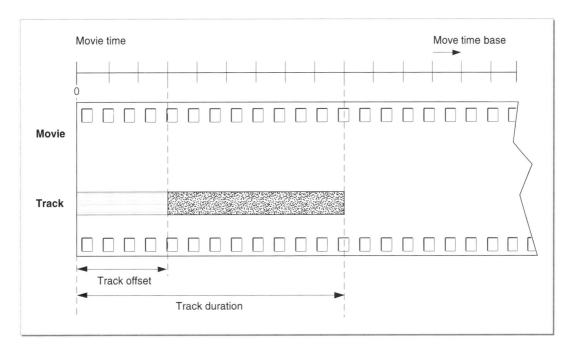

A track is always associated with one media structure. The media structure contains control information that refers to the data that constitutes the track. The track contains a list of references that identify portions of the media structure that are used in the track. Consequently, a track can play the data in its media structure in any order and any number of times. Figure 2.6 shows how a track maps data from a media structure into a movie.

When a movie is flattened and made self-contained, it can remove all of its media sources that are not used by a track. Thus, one can have large amounts of data that are available when capturing and creating movies, but the movie itself represents a snapshot of all the media structures it uses and only the media structures it uses.

FIGURE 2.6   *A track and its media*

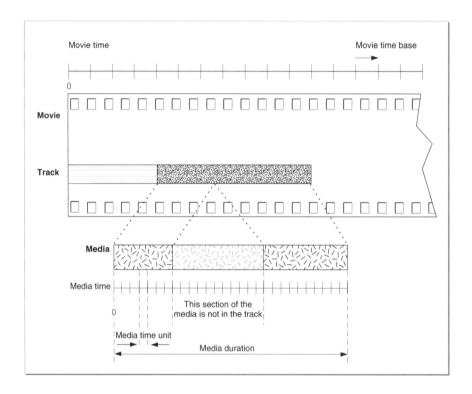

MEDIA STRUCTURES

A media structure describes the data for a track. The data is not actually stored in the media. Rather, the media contains references to its media data, which may be stored in disk files, on CD-ROM discs, or other storage devices. Note that the data referred to by one media may be used by more than one movie, with each movie containing unique media objects that document the media data it uses.

Each media has its own time coordinate system, which defines the media's time scale and duration. A media's time coordinate system always starts at time 0, and it is independent of the time coordinate system of the movie that uses its data. Tracks map data from the movie's time coordinate system to the media's time coordinate system.

Each supported data type has its own *media handler.* The media handler interprets the media's data. The media handler must be able to randomly access the data and play segments at rates specified by the movie. The track determines the order in which the media is played; the media handler is responsible for playing those segments. Figure 2.7 shows the final link to the data. The media in the figure references digital video frames on a CD-ROM disc.

Figure 2.7   *A media and its data*

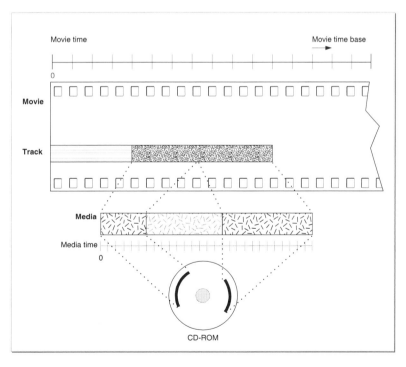

MEDIA HANDLERS AND THE MOVIE TOOLBOX

The QuickTime Movie Toolbox is a generic movie-building kit; it does not provide direct support for manipulating specific media types. This work is performed by media handler components, which are responsible for interpreting and manipulating a media's sample data.

For each media type there is a specific media handler that deals with the characteristics of that media type. Apple provides media handlers for video, sound, text, sprites, timecodes, tweening, models constructed using QuickDraw 3D, and music constructed with the QuickTime Music Architecture. Because media handlers are implemented as components, new media handlers can be created to support new media types or to add new features to the ways they handle existing media.

Applications do not normally interact with media handlers directly; applications make calls to the Movie Toolbox, which calls media handlers as needed. This means that you don't need to account for the various data formats that your application might encounter when using QuickTime. You just tell the Toolbox to do a certain job, and it calls the components it needs to get the job done.

DATA HANDLERS

Media handlers delegate the actual work of retrieving the media data to another type of component—a data handler. QuickTime's data handlers can retrieve data from local files and provide support for different file systems such as Mac OS, Windows, and CD-ROM file systems. With QuickTime 4, there are also data handlers that can retrieve stored data from remote locations using the FTP (File Transfer Protocol) and HTTP (Hypertext Transfer Protocol) Internet protocols and also data handlers that can retrieve data from a live broadcast stream using the RTP (Real Time Protocol) and RTSP (Real Time Streaming Protocol). This gives QuickTime the capability of presenting media that is sourced from different locations or even of mixing stored and broadcast media data.

TRANSFORMATION MATRICES

QuickTime makes extensive use of transformation matrices to define graphical operations on movies as they are displayed. A *transformation matrix* defines how QuickTime maps points from one coordinate space into another coordinate space. By modifying the values in a transformation matrix, you can perform a variety of graphical operations, including translation, rotation, scaling, stretching, and perspective. Figure 2.8 shows an example of a matrix that translates the points in a movie coordinate system to the display coordinate system.

FIGURE 2.8   *A translation matrix*

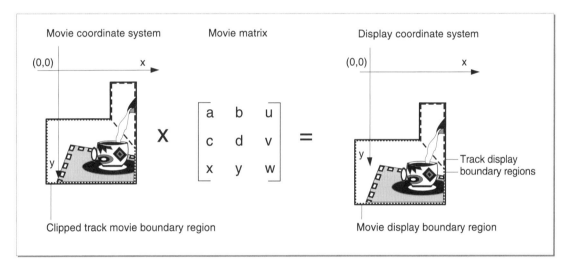

DEFINING QUICKTIME ATOMS AND ATOM CONTAINERS

QuickTime stores most of its data using specialized structures in memory, called *atoms*. Movies themselves are atoms, as are tracks, media, and data samples. There are two kinds of atoms: *chunk atoms*, which your code accesses by offsets, and *QT atoms*, for which QuickTime provides a full set of access tools.

Each atom carries its own size and type information as well as its data. A *container atom* is an atom that contains other atoms, including other container atoms. There are several advantages to using QT atoms for holding and passing information:

- QT atoms can nest indefinitely, forming hierarchies that are easy to pass from one process to another.

- QuickTime provides a single set of tools by which you can search and manipulate QT atoms of all types.

Each atom has a four-character type designation that describes its internal structure. For example, movie atoms are type `'moov'`, while the track atoms inside them are type `'trak'`.

Atoms that contain only data, and not other atoms, are called *leaf atoms*. A leaf atom simply contains a series of data fields accessible by offsets. You can use QuickTime's atom tools to search through QT atom hierarchies until you get to leaf atoms, then read the leaf atom's data from its various fields. With chunk atoms, you read their size bytes and access their contents by calculating offsets. For more information about atoms and atom containers, see *Inside Macintosh: QuickTime*, which is available as an Acrobat PDF on the CD-ROM at the back of this book.

Figure 2.9 shows an example of the atom structure of a simple QuickTime movie that has one track containing video data. Both the atoms in Figure 2.9 are chunk atoms, so you create and read them through your own code.

FIGURE 2.9   *Atom structure of a simple QuickTime movie*

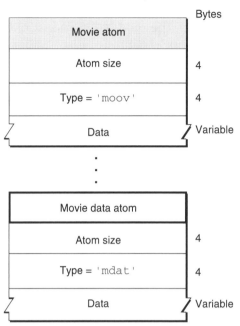

QUICKTIME MOVIE FILE FORMAT

A QuickTime movie file is in an open file format that is used to store all of the movie data as a file. This file format forms the basis of the emerging MPEG-4 file specification. The contents of a movie file are completely self-describing; the media data in the file is described by meta-data structures called sample descriptions. As the contents of a movie file are self-describing, the format is extensible.

On platforms where QuickTime is not present, applications are able to parse a movie file and even present the contents of a QuickTime file if they understand the means that have been used to encode the media in a particular movie. Thus, on UNIX systems there is XAnim that can play and present many QuickTime movies, as can the Java Media Framework.

Compressors and decompressors (codecs) encode and decode media data. Compressors can be either lossless (i.e., none of the media data is lost) or lossy (some of the media data is lost in the compression process), or in some cases both. Compressing data is done for many reasons, and many compressors provide customized settings to control various parameters of the compression process, such as how much data is lost, how big the resulting compressed data will be, the data rate that will be required to read the data back, and so forth. Decompression is the process of decoding the previously compressed data and rendering it.

QuickTime provides support for many codecs that are industry standards or are widely available, as well as providing its own codecs. Widely available codecs supported by QuickTime include JPEG, H263, MPEG, AVI, CinePak, MIDI, and WAV. QuickTime also provides and supports proprietary codecs such as Sorenson Video and QDesign Music that offer solutions to many problems presenting media.

Thus, QuickTime can be used to capture, author, and create movies that can be presented and viewed by users on platforms where QuickTime itself is not available. When used to present media, however, QuickTime provides the content creator with many advantages in performance, predictable and reliable playback, integration, and synchronization that are not available with other media platforms.

ADOPTING THE QUICKTIME FILE FORMAT AS THE STANDARD FOR MPEG-4

In February 1998, the International Standards Organization (ISO) formally adopted the QuickTime file format as the starting point for *MPEG-4*, the latest in a series of standards for transmitting video and audio information. ISO's Motion Picture Experts Group (MPEG) is currently working on the new standard, with input from Apple, IBM, Microsoft, Netscape, Oracle, Silicon Graphics, and Sun Microsystems. ISO plans to publish a final specification in 1999.

MPEG-4 differs from MPEG-1 and MPEG-2 by adopting a component-based architecture for multimedia, an approach derived from

QuickTime's file format. Other existing standards have less flexibility and treat multimedia as just an array of picture elements.

A number of products based on MPEG-4 are in the works, including hardware from IBM, Java support from Sun, video server products from SGI, and media software from Oracle. Most new and existing hardware, software, and media content products that use QuickTime should operate seamlessly with MPEG-4, as QuickTime forms the basis of the MPEG-4 sandard.

ENDIAN ORDERING

There are two ways that multibyte data fields may be referenced in memory: big-endian addressing, where the address for a field points to its most significant byte, and little-endian addressing, where the address for a field points to its least significant byte.

These two types of data referencing are illustrated in Figure 2.10, which shows a region of memory containing fields that are 4 and 2 bytes long. In Figure 2.10, MSB and LSB indicate the most significant and least significant bytes in each field, respectively. Notice that the pointers access different bytes in the two schemes, although they point to the same fields.

FIGURE 2.10 *Big-endian and little-endian addressing*

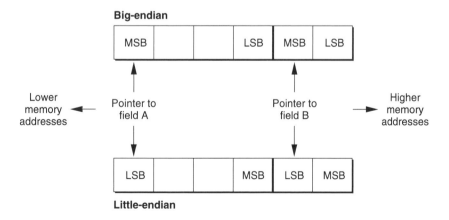

Generally speaking, native QuickTime software uses big-endian addressing (because of its origins in the Mac OS), while most data accessed by Windows software is little-endian:

- *Big-endian* (also called *Motorola* or *Network* order)
  - ❑ Mac OS
  - ❑ Motorola and IBM PowerPC processors
  - ❑ Motorola 680x0 processors
  - ❑ Many RISC workstations (often big/little switchable)
- *Little endian* (also called *Intel* order)
  - ❑ Windows 95, Windows 98, Windows NT
  - ❑ Intel x86, Pentium, Celeron, and related processors
  - ❑ DEC Alpha processor

In general, data in a QuickTime movie is big-endian. While QuickTime can take care of most of the data contained in a QuickTime movie, data that is explicitly contained in atom containers will generally need to be flipped by your application. The QuickTime API documentation specifies the situations when an application is required to deal with this issue. QuickTime for Java provides a set of classes that are context-sensitive. See Chapter 8, "Creating, Editing, and Importing QuickTime Movies," for an example where endian conversion is used.

THE QUICKTIME COMPONENT ARCHITECTURE

QuickTime is highly modular in its architectural design. It is made up of more than 200 discrete components, each of which performs a specific task and has specific interfaces to other components. QuickTime's components fall into a number of different categories:

- *Media handlers* interpret and manipulate a media's sample data in various formats.

- *Capture* components include video digitizers and sequence grabbers with their associated channel and panel components. They let you obtain digitized data from external sources, such as video and audio sources.

- *Movie data exchange* components let you import data from nonmovie sources (such as CD tracks) into QuickTime movies and export data to nonmovie formats.

- *Codecs* (compressor/decompressors) provide compression and decompression services for different media types.

- *Transcoders* translate data from one compressed format to another.

- *Effects* components provide real-time effects and transitions (such as wipes and dissolves) between images in QuickTime movies.

- *Video output* components let you send QuickTime video to devices that are not recognized as displays by the computer's operating system.

- *Graphics importers* display still images obtained from data in various formats.

- *Graphics exporters* create and display previews of QuickTime movie files.

- *Tween* components perform interpolations between values in various data types.

- *The sprite toolbox* and *sprite media handler* let you create and manipulate animated graphics called *sprites*.

- *Clock* components generate timing information and schedule time-based callback events.

This modularity is useful in several important ways. First, it provides a relatively clean programming model for an inherently complex technology. Second, it makes it easy to modify or update QuickTime's behavior. The interfaces and operating rules for most components are defined in QuickTime's detailed documentation. Using this information, you can write software to introduce a custom component and a module, and it will work with the rest of QuickTime.

GRAPHICS ENVIRONMENTS

The way in which QuickTime displays images on the screen is dependent on the characteristics of the graphics device used to present the movies. Such factors as the device's pixel resolution, its color depth, and the capacity of its color table must be taken into account.

Ordinarily, the results of a program's drawing operations depend on the graphical capabilities of the display device connected to the user's computer at runtime. If there is more than one such device attached to the same system, QuickTime figures out which screen is being drawn to and displays all the results correctly, according to the characteristics of each device. This happens automatically and is transparent to the running program.

There may be times, however, when a program needs to take a more active role in controlling the graphics environment for its drawing operations. If you're creating a QuickTime movie, for instance, you probably don't want to define the movie's appearance in terms of the display characteristics of a particular graphics device. Rather, you want the movie's content to be device-independent, with its own inherent dimensions, pixel depth, colors, and so on. Then, when the movie is displayed on a user's computer, QuickTime automatically adapts its graphical characteristics to those of the available display device and presents the movie as faithfully as it can on the given device.

GRAPHICS PORTS

QuickTime uses QuickDraw's graphics structures when drawing on both Mac OS and Windows. This allows QuickTime routines to use QuickDraw calls internally for their drawing operations. To use QuickTime properly, you have to understand a little about QuickDraw.

The fundamental QuickDraw data structure is the *graphics port*. This is a complete drawing environment that specifies all of the parameters needed to control QuickDraw's drawing operations. The port includes such things as the size and location of the line-drawing pen; colors and patterns (like brushes in Windows) for drawing, area fill, and background; the font, size, and style for text display; clipping boundaries; and so forth. All of this information is held in a data structure of type CGrafPort. See *Mac OS for QuickTime Programmers* for a complete description of this data structure and its contents.

The main purpose of a graphics port is to serve as the environment in which to perform QuickDraw graphics operations. Unlike the Windows GDI routines, which always accept a device context as an explicit parameter, most QuickTime QuickDraw routines operate implicitly on the *current port*. At any given time, exactly one graphics port is current. Graphics ports are intimately associated with windows on the screen; the current port for QuickDraw drawing operations is typically a window.

GRAPHICS WORLDS

A *graphics world* is a device-independent environment for preparing images before displaying them on the screen. A graphics world (often called a GWorld) combines a graphics port and a device record, which together completely determine the graphics environment in which QuickTime does its drawing. The data structure representing a graphics world is an extended graphics port with some additional fields appended at the end. The exact details are private to QuickTime. Because the underlying structure is based on a graphics port, however, this pointer is equated to a graphics port pointer.

This means that a graphics world can be used anywhere a graphics port would be expected: for instance, as an argument to the MacSetPort function that sets the current port for subsequent drawing operations.

A graphics world's device record can represent an existing physical graphics device, but it need not. It can also describe a fictitious "offscreen" device with any graphical characteristics you choose. All of QuickTime's objects that draw expect to draw into a destination graphics port, whether this is onscreen (a CGrafPort) or offscreen (a GWorld).

Sound

As is the case with video data, QuickTime movies store sound information in tracks. QuickTime movies may have one or more sound tracks. The Movie Toolbox can play more than one sound at a time by mixing the enabled sound tracks together during playback. This allows you to put together movies with separate music and audio tracks. You can then manipulate the tracks separately but play them together.

There are two main attributes of sound in QuickTime movies: volume and balance. You can control these attributes using the facilities of the Movie Toolbox.

The volume setting controls the loudness of the movie's sound. Every QuickTime movie has a current volume setting which you can adjust. In addition, you can set a preferred volume setting for a movie. The Movie Toolbox saves this value when you store a movie into a movie file. When you load a movie from a movie file, the Movie Toolbox sets the movie's current volume to its preferred volume.

Each track in a movie also has a volume setting. A track's volume governs its loudness relative to other tracks in the movie.

In the Movie Toolbox, movie and track volumes are represented as 16-bit, fixed-point numbers that range from -1.0 to $+1.0$. Positive values denote volume settings, with 1.0 corresponding to the unity gain on the user's computer. Negative values are muted, but they retain the magnitude of the volume setting so that, by toggling the sign of a volume setting, you can turn off the sound and then turn it back on at the previous level (something like pressing the mute button on a remote control).

A track's volume is scaled to a movie's volume, and the movie's volume is scaled to the value the user specifies for speaker volume using the Sound control panel. That is, a movie's volume setting represents the maximum loudness of any track in the movie. If you set a track's volume to a value less than 1.0, that track plays proportionally quieter, relative to the volume of other tracks in the movie.

Each track in a movie has its own balance setting. The balance setting controls the mix of sound in a stereo field. If the source sound is stereo, the balance setting governs the mix of the right and left channels. When you save the movie, the balance setting is stored in the movie file.

In the Movie Toolbox, balance values are represented as 16-bit, fixed-point numbers that range from –1.0 to +1.0. Negative values weight the balance toward the left speaker; positive values emphasize the right speaker. Setting the balance to 0 corresponds to a neutral setting.

ADDING SOUND TO VIDEO

Most QuickTime movies contain both sound data and video data. If you are creating an application that plays movies, you do not need to worry about the details of how sound is stored in a movie. However, if you are developing an application that creates movies, you need to consider how you store the sound data.

There are two ways to store sound data in a QuickTime movie. The simplest method is to store the sound track as a continuous stream. For larger movies, a technique called *interleaving* must be used so that the sound and video data may be alternated in small pieces and the data can be read off disk as it is needed. Interleaving allows for movies of almost any length with little delay on startup. However, you must tune the storage parameters to avoid a lower video frame rate and breaks in the sound that result when sound data is read from slow storage devices.

In general, the Movie Toolbox hides the details of interleaving from your application. The `FlattenMovie` and `FlattenMovieData` functions allow you to enable and disable interleaving when you create a movie. These functions then interact with the appropriate media handlers to correctly interleave the sound and video data for your movie. For more information about working with sound, see *Inside Macintosh: Sound*.

QUICKTIME MUSIC ARCHITECTURE

The QuickTime API provides a highly sophisticated music architecture (QTMA). Among its many features, it lets you

- create and play notes and sequences of notes

- synthesize instruments in software of virtually any description, with fine control of their timbre, attack, velocity, duration, and other characteristics

- import MIDI into QuickTime movies, including any number of parts playing simultaneously

- access a wide variety of synthesizers through a hardware-independent interface

- play sounds through the sound capabilities of any PC or Macintosh computer

- work with MIDI devices of all kinds

- convert sound data from one format to another

The QuickTime Music Architecture is implemented as Component Manager components, which is the standard mechanism that QuickTime uses to provide extensibility.

Different QTMA components are used by a QuickTime movie, depending on if you are playing music or sounds through the computer's built-in audio device, or if you are controlling, for example, a MIDI synthesizer. During playback of a QuickTime movie, the music media handler component isolates your application and the Movie Toolbox from the details of how to actually play a music track and allows the user to specify through the QuickTime Settings control panel whether the built-in software synthesizer or an external MIDI synthesizer is used. The task of processing the data in a music track is taken care of for you by the media handler through Movie Toolbox calls.

OVERVIEW OF QTMA COMPONENTS

The QuickTime Music Architecture includes the following components:

- the note allocator, which plays individual musical notes

- the tune player, which plays sequences of musical notes

- the music media handler, which processes data in music tracks of QuickTime movies

- the QuickTime Music Synthesizer, a software-based music synthesizer included with QuickTime, which plays sounds using the built-in audio of a Macintosh or the sound card or built-in audio circuitry of other computers

- the General MIDI synthesizer, which plays music on a General MIDI device connected to the computer

- the MIDI synthesizer component, which controls a MIDI synthesizer connected to the computer using a single MIDI channel

- other music components that provide interfaces to specific synthesizers

Figure 2.11 illustrates the relationships among the various QTMA components.

FIGURE 2.11 *QTMA components and their various relationships*

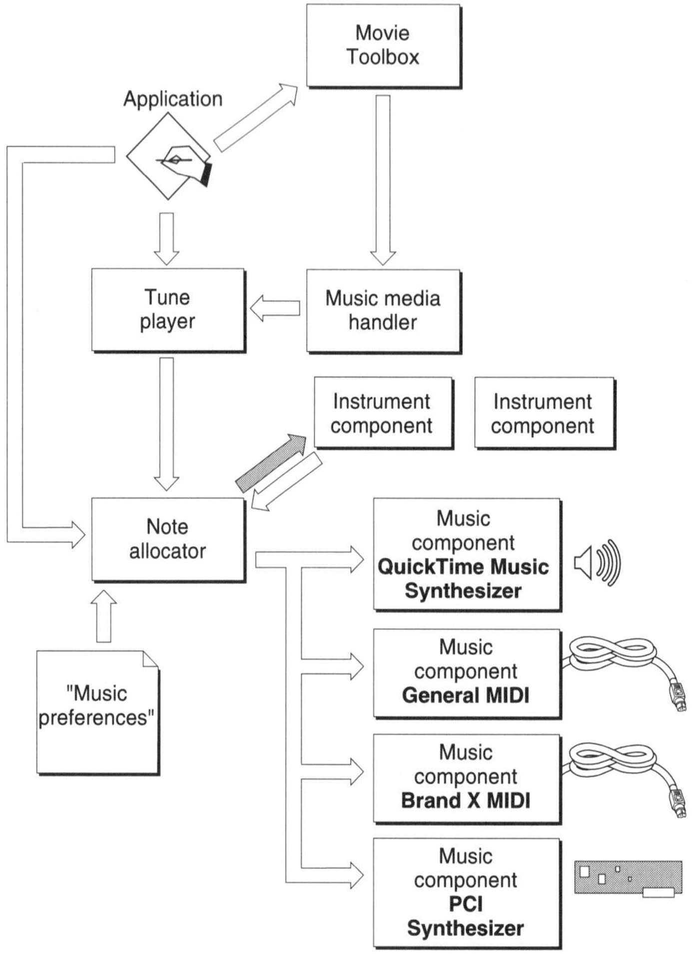

NOTE ALLOCATOR COMPONENT

You use the *note allocator component* to play individual notes. Your application can specify which musical instrument sound to use for a particular note channel and exactly which music synthesizer to play the notes on. The note allocator component can also display an Instrument Picker, which allows the user to choose instruments. The note allocator, unlike the tune player, provides no timing-related features to manage a sequence of notes. It provides the raw capability to turn notes on and off and control various parameters such as volume, pitch blend, and modulation of individual notes as they are playing.

To play a single note, your application must open a connection to the note allocator component and call NANewNoteChannel with a note request to request a particular instrument. A note channel is similar in some ways to a Sound Manager sound channel in that it needs to be created and disposed of and can receive various commands. The note allocator and note channel components provide an application-level interface for requesting note channels with particular attributes. The client specifies the desired polyphony and the desired tone. The note allocator returns a note channel that best satisfies the request.

TUNE PLAYER COMPONENT

The *tune player component* can accept entire sequences of musical notes and play them start to finish, asynchronously, with no further need for application intervention. It can also play portions of a sequence. An additional sequence or sequence section may be queued up while one is currently being played. Queuing sequences provides a seamless way to transition between sections.

The tune player negotiates with the note allocator to determine which music component to use and allocates the necessary note channels. The tune player handles all aspects of timing, as defined by the sequence of *music events.* The tune player also provides services to set the volume, to control the mixing parameters of a particular part, and to stop and restart an active sequence.

A tune player can be used directly by an application assembling the appropriate music data. The tune player is also used by the music media handler to play the stored music data of a music media track in a movie.

SYNTHESIZER COMPONENTS

Individual music components act as device drivers for each type of synthesizer attached to a particular computer. Three music components are included in QuickTime:

- the QuickTime Music Synthesizer component, for playing music out of a computer's built-in audio capabilities

- the General MIDI synthesizer component, for playing music on a General MIDI device attached to the computer

- the MIDI synthesizer component, which allows QuickTime to control a particular synthesizer that is connected to a single MIDI channel

You can add other music components for specific hardware and software synthesizers.

Applications do not usually call synthesizer components directly. Instead, the note allocator or tune player handles synthesizer component interactions. Synthesizer components are mainly of interest to application developers who want to access the low-level functionality of synthesizers and for developers of synthesizers (internal cards, MIDI devices, or software algorithms) who want to make the capabilities of their synthesizers available to QuickTime.

In order for an application to call a synthesizer component directly, you must first allocate a note channel and then use `NAGetNoteChannelInfo` and `NAGetRegisteredMusicDevice` to get the specific music component and part number.

You can use music component functions to

- obtain specific information about a synthesizer

- find an instrument that best fits a requested type of sound

- play a note with a specified pitch and volume

- change knob values to alter instrument sounds

SPRITES AND SPRITE ANIMATION

A *sprite* is an animated graphic created by QuickTime. With traditional video animation, you describe a frame by specifying the color of each pixel in it, and the source data for video tracks are generally some form of external video, film, or DVD data. With sprite animation, you describe a frame by specifying the images that appear at various locations. Sprites may be parts of movies or they may exist independently. A sprite in a movie is defined by its own track. Using sprites in QuickTime, you can

- create animated figures

- integrate sprites into QuickTime movies as animated sequences, overlays, buttons, or images combined with existing video

- dynamically convert images from bitmaps, MPEG, or live video into sprite figures

- detect user actions (such as mouse clicks) on "wired" sprites

A sprite has *properties* that describe its location and appearance at a given point in time. During the course of an animation, you modify a sprite's properties to cause it to change its appearance and move around. Each sprite has a corresponding *image*. During the animation, you can change a sprite's image. For example, you can assign a series of images to a sprite in succession to perform cell-based animation.

A *sprite world* is a graphics world for a sprite animation. To create a sprite animation in an application, you must first create a sprite world. You do not need to create a sprite world to create a sprite track in a QuickTime movie. Once you have created a sprite world, you create sprites associated with that sprite world. You can think of a sprite world as a stage on which your sprites perform. When you dispose of a sprite world, its associated sprites are disposed of as well.

SPRITE MEDIA HANDLERS

The sprite media handler is a media handler that makes it possible to add a track containing a sprite animation to a QuickTime movie. The sprite media handler provides routines for manipulating the sprites and images in a sprite track. The sprite media handler makes use of routines provided by the sprite toolbox.

As with sprites created in a sprite world, sprites in a sprite track have properties that define their locations, images, and appearance. However, you create the sprite track and its sprites differently than you create the sprites in a sprite world.

A *sprite track* is defined by one or more key frame samples, each followed by any number of override samples. A key frame sample and its subsequent override samples define a scene in the sprite track. A key frame sample is a QT atom container that contains atoms defining the sprites in the scene and their initial properties. The override samples are other QT atom containers that contain atoms that modify sprite properties, thereby animating the sprites in the scene.

WIRED SPRITES

In QuickTime, you can take advantage of *wired sprites*. Wired sprites extend QuickTime's interactive capabilities, enabling you to create movies that respond to user interaction. For example, you may "wire" sprite buttons to a QuickTime movie, so that the buttons link to specific URLs, start or stop the movie, or play a custom sound when pressed. These interactive movies can then be played in any Web browser using the QuickTime plug-in and in all applications as long as they use the QuickTime movie controller API.

When you wire a sprite track, you add *actions* to it. These actions are not provided only by sprite tracks. In principle, you can "wire" any QuickTime media handler. Wired sprite tracks may be the only tracks in a movie, but they are commonly used in concert with other types of tracks. Actions associated with sprites in a sprite track, for example, can control the audio volume and balance of an audio track or the graphics mode of a video track.

Wired sprite tracks can also be used to implement a graphical user interface for an application. Applications can find out when actions are executed and respond however they wish. For example, a CD audio controller application could use an action sprite track to handle its graphics and user interface.

SPRITE TRACK AND SPRITE WORLD LOCAL COORDINATE SYSTEM

A sprite's *local coordinate system*—where a sprite is displayed within a sprite world or a sprite track—is defined by the sprite's matrix and its image's registration point. This is the coordinate system, shown in Figure 2.12, that results when the sprite world's matrix and the movie matrix are both ignored. The origin is the sprite world's upper left corner.

For example, if a sprite's matrix contains a horizontal translation of 50 and a vertical translation of 25, the sprite will be positioned such that its current image's registration point is located 50 pixels to the right of the sprite world's left side, and 25 pixels down from the top of the sprite world.

For sprites in a sprite world, the registration point is always 0,0 of the sprite's matrix. The sprite media handler has the capability to set a different location for the registration point.

FIGURE 2.12 *A local coordinate system of a sprite*

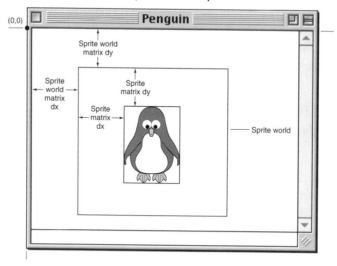

Source Box

A sprite's source box, as shown in Figure 2.13, is defined as a rectangle with a top-left point of (0,0) and its width and height set to the width and height of the sprite's current image. When a sprite is translated to a location by setting the x and y translation elements of its source matrix, the sprite's upper left corner is placed at the given location.

FIGURE 2.13 *A sprite's source box*

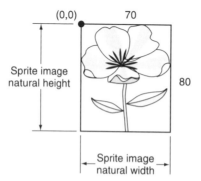

FIGURE 2.14   *A bounding box in a sprite track's local coordinate system*

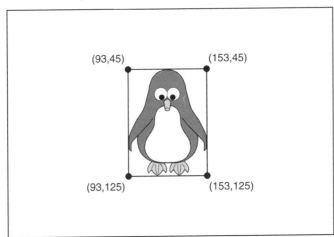

Sprite's Bounding Box

A sprite's bounding box and its four corners are both expressed in its local coordinate system. The bounding box of a sprite, shown in Figure 2.14, is the smallest rectangle that encloses the sprite's area after its matrix is applied. If a sprite is only translated, its bounding box will have the same dimensions as its source box. However, if the sprite is rotated 45 degrees, the bounding box may be larger than its source box.

Sprite's Four Corners

Some sprite actions and operands refer to a sprite's "four corners." These four corners are expressed in its local coordinate system. They are the points derived by taking the four corners of the sprite's source box and applying the current image's registration point and the sprite's source matrix. The first corner is the top left; the second corner is the top right; the third corner is the bottom right, and the fourth corner is the bottom left. Figure 2.15 shows a rotated bounding box in a sprite's local coordinate system.

FIGURE 2.15 *The rotated bounding box becomes the sprite's four corners*

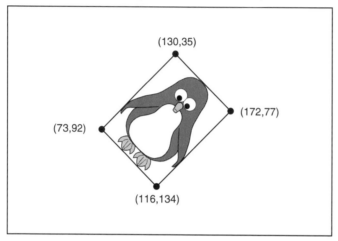

Registration Points and the Sprite Media Handler

QuickTime defines sprite image *registration points*. These image registration points, shown in Figure 2.16, define an offset that is applied to a sprite's source matrix. A sprite's default registration point is (0,0), or the top left of its source box. The sprite world and sprite only support a 0,0 registration point. However, the sprite media handler has capabilities for an application to define a custom registration point for individual sprites and their image data.

Figure 2.16 shows the same sprite displaying three different-sized images. As you can see, this changes the size of the sprite, and the image is drawn from this default registration point of 0,0.

FIGURE 2.16 *Default sprite image registration points*

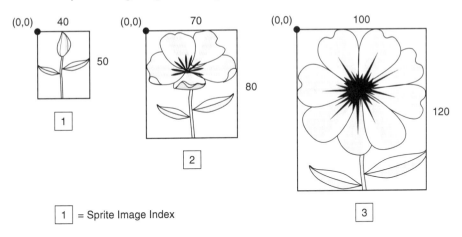

TWEENING

A tween operation lets you algorithmically generate an output value for any point in a time interval. The input for a tween is a small number of values, often as few as one or two, from which a range of values can be derived. You can use output from a tween to modify tracks in a QuickTime movie. You can also use the output values in your application to perform other actions, unrelated to movies.

SEQUENCE GRABBING AND VIDEO CAPTURE

Sequence grabber components allow you to obtain digitized data from sources that are external to a computer. For example, you can use a sequence grabber component to record video data from a video digitizer. Your application can then request that the sequence grabber store the captured video data in a QuickTime movie. In this way, you can acquire movie data from various sources that can augment the movie data you create by other means, such as computer animation. You can also use sequence grabber components to obtain and display data from external sources without saving the captured data in a movie. The sequence grabber component provided by Apple allows you to capture both audio and video data easily, without concern for the details of how the data is acquired.

When capturing video data, the sequence grabber uses a video digitizer component to supply the digitized video images. When working with audio data, Apple's sequence grabber component retrieves its sound data from a sound input device.

Sequence grabber components use sequence grabber channel components (or, simply, channel components) to obtain data from the audio- or video-digitizing equipment. These components isolate the sequence grabber from the details of working with the various types of data that can be collected. The features that a sequence grabber component supplies are dependent on the services provided by sequence grabber channel components. The channel components, in turn, may use other components to interact with the digitizing equipment. You can use the sequence grabber component to play captured data for the user or to save captured data in a QuickTime movie. The sequence grabber component provides functions that give you precise control over the display of the captured data.

PREVIEWING AND RECORDING CAPTURED DATA

You can use sequence grabber components in one of two ways: either to play digitized data for the user or to save captured data in a QuickTime movie. The process of displaying data that is to be captured is called *previewing*; saving captured data in a movie is called *recording*.

You can use previewing to allow the user to prepare to make a recording. If you do so, your application can move directly from the preview operation to a record operation, without stopping the process.

RECORDING

During a record operation, a sequence grabber component collects the data it captures and formats that data into a QuickTime movie. During recording, the sequence grabber can also play the captured data for the user. The sequence grabber tries to prevent the playback from interfering with the quality of the recording process. Figure 2.17 illustrates the process of capturing and playing a movie.

FIGURE 2.17 *Capturing and playing back movies*

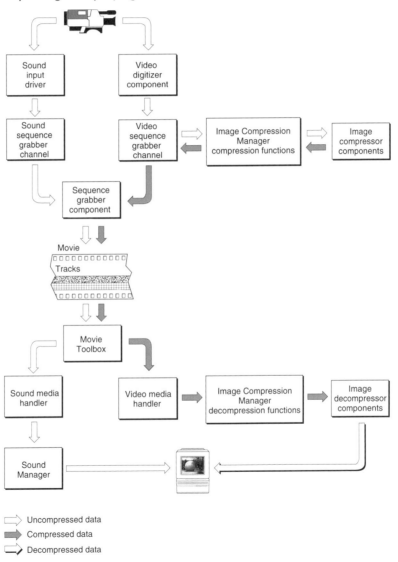

STORING CAPTURED DATA IN MULTIPLE FILES

In QuickTime, the sequence grabber allows a single capture session to store the captured data across multiple files. Each channel of a capture can be placed in a separate file. In this way, sound and video can be captured to separate files, even on separate devices. It is also possible to have a single capture session place its data on several different devices in sequence. As a result, several different devices can be used in a single capture session. This enables data capture to exceed any file size limitation imposed by a file system.

GRAPHICS IMPORTER AND EXPORTER COMPONENTS

In QuickTime, graphics importer components provide a standard mechanism for applications to open and display still images contained within graphics files. They also allow you to work with any type of image data, regardless of the file format or compression used in the file. You specify the file that contains the image and the destination rectangle that the image should be drawn into, and QuickTime handles the rest.

SUPPORTED IMAGE FILE FORMATS

QuickTime supports a wide range of image file formats: GIF, JFIF/JPEG, BMP, PNG, Targa, and TIFF, as well as those that are native to QuickDraw, QuickTime, MacPaint, Photoshop, Silicon Graphics, and QuickDraw GX. QuickTime 4 adds support for the FlashPix file format on Macintosh and Windows platforms.

BASE GRAPHICS EXPORTER

QuickTime provides a base graphics export component, which provides abstractions that greatly simplify the work of format-specific graphics exporter components, while offering applications a rich interface.

The input image for an export operation can come from a Quick-Draw Picture, a GWorld or PixMap, a QuickTime graphics importer component instance, or a segment of compressed data described by a QuickTime image description. In the last case, the compressed data may be accessed via a pointer, handle, file, or other data reference. The output image for an export operation can be stored in memory, a file, or other data reference. Different image file formats support a wide range of configurable features, such as depth, resolution, and compression quality.

How Graphics Export Components Work

Format-specific graphics exporters, such as the exporters for JPEG, PNG, and TIFF, are relatively simple components. When a format-specific exporter is opened, it opens and targets an instance of the base graphics exporter. Subsequently, it delegates most of its calls to the base exporter instance. The base exporter communicates with data handler components to negotiate access to image file data. If necessary, it calls the Image Compression Manager to perform compression operations.

QUICKTIME VR

The data for a QuickTime VR virtual world is stored in a QuickTime VR movie. A QuickTime VR movie contains a single scene, which is a collection of one or more nodes. A *node* is a position in a virtual world at which an object or panorama can be viewed. For a panoramic node, the position of the node is the point from which the panorama is viewed. QuickTime VR scenes can contain any number of nodes, which can be either object or panoramic nodes.

Note that QuickTime uses the term *movie* to emphasize the time-based nature of QuickTime data (such as video and audio data streams). QuickTime VR uses the same term solely as an analogy with QuickTime movies; in general, QuickTime VR data is not time-based.

An *object* node provides a view of a single object or a closely grouped set of objects. You can think of an object node as providing a view of an object from the outside looking in. The user can use the mouse or keyboard to change the horizontal and vertical viewing angles to move around the object. The user can also zoom in or out to enlarge or reduce the size of the displayed object. Object nodes are often designed to give the illusion that the user is picking up and turning an object and viewing it from all angles. Figure 2.18 illustrates the pan and tilt angles of an object view.

A panoramic node provides a panoramic view of a particular location, such as you would get by turning around on a rotating stool. You can think of a panoramic node as providing a view of a location from the inside looking out. As with object nodes, the user can use the mouse (or keyboard) to navigate in the panorama and to zoom in and out. QuickTime VR panoramas are often made by the process of stitching together photographs that capture a 360 degree view of a location from a central point.

FIGURE 2.18 *Pan and tilt angles of a virtual reality object*

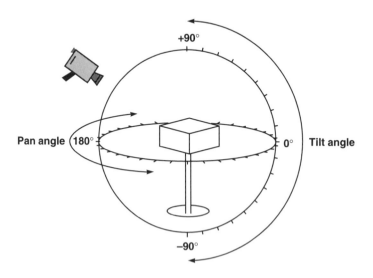

QuickDraw 3D

QuickDraw 3D is a graphics library developed by Apple Computer that you can use to create, configure, and render three-dimensional objects. It is specifically designed to be useful to a wide range of software developers, from those with very little knowledge of 3D modeling concepts and rendering techniques to those with very extensive experience with those concepts and techniques.

At the most basic level, you can use the file format and file-access routines provided by QuickDraw 3D to read and display 3D graphics created by another application. For example, a word-processing application might want to import a picture created by a 3D modeling or image-capturing application. QuickDraw 3D supports the 3D Viewer, which you can use to display 3D data and objects in a window and allow users limited interaction with that data, without having to learn any of the core QuickDraw 3D application programming interfaces.

You can also use QuickDraw 3D for more sophisticated applications, such as interactive 3D modeling and rendering, animation, and data visualization. To create images, you typically engage in at least two main tasks: modeling and rendering. *Modeling* is the process of creating a representation of real or abstract objects, while *rendering* is the process of creating an image (on the screen or some other medium) of a model. QuickDraw 3D subdivides each of these tasks into a number of subtasks.

QuickDraw 3D defines a platform-independent metafile format—3DMF—for storing and interchanging 3D data. 3DMF is intended to provide a standard format according to which applications can read and write 3D data, even applications that use 3D graphics systems other than QuickDraw 3D. QuickDraw 3D itself includes routines that you can use to read and write data in the metafile format. Apple also supplies a parser that you can use to read and write metafile data on operating systems that do not support QuickDraw 3D.

3

Integrating QuickTime with Java

As we've seen in Chapter 1, QuickTime for Java represents a library of classes that are designed to bring the power and functionality of QuickTime to Java. The core library of these classes provides you with the ability to access many features and capabilities in the QuickTime API. The second set of classes—an Application Framework—lets you integrate those capabilities into your Java programs.

This chapter discusses how that integration works. The topics discussed include the following:

- a brief introduction to some Java terminology

- grouping QuickTime for Java classes into a set of packages based on common functionality and usage

- classes in the Application Framework built on top of QuickTime for Java native binding classes

- the `QTSimpleApplet` and `PlayMovie` programs explained method by method

In this and the following chapters, many code listings are given that use the various QuickTime components and structures. A brief introduction to QuickTime is given and its major components and structures discussed in Chapter 2, "QuickTime Basics." More information is available in the various books and reference material for QuickTime that is presented on the CD-ROM at the back of this book and at the QuickTime website `http://www.apple.com/quicktime`, where the complete QuickTime reference documentation and SDK are available.

SOME JAVA TERMINOLOGY

If you're a C or C++ programmer, you'll need to understand some of the key terms in the Java programming language before proceeding with the QuickTime for Java API.

In Java, you can think of an *object* as a collection of data values, or *fields*. In addition, there are *methods* that operate on that data. The data type of an object is called a *class*; and an object is referred to as an *instance* of its class. In object-oriented programming, the class defines the type of each field in the object. The class also provides the methods that operate on data that is contained in an instance of the class. You create an object using the *new* keyword. This invokes a constructor method of the class to initialize the new object. You access the fields and methods of an object by using the dot (.) operator.

In Java, methods that operate on the object itself are known as *instance methods*. These are different from the *class* methods. Class methods are declared static; and they operate on the class itself rather than on an individual instance of the class. The fields of a class may also be declared static, which makes them *class fields* instead of *instance fields*. Each object that you instantiate in Java has its own copy of each instance field, but there is only one copy of a class field, which is shared by all instances of the class.

Fields and methods of a class may have different *visibility levels*, namely, public, protected, package, and private. These different levels allow fields and methods to be used in different ways.

Every class has a *superclass*. And from that superclass it inherits fields and methods. When a class inherits from another class, it is called a *subclass* of that class. This inheritance relationship forms what is known as a *class hierarchy*. The java.lang.Object class is the root class of all Java classes; Object is the ultimate superclass of all other classes in Java.

An *interface* is a Java construct that defines methods, like a class. However, it does *not* provide implementations for those methods. A class can implement an interface by defining an appropriate implementation for each of the methods in the interface. An interface expresses the methods an object can perform—what a class can do—while making no assumptions about how the object implements these methods.

When compiled, Java classes generate a class file that is a byte-coded representation of the class. When a Java program is run, these byte codes are interpreted and often compiled (with a Just-in-Time Compiler) into the native or machine code of the runtime environment and then executed. This is the part of the work done by the Java Virtual Machine (VM). These byte codes are platform-independent and can be executed on any platform that has a Java VM.

A method in a Java class can be declared to be a *native* method. A native method has no Java code; it assumes that the method is actually defined in a native library, typically in C. Native methods are used for a number of reasons: performance, access to native services provided by the operating system, and so on. In fact, many of the classes in the `java.*` packages contain native methods in order for the Java classes to intergrate with an existing operating system.

Part of the distribution of QuickTime for Java is a framework of classes. A package name (package and import) is a qualification that precedes the name of a class, i.e., it defines a name-space. The `java.*` packages are the standard set available on any distribution. QuickTime for Java uses `quicktime.*` to delineate the QuickTime for Java name-space.

You may want to refer to Appendix A for an explanation of the nomenclature that is used in the QuickTime for Java API. Appendix A also discusses some of the guidelines used in naming methods and classes.

A VIEW OF THE QUICKTIME TO JAVA INTEGRATION

Figure 3.1 illustrates a top-level view of the QuickTime to Java integration.

FIGURE 3.1 *The QuickTime and Java integration*

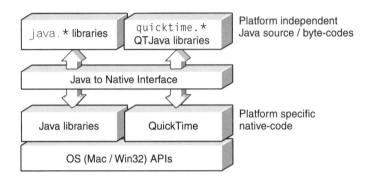

BINDING QUICKTIME FUNCTIONS TO JAVA METHODS

Java classes are created from structures and data types found in the standard QuickTime C language header files. These data types provide the basic class structure of the QuickTime for Java API. For example, the Movie data type in Movies.h becomes the Movie class. In general, the C function calls list the main data structure they operate on as the first parameter of the function. These calls become methods in this class. In line with Java conventions, all class names are capitalized, while method names are not.

Functions to Methods

The methods of a class are created from C functions. There is generally a one-to-one relationship between a native function call and a Java method. The Java method's name is derived by the following procedure:

The QuickTime native function

SetMovieGWorld

logically translates (or is bound by) the Java method

setGWorld on the Movie class.

The QuickTime native function

`MCSetControllerPort`

logically translates (or is bound by) the Java method

`setPort` on the `MovieController` class.

A complete list of the QuickTime functions that QuickTime for Java binds is provided on the CD-ROM at the back of this book. The java-doc-generated documentation in HTML, also on the CD-ROM, lists for each method the related QuickTime function call in **bold**. For example:

QuickTime::EnterMovies()

The supplied HTML documentation for these binding calls provides only brief descriptions. You need to refer to the QuickTime documentation both for specific details of a particular API, as well as for general discussions on the usage of particular services. QuickTime documentation is available on the QuickTime website.

GARBAGE COLLECTION

As Java has a built-in garbage collection mechanism, the QuickTime for Java classes perform their own memory management. There are no explicit dispose calls in the QuickTime for Java API. These calls are called by the objects themselves when they perform garbage collection. The `quicktime.util.QTUtils.reclaimMemory()` method requests that the garbage collector run and can be used to help ensure disposed of memory that is no longer referenced.

The QuickTime for Java API contains no direct access to pointers or other features that are common in a C-based API. The Java method calls provide very little overhead to the native call; they do parameter marshalling and check the result of the native call for any error conditions. If an error is returned by the native call, then an exception is thrown.

THREADS

Although Java is a multithreaded environment, the method calls that map a QuickTime function to a Java method do not provide any implicit synchronization support. If you share any QuickTime object between threads, you are responsible for dealing with any synchronization issues that may arise. The Java language provides easy services to let you do this by means of the following syntax as well as synchronized method calls:

```
synchronize (aJavaObject) { /*synchronized block of code*/ }
```

THE QUICKTIME FOR JAVA PACKAGE STRUCTURE

The QuickTime for Java classes are grouped into a set of packages. The grouping is based on common functionality and usage and on their organization in the standard QuickTime header files. The packages provide both an object model for the QuickTime API and a logical translation or binding of the native function calls into Java method calls. A number of packages also have subpackages that group together smaller sets of functionality.

The major packages generally have a constants interface that presents all of the constants that relate to this general grouping and an exception class that all errors that derive from a call in this package group will throw. The packages, with descriptions of their principal classes and interfaces, are shown in Table 3-1.

TABLE 3-1   *QuickTime for Java packages*

Package	Principal classes and interfaces	Description
quicktime	QTSession, QTException	The QTSession class has calls that set up and intialize the QuickTime engine, such as initialize, gestalt, and enterMovies.
quicktime.io	OpenFile, QTFile, OpenMovieFile, QTIOException	Contains calls that deal with file I/O. These calls are derived from the Movies.h file.
quicktime.qd	QDGraphics, PixMap, Region, QDRect, QDColor, QDConstants, QDException	Contains classes that represent the QuickDraw data structures that are required for the rest of the QuickTime API. These calls are derived from the QuickDraw.h and QDOffscreen.h files. The QuickTime API expects data structures that belong to QuickDraw, such as graphics ports, GWorlds, rectangles, and points.
quicktime.qd3d	CameraData, Q3Point, Q3Vector	Contains classes that represent the QuickDraw 3D data structures that are required for the rest of the QuickTime API, predominantly the tweener and 3D media services.
quicktime.sound	SndChannel, Sound, SPBDevice, SoundConstants, SoundException	Contains classes that represent the Sound Manager API. These calls are derived from the Sound.h file. While some basic sound recording services are provided, for more demanding sound input and output the sequence grabber components and movie playback services should be used.

3

Integrating QuickTime with Java

Package	Principal classes and interfaces	Description
quicktime.std	StdQTConstants, StdQTException	The original QuickTime interfaces on the Mac OS are contained in a collection of eight header files that describe the standard QuickTime API. As such, nearly all of the functions defined in these files are to be found in classes in the quicktime.std group of packages.
quicktime.std. anim	Sprite, SpriteWorld	Classes that provide support for animation. QuickTime can be used as a real-time rendering system for animation, distinct from a data format—that is, the movie. Thus, you can create a graphics space (SpriteWorld) within which characters (Sprite objects) can be manipulated.
quicktime.std. clocks	Clock, TimeBase, QTCallback **and** subclasses	Contains classes that provide timing services, including support for the creation of hierarchical dependencies between time bases, the usage of callbacks for user scheduling of events or notification, and the capability of instantiating the system clocks that provide the timing services.
quicktime.std. com	Component, Component-Description	QuickTime is a component-based architecture, with much of its funtionality being provided through the creation and implementation of a particular component's API. This package contains classes that provide basic support for this component architecture; a full implementation is forthcoming.

Package	Principal classes and interfaces	Description
quicktime.std. image	CodecComponent, QTImage, CSequence, Matrix	Contains classes that present the Image Compression Manager. These classes provide control for the compression and decompression of both single images and sequences of images. It also contains the Matrix class, which (like the Region class in the qd package) is used generally throughout QuickTime to alter and control the rendering of 2D images.
quicktime.std. movies	AtomContainer, Movie, MovieController, Track	Contains the principal data structures of QuickTime, including classes that represent QuickTime atom containers, movies, movie controllers, and tracks—all essential for creating and manipulating QuickTime movies. A movie containing one or more tracks is the primary way that data is organized and managed in QuickTime. A Movie object can be created from a file or from memory and can be saved to a file. The MovieController class provides the standard way that QuickTime data (movies) are presented and controlled. AtomContainer objects are the standard data structures used to store and retrieve data in QuickTime.
quicktime.std. movies.media	DataRef, Media and subclasses, MediaHandler and subclasses, Sample Description and subclasses	A Track object is a media neutral structure, but it contains a single Media type that defines the kind of data that a Track is representing. The Media, MediaHandler and SampleDescription subclasses describe the various media types that QuickTime can present. Media classes control references to data that comprise the raw media data.

Package	Principal classes and interfaces	Description
quicktime.std. music	AtomicInstrument, NoteChannel, NoteAllocator	Contains classes that deal with the general music architecture provided by QuickTime. This architecture can be used to capture and generate music (MIDI) events in real time, customize and create instruments, and eventually provide your own algorithmic synthesis engines.
quicktime.std. qtcomponets	MovieExporter, MovieImporter, TimeCoder	Contains classes that interface with some of the components that are provided to supply different services. The import and export components are supported, as are tween and timecode media components.
quicktime.std.sg	SequenceGrabber, SGVideoChannel, SGSoundChannel	Contains classes that implement the sequence grabber component for capturing video and audio media data.
quicktime.util	QTHandle, QTByteObject, QTPointer, UtilException	Contains classes that represent utility functionality required by the general QuickTime API. The most commonly used feature of this package is set of classes for memory management from Memory.h. These classes typically form the base class for actual QuickTime objects.
quicktime.vr	QTVRConstants, QTVRInstance, QTVRException	Contains classes that represent the QuickTime Virtual Reality API. The package contains all the QuickTime VR interface constants, the QTVRInstance class and some QTVR callbacks for presentation of QTVR content.

QuickTime Headers and Java Classes

As we've seen, Java classes are created from structures and data types found in the standard QuickTime C language header files. These provide the basic class structure of the QuickTime for Java API. The original QuickTime interfaces on the Mac OS are contained in a collection of eight header files that describe the standard QuickTime API. As such, nearly all of the functions defined in these files are to be found in classes in the `quicktime.std` group of packages.

The standard QuickTime C header files with their corresponding packages in the QuickTime for Java API are shown in Table 3-2.

TABLE 3-2 *C header files and corresponding QuickTime for Java packages*

QuickTime C header files	Description
`Components.h`	Calls from this file are in the `quicktime.std.comp` package.
`ImageCompression.h` and `ImageCodec.h`	Calls from this file are in the `quicktime.std.image` package.
`MediaHandlers.h`	Not required in QuickTime for Java.
`Movies.h`	This file has been separated into a number of packages to present a finer degree of definition and functional grouping. Sprite animation calls are in the `quicktime.std.anim` package. Callback and time-base calls are in the `quicktime.std.clocks` package. File I/O calls are in the `quicktime.io` package. All media-related calls are in the `quicktime.std.movies.media` package. Movies, movie controllers, tracks, and atom containers are in the `quicktime.std.movies` package.

QuickTime C header files	Description
MoviesFormat.h	Not required in QuickTime for Java.
QuickTimeComponents.h	This file has been separated into a number of packages to present a finer degree of definition and functional grouping. The clocks component is found in the quicktime.std.clocks package. Sequence grabber components calls are found in the quicktime.std.sg package. The remaining components are found in the quicktime.std.qtcomponents package.
QuickTimeMusic.h	All calls from this file are in the quicktime.std.music package.

THE APPLICATION FRAMEWORK

The classes in the QuickTime for Java Application Framework are built entirely on top of QuickTime for Java native binding classes.

The Application Framework classes are designed to simplify the usage of the QuickTime for Java API and to provide a close integration with Java's display and event distribution system. They offer a set of services that are commonly used by QuickTime programs. In addition, they provide useful abstractions and capabilities that make the use of these services simpler and easier for the developer.

The Framework itself is also designed with reusability and extensibility of classes in mind. It uses Java interfaces to express some of the functionality that can be shared or is common among different classes. You can also implement your own versions of these interfaces, or extend existing implementations, to more specifically meet a particular requirement, and in so doing, use these custom classes with other classes of the Framework itself. Table 3-3 describes the various Framework packages and their principal classes.

TABLE 3-3   *QuickTime for Java Application Framework packages*

Package	Description
quicktime.app	Provides a set of "factory" methods for creating classes that you can use to present media that QuickTime can import. In addition, it provides some utility methods for finding directories and files in the local file system.
quicktime.app.action	Contains a large number of useful controller classes for mouse drags and for handling mouse events. It also contains action classes that can be used to apply actions to target objects.
quicktime.app.anim	Contains classes that present all of the functionality of the Sprite and SpriteWorld.
quicktime.app.audio	Contains a number of interfaces and classes that deal specifically with the audio capabilities of QuickTime.
quicktime.app.display	Contains a number of classes that are important for using the QuickTime for Java API. QTCanvas and QTDrawable negotiate with java.awt classes to allow the presentation of QuickTime content within a Java window or display space.
quicktime.app.image	Handles the presentation and manipulation of images. Included are utility classes for setting transparent colors in images, applying visual effects, creating objects for handling sequences of images, and QTDrawable objects that read image data from a file or load the data into memory.
quicktime.app.players	QTPlayer and MoviePlayer define a set of useful methods that enables you to present QuickTime movies, using QTCanvas objects and the QTDrawable interface.
quicktime.app.sg	Contains a single class, SGDrawer.
quicktime.app.spaces	Interfaces in this package provide a uniform means of dealing with a collection of objects in QuickTime for Java.
quicktime.app.time	Provides a set of useful classes to handle timing services used to schedule regular tasks that need to be performed on an ongoing basis.

THE QTSIMPLEAPPLET

The sample code on the accompanying CD-ROM includes QTSimpleApplet, a QuickTime for Java applet you can create that presents any of the media file formats that QuickTime supports. QuickTime includes support for a vast array of common file formats: QuickTime movies (including QuickTime VR), pictures, sounds, MIDI, and QuickDraw 3D.

The applet tag for this applet is

```
<applet code="QTSimpleApplet.class" width=200 height=100>
    <param name="file" value="media/crossfad.gif">
</applet>
```

The test.html file on the CD-ROM contains the complete HTML listing, including the use of a JavaScript script to generate the appropriate tag. The QTSimpleApplet code takes any of the media file types supported by QuickTime as a parameter in the HTML applet tag and creates the appropriate object for that media type:

```
param name=file value="MyMediaFile.xxx"
```

The QTCanvas, QTDrawable, and QTFactory classes, which are part of the QTSimpleApplet code, are discussed in greater detail in Chapter 4, "QTCanvas, QTDrawable, and QTFactory."

As with all Java applets, we begin in the QTSimpleApplet code by declaring a list of Java packages and QuickTime for Java packages that contain the required classes you need to import:

```
import java.applet.Applet;
import java.awt.*;
import quicktime.QTSession;
import quicktime.io.QTFile;

import quicktime.app.QTFactory;
import quicktime.app.display.QTCanvas;
import quicktime.app.display.Drawable;
import quicktime.QTException;
```

To get the resources for the simple applet and set up the environment, including the creation of the QTCanvas object, you use the init() method, as shown in the snippet below. QTCanvas is the object responsible for handling the integration from the java.awt side between Java and QuickTime. The QTCanvas also has parameters that let you control the resizing of the client that it presents. In this case, we tell the canvas to center the client within the space given by the applet's layout manager. This ensures that the client is only as big as its initial size (or smaller if you make the canvas smaller).

The QTSession.open() call performs a gestalt check to make sure that QuickTime is present and is initialized. Note that this is a *required* call before any QuickTime for Java classes can be used:

```
public void init () {
    try {
        QTSession.open()
```

To set up a QTCanvas object that displays its content at its original size or smaller and is centered in the space given to the QTCanvas when the applet is laid out, we do the following:

```
        setLayout (new BorderLayout());
        myQTCanvas = new QTCanvas (QTCanvas.kInitialSize, 0.5F,
                0.5F);
        add (myQTCanvas, "Center");

        QTFile file = new QTFile (getCodeBase().getFile() +
                            getParameter("file"));
        myQTContent = QTFactory.makeDrawable (file);
    } catch (Exception e) {
        e.printStackTrace();
        . . .

    }
}
```

The QTFactory.makeDrawable() method is used to create an appropriate QuickTime object for the media that is specified in the <PARAM> tag.

If a QTException is thrown in the init() method, an appropriate action should be taken by the applet, depending on the error reported.

In the start() method shown in the next code snippet, you set the client of the QTCanvas. This QTCanvas.client is the QuickTime object (i.e., an object that implements the QTDrawable interface) that draws to the area of the screen that the QTCanvas occupies. This is the QuickTime side of the integration between Java and QuickTime:

```
public void start () {
    try { myQTCanvas.setClient (myQTContent, true);
    } catch (Exception e) {
        e.printStackTrace();
    }
}
```

You use the stop() method to remove the client from the QTCanvas. It will be reset in the start() method if the applet is restarted. destroy() is used to close the QTSession. This protocol enables the applet to be reloaded, suspended, and resumed—for example, if the user is leaving and returning to the page with the applet. The init()/destroy() and start()/stop() methods are reciprocal in their activities:

```
public void stop () {
    myQTCanvas.removeClient();
}

public void destroy () {
    QTSession.close();
}
```

You need to call QTSession.close() if you have previously called QTSession.open() in order to shut down QuickTime properly.

The QTTestApplet on the accompanying CD-ROM at the back of this book lists a version of the simple applet that allows for the contingencies of QuickTime or QuickTime for Java not being present when an applet is launched. The init() method may throw exceptions because the required file was not found or the applet does not have permission from Java's security manager to read that file. Alternatively, the required version of QuickTime may not be installed. The applet should deal with these issues appropriately.

COMPARING QUICKTIME C AND JAVA CODE

Much of the sample code available for QuickTime is presented in the C programming language. Comparing Example 3.1 and Example 3.2 in C with the Java version shown in Example 3.3 can aid in understanding how to translate C to Java code.

GETTING A MOVIE FROM A FILE

Before your application can work with a movie, you must load the movie from its file. You must open the movie file and create a new movie from the movie stored in the file. You can then work with the movie. You use the OpenMovieFile function to open a movie file and the NewMovieFromFile function to load a movie from a movie file. The code in Example 3.1 shows how you can use these functions.

EXAMPLE 3.1 *Getting a movie from a file using C code*

```
Movie GetMovie (void)
{
    OSErr               err;
    SFTypeList          typeList = {MovieFileType,0,0,0};
    StandardFileReply   reply;
    Movie               aMovie = nil;
    short               movieResFile;

    StandardGetFilePreview (nil, 1, typeList, &reply);
    if (reply.sfGood)
    {
        err = OpenMovieFile (&reply.sfFile, &movieResFile,
                        fsRdPerm);

        if (err == noErr)
        {
```

```
        short movieResID = 0; /* want first movie */
        Str255 movieName;
        Boolean wasChanged;
        err = NewMovieFromFile (&aMovie, movieResFile,
                                &movieResID,
                                movieName,
                                newMovieActive, /* flags */
                                &wasChanged);
        CloseMovieFile (movieResFile);
    }
  }
  return aMovie;
}
```

The Movie Toolbox uses Alias Manager and File Manager functions to manage a movie's references to its data. A movie file does not necessarily contain the movie's data. The movie's data may reside in other files, which are referred to by the movie file. When your application instructs the Movie Toolbox to play a movie, the Toolbox attempts to collect the movie's data. If the movie has become separated from its data, the Movie Toolbox uses the Alias Manager to locate the data files. During this search, the Movie Toolbox automatically displays a dialog box. The user can cancel the search by clicking the Stop button.

The code in Example 3.2 shows the steps your application must follow in order to play a movie. This program retrieves a movie, sizes the window properly, plays the movie forward, and exits. This program uses the GetMovie function shown in Example 3.1 to retrieve a movie from a movie file.

EXAMPLE 3.2 *Playing a movie*

```
#include <Types.h>
#include <Traps.h>
#include <Menus.h>
#include <Fonts.h>
#include <Packages.h>
#include <GestaltEqu.h>
#include "Movies.h"
#include "ImageCompression.h"
```

```c
/* #include "QuickTimeComponents.h" */

#define doTheRightThing 5000

void main (void)
{
    WindowPtr aWindow;
    Rect windowRect;
    Rect movieBox;
    Movie aMovie;
    Boolean done = false;
    OSErr err;
    EventRecord theEvent;
    WindowPtr whichWindow;
    short part;

    InitGraf (&qd.thePort);
    InitFonts ();
    InitWindows ();
    InitMenus ();
    TEInit ();
    InitDialogs (nil);
    err = EnterMovies ();
    if (err) return;

    SetRect (&windowRect, 100, 100, 200, 200);
    aWindow = NewCWindow (nil, &windowRect, "\pMovie",
                        false, noGrowDocProc, (WindowPtr)-1,
                        true, 0);

    SetPort (aWindow);
    aMovie = GetMovie ();
    if (aMovie == nil) return;

    GetMovieBox (aMovie, &movieBox);
    OffsetRect (&movieBox, -movieBox.left, -movieBox.top);
    SetMovieBox (aMovie, &movieBox);

    SizeWindow (aWindow, movieBox.right, movieBox.bottom, true);
    ShowWindow (aWindow);

    SetMovieGWorld (aMovie, (CGrafPtr)aWindow, nil);
```

```
    StartMovie (aMovie);
while ( !IsMovieDone(aMovie) && !done )
{
    if (WaitNextEvent (everyEvent, &theEvent, 0, nil))
    {
        switch ( theEvent.what )
    {
            case updateEvt:
                whichWindow = (WindowPtr)theEvent.message;
                if (whichWindow == aWindow)
                {
                    BeginUpdate (whichWindow);
                    UpdateMovie(aMovie);
                    SetPort (whichWindow);
                    EraseRect (&whichWindow->portRect);
                    EndUpdate (whichWindow);
                }
                break;

            case mouseDown:
                part = FindWindow (theEvent.where,
                                        &whichWindow);
                if (whichWindow == aWindow)
                {
                    switch (part)
                    {
                        case inGoAway:
                            done = TrackGoAway (whichWindow,
                                                    theEvent.where);
                            break;
                        case inDrag:
                            DragWindow (whichWindow,
                                            theEvent.where,
                                            &qd.screenBits.bounds);
                            break;
                    }
                }
                break;
        }
}

            MoviesTask (aMovie, DoTheRightThing);
```

```
}
DisposeMovie (aMovie);
DisposeWindow (aWindow);
}
```

PLAYING A QUICKTIME MOVIE

Example 3.3 shows how to display any QuickTime content within a java.awt display space using the QTCanvas. It also demonstrates the use of the different resize options of the QTCanvas (with the alignment set to center it in the display space). You use the movie controller to select and then play a QuickTime movie, which can be a local file or a URL specified by the user.

You call QTSession.open() to perform a gestalt check to ensure that QuickTime is present and is initialized. This is a required call before any QuickTime Java classes can be used.

The window is the size of the movie and resizing the window will resize the movie. The QTCanvas is set to allow any size and is the central component in a java.awt.BorderLayout of its parent Frame.

You use the following methods to lay out and resize the Frame to the size of the Movie:

```
pm.pack();
pm.show();
pm.toFront();
```

You now prompt the user to select a movie file:

```
QTFile qtf = QTFile.standardGetFilePreview(QTFile.kStandardQTFileTypes);
```

You open the selected file and make a movie from it, using these calls:

```
OpenMovieFile movieFile = OpenMovieFile.asRead(qtf);
Movie m = Movie.fromFile (movieFile);
```

You construct a movie controller from the resultant movie, enabling the keys so the user can interact with the movie using the keyboard:

```
MovieController mc = new MovieController (m);
mc.setKeysEnabled (true);
```

You create a QTCanvas so that the MovieController has somewhere to draw and add it to the Frame:

```
QTCanvas myQTCanvas = new QTCanvas();
add (myQTCanvas);
```

You construct the QTDrawable object to present a movie controller:

```
QTPlayer myQTPlayer = new QTPlayer (mc);
```

Now you set it as the drawing client of the QTCanvas for a QTPlayer. This also registers interests for both mouse and key events that originate in the QTCanvas:

```
myQTCanvas.setClient (myQTPlayer, true);
```

You add a WindowListener to this frame that will close down the QTSession. Finally, you dispose of the Frame that closes down the window and you exit:

```
addWindowListener(new WindowAdapter () {
    public void windowClosing (WindowEvent e) {
        QTSession.close();
        dispose();
    }

    public void windowClosed (WindowEvent e) {
        System.exit(0);
    }
});
```

When the user closes the window, the program quits, first calling QTSession.close to terminate QuickTime. You need to call QTSession.close() if you have previously called QTSession.open() in order to shut down QuickTime properly. QTSession.close() is called before the canvas that the QuickTime object is attached to is disposed of. This enables QuickTime to clean up its graphics objects, which it attaches to the native implementation of the QTCanvas.

EXAMPLE 3.3 *PlayMovie.java*

```java
import java.awt.*;
import java.awt.event.*;

import quicktime.*;
import quicktime.io.*;
import quicktime.std.movies.*;
import quicktime.app.display.QTCanvas;
import quicktime.app.players.QTPlayer;

public class PlayMovie extends Frame {

    public static void main (String args[]) {
        try {
            QTSession.open ();
            PlayMovie pm = new PlayMovie("QT in Java");
            pm.pack();
            pm.show();
            pm.toFront();
        } catch (QTException e) {
                // handle errors
                . . .
        }
    }

    PlayMovie (String title) throws QTException {
        super (title);

        QTFile qtf = QTFile.standardGetFilePreview(QTFile.kStandardQTFileTypes);

        OpenMovieFile movieFile = OpenMovieFile.asRead(qtf);
        Movie m = Movie.fromFile (movieFile);

        MovieController mc = new MovieController (m);
        mc.setKeysEnabled (true);

        QTCanvas myQTCanvas = new QTCanvas();
        add (myQTCanvas);

        QTPlayer myQTPlayer = new QTPlayer (mc);
```

```
    myQTCanvas.setClient (myQTPlayer, true);

    addWindowListener(new WindowAdapter () {
        public void windowClosing (WindowEvent e) {
            QTSession.close();
            dispose();
        }

        public void windowClosed (WindowEvent e) {
            System.exit(0);
        }
    });
    }
}
```

SUMMARY COMPARISION

We've seen two bodies of code illustrated in several examples, one in C and the other in Java. In summary, we could note the following points:

■ Both pieces of code can open and play a vast number of media files.

■ The C code is specific to the Macintosh; the Windows version (not shown) is different—though only slightly. Of course, as an application in C is developed around QuickTime, more and more platform-specific code needs to be written, whereas with Java, a framework is provided that is a cross-platform API as well as a cross-platform execution model.

■ The Java code benefits from the Java class framework with which a developer may already be familiar.

■ Java runs anywhere, unchanged, so long as QuickTime is available. As other client operating systems gain QuickTime support, the QuickTime for Java code will run there, too.

■ The Java code is arguably simpler.

4 QTCanvas, QTDrawable, and QTFactory

This chapter discusses the usage of two principal classes and one principal interface in the QuickTime for Java API. These are the QTCanvas, QTDrawable, and QTFactory. As we saw in the Chapter 3, "Integrating QuickTime with Java," the QTCanvas is a subclass of the java.awt.Canvas and represents primarily a way to gain access to the underlying native graphics structure of the platform. QuickTime requires this in order to draw to the screen. QTDrawable is an interface that expresses this requirement of QuickTime objects to draw to this native graphics structure. QTFactory is a class that uses the importing capabilities of QuickTime to "manufacture" QTDrawable objects to present that media.

In this chapter, we discuss how to

- use the QTCanvas class to interact with the Java display and event system

- use the QTDrawable interface to encapsulate common operations that can be applied to a QuickTime drawing object

- present media that QuickTime can import by using "factory" methods provided by the QTFactory class

The chapter also introduces briefly an abstraction known as a *space*, which is part of the QuickTime for Java spaces and controllers architecture. A space defines and organizes the behavior of objects and allows for the complex representation of disparate media types. The concept is discussed in detail in Chapter 13, "Spaces and Controllers."

THE QTCANVAS CLASS

To present QuickTime content within Java, you need a mechanism for interacting with the Java display and event system. This is provided through the services of the QTCanvas class and its client, an object that implements the Drawable interface. QTCanvas is a specialized canvas that supplies access to the native graphics environment and offers expanded display functionality.

QTCanvas encapsulates much of the display and presentation functionality of the QuickTime for Java API. It is responsible for "punching a hole" within the Java display surface and telling its client that it can draw to this display surface and receive events that occur therein. Its clients are generally some kind of QuickTime object, and the events it receives may be mouse or key events. An instance of a QTCanvas object can display any object that implements the Drawable interface.

The client of a QTCanvas object is called Drawable because QuickTime generally uses the word "draw"—for example, MCDraw. Java uses the word "paint," so this enables us to make a distinction between Java objects that "paint" and QuickTime objects that "draw."

Your code can interact with the QTCanvas methods as with those of any java.awt.Component. The QTCanvas delegates calls as appropriate to its drawing client. A client essentially draws itself in the display area of a QTCanvas. If the client is a QTDrawable, the QTCanvas also gets the graphics structure (QDGraphics) of the native implementation of the canvas's peer and sets this QDGraphics as the destination QDGraphics of such a client. All QTDrawable objects require a destination QDGraphics in which to draw.

Using the setClient() method, you can associate a new client, a Drawable object, with this QTCanvas. The flag determines if awt performs a layout and how the client is integrated with the canvas. If the flag is false, the new client takes on the current size and position of the canvas. If the flag is true, then awt lays out the canvas again, using the initial size of the client and the resize flags to resize the canvas and its client. The getClient() method returns the Drawable object currently associated with this QTCanvas.

INTERACTING WITH JAVA LAYOUT MANAGERS

QuickTime media content is often sensitive to the size and proportions of screen space that it uses—for instance, a movie that is made to display at 320 × 240 pixels can look bad or have serious performance repercussions if drawn at 600 × 60 pixels on the screen.

The QTCanvas provides flags for controlling how the Java layout managers allocate space to it (resizeFlags) and where, within that space, the QTCanvas client actually draws (alignmentFlags). You can also set the minimum, preferred, and maximum sizes of the QTCanvas, as with any other java.awt.Component. The preferred size is automatically set for you as the initial size of the QTCanvas client if your application does not specifically set the preferred size itself.

THE QTDRAWABLE INTERFACE

The QTDrawable interface encapsulates the common operations that can be applied to a QuickTime drawing object. It also presents an interface that expresses the required methods that the QTCanvas needs to call upon its drawing client.

Objects that implement the QTDrawable interface draw into the QDGraphics object presented to the client by its QTCanvas. As a consequence, this is not an appropriate interface for objects that are not QuickTime-based drawing objects. QTExceptions can be thrown by any of the methods in this interface and would indicate that either the graphics environment has changed in some unexpected way or that the media object itself is in some unexpected state.

Figure 4.1 represents the QTDrawable interfaces and the classes in QuickTime for Java that implement this interface. The QTDisplaySpace interface and the classes that implement that interface are discussed in Chapter 13, "Spaces and Controllers," and Chapter 14, "Using Spaces and Controllers: QTDisplaySpace."

WORKING WITH THE QTDRAWABLE INTERFACE

As we've seen, the QTDrawable interface is used to handle the negotiation between the QTCanvas and one of several QuickTime objects. The QuickTime objects that implement the QTDrawable interface are extensive and include the following:

- the QTPlayer class, which presents the movie controller

- the MoviePlayer or MoviePresenter classes, which present the Movie data type

- the GraphicsImporterDrawer class, which wraps the graphics importer to present images from a data source, typically image files

- the ImagePresenter class, which presents the DSequence but for a single image only, allowing image data to be loaded and kept in memory, providing a faster redraw than the GraphicsImporter object

- the SWCompositor class, which presents the sprite world

- the SGDrawer class, which presents the sequence grabber and sequence grabber channel (video) components

- the GroupDrawable class, which groups QTDrawable objects into the same canvas

- the QTEffect class, which wraps the visual effects architecture of QuickTime

- the QTImageDrawer class, which allows the results of Java painting into a java.awt.Image to be captured and drawn by QuickTime

FIGURE 4.1   *The QTDrawable implementation*

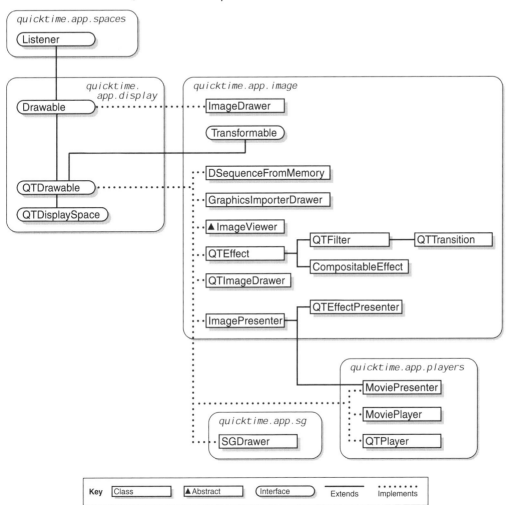

The QTDrawable interface is designed to work hand-in-hand with a QTCanvas object. The class that implements this interface draws into the supplied QDGraphics object. The QTCanvas will call the methods of its client (setting its destination QDGraphics, display bounds, and redrawing it) as required.

QTDRAWABLE METHODS

The QTDrawable interface expresses the capabilities that all QuickTime drawing objects possess. The QTCanvas uses the following methods of the QTDrawable interface:

- addedTo(), removedFrom()

    These methods are used by the QTCanvas to notify the client object that it has been added to or removed from the QTCanvas. Various clients require this notification:

    - QTPlayer, so it can declare its interest in mouse and key events

    - QTImageDrawer, so that it can create an java.awt.Image object to paint into

    - QTDisplaySpaces, to allow the attachment of controllers that are interested in receiving events whose source is the QTCanvas

- setDisplayBounds(), getDisplayBounds()

    These methods are used to get the current size of a QTCanvas client and set its size. The QTCanvas determines the size of itself and its client based on a complex interaction between the size the QTCanvas parent container allocates to the QTCanvas, the initial (or best) size of its client, and the setting of the resize and alignment flags of the QTCanvas itself.

    Once the QTCanvas has determined the correct size of itself and its client, it uses the setDisplayBounds() method to resize and locate its client. The size and location of a QTCanvas and its client is always the same.

- redraw()

    This method is used to tell the client to redraw itself.

    Both the setDisplayBounds() and redraw() methods of a client are only called by the QTCanvas paint() method, with the setDisplayBounds() call, if required, being always called before a redraw() call.

- getGWorld(), setGWorld()

These methods are used to set the `QTDrawable` client's destination `QDGraphics` if the client of a `QTCanvas` is a `QTDrawable`, as is normally the case. All `QTDrawable` objects must have a destination `QDGraphics` at all times. As such, if a `QTDrawable` client is removed from a `QTCanvas` or the `QTCanvas` has been hidden

```
myQTCanvas.setVisible (false);
```

then a special `QDGraphics`, `QDGraphics.scratch()`, is used to indicate to the `QTDrawable` that it is invisible and basically disabled.

While the following methods are not used specifically in the relationship between `QTCanvas` and its client, they are presented here for the sake of completeness and also express capabilities that all `QTDrawable` objects possess:

- `getClip()`, `setClip()`

    All `QTDrawable` objects have the ability to clip their drawn pixels to a specified region. The `getClip()` and `setClip()` methods are used to get and set a clipping region. `null` can be used and returned, and it indicates that the `QTDrawable` currently has no clipping region set.

    The `DirectGroup` display space enables one or more `QTDrawable` objects to draw into the same `QTCanvas` destination `QDGraphics`. It provides the capability to layer the objects in such a group, so that the objects do not draw over each other. This layering is achieved through the use of clipping regions. The `DirectGroup` clips its members so that members that are behind others cannot draw into the area where those in front are positioned. As this group by definition draws directly to the screen, this is the only means that can be used to avoid the flickering that would occur if the `QTDrawable` objects could not be clipped. For more information, see Chapter 14, "Using Spaces and Controllers: QTDisplaySpace."

- `getMatrix()`, `setMatrix()`, `getInitialSize()`

    The `QTDrawable` interface also extends the `Transformable` interface. The `Transformable` interface expresses the ability of QuickTime drawers to have a matrix applied that will map the source pixels of a drawing object to some transformed destination appearance. A matrix allows the following transformations to be applied in the rendering process:

- ❑ *translation*. Drawing pixels from an x or y location
- ❑ *scaling*. Scaling the image by an x or y scaling factor
- ❑ *rotation*. Rotating the image a specified number of degrees
- ❑ *skew*. Skewing the image by a specified amount
- ❑ *perspective*. Applying an appearance of perspective to the image

Your application can freely mix and match these different transformations at its own discretion.

All QTDrawable objects can have a matrix applied to them that will transform their visual appearance. A Sprite in a SpriteWorld can also have matrix transformations applied to it, as can a 3D model. The TwoD-Sprite also implements the Transformable interface.

The Transformable interface allows for applications to define behaviors that can be applied to any of these objects. For example, the quicktime.app.actions.Dragger, which will position objects in response to a mouseDragged event, is defined totally in terms of the Transformable interface. Thus, the Dragger can reposition any TwoD-Sprite in a SWCompositor or any QTDrawable in a GroupDrawable. For more details, see Chapter 14, "Using Spaces and Controllers: QTDisplaySpace."

Using interfaces to express common functionality is a powerful concept and is relied upon extensively in the QuickTime for Java Application Framework.

THE QTFACTORY CLASS

The QTFactory class provides "factory" methods for creating classes used to present media that QuickTime can import. The makeDrawable() methods of QTFactory use the QuickTime importers to return an appropriate QuickTime object that can present any of a wide range of media types (images, movies, sounds, MIDI, and so on) that QuickTime can import.

Given a file, a Java `InputStream` object, or URL, the `makeDraw-able()` methods that belong to the `QTFactory` class examine the contained media and return an object that best presents that kind of media. For example:

- movies—a `QTPlayer` object

- images—a `GraphicsImporterDrawer` object

- sound media—a `QTPlayer` object

- MIDI media—a `QTPlayer` object

Once you have the `QTDrawable` object, you merely add it to the canvas, and the visual component of the media is presented in the canvas's display space.

There are three versions of the `makeDrawable()` method. The first two methods deal with a file, either local or remote:

- `QTFactory.makeDrawable( QTFile, . . .)`
- `QTFactory.makeDrawable( String URL, . . .)`

The `QTFile` version is for a local file, whereas the URL version can use any of the protocols known to QuickTime:

- ❑ file: for a local file

- ❑ HTTP: for a remote file

- ❑ FTP: for a remote file

- ❑ RTP and RTSP: for a movie with streaming content

- `QTFactory.makeDrawable (InputStream, . . . )`

In this method, the media data can be derived from any source—for example, from a `ZipEntry`, from a local or remote file, or from memory. The `readBytes()` method of the input stream is used to read all of the source object's bytes into memory. Then this memory is used to create the appropriate `QTDrawable`.

In the first two cases, QuickTime can use details about the file to determine the type of media that the file contains. Many media formats are not self-describing. That is, they don't have information in the data that describes what they are. Usually, the file type describes to QuickTime this important detail.

In the case of the `InputStream`, however, because the data can come from an unknown or arbitrary source, your application must describe to QuickTime the format of the source data so that it can import it successfully. As such, these methods require the provision of a `hintString` and `hintType`. You can specify that the hint is either the file extension, Mac OS file type, or MIMEType of the source data.

Once the `makeDrawable()` methods determine the media, they create either a `Movie` or a `GraphicsImporter` as the QuickTime object to present that media. They then pass off this `Movie` or `GraphicsImporter` to a `QTDrawableMaker` to return a `QTDrawable` object to present that `Movie` or `GraphicsImporter`.

Your application uses the default `QTDrawableMaker` if you do not specify one. This returns a `QTPlayer` that creates a `MovieController` for the `Movie` or a `GraphicsImporterDrawer` for the `GraphicsImporter`. An application can also specify a custom `QTDrawableMaker` that will create a required object for one or both of these two cases.

The `QTFactory` also provides methods to locate files in the known directories of the Java application when it executes. In order for QuickTime to open a local file, it must have the absolute path and name of the file. Your application may want to open files where it can know the relative location of the file from where it is executing. For instance, many of the code samples in the QuickTime for Java SDK will look for files in the media directory that is in the SDK directory. This media directory is added to the class path when the application is launched. The `QTFactory.findAbsolutePath()` method is used by the application to find the absolute path of the file, and to find those files, at runtime.

- `addDirectory()`

  Allows your application to specify a directory that is added to the known directories that are used in searching for files

■ `removeDirectory()`

Allows your application to remove directories where it doesn't want files to be found. This can shorten the search process, as the application can remove the specified directory from the search paths that the `find()...` methods will search for specified files in.

■ `findAbsolutePath()`

Given a relative file (or directory), this method will search for this specified path in

❑ application-specified directories

❑ `user.dir`, which is a directory that is one of the system properties of the Java runtime

❑ any directory known in the class path directories. `class.path` is also a system property of the Java runtime.

This method searches for the specified path as this path is appended to these known directories. It returns the first occurrence of the file (or directory) that exists in these locations. If the specified file is not found, a `FileNotFoundException` is thrown.

■ `findInSystemPaths()`

Whereas the `findAbsolutePath()` will look for the specified file by appending that file to the known directories, this method will do a recursive search for the specified file or subdirectory of all of the known or registered directories and their parents. This can be a time-consuming search, and typically your application will only use this method to find a file that the user has misplaced or is not found in the `findAbsolutePath()` method. If the specified file is not found, a `FileNotFoundException` is thrown.

SPACES AND CONTROLLERS ARCHITECTURE

The QuickTime for Java API introduces an abstraction known as a *space*. A space defines and organizes the behavior of objects and allows for the complex representation of disparate media types. Spaces provide a powerful and useful means to assemble and control a complex presentation.

You use a space to create a "world" that can be controlled dynamically from Java at runtime. This world could have certain characteristics that define how the objects exist and interact with others. Your application assembles the space with its objects or *members* and uses Java's event model to allow for user interaction with those objects. Because it is a dynamic environment, decisions about behavior and even which members belong to the space can be deferred until runtime. The Space interface, which is part of the `quicktime.app.spaces` package, provides the standard API that all spaces support.

QuickTime for Java controllers manipulate Java objects in spaces. These controllers can define the standard behavior for a group of objects by defining the behavior of objects over time, by monitoring objects, and by responding to user events. Controllers provide a uniform way of enforcing the same behavior on a group of objects. The behavior of a controller depends upon the support protocols defined by a space and by a controller itself.

The QuickTime for Java API provides a `Controller` interface and defines a protocol for the interaction between spaces and controllers. While the focus in this release of QuickTime for Java is in presentation, the architecture is general enough to be applied in the model space for generating data. The spaces and controllers architecture is discussed in detail in Chapter 13, "Spaces and Controllers."

Using QuickTime From Java

Part II is a hands-on introduction to QuickTime for Java programming.

Each chapter works through a series of code examples that illustrate various techniques you can use in QuickTime for Java programming. It builds on many of the concepts and examples discussed in Chapters 2, 3, and 4.

Part II contains the following chapters:

Chapter 5, "Displaying and Streaming Movies"

Chapter 6, "QuickTime Media and Presenters"

Chapter 7, "QuickTime and Java Imaging and Effects"

Chapter 8, "Creating, Editing, and Importing QuickTime Movies"

Chapter 9, "Capturing Media with QuickTime"

Chapter 10, "Playing Music with QuickTime"

5 Displaying and Streaming Movies

QuickTime provides a set of APIs that enable you to stream multimedia content over a network in real time, as opposed to downloading that content and storing it locally prior to presentation. With streaming, the timing and speed of transmission as well as the display of data are determined by the nature of the content rather than the speed of the network, server, or the client. Thus, a one-minute-long QuickTime movie is streamed over a network so that it can be displayed or presented in real time.

In the QuickTime streaming architecture, a *stream* is, simply, a track in a movie. QuickTime lets you stream a broad variety of content—audio, video, text, and MIDI; the output of any audio or video codec supported in QuickTime can be streamed, in fact. If your application is QuickTime-savvy, you can automatically take advantage of this multimedia streaming capability.

In addition to demonstrating some useful techniques for displaying QuickTime movies, this chapter shows you how to play a streaming movie from a URL. It builds on the concepts and examples discussed in Chapter 3, "Integrating QuickTime with Java," and Chapter 4, "QTCanvas, QTDrawable, and QTFactory," and shows you how to

- select and then play a QuickTime movie with its controller detached
- convert a screen to full-screen mode and back to normal mode

■ display a QuickTime movie within a window and add callbacks that are triggered at some specific time during movie playback

PLAY A STREAMING MOVIE

Example 5.1 builds on the QTSimpleApplet example discussed in Chapters 1 and 3. This applet enables you to play a steaming movie from a URL.

You define the instance variables for the applet:

```
private Drawable myQTContent;
private QTCanvas myQTCanvas;
```

Just as with the QTSimpleApplet code sample, you can use the standard init(), start(), stop(), and destroy() methods to initialize, execute, and terminate the applet. Likewise, you call QTSession.open() in order to make sure that QuickTime is present and initialized. Again, this is a *required* call before any QuickTime for Java classes can be used. It is called first in the init() method. In order to shut down QuickTime properly, you also need to call QTSession.close() if you have previously called QTSession.open(). This is called in the destroy() method.

QTCanvas, as we've seen, is a display space into which QuickTime can draw and receive events. QTCanvas provides the output destination for QuickTime drawing. You set up a QTCanvas to display its content at its original size or smaller and centered in the space given to the QTCanvas when the applet is laid out. The QTCanvas is initialized to display its client up to as large as that client's initial size. And 0.5F flags are used to position the canvas at the center of the space allocated to it by its parent container's layout manager:

```
setLayout (new BorderLayout());
myQTCanvas = new QTCanvas (QTCanvas.kInitialSize, 0.5F, 0.5F);
add (myQTCanvas, "Center");
```

You need to set the client as a `Drawable` object that can display into the canvas. The QuickTime logo is displayed when there is no movie to display. Thus, `ImageDrawer` is set up as the initial client of `QTCanvas`.

```
myQTContent = ImageDrawer.getQTLogo();
```

You enter the URL to a QuickTime movie to be displayed in a text field:

```
final TextField urlTextField = new TextField (
                    "file:///. . . Enter an URL to a movie",
                    30);
```

You set the font and font size in the text field for the URL. The initial string is displayed in the text field. You add an `ActionListener` so that the events taking place on the text field are captured and executed. `tf.getText()` returns the URL that the user has entered:

```
urlTextField.setFont (new Font ("Dialog", Font.PLAIN, 10));
urlTextField.setEditable (true);
urlTextField.addActionListener (new ActionListener () {
    TextField tf = urlTextField;

    public void actionPerformed (ActionEvent ae) {
        myQTContent = QTFactory.makeDrawable (tf.getText());
        myQTCanvas.setClient (myQTContent, true);
    }
});
```

The URL can support the following protocols:

■ file—a local file on the user's computer

■ HTTP—HyperText Transfer Protocol

■ FTP—File Transfer Protocol

■ RTP and RTSP—Real Time Streaming Protocols

The URL can also point to any media file (movies, images, and so on) that QuickTime can present. The single `makeDrawable()` method will return the appropriate QuickTime object to present the specified media. Once created, this QuickTime object is set as the client of the `QTCanvas` and can then be viewed and/or played by the user.

Note that no error handling is done in the code in Example 5.1.

EXAMPLE 5.1 *QTStreamingApplet.java*

```java
import java.applet.Applet;
import java.awt.*;
import java.awt.event.*;

import quicktime.*;
import quicktime.io.QTFile;

import quicktime.app.QTFactory;
import quicktime.app.display.*;
import quicktime.app.image.ImageDrawer;

public class QTStreamingApplet extends Applet {
    private Drawable myQTContent;
    private QTCanvas myQTCanvas;

    public void init () {
        try {
            QTSession.open();
            setLayout (new BorderLayout());
            myQTCanvas = new QTCanvas (QTCanvas.kInitialSize, 0.5F, 0.5F);
            add (myQTCanvas, "Center");

            myQTContent = ImageDrawer.getQTLogo();

            final TextField urlTextField = new TextField ("Enter URL to movie here",
                                                        30);
            urlTextField.setFont (new Font ("Dialog", Font.PLAIN, 10));
            urlTextField.setEditable (true);
            urlTextField.addActionListener (new ActionListener () {
                TextField tf = urlTextField;

                public void actionPerformed (ActionEvent ae) {
                    if (myQTCanvas != null) {
                        try {
                            myQTContent = QTFactory.makeDrawable (tf.getText());
                            myQTCanvas.setClient (myQTContent, true);
                        } catch (QTException e) {
                            e.printStackTrace();
```

```
                    }
                }
            }
        });
        add (urlTextField, "South");
    } catch (QTException qtE) {
        throw new RuntimeException (qtE.getMessage());
    }
}

public void start () {
    try {
        if (myQTCanvas != null)
            myQTCanvas.setClient (myQTContent, true);
    } catch (QTException e) {
        e.printStackTrace();
    }
}

public void stop () {
    if (myQTCanvas != null)
        myQTCanvas.removeClient();
}

public void destroy () {
    QTSession.close();
}
}
```

USING THE DETACHED CONTROLLER

The code sample in this section shows how to select and then play a QuickTime movie with its controller detached. The media required is a QuickTime movie of the user's choice.

You are prompted to select a movie file. If you make the selection, a window is constructed, and the movie and its controller are presented, as shown in Figure 5.1.

FIGURE 5.1   *The detached controller*

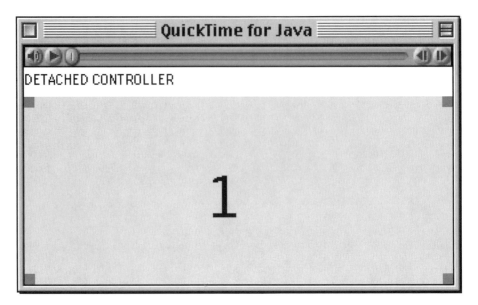

The movie and its controller are displayed separately in the same window, with the controller at the top and the actual movie at the bottom. They are separated by a label. Though the movie and its controller are shown here in the same window, they could also be displayed in different windows, even on different monitors. Figure 1.1 shows the same movie with its controller attached, which is the normal mode of presenting a movie and its movie controller.

You use a QTPlayer object to play the movie in its canvas, and you can use a MoviePlayer object to present the movie.

```
void setControllerCanvas(Movie mMovie) throws QTException {
    QTCanvas controllerCanvas = new QTCanvas();

    MovieController mController = new MovieController(mMovie,
                                            mcScaleMovieToFit);

    mController.setAttached(false);

    QTPlayer qtPlayer = new QTPlayer(mController);
```

```
    add(controllerCanvas, "North");
    controllerCanvas.setClient(qtPlayer, true);
}
```

You can attach or detach the movie from its controller using this method:

```
mController.setAttached(false);
```

Once the controller is a client of its canvas, if the movie is reattached to the controller, you need to notify the canvas of this change in the client's display characteristics. The TimeCode sample on the CD-ROM at the back of this book, which adds and removes timecode display from a movie, illustrates this requirement.

Now you create the canvas for the detached movie:

```
void setMovieCanvas(Movie mMovie) throws QTException{
    QTCanvas movieCanvas = new QTCanvas();

    MoviePlayer mPlayer = new MoviePlayer(mMovie);

    add(movieCanvas, "South");
    movieCanvas.setClient(mPlayer, true);
}
```

The following snippet shows the code that assembles the Detached-Controller window. Resizing the window resizes the movie and the width of the controller but not its height.

```
DetachedController(Movie mMovie) throws QTException {
    super ("QT in Java");

    setControllerCanvas(mMovie);

    setMovieCanvas(mMovie);

    add (new Label("DETACHED CONTROLLER"), "Center");
    . . .
}
```

CONVERTING TO FULL SCREEN

The FullScreen class provides the capability for converting a screen to full-screen mode and back to normal mode. The QuickTime for Java API allows you to put the specified screen into full screen mode and then use a Java window to fill the screen.

To do this, you use the FullScreenWindow class, discussed in Chapter 21, "The quicktime. app.display Package," which is a subclass of the java.awt.Window object. The FullScreenWindow class internally manages a FullScreen object, and when the show() method is called, it puts the screen into full-screen mode and fills up the screen with an awt.Window. This is very useful because you can get the complete functionality of using a Java AWT Window but in full-screen mode.

The movie is created in a similar fashion as the QTStreamingApplet. The program also creates a menu that allows the user to select a movie and once opened provides a **Present Movie** menu item to present the movie in full screen mode.

The full code listing is shown in Example 5.2. You present the movie in full screen mode and use the current screen resolution and current movie. The QTCanvas is created using the performance resize flag. This ensures that the movie is displayed at its original size or at a multiple of 2:

```
FullScreenWindow w = new FullScreenWindow(new FullScreen(),
                                          myPlayMovie);
MoviePlayer mp = new MoviePlayer (myPlayMovie.getMovie());
QTCanvas c = new QTCanvas (QTCanvas.kPerformanceResize, 0.5F, 0.5F);
w.add (c);
w.setBackground (Color.black);
```

You remove the movie from its current QTCanvas and put the movie into the new canvas of the FullScreenWindow. You do this because a QTDrawable can only draw to a single destination QDGraphics:

```
myPlayMovie.getCanvas().removeClient();
c.setClient (mp, false);
```

HideFSWindow is a MouseListener. A MouseListener is installed on both the QTCanvas and the Window. The window is then shown, which will put the window into full-screen mode:

```
w.show();
HideFSWindow hw = new HideFSWindow (w, myPlayMovie, c);
w.addMouseListener (hw);
c.addMouseListener (hw);
```

As MoviePlayer object is used to present the movie, this shows just the movie and not a controller. So finally, you start the movie playing:

```
mp.setRate (1);
```

When the user presses the mouse, the movie is restored to its previous QTCanvas and the full-screen window is hidden:

```
public void mousePressed (MouseEvent me) {
    try {
        c.removeClient();
        pm.getCanvas().setClient (pm.getPlayer(), false);
    } catch (QTException e) {
        e.printStackTrace();
    } finally {
        w.hide();
    }
}
```

The user must explicitly press the mouse to hide the FullScreen-Window. However, your application could also define an ExtremeCall-Back that would automatically hide the FullScreenWindow when the movie is finished playing. Callbacks are discussed in the next section.

EXAMPLE 5.2 *FileMenu.java*

```
presentMovieMenuItem.addActionListener (new ActionListener () {
    public void actionPerformed(ActionEvent event) {
        try {
            if (myPlayMovie.getPlayer() == null) return;

            FullScreenWindow w = new FullScreenWindow(new FullScreen(), myPlayMovie);
            MoviePlayer mp = new MoviePlayer (myPlayMovie.getMovie());
```

```
        QTCanvas c = new QTCanvas (QTCanvas.kPerformanceResize, 0.5F, 0.5F);
        w.add (c);
        w.setBackground (Color.black);

        myPlayMovie.getCanvas().removeClient();
        c.setClient (mp, false);

        w.show();
        HideFSWindow hw = new HideFSWindow (w, myPlayMovie, c);
        w.addMouseListener (hw);
        c.addMouseListener (hw);

        mp.setRate (1);
    } catch (QTException err) {
        err.printStackTrace();
    }
}

static class HideFSWindow extends MouseAdapter {
    HideFSWindow (FullScreenWindow w, PlayMovie pm, QTCanvas c) {
        this.w = w;
        this.pm = pm;
        this.c = c;
    }

    private FullScreenWindow w;
    private PlayMovie pm;
    private QTCanvas c;


    public void mousePressed (MouseEvent me) {
        try {
            c.removeClient();
            pm.getCanvas().setClient (pm.getPlayer(), false);
        } catch (QTException e) {
            e.printStackTrace();
        } finally {
            w.hide();
        }
    }
}
```

USING MOVIE CALLBACKS

This section explains how to display a QuickTime movie within a window and add callbacks. The callbacks are QuickTime calling back into Java through the movie controller, movie, and QuickTime VR APIs.

Callbacks can be used by an application to perform its own tasks when certain conditions occur within QuickTime itself. The callbacks used in the MovieCallbacks program on the accompanying CD-ROM are invoked when some condition having to do with the presentation of a movie is changed:

- In the movie, the DrawingComplete procedure is used to notify the Java program whenever QuickTime draws to the screen.

- ActionFilter procedures are used. This subclass overrides those actions that pass on no parameters and a float parameter.

- The movie contains QuickTime VR content, and a number of QTVR callbacks are installed for panning and tilting, for hot spots, and for entering and leaving nodes.

The QTCallBack, ActionFilter, and DrawingComplete callbacks are invoked through a direct or indirect call of the QuickTime MoviesTask function.

Many of the callback methods in QuickTime in Java are required to execute in place, in that QuickTime requires a result code in order to proceed. These callbacks provide meaningful feedback when their execute() method returns. The subclasses of QTCallBack, however, can execute asynchronously, in which case QuickTime does not require a result code in order to proceed. This is also true of any of the execute() methods with no return value.

The program just prints out details about the callback when it is invoked. The QuickTime API documentation on the CD-ROM accompanying this book provides examples and discussions on the usage of these. The full code listing for this example is available on the CD-ROM.

To set up a movie drawing callback:

```
static class MovieDrawing implements MovieDrawingComplete {
    public short execute (Movie m) {
        System.out.println ("drawing:" + m);
        return 0;
    }
}
```

To set up an action filter:

```
static class PMFilter extends ActionFilter {
    public boolean execute (MovieController mc, int action) {
        System.out.println (mc + "," + "action:" + action);
        return false;
    }

    public boolean execute (MovieController mc, int action, float value) {
        System.out.println (mc + "," + "action:" + action + ",value=" + value);
        return false;
    }
}
```

The following code sets up callbacks for QuickTime VR content:

```
Track t = m.getQTVRTrack (1);
if (t != null) {
    QTVRInstance vr = new QTVRInstance (t, mc);
    vr.setEnteringNodeProc (new EnteringNode(), 0);
    vr.setLeavingNodeProc (new LeavingNode(), 0);
    vr.setMouseOverHotSpotProc (new HotSpot(), 0);
    Interceptor ip = new Interceptor();
    vr.installInterceptProc (QTVRConstants.kQTVRSetPanAngleSelector, ip, 0);
    vr.installInterceptProc (QTVRConstants.kQTVRSetTiltAngleSelector, ip, 0);
    vr.installInterceptProc (QTVRConstants.kQTVRSetFieldOfViewSelector, ip, 0);
    vr.installInterceptProc (QTVRConstants.kQTVRSetViewCenterSelector, ip, 0);
    vr.installInterceptProc (QTVRConstants.kQTVRTriggerHotSpotSelector, ip, 0);
    vr.installInterceptProc (QTVRConstants.kQTVRGetHotSpotTypeSelector, ip, 0);
}

static class EnteringNode implements QTVREnteringNode {
    public short execute (QTVRInstance vr, int nodeID) {
        System.out.println (vr + ",entering:" + nodeID);
```

```
        return 0;
    }
}

static class LeavingNode implements QTVRLeavingNode {
    public short execute (QTVRInstance vr, int fromNodeID, int toNodeID, boolean[]
                          cancel) {
        System.out.println (vr + ",leaving:" + fromNodeID + ",entering:" +
                            toNodeID);
            // cancel[0] = true;
        return 0;
    }
}

static class HotSpot implements QTVRMouseOverHotSpot {
    public short execute (QTVRInstance vr, int hotSpotID, int flags) {
        System.out.println (vr + ",hotSpot:" + hotSpotID + ",flags=" + flags);
        return 0;
    }
}

static class Interceptor implements QTVRInterceptor {
    public boolean execute (QTVRInstance vr, QTVRInterceptRecord qtvrMsg) {
        System.out.println (vr + "," + qtvrMsg);
        return false;
    }
}
```

The following code shows how to install a QTRuntimeException handler:

```
QTRuntimeException.registerHandler (new Handler());
```

Runtime exceptions can be thrown by many methods and are thrown where the method does not explicitly declare that it throws an exception. Using the QTRuntimeHandler allows your application to examine the exception and determine if it can be ignored or recovered from.

An example of this is the paint() method of a Java component. Its signature is

```
public void paint (Graphics g);
```

It is declared not to throw any exceptions. However, the QTDrawable redraw() or setDisplayBounds() calls (which are both invoked on a QTCanvas client) are defined to throw QTExceptions.

If the QTCanvas client does throw an exception in this case, it passes it off to a QTRuntimeHandler if the application has registered one, with details about the cause of the exception. The application can then either throw the exception or rectify the situation. If no runtime exception handler is registered, the exception is thrown and caught by the Java VM thread itself.

6 QuickTime Media and Presenters

QuickTime understands media through the pairing of media data and a meta-data object that describes the format and characteristics of that media data. This media data can exist either on some external storage device or in memory. The media data can further be stored in the movie itself or can exist in other files, either local or remote. The meta-data object that describes the format of the media data is known as a `SampleDescription`. There are various extensions to the base-level `SampleDescription` that are customized to contain information about specific media types (e.g., `ImageDescription` for image data).

This chapter discusses the following topics:

- retrieving media data and QuickTime's use of this complex and powerful capability, particularly with the introduction of multimedia streaming

- using presenters to express an object that renders media data loaded into or residing in memory

- the `ImagePresenter` class, which is the principal class in the QuickTime for Java API that presents such image data

MEDIA DATA AND MOVIES

With the introduction of QuickTime streaming, QuickTime has extended its ability to retrieve data. Traditionally, media data had to exist as local data. With streaming, media data can now exist on remote servers and retrieved using the HTTP or FTP Internet protocols, as well as

125

the more traditional file protocol of previous releases. The location of media is contained in a structure called a `DataRef`. This tells QuickTime where media data is and how to retrieve it.

QuickTime streaming also adds support for broadcast media data, using the RTP and RTSP protocols. Media data of this format is delivered through network protocols, typically sourced through the broadcast of either live or stored video. It requires the creation of streaming datahandlers to deal with the mechanics of retrieving media data using this protocol.

The tracks in a single movie can have data in different locations. For example, one track's media data might be contained in the movie itself; a second track's media data might exist in another local file; and a third track's media data might exist in a remote file and be retrieved through the FTP protocol. In these two cases, the movie references the media data that is stored elsewhere. A fourth track might retrieve broadcasted media data through a network using the RTSP protocol.

Your application is free to mix and match these data references for tracks' media data as appropriate. QuickTime presents a complex and powerful capability to deal with media data, a complexity that provides the user of QuickTime with a powerful tool in both the development and delivery of media content.

DEALING WITH MEDIA

Despite the complexity of the data retrieval semantics of QuickTime, the process of dealing with media in QuickTime is quite simple. In the `CreateMovie` sample code on the CD-ROM, the movie's data is constructed by inserting the media sample data and its description into the media object and then inserting the media into the track.

The following is a printout of the `ImageDescription` for the last frame of the image data that is added to the movie. As you can see, the `ImageDescription` describes the format, the size, and the dimensions of the image itself:

```
quicktime.std.image.ImageDescription[
        cType=rle ,
        temporalQuality=512,
        spatialQulity=512,
        width=330,
        height=140,
        dataSize=0,
        frameCount=1,
        name=Animation,
        depth=32]
```

The following is the SoundDescription of the sound track added in this sample code. It describes the sample rate, the sample size, and its format:

```
quicktime.std.movies.media.SoundDescription[
        format=twos,
        numChannels=1,
        sampleSize=8,
        sampleRate=22050.0]
```

If the data is not local to the movie itself, one inserts a sample description (as previously to describe the data) and a DataRef that describes to QuickTime both the location of the data and the means it should use to retrieve the data when it is required. Once assembled, QuickTime handles all of the mechanics of retrieving and displaying the media at runtime.

When media is displayed, the media handlers use the various rendering services of QuickTime. These rendering services are based on the same data model, in that the sample description is used to both describe the media and to instantiate the appropriate component responsible for rendering data of that specific format. These rendering components are also available to the application itself outside of movie playback.

For example, the DSequence object is used to render image data to a destination QDGraphics and used throughout QuickTime to render visual media. Your application can also use the DSequence object directly by providing both the image data and an ImageDescription that describes the format and other characteristics of this data and, of course, a destination QDGraphics where the data should be drawn. Like QuickTime itself, your application can apply matrix transformations, graphics modes, and clipping regions that should be applied in this rendering process.

Similar processes are used and available for all of the other media types (sound, music, and so on) that QuickTime supports, with each of these media types providing their own extended sample descriptions, media handlers, and rendering services.

THE IMAGESPEC INTERFACE

The ImageSpec interface expresses the close relationship between image data and an ImageDescription that describes it. Figure 6.1 illustrates all of the ImageSpec-derived classes in the QuickTime for Java API.

The image data itself is represented by an object that implements the EncodedImage interface. This interface allows image data to be stored in either raw memory, accessed using pointers, or in a Java int or byte array. Any object that implements the ImageSpec interface can have its image rendered by either the ImagePresenter to a destination QDGraphics or by a TwoDSprite to its container SWCompositor.

The ImageSpec interface expresses the commonality of QuickTime's media model, specifically with regard to image data, and unifies the many possible constructions and imaging services that QuickTime provides.

If your application requires a particular format for generating image data, then it can implement the ImageSpec interface and thus have QuickTime use this custom class wherever the QuickTime for Java API uses existing ImageSpec objects.

Figure 6.1 *Image implementations*

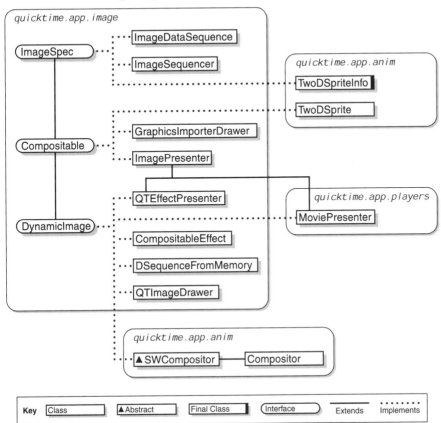

THE COMPOSITABLE AND DYNAMICIMAGE INTERFACES

The Compositable and DynamicImage interfaces extend the ImageSpec interface. The Compositable interface captures the ability of image data to have a graphics mode applied to it when it is rendered. Graphics modes include rendering effects such as transparency, where any pixels of a particular color in the image data won't be drawn, and blending, where all of the drawn colors of an image are blended with a blend color to alter the rendered image.

The `DynamicImage` interface extends `Compositable` and expresses the fact that some pixel data may change. This interface is used by the `Compositor`, as a `TwoDSprite` must invalidate its `Sprite` if the pixel data changes. This is discussed in more detail in Chapter 15, "Animation and Compositing."

QUICKTIME FOR JAVA PRESENTERS

When QuickTime plays back a movie, it does not generally read all of its media data into memory but rather reads chunks of data as required. A movie can be constructed that requires the media data to be loaded into memory or other parameters that will require more memory to be used but will generally improve the quality of the rendered movie. The QuickTime API documentation covers these customizations that a movie's author can make.

Due to the usefulness of, and in some cases requirement for, loading media data into memory, QuickTime for Java provides *presenters*. A presenter is an object that renders media data that is loaded or resides in memory. A presenter also uses a QuickTime service to render this media data.

QuickTime for Java ships with an `ImagePresenter` for rendering image data. The `ImagePresenter` class implements the `QTDrawable` interface. The `ImagePresenter` uses a `DSequence` to perform the rendering of the image data. It is the primary object that is used in QuickTime for Java to render image data. The `TwoDSprite` is also a presenter that presents image data loaded into memory. However, its role is specific to the membership of its `Sprite` in a `SpriteWorld` (which is represented in QuickTime for Java by the `SWCompositor`).

Though only an `ImagePresenter` is provided in this release, a similar design strategy could be employed with other media types. For example, let's consider the music media type. `MusicMedia` is rendered in QuickTime by the `TunePlayer` class. A `MusicPresenter` class could be created that used the `TunePlayer` to render the `MusicData`. A `MusicSpec` interface could be described that returns a MusicDescription and the raw MusicData of the tune events. The PlayTune sample code in Chapter 10, "Playing Music with QuickTime," shows the usage of these classes and can serve as a guide to the construction of these design classes.

THE IMAGEPRESENTER CLASS

The ImagePresenter manages the varying state and conditions of use of QuickTime's DSequence renderer. It is a useful abstraction because it hides such details from the user, creating a robust and reusable class.

The ImagePresenter is able to render its data faster than its corollary GraphicsImporterDrawer, which also implements the QTDrawable interface, for two reasons. First, the data is kept in memory and so it is quicker to read. (The GraphicsImporterDrawer reads its image data from its DataRef, typically a file.) Second, the image data of an ImagePresenter can be (and often is) kept in a format that is optimized for rendering or decompression. However, a GraphicsImporterDrawer will use less memory and is often more than sufficient for presenting an image where no demanding rendering tasks are required, such as constant, time-sensitive redrawing.

An ImagePresenter object can be created from many sources. For example, from a file:

```
ImagePresenter myImage = ImagePresenter.fromFile(imageFile);
```

In this case, the ImagePresenter will create a GraphicsImporter to read and load into memory the image data from the file. It will then decompress the image if necessary to a format optimized for rendering.

You can also create an ImagePresenter from generated image data and an ImageDescription that describes it:

```
int width = 100;
int height = 100;

IntEncodedImage myImageData = new IntEncodedImage (width * height);
//...fill in pixel values using standard java ARGB ordering
```

```
ImageDescription myDescription =
        ImageDescription.getJavaDefaultPixelDescription (width,
                                                         height);
myDescription.setDataSize (myImageData.getSize());

ImagePresenter myPresenter = ImagePresenter.fromQTImage(myImageData,
                                        myDescription);
```

You can also create an ImagePresenter object from an onscreen or offscreen QDGraphics that you have previously drawn into:

```
QDGraphics gWorld = ....
Rect rect = ....
int colorDepth = ....
int quality = ....
int codecType = ....
CodecComponent codec = ....

ImagePresenter myIP = ImagePresenter.fromGWorld (myGWorld,
                            myGWorld.getBounds(),
                            myGWorld.getPixMap().getPixelSize(),
                            myDerivedCompressionQuality,
                            myDerivedCompressionType,
                            myDerivedCodecComponent);
```

Subclasses of ImagePresenter

There are two basic subclasses of ImagePresenter, which inherit from and build on the features of ImagePresenter: MoviePresenter and QTEffectPresenter. Both of these subclasses work in a similar fashion. They render their target objects (a movie or an effect) into an offscreen QDGraphics object. The pixel data from this QDGraphics is then set as the EncodedImage data of the superclass. An ImageDescription is created that describes this raw pixel data and this description is given to the superclass. Thus, retrieving the image data (getImage()) returns the raw pixel data that the movie has drawn into.

The ImagePresenter superclass then blits this raw pixel data to its destination QDGraphics. If this presenter is added as a Sprite, the raw pixel data becomes that sprite's image data.

MoviePresenter takes a Movie object and implements the same interfaces as MoviePlayer, but it has the extra capability of being a presenter and having a graphics mode set for its overall appearance.

QTEffectPresenter is similar to MoviePresenter but takes a QTEffect object. You could use this presenter to capture the results of applying a filter to a source image. You could then discard the filter object and just present the resultant image. You can also use this presenter to present a character in a sprite animation that could transition on and off the stage.

Some examples of the usage of these classes are presented in Chapter 15, "Animation and Compositing."

7

QuickTime and Java Imaging and Effects

The QuickTime for Java Application Framework provides a number of classes that handle the presentation of images within a Java display space. These classes provide utility methods that you can use to set transparent colors in images, apply visual effects, or create objects for handling sequences of images (such as slide shows). Other methods enable you to create QTDrawable objects that read image data from a file or load the data into memory.

This chapter shows you how to

- draw an image file using the GraphicsImporterDrawer

- create a java.awt.Image out of an image in QuickTime's format

- use the QTImageDrawer class to render Java-painted content in a QuickTime graphics space

- take advantage of QuickTime's visual effects architecture to apply transitions between two images

DRAWING AN IMAGE FILE

Example 7.1 shows how to import and draw an image from a file. This program works with the GraphicsImporterDrawer object to import and display a variety of image file formats. The media required for this sample code is any image file that can be imported using the GraphicsImporterDrawer.

The `quicktime.app.image` package has two primary image display classes: `GraphicsImporterDrawer` and `ImagePresenter`. These classes implement both the `ImageSpec` and the `QTDrawable` interfaces. `GraphicsImporterDrawer` uses `GraphicsImporter` to read, decompress, and display image files.

EXAMPLE 7.1 *ImageFileDemo.java*

```java
import quicktime.*;
import quicktime.std.StdQTConstants;
import quicktime.std.image.GraphicsImporter;
import quicktime.io.QTFile;

import quicktime.app.display.QTCanvas;
import quicktime.app.image.*;

public class ImageFileDemo extends Frame implements StdQTConstants {

    public static void main (String args[]) {
        try {
            QTSession.open();

            int[] fileTypes = { kQTFileTypeGIF, kQTFileTypeJPEG, kQTFileTypePicture };
            QTFile qtf = QTFile.standardGetFilePreview (fileTypes);

            ImageFileDemo ifd = new ImageFileDemo (qtf);
            ifd.pack();
            ifd.show();
            ifd.toFront();
        } catch (QTException e) {
            if (e.errorCode() != Errors.userCanceledErr)
                e.printStackTrace();
            QTSession.close();
        }
    }

    ImageFileDemo (QTFile qtf) throws QTException {
        super (qtf.getName());

        QTCanvas canv = new QTCanvas();
        add (canv, "Center");
```

```
GraphicsImporterDrawer myImageFile = new GraphicsImporterDrawer (qtf);
canv.setClient (myImageFile, true);

addWindowListener(new WindowAdapter () {
    public void windowClosing (WindowEvent e) {
        QTSession.close();
        dispose();
    }

    public void windowClosed (WindowEvent e) {
        System.exit(0);
    }
});
    }
}
```

QuickTime to Java Imaging

The code in this section shows how to create a java.awt.Image from a QuickTime source. The QTImageProducer is used to produce this image's pixel data from the original QuickTime source.

The QuickTime image could come from any one of the following sources:

- an image file in a format that Java doesn't directly support but QuickTime does

- recording the drawing actions of a QDGraphics into a Pict. This can be written out to a file or presented by an ImagePresenter class to the QTImageProducer directly.

- using the services of QuickTime's sequence grabber component. A sequence grabber can be used to capture just one individual frame from a video source.

In the sample code, the user is prompted to open an image file from one of 20 or more formats that QuickTime's GraphicsImporter can import.

The program then uses the QTImageProducer to create a java.awt.Image that is then drawn in the paint() method of the Frame.

You prompt the user to select an image file and import that image into QuickTime. You then create a GraphicsImporterDrawer that uses the GraphicsImporter to draw. This object produces pixels for the QTImageProducer:

```
QTFile imageFile =
        QTFile.standardGetFilePreview(QTFile.kStandardQTFileTypes);
GraphicsImporter myGraphicsImporter = new GraphicsImporter
                                        (imageFile);
GraphicsImporterDrawer myDrawer = new GraphicsImporterDrawer
                                        (myGraphicsImporter);
```

You create a java.awt.Image from the pixels supplied to it by the QTImageProducer:

```
QDRect r = myDrawer.getDisplayBounds();
imageSize = new Dimension (r.getWidth(), r.getHeight());
QTImageProducer qtProducer = new QTImageProducer (myDrawer,
                                        imageSize);
javaImage = Toolkit.getDefaultToolkit().createImage(qtProducer);
```

Note that to do Java drawing, your application uses the java.awt.Graphics.drawImage(...) calls, which must be defined in a paint() method. When using a QTCanvas client, this detail is taken care of by the QTCanvas itself by establishing the QTCanvas QTDrawable client relationship, as the above code demonstrates.

In the paint() method of the frame, the image that we produced in the above code is drawn, using this drawImage call. This method will correctly resize the image to the size of the frame.

```
public void paint (Graphics g) {
    Insets i = getInsets();
    Dimension d = getSize();
    int width = d.width - i.left - i.right;
    int height = d.height - i.top - i.bottom;
    g.drawImage (javaImage, i.left, i.top, width, height, this);
}
```

This returns the size of the source image, so the `pack()` will correctly resize the frame:

```
public Dimension getPreferredSize () {
    return imageSize;
}
```

The complete code, `QTtoJavaImage`, is available on the CD-ROM.

IMAGE PRODUCING

The code in this section, available on the CD-ROM at the back of this book, shows how to display any QuickTime drawing object using Java's `ImageProducer` model.

The program works with the `QTImageProducer` and with Swing components. The `QTImageProducer` in this case is responsible for getting the QuickTime movie and producing the pixels for a `java.awt.Image`. It draws the movie into its own `QDGraphics` world and then feeds the pixels to any `java.image.ImageConsumer` objects that are registered with it in a format that they are able to deal with. The Swing buttons control the movie playback.

The Swing `JComponent` is the `ImageConsumer` of the `QTImageProducer`. It will automatically repaint itself if the `QTImageProducer` source is multiframed media, such as a movie. This is a feature of the `ImageProducer` model of the Java API.

Placing a QuickTime movie within a Swing `JComponent` requires the usage of Java's Image producing API. Swing is a framework that uses lightweight components. As such, a heavyweight component, such as a `QTCanvas`, is generally not added to the lightweight components. To put QuickTime content into a lightweight component a `java.awt.Image` is used to capture the pixel data generated by QuickTime. As the previous example showed, the Java image producing API is used, with the `QTImageProducer` implementing the `ImageProducer` interface used for this purpose. More information about Swing and the image producing

API can be found in Java documentation and at the Java website: `http://java.sun.com/`.

We open the movie and set looping of its time base. We make a `MoviePlayer` out of the movie to pass to the `QTImageProducer`, which takes any `QTDrawable` object as a source of pixel data. We pass in the original size of the movie to the `QTImageProducer`, which will notify the producer how big a `QDGraphics` it should create.

Once the `QTImageProducer` is made, we need to redraw it when each frame of the movie is drawn. To optimize this process, we install a `MovieDrawingComplete` callback. This callback notifies us when the movie draws a complete frame, and in the `execute()` method we redraw the `QTImageProducer`. The `QTImageProducer redraw()` method will pass on the changed pixel data to the registered `ImageConsumer` objects. The `ImageConsumer` is registered with the `QTImageProducer` when we create the `IPJComponent,` as shown in the code below:

```
OpenMovieFile openMovieFile = OpenMovieFile.asRead(movFile);
Movie m = Movie.fromFile (openMovieFile);
m.getTimeBase().setFlags (loopTimeBase);
MoviePlayer moviePlayer = new MoviePlayer (m);
QDRect r = moviePlayer.getDisplayBounds();
Dimension d = new Dimension (r.getWidth(), r.getHeight());
ip = new QTImageProducer (moviePlayer, d);

    //this tells us that the movie has redrawn and
    //we use this to redraw the QTImageProducer - which will
    //supply more pixel data to its registered consumers
m.setDrawingCompleteProc (movieDrawingCallWhenChanged, this);

IPJComponent canv = new IPJComponent (d, ip);
pan.add("Center", canv);
```

The following is the `execute()` method of the `MovieDrawingComplete` interface. This `execute()` method is invoked whenever the movie draws. We use the `updateConsumers()` method of the `QTImageProducer` as the movie has already drawn when this callback is executed, so we only need to notify the image consumers and give them the new pixel data. If the movie hadn't drawn, then the `QTImageProducer redraw()`

method would be called. This both redraws the QTDrawable source and updates the image consumers' pixel data:

```
public int execute (Movie m) {
    try {
        ip.updateConsumers (null);
    } catch (QTException e) {
        return e.errorCode();
    }
    return 0;
}
```

The following shows the construction of the IPJComponent. This JComponent is a Swing component and its paint() method will draw the image that is the consumer of the QTImageProducer. The constructor creates a java.awt.Image, the createImage() method establishing the QTImageProducer as the producer of pixel data for this image. The prepareImage() call establishes the IPJComponent as the ImageObserver of this process. The paint() method uses the supplied java.awt.Graphics drawImage() call to draw the image, also passing the IPJComponent as the ImageObserver. Each time the QTImageProducer is redrawn, it notifies its image consumers that it has more pixel data. This will, in turn, notify the ImageObserver, which is the IPJComponent, that it should repaint itself. The paint() method is consequently called and drawImage() will draw the new pixel data to the screen.

```
static class IPJComponent extends JComponent {
    IPJComponent (Dimension prefSize, QTImageProducer ip) {
        pSize = prefSize;
        im = createImage (ip);
        prepareImage (im, this);
    }

    private Dimension pSize;
    private Image im;


    public Dimension getPreferredSize() {
        return pSize;
    }
```

7 QuickTime and Java Imaging and Effects

```
public void paint (Graphics g) {
    g.drawImage (im, 0, 0, pSize.width, pSize.height, this);
}
// stops flicker as we have no background color to erase
public void update (Graphics g) {
    paint (g);
}
}
```

USING THE QTIMAGEDRAWER CLASS

The QTImageDrawer class enables standard Java drawing commands and graphics objects to have their content rendered by QuickTime within a QuickTime graphics space (QDGraphics). Standard AWT paint() calls can be made on the Graphics object supplied to the paint() call of the Paintable interface attached to the QTImageDrawer. Because the QTImage-Drawer implements the ImageSpec interface, you can add it to a quicktime.app.display.Compositor object and thus draw into the same display space as QuickTime-generated content. It also implements the QTDrawable interface and can thus also be a client of a QTCanvas.

A QTImageDrawer object is used to convert the results of painting into a java.awt.Image object using a java.awt.Graphics object to a format that QuickTime can render.

When the java.awt.Image object is created and painted into (using the QTImageDrawer Paintable object) the QTImageDrawer uses Java's PixelGrabber to grab the raw pixel values that resulted from this painting. It then constructs an ImageDescription object that describes to QuickTime the format, width, and height of this pixel data, and an ImagePresenter is used internally to render the image using QuickTime imaging services.

If the QTImageDrawer is used to grab the results of a single paint, then it can make optimizations on the amount of memory that it uses. A single frame is indicated by the kSingleFrame flag when constructing it. In this case, your application can grab the resultant image data (get-

Image()) and its description (getDescription()) and then discard the QTImageDrawer object completely. This is preferable in many situations where both performance and memory usage are a consideration; performance is enhanced because once the image is retrieved in this way, it is already in a format that is suitable and can be drawn very efficiently by QuickTime. The extra memory and overhead of Java's imaging model and the translation to a format QuickTime can render can thus be discarded.

The paint() method of the QTImageDrawer Paintable object returns an array of rectangles that tells the drawer which areas of its drawing area were drawn. This optimizes the amount of copying and can greatly increase performance when composited.

The QTImageDrawer is used in the CreateMovies sample code in Chapter 8, "Creating, Editing, and Importing QuickTime Movies," and it is also used in the DirectGroup and compositing examples in Chapter 15, "Animation and Compositing." In the description in Chapter 8, an important consideration is discussed that your application should be aware of when using the QTImageDrawer that arises out of the nature of Java's imaging model.

VISUAL EFFECTS

QuickTime provides a wide range of sophisticated visual effects, as demonstrated by the sample movies on the CD-ROM at the back of this book. QuickTime's visual effects architecture can be applied to visual media in a movie or can be used in real time—that is, applied to image sources that are not contained in a movie. The code listed here and the QuickTime for Java classes are designed with this second usage in mind. Example code to apply effects to a movie can be found in the QuickTime SDK.

The QTEffect class forms the base class for visual effects. Depending on the effect itself, you can apply visual effects over a length of time or once only. Effects can be applied to no source images (i.e., the effect acts on a background QDGraphics object), such as the ripple effect. An effect can also be applied to a single source image (typically, color correction or embossing) using the QTFilter class. Finally, an effect can be applied to two sources (such as wipes and fades), using the QTTransition class that transitions from the source to the destination image.

APPLYING QUICKTIME VISUAL EFFECTS

The code snippets in this section show how to use QuickTime's visual effects architecture. The effects in the code are applied, in real time, to two images. The rendering of the transitions is controlled by the user settings in the window's control panel.

Changes to any one of these three fields of the transition can affect the values of the other. Thus, changing the duration or frames per second (fps) will alter how many frames are rendered. The code updates the values in the other fields to reflect these dependencies.

You set the duration of the transition if it is running using the time mode of the QTTransition class:

```
timeField.addActionListener (new ActionListener () {
    public void actionPerformed (ActionEvent event) {
        int output = ...//get value from field
        transition.setTime (output);
    }
});
```

You set the number of frames the transition will take to render:

```
frameField.addActionListener (new ActionListener () {
    public void actionPerformed (ActionEvent event) {
        int output = ...//get value from field
        transition.setFrames (output);
    }
});
```

You set the number of frames per second that the transition should be rendered in:

```
fpsField.addActionListener (new ActionListener () {
    public void actionPerformed (ActionEvent event) {
        int output = ...//get value from field
        transition.setFramesPerSecond (output);
    }
});
```

You use this code snippet to make the transition run based on the settings. If the transition is profiling, some statistics about the transition are printed.

```
runEffectButton.addActionListener (new ActionListener () {
    public void actionPerformed (ActionEvent event) {
        try {
            transition.doTransition();
            if (transition.isProfiled()) {
                String profileString = "Transition Profile:"
                    + "requestedDuration:" + transition.getTime()
                    + ",actualDuration:" + transition.profileDuration()
                    + ",requestedFrames:" + transition.getFrames()
                    + ",framesRendered=" + transition.profileFramesRendered()
                    + ",averageRenderTimePerFrame="
                    + (transition.profileDuration()
                            / transition.profileFramesRendered());
                System.out.println (profileString);
            }

        } catch (QTException e) {
            if (e.errorCode() != userCanceledErr)
                e.printStackTrace();
        }
    }
});
```

You use this code snippet to show QuickTime's Choose Effects dialog box:

```
chooseEffectButton.addActionListener (new ActionListener () {
    public void actionPerformed (ActionEvent event) {
        PlayQTEffectApp.showDialog (transition);
    }
});
```

The two buttons in the following code snippet can change the mode of the transition. If the transition renders using time mode, it will potentially drop frames in order to render itself as close to the specified duration as possible. If the transition is set to doTime(false), it will render the currently specified number of frames as quickly as possible. This mode varies considerably from computer to computer based on the processing and video capabilities of the runtime environment.

```
frameButton.addItemListener (new ItemListener () {
    public void itemStateChanged (ItemEvent event) {
        transition.doTime (false);
    }
});
timeButton.addItemListener (new ItemListener () {
    public void itemStateChanged (ItemEvent event) {
        transition.doTime (true);
    }
});
```

Figure 7.1 shows an explode effect from the program.

FIGURE 7.1   *The explode effect from the QT Effects program*

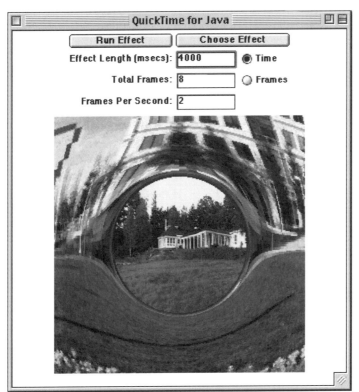

To make an effect, you need to either build one in code or the user can choose an effect from QuickTime's Choose Effects dialog box, as shown in Figure 7.2.

FIGURE 7.2 *QuickTime's Choose Effects dialog box*

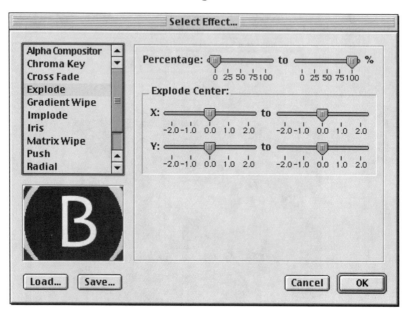

You set up an atom container to use a SMPTE effect. Using SMPTE effects, you set the WhatAtom to SMPTE, ensure the endian order is big-endian, and use SMPTE effect number 74:

```
public AtomContainer createSMPTEEffect (int effectType,
                                        int effectNumber) {
    AtomContainer effectSample = new AtomContainer();

// We are using SMPTE Effects so set the what atom to smpt
    effectSample.insertChild (new Atom(kParentAtomIsContainer),
        kEffectWhatAtom,
        1,
        0,
        EndianOrder.flipNativeToBigEndian32(kWipeTransitionType));

// We are using SMPTE effect number 74  - start at 0%, stop at 100%
    effectSample.insertChild (new Atom(kParentAtomIsContainer),
            effectType,
            1,
            0,
```

```
                    EndianOrder.flipNativeToBigEndian32(effectNumber));

    return effectSample;
}
```

In this example, the dialog box is configured to show only effects that expect two sources, but it can be configured to show effects applied or requiring only a single source.

```
public static void showDialog (QTEffect ef) throws QTException {
    AtomContainer effectSample = ParameterDialog.showParameterDialog
                                    (new EffectsList (2, 2, 0), 0);
    ef.setEffect (effectSample);
}
```

You use the `doTransition()` method, which is part of the `QTTransition` class in the `quicktime.app.image` package, to set parameters to control the rendering behavior of the effect.

```
QTTransition ef = new QTTransition ();
ef.setTime (800);
ef.setSourceImage (sourceImage);
ef.setDestinationImage (destImage);
ef.setEffect (createSMPTEEffect (kEffectWipe, kRandomWipeTransitionType));
```

Your application can also directly control the rendering of each frame of an effect through setting the frame directly and redrawing the effect. The `Transitions` sample code in Chapter 15, "Animation and Compositing," shows an example of this.

8 Creating, Editing, and Importing QuickTime Movies

This chapter demonstrates some of the techniques you can use to create and edit movies using QuickTime for Java. The examples in this chapter show you how to

- create a movie using Java drawing capabilities and a sound file

- present an example of adding a tween track to a movie with a 3D track

- subclass the `quicktime.std.movies.media.Media` class to support any custom media types

- use the import and export capabilities of QuickTime, as well as the flexible data model that a QuickTime movie can support

CREATING MOVIES

The code in this section shows how to create a movie from the results of using Java drawing capabilities and a sound file. The media that uses this sample code is the file `sound.aif`. The code is a rough translation of the `CreateMovie` code in the QuickTime API documentation. Figure 8.1 shows an example of the movie created.

FIGURE 8.1   *The screen output from CreateMovie.mov*

The code snippets that follow provide a general overview of how you construct the movie. You take the following steps:

1. The user is prompted to save and create the new movie file.

2. You create both the new file and a `Movie` object that references that file.

3. You add a video track to this movie.

4. You add a sound track to this movie.

5. You write the new movie out to the file

```
private void makeMovie() {
    FileDialog fd = new FileDialog (this, "Save Movie As...", FileDialog.SAVE);
    fd.show();
    if(fd.getFile() == null)
        throw new QTIOException (userCanceledErr, "");
    QTFile f = new QTFile(fd.getDirectory() + fd.getFile());
    Movie theMovie = Movie.createMovieFile (f, kMoviePlayer,
                createMovieFileDeleteCurFile | createMovieFileDontCreateResFile);

    addVideoTrack( theMovie );
    addAudioTrack( theMovie );

    OpenMovieFile outStream = OpenMovieFile.asWrite (f);
```

```
theMovie.addResource( outStream, movieInDataForkResID, f.getName() );
outStream.close();
}
```

We add a track to the movie and create a `VideoMedia` object as the media for this new track. After adding the video media samples to this `VideoMedia` object, we insert the video media into this track:

```
private void addVideoTrack (Movie theMovie) throws QTException {
    int kNoVolume    = 0;
    int kVidTimeScale = 600;

    Track vidTrack = theMovie.addTrack (kWidth, kHeight, kNoVolume);
    VideoMedia vidMedia = new VideoMedia (vidTrack, kVidTimeScale);

    vidMedia.beginEdits();
    addVideoSample (vidMedia);
    vidMedia.endEdits();

    int kTrackStart = 0;
    int kMediaTime  = 0;
    int kMediaRate  = 1;
    vidTrack.insertMedia (kTrackStart, kMediaTime,
                vidMedia.getDuration(), kMediaRate);
}
```

To compress image data, you need to have some kind of `QDGraphics` object. The code draws into an offscreen `QDGraphics`, which is the source image that is then compressed. The resultant compressed data is then added to the movie. This code is seen in the `addVideoSample()` method.

The animation compressor is used in this example. Animation is an ideal compression format for images that contain large pieces of the same color, typically found in graphics that are generated for animation (thus its name). Animation can be a lossless compressor. That is, none of the image data when compressed is lost, so when decompressing, all of the original pixel data of the source image can be recreated.

Temporal compression is also used in this example. This means that the first frame's compressed data completely describes the image. The

consequent frame's compressed data only contains the differences between that frame and the key frame. This can make the actual data that
is stored considerably smaller and thus faster to read when playing the
movie back. This is particularly pertinent in this example, as the only
difference between each frame is the number that is painted in the center. The following is a part of the printout of the program:

```
f#:1,kf=true,sim=0
f#:2,kf=false,sim=253
f#:3,kf=false,sim=254
f#:4,kf=false,sim=253
. . .
```

As you can see, the first frame is a key frame, and it has a similarity
of 0—that is, its compressed data contains the complete image. The
consequent frames have very high similarity values (255 means that all
of the data is identical to the key frame).

The QTImageDrawer takes the pixels that the NumberPainter paints in
the paint() call and blits them to its destination QDGraphics (the setG-
World call), which is offscreen. We set the QTImageDrawer to draw to an
offscreen QDGraphics, and after each draw the QDGraphics is compressed, and the resultant compressed image data is added to the movie.

After the compression cycle is complete, we reset the QTImageDrawer
gWorld to the QDGraphics of its QTCanvas:

```
private void addVideoSample( VideoMedia vidMedia ) throws QTException {
    QDRect rect = new QDRect (kWidth, kHeight);
    QDGraphics gw = new QDGraphics (rect);
    int size = QTImage.getMaxCompressionSize (gw,
                                               rect,
                                               gw.getPixMap().getPixelSize(),
                                               codecNormalQuality,
                                               kAnimationCodecType,
                                               CodecComponent.anyCodec);
    QTHandle imageHandle = new QTHandle (size, true);
    imageHandle.lock();
    RawEncodedImage compressedImage = RawEncodedImage.fromQTHandle(imageHandle);
    CSequence seq = new CSequence (gw,
                                   rect,
```

```
                                gw.getPixMap().getPixelSize(),
                                kAnimationCodecType,
                                CodecComponent.bestFidelityCodec,
                                codecNormalQuality,
                                codecNormalQuality,
                                numFrames,  //1 key frame
                                null,
                                0);
    ImageDescription desc = seq.getDescription();

//redraw first...
    np.setCurrentFrame (1);
    qid.redraw(null);

//set the destination GWorld of the QTImageDrawer to the QDGraphics
// we compress for the video data
    qid.setGWorld (gw);
    qid.setDisplayBounds (rect);

    for (int curSample = 1; curSample <= numFrames; curSample++) {
        np.setCurrentFrame (curSample);
        qid.redraw(null);
        CompressedFrameInfo info = seq.compressFrame (gw,
                                               rect,
                                               codecFlagUpdatePrevious,
                                               compressedImage);
        boolean isKeyFrame = info.getSimilarity() == 0;
        System.out.println ("f#:" + curSample + ",kf=" + isKeyFrame
                                       + ",sim=" + info.getSimilarity());
        vidMedia.addSample (imageHandle,
                            0, // dataOffset,
                            info.getDataSize(),
                            60, // frameDuration, 60/600 = 1/10 of a second,
                            desc,
                            1, // one sample
                            (isKeyFrame ? 0 : mediaSampleNotSync)); // no flags
    }

//redraw after finishing...
// reset the QTImageDrawer GWorld back to the QTCanvas
    qid.setGWorld (canv.getPort());
```

```
np.setCurrentFrame (numFrames);
qid.redraw(null);
}
```

The code reuses the same (imageHandle) for compressing the data into and then adding this data into the movie. The program creates the imageHandle to be the maximum size that would be required to hold the resultant compressed data and reuses that handle from frame to frame. You can do this because the vidMedia.addSample() method copies the data. The compress call takes an EncodedImage class. The program uses a RawEncodedImage object that references the same memory as is allocated in the (imageHandle). The ImageDescription returned by the compress call tells this addSample() method how much of the incoming imageHandle is valid data. At this point we don't care what is in the rest of the imageHandle.

In the CreateMovie constructor, the QTImageDrawer is used to get the drawing results from the NumberPainter object. The NumberPainter object draws into a java.awt.Image object, using those drawing commands derived from a java.awt.Graphics object. This Image object is an offscreen java.awt.Image object.

```
public CreateMovie (String frameTitle) throws Exception {
    super(frameTitle);
    soundFile = QTFactory.findAbsolutePath ("sound.aif");

    canv = new QTCanvas (QTCanvas.kInitialSize, 0.5F, 0.5F);
    add ("Center", canv);

    np = new NumberPainter(numFrames);
    qid = new QTImageDrawer (np, new Dimension (kWidth, kHeight),
                                    Redrawable.kMultiFrame);
    qid.setRedrawing(true);

    canv.setClient (qid, true);

    pack();
}
```

The QTImageDrawer creates that offscreen Image object from the QTCanvas it is attached to. The image it creates remains unchanged in size and composition once it is created, so the NumberPainter can do less work once it has done an intial paint, where it paints all of the image. In subsequent calls, it only paints the new number and returns a rectangle that tells the QTImageDrawer which area of its pixel data it has changed.

Creating a QTCanvas in the first place and adding it to a Frame may seem like an arbitrary and highly inconvenient and unnecessary restriction in the AWT, but it must be done. The java.awt does *not* allow the creation of an offscreen image at all unless you create it from a java.awt.Component.createImage call. And you can only do this when the component has been added to a Frame (or applet). The native graphics environment must be initialized (this is why the program calls pack()), but it does not need to actually show the frame—it just needs the native graphics environment for it to be initialized. The frame is shown for convenience and visual feedback—it is not required, and the make-Movie() method could be called right after the constructor without showing the number frame at all.

The sound track is constructed and added in a similar fashion as the video track. We add the new track to the movie, create a SoundMedia object for this track, insert the samples of the sound data into this Media object, and then insert the Media object into the track.

```
private void addAudioTrack (Movie theMovie) throws Exception {
    int kFullVolume = 1;

    SoundData theSound = getSound();

    Track sndTrack = theMovie.addTrack (0, 0, kFullVolume);
    SoundMedia sndMedia = new SoundMedia (sndTrack,
                theSound.description.getSampleRateRounded());

    sndMedia.beginEdits();
    sndMedia.addSample (theSound.sampleData,
                        0,
                        theSound.sampleData.getSize(),
                        1, // duration of each sound sample,
```

```
                                     theSound.description,
                                     theSound.numSamples,
                                     0);
        sndMedia.endEdits();

        int kTrackStart = 0;
        int kMediaTime  = 0;
        int kMediaRate  = 1;
        sndTrack.insertMedia (kTrackStart, kMediaTime,
                              sndMedia.getDuration(), kMediaRate);
    }
```

We retrieve the sound data from an AIF file. We also need to retrieve some of the meta-data from this file that describes to QuickTime
the format of the sound data, sample size, and rate. A SoundDescription is created to contain this meta-data.

This method returns a custom SoundData object that has the created
SoundDescription, the number of samples that are in the sound data,
and the sound data itself that has been read into memory. This SoundData object is then used in the above code to insert this sound data into
the SoundMedia object.

```
private SoundData getSound() throws QTException, IOException {
    SndInfo info = SndInfo.parseAIFFHeader (
                       OpenFile.asRead (new QTFile(soundFile)));

    SoundData sd = new SoundData();

    SoundComponentData mySndInfo = info.sndData;

    sd.description = new SoundDescription (mySndInfo.getFormat());
    sd.description.setNumberOfChannels (mySndInfo.getNumChannels());
    sd.description.setSampleSize (mySndInfo.getSampleSize());
    sd.description.setSampleRate (mySndInfo.getSampleRate());

    int mySampleDataSize = mySndInfo.getSampleCount() *
                           (mySndInfo.getSampleSize() / 8);
    FileInputStream fis = new FileInputStream (soundFile);
    byte[] ar = new byte [mySampleDataSize];
    fis.skip (info.dataOffset);
```

```
        fis.read (ar, 0, mySampleDataSize);

        sd.sampleData = new QTHandle (ar);

        sd.numSamples = mySndInfo.getSampleCount();
        return sd;
    }

    static class SoundData {
        QTHandle sampleData;
        SoundDescription description;
        int numSamples;
    }
```

ADDING A TWEEN TRACK

The code in this section shows how to apply camera actions to a 3D model (a 3D media track) in a movie using the tween media type of QuickTime. This code presents an example of adding a tween track to a movie with a 3D track. The media required for this sample code is `jet.mov`.

Movies use big-endian file formats. The types `ints`, `shorts`, and `floats` on Win32 systems are little endian (even in Java). While QuickTime can take care of many of the endian issues when reading and writing movies, it cannot do so with atom containers the user adds to a movie directly. The user must ensure that the data added to atom containers by the `insertChild()` and `setAtomData()` methods be in required endian formats. Thus, we have the need to flip the endian ordering, as shown in the code below.

QuickTime for Java provides a number of utility classes and methods in the `quicktime.util` package for dealing specifically with this issue (see Chapter 44, "The quicktime. util Package," for more information). Endian order is discussed briefly in Chapter 2, "QuickTime Basics," and the QuickTime documentation explains the circumstances where the application must ensure the correct endian order of data—generally when dealing with data contained in atom containers.

QTUTILS.ENDIANFLIP() METHODS

These methods will flip the endian order of the supplied value(s).

Remember, endian order is context sensitive in that there exists no specific indication that a value is ordered in little- or big-endian order. Thus, flipping of the endian order of a value to a big- or little-endian order depends on whether the value is currently in big- or little-endian order, and this can only be ascertained by the context of the value. A native value on Mac OS is in big-endian order, while a native value on Windows is little-endian. Ensuring that a native value is in big-endian order means that on the Mac OS the endian order should not be flipped, but on Windows it should be.

It is the application's responsibility to ensure that these endian methods are applied in the correct context. To assist developers dealing with these issues, a context-sensitive class is provided: `EndianOrder`. This class has two distinct sets of methods:

- `flipNativeToBigEndian()`

  These methods will only flip the endian order of values if the native platform is little-endian (for example, Windows). This method is used when a big-endian value is required and the native format is little-endian. This method will not flip the endian order of the specified value when the native format of the platform is already big-endian (for example, Mac OS). These methods are generally used when adding data to atom containers, as QuickTime expects the data in these containers to be in big-endian formats.

- `flipNativeToLittleEndian()`

  These methods will only flip the endian order of values if the native platform is big-endian (for example, Mac OS). This method is used when a little-endian value is required and the native format is big-endian. This method will not flip the endian order of the specified value when the native format of the platform is already little-endian (for example, Windows). These methods are generally used far less frequently than the `flipNativeToBigEndian`, but for a few data formats that are native to the Windows world, this capability may be required.

■ `EndianDescriptor`

Atom containers may also contain data that is represented as a QuickTime structure, for example, the `CameraData` in the following code example. In this case, a helper class called and `Endian-Descriptor` is provided. An `EndianDescriptor` is a class that describes the endian-flipping requirements of such a structure. For example, the `CameraData` contains embedded structures that are ultimately composed of 32 bit or 4 byte values. To flip the values of a `CameraData` requires that all of these fields be flipped around these 4 byte boundaries. The `EndianDescriptor` for this class uses the constant `EndianDescriptor.flipAll32` to describe its endian- flipping requirements.

■ `EndianFlipSpec`

The `EndianFlipSpec` is a class that is used in conjunction with the `EndianDescriptor` class. It describes the size of the field that must be flipped and the offset within the native structure that a particular `EndianFlipSpec` should be applied to. These objects are added to an `EndianDescriptor` object that describes a native structure that has different-sized fields. For example, the `SampleDescription` family of classes has both 2 and 4 bytes fields, as well as byte[] fields that do not require flipping. In these cases, an `EndianDescriptor` is created using these `EndianFlipSpec` objects that describe which fields need to be flipped and around what size (typically 2 or 4 bytes) that the specified field should be flipped.

QuickTime for Java provides many `EndianDescriptor` objects for those classes that are typically added to atom containers by an application. However, your application may provide custom data formats, or there maybe some classes that do not have an `EndianDescriptor`. If either of these situations arises and the class needs to be flipped, then your application can use the `EndianDescriptor` and `EndianFlipSpec` classes to build their own endian-flipping specifications, and use the resultant `EndianDescriptor` with the methods discussed above to ensure their structures are presented to QuickTime in the appropriate endian order.

ADDING THE TRACK

The steps involved in adding a tween track to a movie with a 3D track are as follows:

1. You create the tween track and media:

```
Track tweenTrack = myMovie.addTrack(0, 0, 0);
TweenMedia tweenMedia = new TweenMedia(tweenTrack,
                              threeDMedia.getTimeScale());
```

2. You create the tween sample and add the tween sample to the tween media. Then you add the tween media to the tween track:

```
AtomContainer tweenSample = new AtomContainer();
   //... see code below

tweenMedia.beginEdits();
tweenMedia.addSample(tweenSample, 0, tweenSample.getSize(),
                          threeDMedia.getDuration(),
                          sampleDescription, 1, 0);
tweenMedia.endEdits();
tweenTrack.insertMedia(0, 0, tweenMedia.getDuration(), 1);
```

3. You establish a link between the tween and 3D tracks and create a new input map for the 3D track. Then you attach the input map to the 3D media handler:

```
int referenceIndex1 = threeDTrack.addReference(tweenTrack,
                              kTrackModifierReference);
AtomContainer inputMap = new AtomContainer();

Atom inputAtom = inputMap.insertChild (
                          new Atom(kParentAtomIsContainer),
                          kTrackModifierInput,
                          referenceIndex1,
                          0);

inputMap.insertChild(inputAtom, kTrackModifierType, 1, 0,
```

```
EndianOrder.flipNativeToBigEndian32(kTrackModifierCameraData));

inputMap.insertChild(inputAtom, kInputMapSubInputID, 1, 0,
                    EndianOrder.flipNativeToBigEndian32(1));

threeDMedia.setInputMap(inputMap);
```

4. You update the movie's file to contain these additions that
we've made:

```
OpenMovieFile outstream = OpenMovieFile.asWrite(movieFile);
myMovie.updateResource(outstream, movieInDataForkResID,
                      movieFile.getName());
```

The program overwrites the original source file, adding a tween
track to it, so keep a copy if you want to go back to it. Also, note that
you need to close the little window that pops up to actually exit the
program properly.

We now build up an `AtomContainer` that is the media data for the
`TweenMedia` track. This data contains an initial `Camera` specification and
the amount the camera view should change over the course of the
tween's duration. We are specifying a `CameraData` action that
QuickTime will use when the movie is played back; specifying the
from, to, and data points for the camera's view of the 3D model:

```
AtomContainer tweenSample = new AtomContainer();

// Construct shared data for the two camera descriptions
Point3D cameraTo = new Point3D (0.0F, 0.0F, 0.0F);
Vector3D cameraUp = new Vector3D (0.0F, 1.0F, 0.0F);

float hither = 0.001F;
float yon = 1000.0F;
CameraRange range = new CameraRange(hither, yon);

QDPoint origin = new QDPoint (-1.0F, 1.0F);
float width = 2.0F;
float height = 2.0F;
CameraViewPort cameraView = new CameraViewPort (origin, width,
                                                height);
```

We add the tween entry to the sample. This sets the type of the tween data, that is to 3D CameraData:

```
Point3D cameraFrom = new Point3D(0.0F, 0.0F, 30.0F);
CameraData tweenCamera = new CameraData(
            new CameraPlacement(cameraFrom, cameraTo, cameraUp),
            range,
            cameraView);


        // create entry for this tween in the sample
Atom tweenAtom = tweenSample.insertChild (
                    new Atom(kParentAtomIsContainer),
                    kTweenEntry, 1, 0);


        // define the type of this tween entry
tweenSample.insertChild(tweenAtom, kTweenType, 1, 0,
    EndianOrder.flipNativeToBigEndian32(kTweenType3dCameraData));


        //Endian flip tweenCamera in place
EndianOrder.flipNativeToBigEndian (tweenCamera, 0,
                            CameraData.getEndianDescriptor());


        // define the 'flipped' data for this tween entry
tweenSample.insertChild(tweenAtom, kTweenData, 1, 0, tweenCamera);
```

The following code sets the initial conditions of the tween data. It is the camera's initial state. Though the only difference is the initial location of the camera, we create a clean copy of the CameraData because it may have been endian-flipped previously. Thus, we have two different camera objects, even though they share common values:

```
Point3D initialLocation = new Point3D (0, 0, 150.0F);
CameraData initialCamera = new CameraData(
        new CameraPlacement(initialLocation, cameraTo, cameraUp),
        range,
        cameraView);


        // look up the tween entry
Atom initialTweenAtom = tweenSample.findChildByID_Atom (
                            new Atom(kParentAtomIsContainer),
                            kTweenEntry, 1);
```

```
        //Endian flip tweenCamera in place
EndianOrder.flipNativeToBigEndian (initialCamera, 0,
                              CameraData.getEndianDescriptor());


        // add in the initial 'flipped' data
tweenSample.insertChild (initialTweenAtom,
            kTween3dInitialCondition, 1, 0, initialCamera);
```

USING CUSTOM MEDIA TYPES

Code on the CD in the back of this book shows how to subclass the `quicktime.std.movies.media.Media` class to support any custom media types. The media required is a QuickTime VR panoramic movie of the user's choice.

Often developers define media types based on their custom requirements. This example code shows how your application can integrate this custom component with the existing QuickTime for Java framework.

FIGURE 8.2   *A QuickTime VR panoramic movie*

To begin with, the user is prompted to select a QTVR panoramic movie file (see Figure 8.2). The code prints out the media object and the SampleDescription of all of the tracks found in the opened movie. The TestVRMedia.zip file also contains the VRMedia class, which is the custom Media subclass. It supplies an Integer constructor. The application should not call this directly; it is called by the Media factory method based on the media type and the vrMediaOSType registered with the Media factory.

The factory methods create Media subclasses based on the media type. If a match is not found for QuickTime's default media types, a search is performed to see if the application itself has registered knowledge of custom or application-specific media types. If a match is still not found, the factory method returns a GenericMedia object.

Standard `Media` calls can still be done on a `GenericMedia` class. It is only if the application requires specific functionality and support for specific media or media handlers that custom media classes have to be written. This mechanism can be used to integrate those custom classes with the existing framework.

The `registerMediaType` static call could easily be done in the static initializer of the `VRMedia` class. It is left as a specific call for the purpose of illustrating the mechanism being used.

The CD-ROM contains the code for the `CustomMedia`, `SampleDescription`, and `MediaHandler` classes. Though they define no methods as such—just the required constructors—they provide a starting point for supporting this functionality. The code below shows the registration of the custom media and then prints out the media and sample description for each track in the target movie.

```
// 0x5354706e is the OSType for a panorama media type
final int vrMediaOSType = 0x5354706e;

//we provide the full class name for the custom media class
Media.addMediaType (vrMediaOSType, "com.vr.VRMedia");
for (int i = 1; i <= n; i++) {
    Media m = Media.getTrackMedia (mov.getIndTrack (i));
    System.out.println (m);
    SampleDescription sd = m.getSampleDescription (1);
    System.out.println (sd);
}
```

IMPORTING AND EXPORTING MEDIA

The code in this section shows some of the import and export capabilities of QuickTime, as well as the flexible data model that a QuickTime movie can support.

The example displays a window with three buttons:

- **Import Media** imports any QuickTime readable content and displays it in the window.

- **Reference Movie** shows how QuickTime can create a movie that references data in the opened movie.

- **Export Movie** shows the exporting of a movie.

Import Movie button. This shows the QTFactory.makeDrawable() method as discussed previously. This method imports any media using the QuickTime importing services. If the source file is an image, a GraphicsImporter is used. If not, then the various Movie.fromFile and MovieImporter options are used to import the media and return a QuickTime movie:

```
void importMedia () {
    FileDialog ifd = new FileDialog (this,
                              "Choose Media to Import...",
                              FileDialog.LOAD);
    ifd.show();
    if (ifd.getFile() == null)
        return;
    QTFile importFile = new QTFile (ifd.getDirectory() +
                                        ifd.getFile());
    QTDrawable media = QTFactory.makeDrawable (importFile);
    if (myQTCanvas == null) {
        myQTCanvas = new QTCanvas();
        add (myQTCanvas, "East");
    }
    myQTCanvas.setClient (media, true);
    pack();
}
```

Reference Movie button. This prompts the user to select a movie. A new movie is created that references this open movie.

```
void makeReferenceMovie (QTFile movieFile, String outputPath) {
    // Create the movie object from the original movie
    Movie theMovie = Movie.fromFile (
                          OpenMovieFile.asRead (movieFile));
    displayMovie (theMovie);
```

```
    QTFile outputMovie = new QTFile (outputPath);
    ...
}
```

The following code snippet creates what is known as a short cut movie. It is a very small movie that contains a data reference to another movie, and when it is opened, it will open the movie it references. The DataRef can be to a local file, HTTP or FTP file, or a RTSP broadcast session.

```
//make a Data ref out of a URL that references the movie
DataRef targetDataRef = new DataRef ("file://" + movFile.getPath());
    //make the very small short cut movie
outputMovie.createShortcutMovieFile (kMoviePlayer,
                            smSystemScript,
                            createMovieFileDeleteCurFile,
                            targetDataRef);
```

This next code snippet creates a movie that gets its media data from another movie. It will create a track in this new movie that references it media data to the existing movie. First, we create the new movie file, then open it and add references to all of the data in the original movie. If we want to copy the referenced data to the new movie, we could open the file we just created as a movie and then flatten it. Flattening a movie makes sure that all of the data it references is copied into the file. The movie becomes a self-contained movie at this point. The flattening code is not shown here but is on the CD-ROM.

```
// create the new movie file, deleting existing file if there
outputMovie.createMovieFile (kMoviePlayer,
createMovieFileDeleteCurFile);

// add a reference to all of the media in the existing media file
// The outputMovie file now contains a reference and dependency
// on the existing media file
OpenMovieFile outStream = OpenMovieFile.asWrite (outputMovie);
theMovie.addResource (outStream, movieInDataForkResID,
                        outputMovie.getName());
outStream.close();
```

Export Movie button. This shows the exporting of a movie to a movie. Exporting copies data from the input or source movie to its destination. This can be a time-consuming task if the media data is large.

The following code snippet is a simple example that uses the Movie.convertToFile call, which prompts the user to save the file and create the destination file itself. The destination file type and format is determined by the type of the file: in this case, kQTFileTypeMovie. This also determines which MovieExporter the code instantiates to perform the export. If we passed in, say, kQTFileTypeAIFF, the method would use the AIFF export component and create an AIF file from the sound tracks in the source movie. We set the defaultProgressProc for the movie so that a progress dialog is displayed to show the progress of the export process. The convertToFile method is passed showUserSettingsDialog to allow the user to choose different formats for the exported data or disable tracks that they do not want to export.

```
int exportType = kQTFileTypeMovie;

theInputMovie.setProgressProc();
theInputMovie.convertToFile (new QTFile ("Export Movie"),
                             exportType,
                             kMoviePlayer,
                             IOConstants.smSystemScript,
                             showUserSettingsDialog);
```

The next code snippet shows the explicit use of a MovieExporter. Though this is very similar to the above example, the capability exists to customize the settings of the export component that is used, either through prompting the user with the settings dialog (the same as the previous example) or through the program itself configuring the settings AtomContainer of the export component itself. The Movie.convertToFile() method can be used with a configured MovieExporter (not shown here) or, as shown here, your application can create the movie file itself and export it directly to that file. In this case, your application would need to define its own progress dialog. Here, we just print out the export progress to the console.

```
FileDialog ofd = new FileDialog (new Frame(), "Export Movie to...",
                                  FileDialog.SAVE);
ofd.show();
if (ofd.getFile() == null)
    return;
QTFile outFile = new QTFile (ofd.getDirectory() + ofd.getFile());
outFile.createMovieFile (kMoviePlayer,createMovieFileDeleteCurFile);

MovieExporter theMovieExp = new MovieExporter (exportType);
theMovieExp.doUserDialog (theInputMovie, null, 0,
                    theInputMovie.getDuration());

theMovieExp.setProgressProc (new MovieProgress () {
    public int execute (Movie mov, int message, int whatOperation,
                                    float percentDone) {
        System.out.println (mov + ",message="
                + Integer.toHexString(message) + "," + ",what="
                + Integer.toHexString(whatOperation)
                + ",%=" + percentDone);
        return 0;
    }
});

theMovieExp.toFile (outFile, theInputMovie, null, 0,
                    theInputMovie.getDuration());
```

9 *Capturing Media with QuickTime*

This chapter demonstrates some of the techniques you can use to capture QuickTime media. It shows you how to

- use the `SequenceGrabber` class to record audio into a movie file

- use Sound Manager Input SPB calls to record audio into memory

- use the `SGDrawable` class to capture and display live video within a `QTCanvas`

The `SequenceGrabber` always records to a movie that it creates. The SPB calls allow the program to record to a preallocated memory buffer.

RECORDING AUDIO

The sample code in this section shows how to use the `SequenceGrabber` for simple audio recording. The program creates a small window with three buttons on it that let you

- show the settings of the audio input

- record audio

- stop recording and display the recorded movie

The `createSGObject()` method creates the `SequenceGrabber`:

```
void createSGObject() throws QTException {
        mGrabber = new SequenceGrabber();
        mAudio = new SGSoundChannel (mGrabber);
        mAudio.setUsage (seqGrabRecord);
        t = new Thread (this,"SoundRecord Idle Method");
}
```

Settings. This button allows the user to specify the source, compression, and format for the recording:

```
settingsButton.addActionListener (new ActionListener () {
    public void actionPerformed (ActionEvent event) {
        try{
            if (mAudio == null) {
                createSGObject();
            }

            if (recording == false)
                mAudio.settingsDialog ();
        } catch (QTException ee){
            ee.printStackTrace();
        }
    }
});
```

Start. This button creates a file to save the recorded information in and start recording:

```
startButton.addActionListener (new ActionListener () {
    public void actionPerformed (ActionEvent event) {
        try{

            createMovie();

            if (mGrabber == null)
                createSGObject();

            mGrabber.setDataOutput (recordFile, seqGrabToDisk);
            mGrabber.prepare(true, true);
            mGrabber.startRecord();
            t.start();
            recording = true;
```

```
        recordNotice = new Frame("Recording");

        recordNotice.setLayout(new GridLayout(1, 3, 2, 2));
        recordNotice.add (stopButton);
    } catch (QTException ee){
        ee.printStackTrace();
    }
  }
});
```

The program creates a thread in order to call the `idle()` method of the `SequenceGrabber`, which is a requirement for the `SGComponent`. This idling is started after the `SequenceGrabber` begins recording and is stopped before stopping the recording. This order ensures that the `idle()` method is only called while the `SequenceGrabber` is actually recording:

```
public void run () {
    try {
        for (;;) {
            mGrabber.idle();
            Thread.sleep(10);
        }
    } catch (Exception e) {
        e.printStackTrace();
    }
}
```

Stop. You use this next code snippet to create a button that stops recording and shows the window with the resultant movie in it.

You need to dispose of your connection to the audio channel before playing back the recorded sound. Otherwise, you won't hear your recorded sound. You don't need to create a movie file to save the recorded data, since the sequence grabber will automatically create a movie file for you based on the file you set in the `setDataOutput()` method.

```
stopButton.addActionListener (new ActionListener () {
    public void actionPerformed (ActionEvent event) {
        if (recording) {
            try {
```

```
                        t.stop();
                        mGrabber.stop();    //stop record
                        recordNotice.hide();
                        recordNotice = null;
                        recording = false;

                        mGrabber.disposeChannel (mAudio);
                        mAudio = null;

                        mGrabber.release();
                        mGrabber = null;
                        showMovie();
                    } catch (QTException ee) {
                        ee.printStackTrace();
                    }
                }
            }
        });
```

RECORDING AUDIO TO MEMORY

This example program, which is available on the CD-ROM at the back of this book, shows how to use Sound Manager SPB calls for simple audio recording to memory. The program creates a window with two buttons in it to record and play the recorded sound.

The program starts by making an SPBDevice that will be used to record from. It then prints out a number of the current settings of the SPBDevice. It then makes a SndHandle, based on some of the state information of the SPBDevice and then resizes the handle to add the desired buffer to record to. At this point you are ready to record into this SndHandle:

```
snd = new SPBDevice (null, siWritePermission);
System.out.println ("OptionsDialog==" + snd.hasOptionsDialog());
System.out.println ("NumChannels=" + snd.getChannelAvailable());
System.out.println ("SampleSize=" + snd.getSampleSize());
printArray("Compression", snd.getCompressionAvailable(), kOSType);
```

```
printArray("SampleSize", snd.getSampleSizeAvailable(), 0);
printArray("SampleRate", snd.getSampleRateAvailable());
snd.setPlayThruOnOff (0);
hdl = new SndHandle (snd.getNumberChannels(),
                                snd.getSampleRate(),
                                snd.getSampleSize(),
                                snd.getCompressionType(),
                                60);
hdl.appendSoundBuffer (sndBufferSize);
```

You make a recorder when the user clicks the **Record** button. The recording will be done synchronously (the false value to the `record()` method). You then reset the header of the `SndHandle` with the number of bytes recorded, and this handle is now ready to play.

The **Record** button starts recording into memory. It records into the buffer you've allocated:

```
startButton.addActionListener (new ActionListener () {
    public void actionPerformed (ActionEvent event) {
        try{
            System.out.println ("StartRecording");
            SPB recorder = new SPB(snd, 0,
                    snd.bytesToMilliseconds(sndBufferSize),
                    hdl.getSoundData());
            recorder.record (false);
            System.out.println ("FinishedRecording");
            hdl.setupHeader (snd.getNumberChannels(),
                                snd.getSampleRate(),
                                snd.getSampleSize(),
                                snd.getCompressionType(),
                                60,
                                recorder.getCount());
        } catch (QTException ee){
            ee.printStackTrace();
        }
    }
});
```

The **Play** button plays what you last recorded:

```
playButton.addActionListener (new ActionListener () {
    public void actionPerformed (ActionEvent event) {
        try{
            if (hdl != null) Sound.play (hdl);
        } catch (QTException ee){
            ee.printStackTrace();
        }
    }
});
```

CAPTURING AND DISPLAYING LIVE VIDEO

This next sample code, also available on the CD-ROM at the back of this book, shows how to use the SGDrawable class to capture and display live video within a QTCanvas.

You need to set the client in the windowOpened() method for the SequenceGrabber because the QDGraphics, which is the source of the capture, needs to be visible. The createMovie() call prompts the user and creates a file and an associated movie into which to record the incoming video and audio.

The recording of the video to the movie is done in a similar manner as above and is listed in the example code SGCapture2Disk on the CD-ROM.

The video and sound channels are created; the user is prompted to configure the video input and desired compression. The usage of the channels and SequenceGrabber is established, and the SequenceGrabber is set up to preview the incoming digitized video signal:

```
public void windowOpened (WindowEvent e) {
    try{
        createMovie();

        SequenceGrabber mGrabber = new SequenceGrabber();

        SGVideoChannel mVideo = new SGVideoChannel(mGrabber);
```

```
            mVideo.settingsDialog ();
            mVideo.setBounds (new QDRect(kWidth, kHeight));
            mVideo.setUsage (seqGrabPreview | seqGrabRecord |
                                    seqGrabPlayDuringRecord);

            mAudio =  new SGSoundChannel(mGrabber);
            mAudio.setUsage (seqGrabPreview | seqGrabRecord |
                                    seqGrabPlayDuringRecord);
            mAudio.setVolume (2);

            mDrawable = new SGDrawer(mVideo);
            myQTCanvas.setClient(mDrawable,true);

            mGrabber.setDataOutput (mFile, seqGrabPreview |
                                        seqGrabRecord |
                                        seqGrabPlayDuringRecord);
            mGrabber.prepare(true,true);
            mGrabber.startPreview();
        } catch (Exception ee) {
            ee.printStackTrace();
        }
}
```

10 *Playing Music with QuickTime*

This chapter demonstrates some of the techniques you can use to play music with QuickTime. The fundamentals of the QuickTime Music Architecture are explained in Chapter 2, "QuickTime Basics."

This chapter shows you how to

- use QuickTime's music components
- use the `TunePlayer` to play a tune and to create and use a movie to store instruments

PLAYING MUSIC

The code example in this section shows a simple usage of QuickTime's music components. There are no required media for this program. The program shows how to use the QuickTime Music Architecture, specifically the `NoteAllocator` component. The user is prompted to pick an instrument, as shown in Figure 10.1.

The tone description, which describes the characteristics of the selected instrument, is then printed out. In this case, the instrument name is Acoustic Grand Piano, and the instrument General MIDI number is 1.

FIGURE 10.1 *Music program*

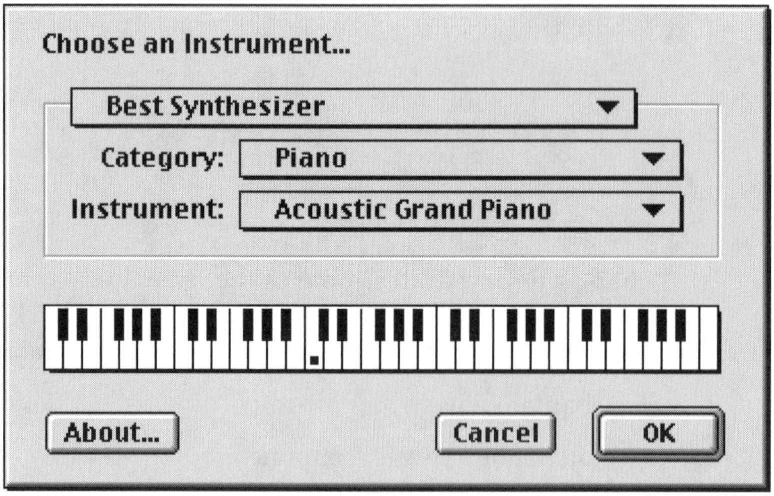

The sample code then makes a NoteChannel of a GM instrument of 25 (Acoustic Guitar) and a polyphony of 1. A NoteAllocator is required for using a NoteChannel. However, QuickTime for Java provides a default NoteAllocator:

```
NoteAllocator na = NoteAllocator.getDefault();
```

This is used for the ToneDescription, NoteRequest, and NoteChannel constructors if your application does not provide one.

```
public class NotesToneTest implements Errors {
    public static void main (String[] args) {
        try {
            QTSession.open();

            ToneDescription td = new ToneDescription ();

            try {
                td.pickInstrument (NoteAllocator.getDefault(),

                                    "Choose an Instrument...", 0);
                System.out.println (td);
            } catch (StdQTException e) {
                if (e.errorCode() != userCanceledErr) return;
```

```
            }

            td = new ToneDescription (25);
            System.out.println (td);

            NoteChannel nc = new NoteChannel(new NoteRequest(td));
            nc.playNote (60, 127);
                try { Thread.sleep (2000); }
                catch (InterruptedException e) {}
            nc.playNote (60, 0);
        }
        catch (QTException qte) {
            qte.printStackTrace();
        }
        finally {
            QTSession.close();
        }
    }
}
```

PLAYING A TUNE

The code example in this section shows how to use the `TunePlayer` to play a tune using the QuickTime Music Architecture. The code snippet also shows you how to make a movie from the `Tune` object that has been constructed.

This `TunePlayer` sample is a translation of the C code example from an article on QuickTime Music Architecture in the magazine *develop*, issue 23.

The user is shown a small window with three buttons on it.

- **Play Tune** plays a specific tune.

- **Save Tune** saves a movie of this tune.

- **Rebuild Tune** reads in this previously created movie and reestablishes the tune with the two instruments swapped.

NoteChannel objects are constructed and given to the TunePlayer to play the tune with. The tune is then constructed using the static methods of the MusicData class to stuff the desired notes, rests, and so on into the data format that the TunePlayer expects.

You make up a tune player and set the note channels that will be used. The order of the note channels in the array when they are added to the TunePlayer is the part those channels take on:

```
aTunePlayer = new TunePlayer();
NoteChannel[] nc = new NoteChannel[2];
myNoteChannel = nc[0] = new NoteChannel (1, 4);

File f = QTFactory.findAbsolutePath ("sin440.aif");
myInstrument = createAtomicInstrument (new QTFile (f));

nc[1] = myInstrument.newNoteChannel (0);
aTunePlayer.setNoteChannels (nc);
```

The second NoteChannel is created from an AtomicInstrument. An AtomicInstrument is a custom instrument your application can define that contains one or more sample data. This instrument specifies a key range and looping points for each of the sample data that is added to the AtomicInstrument container. The format of the sample data is read in from the AIF file that is used for the sample data itself.

A custom instrument is defined by a QuickTime atom structure containing appropriate atoms (hence the name "atomic" instrument):

```
static AtomicInstrument createAtomicInstrument (QTFile f) throws Exception {
        // some constants that are used
    final int kCustomInstAtomID = 11;
    final int
            kMIDINoteValue_Lowest = 0,
            kMIDINoteValue_Highest = 127,
            kMIDINoteValue_A440 = 69;

    // get information about the sound;
    // we'll use this later to construct a sample description atom
    SndInfo info = SndInfo.parseAIFFHeader (OpenFile.asRead (f));
    SoundComponentData mySndInfo = info.sndData;
```

```java
    // assume the AIFF sound data is uncompressed as
    // atomic instruments ONLY accept uncompressed sound
System.out.println (mySndInfo);

    // create an atom container with atoms that describe the custom instrument
AtomicInstrument myInstrument = new AtomicInstrument();

    // insert a tone description atom, which contains a tone description structure
ToneDescription myToneDesc = new ToneDescription ();
myToneDesc.setSynthesizerType (kSoftSynthComponentSubType);
myToneDesc.setInstrumentName ("Sin 440");
myToneDesc.setInstrumentNumber (1);//kInst_Custom
myInstrument.insertChild (Atom.kParentIsContainer, kaiToneDescType, 1, 1,
                          myToneDesc);

    // insert a note request atom, which contains a note request structure;
    // this atom is optional; if it's not present,
    // QTMA assumes some reasonable values
NoteRequestInfo myNoteInfo = new NoteRequestInfo ();
myInstrument.insertChild (Atom.kParentIsContainer, kaiNoteRequestInfoType, 1, 1,
                          myNoteInfo);

    // insert a knob list atom;
    // this atom is optional; if it's not present,
    // QTMA assumes some reasonable values
InstKnobList myKnobList = new InstKnobList ();
myInstrument.insertChild (Atom.kParentIsContainer, kaiKnobListType, 1, 1,
                          myKnobList);

    // insert a key range information atom;
    // this is the parent of the sample description atom
Atom myKeyRangeInfoAtom = myInstrument.insertChild (Atom.kParentIsContainer,
                                               kaiKeyRangeInfoType, 1, 1);

    if (myKeyRangeInfoAtom.getAtom() == 0)
        throw new QTException ("Empty KeyRange Atom");

    // this is defined as a big-endian struct
    // so QTJava automatically flips the fields
InstSampleDesc  mySampleDesc = new InstSampleDesc ();

mySampleDesc.setDataFormat (mySndInfo.getFormat());
```

```
mySampleDesc.setNumChannels (mySndInfo.getNumChannels());
mySampleDesc.setSampleSize (mySndInfo.getSampleSize());
mySampleDesc.setSampleRate (mySndInfo.getSampleRate());

    // define the characteristics of the sampled sound
mySampleDesc.setSampleDataID (kCustomInstAtomID);
mySampleDesc.setOffset (0);
mySampleDesc.setNumSamples (mySndInfo.getSampleCount());

    //set looping characteristics
mySampleDesc.setLoopType (kMusicLoopTypeNormal);
mySampleDesc.setLoopStart (0);
mySampleDesc.setLoopEnd (mySndInfo.getSampleCount());

    // set pitch characteristics
mySampleDesc.setPitchNormal (kMIDINoteValue_A440);
mySampleDesc.setPitchLow (kMIDINoteValue_Lowest);
mySampleDesc.setPitchHigh (kMIDINoteValue_Highest);

    System.out.println (mySampleDesc);

    // insert the sample description atom
myInstrument.insertChild (myKeyRangeInfoAtom, kaiSampleDescType, 1, 1,
                          mySampleDesc);

    // insert a sample information atom;
    // this is the parent of the sample data atom and must have
    // the same atom ID specified by the sampleDataID
    // field of the instrument sample description
Atom mySampleInfoAtom = myInstrument.insertChild (Atom.kParentIsContainer,
                                    kaiSampleInfoType, kCustomInstAtomID, 0);

if (mySampleInfoAtom.getAtom() == 0)
    throw new QTException ("Sample Info Atom is 0");

    // insert a sample data atom into the sample information atom;
    // this atom contains the actual
    // sample data that defines the custom instrument;
    // the format of the sample data is defined
    // by the corresponding sample description atom
    // was using myCompInfo.getBytesPerSample()
    // but as this is not-compressed seems redundant
```

```
    // if worried about dealing with 12/18/20 bit sample sizes
    // we could do (getSampleSize() + 7) / 8 => will truncate to correct value
int mySampleDataSize = mySndInfo.getSampleCount() * (mySndInfo.getSampleSize() / 8);
    // read just the sample data into memory
    // it is sample data size and is found at the data offset location in the file
    // as returned by the ParseAIFF header call
    FileInputStream fis = new FileInputStream (f);
    byte[] ar = new byte [mySampleDataSize];
    fis.skip (info.dataOffset);
    fis.read (ar, 0, mySampleDataSize);
    QTByteObject mySampleData = QTByteObject.fromArray (ar);
myInstrument.insertChild (mySampleInfoAtom, kaiSampleDataType, 1, 0, mySampleData);

    // insert an instrument info atom; this is a parent atom
Atom myInstInfoAtom = myInstrument.insertChild (Atom.kParentIsContainer,
                                                kaiInstInfoType, 1, 0);

if (myInstInfoAtom.getAtom() == 0)
    throw new QTException ("InstInfoAtom is 0");

    // insert a picture atom into the instrument info atom
Pict myPictHandle = Pict.fromFile (QTFactory.findAbsolutePath ("images/
                                   Ship01.pct"));
myInstrument.insertChild (myInstInfoAtom, kaiPictType, 1, 0, myPictHandle);

    // doesn't matter what format we have the strings in
    // because the insert child call for StringHandle will correctly
    // insert just the string character's (bytes)
StringHandle myWriter = new StringHandle ("This space for rent!",
                                          StringHandle.kCStringFormat);
StringHandle myRights = new StringHandle ("Copyright 1998 by Apple Computer, Inc.",
                                          StringHandle.kCStringFormat);
StringHandle myOthers = new StringHandle ("Custom Atomic Instrument.",
                                          StringHandle.kCStringFormat);
    // insert a writer atom into the instrument info atom
myInstrument.insertChild (myInstInfoAtom, kaiWriterType, 1, 0, myWriter);

    // insert a copyright atom into the instrument info atom
myInstrument.insertChild (myInstInfoAtom, kaiCopyrightType, 1, 0, myRights);

    // insert an other info atom into the instrument info atom
myInstrument.insertChild (myInstInfoAtom, kaiOtherStrType, 1, 0, myOthers);
```

```
    return myInstrument;
}
```

The TuneHeader is a MusicData object that contains a NoteRequest for the Piano sound and the AtomicInstrument for the Sine wave.

myInstrument is the previously created AtomicInstrument. We get the NoteRequest from the NoteChannel we created with the Piano instrument of the built-in synthesizer:

```
MusicData makeTuneHeaderFromTunePlayer () throws QTException {
        // we need to find out how many 4byte values are
        //required to fit our ai in
    int instSize = myInstrument.getSize() / 4;
    if (myInstrument.getSize() % 4 != 0)
        instSize++;
        //add 2 for the header and footer music events
    int aiEventLength = instSize + 2;

    int endMarkerSize = 4;

    MusicData musicHeader = new MusicData
                    (MusicData.kNoteRequestHeaderEventLength * 4
                    + aiEventLength * 4 + endMarkerSize);

        // get its note request
    NoteRequest nr = myNoteChannel.getNoteRequest();
        // stuff the note request into the music header
    musicHeader.setNoteRequest (0, 1, nr);

        // 2 is the part number for the instrument
        // offset into music data past the first note request event
    musicHeader.setAtomicInstrument (
                        MusicData.kNoteRequestHeaderEventLength,
                        2,
                        myInstrument);

    return musicHeader;
}
```

The tune is created from a number of note and rest events. The rest events in the tune are used as a cursor. So we add a note to start, then add a rest. The next note will start playing after this rest event. The note events also specify the duration of the note itself:

```
static MusicData testSequenceCreation () throws QTException {

    MusicData tune = new MusicData (our_sequence_length);

    tune.setMusicEvent (0, MusicData.stuffNoteEvent(1, 60, 100, kNoteDuration));
    tune.setMusicEvent (1, MusicData.stuffRestEvent(kRestDuration));
    tune.setMusicEvent (2, MusicData.stuffNoteEvent(2, 60, 100, kNoteDuration));
    tune.setMusicEvent (3, MusicData.stuffRestEvent(kRestDuration));
    tune.setMusicEvent (4, MusicData.stuffNoteEvent(1, 63, 100, kNoteDuration));
    tune.setMusicEvent (5, MusicData.stuffRestEvent(kRestDuration));
    tune.setMusicEvent (6, MusicData.stuffNoteEvent(2, 64, 100, kNoteDuration));
    tune.setMusicEvent (7, MusicData.stuffRestEvent(kRestDuration));
        // • Make the 5th and 6th notes much softer, just for fun.
    tune.setMusicEvent (8, MusicData.stuffNoteEvent(1, 67, 60, kNoteDuration));
    tune.setMusicEvent (9, MusicData.stuffRestEvent(kRestDuration));
    tune.setMusicEvent (10, MusicData.stuffNoteEvent(2, 66, 60, kNoteDuration));
    tune.setMusicEvent (11, MusicData.stuffRestEvent(kRestDuration));
    tune.setMusicEvent (12, MusicData.stuffNoteEvent(1, 72, 100, kNoteDuration));
    tune.setMusicEvent (13, MusicData.stuffRestEvent(kRestDuration));
    tune.setMusicEvent (14, MusicData.stuffNoteEvent(2, 73, 100, kNoteDuration));
    tune.setMusicEvent (15, MusicData.stuffRestEvent(kRestDuration));
    tune.setMusicEvent (16, MusicData.stuffNoteEvent(1, 60, 100, kNoteDuration));
    tune.setMusicEvent (17, MusicData.stuffNoteEvent(1, 67, 100, kNoteDuration));
    tune.setMusicEvent (18, MusicData.stuffNoteEvent( 2, 63, 100, kNoteDuration));
    tune.setMusicEvent (19, MusicData.stuffNoteEvent(2, 72, 100, kNoteDuration));
    tune.setMusicEvent (20, MusicData.stuffRestEvent(kRestDuration));
        // • end-of-sequence marker already in MusicData object

    return tune;
}
```

The **Play Tune** button uses this tune and tune header to create and use a TunePlayer object to play the tune in memory. The construction of the Tune and TuneHeader is discussed below:

```
playTuneButton.addActionListener (new ActionListener () {
    public void actionPerformed (ActionEvent ae) {
        try {
            aTunePlayer.queue (aTune, 1.0F, 0, 0x7FFFFFFF, 0);
        } catch (QTException e) {
            e.printStackTrace();
        }
    }
});
```

We make the movie in the usual manner, following these steps:

- create a `File` and its associated `Movie`

- add a new `Track` to the `Movie`

- create a `MusicMedia` object for that `Track`

- create a `MusicDescription`, setting the tune header of this description to be the `MusicData TuneHeader`

- add the tune data itself to the `MusicMedia`, which of course also includes the `MusicDescription` with the `TuneHeader`

- The `MusicMedia` is then inserted into the `Track` and its updated `Movie` is written out to the file. The code below lists this overall construction process:

```
void makeMovie () {
    try {
        FileDialog fd = new FileDialog (this, "Save Movie As...", FileDialog.SAVE);
        fd.show();
        if(fd.getFile() == null)
            return; //not saving at this time

        movieFile = new QTFile(fd.getDirectory() + fd.getFile());
        Movie theMovie = Movie.createMovieFile (movieFile,
                        kMoviePlayer,
                        createMovieFileDeleteCurFile |
        createMovieFileDontCreateResFile);

        Track t = theMovie.newTrack (0, 0, 1.0F);
        MusicMedia mm = new MusicMedia (t, 600);
        MusicDescription md = new MusicDescription ();
```

```
      // create the TuneHeader from the TunePlayer
      // then add it to the end of the MusicDescription
      md.setTuneHeader (makeTuneHeaderFromTunePlayer());

      // add the MD and the tune to the music media.
      mm.beginEdits();
      mm.addSample (aTune, 0, aTune.getSize(), our_sequence_duration, md, 1, 0);
      mm.endEdits();

      // insert the media into our track
      t.insertMedia (0, 0, our_sequence_duration, 1.0F);

      // save the movie to the created file
      OpenMovieFile outStream = OpenMovieFile.asWrite (movieFile);
      theMovie.addResource (outStream, movieInDataForkResID, movieFile.getName());
      outStream.close();

      System.out.println ("Finished");
   } catch (QTException e) {
      e.printStackTrace();
   }
}
```

We can use a `Movie` just to store instrument data. In the following code, we recreate two `NoteChannel` objects based on the `TuneHeader` data that is contained in the `MusicDescription` we previously wrote out above. For fun, we swap the parts that the `NoteRequest` and `AtomicInstrument` are assigned to. We then use the same tune as we used previously in the **Play Tune** button. That is, we don't read the tune itself from the `Movie`, just the instruments:

```
void rebuildTune () {
   try {
      if (movieFile == null) {
         System.out.println ("Save Tune to Movie first");
         return;
      }

      Movie mov = Movie.fromFile (OpenMovieFile.asRead(movieFile));
      int numTracks = mov.getTrackCount();
```

```
MusicMedia musicMedia = null;

for (int i = 1; i <= numTracks; i++) {
    Track curTrack = mov.getIndTrack(i);
    Media trackMedia = Media.getTrackMedia(curTrack);
    if (trackMedia instanceof MusicMedia)
        musicMedia = (MusicMedia)trackMedia;
}

if (musicMedia == null)
    throw new QTException ("Music Media not found");

MusicDescription mdesc = musicMedia.getMusicDescription(1);
System.out.println (mdesc);

MusicData md = mdesc.getTuneHeader();
System.out.println (md);

    // we know there are two instruments in the file we just created-we could
    // calculate this ourselves from the TuneHeader if we didn't know it
NoteChannel[] nc = new NoteChannel[2];

    // we parse the tune header music data object.
    // pulling out any note requests and atomic instruments
    // we find in the header
int currentEventIndex = 0;
int i = 0;
    // to loop through the entire tune header
    // we loop until the currentIndex is greater than the size (in bytes) of
    // the music data / 4 (gives us the number of music events) - 1 (to ignore
    // the end marker event)
while (currentEventIndex < md.getSize() / 4 - 1) {
    int eventHeader = md.getMusicEvent(currentEventIndex);
        System.out.print ("event header:" + Integer.toHexString(eventHeader));
    int eventLength =  MusicData.generalLength (eventHeader);
        System.out.print (",event length:" + eventLength);
    int eventFooter = md.getMusicEvent (eventLength + currentEventIndex - 1);
        System.out.print (",event footer:" + Integer.toHexString(eventFooter));
    int eventSubtype = MusicData.generalSubtype_Footer (eventFooter);
        System.out.print (",event subtype:" + eventSubtype);
    System.out.println ("");
```

```java
            // based on the event sub type we have either
            // stored a note request or an atomic instrument
            // in the movie -> so we read out from the music data the appropriate
            // type the note request/atomic inst. will start at the index of the
                // general event + 1
                // (to get past the general event header)
            switch (eventSubtype) {
                case kGeneralEventNoteRequest:
                    NoteRequest nr = md.getNoteRequest (currentEventIndex + 1);
                    System.out.println (nr);
                    myNoteChannel = nc[i] = new NoteChannel (nr);
                    break;
                case kGeneralEventAtomicInstrument:
                    AtomicInstrument ai = md.getAtomicInstrument (currentEventIndex +
                                                            1);
                    System.out.println (ai);
                     nc[i] = myInstrument.newNoteChannel (0);
                    break;
                default:
                    break;  //skip this general event
            }
                // move our index to the next general event header
            currentEventIndex += eventLength;
            i++;
        }

    if (nc[0] == null || nc[1] == null)
        throw new QTException ("Problem reading instruments");

        // swap the parts that the note channels play
        // originally we had the piano playing the first note
        // after rebuilding the sin wave will play the first note
    NoteChannel temp = nc[0];
    nc[0] = nc[1];
    nc[1] = temp;

    aTunePlayer.setNoteChannels (nc);

} catch (QTException e) {
    e.printStackTrace();
}
}
```

The QuickTime for Java Software Architecture

Part III introduces you to the QuickTime for Java software architecture.

It discusses isssues related to timing, collections, spaces and controllers, and animation and compositing. A number of programming examples show you how to take full advantage of this architecture in your own code.

11

Timing

We've seen that the primary media types that QuickTime presents are time-based, as discussed in Chapter 2, "QuickTime Basics." Typically, these include movies, sound, and MIDI files. With time-based media, you can play back the media at different rates, where a rate of 1 is normal forward motion playback, a rate of 5 might be fast-forward, –5 rewind, and 0 stopped. You can also set the position within the media—that is, at the start of the media or halfway through and get the duration of a particular media stream.

This time-based, playable capability of objects is represented in the QuickTime for Java Framework by the `Playable` interface, which is part of the `quicktime.app.players` package discussed in Chapter 23. The `QTPlayer`, `MoviePlayer`, and `MoviePresenter`, which also belong to the `quicktime.app.players` package, implement the `Playable` interface. You use an instance of these objects to present movies as well as sound and MIDI files.

This chapter discusses

- QuickTime's timing services

- how to use the `Taskable`, `Timeable`, and `Playable` interfaces to interact with QuickTime's timing services

- using these timing services to control a scrolling Java text object

QuickTime's Timing Services

The `quicktime.std.clocks` package contains the classes that provide the core timing services that QuickTime provides. They include support for the creation of hierarchical dependencies between time bases, the usage of callbacks for user-scheduling of events or notification, and the capability of instantiating the system clocks that provide these timing services.

A Clock object is a pure source of time: It doesn't stop ticking, and a particular instance of a Clock class corresponds to some hardware clock that provides the time information.

A QuickTime TimeBase provides an application with an abstract and powerful way of dealing with time. Unlike a clock, which as a source of time doesn't stop, and its values are always defined, a TimeBase allows the application a view and control of time on its own terms, in whatever resolution (to the resolution of the clock source) the application requires. For instance, a TimeBase allows the setting of start and stop times and looping the time value between these times. The current time value can be set to an arbitrary value. The rate at which the time values change of a TimeBase can be set: A rate of 0 meaning that the time value doesn't change; 1, that it changes in a forward motion at the normal rate (a second equals a second); 2, that the time value changes twice as fast as normal. Rates can also be set to negative values, in which case the time value decreases at the specified rate.

QuickTime TimeBase objects also allow for the construction of hierarchies of time. When a TimeBase is slaved to another, its effective rate is the multiplication of its rate with the rate of its parent, that is master's rate == 2, slave's rate == 4. Thus, the effective rate of the slave (the actual rate its time values are changing) in this case is 8. The depth of a timing hierarchy is at the application's discretion.

Figure 11.1 shows a hierarchy of slaved TimeBase objects.

FIGURE 11.1   *A hierarchy of slaved TimeBase objects*

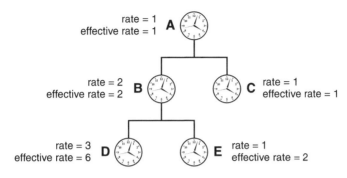

In this diagram `TimeBase` objects D and E are slaved to `TimeBase` B. `TimeBase` objects B and C are in turn slaved to `TimeBase` A, which is the ultimate master `TimeBase` of this hierarchy. The rates and effective rates of each `TimeBase` are shown. The effective rate of a `TimeBase` is calculated by multiplying its rate with the effective rate of its master. Thus, the effective rate of `TimeBase` D is 6, which is its rate (3) multiplied by the effective rate of its master (2).

`QTCallBack` provides users with a means to schedule a callback when a specified condition of the `TimeBase` is met. The class that subclasses a particular callback type must define the `execute()` method. This is the method that will be called when the callback is invoked.

The `TimeRecord` class allows a full description of a QuickTime time specification structure and contains a time value scaled to a time base coordinate system and in certain cases, the `TimeBase` from which the `TimeRecord` was retrieved.

These timing services are discussed in more detail in Chapter 2, "QuickTime Basics," and in the general QuickTime reference material.

11

Timing

TIME AND TASKING

The `quicktime.app.time` package provides a set of classes to handle timing services used to schedule tasks that need to be performed on an ongoing basis. Certain QuickTime objects (such as the `QTPlayer` and `SGDrawer`) need to be given regular slices of time in order to perform their work.

The `Timeable` interface, discussed in Chapter 26, "The quicktime. app.time Package," defines a protocol for dealing with time bases. The `Timer`, `QTPlayer`, `MoviePlayer`, and `MoviePresenter` objects all have a `TimeBase` as the foundation upon which their sense of time is founded. This interface provides a way to get this `TimeBase` and to set and get its current rate.

THE TASKABLE INTERFACE

Because QuickTime can present content that takes place over a period of time, some QuickTime objects require that a regular slice of time be given to them in order for them to marshall their resources and generally do their work. The `Taskable` interface, discussed in Chapter 26, "The quicktime. app.time Package," is provided for this purpose, and it is used in conjunction with a `Tasker` object. The `Tasker` class wraps a `java.lang.Thread` object, calling the `task()` method of each of its `Taskable` objects, and then goes to sleep for a specified sleep time. The `Taskable` interface defines a default `Tasker`, in the static variable `tasker`, that can be used for tasking purposes.

Your application can have a number of `Tasker` objects if it requires them, though typically only one `Tasker` object will be required. The `Taskable` interface provides a `Tasker` object for general use. The following classes implement the `Taskable` interface: `QTPlayer` calls `MCIdle`, `SGDrawer` calls `SGIdle`, and `TaskAllMovies` calls `MoviesTask` in its `task()` method.

The abstract `Tasking` class defines a default implementation of the `Taskable` interface and is the superclass for the above three classes. Your application can use the `Tasking` class as a foundation for application-specific tasking requirements. An object can be based on the `Tasking` class to provide a managed periodic call of a `task()` method from the `TaskThread` class.

Figure 11.2 illustrates the relationships among the various classes and interfaces that deal with timing in the QuickTime for Java API.

FIGURE 11.2   *Time and tasking relationships*

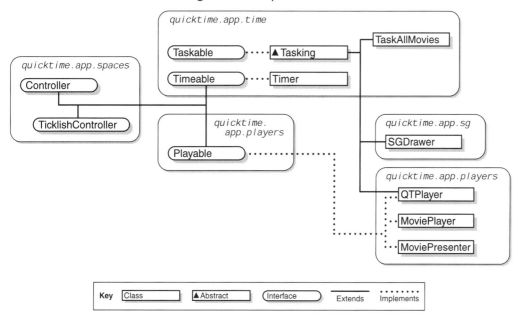

The Timeable Interface

The `Timeable` interface defines a protocol for dealing with time bases. The `Timer`, `QTPlayer`, `MoviePlayer`, and `MoviePresenter` classes all have a `TimeBase` as the foundation upon which their sense of time is based. This interface provides a uniform means to retrieve this `TimeBase` and to get and set its current rate.

■   `getRate()`, `setRate()`

A rate of 1 indicates a normal playback rate where 1 second equals 1 second. A rate of zero indicates that the `TimeBase` is stopped, that is, its time values are not changing. A rate less than zero indicates that the time values are decreasing.

■ `getTimeBase()`

This method is used to retrieve the `TimeBase` of the `Timeable` object. The `TimeBase` can be used to retrieve and set all of the current state and behavior of timing using the `TimeBase` API as discussed in Chapter 36, "The quicktime. std.clocks Package."

Tasking Requirements of Time-Based Objects

In QuickTime, an object with a `TimeBase` can have the requirement of being tasked. That is, there exist tasks that these objects must perform on a regular basis as their time values change. The `TimeBase` provides the changing time values and is itself driven by a system-provided clock.

Think of a movie playing: The new frames of the movie must be drawn as time changes. Drawing is one of the tasks of the movie object. This relationship can be handled in one of two ways: The object in question specifically tasks itself or it delegates its tasking requirements to a helper object.

First, a QuickTime object with time behavior requires specific tasking. The `QTPlayer`/`MovieController` pairing is one such, as any particular instance of the `MovieController` must periodically update the visual presentation of its control bar (among other `MovieController`-specific tasks). Many `MovieController` methods will also task the movie that is attached to a particular controller. The `SGDrawer`/`SequenceGrabber` pairing also requires specific tasking. Both of these classes (`QTPlayer` and `SGDrawer`) implement the `Taskable` interface.

Second, the tasking requirements can be delegated to another object. Thus any tasking requirements of a `Movie` object (through the `MoviePlayer` and `MoviePresenter`) or a `TimeBase` (through the `Timer`) are delegated to the `TaskAllMovies` class. QuickTime has the capability of tasking all currently active movies and time bases through a specialized use of the MoviesTask function. The TaskAllMovies class uses this, allowing QuickTime itself to determine the tasking needs of open movies and time bases. As the classes are used, they register their tasking requirements with the TaskAllMovies class, which will control the creation and destruction of the TaskThread object the TaskAllMovies class manages. Calling the task() method of the TaskAllMovies object will thus service all currently active movies and time bases.

Working with a TaskThread Object

Whenever a TaskThread object creates a Thread—it only does so when the application calls start() or addAndStart()—the thread is added to an internal thread group. This thread group will not be exposed to the developer.

As we've discussed, calling the QTSession.close() method is a required call by an application. If you are the only current client of QuickTime when you call this, this call destroys all of the exisiting QuickTime objects and closes down the QuickTime environment. One of the first things that QTSession.close does when it executes is to stop all of the threads in the TaskThread group. This ensures that these threads will not continue to execute after QuickTime itself has been terminated.

THE PLAYABLE INTERFACE

The Playable interface defines a protocol for dealing with time-based media and allows you to get the duration, set and get the current time position of playback of the media, retrieve the time scale (i.e., how many ticks per second) of the media, and set and get the playback rate and the inherited functionality of the Timeable interface, which it extends.

Three playable classes—MoviePlayer, MoviePresenter, and QTPlayer—discussed in Chapter 23, "The quicktime. app.players Package," define a large number of methods that enable you to display, play, and control any QuickTime movie.

The setTime() method sets the player's current time value to the time specified. This is a totally arbitrary time value, however.

This time value is best expressed in units that correspond to the player's time scale. Thus, the getScale() method returns the resolution of the player's time base. For example, if the getScale() returns a value of 600, a setTime(1200) will set the current time to a position that is 2 seconds from the start of the movie. getDuration() returns the duration of the media attached to the player. This value is also expressed in the units as specified by the scale value returned by the getScale() method. If the player has no media, or does not know the duration of its media, it can return the constant kDurationUnknown.

TIME SLAVING

The code in this section shows how to use timing information to control a scrolling Java text object and how slaving its TimeBase to a movie alters its behavior. The only media required is the jumps.mov file. The full code listing for TimeSlaving is on the CD-ROM at the back of this book.

Figure 11.3 shows the screen output from the TimeSlaving program.

The program opens up with the scrolling Java text object (QTImage-Drawer). Setting the playback rate to 1 starts scrolling the text. The scrolling text object is set up to position the scrolling text based on the incoming time values; the scale of 110 is the number of pixels that the text scrolls. To get a smooth scroll on less powerful machines, the rate can be set to a slower rate (0.1, . . .), and a negative rate will reverse the direction of the scroll. Changing the scale changes the scrolling behavior, with a smaller number having the text jump pixels—a pixel more than 1 pixel from where it is.

FIGURE 11.3   *Window displayed by the time-slaving sample code*

When the **Make Movie** button is pressed, the scrolling text's time base is slaved to the time base of the movie. As the movie is initially stopped, the text stops scrolling, and the text will jump to correspond to the current time of the movie. Playing the movie starts the text scrolling again (provided that the rate of the text is still not equal to 0). Changing the rate to a negative value will *not* change the scrolling behavior once it is slaved (only starting (rate does not equal 0) and stopping (rate equals 0)). The reason for this is that the text is positioned solely on the incoming time value, and the master time base determines the time values. This is embedded in the calculations of the text positioning, where you can see that the rate parameter of the tickle() method is ignored.

Playing the movie backwards makes the text scroll backwards, as the master time base is now feeding in time values that decrease in value.

The program creates a ScrollingText object that implements the Paintable interface. We then give this ScrollingText object to the QTImageDrawer subclass TimeableID (see below), which will coordinate the drawing. We create a Timer with a scale of 110 (this is the number of pixels that the text scrolls from top to bottom with a height of 150), and we use the TimeableID object (which implements the Ticklish interface) to this Timer. When the Timer is active, it will tickle this TimeableID at a scale of 110 times a second at a rate of 1.

Timing

The Timer itself that will drive the ScrollingText is activated in the windowOpened() method.

```
private void setUpWindow () throws QTException, IOException {
    ScrollingText t = new ScrollingText();

    Dimension d = new Dimension (300, 150);
    TimeableID qid = new TimeableID (t, d);
    ti = new Timer (110, 1, qid);    //110 frames a second
    qid.setTimer(ti);

    //...
    textCanv.setClient (qid, true);
}

public void windowOpened (WindowEvent ev) {
    try {
        ti.setActive (true);
        cp.setDisplay();
    } catch (QTException e) {
        e.printStackTrace();
    }
}
```

The following class extends QTImageDrawer and implements the Ticklish interface. The tickle() method is called by the Timer it is attached to. We perform calculations in the tickle() method to get the time value and position the scrolling text's y value to this calculated position. Once we set the y value, we redraw ourselves, which will invoke the ScrollingText paint() call. This moves the scrolling text to the y value we've set. The rate of the Timer is ignored.

```
class TimeableID extends QTImageDrawer implements Ticklish {
    TimeableID (ScrollingText p, Dimension size) throws QTException {
        super (p, size, kMultiFrame);
        st = p;
        setRedrawing(true);
    }

    ScrollingText st;
    Timer t;
```

```
    public void setTimer (Timer t) throws QTException {
        this.t = t;
    }

    public boolean tickle (float er, int time) throws QTException {
        return doTickle ();
    }

    public void timeChanged (int time) throws QTException {
        doTickle();
    }

// Has an offset of 18 at the bottom and 22 at the top == 40
    private boolean doTickle () throws QTException {
        st.oldy = st.y;
        TimeBase tb = t.getTimeBase();
        TimeBase master = tb.getMasterTimeBase();
        if (master != null) {
            int timeSpan = master.getStopTime(Ticklish.kScale) -
                        master.getStartTime(Ticklish.kScale);
            st.y = (int)((master.getTime(Ticklish.kScale) /
                        (float)timeSpan) * (st.height - 40) + 22);
        } else
            st.y = (tb.getTime((st.height - 40))) % (st.height - 40) + 22;

        redraw(null);
        return true;
    }
}
```

The ControlPanel allows the user to alter the rate and scale of the Timer that drives the rendering of the ScrollingText. It also has a make-Movie button that will place a movie in the window and slave the TimeBase of TimeableID to this movie.

First, we make the movie, then get the TimeBase from t (the TimeableID object we created above) and set the movie's TimeBase as the master time base of the TimeableID TimeBase. Then we display the movie in the same window.

```
makeMovie.addActionListener (new ActionListener () {
    public void actionPerformed (ActionEvent event) {
        QTCanvas movCanv = new QTCanvas(QTCanvas.kInitialSize,
                                                0.5f, 0.5f);
        f.add ("West", movCanv);
        File fl = QTFactory.findAbsolutePath ("jumps.mov");
        OpenMovieFile movieFile = OpenMovieFile.asRead(
                                            new QTFile(fl));
        Movie mov = Movie.fromFile (movieFile);
        t.getTimeBase().setMasterTimeBase(mov.getTimeBase(), null);
        MovieController mc = new MovieController (mov);
        mc.setLooping (true);
        p = new QTPlayer (mc);
        movCanv.setClient (p, true);
    }
});
```

12 *Collections*

The QuickTime for Java API provides a common interface for defining the use of collections of objects. This interface is designed to provide developers with a uniform means of implementing and accessing collections. As specified in the API, all objects within the `quicktime.app` framework that are collections of objects are required to implement the `Collection` interface. This interface defines the standard way of adding or removing members that belong to a collection by using the `addMember()` or `removeMember()` methods.

This chapter, along with Chapter 13, "Spaces and Controllers," discusses a set of abstractions that are important for understanding the underlying architecture of the QuickTime for Java Application Framework. In this chapter, we discuss briefly the methods defined in the `Collection` interface with an example of using the interface. We also discuss the `DynamicCollection` interface and the `Protocol` class. For more information about the `Collection` interface, see Chapter 25, "The quicktime. app.spaces Package," which describes the classes and interfaces that are part of the `quicktime.app.spaces` package.

DEFINING THE COLLECTION INTERFACE

A collection can be thought of as an *aggregation of objects*. The objects within a particular collection can be of any type of object.

Items in a collection are called *members*. A collection maintains a set of data and provides methods for managing the data or members it contains. A collection allows a set of members to be added together, removed, counted, and verified as appropriate candidates for membership. As specified, the Collection interface defines methods that must be implemented by an object that wants control over its members.

The Collection interface lets you define a test to determine if the provided object is an "appropriate" candidate for membership in a collection. By implementing the isAppropriate() method, the Collection itself decides if an object is an appropriate member of the collection. The Collection implementation provides eligibility criteria and definitions to determine a prospective candidate.

One of the goals of the QuickTime for Java model is to make a collection more *restrictive*, that is, to provide a means to define and limit, as necessary, its members, by using the various methods defined in Collection. Thus, a collection implementation can make assumptions about the type of objects it contains.

The isAppropriate() method returns a boolean if the object argument conforms to the type of object that the Collection is a collector of. This method typically uses the compile or runtime version of the instanceof operator, ensuring that members are instances of a particular class or set of classes and that the type of object can be, in fact, added to a collection. The DynamicCollection extension of Collection provides a mechanism for dynamically customizing the membership requirments for individual collections.

addMember() methods call isAppropriate() and return true if the object is an appropriate member (and is therefore added to or already a member of the collection). In practice, the implementations of this interface provide both their own storage mechanism and semantics about the default position and characteristics of the addMember() method.

Note that this is a *static* as opposed to a dynamic collection. The individual collection classes explain the customizations and restrictions on membership that they enforce.

hasMember() returns true if the provided object is a member of the collection. isEmpty() returns true if the collection contains no members or false if it has one or more members. members() returns an enumeration to iterate over the current members of a collection. size()

returns the number of members in the collection, that is, the collection's size.

Take, for example, the TaskThread object. This object must be a collection of Taskable objects. To add a Taskable object to a TaskThread, you use the myTaskThread.addMember(myTaskable) method. This ensures that members of a TaskThread collection implement the Taskable interface before they are added. Thus, in the run() method, the members are cast to a Taskable object, and their task() method is called.

THE DYNAMICCOLLECTION INTERFACE

The DynamicCollection interface, which is also part of the quicktime.app.spaces package discussed in Chapter 25, uses the Protocol class to enable an application to dynamically type members on a collection-by-collection basis. Dynamic collections use the protocol to test to see if an object is appropriate before it is accepted as a candidate for membership of the collection.

This enables you to tighten the restrictions on membership on a case-by-case basis. For example, the DirectGroup is a Dynamic-Collection, of which the fundamental requirement is that the member must implement the QTDrawable interface. The fundamental requirement of a Protocol cannot be altered.

However, if you want to ensure that for a particular group only movies are in the collection, your application could get the Protocol object for that particular DirectGroup object and add the MoviePlayer class to the collection of class objects that make up the Protocol. Consequent uses of that DirectGroup would ensure that the object being added was both a QTDrawable and MoviePlayer before the object was added. Your code (having specified this protocol, as shown below) can then make certain assumptions about the type of object that is a member of the collection.

Note that changing a protocol after a member has been added to the collection does not mean that existing members are removed if they don't match the new protocol, only that new members must match the new protocol.

You use the getProtocol() method to return the Protocol class that is used when testing an object's appropriateness for membership of a collection.

Dynamic Collections and Controllers

A DynamicCollection allows an application to specialize the membership requirements of a Collection on a case-by-case basis without the need to subclass. This technique can also be used with controllers in an effective manner.

A controller that is also a collection will return a selected object if that object is an appropriate object for that controller. This test is performed upon the selection if the isWholespace method of such a controller returns true. If isWholespace() returns false, the selected object must already be a member of the controller's collection and thus has already passed the isAppropriate() test when added to the controller's collection.

In the first case, when isWholespace() returns true, a controller can be specialized to control only a selected subset of potential objects. In this case the application can specialize the controller, defining its own semantics for the isAppropriate() method by implementing the DynamicCollection interface and providing specific protocols for different instances of the controller. Because the selected object must pass the isAppropriate() test, different controllers can be defined to control all objects of a particular type. Thus, isWholespace() means that any object that matches the specified protocol can be controlled by the controller.

Controllers are discussed in more detail in Chapter 13, "Spaces and Controllers."

THE PROTOCOL CLASS

As implemented in the QuickTime for Java API, a Protocol, which is part of the quicktime.app.spaces package, is a collection of classes used to test an object against. Notably, the passProtocol() method in this class uses the Class.instanceOf() method on each of the classes in its collection. If the incoming object is not an instance of all of the classes in the `Protocol`, the `passProtocol()` method returns `false`. If the incoming object is, then it returns `true`.

For a `DynamicCollection` your application can dynamically assign or add classes to a `Protocol` to tighten the membership requirements of its collection. When an object is added to a dynamic collection, the dynamic collection will first test the object against its `Protocol` `passProtocol()` method. Only if it passes this test is the object allowed to be added to the `Collection`. This test is encapsulated in the `Dynamic-Collection` `isAppropriate()` method.

You can add a class to a `Protocol` by using the following code, taking the previous example:

```
Protocol p = myDirectGroup.getProtocol();
p.addMember(Class.forName("quicktime.app.players.MoviePlayer"));
```

13

Spaces and Controllers

One of the keys to a viable multimedia standard is the rich representation of time-based media. This representation must take into account the interaction among different media types as well as different time scales. QuickTime itself provides a rich and complex architecture that deals with both disparate media types and timescales. One of the main focuses of QuickTime for Java is to allow for the presentation of QuickTime media in complex and interesting ways, using QuickTime itself to achieve this.

Toward that end, QuickTime for Java relies on an authoring abstraction, similar to that in the ScriptX programming language, known as a space. ScriptX, though no longer a supported product, was a language jointly developed by Kaleida Labs, a wholly owned subsidiary of IBM and Apple. It was an object-oriented language that generated byte-code executables that ran on both Mac OS and Windows, as does Java. Its main focus was on the authoring of multimedia titles and tools for doing this, and it incorporated a powerful graphics engine and class framework.

A *space* defines and organizes the behavior of objects. It is a container class for holding member objects, with a clock for timing and controllers to manipulate the objects. A space is thus an environment with a clock where objects live, interact, and can be controlled. In a very real sense it defines a created world with a predictable set of members and behaviors.

QuickTime for Java's concept of a space is one that is dynamically created by a program at runtime. The program assembles the space with its members and controllers and uses Java's event model to allow for interaction with those members. This can be a very dynamic environment, indeed, with decisions made about behavior and even membership deferred until runtime.

In Chapter 12, "Collections," we discussed the basics of the `Collection` interface. A solid understanding of spaces and controllers is also important for developing applets and applications with the QuickTime for Java API. This chapter covers these topics:

- the Model-View-Controller (MVC) abstraction. This concept is useful in understanding the various characteristics of a space, including its members, controllers, and clocks that handle timing.

- the `Space` interface. This interface represents a container in which objects can interact with each other and, indirectly, with the user.

- the behavior of a controller. Controllers provide a uniform way of enforcing the same behavior on a group of objects.

- how controllers work together with spaces.

AN INTRODUCTION TO SPACES

Model-View-Controller (MVC) is a broadly used concept in software engineering and is particularly associated with object-oriented design. As defined, *model* generally refers to the generation of data, *view* to the presentation of that data, and *control* to the services provided to control both the generation and presentation of the model.

The concept of a space, as introduced originally in the ScriptX programming language and presented in QuickTime for Java, is an abstraction that embodies this approach to object-oriented design. As such, it possesses no intrinsic assumptions about usage in the modeling or presentation of this model. The concept is provided as a useful encapsulation of the various characteristics of members, controllers, and the special case of a clock that in many contexts can be seen to drive the behavior of the space.

A space is often used to create a "world" that has certain characteristics that define how the members exist in it. For example, a model space can be used to generate data that then affects a visual representation of an accompanying display space. Through the separation of the generation of data from its presentation, an application is given the power to do more. Thus, a single data source can be presented in different views. Alternate data sources can be used to provide data for the same viewing constructs.

MVC is a generally used design tool, and a more detailed discussion can be found in any number of books on software design models. If you would like more information, you should refer to alternate sources.

Imagine displaying the movie discussed in the tweening example where a 3D model track is controlled by a tween track. Using the Model-View-Controller concept, we can look at the display of this interaction as presented in the next sections. Figure 13.1 illustrates the Model-View-Controller relationships.

Model

The movie itself is responsible for displaying the contents of its tracks. It has two tracks: The 3D track contains a 3D model of an airplane; this media data (3D model) represents the model component.

View

The movie is responsible for displaying its media data, which in this case will also involve the internals of the Movie Toolbox applying `CameraView` to the 3D model contained in the 3D track.

The `MovieController` delegates to its movie the task of displaying the movie. The `MovieController` is represented by the `QTPlayer`, which implements the `QTDrawable` interface. The `QTPlayer` is a client of the `QTCanvas`, where the movie is presented.

FIGURE 13.1 *The Model-View-Controller relationships*

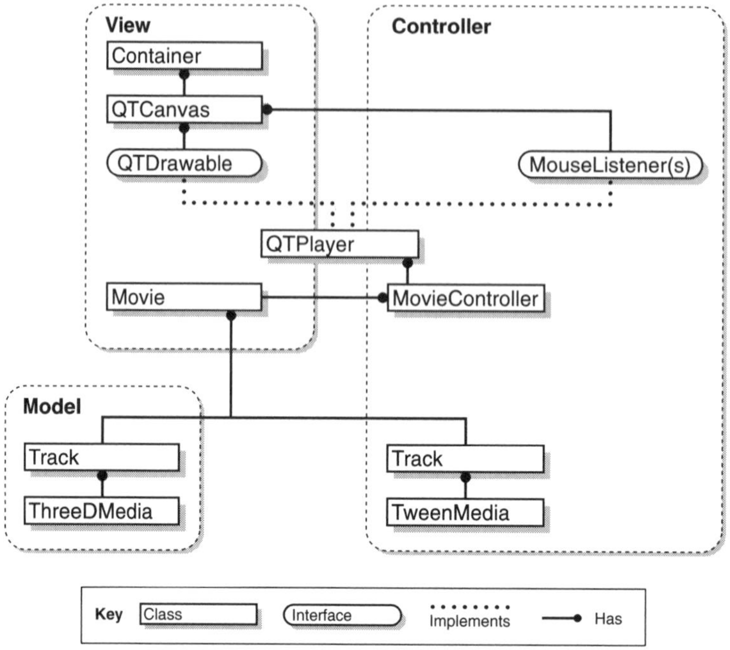

Controller

The movie also contains a tween track that controls how the 3D model is viewed. As the movie is played, the tween track applies different camera views over the duration of the movie itself—in effect, zooming out our view of the 3D model.

The movie controller also represents a means for the user to control the view of the movie. The user can play the movie, step through each frame, stop it, and so forth. The MovieController is represented by the QTPlayer, which implements the MouseListener interface to receive mouse events that occur in the QTCanvas display space. This is the controller aspect of the QTPlayer.

Chapter 15, "Animation and Compositing," illustrates the construction of an animation using the Compositor space with this Model-View-Controller technique. It presents a similar diagram and analysis to aid in understanding the application of the Model-View-Controller technique with spaces.

THE STATE OF A SPACE

In general, a space has a state represented by four characteristics:

- *members*—A space is first and foremost a collection of objects or members. Members are objects added to a space.

- *protocols*—Protocols are used to determine eligibility for membership in a space. A protocol provides an ability to define custom spaces with particular requirements for membership.

- *controllers*—Controllers define the standard behavior, or natural laws, governing some or all members of the space.

- *timer*—A space's time source; it often drives the model.

THE SPACE INTERFACE

The `Space` interface, discussed in Chapter 25, "The quicktime. app.spaces Package," represents this abstraction and provides the standard API that all spaces should support. The `quicktime.app.spaces` package was introduced to include a `Space` interface and a collection of Controller interfaces.

In the QuickTime for Java architecture, a `Space` is a dynamic collection of members. It has a `Timer` that provides basic timing services and tickling requirements. The `Timer` object provides the parent `TimeBase` for all members and controllers within a `Space` that have a `TimeBase`. You add and remove member objects to a `Space` just as you would to any collection, using the `addMember()` and `removeMember()` methods of the `Collection` interface.

A `Space` also has controllers attached to it that provide differing mechanisms for controlling the members of that `Space`.

The `Space` interface extends the `Listener`, `Ticklish`, and `DynamicCollection` interfaces. Figure 13.2 shows the overall structure of the `Space` interface and its implementation in QuickTime for Java.

FIGURE 13.2 *Structure of the Space interface*

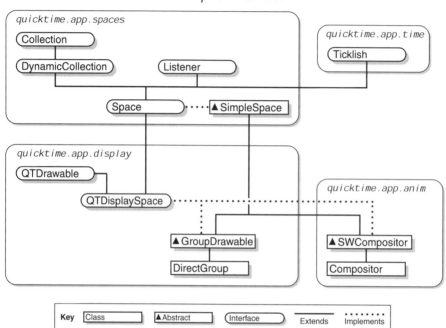

Space Methods

Some of the methods that belong to the Space interface and their common uses include

- the addController() method. You use this method to add a controller to the Space. That controller will control the members of the Space you've defined. Conversely, the removeController() removes a controller previously added to the Space.

- the controllers() method. This method returns a list of all controllers currently attached to the Space.

- the tickleList() method. This returns a list of all of the Ticklish-Controller objects that have been added to the Space. These controllers are tickled each time the Space itself is tickled by its Timer.

■ the getTimer() method. This returns the Timer of the Space, which provides a TimeBase for the Space and, if active, tickles and sends timeChanged calls to the Space.

■ the getSource() method. This method returns the Listener source object. The object is the source of events for all the members of the Space that implement the Listener interface and ListenerController objects.

QTDISPLAYSPACE

QTDisplaySpace is an interface that extends the Space interface and provides an API that allows an application to deal with a display space without necessarily knowing anything about its implementation. In particular, this enables your application to define controllers that can deal with both implementations of this interface provided in QuickTime for Java. There is a more specific discussion of this capability in Chapter 14, "Using Spaces and Controllers: QTDisplaySpace."

The QTDisplaySpace interface implies that a display space contains members that can be displayed using layers to determine their front-to-back ordering. Members of a display space also have some visual presentation area of the space that they occupy. This display area is completely described by a member's matrix. Thus, members of such a Space can be presented in front of or behind other members.

How a particular Space implements these characteristics for its members is defined by the space itself and is very dependent on the characteristics of the presentation display space. The QTDisplaySpace interface defines methods for both the layering and positioning of its members.

CONTROLLERS

Controllers manipulate objects in spaces. The behavior of a controller depends upon the support protocols defined by a space and by a controller itself. Controllers can define standard behavior for a group of objects by defining the behavior of objects over time, by monitoring objects, or by responding to user events. Controllers provide a uniform way of enforcing the same behavior on a group of objects.

The Controller interface is very abstract and makes no assumptions about the type of controller it is, allowing you to extend or specialize its particular function. It provides two methods:

- addedToSpace(Space s), which is a notification method called to inform the controller that it has been added to a space. The space it has been added to is passed in as a parameter.

- removeFromSpace(), which is a notification method called by the space when the controller has been removed from it. The space it is removed from is the space it was previously added to. By implication a controller can only be attached to a single space at any one time.

EXTENSIONS TO THE INTERFACE

There are four extensions to the Controller interface in the QuickTime for Java API. These extensions mix in the Controller interface and the interface as signified by the first part of their name. When controllers of these types are added to a Space object, the Space is expected to support the controller in the following manner:

- CollectionController—a controller that controls a collection of objects, which are members of a space. When added, the space will add existing and any new members to such a controller if that controller's isWholespace() method returns true.

- ListenerController—a controller that has a specific interest in events implements this interface. When added to the space, the space will indicate to this controller that it has been addedTo the source object that is the source of interest or events for the space itself.

■ TicklishController—a controller that performs time-based control actions at the same rate as the space's Timer ticks. When the space itself is tickled by its Timer, it will tickle any of the Ticklish-Controller objects attached to it.

■ TimeableController—a controller that provides its own TimeBase. This gives such a controller its own sense of time. The TimeBase of this controller should be slaved to the Space when it is added to it, allowing for changes in the space's time states to also affect this controller. Whereas the TicklishController will always tick at the same rate as its space, a TimeableController has more independence and can tick at any appropriate rate. By slaving the Timeable-Controller to the space's Timer, there will exist a proportional relationship between these tick rates.

Your application is not restricted to just these four controller types, however, even though these are the only known types in the Simple-Space class. You can mix or extend these interfaces in any way appropriate.

For instance, you might also want a controller that is a Ticklish-Controller to control a collection of members. Thus, a controller could implement both the TicklishController and CollectionController interfaces, and the behavior for these types of controllers would also apply to this controller. The TickleList controller is an example of this polymorphism.

Alternatively, a controller may be a collection but not wish to delegate to the space the adding and removing of its members. In such a case, it can circumvent this delegation by still implementing the Collection interface but not the CollectionController interface. The MouseController in QuickTime for Java behaves in this manner.

Though the most common usage of the classes that implement the Controller interface is in conjunction with a space, these classes are not limited to this usage. For instance, the TickleList class, which implements the `Ticklish` interface, can be used in conjunction with a `Timer` for tickling its collection of `Ticklish` objects.

The specific details of these controllers and the provided classes that implement some of these interfaces are discussed in the next section. Figure 13.3 illustrates all of the `Controller` interfaces and classes that provide implementations for these in QuickTime for Java.

FIGURE 13.3 *Controllers implementation*

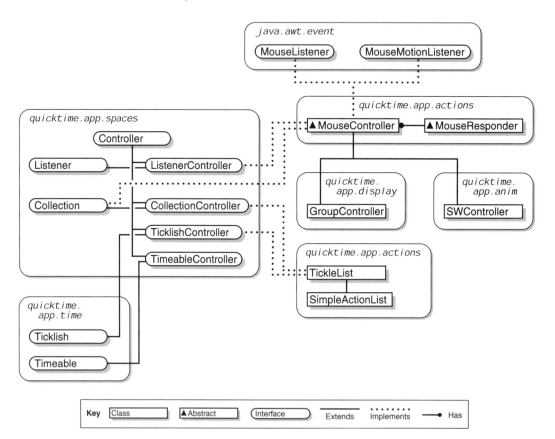

How Controllers Work

Controllers, as we've seen, operate on objects in spaces. Spaces and controllers work closely together; to understand controllers, it is important to understand how they work with spaces.

To attach a controller to a space, you use the `addController()` method. The space in turn automatically adds the controller to the `protected controllers` instance variable. It then notifies the controller of the space that it has been added to through the `addedToSpace()` method. To remove a controller from a space, you use the `removeController()` method. The space then notifies the controller itself that it has been removed from the space by calling the `removedFromSpace()` method.

As discussed below, the actions that occur after a controller is added to a space, in this instance the `SimpleSpace` implementation, depend very much on the type of controller. In this implementation, it is not enough that a controller implements one of the parent interfaces, such as `Collection`, for this behavior to be established. The controller must implement the `CollectionController` interface, for example, in order for this behavior to occur. In this way, the `SimpleSpace` implementation does not do more than your application would expect.

COLLECTIONCONTROLLER

The `CollectionController` interface mixes in the `Collection` and `Controller` interfaces. When such a controller is added to a `SimpleSpace`, the `Space` asks the controller if `wholespace` is `true` by calling `isWholespace()`. If this method returns `true`, then the `SimpleSpace` calls the `CollectionController addMember()` method with every member of the space it currently has. Also, as new members are added if the `isWholespace()` returns `true`, those members will be added to the `CollectionController`.

It is the responsibility of the particular `CollectionController` to ensure that the candidate member in such a case is an object that is suitable to be added. If not, then the `addMember()` returns `false`. The intention of the `isWholespace()` capability is to provide an easy mecha-

13

Spaces and Controllers

nism for a controller to control all of the members, or all of the appropriate members, of a space, without your application having to specifically add these members to the controller.

If isWholespace() returns false, then the space will not attempt to add existing or new members, and the application must explicitly add those members to the controller.

The TickleList and its subclass, the SimpleActionList, implement this interface. Their membership requirement is that their members implement the Ticklish interface. So in this case if the controller's isWholespace() returns true, then any members of the Space that also implement the Ticklish interface could become members of a controller of this type when they are added to the Space.

LISTENERCONTROLLER

When a ListenerController is added to a space, the source of the Space's interest is indicated to this controller using the Listener interface's addedTo() method. All members and controllers of a space are considered to have the same source object as its source of interest. In the case of the QTDisplaySpace, this source is the QTCanvas to which the top-level QTDisplaySpace object is attached. The QTCanvas object is the source of events derived from Java's event model as it relates to AWT components. For example, mouse events in the QTCanvas that a space is attached to will be sent to these interested controllers.

MouseController

The MouseController, though a Collection, does not implement the CollectionController interface, so it does not automatically have members added to it. The reason is that in both the GroupController and SWController subclasses, it is more efficient to return the frontmost member at the location of the user's mouse, rather than to query each member in turn and to maintain a separate list for the situation of controlling every object in its respective QTDisplaySpace. Internally, these controllers use the isWholespace() setting to decide which member should be returned in response to a mouse event. This is a detail that the space itself does not need to know about, and thus their status as a collection of objects is shielded from the space.

The MouseController is a ListenerController. When it is added to a Space, it calls the source object's addMouseListener() and/or addMouseMotionListener() methods, depending on the type of events the MouseController will respond to.

The MouseController is an abstract class and itself acts as a dispatch object. The subclasses' primary task is to extract a member from their respective space where the mouse event occurred. They return as the target of the member (in the case of the QTDisplaySpace) the frontmost object at the mouse location if isWholespace() returns true, or the frontmost object of the members of the MouseController if isWholespace() returns false.

The MouseController then dispatches the mouse event to its MouseResponder, which is responsible for performing the action desired for that particular type of mouse event. To put it another way, the MouseController delegates its responses to a mouse event to its MouseResponder.

The MouseController-MouseResponder pairing is a powerful abstraction, allowing the application to define responses to mouse events without being concerned about acquiring a target, if appropriate, for a particular mouse event. These classes also make no assumptions about the type of Space or target object that they operate on. The concrete classes provided in QuickTime for Java deal specifically with the manipulation and presentation of members of a QTDisplaySpace. But these abstract classes could just as easily be used to target objects in a model space.

The SimpleActionList, discussed more fully in the following chapters, provides a container for PeriodicAction objects, allowing your application to apply time-based behaviors to members of a space.

TicklishController

When a TicklishController is added to a SimpleSpace, it is added to a special list, the tickleList, that is maintained by the Space. Controllers that are members of this list are tickled whenever the Space itself is tickled—that is, the SimpleSpace tickle() method tickles its tickleList.

There are two TicklishController classes in QuickTime for Java: TickleList and SimpleActionList. These classes also implement the CollectionController interface discussed above. They are also abstract in their design: The requirement for membership of a TickleList is that the candidate implement the Ticklish interface. With each tickle that the TickleList receives, it tickles all of its members in turn. If those members return true from their tickle, they are kept in an active state and will receive a consequent tickle. When or if the tickle method returns false, the TickleList will deactivate this member. The TickleList will only tickle active members.

The Ticklish classes provided in QuickTime for Java include an abstract PeriodicAction class and concrete subclasses that operate on display characteristics of its assigned object. The PeriodicAction, like the Ticklish interface itself, is abstract in that it doesn't define a particular characteristic of the action that is performed. This is left to the subclass itself to define.

TimeableController

When a TimeableController is added to a SimpleSpace, its TimeBase is slaved to the TimeBase of the SimpleSpace. A TimeableController, having its own TimeBase, has its own sense of time and can perform its actions independaently of the time conditions of its space. This differs from the TicklishController, as the TicklishController is only tickled when the space itself is tickled by its Timer.

The establishment of the master-slave relationship between the space's TimeBase and the TimeBase of the TimeableController ensures a synchronization of the sense of time between the space and the controller. However, the TimeBase of the controller can have any rate it desires; the effective or actual rate of the Timeable objects TimeBase will depend on its rate and the rate of the space's `TimeBase`. An application can of course remove this relationship if this is not desired, but in most situations this relationship correctly encapsulates the connection between the `Space` and its controller.

In the current release of QuickTime for Java, there are no controllers that implement this interface; however, the `SimpleSpace` has been designed to support this capability.

SPECIFYING OBJECTS TO BE CONTROLLED

As a general rule, your application must establish the relationship between the objects that it wants to control and the controller itself.

The exception to this rule is when a controller is a `CollectionController` and the `isWholespace()` method returns `true`. In this situation, the `Space` itself adds its members to the `CollectionController`. The discussion above on `CollectionController` explains some of the finer details of this capability.

DEFINING YOUR OWN CONTROLLER

If none of the controllers in the core classes performs the task you need, you can define a subclass of `Controller` for that task.

Chapter 15, "Animation and Compositing," contains example code that defines some controllers: a specialized `TicklishController` and a `KeyController`. There are, however, some general points that should be discussed.

MouseController Classes

There are two `MouseController` classes in the existing QuickTime for Java. `GroupController` extracts a `QTDrawable` member from the `GroupDrawable` space, and `SWController` extracts a `TwoDSprite` member from the `SWCompositor` space. These two controllers implement the following abstract methods of `MouseController`:

```
protected abstract void setTargetSpace (Space s);
```

The MouseController calls this method when it is added to a Space, passing in the Space it has been attached to. A subclass can cast the Space to the particular type of Space that it is able to act upon. If the Space is not of the appropriate type, a ClassCastException is generated by this action, and the controller will not be added to that Space. Your application is then informed that it has mismatched a particular Mouse-Controller and Space.

```
public abstract Space getSpace ();
```

A corollary to the setTargetSpace() method, this enables the Control-ler to return the Space it is attached to. Typically, the subclass will cache the Space it is attached to; the MouseController itself does not.

```
protected abstract Object getSelected (MouseEvent event)
                                        throws QTException;
```

This method returns an object that is a member of the space—typi-cally, the frontmost object at the location of the MouseEvent. The Mouse-Controller calls this method for mouse events that could potentially target a specific member (such as mouseClicked, mousePressed).

THE SIMPLESPACE CLASS

The abstract SimpleSpace class provides a default implementation for the Space interface. In addition to the public interface and implementa-tion, there are protected methods that a subclass needs to interact with for the default behavior of this Space to be realized.

MEMBERS AND SPACES

In the memberAdded() and memberRemoved() methods of the Simple-Space, certain actions are defined to happen based on the interfaces that the new member implements.

Member Spaces

A space, if appropriate, can be a member of a parent space, enabling the embedding of spaces. When a member space is added to the SimpleSpace, the timer's TimeBase of the member space is slaved to the parent space. The source of interest for the member space is set to the source of interest for the parent space. All of the TimeableController objects of the member space will indirectly be slaved to the TimeBase of the parent space through the slaving of the member space's TimeBase. All of the ListenerController objects of the member space will have the same source of interest as the parent space.

In QuickTime for Java, it is possible for a SWCompositor to be a member of a parent of an SWCompositor or a GroupDrawable display space. It is not possible for a GroupDrawable to be a member of the SWCompositor display space, as it does not satisfy the requirements for membership of a SWCompositor. A GroupDrawable can be a member of a parent GroupDrawable display space.

Listener

Members that implement the Listener interface have their source of interest set to the parent Space.

In QuickTime for Java, all of the QTDrawable classes are Listener classes as is the MouseController. The action taken by the QTDrawable is very dependent on the class. For instance, a QTPlayer will register interests in mouse and key events, a QTImageDrawer will create an offscreen java.awt.Image object to use when calling its Paintable paint() method. A MouseController will declare an interest in mouse and/or mouse-motion events, depending on the requirements of its MouseResponder.

Timeable

Members that implement the Timeable interface have their TimeBase slaved to that of the parent Space.

QTPlayer, MoviePlayer, MoviePresenter all implement this interface and can be members of QTDisplaySpace objects in QuickTime for Java, so they will, when added to a space, have their respective TimeBase objects slaved to the TimeBase of the containing space.

An important implication of this for the GroupDrawable/ DirectGroup is as follows. The master-slave relationship established between the members and its space means that the clocks of the members will not tick if the rate of the parent space's TimeBase is zero. Thus, in the DirectGroup sample code on the CD-ROM, the rate of the DirectGroup Timer is set to 1, even though the DirectGroup itself may have no tickling requirements. The initial state of a Timer is inactive, so the Timer in this case will not tickle or send timeChanged messages to the DirectGroup space unless the application specifically activates the Timer because it has some tickle requirements.

The relationship of time values changing and tickling is discussed in Chapter 11, "Timing." Chapter 14, "Using Spaces and Controllers: QTDisplaySpace," has sample code where this requirement is illustrated.

Extending the SimpleSpace Class

Your application can define its own specializations of spaces, whether in the display or model space areas. To do this, you need to define the methods of the Collection interface, particularly the storage implementation of its members, as the SimpleSpace makes no assumptions about how members are stored. Your application may also require a new type of Controller and need to add the logic to deal with setting up the relationship between this new Controller class and the space.

If the existing semantics of the Controller and Space relationship are suitable, then the subclasses' addController() method can call the SimpleSpace addController() method. This ensures that the existing actions are performed when a Controller is added, including the addition of the Controller to the SimpleSpace controller Vector. Once added, the subclass can then perform the specific actions it requires for this new type of controller:

```
class MySpace extends SimpleSpace {
    public synchronized void addController (Controller c)
                                        throws QTException {
```

```
            if (controllersVec.contains (c)) return;
            super.addController (c);
            if (c instanceof MySpeciailisedController) {
                //... do whatever is appropriate
        }

        public synchronized void removeController (Controller c)
                                            throws QTException {
            if (controllersVec.contains (c) == false) return;
            super.removeController (c);
            if (c instanceof MySpeciailisedController) {
                //... do whatever is appropriate
        }
}
```

The removeController() method should, of course, undo the actions taken when the controller was added. The application might also want to test to see if the controller has already been added (or is a member in the case of the remove method) before doing anything.

Protected Methods

The memberAdded() method should be called by a subclass after it has successfully added a member. This method will perform the above documented procedures for the new member, such as setting the Listener source, slaving the TimeBase of a Timeable member. It will also correctly embed a member that is also a space, allowing for spaces to contain other spaces.

The memberRemoved() method should be called by a subclass after it has successfully removed a member. It will undo all of the actions that are taken when a member is added, leaving the removed member in an appropriately unconnected state.

Chapter 14, "Using Spaces and Controllers: QTDisplaySpace," and Chapter 15, "Animation and Compositing," contain examples of using the two QTDisplaySpace classes and the controllers that are provided in QuickTime for Java.

14

Using Spaces and Controllers: QTDisplaySpace

By definition, a display space is a collection of objects that has some kind of visual appearance. The display space manages the layering of those objects within its visual presentation. The QTDisplaySpace interface defines the minimum API that a display space provides. A QTDisplaySpace is also a kind of QTDrawable, which means that it can be set as a client for a QTCanvas object.

This chapter shows you how to

- group QuickTime drawing-capable objects into the same display space of the QTCanvas

- customize user control of the playback of a movie that is a member of a Compositor using the keyboard

THE QTDISPLAYSPACE INTERFACE

The QTDisplaySpace interface provides an API for retrieving the current frontmost and backmost layers of its members. It also provides a way of retrieving the Layerable object for a member that allows the member to both get and set its layer within the display space. A member can be added to the display space, specifying the layer at which it should be added. The lower the layer (or z) value, the more frontmost the object is displayed. The backmost layer of a `QTDisplaySpace` is `Short.MAX_VALUE`. This interface abstracts out where the layering is managed. This can be defined in the implementation.

Members of display spaces may or may not know about their position and two-dimensional display matrix. As such, the `QTDisplaySpace` also provides an API for retrieving a member's `Transformable` interface, which allows a member to get and set its display matrix.

Two display spaces are provided in QuickTime for Java. These are the abstract `GroupDrawable` class and its concrete `DirectGroup` subclass and the abstract `SWCompositor` and its concrete `Compositor` subclass. These classes have a different manner of dealing with their member objects, specifically in dealing with how objects are positioned within their space's x, y, and z coordinates. As such, the `QTDisplaySpace` enables you to retrieve the `Layerable` object that allows you to get and set the layer of a display space's member and a `Transformable` object that allows you to alter the display matrix of the member. Figure 14.1 shows an implementation of the `Layerable` interface.

FIGURE 14.1 *The Layerable implementation*

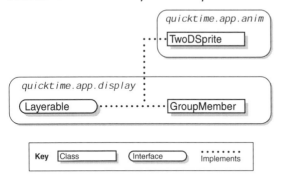

PRESENTING MEMBERS

There is one major difference between display spaces in how they present their members: "direct to screen" versus "indirect," or composited, drawing. Members of a `SWCompositor` are composited into an off-screen `QDGraphics`, and the `Space` is responsible for drawing this composited image to the destination (generally onscreen) `QDGraphics` of the `QTCanvas` the space is a client of. This allows for transparency and alpha-blending modes to be applied to members because all of the members of such a space draw unrestricted into this buffer.

Members of a `GroupDrawable` space draw directly to the destination `QDGraphics` of the `QTCanvas` the space is a client of. This can give better drawing performance because the members draw directly, rather than through the offscreen buffer of the `Compositor`. The layering capabilities of such a space are achieved through clipping out the areas of the destination `QDGraphics` of members that are behind other members. Thus, transparency and blend effects are not possible with such a display mode.

Another characteristic of the different implementations of these types of display spaces is how they store the layering and visual presentation area of their members. As such, the `QTDisplaySpace` removes the need for a `QTDisplaySpace` to provide a specific implementation of both characteristics by delegating the implementation of the `Layerable` and `Transformable` functionality. The `QTDisplaySpace` interface provides methods that return the `Layerable` and the `Transformable` (visual display matrix property) characteristics of a given member. Depending on the space itself, these methods can return the same object (the given member is the object that contains information about its layer, for instance), or it may return a helper object that the space uses to contain this information. In both cases, these methods return an object that can then be interacted with either to change the layer or to transform the visual presentation area of the member.

A `QTDrawable` is a general presentation object that has no concept of being presented in a layered space. As such, the `GroupDrawable` uses a helper class (`GroupMember`) to encapsulate the layering information for each of its members. Members of a `SWCompositor` objects, on the other hand, are `TwoDSprite`, and a `TwoDSprite` itself contains the layering information. Of course, both of these display spaces deal with the actual mechanics of layering their members.

You should use these methods to ensure that your application is dealing with the correct and appropriate object to achieve the desired behavior, as well as to generalize and ensure the reusability of the class that performs these actions. The example code in this chapter discusses how to utilize these interfaces.

Using DirectGroup

A `DirectGroup` object contains a set of `QTDrawable` objects that present their visual contents directly to the screen. Items that overlap screen space could draw over each other and thus cause flickering. To avoid this problem, the front object will clip the rear object so that the rear object does not draw in the area occupied by the front object. As such, none of the overlaying transparency or blending effects that are possible between a compositor's members are possible between members of a `DirectGroup`.

The general constraints of the `DirectGroup` are handled by the `GroupDrawable` abstract class. The particular clipping mechanism that QuickTime for Java employs is encapsulated within the `DirectGroup` class itself. If you wish to use a different layering technique, you could subclass `GroupDrawable`.

The members of `DirectGroup` are `QTDrawable` objects, which know how to draw but have no information about the layer within the group. This information is kept and managed by the space and the `Group-Member` class.

```
addMember (member)
addMember (member, layer)
```

The default `addMember()` call uses the pixel location of the `QTDrawable` itself to position the drawer within the space; this is the default positioning mechanism. When the group is resized the group's items will not be resized or repositioned.

The `addMember (member, layer)` method allows your application to specify at which layer the member should be positioned. This determines which members of the group will be in front of the new member or behind it.

GROUP DRAWING

The sample code in this section shows how to group QuickTime drawing-capable objects into the same display space of the `QTCanvas`. The media you need for this program are `ShipX.pct` files (where X is a number indicative of a frame order), the `house.jpg` picture file, and the `jumps.mov` movie. Figure 14.2 shows a screenshot from the program, with the various layers of each of the members notated. Each member both draws completely its visible region and does not draw in any area that a member in front of it occupies.

Thus, the `Movie`, which is in layer 1, has the ability to draw completely to any area of the space occupied by the `QTCanvas`. There is no specific clip region that is applied to this frontmost member.

The contained animation is in layer 2. It is able to draw anywhere except where the layer 1 members are—in this case the `Movie`. The clip region for this member is set so that it excludes that display area of the `Movie`.

The still image is placed in layer 3; it is behind the other two members. Its clip region is set to exclude the areas that are occupied by both the `Movie` and the animation.

As these objects are dragged around or otherwise resized or repositioned, the `DirectGroup` is notified that the display characteristics of a member have been changed and resets the clipping of those members behind it accordingly. The `GroupController` will do this automatically in its `mouseDragged` method, by calling the `DirectGroup.memberChanged` method supplying the member that has been changed. If an application itself performs any such alterations of members, then it must notify the `DirectGroup` accordingly.

The primary distinction between a `DirectGroup` and a `Compositor` can also be seen here. The animation in layer 2 shows both a blending `GraphicsMode` and transparency. The vertical spaceship is translucent and thus you can see the other spaceship behind it. All of the spaceships have also had transparency applied to them, so you only see the spacehip image and not its surrounding color. This is discussed fully in the next chapter, "Animation and Compositing."

FIGURE 14.2 *Group drawing in same display space as QTCanvas*

The `DirectGroup` allows for groups of `QTDrawable` objects to be added to the same `QTCanvas`. There are also controllers attached to the space, allowing you to

- Drag any object around—the picture is restrained to the bounds of the `DirectGroup` (see dragger 2 and controller 2). The other two objects can be dragged outside the group to within a single pixel showing (see dragger and controller 1).

■ Option-click to send an object to the back layer

■ Shift-drag any spaceship around within its own space

At the code level, you begin by setting up the DirectGroup, specifying width and height, and then adding members. The addMember() method used in this sample uses an addMember() specific to the DirectGroup. It allows your application to specify the x and y origin by using a range of 0 → 1.0F, where 0 is the top or left and 1 is the bottom or right of the enclosing space.

```
int kWidth = 300, kHeight = 300;
Dimension d = new Dimension (kWidth, kHeight);
DirectGroup drawer = new DirectGroup(d, QDColor.gray);
QTPlayer p1 = makePlayer (new QTFile (QTFactory.findAbsolutePath
                                        ("jumps.mov")));
drawer.addMember (p1, 1, 0.1F, 0.2F);
```

You use an ImagePresenter as a member of the group because dragging will be much faster:

```
ImagePresenter ip = ImagePresenter.fromGraphicsImporterDrawer (if1);
drawer.addMember (ip, 3);
```

You create the Spaceship animation by making a Compositor and adding sprites to it. The addSprites code is discussed in Chapter 15, "Animation and Compositing."

```
Compositor shipAnimation = new Compositor (
                    new QDGraphics (new QDRect(200, 200)),
                    QDColor.lightGray, 20, 1);
addSprites (shipAnimation);
shipAnimation.setLocation (kWidth - 160, kHeight - 160);
drawer.addMember (shipAnimation, 2);
```

You add the controllers for dragging the members around and changing their layers. Since the wholespace setting is false for this controller, we explicitly add the members to the controller that we want this controller to control. We also use the built-in Dragger, which is a MouseResponder that allows your application to drag around user-selected members of a space.

```
Dragger dragger = new Dragger (MouseResponder.kNoModifiersMask);
dragger.setConstrained(Dragger.kConstrainNone);
GroupController controller1 = new GroupController (dragger, false);
controller1.addMember (p1);
controller1.addMember (shipAnimation);
drawer.addController (controller1);

Dragger dragger2 = new Dragger (MouseResponder.kNoModifiersMask);
GroupController controller2 = new GroupController (dragger2, false);
controller2.addMember (ip);
drawer.addController (controller2);

LayerChanger lc = new LayerChanger (InputEvent.ALT_MASK);
GroupController controller3 = new GroupController (lc, true);
drawer.addController (controller3);
```

Then we set the drawer as the client of the QTCanvas and set the rates of both the animation and the top-level group to one. Even though there are no time-based behaviors defined for the top group, we still need to set the rate of its Timer to 1 so that any members that do have time requirements (like the member movie and animation) will play back.

```
myQTCanvas.setClient (drawer, true);

shipAnimation.getTimer().setRate(1);
drawer.getTimer().setRate (1);
```

The LayerChanger represents a customized MouseResponder and is defined in terms of the Layerable interface. This means that this controller could change the layer of a member of either of the two kinds of QTDisplayGroup objects: the DirectGroup, where the members are some kind of QTDrawable, and the Compositor, where the members are sprites. The Layerable interface provides an abstraction that allows us to deal with the layer placement of members of these groups without knowing anything more about the members.

The MouseController that this MouseResponder is attached to will set the target for the LayerChanger when the user clicks on a member of the QTDisplaySpace. We are given this member by the MouseController, and we get that member's Layerable object.

In the mouseClicked() method we get the backmost layer of the QTDisplaySpace and set our target's layer to this backmost layer + 1, thus moving the member behind any other member in the display space.

The isAppropriate() method returns true. We could do this test:

```
return group.getLayerable(object) != null;
```

to ensure that the incoming object is a member of the group and thus has a Layerable representation. However, in the normal course of operation of the MouseController, it will only return members of a display space, and by definition these all have a Layerable representation. So for this usage, returning true is quite acceptable.

```
public class LayerChanger extends MouseResponder {
    //CONSTRUCTORS...

    private Layerable current;
    private QTDisplaySpace group;

    // This will throw a ClassCastException if the Space
    // is incorrect. It is called by the MouseController constructor
    // and thus if this cast fails then it won't be constructed.
    protected void setTargetSpace (Object space) {
        group = (QTDisplaySpace)space;
    }

    protected void setTarget (Object t) {
        current = group.getLayerable(t);
    }

    protected void removeTarget () {
        current = null;
    }
```

```
public boolean isAppropriate (Object object) {
    return true;
}

public void mouseClicked (MouseEvent e) {
    try {
        int layer = group.getBackLayer();
        current.setLayer (layer+1);
    } catch (QTException ex) {
        throw new QTRuntimeException (ex);
    } finally {
        current = null;
    }
}
}
```

This example also shows the ability to embed spaces within spaces with the contained space retaining its own sense of a space for its members.

The blue border that appears around the picture after you make the window bigger is the background color of the DirectGroup. You could restrain the size of the canvas to the picture's size by using new QT-Canvas (kInitialSize,...) when making the QTCanvas.

The addSprites() method, which defines a cell-based animation and a set of actions to control this animation, is discussed in Chapter 15, "Animation and Compositing."

CUSTOMIZING USER CONTROL OF MOVIE PLAYBACK

The example code in this section shows how you can customize user control of the playback of a movie that is a member of a Compositor using the keyboard.

The following code sets up the Compositor that will have both the movie and a picture as its members.

We make an ImagePresenter to ensure that the image is in a format optimized for rendering, as the image will have to be rendered each time the movie draws. We set its graphics mode to a blend, which enables a mixing of the image with the movie.

We then make the MoviePresenter, which is how we can have a movie as a member of a Compositor. This is more fully discussed in Chapter 15, "Animation and Compositing."

A key controller is created that allows the user to control the movie playback with the keyboard, as shown below.

The Compositor is added to the QTCanvas and its rate is set to 1 so that the movie will play back.

```
Dimension d = new Dimension (300, 300);
QDGraphics gw = new QDGraphics (new QDRect(d));
Compositor comp = new Compositor (gw, QDColor.gray, 20, 1);

GraphicsImporterDrawer if1 = new GraphicsImporterDrawer (
        new QTFile (QTFactory.findAbsolutePath ("pics/house.jpg")));
if1.setDisplayBounds (new QDRect (d));
ImagePresenter id = ImagePresenter.fromGraphicsImporterDrawer (if1);
id.setGraphicsMode (new GraphicsMode (blend, QDColor.gray));
comp.addMember (id, 1);

QTFile qtf = new QTFile (QTFactory.findAbsolutePath ("jumps.mov"));
OpenMovieFile movieFile = OpenMovieFile.asRead(qtf);
Movie mv = Movie.fromFile (movieFile);
MoviePresenter mvp = new MoviePresenter(mv);
mvp.setLocation (80, 80);
comp.addMember (mvp, 2);

KBDController keyController = new KBDController(mvp);
comp.addController(keyController);

myQTCanvas.setClient (comp, true);
comp.getTimer().setRate(1);
```

The KBDController code is listed below. It is a KeyListener and implements the ListenerController so that the Compositor will register its interest in events and pass on to it the QTCanvas when it is set as the client of QTCanvas. To do this, the QTDisplaySpace calls this controller's addedTo() and removedFrom() methods, as the space itself is added to or removed from a QTCanvas. In these methods, we declare our interest in key events that are generated by the source of interest, in this case a QTCanvas.

The controller deals with a Playable object, so it can be used to send the appropriate notifications to any object that implements this interface.

The keyPressed() method is used to set the rate and time values appropriately according to the key the user presses.

One could customize this controller to deal specifically with movies with QuickTimeVR content, using the same methodology to set pan, rotate, tilt angles, and so forth, as well as extending the key controls for a normal movie that are presented here.

```java
class KBDController implements ListenerController, KeyListener {

    private Playable player;
    private float savedRate = 1;
    KBDController (Playable player) {
        this.player = player;
    }

    public void addedTo (Object interest){
        if (interest instanceof Component)
            ((Component)interest).addKeyListener (this);
    }

    public void removedFrom (Object interest){
        if (interest instanceof Component)
            ((Component)interest).removeKeyListener (this);
    }

    public void keyPressed (KeyEvent e) {
        try {
            switch (e.getKeyCode()) {
                case KeyEvent.VK_SPACE:
                    if (player.getRate() != 0)
                        player.setRate (0);
```

```
                else
                    player.setRate (savedRate);
                break;
            case KeyEvent.VK_UP:
                player.setTime (player.getDuration());
                break;
            case KeyEvent.VK_DOWN:
                player.setTime (0);
                break;
            case KeyEvent.VK_LEFT:
                player.setRate (-1);
                savedRate = -1;
                break;
            case KeyEvent.VK_RIGHT:
                player.setRate (1);
                savedRate = 1;
                break;
        }
    } catch (QTException ee) {
        throw new QTRuntimeException (ee);
    }
}
//...
}
```

15 Animation and Compositing

With animation, you are working essentially with a time-based script of composited images, which simply means that the images will change over time. With compositing, you are using images from different sources and layering them and generating a composited image.

This chapter introduces you to some of the techniques that you can use to animate and composite images in QuickTime for Java programs. It shows you how to

- composite a presentation out of disparate media sources, applying compositing effects such as blend and transparency

- construct a simple animation and apply compositing (graphics mode) effects to the sprites

- define MouseResponder objects to customize the behavior of mouse actions

- create composited effects, such as ripple effects

- build a transition effect and apply it to a character in an animation, using the QuickTime effects architecture

USING THE SWCOMPOSITOR

The SWCompositor class provides the capability to compose a complex image from disparate image sources and then treat the result as a single image, which is presented to the user. It also provides a time base that controls the rendering cycle and allows your application to attach time-based behaviors or actions.

The SWCompositor uses the QuickTime SpriteWorld internally to perform its compositing tasks and its TimeBase for its timing services. All of the actual drawing of the members of a SWCompositor is handled through the interaction between the SpriteWorld and Sprite classes of QuickTime.

The SpriteWorld itself is wrapped by the SWCompositor class, and to represent the Sprite class, it uses the TwoDSprite. The TwoDSprite is a presenter, that is, it presents image information. The presentation of image information within the context of the SpriteWorld is determined by the matrix, graphics mode, layer, and visibility of the Sprite object.

To create a Sprite, you need a valid SpriteWorld. To create a SpriteWorld, you need a valid QDGraphics destination. Depending on whether a SWCompositor is visible, you may or may not have a valid destination QDGraphics. The interaction between the SWCompositor and its TwoDSprite presenters handles the saving and creating of SpriteWorld and Sprite objects—your application does not need to deal specifically with this issue.

The SWCompositor object presents the functionality of the SpriteWorld within the context of the QTDisplaySpace interface. The TwoDSprite object wraps the QuickTime Sprite object, giving it a Transformable interface so that its visual characteristics can have matrix transformations applied to them. It also implements the Compositable interface, as graphics modes can be applied when a sprite's image data is rendered. You can save the current display state of an individual sprite and recreate a sprite from the information you saved; the TwoDSpriteInfo object is a helper class created for this purpose.

The SWCompositor supports two important characteristics of members. If the member implements a DynamicImage, this indicates to the Compositor that the image being presented by the member is apt to change. For example, the member is a MoviePresenter, in which case the member needs to create a special object—an Invalidator—that will invalidate the sprite that is presenting the member, so that the composite cycle will redraw that sprite, and you will see the changing image data of a movie as it plays back. This is discussed in more detail below.

A further service that the SWCompositor renders to its new members is the handling of members that implement the Notifier interface. If a member implements this interface, the Compositor establishes the connection between the Notifier (the new member) and its Notify-Listener (the new member's TwoDSprite). When the new member's image data is complete, it can then automatically notify its registered NotifyListener—its TwoDSprite. This is used with QTImageDrawer members where the QTImageDrawer won't have valid image data until the Java offscreen image is created. It could also be used with images that may reside on a remote server, or interactively where the user may choose or draw an image that is part of an animation.

THE SWCONTROLLER

The SWController deals with SpriteWorldHitTest calls on the SpriteWorld that is contained by the SWCompositor's subclasses. By default, it performs hit-testing on the actual sprite image itself. However, your application can set the hit-test flags to support any mode of hit-testing appropriate. As a subclass of the MouseController, it will return any member of the SWCompositor that is hit only if isWholespace() is true. If isWholespace() is false, the hit sprite must be a member of the SWController itself.

THE COMPOSITOR

The Compositor class is a subclass of SWCompositor, with its primary role being the relaxation of membership requirements of its members. The member object of a Compositor is only required to implement the ImageSpec interface, in which case, the Compositor creates the TwoD-Sprite that presents that image data in its display space. If a TwoD-Sprite itself is added to the Compositor, it is added directly as a member, since TwoDSprite also implements the ImageSpec interface.

If the new member implements the Transformable interface, then its current matrix will be set on its TwoDSprite presenter. If the new member implements the `Compositable` interface, then its current `GraphicsMode` is applied to its `TwoDSprite` presenter. These actions simplify the adding of members to the `Compositor`. However, once added, your application will need to deal directly with the member's `TwoDSprite` presenter to alter the `Matrix` or `GraphicsMode` of the sprite.

Note that most of the functionality of the `Compositor` is within the `SWCompositor` abstract class. It is only in the membership requirements that the `Compositor` specializes the `SWCompositor`—specifically in the creation, removal, and retrieval of a member's `TwoDSprite` presenter.

COMPOSITION AND TIME-BASED SERVICES

One of the primary requirements of assembling an animation is to have a means of scheduling actions that should occur over time. For example, a character in a cell-based animation is animated by flipping through different still images that show the character performing some action. In previous examples, such as those in Chapter 14, "Using Spaces and Controllers: QTDisplaySpace," we've seen a standard cell-based animation of a spinning spaceship. The spinning spaceship is made up of 24 individual pictures, and the appearance of the spinning is achieved by flipping through these images in an ordered manner. Though this is a simple example, the principle applies to any generation of an animated character. This kind of requirement is generally handled through the `quicktime.app.actions.PeriodicAction` subclasses.

A second requirement has more to do with the mechanics of the actual rendering process. Optimizations to the rendering of any given state of the `Compositor` are made to ensure that the rendering is as efficient as possible. A sprite is only redrawn if some known property of the sprite is changed—for example, if its display matrix has been altered. In the case of sprites that present changing pixel data—for example, a movie that is playing back—the `SpriteWorld render()` method will not know that it needs to be redrawn because none of its explicit properties have been changed, just the values of its image data. In order to see this sprite's changing image, the `Sprite` itself has to be explicitly invalidated. The `DynamicImage` interface is provided to express this requirement, and the `Invalidator` set of classes deal specifically with this issue. Figure 15.1 illustrates these two timing services.

FIGURE 15.1 *Time-based actions*

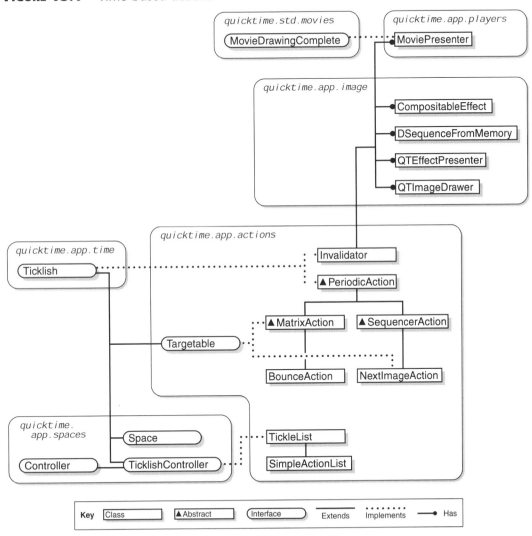

PERIODICACTION

The `PeriodicAction` class implements the `Ticklish` interface. `Periodi-cAction` objects are generally added to a `TicklishController`, such as the `SimpleActionList`. During the render cycle of the `SWCompositor`, it will tickle any of its `TicklishController` objects. The `PeriodicAction` objects in a `SimpleActionList` will be tickled. If enough time has elapsed according to the specified scale and period of the `PeriodicAc-tion`, then the `PeriodicAction` will "fire" through, invoking the protect-ed abstract `doAction()` method. Subclasses of `PeriodicAction` define this method to implement the particular behavior associated with this action.

The `SimpleActionList` and periodic actions do not really provide an ordering based on a time line. Periodic actions are fired based on the elapsed time from the last time they fired and the current rate and time of the current tickle invocation. However, while this time-line service is not provided, your application could provide its own implementation of this service by providing a `TicklishController` that could order and schedule the firing of member actions based on the their time position and the time value that is passed in to its `tickle()` method.

MatrixAction

The `MatrixAction` class is defined to operate on the matrix of an object that implements the `Transformable` interface. As such it can be applied to `QTDrawable` members of a `DirectGroup` as well as `TwoDSprite` mem-bers of a `Compositor`, as both implement this interface. A single sub-class of `MatrixAction`—`BounceAction`—is provided in QuickTime for Java. However, it is a simple task to write a subclass of `MatrixAction` to apply desired matrix transformations as required. The `Dragging-Sprites` sample code, which is discussed below, shows an example of defining a `RotateAction`.

Constructing Cell-Based Sprites and SequencerAction

A cell-based sprite is constructed by flipping through an ordered col-lection (sequence) of images that typically describe an action of a character. To construct a sprite with these characteristics, you follow these steps:

First, the image data is read into memory, generally into an ImageDataSequence:

```
File matchFile = QTFactory.findAbsolutePath ("images/Ship01.pct");
ImageDataSequence seq = ImageUtil.createSequence (matchFile);
```

The ImageDataSequence is a sequence of EncodedImage objects that are all described by a single ImageDescription. The ImageUtil.controllers:createSequence calls enable your application to create a sequence easily out of a specified match file.

You then can explicitly create a TwoDSprite using one of the frames of this image sequence as the initial image of that sprite:

```
Matrix matrix1 = new Matrix();
matrix1.setTx(20);
matrix1.setTy(30);
TwoDSprite sprite = new TwoDSprite(seq, 4, matrix1, true, 1);
myCompositor.addMember (sprite);
```

This will create a sprite with an initial location of 20, 30. It uses frame 4 of the image sequence, is initially visible (true), and will be put in layer 1.

Now your application must create a mechanism where the images of this sprite can be flipped through:

```
SimpleActionList actionList = new SimpleActionList();
ImageSequencer sequencer = new ImageSequencer (seq);
sequencer.setLooping (ImageSequencer.kLoopForwards);
actionList.addMember (new NextImageAction (20, 1, sequencer,
                                                      sprite));
//...
myCompositor.addController(actionList);
```

An action list is created that contains a collection of actions that will be applied to the sprites. An ImageSequencer is similar to a java.util.Enumeration in that it iterates over a collection's members. Howver, a Sequencer introduces the concept of a cursor or current frame. Thus, you can advance a sequencer forwards or backwards; it also has looping behavior. The ImageSequencer is created to iterate over the members of the ImageDataSequence we created earlier.

We then add a SequencerAction to the action list, in this case a NextImageAction. A NextImageAction will, when fired, set its Sequencer to display the next image of its sequence to its target sprite. If the rate is less than zero when it is fired, it will display the previous image. It is set to fire 20 frames a second at a rate of 1.

After we've set up the action list, we add it as a controller to the compositor.

A common feature of the sample code that is listed in this book is the sharing of image data by more than one sprite. This is achieved through creating a separate ImageSequencer for each sprite, but the ImageSequencer is set to iterate over the same ImageDataSequence, which contains the actual image data. Then a separate image action is created to trigger this flipping process. So in the //... commented section above, we could insert the following lines that apply to a second sprite previously created (not shown here):

```
ImageSequencer sequencer2 = new ImageSequencer (seq);
sequencer2.setLooping (ImageSequencer.kLoopForwards);
actionList.addMember (new NextImageAction (5, 1, sequencer2,
                                                sprite2));
```

As you can see, the sequencer2 acts on the same image data as the first sprite but with a new NextImageAction to control this sequencer and a different firing scale (five times a second).

INVALIDATION

The DynamicImage interface was introduced to capture the requirement of some sprite members to explicitly invalidate their presenting sprites.

Imagine a sprite that is presenting a movie that is playing back. The movie will be presented to the Compositor as a MoviePresenter. That is, the movie draws into an offscreen QDGraphics, and the pixel data of this QDGraphics becomes the image data of its sprite. As the movie plays back, it will of course alter this pixel data, but it is only altering the internal values of the pixels—the actual image data as far as the sprite is concerned is the same. Thus, to see this movie playing back in a compositor, the presenting sprite must be explicitly invalidated so that the compositor's SpriteWorld will ensure that that sprite is redrawn and thus the new pixels the movie has generated will be seen.

There is a MovieDrawingComplete callback that can be added to a movie so that the movie can notify interested parties that it has drawn to its destination QDGraphics. As MoviePresenter implements DynamicImage, it will create an Invalidator, which the Compositor will invoke each time through its render cycle. This Invalidator will invalidate the sprite presenter of MoviePresenter if the movie it is presenting has actually drawn—that is, if the MovieDrawingComplete execute method has set this invalidation flag.

Other invalidators work in a similar manner, though without the notification services of a callback. Invalidators exist for the effect classes that can be added to a Compositor. In these cases the invalidator will invalidate its sprite if the isRedrawing method returns true. The TransitionEffects sample code at the end of this chapter defines a controller that controls a transitioning member. As part of this control, it sets the redrawing state of the QTEffectPresenter to true or false, thus directly controlling this invalidation process.

SPACE CONSTRUCTION

The overall assemblage of the Compositor or DirectGroup display spaces is basically descriptive, and many behaviors can be used in both situations.

Your application describes how these spaces should be assembled and the control aspects they require. The spaces themselves look after all of the details of assembling and coordinating the various requirements of their members and controllers.

Figure 15.2 illustrates a fairly typical construction of an animation. It presents the `Compositor` in the Model-View-Controller design to aid in understanding the overall construction and control semantics that are inherent in its use. The diagram illustrates both the addition and construction of time-based actions in a `SimpleActionList` as described above, as well as a `MouseController` that enables the user to drag a sprite around.

The overall intention of the spaceship example and the `Dragging-Sprites` example later in this chapter is to present the image data of the sprites (the spaceships). This is presented as an animation that is assembled and controlled through the construction of the `Compositor` space and its various controllers. QuickTime is used to provide both the time base that controls the animation's rendering and the rendering services of its `Sprite` and `SpriteWorld` objects. The user is also able to interact with the animation, dragging the sprites around, and through the provision of custom `MouseResponder` objects, resize and skew the presentation of the sprite's images.

FIGURE 15.2 *Construction of an animation using the Model-View-Controller design*

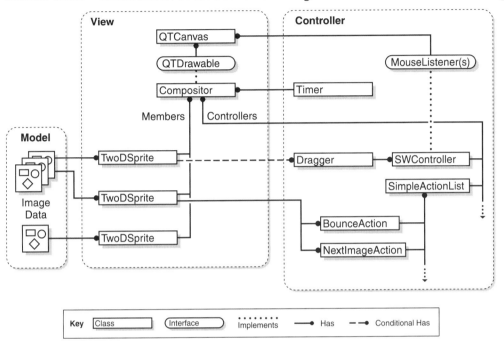

The various components of Figure 15.2 are explained as follows:

Model: The image data of the sprites is the "Model" aspect of this construction.

View: The image data is presented by TwoDSprite objects in the context of their Compositor. The Compositor coordinates the rendering of each member TwoDSprite. It implements the QTDrawable interface and thus a client of a QTCanvas. This is the "View" aspect of this construction.

Controller: As this construction is built using Java objects, the "Controller" aspect of this is quite visible. Much of this construction is coordinated by the Compositor itself. It creates its Timer and passes on to its controllers the QTCanvas when it is addedTo the QTCanvas as its client. There are two primary aspects of control illustrated:

1. Timer: The Timer controls the rendering process of the Compositor. In the rendering process, the Compositor will tickle any Ticklish-Controller, such as the SimpleActionList. The SimpleActionList

contains actions that, when fired, will alter the display matrix of its TwoDSprite target or change the image from a sequence of images that are presented by a TwoDSprite target.

2. The user is able to drag the TwoDSprite objects through altering a TwoDSprite display matrix. Mouse events that occur in the QTCanvas are passed through to its registered MouseListener, in this case a SWController. When the user presses on a TwoDSprite to drag it, the SWController sets this TwoDSprite as the selected target of its attached MouseResponder (the Dragger). As the user drags, the Dragger alters the display matrix of this target TwoDSprite accordingly.

The separation between Model-View-Controller in this example is quite powerful. The image data can be changed or substituted at any time, and the same control structures can still be used. Different TwoDSprites can access the same image data but present it in different modes.

Because the Compositor coordinates the establishment of these relations (its associated members and controllers), it can be detached from one QTCanvas and added to another simply through the setClient() method of the QTCanvas.

Your application or the user can control both the rendering scale and rate of the Compositor through its Timer setRate() and rescheduleTickle() methods.

IMAGE COMPOSITING

The code in this section shows how to composite a presentation out of disparate media sources, applying compositing effects such as blend and transparency. Recording a movie from the activities of the Compositor is also shown. You use the offscreen Compositor to present multiple QuickTime content in a single image. Figure 15.3 shows a screenshot from the program.

FIGURE 15.3 *Compositing a presentation from disparate media sources*

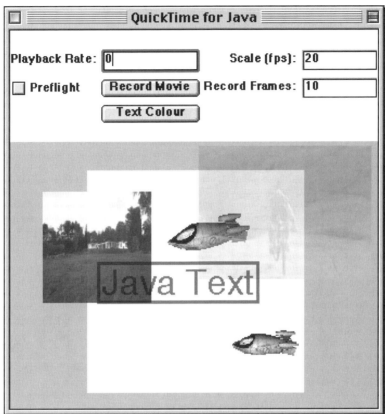

To start with, you add different types of objects as members to the top-level compositor. These objects include

- a `Compositor` made up of cycling image-based sprites

- a `Movie` added through the use of the `MoviePresenter` class. A blend effect is applied to this member. A `MoviePresenter` is used because it implements the `ImageSpec` interface, returning as the image the off-screen pixel data that the movie draws into.

- an image that has a blend effect also applied to it (`ImagePresenter`)

■ a `QTImageDrawer`. This object takes any drawing that is done using Java drawing APIs and draws the resultant image in the QuickTime-owned space. It has a transparent graphics mode applied to it.

Controllers are attached to the `Compositor` in the same way they are for the `GroupDrawing` program shown in Chapter 14, "Using Spaces and Controllers: QTDisplaySpace," with dragging and layering responders.

In the following code, `comp` is the top-level `Compositor` that is created for these calls.

The `JavaTextDrawer` is a `QTImageDrawer` that will draw a small piece of Java text. It is discussed more fully below.

```
JavaTextDrawer jtDrawer = new JavaTextDrawer (new JavaText(),
                                    new Dimension (150, 38), true);
    // apply a tinge of pink to the java text that is drawn
jtDrawer.setGraphicsMode (new GraphicsMode (blend, QDColor.gray));
comp.addMember (jtDrawer, 1);
```

Next, we add another `Compositor` to `comp`. This `Compositor` presents cell-based animated sprites (our spinning spaceships). The `addSprites()` method is discussed below.

```
Compositor sh = new Compositor (
                    new QDGraphics (new QDRect(200, 200)),
                    QDColor.white, 20, 1);
addSprites (sh);
sh.setLocation (10, 10);
sh.getTimer().setRate(1);
comp.addMember (sh, 3);
```

Next, we make a `Movie` and a `MoviePresenter`. We set a graphics mode on the presenter to provide a magenta blend mode to the composited movie. When the `MoviePresenter` is added to the `Compositor`, it establishes the invalidation requirements as discussed above.

```
Movie m = makeMovie (new QTFile (QTFactory.findAbsolutePath
                                    ("jumps.mov")));
MoviePresenter md = new MoviePresenter (m);
md.setLocation (120, 120);
```

```
md.setGraphicsMode (new GraphicsMode (blend, QDColor.magenta));
md.setRate(1);
comp.addMember (md, 2);
```

Next, we make and add an `ImagePresenter`, also setting a graphics mode that will apply a yellow blend mode to the composited image.

```
ImagePresenter id = makeImagePresenter (new QTFile
                 (QTFactory.findAbsolutePath ("pics/house.jpg")),
                 new QDRect (100, 100));
id.setLocation (20, 20);
id.setGraphicsMode (new GraphicsMode (blend, QDColor.yellow));
comp.addMember (id, 2);
```

Now we set up the controllers for this `Compositor`. First, we create a `Dragger` that allows the user to drag any of these members around within the confines of the `Compositor` and a `LayerChanger` that allows the user to Option-click a member to send it to the back.

```
Dragger dragger = new Dragger (MouseResponder.kNoModifiersMask);
SWController controller2 = controller2 = new SWController (dragger,
                                                    true);
comp.addController (controller2);

LayerChanger lc = new LayerChanger (InputEvent.ALT_MASK);
SWController controller3 = new SWController (lc, true);
comp.addController (controller3);
```

We also create a `SimpleActionList` that will bounce three of the compositor's members around. Because we did not explicitly create the sprites that present these members, we ensure that the `BounceAction` objects act upon the `Transformable` object that presents this information for a member in the `Compositor`. In these cases, it will be the member's `TwoDSprite` presenter.

```
SimpleActionList al2 = new SimpleActionList ();
al2.addMember (new BounceAction (2, 1, comp,
comp.getTransformable(jtDrawer), 1,
                                      1));
al2.addMember (new BounceAction (10, 1, comp,
                          comp.getTransformable(id), 1, 1));
```

```
al2.addMember (new BounceAction (10, 1, comp,
                                 comp.getTransformable(md), -1, -1));
comp.addController (al2);
```

Finally, we set the rate of the Compositor to one for normal play-back rate:

```
comp.getTimer().setRate(1);
```

The following code shows the assemblage of the cell-based spin-ning spaceships. This is the addedSprites() method mentioned above.

First, we find our match file and build a ImageDataSequence to hold the EncodedImage data for each file that matches this match file. We also post-process this data sequence by recompressing the images to ensure that any blue color in them is not drawn. This gives us just the space-ship images themselves.

```
File matchFile = QTFactory.findAbsolutePath ("images/Ship01.pct");
ImageDataSequence isp = ImageUtil.createSequence (matchFile);
ImageDataSequence seq = ImageUtil.makeTransparent (isp, QDColor.blue);
```

We create the two sprites, using the fourth frame of the image se-quence for the first sprite and the first frame of the sequence for the sec-ond. Though both sprites use the same image data source, they can display different frames from that source.

```
Matrix matrix1 = new Matrix();
matrix1.setTx(20);
matrix1.setTy(20);
matrix1.setSx(0.8F);
matrix1.setSy(0.8F);
TwoDSprite s1 = new TwoDSprite(seq, 4, matrix1, true, 1);
sh.addMember (s1);

Matrix matrix2 = new Matrix();
matrix2.setTx(4);
matrix2.setTy(4);
TwoDSprite s2 = new TwoDSprite(seq, 1, matrix2, true, 10);
sh.addMember (s2);
```

We next add an action list that contains actions to move the sprites around and cycle through their images using ImageSequencer objects:

```
SimpleActionList al = new SimpleActionList();
ImageSequencer is = new ImageSequencer (seq);
is.setLooping (ImageSequencer.kLoopForwards);
al.addMember (new NextImageAction (20, 1, is, s1));
al.addMember (new BounceAction (20, 1, sd, s1, 3, 2));
ImageSequencer is2 = new ImageSequencer (seq);
is2.setLooping (ImageSequencer.kLoopForwards);
al.addMember (new NextImageAction (15, 1, is2, s2));
al.addMember (new BounceAction (40, 1, sd, s2, 4, 3));
sh.addController (al);
```

USING THE RECORDMOVIE CLASS

The ImageCompositing sample code on the CD-ROM also shows the usage of the RecordMovie class. This class can be used to record and make a single video track from any existing QDGraphics. You can use this class for both preflighting and recording. The user can enable recording and select the number of frames to record. Because the compression of each frame can take longer than the composite cycle, the rate of the compositor's playback may need to be slower to ensure that frames are not missed when compressing. This does not affect the ultimate recorded output, which is recorded to play back at the same scale as the Compositor itself, regardless of the time it takes to record each frame.

To set up the record movie class:

```
recMovie = new MovieRecording();
recMovie.setCompressionSettings (framesPerSecond,
                 codecNormalQuality,
                 codecNormalQuality,
                 0,
                 kAnimationCodecType,
                 CodecComponent.bestSpeedCodec);
```

This is the code that records the compositor's output. It prompts the user to save the file, sets the movie to the new movie we create from this file, and begins the record. After recording is completed, the Clean-upMovie class is called to ensure the movie is written out.

```
recordMovieButton.addActionListener (new ActionListener () {
    public void actionPerformed (ActionEvent event) {
        FileDialog fd = new FileDialog (ImageCompositing.pm,
                                        "Save Movie As...",
                                        FileDialog.SAVE);
        fd.show();
        if(fd.getFile() == null)
            throw new QTIOException (userCanceledErr, "");

        QTFile f = new QTFile(fd.getDirectory() + fd.getFile());
        Movie theMovie = Movie.createMovieFile (f,
                            kMoviePlayer,
                            createMovieFileDeleteCurFile |
                            createMovieFileDontCreateResFile);

        preflightCheck.setState(false);

        //Setup the record movie class
        recMovie.setMovie(theMovie, new CleanupMovie (f));
        recMovie.recordMode (numRecordFrames);
        comp.setRecordMovie (recMovie);

        System.out.println ("Start Recording");
    }
});

private class CleanupMovie implements RecordMovieCallback {
    CleanupMovie (QTFile f) {
        this.f = f;
    }

    private QTFile f;

    public void finish (Movie m) {
        try {
            OpenMovieFile outStream = OpenMovieFile.asWrite (f);
            m.addResource (outStream, movieInDataForkResID,
                            f.getName());
            outStream.close();
```

```
        } catch (QTException e) {
            e.printStackTrace();
        }
        System.out.println ("Finished Recording");
    }
}
```

The JavaTextDrawer Class

The following code shows an excerpt from the `JavaTextDrawer` class. This class is listed completely in the CD-ROM at the back of the book. This class supports the `Notifier` interface and can be a very useful mechanism for supplying image data to a sprite. For example, you may be downloading an image from a remote location and want to then supply the image to the presenting sprite when it has arrived. Or you could be calculating image data, and this calculation may be a lengthy and repetitive process. In these and other situations, this notification mechanism is useful because the class that supplies this image data (the `Notifier`) can automatically be hooked up by the `Compositor` to the `TwoDSprite` that is the `NotifyListener`.

The `Compositor` will call the `Notifier addNotifyListener()` method when a `Notifier` is added to the `Compositor`. We set ourselves up as the notifier for the `NotifyListener`. If the image data has been prepared (`ids` is the `ImageDataSequence` that contains the image data the `JavaTextDrawer` generates), then we notify the `NotifyListener` that we are complete. If the image data has not been established yet, we do nothing.

```
public boolean addNotifyListener (NotifyListener nl) {
    if (nl.setNotifier (this) == false)
        return false;

    fListener = nl;

    if (ids != null) {
        nl.notifyComplete();
    }
```

```
        return true;
}
```

We must ensure that we have been addedTo a QTCanvas, as the QT-ImageDrawer is not able to create an offscreen image until it has a java.awt.Component upon which to do this.

```
public void addedTo(Object interest) {
    fInterest = interest;
    doWork();
}
```

The doWork() method is called either when the Compositor is finally addedTo the presenting QTCanvas or when the user clicks the Change **Text Color** button. In this method, we create a QTImageDrawer with our fRenderer which implements the Paintable interface. It will use the paint commands on a java.awt.Graphics to generate pixel data (in this case "Java Text"), which the QTImageDrawer will capture. The getImage() and getDescription() calls on the QTImageDrawer object return this captured image data and a description in a format that QuickTime can render. If we have a listener, we notify it that we are completed, and the NotifyListener will retrieve the image data and description from us calling our getImage() and getDescription() methods:

```
public void doWork() {
    if (fInterest != null) {
        // qid is only kept as a local as we only need it to produce
        // a single frame then we throw it away
        QTImageDrawer qid = new QTImageDrawer (fRenderer, fSize,
                                    Redrawable.kSingleFrame);
        // this will capture the result of the Java drawing
        qid.addedTo (fInterest);

        ids = new ImageDataSequence (qid.getDescription());
        ids.addMember (qid.getImage());

        if (fListener != null)
            fListener.notifyComplete();
    }
}
```

```
public EncodedImage getImage() {
    return (ids != null ? ids.getImage() : null);
}

public ImageDescription getDescription() {
    return (ids != null ? ids.getDescription() : null);
}
```

DRAGGING SPRITES

The code in this section shows how to define a MouseResponder to customize the behavior of mouse actions and to define custom matrix transformations on a sprite. The media required for this sample code is contained in the Ships.mov file.

A movie is used as the container for the images that are used to create the spinning spaceships. We extract the first track from this movie, which contains the image data, and use the ImageUtils.createSequence to return an ImageDataSequence from this image data. We then pass this sequence to the following create sprites call, after making the images transparent so that the blue background color of these images doesn't draw:

```
File matchFile = QTFactory.findAbsolutePath ("Ships.mov");
OpenMovieFile movieFile = OpenMovieFile.asRead(
                                    new QTFile(matchFile));
Movie mov = Movie.fromFile (movieFile);
Track shipTrack = mov.getIndTrack (1);
ImageDataSequence is = ImageUtil.createSequence (shipTrack);
is = ImageUtil.makeTransparent (is, QDColor.blue);
```

A screenshot of the program is shown in Figure 15.4.

FIGURE 15.4 *Dragging sprites*

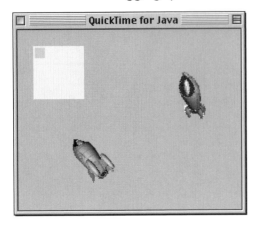

This program demonstrates the use of the SWController with sprites as the target objects to be dragged. It also uses the setActionable() method on actions that allow the program to trigger an action when a constraining condition is reached. The NoteChannelPart allows one NoteChannel to play all of the different sounds of the drumkit; each "noisy" action just triggers a different drum sound.

The program uses three drag actions:

- All the sprites are draggable by just pressing them—this is the action of the Dragger object.

- Two sprites are scalable if you Shift-drag them—this is the action of the ScalerAction object.

- The yellow box sprite is skewable by holding down the Alt or Option keys while dragging the enclosed green square.

The yellow box sprite also shows the use of a hit-test region that is a smaller visible area of sprite's visible area. In the normal makeTransparent calls, the hit-test region is the visible area of the sprite. In this case, we define the green rectangle as the hit-test area of the sprite through using the makeTransparent call that passes in a region.

The makeTransparent call is used because in both cases the image is recompressed using the animation codec. If a hit-test region is required but transparency isn't, then a keyColor must still be specified. But in this case, we use a `keyColor` that is *not* contained in the source image. This is the code that creates a hit-test region:

```
// paint a sprite and set a hot spot region for it
// the green region is the hot spot
matrix = new Matrix();
matrix.setTx(20);
matrix.setTy(20);
QDRect r40 = new QDRect (40, 40);
QDRect r8 = new QDRect (1, 1, 8, 8);
QDGraphics y = new QDGraphics (r40);
y.setBackColor (QDColor.yellow);
y.eraseRect (null);
y.setForeColor (QDColor.green);
y.paintRect (r8);
EncodedImage ei = RawEncodedImage.fromPixMap (y.getPixMap());
ImageDescription id = new ImageDescription (y.getPixMap());
ImageDataSequence idsy = new ImageDataSequence (id);
idsy.addMember (ei);
idsy = ImageUtil.makeTransparent (idsy, QDColor.black,
                                  new QDGraphics (16, r40),
                                  new Region (r8));
TwoDSprite s2 = new TwoDSprite(idsy, matrix, true, 10);
sd.addMember (s2);
```

The program also provides two mouse-over actions:

- Over any sprite will apply blend graphics mode to it.

- Over any sprite will play notes:
  - Snare drum when the mouse enters a sprite
  - Closed hi-hat when the mouse moves over the sprite
  - Open hi-hat when the mouse leaves the sprite (or the display space)

These mouse-over actions are defined using the `QTMouseListener`. This `Listener` is added as a listener to the `GenericResponder`. The `GenericResponder` receives these events from the `SWController`.

The Responder responds to rollover-type events on sprites when no modifiers are pressed. After creating the SWController, we add it to the Compositor created earlier, myCompositor:

```
final GenericResponder gr = GenericResponder.asRolloverListener
                (MouseResponder.kNoModifiersMask, MouseResponder.kModifiersExactMatch);
gr.addQTMouseMotionListener (new QTMouseMotionAdapter () {
    GenericResponder g = gr;
    GraphicsMode savedGM;
    GraphicsMode setGM = new GraphicsMode (QDConstants.blend, QDColor.lightGray);

    public void mouseDragged (MouseEvent event) {
        try {
            nc.playNoteFor (kClosedHiHat, 127, 80);
        } catch (QTException e) {
            e.printStackTrace();
        }
    }

    public void mouseMoved (MouseEvent event) {
        try {
            nc.playNoteFor (kClosedHiHat, 127, 80);
        } catch (QTException e) {
            e.printStackTrace();
        }
    }

    public void mouseEnteredTarget (MouseEvent event) {
        try {
            if (g.getTarget() instanceof TwoDSprite) {  // just for sanity
                TwoDSprite sprite = (TwoDSprite)g.getTarget();
                savedGM = sprite.getGraphicsMode();
                sprite.setGraphicsMode (setGM);
            }
            nc.playNoteFor (kSnareDrum, 127, 80);
        } catch (QTException e) {
            throw new QTRuntimeException (e);
        }
    }

    public void mouseExitedTarget (MouseEvent event) {
        try {
```

```
            if (g.getTarget() instanceof TwoDSprite) {  // just for sanity
                TwoDSprite sprite = (TwoDSprite)g.getTarget();
                sprite.setGraphicsMode (savedGM);
            }
            nc.playNoteFor (kOpenHiHat, 127, 80);
        } catch (QTException e) {
            throw new QTRuntimeException (e);
        }
    }
});

SWController ctr = new SWController (gr, true);
myCompositor.addController (ctr);
```

The controllers are SWControllers, a subclass of MouseController.
An SWController knows how to extract a QuickTime sprite from a
sprite world if there is one where the user pressed the mouse and will
return the TwoDSprite that is using that sprite in the SWCompositor.

The first controller has its wholespace set to true. Thus, any objects
that are members of the Compositor will be dragged by their Dragger.

```
SWController ct = new SWController (dragger, true);
myCompositor.addController (ct);
```

The second controller has its wholespace set to false, so you have
to explicitly add objects to this controller for them to be controlled by
it. This controller is given a Scaler responder that rescales the sprite
according to how far the mouse is moved. This scale action only occurs when the user is holding the Shift key down when the mouse-
Pressed is received. These are the conditions under which the
responder is activated.

We explicitly add the two sprites (s2 and s3) to this controller.
These two sprites were created in a similar manner to the sprites in the
addSprites() method discussed in the previous section:

```
MouseController controller = new SWController (
                    new Scaler (400, InputEvent.SHIFT_MASK), false);
controller.addMember (s3);
controller.addMember (s2);
myCompositor.addController (controller);
```

The third controller also has its wholespace set to false, so you have to explicitly add objects to this controller for them to be controlled by it. This controller is given a Skewer that skews the sprite according to how far the mouse is moved. This skew action's magnitude is controlled by the values supplied—larger values give a finer degree of control. The skew action occurs only when the user is holding the Option or Alt key down when the mousePressed is received.

We explicitly add the sprite (s2) to this controller:

```
controller = new SWController (
              new Skewer (200, 200, InputEvent.ALT_MASK), false);
controller.addMember (s2);
myCompositor.addController (controller);
```

The Scaler and Skewer are custom draggers that your application has defined.

```
public class Scaler extends Dragger {
    public Scaler (int scaleFactor, int modifierKeyMask) {
        this (scaleFactor, modifierKeyMask, MouseResponder.kModifiersExactMatch, 0);
    }

    public Scaler (int scaleFactor, int modifierKeyMask, int modifierTestConditions,
                                                         int addedEventInvoker) {
        super (modifierKeyMask, modifierTestConditions, addedEventInvoker);
        this.scaleFactor = scaleFactor;
    }

    private int xOrigin, yOrigin;
    private int scaleFactor;

    public void mousePressed (MouseEvent event) {
        xOrigin = event.getX();
        yOrigin = event.getY();
    }

    public void mouseDragged (MouseEvent event) {
        try {
            Matrix mat = target.getMatrix();

            float x = (event.getX() - xOrigin) / (float)scaleFactor;
```

```
        float y = (event.getY() - yOrigin) / (float)scaleFactor;
        xOrigin = event.getX();
        yOrigin = event.getY();

        mat.setSx (mat.getSx() + x);
        mat.setSy (mat.getSy() + y);

        target.setMatrix (mat);
    } catch (QTException e) {
        throw new QTRuntimeException (e);
    }
  }
 }
}
```

One sprite is also given a `RotateAction` that rotates the sprite in a circle. The rotate action is a subclass of `quicktime.app.actions.MatrixAction`. `MatrixAction` takes care of most of the details of manipulating its target—an object that implements the `Transformable` interface (which the `TwoDSprite` does). The `MatrixAction` subclass thus only needs to define the matrix transformation that is applied when the action is invoked by the `tickle()` method of the `PeriodicAction` superclass.

The `transformMatrix()` method is the protected method invoked by the `MatrixAction` superclass to transform the matrix. We use the `deltaDegree` to alter the direction of the rotation according to the rate that the action is invoked by. The `rateDirectionChanged()` method is invoked by the `PeriodicAction` base class when the action's time source changes direction. The `doConstraintBoundsTesting` is a protected variable that indicates to the superclass whether it should constrain the transformed object to the bounds of the enclosing space after the matrix transformation has been performed.

```
public class RotateAction extends MatrixAction {
    public RotateAction (int scale, int period, QTDrawable space, Transformable t) {
        super (scale, period, space, t);
        doConstraintBoundsTesting = false;
    }

//_____ INSTANCE VARIABLES
    private float deltaDegree = 1;
```

```
//_____ INSTANCE METHODS
    protected void rateDirectionChanged (boolean forwards) throws QTException {
        deltaDegree = -deltaDegree;
    }

    protected void transformMatrix (Matrix theMatrix) throws QTException {
        theMatrix.rotate (deltaDegree, theMatrix.getTx(), theMatrix.getTy());
    }
}
```

The `BounceAction` class provides the capability of moving and bouncing a `Transformable` object around within the space provided by the `QTDisplaySpace`. It moves within the space it is a member of by the amount specified by the `deltaMatrix` object.

COMPOSITED EFFECTS

The example code in this section, which is available on the CD-ROM, shows the use of a `Compositor` to create a composited image out of effects, sprites, and Java text. It also shows you how to use this as a backdrop for a QuickTime movie that draws directly to the screen. You construct a composited image containing the layering of an image file, a ripple effect, an animation, and some Java text. Over this, you place a movie and its `MovieController`, which is drawn in front of the composited image.

The `Compositor` is used to combine multiple-image objects, including a `CompositableEffect` (the ripple effect), into a single image that is then blitted on screen. Both the `Compositor` and the `QTPlayer` are added as members of the top-level `DirectGroup` client of a `QTCanvas`. The code also shows you how timing hierarchies can be established when spaces are contained within each other.

The media required for this sample code include

- `ShipX.pct` files (where X is a number indicative of a frame order)
- `Water.pct`
- `jumps.mov`

The compositing services of the Compositor (that is, transparent drawing, alpha blending, and so on) are not available with a DirectGroup. A DirectGroup does allow for its member objects to be layered. Thus, the movie can draw in front of the Compositor unheeded. It shows the embedding of a Compositor space in a parent Compositor and then the embedding of this Compositor in a parent DirectGroup display space.

We create the parent Compositor that will contain the background image, ripple effect, Java text, and the spaceship compositor. The spaceship compositor is created similarly to preceding examples:

```
Dimension d = new Dimension (kWidth, kHeight);
QDRect r = new QDRect(d);
QDGraphics gw = new QDGraphics (r);
Compositor comp = new Compositor (gw, QDColor.green,
                                  new QDGraphics (r), 10, 1);
```

We add the background image, setting it to the same size as the Compositor. The ripple effect will ripple the pixels that this image draws:

```
QTFile bgFile = new QTFile(
                QTFactory.findAbsolutePath("pics/water.pct"));
GraphicsImporterDrawer if1 = new GraphicsImporterDrawer (bgFile);
if1.setDisplayBounds (r);
ImagePresenter background =
                ImagePresenter.fromGraphicsImporterDrawer (if1);
comp.addMember (background, Layerable.kBackMostLayer);
```

The ripple effect is layered to apply on top of the background image, and its bounds are set to only the top part of the compositor's display bounds. A ripple effect is applied only to what is behind it, not to sprites or text drawn in front of it. The QuickTime ripple effect codec works by moving pixels around on the destination QDGraphics that it is set to. By placing it in a Compositor, your application can control which part of an image it ripples—in this case, the water picture that is behind it.

```
CompositableEffect e = new CompositableEffect ();
AtomContainer effectSample = new AtomContainer();
effectSample.insertChild (new Atom(kParentAtomIsContainer),
```

```
                kEffectWhatAtom,
                1,
                0,
                EndianOrder.flipNativeToBigEndian32(kWaterRippleCodecType));
e.setEffect (effectSample);
e.setDisplayBounds (new QDRect (0, kHeight - 100, kWidth, 100));
comp.addMember (e, 2);
```

We add the contained `Compositor`. Yellow is set as the background color, which is then not drawn, as we set the graphics mode of the `Compositor` to transparent with yellow as the transparent color.

We also add a `Dragger` so that members of this compositor can be dragged around when any modifier key is pressed when the `mouse-Pressed` event is generated. We also add a `Dragger` to the parent `Compositor` so that we can drag any of its top-level members when no modifier keys are pressed:

```
Compositor sh = new Compositor (
                        new QDGraphics (new QDRect(160, 160)),
                        QDColor.yellow, 8, 1);
addSprites (sh);
sh.setLocation (190, 90);
sh.setGraphicsMode (new GraphicsMode (transparent, QDColor.yellow));
sh.getTimer().setRate(1);
sh.addController(new SWController (new Dragger (

MouseResponder.kAnyModifiersMask,

MouseResponder.kAnyModifiers), true));
comp.addMember (sh, 1);

comp.addController(new SWController (
            new Dragger (MouseResponder.kNoModifiersMask), true));
```

You use the `QTImageDrawer` object using the Java-drawing APIs to draw the Java text, which is then given a transparency so that only the text characters themselves are displayed by QuickTime. Note that you set the background color to white, so the Java text appears transparent. White provides a reliable transparent background for different pixel depths.

```
myQTCanvas.setBackground (Color.white);
```

You add the Java text in front of the background image and ripples and set its transparency to the background color of the QTCanvas, so that only the text is seen.

```
QTImageDrawer qid = new QTImageDrawer (jt, new Dimension (110, 22),
                                       Redrawable.kSingleFrame);
Paintable jt = new JavaText ();
qid.setGraphicsMode (new GraphicsMode (transparent, QDColor.white));
qid.setLocation (200, 20);
comp.addMember (qid, 1);
```

The code here provides a good demonstration of the timing hierarchy that is built using the display spaces of the Compositor and DirectGroup.

We make a DirectGroup as the top-level container space, adding both the containing Compositor as a member of this group and the movie jumps.mov. Finally, we set the rates of both the Compositor and the DirectGroup to 1 so that they are playing when the window is shown:

```
DirectGroup dg = new DirectGroup (d, QDColor.white);
dg.addMember (comp, 2);

QTFile movieFile = new QTFile (
                     QTFactory.findAbsolutePath ("jumps.mov"));
QTDrawable mov = QTFactory.makeDrawable (movieFile);
mov.setDisplayBounds (new QDRect(20, 20, 120, 106));
dg.addMember (mov, 1);

myQTCanvas.setClient (dg, true);

comp.getTimer().setRate(1);
dg.getTimer().setRate(1);
```

The top DirectGroup is the master time base for all of its members; the rate at which its time base is set (the top text box) determines the overall rate of its members. The members can have their own rates that become offset based on the rates of their parent groups. To start the program, you set the top rate to 1.

TRANSITION EFFECTS

We end this chapter with a program that demonstrates how to use the QuickTime effects architecture and apply it to a character in an animation scene.

The code in this section shows how you can build a transition effect and apply it to a character in a realistic animation of a UFO encounter! In the program, a fading effect is applied to transition to the spaceship image. The image fades in and out as per the rate and the number of frames set for the transition.

It shows the usage of effects and effects presenters. The kCrossFadeTransitionType effect is applied to the source and the destination images, which makes them fade as per the number of frames set for the transition.

The QTEffectPresenter is used to embed the QTTransition effect and present it to the Compositor, which draws it to the canvas. Note that the QTTransition effect cannot be directly added to the Compositor; instead, it is given to the QTEffectPresenter, which is added to the Compositor. If a filter were applied, it would have the same limitations as a transition when added to a Compositor. It must be added using the QTEffectPresenter.

A ripple effect is applied to the water image (in front of the water image taking up the same location), using the CompositableEffect class. Zero sourced effects, such as the ripple effect, can be added directly to a Compositor.

```
CompositableEffect ce = new CompositableEffect ();
AtomContainer effectSample = new AtomContainer();
effectSample.insertChild (new Atom(kParentAtomIsContainer),
        kEffectWhatAtom,
        1,
        0,
        EndianOrder.flipNativeToBigEndian32(kWaterRippleCodecType));
ce.setEffect (effectSample);
ce.setDisplayBounds (new QDRect(0, 220, 300, 80));
comp.addMember (ce, 3);
```

The Fader class is used to create the QTTransition and return the QT-EffectPresenter that will supply the pixel data that becomes the image data for this member's sprite:

```
class Fader implements StdQTConstants {
    Fader() throws Exception {
        File file = QTFactory.findAbsolutePath ("pics/Ship.pct");
        QTFile f = new QTFile (file.getAbsolutePath());

        QDGraphics g = new QDGraphics (new QDRect (78, 29));
        g.setBackColor (QDColor.black);
        g.eraseRect(null);
        ImagePresenter srcImage = ImagePresenter.fromGWorld(g);
        Compositable destImage = new GraphicsImporterDrawer (f);

        ef = new QTTransition ();
        ef.setRedrawing(true);
        ef.setSourceImage (srcImage);
        ef.setDestinationImage (destImage);
        ef.setDisplayBounds (new QDRect(78, 29));
        ef.setEffect (createFadeEffect (kEffectBlendMode, kCrossFadeTransitionType));
        ef.setFrames(60);
        ef.setCurrentFrame(0);
    }

    private QTTransition ef;

    public QTEffectPresenter makePresenter() throws QTException {
        QTEffectPresenter efPresenter = new QTEffectPresenter (ef);
        return efPresenter;
    }

    public QTTransition getTransition () {
        return ef;
    }

    AtomContainer createFadeEffect (int effectType, int effectNumber)
                                                    throws QTException {
        AtomContainer effectSample = new AtomContainer();
        effectSample.insertChild (new Atom(kParentAtomIsContainer),
                    kEffectWhatAtom,
                    1,
```

```
                        0,
                        EndianOrder.flipNativeToBigEndian32(kCrossFadeTransitionType));

    effectSample.insertChild (new Atom(kParentAtomIsContainer),
                        effectType,
                        1,
                        0,
                        EndianOrder.flipNativeToBigEndian32(effectNumber));
    return effectSample;
  }
}
```

We then create the QTEffectPresenter for the transition and add it as a member of the Compositor:

```
Fader fader = new Fader();
QTEffectPresenter efp = fader.makePresenter();
efp.setGraphicsMode (new GraphicsMode (blend, QDColor.gray));
efp.setLocation(80, 80);
comp.addMember (efp, 1);

comp.addController(new TransitionControl (20, 1,
fader.getTransition()));
```

The controller object implements the TicklishController and subclasses the PeriodicAction class that has a doAction() method, which gets invoked on every tickle call.

```
class TransitionControl extends PeriodicAction
                                implements TicklishController {
    TransitionControl (int scale, int period, QTTransition t) {
        super (scale , period);
        this.t = t;
    }
```

The doAction() call is overidden to set the current frame and redraw the TransitionEffect. The source and the destination images of the transition effect are swapped when the number of set frames is reached. The transition's controller then rests for a few seconds before it is awakened again and reapplied. The incoming time values to the doAction method (called by PeriodicAction.tickle()) are used to calculate the rest and transition, ensuring that if the rate of playback changes, the transition controller will react to these changes.

When the transition is quiescent, we set the redrawing state of the QTEffectPresenter to false. This ensures that when the Compositor invalidates this presenter it will not invalidate the sprite, as we are not currently drawing into the QTEffectPresenter. When the transition is being applied, that is when the current frame is set, then the isRedrawing method will return true. The Invalidator for the QTEffectPresenter will then redraw the effect and invalidate its sprite presenter. Thus, this controller is also able to control the redrawing of both itself and its sprite through the use of the redrawing state and ensure that the Compositor only renders the sprite that presents this QTEffectPresenter when it actually changes its pixel data—that is, the image data of the effect's presenter.

```
protected void doAction (float er, int tm) throws QTException {
    if (waiting) {
        if ((er > 0 && ((startWaitTime + waitForMsecs) <= tm))
            || (er < 0 && ((startWaitTime - waitForMsecs) >= tm))) {

            waiting = false;
            t.setRedrawing(true);
        } else
            return;
    }
    int curr_frm = t.getCurrentFrame();
    curr_frm++;
    t.setCurrentFrame(curr_frm);
    if (curr_frm > t.getFrames()) {
        curr_frm = 0;
        t.setRedrawing(false);
        t.setCurrentFrame(curr_frm);
        t.swapImages();
        waiting = true;
        startWaitTime = tm;
    }
```

QuickTime for Java Reference

Part IV is a complete reference for the QuickTime for Java API. Each chapter discusses a separate package that is part of the API. Chapters 16 through Chapter 26 focus on the classes and interfaces belonging to the Application Framework. Chapters 27 through Chapter 45 discuss the core QuickTime for Java packages.

The packages are listed alphabetically. The first package is the `quicktime` package, and the last is the `quicktime.vr` package. Each chapter starts with a brief overview of the package and describes those classes and interfaces that are most useful. A diagram illustrates the class hierarchy of each package. All the classes and interfaces belonging to each package are listed alphabetically.

This structure corresponds to the `javadoc` HTML documentation, which is on the CD-ROM at the back of this book.

This is the complete API for the current QuickTime for Java release. As new classes and interfaces are added, you'll want to check the QuickTime website at `http://www.apple.com/quicktime` for the latest updates and changes.

Chapter 16, "The quicktime Package"

Chapter 17, "The quicktime.app Package"

Chapter 18, "The quicktime.app.actions Package"

Chapter 19, "The quicktime.app.anim Package"

Chapter 20, "The quicktime.app.audio Package"

Chapter 21, "The quicktime.app.display Package"

Chapter 22, "The quicktime.app.image Package"

Chapter 23, "The quicktime.app.players Package"

Chapter 24, "The quicktime.app.sg Package"

Chapter 25, "The quicktime.app.spaces Package"

Chapter 26, "The quicktime.app.time Package"

Chapter 27, "The quicktime.io Package"

Chapter 28, "The quicktime.qd Package"

Chapter 29, "The quicktime.qd3d Package"

Chapter 30, The quicktime.qd3d.camera Package"

Chapter 31, "The quicktime.qd3d.math Package"

Chapter 32, "The quicktime.qd3d.transform Package"

Chapter 33, "The quicktime.sound Package"

Chapter 34, "The quicktime.std Package"

Chapter 35, "The quicktime.std.anim Package"

Chapter 36, "The quicktime.std.clocks Package"

Chapter 37, "The quicktime.std.comp Package"

Chapter 38, "The quicktime.std.image Package"

Chapter 39, "The quicktime.std.movies Package""

Chapter 40, "The quicktime.std.movies.media Package"

Chapter 41, "The quicktime.std.music Package"

Chapter 42, "The quicktime.qtcomponents Package"

Chapter 43, "The quicktime.std.sg Package"

Chapter 44, The quicktime.util Package"

Chapter 45, "The quicktime.vr Package"

16

The quicktime Package

The `quicktime` package contains a number of useful classes that define methods for setting up and initializing the QuickTime runtime. The classes in this package also provide unique identifiers for QuickTime objects.

`QTSession` provides a number of methods for initializing and terminating QuickTime, QuickTime VR, and QuickDraw 3D, and for querying the runtime availability of these different components of QuickTime.

Among the other classes, `QTObject` defines a unique identifier for many QuickTime objects. The `Errors` interface contains a complete list of errors. `QTException` is a general catch-all class used to signal errors that occur from QuickTime calls. `QTRuntimeExceptions` are thrown by the QuickTime for Java classes when an exceptional condition is caused at runtime.

A complete list of QuickTime errors, which is also in this package, is provided on the CD-ROM at the back of this book.

Figure 16.1 shows the class hierarchy for this package.

FIGURE 16.1 *The* quicktime *package*

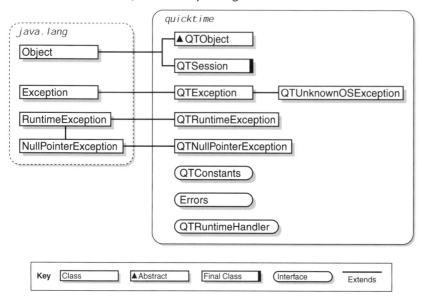

Interface quicktime.Errors

This interface provides a complete list of errors.

The full listing is available on the CD-ROM at the back of this book.

Interface quicktime.QTConstants

This class represents all the constants in the QuickTime interfaces.

Note that all constants, except for those beginning with an acronym such as MPEG, start with a lowercase letter (not a capital one).

The full listing is available on the CD-ROM at the back of this book.

Class quicktime.QTException

This is a general catch-all class used to signal errors that occur from QuickTime calls.

The `QTException()` constructor creates an exception with a message that could contain information displayed to the user or a constructor that creates an exception with a specific error number.

`errorCodeToString()` returns a string representation of the error code that can inform the user of the meaning of the error.

```
public class QTException extends Exception implements Errors {
//Constructors
    public QTException(String str);
    public QTException(int val);

//Static Methods
    public static void checkError(int err);
    public static String errorCodeToString(int eCode);
    public static int isDrawingError(int err);

//Instance Methods
    public int errorCode();
    public String errorCodeToString();
    public String toString();
}
```

CLASS HIERARCHY:

Object→Throwable→Exception→QTException

Class quicktime.QTNullPointerException

This exception is thrown if `QTObject` is used after its native data structure has been disposed of. Typically, this exception is thrown when trying to use a `QTObject` after `QTSession.close()` has been called by an application.

The `QTNullPointerException()` constructor creates an exception with the name of the class that caused the exception to be thrown.

```
public class QTNullPointerException extends NullPointerException {
//Constructors
    public QTNullPointerException(String str);
}
```

CLASS HIERARCHY:

Object→Throwable→Exception→RuntimeException→NullPointerException→ QTNullPointerException

Class quicktime.QTObject

This abstract class defines an unique identifier for QuickTime objects.

```
public abstract class QTObject extends Object implements Errors {
//Static Methods
    public static final int ID(QTObject id);

//Instance Methods
    public boolean equals(Object anObject);
    public String toString();
}
```

CLASS HIERARCHY:

Object→QTObject

Class quicktime.QTRuntimeException

`QTRuntimeExceptions` are thrown by the QuickTime for Java classes when an exceptional condition is caused at runtime. This usually occurs within a Java method (for example, `clone()`) that does not have an API for throwing an exception. In the `clone()` method, for instance, this exception is thrown if there is an Out of Memory condition.

The `errorCodeToString()` method returns a string that represents the error code of the current `QTException`. This returns the name of the error code as represented in the `quicktime.Errors` interface. If the error code is unknown, the string "Unknown Error Code" is returned.

```
public class QTRuntimeException extends RuntimeException {
//Constructors
    public QTRuntimeException(QTException e);
    public QTRuntimeException(Exception e);
    public QTRuntimeException(int val);
    public QTRuntimeException(String str);

//Static Methods
    public static void handleOrThrow(QTRuntimeException e, Object eGenerator,
                                     String methodNameIfKnown);
    public static void registerHandler(QTRuntimeHandler h);

//Instance Methods
    public final int errorCode();
    public String errorCodeToString();
    public String toString();
}
```

CLASS HIERARCHY:

Object→Throwable→Exception→RuntimeException→QTRuntimeException

Interface quicktime.QTRuntimeHandler

Your application can implement this interface to register a handler object of runtime exceptions. QTRuntimeExceptions occur in methods of which there is no means for an application to try/catch an exception—for example, if a QTDrawable object threw an exception when invoked from the QTCanvas.paint() method.

By registering a handler, your application can deal with the exception rather than having the exception thrown as a matter of course. If the exception cannot be dealt with, then the handler should throw the exception. In the case of an unrecoverable-Flag being set to true, it is imperative that the exception be thrown.

If the handler is able to deal with the exception, then the exceptionOccurred() method should return normally—in which case, the exception is considered to have been harmless, innocuous, or dealt with, and the calling code will assume that basically the exception never occurred.

```
public interface QTRuntimeHandler {
//Instance Methods
    public abstract void exceptionOccurred(QTRuntimeException e, Object eGenerator,
                        String methodNameIfKnown, boolean unrecoverableFlag);
}
```

Class quicktime.QTSession

This class provides a number of methods for initializing and terminating QuickTime, QuickTime VR, and QuickDraw 3D. It also provides methods for querying the runtime availability of these QuickTime components.

QTSession.open() will initialize QuickTime, perform a gestalt check and call enterMovies. Calls to the initialize routine are accumulative. Thus, if your code calls QTSession.open (which calls QTSession.initialize()) and/or QTSession.initialize(), the current session of QuickTime will only be closed down when it gets the same number of calls to QTSession.close() (which calls QTSession.terminate) and/or QTSession.terminate. This ensures that if you have other applets (or beans, for example) running in the same process, the QuickTime session will be terminated only when all of the current Java QTSession objects in that process have been destroyed.

initialize() opens a QTSession and performs any initialization of the QuickTime environment. If you use this call (and not the open() calls), you should also ensure that you check that QuickTime is present through the gestalt call, and call enterMovies to initialize the Movie Toolbox.

Note that QTSession.open() must be called before any QuickTime Java objects are instantiated. After calling QTSession.close(), no QuickTime Java objects can be used because the runtime services of QuickTime are no longer available. QTSession.close() ensures that a proper termination of QuickTime is performed. Any QuickTime Java objects become invalid after a QTSession.close() call is successful, and those objects cannot be reused even if QuickTime is reinitialized.

A typical usage of QTSession calls by an Java applet is shown in Example 16.1.

EXAMPLE 16.1 *Using QTSession*

```
public class MyApplet extends Applet {
    public void init () {
        QTSession.open();

            . . .

                            }
    public void destroy () {
        QTSession.close();
    }
}
```

As shown in Example 16.1, the applet initializes the QTSession in its init() method and closes it down in its destroy() method.

open() will also open a QTSession and perform any initialization of the QuickTime environment. This ensures that any required initializations are performed and that the required version of QuickTime is present. The minimal version of QuickTime required is version 3.02. This also calls EnterMovies.

```
public final class QTSession extends Object
      implements QTConstants, Errors, QuickTimeLib, QuickTimeVRLib, QuickDraw3DLib {
//Static Fields
    public static final int kInit3D;
    public static final int kInitVR;
    public static final int kMacOS;
```

```
    public static final int kWin32;

//Static Methods
    public static void addActiveCanvas(QTCanvas c);
    public static void close();
    public static final void enterMovies();
    public static final void exitMovies();
    public static final int gestalt(int selector);
    public static final int getBugFixVersion();
    public static final int getDeveloperVersion();
    public static int getJavaVersion();
    public static final int getMajorVersion();
    public static final int getMinorVersion();
    public static int getQTMajorVersion();
    public static int getQTMinorVersion();
    public static int getQTVersion();
    public static void initialize(int flag);
    public static void initialize3D();
    public static void initializeVR();
    public static boolean is3DInitialized();
    public static boolean isCurrentOS(int osName);
    public static boolean isInitialized();
    public static boolean isQD3DAvailable();
    public static boolean isQTVRAvailable();
    public static boolean isVRInitialized();
    public static void open(int initFlag);
    public static void open(int version, int minorVersion, int initFlag);
    public static void open();
    public static void removeActiveCanvas(QTCanvas c);
    public static void terminate();
    public static void terminate3D();
    public static void terminateVR();
    public static Object terminationLock();
}
```

CLASS HIERARCHY:

Object→QTSession

Class quicktime.QTUnknownOSException

This exception is thrown if the QuickTime for Java library is used on an operating system that does not have QuickTime available.

```
public class QTUnknownOSException extends QTException {
//Constructors
    public QTUnknownOSException();
}
```

CLASS HIERARCHY:

Object→Throwable→Exception→QTException→QTUnknownOSException

17

The quicktime.app Package

The `quicktime.app` package contains three classes and one interface. The `QTFactory` class in this package, however, is one of the most useful in the QuickTime for Java API. It provides a set of factory methods for creating classes that you can use to present any media that QuickTime can import. In addition, it provides some utility methods for finding directories and files in the local file system. Using this class, for example, you can create `quicktime.app.display.QTDrawable` objects from a file, a Java `InputStream` or a URL that specifies a local or remote file.

The `QTDrawableMaker` class provided in this package is useful for making custom `QTDrawable` objects when used in conjunction with `QTFactory.makeDrawable()` methods.

You can use the `RecordMovie` class in this package to record a movie from a source `QDGraphics`. This class provides a profiling mode for estimating the compression time for each frame captured. You use this class to enable a movie to be recorded where the record rate is unrelated to the capture rate.

Figure 17.1 shows the class hierarchy for this package. See Chapter 3, "Integrating QuickTime with Java," for more information on using the classes and methods defined in this package.

FIGURE 17.1 *The* quicktime.app *package*

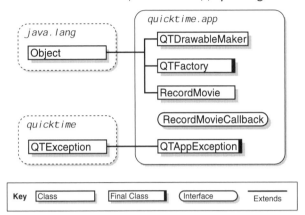

Class quicktime.app.QTDrawableMaker

This class works alongside the QTFactory.makeDrawable() methods to return QTDrawable objects from a GraphicsImporter or a movie.

You can subclass the QTDrawableMaker class if you need a QTDrawable object more suited for your requirements. For example, an ImagePresenter could be returned from a GraphicsImporter that yields better performance at the expense of using more memory. (The default QTDrawable objects for a GraphicsImporter and Movie are an ImageFile and a QTPlayer, respectively.) The following is an example of subclassing the QTDrawable class:

```
class MyQTDrawableMaker extends QTDrawableMaker {
    public QTDrawable fromGraphicsImporter (GraphicsImporter gi)
                                    throws QTException {
        return ImagePresenter.fromGraphicsImporter (gi);
    }
}
```

You use your subclass with the QTFactory methods as follows:

```
QTDrawable d = QTFactory.makeDrawable (..., new MyQTDrawable());
```

```
public class QTDrawableMaker extends Object {
//Constructors
    public QTDrawableMaker();
```

```
//Instance Methods
    public QTDrawable fromGraphicsImporter(GraphicsImporter gi);
    public QTDrawable fromMovie(Movie m);
}
```

CLASS HIERARCHY:

Object→QTDrawableMaker

Class quicktime.app.QTFactory

This class provides factory methods for creating classes used to present media that QuickTime can import. It also provides some utility methods for finding directories and files in the local file system. Since all of the methods are static, you cannot instantiate objects of this type.

Given a filename, the `findAbsolutePath()` method searches exhaustively all paths found in `user.dir` and `classPath` and returns a file object that contains an absolute path to the first occurrence of the specified argument. Use the `findInSystemPaths()` method to locate the first instance of the file (i.e., the last name in the path) that it finds within the directories known to Java at runtime.

`makeDrawable()` returns a `QTDrawable` object from the specified sources, as follows:

- The file methods return `QTDrawable` based on the type of the file. If a Security Manager is present, the applet must have read-access to the file and its directory.

- The input stream will be read in its entirety to a byte array, which is then used as the source of the data to import. The supplied `fileExt` is used by the importers to determine the format of the data contained within the input stream. It uses the default `QTDrawableMaker` to return objects from a `GraphicsImporter` or a `Movie`.

- The `DataRef` returns a `QTDrawable` based on the type of file the URL points to (whether local or remote) or an RTSP session. Any URL protocol that QuickTime's data handlers can deal with can be parsed into this version of the `makeDrawable` method.

An example usage of some of the factory methods is as follows:

```
                 File mediaFile = QTFactory.findAbsolutePath ("media/myMovie.mov");
                 QTDrawable d = QTFactory.makeDrawable(new QTFile(mediaFile));
                 myQTCanvas.setClient (d);
                 ...
                 // from an URL
                 QTDrawable d2 = QTFactory.makeDrawable (
                                   "http://www.mywebsite.com/movies/myMovie.mov");
                 myOtherQTCanvas.setClient (d2);
```

```
public final class QTFactory extends Object implements StdQTConstants, Errors {
//Static Methods
    public static void addDirectory(File dir);
    public static File findAbsolutePath(String fileName);
    public static File findInSystemPaths(String fileName);
    public static QTDrawable makeDrawable(QTFile qtFile, QTDrawableMaker maker);
    public static QTDrawable makeDrawable(InputStream is, int hintType,
                                String hintString);
    public static QTDrawable makeDrawable(InputStream is, int hintType,
                                String hintString, QTDrawableMaker maker);
    public static QTDrawable makeDrawable(String url);
    public static QTDrawable makeDrawable(String url, QTDrawableMaker maker);
    public static QTDrawable makeDrawable(QTFile qtFile);
    public static void removeDirectory(File dir);
}
```

CLASS HIERARCHY:

Object→QTFactory

Class quicktime.app.QTAppException

QTAppExceptions **are thrown by** quicktime.app **classes when some condition is not as** expected. They are a general exception type with specific subclasses for specific situations.

```
public class QTAppException extends QTException {
//Constructors
    public QTAppException(String message);
    public QTAppException();
}
```

CLASS HIERARCHY:

Object→Throwable→Exception→QTException→QTAppException

Class quicktime.app.RecordMovie

This class is used to record a movie from a source `QDGraphics`. It provides a profiling mode with an estimate of the compression time for each frame captured. This class enables a movie to be recorded where the record rate is unrelated to the capture rate. That is, a recorded rate of 10 frames a second can be specified, and each frame that is captured will have a duration of $1/_{10}$ of a second regardless of how long the compression process takes or how often the `frameReady()` method is called.

Typically, this class is used as a utility service by some other class that wants to provide recording capabilities. When a `RecordMovie` object is set in the target class, the target class notifies the `RecordMovie` object that it now has a source `QDGraphics`. Whenever appropriate, the target class then notifies the `RecordMovie` object that a frame is ready to be captured from the `QDGraphics` object, and the `RecordMovie` object either captures that frame or profiles the compression based on its current mode of operation. After the specified number of frames to be recorded has elapsed, the `frameReady()` method returns false to indicate that it is no longer interested in capturing frames. The target class can discard the `RecordMovie` object and cancel notification of frame readiness.

In its turn, the `RecordMovie` disavows any knowledge of the `QDGraphics` object it was compressing until the next time it receives notification that it has been added to a source.

Once a movie has completed recording, the `RecordMovie` object will spawn a thread and call the `RecordMovieCallback finish()` method with the movie that has just been recorded. The recorded movie will have a video track added with all of the data captured; at this point, your application can do whatever is appropriate with the movie—save it, play it back, and so on. Each record operation adds a new video track with the specified compression and visual media characteristics.

The `RecordMovie()` constructor creates a default `RecordMovie` object. No movie or callback object is specified, so in this state the object can only be used for profiling. If a recording is desired, your application must specify the movie with the `setMovie()` method. In order for profiling to be enabled, you must also set the compression settings, describing the type of compression to be applied.

The `Compositor` class provides an API for the usage of this class.

```
public class RecordMovie extends Object implements StdQTConstants {
//Constructors
```

```
    public RecordMovie();
    public RecordMovie(Movie theMovie, RecordMovieCallback cBack);
    public RecordMovie(Movie theMovie, RecordMovieCallback cBack, QDRect rectBounds);

//Instance Methods
    public void abortRecording();
    public void addedToSource(QDGraphics g);
    public synchronized boolean frameReady();
    public boolean isPreflighting();
    public synchronized void recordMode(int numRecordFrames);
    public void setCompressionSettings(int scale, int spatialQuality,
                              int temporalQuality, int keyFrameRate,
                              int codecType, CodecComponent codec);
    public void setMovie(Movie theMovie, RecordMovieCallback cBack);
    public synchronized void setPreflighting(boolean flag);
}
```

CLASS HIERARCHY:

Object→RecordMovie

Interface quicktime.app.RecordMovieCallback

An object that implements this interface can be given to the RecordMovie class to notify the caller when recording is complete.

The movie returned in the parameter of the finish() method is the movie to which a video track was added. The finish() method is called when the movie has completed recording.

```
public interface RecordMovieCallback {
//Instance Methods
    public abstract void finish(Movie m);
}
```

18

The quicktime. app.actions Package

The `quicktime.app.actions` package contains a large number of controller classes for mouse drags and for handling mouse events. It also contains action classes that can be used with objects that implement the `quicktime.app.image.Transformable` interface.

Implementing the `Ticklish` interface, an object can be defined to invoke an action on its target according to the time constraints supplied by the caller of the `tickle()` method. Objects that implement the `Targetable` interface are actions that act on a specific target.

Among the controller classes, the `Dragger` defines a particular type of `MouseResponder` that performs the action of moving the dragger's target (a `Transformable` object) according to the drag movements of the mouse.

The `MouseController` is a useful class in this package. You can use it to marshal mouse events that occur within a display space and activate the responder attached to it if the received events are of interest to the responder. `MouseResponder` is an abstract class used to provide a base-level functionality for objects that respond to mouse events. This split between controller and responder allows your application to easily customize a particular response to mouse events.

Another useful class is `PeriodicAction`, which serves as the base class for all periodically reoccuring time-based actions.

Figure 18.1 shows the class hierarchy for this package. See Chapter 13, "Spaces and Controllers," for more information on using these classes.

FIGURE 18.1 *The quicktime.app.actions Package*

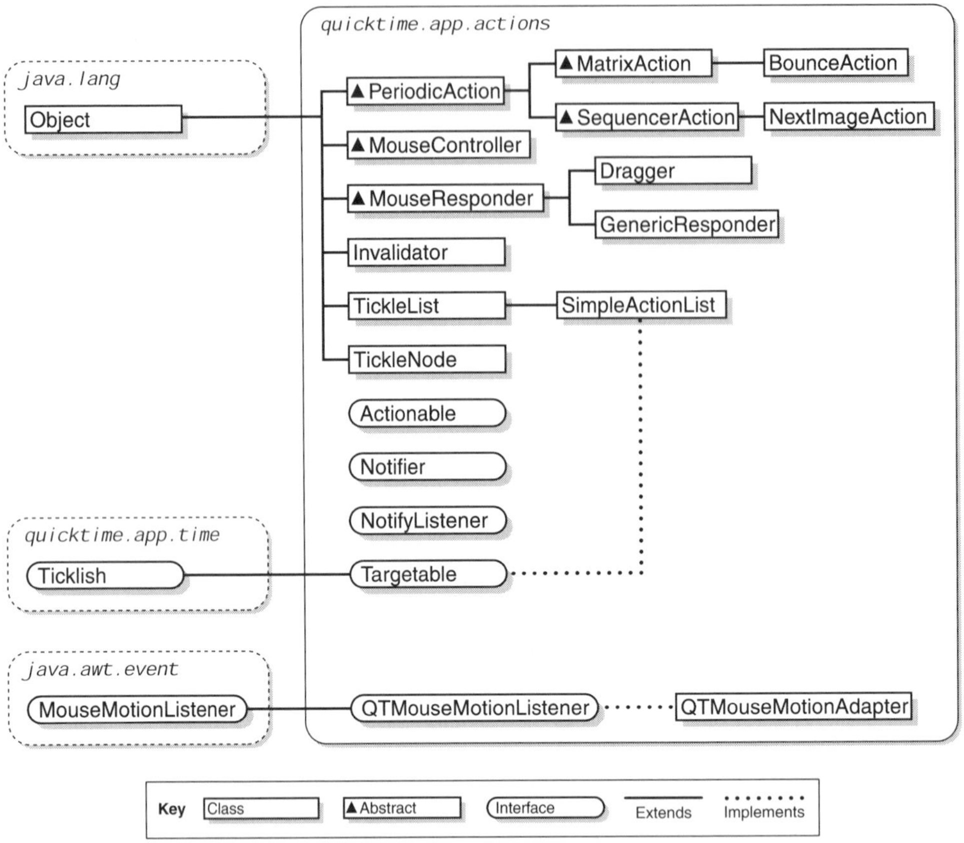

Interface quicktime.app.actions.Actionable

This interface, which contains a single method, provides a way for actions to invoke actions on objects when their particular constraining condition has been reached. The trigger() method is called by the action that the Actionable object is attached to.

See also BounceAction and Dragger.

```
public interface Actionable {
//Instance Methods
    public abstract void trigger();
}
```

Class quicktime.app.actions.BounceAction

This class provides the capability to move and bounce around a `Transformable` object within the space provided by the space within which the object is a member by the amount specified by the `deltaMatrix` object.

```
public class BounceAction extends MatrixAction {
//Constructors
    public BounceAction(int scale, int period, QTDrawable space, Transformable t,
                        float deltaX, float deltaY);

//Instance Fields
    public float deltaX;
    public float deltaY;

//Instance Methods
    public boolean equals(Object obj);
//protected
    protected void boundsReached(int whichSide);
    protected void rateDirectionChanged(boolean forwards);
    protected void transformMatrix(Matrix theMatrix);
}
```

CLASS HIERARCHY:

Object→PeriodicAction→MatrixAction→BounceAction

Class quicktime.app.actions.Dragger

A `Dragger` is a particular type of `MouseResponder` that performs the action of moving its target (a `Transformable` object) according to the drag movements of the mouse.

Draggers can be constrained to keep their target object completely within their enclosing space or allow the target to be dragged out of that space to a minimum view of one row or column of pixels of the target. The `setConstrained()` method, if `true`, sets the `Dragger` to constrain the target to be completely within the bounds of the space. If `false`, the target can be dragged outside of the space to a maximum of still showing 1 pixel. When a constraining condition is reached, the `Dragger` invokes the `trigger` (theDragger) method of an attached `Actionable` object.

The `mousePressed()` method is used by the `Dragger` when the mouse is first pressed down on the draggable object. It calculates the offset between where the user clicked in the target and the target's actual origin. The `mouseDragged()` method allows the user to drag the `Transformable` object around. Note that subclasses can define custom behaviors that occur when the target is dragged.

setActionable() sets the `Actionable` object of the action, while the getActionable() method retrieves the current actor attached to the action.

```
public class Dragger extends MouseResponder implements StdQTConstants {
//Static Fields
    public static final int kConstrainAll;
    public static final int kConstrainBottom;
    public static final int kConstrainHorizontal;
    public static final int kConstrainLeft;
    public static final int kConstrainNone;
    public static final int kConstrainRight;
    public static final int kConstrainTop;
    public static final int kConstrainVertical;

//Constructors
    public Dragger(int modifierKeyMask);
    public Dragger(int modifierKeyMask, int modifierTestConditions);
    public Dragger(int modifierKeyMask, int modifierTestConditions,
              int additionalEvents);

//Instance Fields
//protected
    protected Actionable actor;
    protected QTDrawable space;
    protected Transformable target;
    protected int xBufferIfUnConstrained;
    protected int yBufferIfUnConstrained;

//Instance Methods
    public Actionable getActionable();
    public int getConstrained();
    public boolean isAppropriate(Object object);
    public void mouseDragged(MouseEvent event);
    public void mousePressed(MouseEvent event);
    public void setActionable(Actionable actor);
    public void setConstrained(int flag);
//protected
    protected void removeTarget();
    protected void setTarget(Object t);
    protected void setTargetSpace(Object o);
}
```

CLASS HIERARCHY:

Object→MouseResponder→Dragger

Class quicktime.app.actions.GenericResponder

This is a generic responder for MouseEvent objects. It places no conditions on the containing space or target. Your application can also register QTMouseListener objects and MouseListener objects with this responder, in which case the GenericResponder invokes the appropriate method on the registered listeners.

```
public class GenericResponder extends MouseResponder {
//Constructors
    public GenericResponder(int modifierKeyMask, int modifierTestConditions,
                            int eventTypes);

//Static Methods
    public static GenericResponder asAnyMouseListener(int modifierKeyMask,
                                        int modifierTestConditions);
    public static GenericResponder asMouseListener(int modifierKeyMask,
                                        int modifierTestConditions);
    public static GenericResponder asMouseMotionListener(int modifierKeyMask,
                                        int modifierTestConditions);
    public static GenericResponder asMouseOrMouseMotionListener(int modifierKeyMask,
                                        int modifierTestConditions);
    public static GenericResponder asQTMouseMotionListener(int modifierKeyMask,
                                        int modifierTestConditions);
    public static GenericResponder asRolloverListener(int modifierKeyMask,
                                        int modifierTestConditions);

//Instance Fields
//protected
    protected Object space;
    protected Object target;

//Instance Methods
    public void addMouseListener(MouseListener ml);
    public void addQTMouseMotionListener(QTMouseMotionListener ql);
    public Object getSpace();
    public Object getTarget();
    public boolean isAppropriate(Object object);
    public void mouseClicked(MouseEvent e);
    public void mouseDragged(MouseEvent e);
    public void mouseEntered(MouseEvent e);
    public void mouseEnteredTarget(MouseEvent e);
    public void mouseExited(MouseEvent e);
    public void mouseExitedTarget(MouseEvent e);
    public void mouseMoved(MouseEvent e);
    public void mousePressed(MouseEvent e);
    public void mouseReleased(MouseEvent e);
    public void removeMouseListener(MouseListener ml);
    public void removeQTMouseMotionListener(QTMouseMotionListener ql);
//protected
    protected void removeTarget();
```

```
    protected void setTarget(Object target);
    protected void setTargetSpace(Object s);
}
```

CLASS HIERARCHY:

Object→MouseResponder→GenericResponder

Class quicktime.app.actions.Invalidator

This class is used as a helper class when compositing objects with a dynamic image source.

The SWCompositor uses QuickTime's SpriteWorld to draw a member's image. If the member's image data is dynamic but there are no changes in the presentation of the member's Sprite image data (a QuickTime Sprite is used to represent the member in the SpriteWorld of the SWCompositor), then the compositing cycle of the SpriteWorld will not redraw the Sprite. Thus, in order to force the SpriteWorld to redraw a Sprite of this nature, the Sprite presenting the member must be invalidated.

For example, the CompositableEffect and QTImageDrawer classes explicitly use the Invalidator class in QuickTime for Java. Implicit invalidation is done in other classes (MoviePresenter, the SWCompositor itself if a member of a parent SWCompositor), since they possess their own drawing logic.

If an Invalidator is required, it is returned by the addedToCompositor() method, and the SWCompositor keeps a list of the invalidators and invokes the invalidator's composite cycle. Subclasses of the Invalidator class can override the tickle() method more efficiently, invalidating based on the explicit conditions under which the Two-DSprite is invalidated. For example, if a QTImageDrawer is not redrawing every time, the TwoDSprite needs only be invalidated when the QTImageDrawer signifies that it is redrawing. Thus, the Invalidator for the QTImageDrawer checks isRedrawing() and only redraws and invalidates the presenting sprite if the QTImageDrawer returns true from the isRedrawing() call. It will still ask the QTImageDrawer if it requires redrawing upon each composite loop when the Invalidator itself is activated.

The Invalidator() constructor takes the TwoDSprite, which presents the Image requiring invalidation. getTarget() returns the target TwoDSprite of the Invalidator. The timeChanged() call is ignored by the default Invalidator.

Invalidators typically ignore time and rate values when invalidating their sprite. However, an Invalidator subclass could, of course, use the time and rate values.

See also SWCompositor, QTImageDrawer, and MoviePresenter for more detailed explanations about handling invalidators.

```
public class Invalidator extends Object implements Ticklish {
//Constructors
    public Invalidator(TwoDSprite s);

//Instance Fields
//protected
    protected TwoDSprite s;

//Instance Methods
    public TwoDSprite getTarget();
    public boolean tickle(float er, int t);
    public void timeChanged(int newTime);
}
```

CLASS HIERARCHY:

Object→Invalidator

Class quicktime.app.actions.MatrixAction

This abstract class provides the means for basic matrix actions. Each time the tickle() method is called, it retrieves the matrix from the target and invokes the transformMatrix() method, which the subclass must implement. The subclass defines the transformMatrix() method to apply a transformation to the matrix of the target of the action.

The MatrixAction also notifies the subclass of any changes of rate direction, and if the subclass is interested in constraint testing, it will notify the subclass which side(s) a target's matrix has collided with after the transformation has been applied. These two states are notified with the rateDirectionChanged() and boundsReached() methods, respectively.

Though the Space is generally specified, it is only used in the bounds testing.

If the matrix action is doing constraint bounds testing, and a bounding condition is reached, the matrix action calls the boundsReached() method with one of four flags to indicate which side of the enclosing space the target collided with.

Using the constraintReached() method, subclasses should return true if after an action is triggered (the doAction() method is called), the action has reached one of its specified constraint conditions, and the Actionable object should be triggered.

The doAction() method when called performs three primary tasks:

- Checks to see if rate direction has changed. If so, calls the rate-DirectionChanged() method.

- Calls the transformMatrix() method, which the subclass defines.

- If doConstraintBoundsTesting is true, it does bounds testing of the target within the enclosing space and notifies of any collisions of the target with the space's sides.

```
public abstract class MatrixAction extends PeriodicAction implements Targetable {
//Static Fields
//protected
    protected static final int kBottomSide;
    protected static final int kLeftSide;
    protected static final int kRightSide;
    protected static final int kTopSide;

//Constructors
//protected
    protected MatrixAction(int scale, int period, QTDrawable space, Transformable t);

//Instance Fields
//protected
    protected boolean doConstraintBoundsTesting;
    protected Transformable target;

//Instance Methods
    public boolean equals(Object obj);
    public QTDrawable getSpace();
    public Object getTarget();
    public void setSpace(QTDrawable space);
    public void setTarget(Object target);
    public String toString();
//protected
    protected void boundsReached(int whichSide);
    protected boolean constraintReached();
    protected void doAction(float er, int t);
    protected void rateDirectionChanged(boolean forwards);
    protected void setTargetMatrix(Matrix transformedMatrix);
    protected abstract void transformMatrix(Matrix theMatrix);
}
```

CLASS HIERARCHY:

Object→PeriodicAction→MatrixAction

Class quicktime.app.actions.MouseController

This abstract class defines methods for marshalling mouse events that occur within a display space and activates its MouseResponder if the received events are of interest to that responder. Thus, the MouseController delegates the response to a mouse event to its MouseResponder.

The test to see if an object is a valid candidate is controlled through the setting of the wholespace variable. If wholespace is true, any object in the controller's space is a candidate for response. If wholespace is false, the object must be a member of the controller's list of objects. By default, wholespace is true.

Subclasses define specialized controllers that deal with some kind of Space knowhow to extract target member objects that are from that Space. The controller and responder are deliberately left abstract; the subclasses define the specifics of the kind of Space and its member that they deal with.

The two QTDisplaySpaces both provide MouseController subclasses for extracting an object the user clicks on: SWController for SWCompositor and GroupController for GroupDrawable. The type of object these controllers return is documented in those classes. The responders that can deal with these members can be defined by the application. A dragger responder is provided that drags a Transformable selection within a QTDrawable space.

In the MouseController addedTo() and removedFrom() methods, it registers its interest in the mouse events generated by that java.awt.Component that is the source of these events. Typically, the top-level Space is addedTo() some kind of component, and the Space itself propagates this to its contained members and controllers, so your application generally has no need to call these methods explicitly.

See also MouseResponder and SWController for an explanation of the general conditions under which a responder may become active.

```
public abstract class MouseController extends Object
                    implements ListenerController, Collection, StdQTConstants,
                        MouseListener, MouseMotionListener {
//Constructors
//protected
```

```
    protected MouseController(MouseResponder mr, boolean wholespace);

//Instance Methods
    public boolean addMember(Object member);
    public void addedTo(Object interest);
    public final void addedToSpace(Space s);
    public abstract Space getSpace();
    public boolean hasMember(Object object);
    public boolean isAppropriate(Object object);
    public boolean isEmpty();
    public boolean isWholespace();
    public Enumeration members();
    public void mouseClicked(MouseEvent e);
    public void mouseDragged(MouseEvent e);
    public void mouseEntered(MouseEvent e);
    public void mouseExited(MouseEvent e);
    public void mouseMoved(MouseEvent e);
    public void mousePressed(MouseEvent e);
    public void mouseReleased(MouseEvent e);
    public void removeMember(Object member);
    public void removedFrom(Object interest);
    public void removedFromSpace();
    public void setWholespace(boolean flag);
    public int size();
//protected
    protected void deactivateResponder();
    protected MouseResponder getResponder();
    protected abstract Object getSelected(MouseEvent event);
    protected abstract void setTargetSpace(Space s);
}
```

CLASS HIERARCHY:

Object→MouseController

Class quicktime.app.actions.MouseResponder

This abstract class is used to provide a base-level functionality for objects that respond to mouse events.

A responder responds to a mouse event based on three conditions being met.

- Modifier keys (or none) that determine if the responder is activated.

- Matching conditions for the specified modifier keys. The default is kExactMatch.

- Events that the particular responder is interested in. Some responders may only be interested in particular mouse events; for instance, the Dragger is only interested in kPressReleaseEvent | kDragEvent.

A responder is associated with a controller, and when the event and modifiers are matched, the controller activates the responder and sends events to the responder while the responder is active.

A responder, in turn, has a target for many mouse events (i.e., click, press, drag, or release). In these event types, the responder is only activated if the controller finds a target at the position of the mouse event. Mouse move, enter, and exit events do not have a target: They relate to the space within which the controller has a declared interest.

You pass in to the MouseResponder() constructor the modifier keys and the conditions of the modifier test that will trigger the activation of the responder object. By default, it sets the modifier test parameters to kModifiersExactMatch.

See also MouseController.

```
public abstract class MouseResponder extends Object {
//Static Fields
    public static final int kAnyModifiers;
    public static final int kAnyModifiersMask;
    public static final int kAnyMouseEvent;
    public static final int kAnyOneOfModifiers;
    public static final int kClickEvents;
    public static final int kDragEvents;
    public static final int kEnterEvents;
    public static final int kExitEvents;
    public static final int kModifiersDisregarded;
    public static final int kModifiersExactMatch;
    public static final int kMouseEvents;
    public static final int kMouseMotionEvents;
    public static final int kMouseOrMouseMotionEvents;
    public static final int kMoveEvents;
    public static final int kNoModifiers;
    public static final int kNoModifiersMask;
    public static final int kPressReleaseEvents;
    public static final int kQTMouseMotionEvents;
    public static final int kRolloverEvents;
    public static final int kSpecifiedModifiersOrNone;
    public static final int kTargetMoveEvents;

//Constructors
//protected
    protected MouseResponder(int modifierKeyMask, int modifierTestConditions,
                    int eventTypes);
```

```
//Instance Fields
    public int modifierKeyMask;
    public int modifierTestConditions;

//Instance Methods
    public int activationEventType();
    public MouseController getMouseController();
    public boolean isActive();
    public abstract boolean isAppropriate(Object object);
    public boolean isInterested(int eventType);
    public boolean isInterested(int eventType, int eventModifiers);
    public void mouseClicked(MouseEvent e);
    public void mouseDragged(MouseEvent e);
    public void mouseEntered(MouseEvent e);
    public void mouseEnteredTarget(MouseEvent e);
    public void mouseExited(MouseEvent e);
    public void mouseExitedTarget(MouseEvent e);
    public void mouseMoved(MouseEvent e);
    public void mousePressed(MouseEvent e);
    public void mouseReleased(MouseEvent e);
//protected
    protected void deactivate();
    protected abstract void removeTarget();
    protected abstract void setTarget(Object target);
    protected abstract void setTargetSpace(Object s);
}
```

CLASS HIERARCHY:

Object→MouseResponder

Class quicktime.app.actions.NextImageAction

This class displays the next image of its sequence of images.

The NextImageAction() constructor creates a NextImageAction object. Scale and period define how many calls are made before the doAction call is made. doAction() increments (or decrements if the rate is less than zero) so that subsequent calls to setImage() and setDescription() set the correct image data. Thus the ImageSequencer iterates over a sequence of images, with the doAction method setting the current image of the ImageSettable target.

```
public class NextImageAction extends SequencerAction implements Targetable {
//Constructors
    public NextImageAction(int scale, int period, ImageSequencer images,
                     ImageSettable target);

//Instance Fields
```

```
//protected
    protected ImageSettable target;

//Instance Methods
    public Object getTarget();
    public void setTarget(Object target);
//protected
    protected void doAction(float er, int t);
}
```

CLASS HIERARCHY:
Object→PeriodicAction→SequencerAction→NextImageAction

Interface quicktime.app.actions.Notifier

The Notifier and NotifyListener interfaces provide a way for objects to deal with some state that is not available immediately but can be acquired. The Notifier represents the class waiting for some condition to be set or established. When this condition is met, it notifies its listener that the state is established.

The classes that interact this way generally have some interdependence, and so the NotifyListener generally expects its Notifier to be a particular type of object. When a NotifyListener is added to a Notifier, if the NotifyListener and Notifier are compatible, the addNotifyListener() method returns true. At that point the Notifier can notify its Listener when the condition it is awaiting is fulfilled.

For instance, the QTImageDrawer is a Notifier and the TwoDSprite is a Notify-Listener. A TwoDSprite requires valid image data before it can present an image in a SWCompositor. A QTImageDrawer does not have valid image data until it has been added to a java.awt.Component. Thus, the QTImageDrawer has a need to notify its TwoD-Sprite when its image data is complete and valid. The TwoDSprite is a NotifyListener that expects its Notifiers to also implement the ImageSpec interface. When the QT-ImageDrawer has valid image data, it notifies its TwoDSprite listener, and the TwoD-Sprite can retrieve that image data and present it within the context of its Compositor.

This type of pairing can be used in other situations where some deferral of resources is an issue. For example, a class could be defined that downloads image data through a network connection. When the image data is completely retrieved, this type of Notifier could then notify, for instance, a TwoDSprite that its image data is now complete.

An established relationship between a Notifier and its Listener can be ongoing; it need not be a one-time-only notification. For instance, image data may be generated at arbitrary times; your application can use this pairing to notify new image data.

```
public interface Notifier {
//Instance Methods
    public abstract boolean addNotifyListener(NotifyListener nl);
}
```

Interface quicktime.app.actions.NotifierListener

This is an interface for those Listener objects that are not valid until the source of the events that the object is interested in becomes valid.

The setNotifier() method registers the Notifier for this listener. If the notifier is not an appropriate Notifier for this listener, the setNotifier() method should return false so the Notifier knows the listener is inappropriate. The Notifier calls the notifyComplete() method when it has completed its task. When the Notifier calls this method on a NotifyListener, the listener can assume that whatever information or state the Notifier possesses is now complete and can take whatever actions are appropriate.

See also Notifier.

```
public interface NotifyListener {
//Instance Methods
    public abstract void notifyComplete();
    public abstract boolean setNotifier(Notifier notifier);
}
```

Class quicktime.app.actions.PeriodicAction

This abstract class is the base class for all periodically recurring time-based actions. The Actionable object (if defined) is an object that has its trigger() method called when the PeriodicAction subclass action is executed or when a constraining condition of the action is reached. The action is tickled periodically based upon the time interval as specified by the scale, period time, and effective rate of the tickle call.

- scale == 10, period = 1 => action executed 10 times a second at effective rate == 1

- scale == 2, period = 1 => action is executed 2 times a second at effective rate == 1

- scale == 1, scale = 2 => action is executed once every 2 seconds at effective rate == 1

Every time the action is executed, the time is saved, and consequent calls to tickle compare the new time rate with the last time the action was executed.

The `tickle()` method is not called with an `effectiveRate` of 0. Whether the `doAction()` method is called can also be affected by a flag that controls whether an action is triggered depending on rate settings. The `tickle()` method can be called as often as you like, though effective rate cannot be zero. If the time specified has elapsed from the last time value that the `tickle()` method was called, then the action will be triggered. The provided time and rate values are used to calculate whether an action should be executed.

The `doAction()` method is called by the `tickle()` method when an action becomes active. Subclasses should do the action performed by the subclass when this method is called.

```
public abstract class PeriodicAction extends Object
                                    implements Ticklish, StdQTConstants {
//Constructors
//protected
    protected PeriodicAction(int scale, int period);

//Instance Fields
//protected
    protected Actionable actor;
    protected boolean reschedule;

//Instance Methods
    public boolean equals(Object obj);
    public Actionable getActionable();
    public int getPeriod();
    public int getScale();
    public int getTriggerCondition();
    public void setActionable(Actionable actor);
    public void setPeriod(int period);
    public void setScale(int s);
    public void setTriggerCondition(int cond);
    public boolean tickle(float effectiveRate, int currentTime);
    public void timeChanged(int newTime);
    public String toString();
//protected
    protected abstract boolean constraintReached();
```

```
    protected abstract void doAction(float er, int t);
}
```

CLASS HIERARCHY:

Object→PeriodicAction

Class quicktime.app.actions.QTMouseMotionAdapter

This abstract class is an adapter that receives mouse events. The methods in this class are empty; the class is provided as a convenience for easily creating listeners by extending this class and overriding only the methods of interest.

```
public abstract class QTMouseMotionAdapter extends Object
                                    implements QTMouseMotionListener {
//Constructors
    public QTMouseMotionAdapter();

//Instance Methods
    public void mouseDragged(MouseEvent e);
    public void mouseEnteredTarget(MouseEvent e);
    public void mouseExitedTarget(MouseEvent e);
    public void mouseMoved(MouseEvent e);
}
```

CLASS HIERARCHY:

Object→QTMouseMotionAdapter

Interface quicktime.app.actions.QTMouseMotionListener

This interface extends the MouseMotionListener interface to notify its listeners of mouse motion events that enter or exit a particular target.

```
public interface QTMouseMotionListener extends MouseMotionListener {
//Instance Methods
    public abstract void mouseEnteredTarget(MouseEvent e);
    public abstract void mouseExitedTarget(MouseEvent e);
}
```

Class quicktime.app.actions.SequencerAction

This abstract class is for actions that interact with some kind of Sequencer. The doAction() method is left for the subclass to define so that it can define the type of a

Sequencer the action deals with. The constraining conditions of the Sequencer are dealt with by this class. The class sets the displayed image of its target. Subclasses implement the three abstract methods that perform the action of setting the image and then returning the image data.

The constructor SequencerAction() creates an ImageAction with a constraining condition not set. Using the constraintReached() method, subclasses should return true if after an action is triggered (the doAction() method is called), the action has reached one of its specified constraint conditions and the Actionable object should be triggered.

```
public abstract class SequencerAction extends PeriodicAction {
//Static Fields
    public static final int kConstraintAny;
    public static final int kConstraintFirst;
    public static final int kConstraintFirstOrLast;
    public static final int kConstraintLast;

//Constructors
//protected
    protected SequencerAction(int scale, int period, Sequencer seq);

//Instance Fields
//protected
    protected Sequencer seq;

//Instance Methods
    public boolean equals(Object obj);
    public int getConstraint();
    public void setConstraint(int cons);
//protected
    protected boolean constraintReached();
}
```

CLASS HIERARCHY:

Object→PeriodicAction→SequencerAction

Class quicktime.app.actions.SimpleActionList

This class extends the TickleList to provide a list of Targetable objects. The Targetable interface extends the Ticklish interface, providing a Ticklish object with the concept of a target that is acted upon by in its tickle() method. By providing a list that requires members to be Targetable objects, the list can remove all of the actions associated with a particular target and return an enumeration that is capable of enumerating over the list member's targets.

See also `Targetable`.

```
public class SimpleActionList extends TickleList {
//Constructors
    public SimpleActionList();

//Instance Methods
    public boolean isAppropriate(Object object);
    public synchronized void removeTarget(Object target);
    public Enumeration targets();
}
```

CLASS HIERARCHY:

Object→TickleList→SimpleActionList

Interface quicktime.app.actions.Targetable

An object that implements this interface is an object defined to invoke some action upon a target according to the time constraints supplied by the caller of the `tickle()` method. How the `Targetable` interprets and acts upon these time constraints is up to the object itself.

A `Targetable` object is a one-to-one relationship between the target of the action and the action (`Targetable`) object itself. The `getTarget()` method returns the current target of the `Targetable` object—this is the object that the `Targetable` will act upon. `setTarget()` sets the target.

```
public interface Targetable extends Ticklish {
//Instance Methods
    public abstract Object getTarget();
    public abstract void setTarget(Object target);
}
```

Class quicktime.app.actions.TickleList

A `TickleList` is a list that contains `Ticklish` members. Each time the `TickleList` is tickled (it itself implements the `Ticklish` interface and can be a member of a `TickleList`) it will tickle all of its members. If the member's `tickle()` method returns true, the `Ticklish` member is kept active. If the `tickle()` method returns `false`, the member must be re-enabled for it to be tickled.

Members of a `TickleList` are kept in a `TickleNode` object, which is where the active state of the node is kept. This information is only relevant for the list itself. When a `Ticklish` member is added to a `TickleList`, the `addMember()` method calls the `makeTickleNode()` method. A subclass can define this method to make a subclass of `TickleNode` to store extra information about `Ticklish` members in a `TickleList`.

A singly linked list is used to implement the `TickleList`. A list is used for fast iteration through the list whenever the `tickle()` method is called. Insertion or removal of members is, of course, a more expensive operation.

The `TickleList` also implements the `TicklishController` interface, thus enabling it to be added to a space as a controller for objects in that space. It implements the `Collection` interface to indicate that it contains a collection of objects. The `TicklishController` aspect of the `TickleList` is generally used to schedule `PeriodicActions` that control aspects of a space's members.

```
public class TickleList extends Object
                    implements TicklishController, CollectionController {
//Constructors
    public TickleList();

//Instance Fields
//protected
    protected TickleNode list;

//Instance Methods
    public synchronized boolean addMember(Object member);
    public void addedToSpace(Space s);
    public TickleNode findNode(Object object);
    public boolean hasMember(Object object);
    public boolean isAppropriate(Object object);
    public boolean isEmpty();
    public boolean isMemberActive(Ticklish member);
    public boolean isWholespace();
    public Enumeration members();
    public Enumeration nodes();
    public synchronized void removeMember(Object member);
    public void removedFromSpace();
    public void setMemberActive(Ticklish member, boolean flag);
    public void setWholespace(boolean flag);
    public int size();
    public synchronized boolean tickle(float effectiveRate, int currentTime);
    public synchronized void timeChanged(int newTime);
    public String toString();
```

```
//protected
    protected TickleNode makeTickleNode(Ticklish t);
}
```

CLASS HIERARCHY:

Object→TickleList

Class quicktime.app.actions.TickleNode

This class is used by the `TickleList` to contain its `Ticklish` members.

`isActive()` allows your application to determine if this node of a `TickleList` is currently active and thus if its `Ticklish` will be tickled by the list. `setActive()` allows your application to activate or deactivate a `TickleNode` that is currently a member of a list.

See also `TickleList`.

```
public class TickleNode extends Object {
//Constructors
//protected
    protected TickleNode(Ticklish action);

//Instance Methods
    public Ticklish getTicklish();
    public boolean isActive();
    public void setActive(boolean flag);
    public void setTicklish(Ticklish action);
    public String toString();
}
```

CLASS HIERARCHY:

Object→TickleNode

19

The quicktime. app.anim Package

The `quicktime.app.anim` package contains classes that present some of the functionality of the `Sprite` and `SpriteWorld`. The `SWCompositor` and the `Compositor` are the two most useful classes in this package.

The `SWCompositor` enables you to create a complex image from disparate image sources and then treat the result as a single image. This is then presented to the user. `SWCompositor` uses the services of the QuickTime `SpriteWorld` internally to perform its compositing tasks. As a consequence, all of the actual drawing of the members of a `SWCompositor` is handled through the interaction between the `SpriteWorld` and `Sprite` classes of QuickTime, which improves the performance and image rendering onscreen.

The `Compositor` uses the `SpriteWorld` compositing services of the `SWCompositor` to composite an image out of its member objects. Because the `Compositor` composites an image offscreen, various graphics modes such as alpha blending and transparency can be applied to its members.

The `SWController` class deals with `SpriteWorldHitTest` calls on the `SpriteWorld` contained by the subclasses of `SWCompositor`.

Figure 19.1 shows the class hierarchy for this package. See Chapter 15, "Animation and Compositing," for more information on using sprites.

FIGURE 19.1 *The* quicktime.app.anim *package*

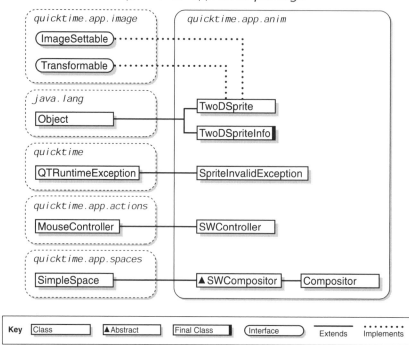

Class quicktime.app.display.Compositor

This class uses the SpriteWorld compositing services of the SWCompositor to composite an image out of its member objects. The member object of a Compositor is required to at least implement the ImageSpec interface—in which case the Compositor creates an instance of the TwoDSprite object that presents image data in its display space. If a TwoDSprite itself is added to the Compositor, it is added directly as a member, since TwoDSprite also implements the ImageSpec interface. Items that overlap draw in front of each other, based on their layer number.

The Compositor can have its composited image recorded into a movie. There are two ways this can be done. The fastest is to temporarily disable the transfer of the composited image to the screen and just add each image to the movie. Alternatively, if some interaction with the Compositor is desired and the results are to be recorded, then the Compositor will blit each frame to the screen, and any changes made to the compositor's image (for example, through dragging an item around) will be faithfully recorded. Bear in mind that compressing a frame and adding it to a movie will take more time. So to gain an accurate rendering of the compositor's image, the rate at which the Compositor ticks should be slow enough to allow for this extra work to be performed.

members() returns an enumeration to enumerate over all of the members that have been added to the Compositor. The sprites() method returns an enumeration that allows your application to iterate over the TwoDSprite presenters that are responsible for presenting the image data within the Compositor. isEmpty() returns true if there are no members of the Compositor.

addMember() adds a member to the Compositor. The member must be some kind of ImageSpec object. The member is added with default settings of visibility set to true. size() returns the number of members of the collection. The removeMember() method removes a sprite from the Compositor and removes it visually. If applications have defined control actions to this member, these actions should be disabled before the member is removed from the Compositor.

See also SWCompositor.

```
public class Compositor extends SWCompositor {
//Constructors
    public Compositor(QDGraphics spriteGWorld, QDColor backgroundColor);
    public Compositor(QDGraphics spriteGWorld, QDColor backgroundColor,
            QDGraphics background);
    public Compositor(QDGraphics spriteGWorld, QDColor backgroundColor,
            int scale, int period);
    public Compositor(QDGraphics spriteGWorld, QDColor backgroundColor,
            QDGraphics background, int scale, int period);
//protected
    protected Compositor(QDGraphics spriteGWorld, QDColor backgroundColor,
            QDGraphics background, int scale, int period, Protocol defaultProtocol);

//Instance Fields
//protected
    protected Hashtable membersTable;
    protected Hashtable spritesTable;

//Instance Methods
    public boolean addMember(Object member);
    public boolean addMember(Object member, int layer);
    public boolean addMember(Object member, int layer, boolean initiallyVisible);
    public int getBackLayer();
    public int getFrontLayer();
    public TwoDSprite getMemberSprite(Object member);
```

```
    public Object getSpriteMember(TwoDSprite sprite);
    public boolean isEmpty();
    public Enumeration members();
    public void removeMember(Object member);
    public int size();
    public Enumeration sprites();
}
```

CLASS HIERARCHY:

Object →SimpleSpace →SWCompositor →Compositor

Class quicktime.app.anim.SpriteInvalidException

Certain actions, such as invalidate, can only be performed on a TwoDSprite when the Sprite that it uses is an active member of its SpriteWorld. If a method is called on the TwoDSprite when its Sprite is invalid, this runtime exception is thrown.

```
public class SpriteInvalidException extends QTRuntimeException {
//Constructors
    public SpriteInvalidException(String s);
}
```

CLASS HIERARCHY:

Object →Throwable →Exception →RuntimeException →
QTRuntimeException →SpriteInvalidException

Class quicktime.app.display.SWCompositor

This class provides the capability to composite a complex image of disparate image sources and then treat the result as a single image presented to the user. It uses the QuickTime SpriteWorld internally to perform the compositing tasks. Thus, all of the actual drawing of the members of a SWCompositor is handled through the interaction between the SpriteWorld and Sprite classes of QuickTime.

The SpriteWorld itself is wrapped by the SWCompositor class, and to represent the Sprite class, it uses the TwoDSprite. The TwoDSprite is a *presenter*—it presents image information. The presentation of the image information within the context of the SpriteWorld of the SWCompositoris determined by the matrix, graphics mode, layer, and visibility of the Sprite object of the TwoDSprite.

To create a `Sprite`, you need a valid `SpriteWorld`. To create a `SpriteWorld`, you need a valid `QDGraphics` destination. Depending on whether a `SWCompositor` is visible, you may or may not have a valid destination `QDGraphics`. The interaction between the `SWCompositor` and its `TwoDSprite` presenters handles the saving and creating of sprite worlds and their sprites—the application does not need to deal specifically with this issue.

The `SWCompositor` has been designed without the requirement that its members be `TwoDSprite` objects. It may be more convenient for your application to add members of a `Compositor` that are a source of image data and have the `addMember()` method deal with the mechanics of creating the `TwoDSprite` presenter. Thus, there are also methods that must be defined by the subclass for getting a member's `TwoDSprite` and getting a `TwoDSprite` object's member.

This is important to understand for the following reason: Once a member has been added to a `SWCompositor`, it is the presenter within the `SWCompositor` itself (i.e., the `TwoDSprite`) that must be interacted with to effect the display characteristics of the member in the `SWCompositor`. While a subclass may provide the capability to create the `TwoDSprite` presenter with display characteristics like `Matrix` and `GraphicsMode`, once the member is added, altering the member's display characteristics directly may or may not affect the display characteristics of the member in the `SWCompositor`. Thus, your application should always interact with the member's `TwoDSprite` presenter.

After a member is added, the subclass should call the `postProcessAdd()`method and `postProcessRemove()` in the case of a `removeMember()` call. This call will look at the member being added and will perform two services. If the new member is an instance of the `Notifier` class, then the `SWCompositor` registers the `Notifer` with the `TwoDSprite` presenter as the `NotifyListener`. That way, a `Sprite` that presents image data not available at the time the member is added can still prepare itself for displaying an image when its `Notifier` notifies the `TwoDSprite` that its image data is valid. If the new member is an instance of `DynamicImage`, then this method will also call that member's `addedToCompositor()` method to allow this new member to establish the invalidation mechanism it uses. Explicit invalidation is required for the `SpriteWorld` to redraw a sprite that presents image data that is changing (such as a movie) when nothing else about the sprite's presentation has changed.

The subclass defines completely the storage mechanism and protocols of its members. The `Compositor` subclass allows members that implement the `ImageSpec` interface and takes care of the details of creating the TwoDSprite needed to present the member's image data.

getMemberSprite() returns the TwoDSprite presenter that is presenting the image data of the given member. It returns null if the object is not a member. The getSpriteMember() method returns the member that is being presented by the supplied TwoDSprite presenter. It returns null if the TwoDSprite is not present in the Compositor. It returns the member being presented by the supplied TwoDSprite presenter.

getFrontLayer() returns the frontmost layer of all of the TwoDSprite presenters of the Compositor. getBackLayer() returns the backmost layer of all of the TwoDSprite presenters of the Compositor.

saveMembers() is called if a SpriteWorld has previously been created and the destination QDGraphics or the QDGraphics that the members are a part of, is about to go away (such as removing a SpriteWorld from a QTCanvas). Any Sprite objects attached to the sprite world will be invalid after this call, so you should ensure that you remove any possibility of a method being called on any of these sprites. If sprites and/or an action list has been added to the Compositor, then those sprites will be saved and re-instantiated if a consequent createSprites() method is received.

createMembers() is called after the Compositor has been added to a valid QDGraphics, and the sprites can be added to the sprite world. Any sprites that the Compositor knows about through an action list or sprites being explicitly added will be recreated at this point. If a subclass overrides this method to create sprites on an initial call and add them to the Compositor, then on subsequent calls the subclass should call super.createSprites to ensure that the previous sprites are recreated.

See also SpriteWorld, Sprite, TwoDSprite, Compositor.

```
public abstract class SWCompositor extends SimpleSpace
                          implements QTDisplaySpace, DynamicImage, StdQTConstants {
//Constructors
//protected
    protected SWCompositor(QDGraphics spriteGWorld, QDColor backgroundColor,
              QDGraphics background, int scale, int period, Protocol defaultProtocol);

//Instance Fields
    public int taskFlag;

//Instance Methods
    public abstract boolean addMember(Object member, int layer);
    public Invalidator addedToCompositor(SWCompositor c, TwoDSprite s);
    public abstract int getBackLayer();
```

```
    public Region getClip();
    public Compositable getCompositable(Object member);
    public ImageDescription getDescription();
    public QDRect getDisplayBounds();
    public abstract int getFrontLayer();
    public QDGraphics getGWorld();
    public GraphicsMode getGraphicsMode();
    public EncodedImage getImage();
    public Dimension getInitialSize();
    public Enumeration getInvalidatorList();
    public Layerable getLayerable(Object member);
    public Matrix getMatrix();
    public synchronized Invalidator getMemberInvalidator(Object member);
    public abstract TwoDSprite getMemberSprite(Object member);
    public abstract Object getSpriteMember(TwoDSprite sprite);
    public SWCompositor getParent();
    public float getStatistics();
    public Transformable getTransformable(Object member);
    public boolean hasRecordMovie();
    public final void redraw(Region invalidRgn);
    public synchronized void removedFromCompositor(SWCompositor c);
    public void resetStatistics();
    public void setClip(Region clipRgn);
    public synchronized void setDisplayBounds(QDRect bounds);
    public synchronized void setGWorld(QDGraphics cgp);
    public void setGraphicsMode(GraphicsMode mode);
    public void setLocation(int x, int y);
    public void setMatrix(Matrix matrix);
    public void setRecordMovie(RecordMovie rm);
    public abstract Enumeration sprites();
    public boolean tickle(float er, int time);
    public String toString();
//protected
    protected void createMembers();
    protected void idle();
    protected synchronized void postProcessAdd(Object member, TwoDSprite s);
    protected synchronized void postProcessRemove(Object member, TwoDSprite s);
    protected void saveMembers();
}
```

CLASS HIERARCHY:

Object →SimpleSpace →SWCompositor

Class quicktime.app.anim.SWController

This class deals with SpriteWorldHitTest calls on the SpriteWorld contained by the subclasses of SWCompositor. By default, it performs hit-testing on the actual sprite image itself. However, your application can set the hit-test flags to support any mode of hit-testing that is appropriate.

See also SWCompositor, SpriteWorld.

```
public class SWController extends MouseController implements StdQTConstants {
//Constructors
    public SWController(MouseResponder mr, boolean wholeSpace);
    public SWController(MouseResponder mr, boolean wholeSpace, int flags);

//Instance Methods
    public int getFlags();
    public Space getSpace();
    public void setFlags(int flags);
//protected
    protected void deactivateResponder();
    protected Object getSelected(MouseEvent event);
    protected void setTargetSpace(Space target);
}
```

CLASS HIERARCHY:

Object →MouseController →SWController

Class quicktime.app.anim.TwoDSprite

This class is a specialized presenter for image data within the context of a SpriteWorld. It contains information about the layer within the SpriteWorld that the image presented by the Sprite is drawn. It also contains information about visibility, matrix transformations, and GraphicsMode drawing that is applied to the image data when the Sprite is drawn in the SpriteWorld.

Typically, an application will provide the image data and presentation characteristics. The SWCompositor assumes the responsibility of creating the actual TwoDSprite object Sprite that is used to present this data in the internal SpriteWorld that the SWCompositor uses to render and construct its image. The TwoDSprite uses the quicktime.std.anim.Sprite class to draw the image in a quicktime.std.anim.SpriteWorld.

See also Compositor, TwoDSpriteInfo.

```
public class TwoDSprite extends Object
                implements NotifyListener, Transformable, Layerable,
                    ImageSettable, Compositable, StdQTConstants, QDConstants {
//Constructors
    public TwoDSprite(TwoDSpriteInfo spriteInfo);
```

```
    public TwoDSprite(Matrix matrix, int layer, GraphicsMode graphicsMode);
    public TwoDSprite(ImageSpec image, Matrix matrix, boolean visibility, int layer);
    public TwoDSprite(ImageSpec image, Matrix matrix, boolean visibility,
                        int layer, GraphicsMode graphicsMode);
    public TwoDSprite(ImageDataSequence images, int frame, Matrix matrix,
                        boolean visibility, int layer);
    public TwoDSprite(ImageDataSequence images, int frame, Matrix matrix,
                        boolean visibility, int layer, GraphicsMode graphicsMode);

//Instance Methods
    public void createSprite(SpriteWorld sw);
    public boolean equals(Object obj);
    public ImageDescription getDescription();
    public GraphicsMode getGraphicsMode();
    public EncodedImage getImage();
    public Dimension getInitialSize();
    public int getLayer();
    public Matrix getMatrix();
    public TwoDSpriteInfo getSpriteInfo();
    public SWCompositor getParent();
    public boolean getVisible();
    public boolean hitTest(int flags, QDPoint loc);
    public final void invalidate();
    public boolean isValid();
    public void notifyComplete();
    public void remove();
    public void setDescription(ImageDescription idh);
    public void setImageData(EncodedImage im, ImageDescription id);
    public void setGraphicsMode(GraphicsMode gMode);
    public void setImage(EncodedImage image);
    public void setLayer(int layer);
    public void setMatrix(Matrix matrix);
    public boolean setNotifier(Notifier notifier);
    public void setVisible(boolean visible);
    public String toString();
//protected
    protected void removeNotify();
}
```

CLASS HIERARCHY:

Object →TwoDSprite

Class quicktime.app.anim.TwoDSpriteInfo

This class can be used to retain the current sprite settings, which can be used at a later stage to reset the TwoDSprite to those settings. The image data and ImageDescription of a TwoDSprite cannot be serialized, rather the application would typically use a

QuickTime Movie to transport such image data. However, the current display characteristics of a TwoDSprite, its Matrix and GraphicsMode for instance, are legitimate and useful characteristics of a TwoDSprite to serialize. As such, this class is Serializable.

See also TwoDSprite.

```
public final class TwoDSpriteInfo extends Object implements ImageSpec, Serializable {
//Constructors
    public TwoDSpriteInfo(EncodedImage im, ImageDescription d, Matrix m, boolean v,
                    int l);
    public TwoDSpriteInfo(EncodedImage im, ImageDescription d, Matrix m, boolean v,
                    int l, GraphicsMode gm);

//Instance Methods
    public ImageDescription getDescription();
    public GraphicsMode getGraphicsMode();
    public EncodedImage getImage();
    public int getLayer();
    public Matrix getMatrix();
    public boolean getVisible();
}
```

CLASS HIERARCHY:

Object →TwoDSpriteInfo

20

The quicktime. app.audio Package

The `quicktime.app.audio` package contains a number of interfaces and classes that deal specifically with the audio capabilities of QuickTime. You can use a variety of QuickTime objects as audio objects (for example, to build an audio mixer).

Both `AudioSpec` and `ExtendedAudioSpec` provide standard interfaces that all audiocapable QuickTime objects can implement. The `AudioMediaControl` class provides a simple implementation of the `ExtendedAudioSpec` interface to control media that has an audio media component.

The `MusicPart` interface extends the capability of audio control objects as they provide an instrument that will play or render the control information (i.e., notes, etc.) of that particular part. The `MusicScore` interface defines methods that abstract the usage of a collection of `MusicPart` objects. These typically make up the collection of instruments that play a set of music notes.

Figure 20.1 shows the class hierarchy for this package. See Chapter 10, "Playing Music with QuickTime," for more information on using audio interfaces.

FIGURE 20.1 *The* quicktime.app.audio *package*

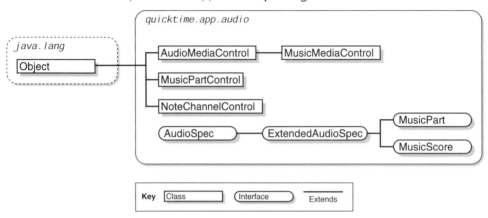

Class quicktime.app.audio.AudioMediaControl

This is a very simple implementation of the ExtendedAudioSpec interface to control media that has an audio media component.

```
public class AudioMediaControl extends Object implements ExtendedAudioSpec {
//Constructors
    public AudioMediaControl(Media media);

//Instance Fields
//protected
    protected AudioMediaHandler audioHandler;
    protected Media audioMedia;

//Instance Methods
    public float getBalance();
    public Media getMedia();
    public float getVolume();
    public boolean isMuted();
    public void setBalance(float val);
    public void setMuted(boolean mute);
    public void setVolume(float vol);
}
```

CLASS HIERARCHY:

Object→AudioMediaControl

Interface quicktime.app.audio.AudioSpec

AudioSpec provides a standard interface that all audio-capable objects can support. Volume values for objects that implement this interface are 0 for silence and 1.0 for unity gain (generally the maximum volume for a given object). Values over 1.0 are not guaranteed to result in louder volumes; some objects support overdriving the volume, some don't. If an object does not support a value greater than 1, it sets the volume to its maximum level.

An object may have a volume level, but because it is muted you won't hear anything. Unmuting an AudioSpec object sets it to its current volume setting. If an object is muted and its volume is changed, this does not make the audio object audible—it has to be explicitly unmuted. This is in line with the way most mixing consoles work.

getVolume() returns the volume setting (0 is silent, 1 is unity gain). isMuted() returns the current mute status. setMuted() allows the muting of the specific channel.

```
public interface AudioSpec {
//Instance Methods
    public abstract float getVolume();
    public abstract boolean isMuted();
    public abstract void setMuted(boolean flag);
    public abstract void setVolume(float val);
}
```

Interface quicktime.app.audio.ExtendedAudioSpec

ExtendedAudioSpec provides a standard interface that all audio-capable objects that have the capability of being rendered in stereo can support.

Balance is defined to a range of −1.0 for maximum left, 0 for center, and 1.0 for maximum right.

```
public interface ExtendedAudioSpec extends AudioSpec {
//Instance Methods
    public abstract float getBalance();
    public abstract void setBalance(float val);
}
```

Class quicktime.app.audio.MusicMediaControl

This class is a specialized version of the generic AudioMediaControl class that provides added capability for dealing specifically with MusicMedia through the implementation of the MusicScore interface.

```
public class MusicMediaControl extends AudioMediaControl implements MusicScore {
//Constructors
    public MusicMediaControl(MusicMedia m);

//Instance Methods
    public MusicPart getPart(int part);
    public int getPartCount();
}
```

CLASS HIERARCHY:

Object→AudioMediaControl→MusicMediaControl

Interface quicktime.app.audio.MusicPart

The MusicPart interface extends the capability of audio control objects as they provide an instrument that plays or renders the control information (i.e., notes, etc.) of that particular part. The analogy is an instrument in an orchestra that plays a particular part in a score. The NoteChannel is responsible for producing the sound. In its completeness a MusicPart has a sense of its volume, its balance location in a left-right stereo field, and an instrument that is the sound it produces.

```
public interface MusicPart extends ExtendedAudioSpec {
//Instance Methods
    public abstract String getInstrumentName();
    public abstract NoteChannel getNoteChannel();
    public abstract void selectInstrument(String prompt);
}
```

Class quicktime.app.audio.MusicPartControl

This class provides an implementation of the MusicPart interface for MusicMedia parts.

```
public class MusicPartControl extends Object implements MusicPart, StdQTConstants {
//Constructors
    public MusicPartControl(MusicMediaHandler mh, int partNumber);

//Instance Methods
```

```
    public float getBalance();
    public String getInstrumentName();
    public final NoteChannel getNoteChannel();
    public float getVolume();
    public boolean isMuted();
    public void selectInstrument(String prompt);
    public void setBalance(float val);
    public void setMuted(boolean flag);
    public void setVolume(float volume);
}
```

CLASS HIERARCHY:

Object→MusicPartControl

Interface quicktime.app.audio.MusicScore

This is an interface that defines methods that abstract the usage of a collection of MusicParts. These MusicParts typically make up the collection of instruments that play a set of musical notes.

```
public interface MusicScore extends ExtendedAudioSpec {
//Instance Methods
    public abstract MusicPart getPart(int part);
    public abstract int getPartCount();
}
```

Class quicktime.app.audio.NoteChannelControl

This class provides an implementation of the MusicPart interface for NoteChannel objects.

```
public class NoteChannelControl extends Object implements MusicPart, StdQTConstants {
//Constructors
    public NoteChannelControl(int gmNumber);
    public NoteChannelControl(int gmNumber, int poly);
    public NoteChannelControl(NoteChannel nc);

//Instance Methods
    public float getBalance();
    public String getInstrumentName();
    public final NoteChannel getNoteChannel();
    public float getVolume();
    public boolean isMuted();
    public void playNoteFor(float note, int velocity, int duration);
    public void selectInstrument(String prompt);
    public void setBalance(float val);
    public void setMuted(boolean flag);
```

```
    public void setVolume(float volume);
}
```

CLASS HIERARCHY:

Object→NoteChannelControl

21

The quicktime. app.display Package

The `quicktime.app.display` package contains a number of classes that are essential for using the QuickTime for Java API. These classes negotiate with `java.awt` classes to allow the presentation of QuickTime content within a Java window or display space. The `QTCanvas` class, which is part of this package, is one of the most useful in the QuickTime for Java API. This class serves as a specialized canvas that supplies access to the native graphics environment.

Various objects within the `quicktime.app` framework implement the `Drawable` interface and can be displayed within the confines of the `QTCanvas`. Both the `Drawable` and `QTDrawable` interfaces in this package are designed to work hand-in-hand with a `QTCanvas` object. All classes that interact with a `QTCanvas` object must implement one of these interfaces.

The `DirectGroup` is an object that allows for the grouping of members that draw. It presents its members directly to the screen. The layering of members in a direct group is achieved through setting the display clip regions of the members that are behind others. The members of a `DirectGroup` must be able to draw themselves to a destination `QDGraphics` and thus must implement the `QTDrawable` interface.

Figure 21.1 shows the class hierarchy for this package. See Chapter 3, "Integrating QuickTime with Java," Chapter 4, "QTCanvas, QTDrawable, and QTFactory," and Chapter 15, "Animation and Compositing," for more information on using display objects.

FIGURE 21.1 *The* quicktime.app.display *package*

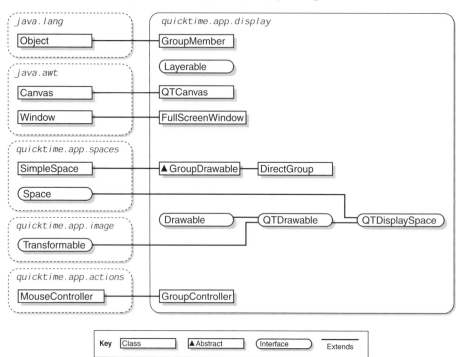

Class quicktime.app.display.DirectGroup

This class contains a set of QTDrawable objects that present their visual contents directly to the screen.

Items that overlap screen space will not draw over each other as the front object clips the rear object so that the rear object does not draw in the area occupied by the front object. When the group is resized, the group's items are not resized but merely repositioned within the group based on their set size, current relative position, and the new display size of the group.

```
public class DirectGroup extends GroupDrawable {
//Constructors
    public DirectGroup(Dimension initialSize, QDColor bc);
//protected
    protected DirectGroup(Dimension initialSize, QDColor bc, int scale, int period,
                Protocol p);
```

```
//Instance Methods
    public boolean addMember(Object member, int layer, float xAlign, float yAlign);
    public boolean addMember(Object member, int layer);
    public boolean addMember(Object member);
    public void addedTo(Object interest);
    public GroupMember memberChanged(QTDrawable d);
    public synchronized void redrawMember(QTDrawable d, Region invalidRgn);
    public void removedFrom(Object interest);
    public void setClip(Region theClip);
    public void setDisplayBounds(QDRect bounds);
    public void setGWorld(QDGraphics cgp);
    public boolean setMemberAlignment(QTDrawable d, float xAlign, float yAlign);
    public boolean setMemberLayer(QTDrawable member, int layer);
}
```

CLASS HIERARCHY:

Object→SimpleSpace→GroupDrawable→DirectGroup

Interface quicktime.app.display.Drawable

This interface is designed to work hand-in-hand with a QTCanvas object. Therefore, all classes that want to interact with a QTCanvas object, referred to as *clients*, must implement this interface. Essentially, these clients become objects that paint in the display space of the QTCanvas.

The Drawable interface is general enough that Java drawing objects can implement it and therefore become a client of the QTCanvas.

Note that a Java applet or application does not generally call the Drawable methods. The QTCanvas object associated with this Drawable object calls these methods as needed, and your application should interact with QTCanvas as with any other AWT component.

QTExceptions can be thrown by any of these methods and indicate that either the graphics environment has changed in some unexpected way or that the media object itself is in some unexpected state.

QTCanvas calls the redraw() method when the client should redraw itself. If the canvas is able to discern that only a part of the client's drawing area needs to be redrawn, then this area shall be passed in using invalidRgn. Otherwise, this region will be null, in which case the client should redraw itself entirely.

```
public interface Drawable extends Listener {
```

```
//Instance Methods
    public abstract QDRect getDisplayBounds();
    public abstract void redraw(Region invalidRgn);
    public abstract void setDisplayBounds(QDRect bounds);
}
```

Class quicktime.app.display.FullScreenWindow

This class is provided for usage when the screen is put into full-screen mode. The class manages a FullScreen object that will hide menu bars, task bars, and so on, thus making available the entire screen for an application to use. The FullScreenWindow is the window that will fill that screen. Because it is an extension of a java.awt.Window, any usage of this window is similar to the usage of a Window in Java applications.

See also quicktime.std.movies.FullScreen.

```
public class FullScreenWindow extends Window {
//Constructors
    public FullScreenWindow();
    public FullScreenWindow(FullScreen fs);
    public FullScreenWindow(FullScreen fs, Frame f);

//Instance Fields
//protected
    protected boolean doNotify;

//Instance Methods
    public void addNotify();
    public int getFlags();
    public FullScreen getFullScreen();
    public GDevice getGDevice();
    public Insets getInsets();
    public Dimension getPreferredSize();
    public void hide();
    public void pack();
    public void setFlags(int flags);
    public void setGDevice(GDevice gDevice);
    public void setPreferredSize(int width, int height);
    public void show();
}
```

CLASS HIERARCHY:

Object→Component→Container→Window→FullScreenWindow

Class quicktime.app.display.GroupController

This controller provides specific semantics for mouse control that deal specifically with GroupDrawable objects. It implements the getSelected() method to extract a QTDrawable member from the group.

The GroupController() constructor constructs a GroupController with a Mouse-Responder that responds to the mouse events of the controller. getSpace() returns the current GroupDrawable space that the controller is controlling. setTargetSpace() sets the target space. If the target object is not a GroupDrawable, a ClassCastException is thrown.

The MouseController calls the getSelected() method when a mouse event occurs in its space. This method returns the frontmost QTDrawable object at the event's location if it finds such an object at the location of the event. In the case of mouse drag actions, the mouseDragged() method ensures that the display logic of the GroupDrawable is kept updated due to any changes in the display characteristics of the selected member.

```
public class GroupController extends MouseController {
//Constructors
    public GroupController(MouseResponder mr, boolean wholeSpace);

//Instance Methods
    public Space getSpace();
    public void mouseDragged(MouseEvent e);
//protected
    protected void deactivateResponder();
    protected Object getSelected(MouseEvent event);
    protected void setTargetSpace(Space target);
}
```

CLASS HIERARCHY:

Object→MouseController→GroupController

Class quicktime.app.display.GroupDrawable

This abstract class forms the base class for grouping QTDrawable objects within a single display space that is controlled by this group.

QTDrawable objects contained within a group are presented according to their xAlignment (0 = left, 1 = right) and yAlignment (0 = top, 1 = bottom) and are drawn in their layer order (Short.minimum value is frontmost, Short.maximum value is furthest back). You can change a position or size of a member by interacting directly with the

QTDrawable member itself, but you must notify the group of any changes in the display characteristics of the QTDrawable by calling memberChanged(). Items use their (initial) size to calculate their relative position in the group.

To reset the layer of an object, you use a Layerable object of the QTDrawable. QTDrawable objects do not contain any sense of layering, so the GroupDrawable uses the GroupMember objects to contain the information about a member's layer and alignment characteristics. The memberChanged() method tells the group that the position or display size of the drawer has changed, and it should recalculate its alignment and clipping based on the new position. If the drawer is not a member of the group, then null is returned; if it is a member, then a group member object is returned that contains the current layout characteristics of the drawer.

See also DirectGroup.

```
public abstract class GroupDrawable extends SimpleSpace implements QTDisplaySpace {
//Constructors
//protected
    protected GroupDrawable(Dimension initialSize, QDColor bc, int scale, int period,
                    Protocol p);

//Instance Fields
//protected
    protected Region clip;
    protected Vector vec;

//Instance Methods
    public abstract boolean addMember(Object member, int layer);
    public int getBackLayer();
    public Region getBackgroundClip();
    public QDColor getBackgroundColor();
    public Region getClip();
    public QDRect getDisplayBounds();
    public int getFrontLayer();
    public QDGraphics getGWorld();
    public GroupMember getGroupMember(Object member);
    public Dimension getInitialSize();
    public Layerable getLayerable(Object member);
    public Matrix getMatrix();
    public Transformable getTransformable(Object member);
    public QTDrawable hitTest(int x, int y);
    public boolean isEmpty();
    public abstract GroupMember memberChanged(QTDrawable d);
    public synchronized Enumeration members();
    public synchronized void redraw(Region invalidRgn);
    public abstract void redrawMember(QTDrawable d, Region invalidRgn);
    public synchronized void removeMember(Object member);
    public void setBackgroundColor(QDColor col);
```

```
    public abstract void setClip(Region theClip);
    public void setDisplayBounds(QDRect bounds);
    public void setGWorld(QDGraphics cgp);
    public void setLocation(int x, int y);
    public void setMatrix(Matrix matrix);
    public boolean setMemberAlignment(QTDrawable d, float xAlign, float yAlign);
    public boolean setMemberLayer(QTDrawable member, int layer);
    public int size();
//protected
    protected void setAlignedMemberLocation(QTDrawable drawer, float xAlign,
                                 float yAlign);
}
```

CLASS HIERARCHY:

Object→SimpleSpace→GroupDrawable

Class quicktime.app.display.GroupMember

This class contains information on QTDrawable objects that are attached to a GroupDrawable object.

```
public class GroupMember extends Object implements Layerable {
//Constructors
//protected
    protected GroupMember(GroupDrawable group, QTDrawable d, int l);

//Instance Methods
    public boolean equals(Object obj);
    public final QTDrawable getDrawer();
    public int getLayer();
    public void setLayer(int l);
    public String toString();
}
```

CLASS HIERARCHY:

Object→GroupMember

Interface quicktime.app.display.Layerable

This is an interface for handling display objects that are members of QTDisplaySpace objects. Using this interface shields both the group and its members from a required implementation of layer characteristics. Thus, the group may use a helper object to contain and manage layers of members, or it may keep the layering information internally and provide a helper object that is not the member itself as the object that will be able to set and get the layer information for a member.

getLayer() returns the current layer of the Layerable object. setLayer() sets the new layer of the Layerable object.

```
public interface Layerable {
//Static Fields
    public static final int kBackMostLayer;

//Instance Methods
    public abstract int getLayer();
    public abstract void setLayer(int layer);
}
```

Class quicktime.app.display.QTCanvas

This class, which is a subclass of java.awt.Canvas, is a specialized canvas that supplies access to the native QuickTime graphics environment and offers expanded display functionality. The QTCanvas object can display any object that implements the Drawable interface.

getClient() returns the Drawable object currently associated with this QTCanvas. getNGLocation() returns the coordinates of a component relative to the native graphics window it is currently placed within. getResizeFlag() returns the current setting of the resize flag being used. removeClient() removes the current client of the canvas.

The setClient() method associates a new client, a Drawable object, with this QTCanvas. A layout flag determines if awt will perform a layout and how the client will be integrated with the canvas. If the flag is false, the new client will take on the current size and position of the canvas. If the flag is true, then awt will lay out the canvas again, using the initial size of the client and the resize flags to resize the canvas and its client. This method can throw a number of exceptions:

- QTUnknownOSException—your application is trying to run on a platform not supported by QuickTime.

- NativeGraphicsException—the native graphics environment is not initialized.

- QTException or subclass—there was a problem within the QuickTime client.

Note that the update() method is overridden, since the background color repaint is not valid for a QTCanvas object.

See also Drawable and QTDrawable.

```java
public class QTCanvas extends Canvas implements Errors {
//Static Fields
    public static final int kAspectResize;
    public static final int kFreeResize;
    public static final int kHorizontalResize;
    public static final int kInitialSize;
    public static final int kIntegralResize;
    public static final int kPerformanceResize;
    public static final int kVerticalResize;

//Constructors
    public QTCanvas();
    public QTCanvas(int resizeFlag, float xAlignment, float yAlignment);

//Instance Methods
    public synchronized void addNotify();
    public void addQTClientListener(ComponentListener e);
    public void clientChanged(int bestWidth, int bestHeight);
    public void clientChanged(Dimension bestSize);
    public float getAlignmentX();
    public float getAlignmentY();
    public Dimension getBestSize();
    public final Drawable getClient();
    public Dimension getMaximumSize();
    public Dimension getMinimumSize();
    public final Point getNGLocation();
    public final NativeGraphics getNativeGraphics();
    public final QDGraphics getPort();
    public Dimension getPreferredSize();
    public int getResizeFlag();
    public void paint(Graphics g);
    public final synchronized void removeClient();
    public synchronized void removeNotify();
    public void removeQTClientListener(ComponentListener e);
    public final void reshape(int x, int y, int width, int height);
    public void setAlignment(float xAlignment, float yAlignment);
    public final void setAlignmentX(float x);
    public final void setAlignmentY(float y);
    public final synchronized void setBounds(int x, int y, int width, int height);
    public synchronized void setClient(Drawable client, boolean layoutFlag);
    public synchronized void setClient(Drawable client, QDRect initialBounds);
    public void setMaximumSize(Dimension maxSize);
    public void setMaximumSize(int width, int height);
    public void setMinimumSize(int width, int height);
    public void setMinimumSize(Dimension minSize);
    public void setPreferredSize(Dimension prefSize);
```

```
    public void setPreferredSize(int width, int height);
    public void setResizeFlag(int rFlag);
    public void setSize(Dimension dim);
    public void setSize(int width, int height);
    public synchronized void setVisible(boolean b);
    public String toString();
    public final QDPoint translatePoint(int x, int y);
    public void update(Graphics g);
//protected
    protected void finalize();
}
```

CLASS HIERARCHY:

Object→Component→Canvas→QTCanvas

Interface quicktime.app.display.QTDisplaySpace

This interface defines the minimum API that a QTDisplaySpace provides. That is, a QTDisplaySpace is some kind of QTDrawable so it can be set as a client for a QTCanvas object and is a collection of members that draw within its confines.

Since a display space is by definition a collection of objects that have some kind of visual appearance, the display space must manage the layering of those objects within the visual presentation of the space. As such, this interface provides an API for retrieving the current frontmost and backmost layers of its members and a way of retrieving the Layerable object for a member that allow your application to both get and set its layer within a display space. Also, a member can be added to the display space specifying the layer at which it should be added. The lower a layer (or z) value, the further to the front the object is displayed. The backmost layer of a QTDisplaySpace is Short.MAX_VALUE, the Layerable.kBackMostLayer value.

Members of display spaces may or may not know about their position and two-dimensional display matrix. As such, the QTDisplaySpace also provides an API for retrieving a member's Transformable interface that allows a member to get and set its display matrix.

getLayerable() returns the Layerable object for a member (or null if the object is not a member) that allows your application to get and set the layer of a member. This may or may not be the member itself, depending both on the type of object the member is and the manner in which the QTDisplaySpace handles the Layer property of its members.

getTransformable() returns the Transformable object that represents the member in the DisplaySpace. The Transformable object allows the application to get and set the two-dimensional display characteristics of a member (i.e., position, size, rotation, skewing, and perspective). If the object is not a member of the Space, this returns null. This may or may not return the member itself, based on the type of the member and how the Space deals with the two-dimensional placement and display of its members.

addMember() adds a member to the QTDisplaySpace at the specified layer. If the member is not an appropriate type of object for the Space, this method returns false, and the member is not added.

See also Transformable, Layerable.

```
public interface QTDisplaySpace extends QTDrawable, Space {
//Instance Methods
    public abstract boolean addMember(Object member, int layer);
    public abstract int getBackLayer();
    public abstract int getFrontLayer();
    public abstract Layerable getLayerable(Object member);
    public abstract Transformable getTransformable(Object member);
}
```

Interface quicktime.app.display.QTDrawable

This interface is designed to work hand-in-hand with a QTCanvas object. The class that implements this interface draws into the supplied QDGraphics. If the class is set as a client of a QTCanvas, the QTCanvas itself sets this property in the normal course of its existence; in this case, your application never needs to call these methods of the QTDrawable object directly.

The QTDrawable interface specifically defines an interface for QuickTime objects that require a destination QDGraphics in order to draw. If the incoming QDGraphics is the QDGraphics.scratch, then the QTDrawable is not visible and can disable itself. If a client is unable to set the graphics world, it should throw an exception. QTExceptions can be thrown by any of these methods and, if thrown, indicate that either the graphics environment has changed in some unexpected way or that the media object itself is in some unexpected state.

QTCanvas calls the getGWorld() method to get the destination QDGraphics of its QuickTime client.

```
public interface QTDrawable extends Drawable, Transformable {
//Instance Methods
```

```
    public abstract Region getClip();
    public abstract QDGraphics getGWorld();
    public abstract void setClip(Region theClip);
    public abstract void setGWorld(QDGraphics cgp);
    public abstract void setLocation(int x, int y);
}
```

22

The quicktime. app.image Package

The `quicktime.app.image` package contains a large number of classes that are among the most useful in the QuickTime for Java API. The purpose of this package is to handle the presentation of images within a Java display space. Included are utility routines for setting transparent colors in images, applying visual effects, and creating objects for handling sequences of images and `QTDrawable` objects that read image data from a file or load the data into memory.

The `QTImageDrawer` class enables standard Java drawing commands and graphics objects to have their content rendered by QuickTime within a QuickTime graphics space. Standard AWT `paint` calls can be made on the graphics object supplied to the `paint()` call of the `Paintable` interface that is attached to the `QTImageDrawer`. The `QTImageDrawer` implements the `Compositable` interface so it can be added to the `quicktime.app.display.Compositor` object and thus be used to draw into the same display space as QuickTime-generated content.

The `QTImageProducer` class implements the `java.awt.image.ImageProducer` interface for a single-source QuickTime object. The QuickTime source can be a single frame (i.e., a still image) or a multiple-frame source, such as a movie, sprite world, or animation. The `QTImageProducer` can be used to produce images for multiple `ImageConsumer` objects.

You can use the `QTTransition` class to apply visual effects to two images, transitioning from the source to the destination image. Figure 22.1 shows the class hierarchy for this package. See Chapter 7, "QuickTime and Java Imaging and Effects," for more information on using images within a Java display space.

FIGURE 22.1 *The* `quicktime.app.image` *package*

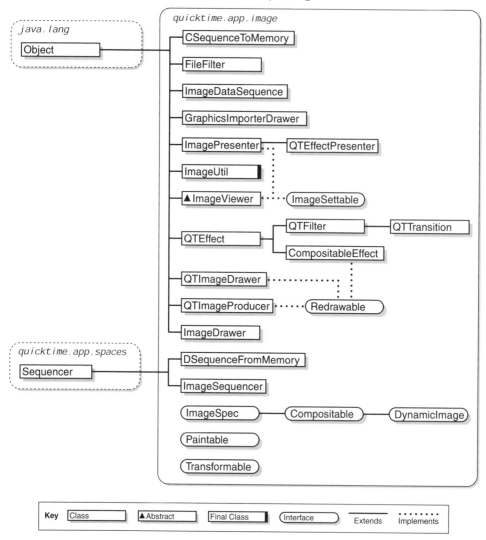

Interface quicktime.app.image.Compositable

A `Compositable` object is an object that is able to apply graphics mode operations to its image data.

```
public interface Compositable extends ImageSpec {
//Instance Methods
    public abstract GraphicsMode getGraphicsMode();
    public abstract void setGraphicsMode(GraphicsMode gMode);
}
```

Class quicktime.app.image.CompositableEffect

This class is used to directly add an effect to a SWCompositor. Only effects of zero source (such as fire or ripple) can be added directly. Filters and transitions act on one or two sources and must be added to a SWCompositor using the QTEffectPresenter.

See also QTEffectPresenter.

```
public class CompositableEffect extends QTEffect implements DynamicImage, Redrawable {
//Constructors
    public CompositableEffect();
    public CompositableEffect(int multiFrameFlag);

//Instance Methods
    public Invalidator addedToCompositor(SWCompositor c, TwoDSprite s);
    public void removedFromCompositor(SWCompositor c);
}
```

CLASS HIERARCHY:

Object→QTEffect→CompositableEffect

Class quicktime.app.image.CSequenceToMemory

This class provides a mechanism for compressing a sequence of images to memory. The compressed images are maintained internally. Use the DSequenceFromMemory class to decompress a sequence of images from a CSequenceToMemory object.

When compressing a sequence of images that you want to keep in memory, you would use the compressFrame() method. This class handles the memory that the compressed image is loaded into. If you call one of the CSequence compressFrame calls, this class does *not* know about the compressed data. See also DSequenceFromMemory.

The CSequenceToMemory(int) constructor creates an instance of this class in order to compress a sequence of frames and store them in memory. You must call begin() before you use any other methods. The begin() method signals the beginning of the process of compressing a sequence of frames. The begin() method is called for you by the second constructor. You call the compressFrame() method to compress one of a sequence of frames. The similarity value is directly returned by this method. The getDescription() method returns an ImageDescription that describes the image data that the class contains.

```
public class CSequenceToMemory extends Object {
//Constructors
    public CSequenceToMemory(int numFrames);
    public CSequenceToMemory(QDGraphics src, QDRect srcRect, int depth, int cType,
                     CodecComponent codec, int spatialQuality, int temporalQuality,
                     int keyFrameRate, ColorTable cTab, int flags);

//Instance Methods
    public void begin(QDGraphics src, QDRect srcRect, int colorDepth, int cType,
                     CodecComponent codec, int spatialQuality, int temporalQuality,
                     int keyFrameRate, ColorTable clut, int flags);
    public int compressFrame(QDGraphics src, QDRect srcRect, int flags);
    public ImageDescription getDescription();
    public CSequence getSequence();
}
```

CLASS HIERARCHY:

Object→CSequenceToMemory

Class quicktime.app.image.DSequenceFromMemory

This class provides a mechanism for decompressing a sequence of images that were previously compressed using the CSequenceToMemory class.

The decompressed sequence is accomplished with a number of default settings:

- It uses no matrix and no mask region.

- It uses ditherCopy as its transfer mode, and it does not use an off-screen buffer or image buffer but writes directly to its destination.

The DSequenceFromMemory() constructor creates a DSequence object from a single piece of data and its description. It will *not* copy the incoming image but merely add it to the internal data storage.

The Movie Toolbox handles the details of decompressing image sequences in QuickTime movies. If you need to decompress other sequences compressed via the CSequenceToMemory class, you can create an instance of this DSequenceFromMemory class.

QTCanvas **calls the** setGWorld() **method to give the** QTDrawable **client the** QDGraphics **object it should draw into.**

See also CSequenceFromMemory.

```
public class DSequenceFromMemory extends Sequencer
                          implements QTDrawable, DynamicImage, StdQTConstants {
//Constructors
    public DSequenceFromMemory(GraphicsImporter importer);
    public DSequenceFromMemory(EncodedImage data, ImageDescription description);
    public DSequenceFromMemory(CSequenceToMemory sequenceInMemory);
    public DSequenceFromMemory(ImageSpec spec);

//Instance Fields
    public int flags;

//Instance Methods
    public void addedTo(Object interest);
    public Invalidator addedToCompositor(SWCompositor c, TwoDSprite s);
    public int drawCurrentFrame(int inFlags);
    public Region getClip();
    public ImageDescription getDescription();
    public QDRect getDisplayBounds();
    public QDGraphics getGWorld();
    public GraphicsMode getGraphicsMode();
    public EncodedImage getImage();
    public Dimension getInitialSize();
    public Matrix getMatrix();
    public DSequence getSequence();
    public final synchronized void redraw(Region invalidRgn);
    public void removedFrom(Object interest);
    public void removedFromCompositor(SWCompositor c);
    public void setClip(Region reg);
    public void setDisplayBounds(QDRect bounds);
    public void setGWorld(QDGraphics cgp);
    public void setGraphicsMode(GraphicsMode mode);
    public void setLocation(int x, int y);
    public void setMatrix(Matrix matrix);
    public int size();
    public String toString();
}
```

CLASS HIERARCHY:

Object→Sequencer→DSequenceFromMemory

Interface quicktime.app.image.DynamicImage

This class enables members of a SWCompositor that presents an image that changes to explicitly invalidate the TwoDSprite that is their presenter in the SWCompositor. This is a requirement of the SWCompositor, due to efficiencies in the composite cycle.

The addedToCompositor() method returns an object that invalidates a sprite. When a DynamicImage is a member of a SWCompositor and the DynamicImage presents a changing image (for example, a movie), the TwoDSprite that presents that image in the SWCompositor must be invalidated so that it will redraw the sprite's image in the next composite cycle. The Invalidator object is used to perform this function by the SWCompositor if the object itself cannot perform the invalidation. It can return null if the DynamicImage does not require the SWCompositor to invalidate it or if the object is in a state where its image won't change.

The invalidators provided with objects that implement the DynamicImage interface will execute at the scale and period of the Compositor. When a dynamic image class is removed from a SWCompositor, the removedFromCompositor() method is called to allow the class to clean up any objects it had allocated in the addedToCompositor() call.

```
public interface DynamicImage extends Compositable {
//Instance Methods
    public abstract Invalidator addedToCompositor(SWCompositor c, TwoDSprite s);
    public abstract void removedFromCompositor(SWCompositor c);
}
```

Class quicktime.app.image.FileFilter

This class is used by the ImageUtil.createSequence call to filter the contents of a directory and return true to those files that match the pattern it expects. After the files are selected, the array of accepted filenames is submitted to the postProcess() method, which returns an array of filenames. The filenames are then used to create a sequence of images in the order of the files in this array.

The filename format that this filter expects is as follows:

- Both prefix and suffix can be empty, but there must be at least one numeric character in the name of the file.

- No sorting is performed on the resulting file list, so generally the files are opened and added to the sequence in alpha/numeric order. For files to appear in proper numeric order, you need to specify leading zeroes in the frame numbers if required.

■ You can also pass in a boolean flag to indicate that the filter should ignore the suffix of the filename when matching.

■ Subclasses can override or extend the methods to provide custom filtering operations.

The extractPrefixAndSuffix() method dissects the incoming fName (the name of a file) into a prefix, which are all the characters of the file name that precede the last occurrence of a number in the filename and a suffix the extracts the characters that immediately follow the last occurrence of a number in the fName. It stores the result of these into the instance variables prefix and suffix, respectively. Subclasses can overwrite this to produce their own semantic for extracting a prefix and suffix—they need to ensure that the instance variables are set with the appropriate values.

testFrameNumber() tests the frame number portion of the filename. If this string does *not* have a number, it will throw a NumberFormatException. It returns the resulting number. accept() is used by the createSequence call to filter the files found in the supplied directory. It returns true if the filename matches the conditions (prefix and suffix are found in the file, and between these there is a number). Both prefix and suffix can be empty, but the frame number is required.

postProcess() is called after the directory has been filtered. The incoming array contains the file list (i.e., files found within the directory that have been accepted as a match) and the order of the files in this list is the order that the files will be added to the sequence. The method can alter this array (or return a new one). The returned array should contain no null values, and the order of the filenames in the returned array is the order that the files will be added to the sequence.

```
public class FileFilter extends Object implements FilenameFilter {
//Constructors
    public FileFilter(boolean testSuffix);
    public FileFilter();

//Instance Fields
//protected
    protected String prefix;
    protected String suffix;
    protected boolean testSuffix;

//Instance Methods
    public boolean accept(File dir, String fName);
```

```
//protected
    protected void extractPrefixAndSuffix(String fName);
    protected String[] postProcess(String[] matchedFiles);
    protected int testFrameNumber(String fName);
}
```

CLASS HIERARCHY:

Object→FileFilter

Class quicktime.app.image.GraphicsImporterDrawer

This class represents an image that is stored as a file that can be read and drawn using the QuickTime graphics importer component.

See also GraphicsImporter.

```
public class GraphicsImporterDrawer extends Object
                              implements QTDrawable, Compositable, StdQTConstants {
//Constructors
    public GraphicsImporterDrawer(GraphicsImporter gi);
    public GraphicsImporterDrawer(QTFile file);
    public GraphicsImporterDrawer(DataRef dataRef);

//Instance Methods
    public void addedTo(Object interest);
    public Region getClip();
    public ImageDescription getDescription();
    public QDRect getDisplayBounds();
    public QDGraphics getGWorld();
    public GraphicsMode getGraphicsMode();
    public EncodedImage getImage();
    public GraphicsImporter getImporter();
    public Dimension getInitialSize();
    public Matrix getMatrix();
    public final synchronized void redraw(Region invalidRgn);
    public void removedFrom(Object interest);
    public void setClip(Region reg);
    public void setDisplayBounds(QDRect bounds);
    public void setGWorld(QDGraphics cgp);
    public void setGraphicsMode(GraphicsMode gMode);
    public void setLocation(int x, int y);
    public void setMatrix(Matrix matrix);
    public String toString();
}
```

CLASS HIERARCHY:

Object→GraphicsImporterDrawer

Class quicktime.app.image.ImageDataSequence

This is a container class for an ordered collection of objects having a single image description and a sequence of picture data. This collection is a 1-based collection.

The append() method adds the image description object to the end of the collection.

getDescription() returns the ImageDescription object that describes the image data in this sequence, while getImage(int) returns the actual image data at the specified index. getNth() gets the image data object at the given position. getSize() determines the number of items. insert() adds the image data object at the specified index. isEmpty() checks if the sequence has any elements. prepend() adds the image description object as the first item in the collection. remove() removes the object at the specified index. removeFirst() removes the object at the specified index.

setDescription() sets the ImageDescription object that describes how the image data objects are to be interpreted by QuickTime.

```
public class ImageDataSequence extends Object implements ImageSpec, Collection {
//Constructors
    public ImageDataSequence();
    public ImageDataSequence(ImageDescription desc);

//Instance Methods
    public boolean addMember(Object member);
    public void addToMovie(Movie theMovie, float framesPerSecond);
    public void append(EncodedImage image);
    public ImageDescription getDescription();
    public EncodedImage getImage();
    public EncodedImage getImage(int index);
    public EncodedImage getNth(int index);
    public boolean hasMember(Object object);
    public void insert(EncodedImage image, int index);
    public boolean isAppropriate(Object object);
    public boolean isEmpty();
    public Enumeration members();
    public void prepend(EncodedImage image);
    public void remove(int i);
    public void removeAll();
    public void removeFirst();
    public void removeLast();
    public void removeMember(Object member);
    public ImageSequencer sequence();
    public void setDescription(ImageDescription desc);
    public int size();
    public String toString();
}
```

CLASS HIERARCHY:

Object→ImageDataSequence

Class quicktime.app.image.ImageDrawer

This class presents a normal java.awt.Image object as a client of the QTCanvas.

The ImageDrawer() constructor makes a default ImageDrawer that will draw nothing as it has no image to present nor a component to present in. The getQTLogo() method returns an ImageDrawer object that presents the standard QuickTime logo. QT-Canvas calls the redraw() method when the client should redraw itself. If the canvas is able to discern that only a part of the client's drawing area needs to be redrawn, then this area shall be passed in using the invalidRgn. Otherwise, this will be null, in which case the client should redraw itself entirely.

```
public class ImageDrawer extends Object implements Drawable {
//Constructors
    public ImageDrawer();
    public ImageDrawer(Dimension initialSize, Image image);

//Static Methods
    public static final ImageDrawer getQTLogo();

//Instance Fields
//protected
    protected Component canv;
    protected Image im;

//Instance Methods
    public void addedTo(Object interest);
    public QDRect getDisplayBounds();
    public Image getImage();
    public void redraw(Region invalidRgn);
    public void removedFrom(Object interest);
    public void setDisplayBounds(QDRect bounds);
}
```

CLASS HIERARCHY:

Object→ImageDrawer

Class quicktime.app.image.ImagePresenter

This class represents an image that is loaded into memory. Its focus is on performance, so if the image data presented to the ImagePresenter is in a format that is non-optimal for drawing, the data is converted to a format that is optimal—at the expense of a greater memory usage.

An ImagePresenter can be made from a number of sources:

- from a file where the file's contents are imported using the Graphics-Importer and then loaded and perhaps converted into memory

- from a QDGraphics object, where the pixel data is used directly on the image data and an ImageDescription is created (by the Image-Presenter) to describe the format of the data

- from a single image data object that is stored in an ImageData-Sequence object

- from any object that implements the ImageSpec interface and thus can return image data and an ImageDescription that describes this data

- from a PICT

- from any encoded image data and an ImageDescription that describes the format of this image data. This option allows an application to fill in values of an Integer or ByteEncoded object directly and have QuickTime render these.

Once the ImagePresenter is created, the standard QuickTime matrix transformations and graphics modes can be applied to the drawn representation of the image data.

```
public class ImagePresenter extends Object
            implements QTDrawable, Compositable, ImageSettable, StdQTConstants,
QDConstants {
//Constructors
    public ImagePresenter(QDRect initialSize);

//Static Methods
    public static ImagePresenter fromFile(QTFile qtFile);
    public static ImagePresenter fromGWorld(QDGraphics grafPort);
    public static ImagePresenter fromGWorld(QDGraphics port, QDRect rect,
            int colorDepth, int quality, int codecType, CodecComponent codec);
    public static ImagePresenter fromGraphicsImporter(GraphicsImporter importer);
    public static ImagePresenter fromGraphicsImporterDrawer(
                                    GraphicsImporterDrawer imageFile);
```

```
    public static ImagePresenter fromImageSequence(ImageDataSequence image, int nth);
    public static ImagePresenter fromImageSpec(ImageSpec image);
    public static ImagePresenter fromPict(Pict p);
    public static ImagePresenter fromQTImage(EncodedImage data, ImageDescription desc);

//Instance Methods
    public void addedTo(Object interest);
    public Region getClip();
    public DSequence getDSequence();
    public ImageDescription getDescription();
    public QDRect getDisplayBounds();
    public QDGraphics getGWorld();
    public GraphicsMode getGraphicsMode();
    public EncodedImage getImage();
    public Dimension getInitialSize();
    public Matrix getMatrix();
    public boolean isRedrawOptimised ();
    public synchronized void redraw(Region invalidRgn);
    public void removeImageData();
    public void removedFrom(Object interest);
    public synchronized void setClip(Region reg);
    public void setDisplayBounds(QDRect bounds);
    public void setGWorld(QDGraphics cgp);
    public void setGraphicsMode(GraphicsMode mode);
    public void setImageData(EncodedImage data, ImageDescription desc);
    public void setImageData(EncodedImage ei);
    public void setLocation(int x, int y);
    public void setMatrix(Matrix matrix);
    public void setRedrawOptimised (boolean flag);
    public String toString();
//protected
    protected final void doDraw();
}
```

CLASS HIERARCHY:

Object→ImagePresenter

Class quicktime.app.image.ImageSequencer

This class handles the obtaining of a specific frame of data and its accompanying description from an ImageDataSequence object.

See also Sequencer.

```
public class ImageSequencer extends Sequencer implements ImageSpec {
//Constructors
    public ImageSequencer(ImageDataSequence images);
```

```
//Instance Methods
    public ImageDescription getDescription();
    public EncodedImage getImage();
    public ImageDataSequence getImageData();
    public void setImageData(ImageDataSequence images);
    public int size();
    public String toString();
}
```

CLASS HIERARCHY:

Object→Sequencer→ImageSequencer

Interface quicktime.app.image.ImageSettable

This interface is used so that objects can have their images flipped to a particular image in their sequence of images.

Use setDisplayedImage() to make the object's current image the specified image.

```
public interface ImageSettable {
//Instance Methods
    public abstract void setImageData (EncodedImage imageData,
                                       ImageDescription desc);
}
```

Interface quicktime.app.image.ImageSpec

Every class that implements this interface holds a common description of one or more image data frames.

getDescription() returns an ImageDescription that describes the image data that the class contains. getImage() returns the actual image data. If the ImageSpec object represents a collection of image data, then getImage() is defined to return that collection's default or current image data object.

```
public interface ImageSpec {
//Instance Methods
    public abstract ImageDescription getDescription();
    public abstract EncodedImage getImage();
}
```

Class quicktime.app.image.ImageUtil

This class provides some utility routines for dealing with images.

The makeTransparent() methods take an ImageSpec object and recompress the images so that the images have the keyColor set as a transparent color that will not draw. It uses the animation codec to do this, and there is no loss in quality. This uses the depth of the source image to map the color into. The makeTransparent() methods can also be used to specify a hit-test region for the image that is different from the transparent areas of the image. If you want to create a hit-test region on some image data without making it transparent, you can specify a keyColor that is not part of the ImageData. In this case, a hit-test region will be created.

If your application does not want any transparency but does want a hit-test region on some ImageData, then it specifies a keyColor that is not in the image data and a hit-test region.

The createSequence() methods create an ImageDataSequence object from either a collection of files in the specified directory that conform to the pattern of the specified filename or data contained in the specified track of a movie. The default FileFilter object is passed in as the filter that can be used by an application in the file matching process.

```
public final class ImageUtil extends Object
                         implements StdQTConstants, Errors, QDConstants {
//Static Fields
    public static final int kHitTestRgnSrc;

//Static Methods
    public static ImageDataSequence createSequence(File matchFile);
    public static ImageDataSequence createSequence(File matchFile, FileFilter ff);
    public static ImageDataSequence createSequence(Track imageTrack);
    public static ImageDataSequence makeTransparent(ImageSpec image, QDColor keyColor);
    public static ImageDataSequence makeTransparent(ImageSpec image, QDColor keyColor,
                         QDGraphics gw);
    public static ImageDataSequence makeTransparent(ImageSpec image, QDColor keyColor,
                         QDGraphics gw, Region r);
    public static ImageDataSequence makeTransparent(ImageDataSequence image,
                         QDColor keyColor, QDGraphics gw, Region[] r);
}
```

CLASS HIERARCHY:

Object→ImageUtil

Class quicktime.app.image.ImageViewer

This class presents a sequence of images that a user can view one at a time. It takes an ImageSequencer object as the source for its images and uses an ImagePresenter object internally to present the current image.

The class is abstract, requiring the subclass to define how the current image of the sequence is selected. For example, your application might have a user click the Image-Viewer to go to the next image, click next/previous buttons, and so on. Your application could also place a QTTransition between the current and next image.

```
public abstract class ImageViewer extends Object implements QTDrawable, ImageSettable {
//Constructors
    public ImageViewer(ImageSequencer images);

//Instance Fields
//protected
    protected ImagePresenter imagePresenter;

//Instance Methods
    public void addedTo(Object interest);
    public Region getClip();
    public QDRect getDisplayBounds();
    public QDGraphics getGWorld();
    public GraphicsMode getGraphicsMode();
    public ImageSequencer getImages();
    public Dimension getInitialSize();
    public Matrix getMatrix();
    public final synchronized void redraw(Region invalidRgn);
    public void removedFrom(Object interest);
    public void setClip(Region theClip);
    public void setDisplayBounds(QDRect bounds);
    public void setImageData(EncodedImage imageData, ImageDescription desc);
    public void setGWorld(QDGraphics cgp);
    public void setGraphicsMode(GraphicsMode mode);
    public void setImages(ImageSequencer images);
    public void setLocation(int x, int y);
    public void setMatrix(Matrix matrix);
}
```

CLASS HIERARCHY:

Object→ImageViewer

Interface quicktime.app.image.Paintable

The Paintable interface is implemented by a class that uses Java's drawing services to produce pixel data drawn by QuickTime. The Paintable object is attached to a QT-ImageDrawer that calls the paint method of the Paintable object and then uses Java's PixelGrabber to obtain the pixels that the paint call of the Paintable object generated. You should not call Paintable methods directly but instead interact with these methods through the QTImageDrawer.

Standard AWT paint calls can be performed on the graphics object passed in the paint call, with the rendered image being drawn by QuickTime. QTImageDrawer of the Paintable tells the paintable object the size of its available drawing surface. Any drawing done outside of these bounds (originating at 0,0) will be clipped.

The paint() method paints on the Graphics context, and the image painted is then rendered by QuickTime. You can supply an array of rectangles that tell the QTImage-Drawer which parts of the image were changed by this call. Only the pixels that are within these rectangles will be changed in the pixel data drawn by the QTImageDrawer.

Typically, your first call to paint() after being notified of a new size will return a rectangle that covers the entire image, with subsequent calls having the option of returning rectangles that describe only those regions of the pixel data that have changed. Returning null indicates that no pixel data has changed. Intelligent use of this can improve drawing performance.

See also QTImageDrawer.

```
public interface Paintable {
//Instance Methods
    public abstract void newSizeNotified(QTImageDrawer drawer, Dimension d);
    public abstract Rectangle[] paint(Graphics g);
}
```

Class quicktime.app.image.QTEffect

This class forms the base class for visual effects. Depending on the effect itself, visual effects can be applied over a length of time, or once only. They can be applied to no source images (i.e., a background QDGraphics), a single image, or multiple images.

The QTEffect class itself will, given a rectangular region, apply some visual effect (like fire or ripples). There are two subclasses: QTFilter, which is an effect applied to a single source image, and QTTransition, which is an effect applied to two separate images, transitioning from the source to the destination image over a period of time.

The setGraphicsMode() method sets the GraphicsMode for the QTEffect when it draws its contents to its destination QDGraphics. getEffect() returns a copy of the atom container that contains the current effect settings. You can alter the values of this container, but you must call setEffect() for those new values to be used by the effect. setEffect() takes the incoming parameters and uses these as the control parameters for the effect. The container will be locked for the duration of the effect object's life or until another effect is set.

```
public class QTEffect extends Object
               implements QTDrawable, Redrawable, StdQTConstants, QDConstants, Errors {
//Constructors
    public QTEffect();
    public QTEffect(Dimension d);
    public QTEffect(int multiFrameFlag);
    public QTEffect(int multiFrameFlag, Dimension d);

//Instance Methods
    public void addedTo(Object interest);
    public void checkForEffect(int effectType);
    public Region getClip();
    public int getCurrentFrame();
    public DSequence getDSequence();
    public ImageDescription getDescription();
    public QDRect getDisplayBounds();
    public AtomContainer getEffect();
    public int getFrames();
    public synchronized QDGraphics getGWorld();
    public GraphicsMode getGraphicsMode();
    public EncodedImage getImage();
    public Dimension getInitialSize();
    public Matrix getMatrix();
    public boolean isRedrawing();
    public boolean isSingleFrame();
    public synchronized void redraw(Region invalidRgn);
    public void removedFrom(Object interest);
    public void setClip(Region r);
    public synchronized void setDisplayBounds(QDRect bounds);
    public void setEffect(AtomContainer effectParams);
    public synchronized void setGWorld(QDGraphics cgp);
    public void setGraphicsMode(GraphicsMode mode);
    public void setLocation(int x, int y);
    public void setMatrix(Matrix matrix);
    public void setRedrawing(boolean redrawFlag);
//protected
    protected synchronized boolean setUpSequence();
}
```

CLASS HIERARCHY:

Object→QTEffect

Class quicktime.app.image.QTEffectPresenter

This class is typically used to present a QTFilter or QTTransition as a member of a SWCompositor. It creates an Invalidator based on whether the effect is a single or multiframed effect, and the Invalidator will redraw the effect based on the effect's current isRedrawing value. If the effect is redrawn, the TwoDSprite presenting the effect in the SWCompositor will be invalidated to update the image it is presenting.

See also SWCompositor.

```
public class QTEffectPresenter extends ImagePresenter implements DynamicImage {
//Constructors
    public QTEffectPresenter(QTEffect ef);
    public QTEffectPresenter(QTEffect ef, QDGraphics g);

//Instance Methods
    public Invalidator addedToCompositor(SWCompositor c, TwoDSprite s);
    public QTEffect getEffect();
    public void redraw(Region invalidRgn);
    public void removedFromCompositor(SWCompositor c);
}
```

CLASS HIERARCHY:

Object→ImagePresenter→QTEffectPresenter

Class quicktime.app.image.QTFilter

This class represents visual effects applied to a single source image. They inherit much of the characteristics of the QTEffect class.

getInitialSize() returns the original size before the transformations specified in the returned matrix are applied. getSourceImage() returns the currently set source image of the QTFilter. The setEffect() method takes the incoming parameters and uses them as the control parameters for the effect. setSourceImage() sets the QuickTime source of the QTFilter, which is the image that the current filter will be applied to when the QTFilter is redrawn.

```
public class QTFilter extends QTEffect {
//Constructors
```

```
    public QTFilter();
    public QTFilter(Dimension d);
    public QTFilter(int isSingleFrame);
    public QTFilter(int isSingleFrame, Dimension d);
//Instance Methods
    public Dimension getInitialSize();
    public ImageSpec getSourceImage();
    public void setEffect(AtomContainer effectParams);
    public void setSourceImage(ImageSpec image);
//protected
    protected synchronized boolean setUpSequence();
}
```

CLASS HIERARCHY:

Object→QTEffect→QTFilter

Class quicktime.app.image.QTImageDrawer

This class enables standard Java drawing commands and graphics objects to have their content rendered by QuickTime within a QuickTime graphics space. The QT-ImageDrawer is a parent container for an object that implements the Paintable interface—which is the object that actually does the drawing using standard java.awt paint commands and graphics objects. The QTImageDrawer implements the DynamicImage interface so it can be added to the quicktime.app.display.Compositor object and thus used to draw into the same display space as other QuickTime-generated content. It can also be a direct client of a QTCanvas.

The isSingleFrame flag specified in the constructor allows optimizations to be made by the QTImageDrawer. If this flag is set to Redrawable.kSingleFrame, then the QT-ImageDrawer will only call its Paintable object once to capture the image its Paintable draws. If kMultiFrame is set, the acquired objects are not discarded, as it is assumed that the Paintable object will present a changing image.

If the QTImageDrawer is a member of the SWCompositor, a similar efficiency can be achieved. If kSingleFrame is specified, then when the drawer is added to the Compositor, it does not require invalidation, and so it does not create an invalidator as its image data is static. If kMultiFrame is specified, then an invalidator is created.

Your application can explicitly call prepaint(), which is the method that calls the Paintable paint() method at any time. If the application is itself controlling the prepaint call, then it will probably want to set and reset the isRedrawing flag , as the redraw() method determines whether to call prepaint or not based on the value of this flag. Once image data has been captured using the prepaint call, to see the results in a destination QDGraphics, the redraw() method must be called. Thus, if an application is calling prepaint itself, it will likely want to then use the setRedrawing method to set redrawing false and would only require redrawing to be set to true if it requires any consequent calls of the redraw() method to recapture image data from the prepaint() call.

The Invalidator determines if the QTImageDrawer requires redrawing and invalidation based on the value of the isRedrawing flag. It redraws and invalidates if isRedrawing returns true. If the application is controlling the prepaint calls (and thus would typically set redrawing to false), then it should invalidate the sprite presenter of the QTImageDrawer. isRedrawing can be set/reset at any time by an application to control this process.

The QTImageDrawer() constructor creates the QTImageDrawer object, which is the parent container of the Paintable object. You supply an initial size—which defines the drawing area that the paintable object has to draw into. Once created, a paintable object's drawing area cannot be resized in relationship to its parent container. If the display area of the QTImageDrawer is changed, then the image that the Paintable object paints will be scaled accordingly. toImagePresenter() returns an ImagePresenter object from the drawing that has been done by the Paintable object. This copies the image data that has been created.

See also Compositor, Paintable.

```
public class QTImageDrawer extends Object
                    implements Notifier, QTDrawable, DynamicImage,
                        Redrawable, QDConstants, StdQTConstants {
//Constructors
    public QTImageDrawer(Paintable painter, Dimension initialSize, int isSingleFrame);

//Instance Methods
    public boolean addNotifyListener(NotifyListener nl);
    public synchronized void addedTo(Object interest);
    public Invalidator addedToCompositor(SWCompositor c, TwoDSprite s);
    public final Region getClip();
    public ImageDescription getDescription();
    public QDRect getDisplayBounds();
    public final QDGraphics getGWorld();
    public GraphicsMode getGraphicsMode();
    public synchronized EncodedImage getImage();
    public Dimension getInitialSize();
    public final Matrix getMatrix();
```

```
    public Dimension getSize();
    public boolean isRedrawing();
    public boolean isSingleFrame();
    public Region prepaint();
    public synchronized void redraw(Region invalidRgn);
    public void removedFrom(Object interest);
    public void removedFromCompositor(SWCompositor c);
    public final void setClip(Region reg);
    public synchronized void setDisplayBounds(QDRect bounds);
    public void setGWorld(QDGraphics cgp);
    public void setGraphicsMode(GraphicsMode mode);
    public void setLocation(int x, int y);
    public final void setMatrix(Matrix matrix);
    public void setRedrawing(boolean redrawFlag);
    public ImagePresenter toImagePresenter();
}
```

CLASS HIERARCHY:

Object→QTImageDrawer

Class quicktime.app.image.QTImageProducer

This class implements the java.awt.image.ImageProducer interface for a single-source QuickTime object. The QuickTime source can be a single frame (i.e., still image) or a multiple-frame source such as a movie, sprite world animation, effect, and so on. The QTImageProducer can produce images for multiple ImageConsumer objects.

```
public class QTImageProducer extends Object
             implements ImageProducer, Redrawable, QDConstants, StdQTConstants {
//Constructors
    public QTImageProducer(QTDrawable qtSource, Dimension initSize);

//Instance Methods
    public synchronized void addConsumer(ImageConsumer ic);
    public Dimension getSize();
    public synchronized boolean isConsumer(ImageConsumer ic);
    public boolean isRedrawing();
    public boolean isSingleFrame();
    public synchronized void redraw(Region invalidRgn);
    public synchronized void removeConsumer(ImageConsumer ic);
    public void requestTopDownLeftRightResend(ImageConsumer ic);
    public synchronized void setRedrawing(boolean redrawFlag);
    public synchronized void startProduction(ImageConsumer ic);
    public synchronized void updateConsumers(Region invalidRgn);
}
```

CLASS HIERARCHY:
Object→QTImageProducer

Class quicktime.app.image.QTTransition

This class implements visual effects between two images and allows transitioning from the source to the destination image. On completion of the transition, the source and destination images are swapped, so you can also transition back to the original source image or set a new destination image.

The QTTransition can run in two modes. In *time mode* the doTransition() method runs the effect in as close as time as possible to the time specified. In *frames mode* the effect runs for the number of frames specified. doTransition() is provided as a means of running the transition according to the time or frames setting. The transition runs as effectively as possible from start to finish: it is a call that blocks the thread of execution that made this call while the transition is running.

If a transition is run with more application control, then the application can control the setting of the current frame of the transition and call redraw after setting each frame. The redraw() method redraws the current frame of the transition. The setEffect() method takes the incoming parameters and uses them as the control parameters for the effect. The container will be locked for the duration of the effect object's life or until another effect is set.

```
public class QTTransition extends QTFilter {
//Constructors
    public QTTransition();
    public QTTransition(Dimension d);

//Instance Methods
    public synchronized void doTime(boolean flag);
    public synchronized void doTransition();
    public ImageSpec getDestinationImage();
    public int getFramesPerSecond();
    public int getTime();
    public boolean isProfiled();
    public boolean isTime();
    public int profileDuration();
    public int profileFramesRendered();
    public void setCurrentFrame(int frame);
    public void setDestinationImage(ImageSpec image);
    public void setEffect(AtomContainer effectParams);
    public synchronized void setFrames(int frames);
    public void setFramesPerSecond(int frames);
```

```
   public void setProfiled(boolean flag);
   public synchronized void setTime(int time);
   public void swapImages();
//protected
   protected synchronized boolean setUpSequence();
}
```

CLASS HIERARCHY:

Object→QTEffect→QTFilter→QTTransition

Interface quicktime.app.image.Redrawable

This interface is used to describe objects that have image data that should be redrawn when a redraw call is issued.

Typically, if you have a static image, there is no extra work that has to be done once you have the image data: It can just be redrawn as is. However, there are some image objects that may have image data that could change, and therefore those objects should do the extra work in their redraw() method to get any potentially changing image data.

The two objects that implement this interface are the QTEffect and the QTImageDrawer: QTEffect, because they may or may not alter the pixel data depending on the type of the effect and the QTImageDrawer, depending on whether its Paintable client will paint a changing image.

The set() and isRedrawing() methods are used to control the redrawing characteristics of the Redrawable object. For instance, you may have an object that is a QTTransition, and while you are transitioning this object, you require that the redraw call redraws the current frame of the transition. So in this case setRedrawing() is set to true. Once the transition is complete and if the transition is now presenting a static image, there is no need to explicitly redraw the object.

The isSingleFrame() method determines if an Invalidator is created when the Redrawable is added to the Compositor. If the Redrawable is a single-frame object, then no Invalidator is created, since the Compositor assumes that the Redrawable is presenting a static image and thus requires no explicit invalidation. The isSingleFrame() method, however, has no actual effect on whether an object will redraw or not—just on the creation of the Invalidator.

See also QTEffect, QTImageDrawer, SWCompositor.

```
public interface Redrawable {
//Static Fields
    public static final int kMultiFrame;
    public static final int kSingleFrame;

//Instance Methods
    public abstract boolean isRedrawing();
    public abstract boolean isSingleFrame();
    public abstract void setRedrawing(boolean redrawFlag);
}
```

Interface quicktime.app.image.Transformable

This interface is used for objects that can have their visual appearance transformed through matrix manipulation. All QuickTime objects that draw can have their visual presentation altered by the application of a display Matrix.

The getMatrix() method returns the current matrix of the Transformable object, while setMatrix() sets the current matrix of the Transformable object to the new matrix. getInitialSize() returns the original size before the transformations specified in the returned matrix are applied.

```
public interface Transformable {
//Instance Methods
    public abstract Dimension getInitialSize();
    public abstract Matrix getMatrix();
    public abstract void setMatrix(Matrix matrix);
}
```

23

The quicktime. app.players Package

The `quicktime.app.players` package, though containing only three classes and one interface, is one of the most useful in the QuickTime for Java API. Both classes, the `QTPlayer` and `MoviePlayer`, define methods that enable you to present QuickTime movies in the `QTCanvas`.

Notably, the `MoviePlayer` class defines a large number of methods that enable you to display, play, and control any QuickTime movie. The `MoviePlayer` object works with the `QTCanvas` to be displayed in a Java AWT container.

The `QTPlayer` class, similar to the `MoviePlayer` class, also allows you to display, play, and control any QuickTime movie but with the standard QuickTime movie controller.

The `Playable` interface defines an important protocol for dealing with time-based media. It defines useful methods for getting and setting the duration, the current time position, and the playback rate of the media. It also lets you retrieve the time scale of the media, that is, the number of ticks per second.

Figure 23.1 shows the class hierarchy for this package. For more information on using the classes in this package, see Chapter 6, "QuickTime Media and Presenters."

FIGURE 23.1 *The* `quicktime.app.players` *package*

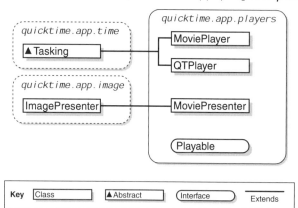

Class quicktime.app.players.MoviePlayer

This class allows your application to display, play, and control any QuickTime movie. The `MoviePlayer` object works with the `QTCanvas` object to be displayed in a Java AWT container.

The `task()` method performs idle processing for the `MoviePlayer` and will be automatically called if this object is added to the `TaskThread` object. `setTime()` sets the player to the time specified. This time value at this level is a totally arbitrary value: What time that means in "real time" is determined by the implementor of the interface; typically, the scale value will determine what a "real" time of 1 second is. `setRate()` sets the player to the playback rate. Typically, a rate of zero will mean that the player is stopped; a positive value that the player is playing forwards; a negative value that the player is playing backwards.

See also `QTCanvas`, `Movie`.

```
public class MoviePlayer extends Object implements QTDrawable, Playable, AudioSpec {
//Constructors
    public MoviePlayer(Movie mov);

//Instance Methods
    public void addedTo(Object interest);
    public Region getClip();
    public QDRect getDisplayBounds();
    public int getDuration();
    public QDGraphics getGWorld();
```

```
    public Dimension getInitialSize();
    public Matrix getMatrix();
    public Movie getMovie();
    public float getRate();
    public int getScale();
    public int getTime();
    public TimeBase getTimeBase();
    public float getVolume();
    public boolean isMuted();
    public final synchronized void redraw(Region invalidRgn);
    public void removedFrom(Object interest);
    public void setClip(Region theClip);
    public synchronized void setDisplayBounds(QDRect bounds);
    public synchronized void setGWorld(QDGraphics cgp);
    public void setLocation(int x, int y);
    public void setMatrix(Matrix matrix);
    public void setMuted(boolean flag);
    public void setRate(float rate);
    public void setTime(int time);
    public void setVolume(float val);
}
```

CLASS HIERARCHY:

Object→MoviePlayer

Class quicktime.app.players.MoviePresenter

This class is primarily used to present a movie as a member of a SWCompositor. It will implicitly invalidate its TwoDSprite that presents the movie in the SWCompositor when the movie draws.

In addition to the use in the SWCompositor, this presenter also gives the ability to apply a GraphicsMode to the overall output of a movie and can be used also for easy manipulation and control of a movie's display characteristics, location, and transformations. For example, if you are moving a movie around the screen (bouncing it around, for instance), you will get better visual performance using a MoviePresenter than doing these kinds of activities with a standard MoviePlayer presentation.

See also SWCompositor.

```
public class MoviePresenter extends ImagePresenter
             implements AudioSpec, Playable, DynamicImage, MovieDrawingComplete {
//Constructors
    public MoviePresenter(Movie m);
    public MoviePresenter(Movie m, QDGraphics g);
```

```
//Instance Fields
//protected
    protected TwoDSprite spritePresenter;

//Instance Methods
    public Invalidator addedToCompositor(SWCompositor c, TwoDSprite s);
    public int execute(Movie m);
    public int getDuration();
    public Movie getMovie();
    public QDGraphics getOffscreenBuffer();
    public float getRate();
    public int getScale();
    public int getTime();
    public TimeBase getTimeBase();
    public float getVolume();
    public boolean isMuted();
    public boolean isPresenting();
    public void movieChanged();
    public void redraw(Region invalidRgn);
    public void removedFromCompositor(SWCompositor c);
    public void setGWorld(QDGraphics cgp);
    public void setMuted(boolean flag);
    public void setRate(float rate);
    public void setTime(int time);
    public void setVolume(float val);
}
```

CLASS HIERARCHY:

Object→ImagePresenter→MoviePresenter

Interface quicktime.app.players.Playable

This interface defines a protocol for dealing with time-based media. It allows you to get the duration, set and get the current time position of playback of the media, retrieve the time scale (i.e., how many ticks per second) of the media, and set and get the playback rate.

setTime() sets the player to the time specified. This time value at this level is a totally arbitrary value: What time that means in "real time" is determined by the implementor of the interface. Typically, the scale value will determine what a "real" time of 1 second is. getDuration() returns the duration of the media attached to the player. If the player has no media, or does not know the duration of its media, it can return the constant kDurationUnknown. The setRate() method sets the player to the playback rate. Typically, a rate of zero means that the player is stopped; a positive value that the player is playing forwards; a negative value that the player is playing backwards.

```
public interface Playable extends Timeable {
//Static Fields
    public static final int kDurationUnknown;

//Instance Methods
    public abstract int getDuration();
    public abstract int getScale();
    public abstract int getTime();
    public abstract void setTime(int time);
}
```

Class quicktime.app.players.QTPlayer

This class allows your application to display, play, and control any QuickTime movie with the standard QuickTime movie controller. The QTPlayer object works with the QTCanvas object to be displayed in a Java AWT container.

The setTime() method sets the player to the time specified. This time value at this level is a totally arbitrary value: What time that means in "real time" is determined by the implementor of the interface. Typically, the scale value determines what a "real" time of 1 second is. setRate() sets the player to the playback rate. Typically, a rate of zero means that the player is stopped; a positive value that the player is playing forwards; a negative value that the player is playing backwards.

setControllerSizeReserved() sets parameters on the resizing of the controller. If true, then the size of controller and its movie will be set with setDisplayBounds(). If false, then setDisplayBounds() will resize the movie to the specified rectangle. Setting this flag causes the movie and its controller to be resized.

See also QTCanvas, MovieController.

```
public class QTPlayer extends Tasking
              implements QTDrawable, Playable, AudioSpec, MouseListener, KeyListener {
//Constructors
    public QTPlayer(MovieController mc);

//Instance Methods
    public void addedTo(Object interest);
    public Region getClip();
    public QDRect getDisplayBounds();
    public int getDuration();
    public QDGraphics getGWorld();
```

```
    public Dimension getInitialSize();
    public Matrix getMatrix();
    public MovieController getMovieController();
    public float getRate();
    public int getScale();
    public int getTime();
    public TimeBase getTimeBase();
    public float getVolume();
    public boolean isControllerSizeReserved();
    public boolean isControllerVisible();
    public boolean isMuted();
    public void keyPressed(KeyEvent e);
    public void keyReleased(KeyEvent e);
    public void keyTyped(KeyEvent e);
    public void mouseClicked(MouseEvent e);
    public void mouseEntered(MouseEvent e);
    public void mouseExited(MouseEvent e);
    public void mousePressed(MouseEvent e);
    public void mouseReleased(MouseEvent e);
    public final synchronized void redraw(Region invalidRgn);
    public void removedFrom(Object interest);
    public void setClip(Region theClip);
    public void setControllerSizeReserved(boolean flag);
    public void setControllerVisible(boolean flag);
    public synchronized void setDisplayBounds(QDRect bounds);
    public synchronized void setGWorld(QDGraphics cgp);
    public void setLocation(int x, int y);
    public void setMatrix(Matrix matrix);
    public void setMuted(boolean flag);
    public void setRate(float rate);
    public void setTime(int time);
    public void setVolume(float val);
    public final synchronized void task();
}
```

CLASS HIERARCHY:

Object→Tasking→QTPlayer

24

The quicktime. app.sg Package

The `quicktime.app.sg` package contains only a single class, `SGDrawer`. This class provides a `SGDrawable` object for presenting the `SGVideoChannel` of a `SequenceGrabber` component in the `QTCanvas`.

Figure 24.1 shows the class hierarchy for this package.

FIGURE 24.1   *The* `quicktime.app.sg` *package*

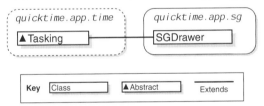

Class quicktime.app.sg.SGDrawer

This class presents the `SequenceGrabber`/`SGVideoChannel` component as a `Drawable` object so that it can be displayed within the confines of the `QTCanvas`.

The `SGDrawer()` constructor creates an `SGDrawer` object from a `SGVideoChannel` component. Only video-based `SGChannels` can be presented by the `SGDrawer`. The `getSGChannel()` method returns the `SequenceGrabber` object presented by this drawable.

```
public class SGDrawer extends Tasking implements QTDrawable, Errors, StdQTConstants {
//Constructors
    public SGDrawer(SGVideoChannel sg);
```

379

```
//Instance Methods
    public void addedTo(Object interest);
    public Region getClip();
    public QDRect getDisplayBounds();
    public QDGraphics getGWorld();
    public Dimension getInitialSize();
    public Matrix getMatrix();
    public SGVideoChannel getSGChannel();
    public SequenceGrabber getSequenceGrabber();
    public final synchronized void redraw(Region invalidRgn);
    public void removedFrom(Object interest);
    public void setClip(Region reg);
    public synchronized void setDisplayBounds(QDRect bounds);
    public synchronized void setGWorld(QDGraphics cgp);
    public void setLocation(int x, int y);
    public void setMatrix(Matrix matrix);
    public final synchronized void task();
    public String toString();
}
```

CLASS HIERARCHY:

Object -> Tasking -> SGDrawer

25

The quicktime. app.spaces Package

The `quicktime.app.spaces` package defines a set of methods and interfaces for dealing with spaces and controllers. A `Space` is a dynamic collection of members. A `Space` also has a `Timer` and a collection of controllers. The `SimpleSpace` class provides a default reference implementation of the `Space` interface.

The `Collection` interface provides a uniform means of dealing with a collection of objects in QuickTime for Java. Similarly, the `CollectionController` interface provides a generic interface for objects that want to control collections of objects and have these objects added to the controller when the objects are added to the space. The `DynamicCollection` interface uses the `Protocol` class to enable the application to dynamically type members on a collection-by-collection basis. `DynamicCollection` objects use the protocol to test to see if an object is appropriate before it is accepted as a candidate for membership of the collection.

The `Controller` interface defines a minimal requirement for all `Controller` objects—that is, they are notified whenever they are added or removed from a `Space`. No particular functionality or *modus operandi* of a controller is assumed.

Figure 25.1 shows the class hierarchy for this package. See Chapter 13, "Spaces and Controllers," and Chapter 15, "Animation and Compositing," for more information on using the classes and interfaces in this package.

FIGURE 25.1 *The* quicktime.app.spaces *package*

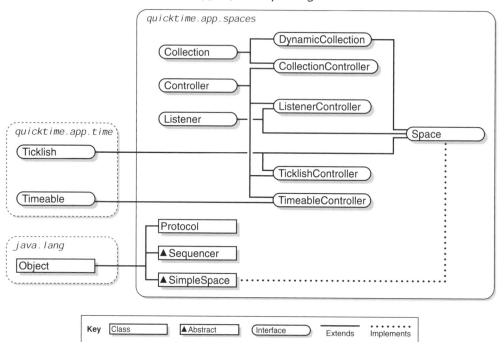

Interface quicktime.app.spaces.Collection

This interface provides a uniform means of dealing with a collection of objects in QuickTime for Java. Particular implementations of this interface provide both their own storage mechanism and semantics about the default position and characteristics of the addMember() method.

The isAppropriate() method returns true if the object argument conforms to the type of object that the Collection is a collector of. The addMember() implementation will call isAppropriate and return true if the object is an appropriate member (and is therefore added to the collection). The individual collection classes explain the customizations and restrictions on membership they enforce. The type of object that a collection contains is statically determined by the isAppropriate() method. The DynamicCollection extension of Collection provides a mechanism for dynamically customizing the membership requirements for individual collections.

hasMember() **returns** true if the provided object is a member of the collection. isAppropriate() **returns** true if the provided object is an appropriate candidate for membership in a collection. The provided QuickTime for Java collections use this method to ensure a minimal requirement of Class or Interface instanceof tests to ensure the type of object that can be added to a collection. Some collections can have a protocol that allows an application to further refine and tighten the type of object allowed within an individual collection.

members() **returns** an enumeration to iterate over the current members of a collection. size() **returns** the number of members in the collection, that is, the collection's size.

See also DynamicCollection.

```
public interface Collection {
//Instance Methods
    public abstract boolean addMember(Object member);
    public abstract boolean hasMember(Object member);
    public abstract boolean isAppropriate(Object object);
    public abstract boolean isEmpty();
    public abstract Enumeration members();
    public abstract void removeMember(Object member);
    public abstract int size();
}
```

Interface quicktime.app.spaces.CollectionController

This interface provides a generic interface for objects that want to control collections of objects and have these objects added to the controller when the objects are added to the space.

When a Space has an object added to it (or a CollectionController is added to a Space) and isWholespace **returns** true, then all members of the space will be added to the CollectionController. It is up to the CollectionController itself to determine through its protocol if the object is an appropriate object to be controlled. If not, the object should not be added to the Controller.

The CollectionController extends Controller, which provides the notification of when the Controller is added to a Space and also to be notified when the Space is added to the object that is the ultimate source of interests. The CollectionController extends Collection, which is how the Space adds and removes the members from the controller.

The `isWholespace()` method returns the current setting of the `wholespace` flag. It returns `true` if any member of the `Space` is a candidate for being controlled by this controller. If `false` then objects must be explicitly added to the space.

```
public interface CollectionController extends Controller, Collection {
//Instance Methods
    public abstract boolean isWholespace();
}
```

Interface quicktime.app.spaces.Controller

A `Controller` is an object that exerts some control over members of a `Space`. The `Controller` interface defines a minimal requirement for all controllers—that is, they are notified whenever they are added or removed from a `Space`. No particular functionality or *modus operandi* of a controller is assumed.

There are a number of interfaces that extend this interface to provide a particular behavior of the `Controller`—particularly in the relationship of the controller to its space. Those interfaces' functionality in terms of the requirements they have when they are added to a `Space` are all supported in the `SimpleSpace` implementation. For example, `TicklishControllers` provide a list of `Ticklish` objects that should be tickled by the space's `Timer`. When a `TicklishController` is added to the `SimpleSpace`, the `SimpleSpace` will tickle this controller.

The extension interfaces provide their own documentation for the actions they require. The provided controller interfaces should provide a comprehensive set of requirements for describing the interaction between controllers and spaces.

The `addedToSpace()` method is called by the `Space` when a controller has been successfully added to the `Space`. `removedFromSpace()` is called by the `Space` when a controller has been removed from a space. This only be called by the `Space` on controllers that have previously been added. Thus, the space they are being removed from is the space they were added to.

See also `Space`.

```
public interface Controller {
//Instance Methods
    public abstract void addedToSpace(Space s);
    public abstract void removedFromSpace();
}
```

Interface quicktime.app.spaces.DynamicCollection

The `DynamicCollection` interface uses the `Protocol` class to enable an application to dynamically type members on a collection-by-collection basis. `DynamicCollection` objects use the protocol to test to see if an object is appropriate before it is accepted as a candidate for membership of the collection.

This enables an application to tighten the restrictions on membership on a case-by-case basis. For example, the `DirectGroup` is a `DynamicCollection`, of which the fundamental requirement is that the member implement the `QTDrawable` interface.

However, if your application wants to ensure that for a particular group only movies are in the collection, you could get the `Protocol` object for that particular `DirectGroup` and add the `MoviePlayer` class to the collection of class objects that make up the `Protocol`. Consequent uses of that direct group would ensure that the object being added was both a `QTDrawable` and `MoviePlayer` before the object was added. Your application (having specified this protocol) can then make certain assumptions about the type of object that is a member of the collection.

Changing a protocol after a member has been added to the collection will not mean that existing members are removed if they do not match the new protocol. Thus, protocols should only be specified when the collection is empty.

The `getProtocol()` method returns the `Protocol` class that is used when testing an object's appropriateness for membership of a collection.

See also `Protocol`.

```
public interface DynamicCollection extends Collection {
//Instance Methods
    public abstract Protocol getProtocol();
}
```

Interface quicktime.app.spaces.Listener

Objects that implement this interface are declaring an interest that is derived or sourced from the object supplied as the argument to the `addedTo` interest. For instance, `java.awt.Component` objects are a source for events that may be used to control the playback of a movie. One such application of this interface is for objects set as the client of a `QTCanvas` to be notified when they have been added to the canvas. However, this interface is more general and can be used to specify a variety of situations and applications depending on the container that the implementor of this interest is added to.

The `Listener` object can cast the incoming source object to an expected class. If the source object is not of that type, a runtime exception is generated. Generally the container and member relationship will enforce the appropriateness of a member for its container.

The `addedTo()` method is called by some kind of container object when the `Listener` is added to the object that is the source of the interest. `removedFrom()` is called by the specified object when the `Listener` object is removed from the object that is the source of the interest.

```
public interface Listener {
//Instance Methods
    public abstract void addedTo(Object source);
    public abstract void removedFrom(Object source);
}
```

Interface quicktime.app.spaces.ListenerController

A `ListenerController` is a controller that is generally invoked or made active by events or notifications from some source object. For example, the `MouseController` is a `ListenerController`: It is activated when its source object (a `java.awt.Component`) broadcasts a mouse event to its listeners. The `MouseController` once activated will act upon the members of the `Space` over which it exerts some kind of control—for example, dragging a visual object around the screen.

A `ListenerController` when added to a `Space` will be notified when the `Space` is added to the object that is to be the source of events for that `Space`. The `Space` will then ensure that the `addedTo()` and `removedFrom()` methods of the `Listener` interface are called on controllers of this type.

```
public interface ListenerController extends Controller, Listener {
}
```

Class quicktime.app.spaces.Protocol

A `Protocol` is a collection of classes used to test an object against. The `passProtocol` `(Object o)` method uses the `Class.instanceOf()` method on each of the classes in its collection. If the incoming object is not an instance of any of the classes in the `Protocol`, then the `passProtocol()` method returns `false`. If the incoming object is, then it returns `true`.

For dynamic collections, your application can dynamically assign or add classes to a `Protocol` to tighten the membership requirements of its collection. When an object is added to a dynamic collection, the dynamic collection will first test the object against its `Protocol passProtocol()` method. Only if it passes this test is the object allowed to be added to the collection. This test is encapsulated in the `DynamicCollection isAppropriate()` method.

```
public class Protocol extends Object implements Collection {
//Constructors
    public Protocol(Class[] defaultProtocols);
    public Protocol(Class defaultProtocol);

//Instance Methods
    public boolean addMember(Object member);
    public Enumeration defaultProtocol();
    public boolean hasMember(Object object);
    public boolean isAppropriate(Object object);
    public boolean isEmpty();
    public Enumeration members();
    public boolean passProtocol(Object o);
    public void removeMember(Object member);
    public int size();
}
```

CLASS HIERARCHY:

Object→Protocol

Class quicktime.app.spaces.Sequencer

This interface defines operations that can control the positioning of a cursor through a sequence of data. Generally a sequencer defines a `get()` method to retrieve the data at the current frame. The type of object returned in a `get()` method is specific to the type of sequencer.

Use `setLooping()` to set the type of looping behavior of the sequencer. `getLooping()` returns the type of looping behavior of the sequencer. `size()` returns the number of frames of the data that the sequencer is sequencing.

```
public abstract class Sequencer extends Object {
//Static Fields
    public static final int kFirstFrame;
```

```
    public static final int kLastFrame;
    public static final int kLoopForwards;
    public static final int kLoopPalindrome;
    public static final int kNoLooping;

//Constructors
    public Sequencer();

//Instance Methods
    public int getCurrentFrame();
    public int getLooping();
    public void setCurrentFrame(int frameNumber);
    public void setFrameNext();
    public void setFramePrevious();
    public void setLooping(int flag);
    public abstract int size();
    public String toString();
}
```

CLASS HIERARCHY:

Object→Sequencer

Class quicktime.app.spaces.SimpleSpace

This class provides a default reference implementation of the Space interface. It also provides a concrete example of the display space concept.

The following actions are taken by the SimpleSpace class when members or controllers are added to the Space.

- If the member is a Space, then the contained Space will have the same source for its Listener members as the parent Space. The TimeBase of the Space will be slaved to the parent Space.

- If the member or controller (TimeableController) implements the Timeable interface, then the TimeBase of the member or controller will be slaved to the Space.

- If the member or controller (ListenerController) implements the Listener interface, then the source of the Listener interest will be the source of the parent Space—that is, all members and controllers will have the same Listener source.

- If the controller implements the `Ticklish` interface (`Ticklish-Controller`), it will be added to the `ticklishList`, and the `tickle()` and `timeChanged()` methods of the `Space` will tickle and change the time of all members of this `ticklishList`.

- If the controller implements the `Collection` interface (`Collection-Controller`) and the `isWholespace` method of the controller returns `true`, then all members added to the `Space` will also be added to the controller. It is the responsibility of the `Controller` to determine if the member is an appropriate member for it to control and, if so, to add it to the collection of objects it controls. If `isWholespace` is `false`, then members must explicitly be added to the controllers. When a member is removed from a `Space`, the `Collection-Controller` will be told to remove that member from the collection of objects it controls (regardless of the `isWholespace()` method).

- All controllers that are added to a `Space` are considered to be active. There is no explicit way for a `Controller` to deactivate itself, though internally a particular implementation of the `Controller` interface may choose to be inactive or active. However, the `Space` knows no such state of the controller and thus treats all attached controllers as active.

The `SimpleSpace` can be used in different settings, that is, it has no predefined application for managing display (presentation) or model contexts. Applications can also use `SimpleSpace` as a parent class for other kinds of spaces, such as model spaces. The `SimpleSpace` has no knowledge or implementation of the type of collection that is used to hold the collection of members.

It is a delegated responsibility of the subclass to implement the `Collection` methods. There are two protected methods that the subclass should call after they have successfully added or removed a member: `memberAdded()` and `memberRemoved()`, respectively. These methods ensure the behavior of members as outlined.

The `timeChanged()` method is invoked by the timer when a time condition of its time base has changed. The `Timer` invokes the `tickle()` method when the invocation constraints of the `Timer` are reached. If the subclass `Space` has its own tickle requirements, then it should override the tickle method. However, to ensure that any ticklish controllers are tickled, the overriding implementation should first call `super.tickle`.

tickleList() returns an Enumeration of all of the Controller objects that implement the Ticklish interface (TicklishControllers) that have been added to the Space. These controllers are tickled each time the Space itself is tickled by its Timer. getProtocol() returns the Protocol object that defines whether a member is an appropriate member of the Space. isAppropriate() returns true if the Object object is an appropriate member of the Space. To be an appropriate member, the object must pass the passProtocol() method of the Protocol object of the Space.

getTimer() returns the Timer of the Space. This Timer provids a TimeBase for the Space and, if active, will tickle and send timeChanged calls to the TicklishController objects that are attached to the Space.

See also SWCompositor, GroupDrawable.

```
public abstract class SimpleSpace extends Object implements Space {
//Constructors
//protected
    protected SimpleSpace(Protocol protocols);
    protected SimpleSpace(Protocol protocols, int scale, int period);

//Instance Fields
//protected
    protected Vector containedSpaces;
    protected Vector controllersVec;
    protected TickleList ticklers;
    protected Timer timer;

//Instance Methods
    public synchronized void addController(Controller c);
    public abstract boolean addMember(Object member);
    public synchronized void addedTo(Object interest);
    public Enumeration controllers();
    public Protocol getProtocol();
    public Object getSource();
    public Timer getTimer();
    public synchronized boolean hasMember(Object object);
    public boolean isAppropriate(Object object);
    public abstract boolean isEmpty();
    public abstract Enumeration members();
    public synchronized void removeAllControllers();
    public synchronized void removeAllMembers();
    public synchronized void removeController(Controller c);
    public abstract void removeMember(Object member);
    public synchronized void removedFrom(Object interest);
    public abstract int size();
    public boolean tickle(float er, int time);
    public Enumeration tickleList();
    public void timeChanged(int newTime);
```

```
//protected
    protected void finalize();
    protected synchronized void memberAdded(Object member);
    protected synchronized void memberRemoved(Object member);
}
```

CLASS HIERARCHY:

Object→SimpleSpace

Interface quicktime.app.spaces.Space

A Space is a dynamic collection of members. A Space also has a Timer and a collection of controllers. The Timer provides the parent TimeBase for all members and controllers within the Space that are themselves spaces or objects that have a TimeBase. The get-Source() method returns the source object that the Space has been added to (i.e., the Space is also a Listener).

The tickleList is the list of TicklishController objects that have been added to the Space and will be tickled by the Space when the Space itself is tickled by its Timer. A default implementation of the Space interface is provided in the SimpleSpace class.

See also SimpleSpace.

```
public interface Space extends Listener, DynamicCollection, Ticklish {
//Instance Methods
    public abstract void addController(Controller c);
    public abstract Enumeration controllers();
    public abstract Object getSource();
    public abstract Timer getTimer();
    public abstract void removeController(Controller c);
    public abstract Enumeration tickleList();
}
```

Interface quicktime.app.spaces.TicklishController

A TicklishController is an object that requires tickling by the space's Timer whenever the Space itself is tickled. A TicklishController when added to a space is also added to a tickleList field that is tickled by the Space whenever it is tickled by its Timer.

A TicklishController has no independence of time from its Space. Whenever a Space is tickled, the TicklishController is also tickled. A TimeableController, on the other hand, can have its own independent sense of time and provide its own timing information for the objects it controls.

See also `TimeableController`.

```
public interface TicklishController extends Ticklish, Controller {
}
```

Interface quicktime.app.spaces.TimeableController

A `TimeableController` is an object that provides its own `TimeBase`, thus allowing it to have an independent sense of time from the `Space` to which it is attached.

When a `TimableController` is added to a `Space`, its `TimeBase` is slaved to the `TimeBase` of the `Space`. However, this still means that the `Controller` can have some independence of time, but its `effectiveRate` depends on the rate of the `Space`. This enables a synchronization to be maintained between the sense of time of a parent `Space` and its `TimeableController` while still allowing the `TimeableController` to provide its own rate and control of its time line.

```
public interface TimeableController extends Timeable, Controller {
}
```

26

The quicktime. app.time Package

The `quicktime.app.time` package provides a set of classes for handling timing services as well as for scheduling periodic tasks. Certain QuickTime objects (such as the `QTPlayer` and `Compositor`) need to be given regular slices of time in order to perform their work. The classes in this package define a number of methods for accomplishing this.

The `TaskThread` class provides a mechanism for maintaining a table of `Taskable` objects that periodically have their `task()` method called. Each time you create an instance of this class a new thread is spawned. The class also defines methods that specify the time a thread will sleep between each task call.

An object can implement the `Taskable` interface in this package to receive a periodic call of its `task()` method from the `TaskThread` class. The system creates a default `TaskThread` used by QuickTime for Java's `Taskable` objects. The `Tasking` class provides a default implementation of many of the `Taskable` interface's methods and is used for this purpose by all of the QuickTime for Java `Taskable` classes.

The `Ticklish` interface is primarily implemented by objects attached to a `Timer`. This association can be used anywhere an object wants to be notified of a time and a rate with which to invoke an action.

Finally, the `Timer` class is useful in providing timing services for either a subclass or a target object that implements the `Ticklish` interface. The `Timer` invokes the `tickle()` method based on its tickling rate and the scale and period of the timer itself.

Figure 26.1 shows the class hierarchy for this package. See Chapter 11, "Timing," for more information on using these classes and interfaces.

FIGURE 26.1 *The* quicktime.app.time *package*

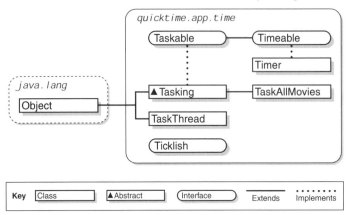

Interface quicktime.app.time.Taskable

An object can implement this interface to have a managed periodic call of the task() method from the TaskThread class. The system creates a default TaskThread, but your application can, of course, create and use its own task threads.

The task() method is defined as a method called periodically to perform regular tasks. getTasker() should return the task thread that the Taskable object is currently being tasked by, or null if not being tasked. addedTo/removedFrom() is called by a TaskThread when a Taskable object is added or removed from it.

```
public interface Taskable {
//Static Fields
    public static final TaskThread tasker;

//Instance Methods
    public abstract void addedToTasker(TaskThread t);
    public abstract TaskThread getTasker();
    public abstract void removedFromTasker();
    public abstract void startTasking();
    public abstract void stopTasking();
    public abstract void task();
}
```

Class quicktime.app.time.TaskAllMovies

QuickTime's MoviesTask call can be called in two ways.

- It can be called on a specific movie—this is, what the Movie-Player.task() method does (and Movie.task).

- It can be called to service all active time bases and movies in a single call.

This class creates a single Taskable object that will use this second alternative, making the single Movie.taskAll() call and allowing the Movie Toolbox to task all of the exisiting and active movies and time bases in a single native call.

The default behavior of some classes in the quicktime.app packages (notably MoviePlayer, Timer, and MoviePresenter) is to not task themselves individually but to register with the TaskAllMovies class that they have a requirement for tasking. The TaskAllMovies call then has a single thread and taskable object (itself) that calls the Movie.taskAll method to let QuickTime's MoviesTask call do the required tasks for any of these active movies and time bases.

Your application can retrieve the Tasking object and set its default thread to a TaskThread object of its choice.

The addMovieAndStart() method informs the TaskAllMovies object that another movie or time base is active and would require tasking. removeMovie() informs the TaskAllMovies object that a movie or time base that was active is no longer active.

See also MoviePlayer, Timer, MoviePresenter.

```
public class TaskAllMovies extends Tasking {
//Static Methods
    public static void addMovieAndStart();
    public static int currentMovieCount();
    public static TaskAllMovies get();
    public static void removeMovie();

//Instance Methods
    public void task();
}
```

CLASS HIERARCHY:

Object→Tasking→TaskAllMovies

Class quicktime.app.time.Tasking

This class provides a default implementation of the `Taskable` interface. Any subclass need only define the `task()` method.

```
public abstract class Tasking extends Object implements Taskable {
//Constructors
    public Tasking();

//Instance Methods
    public void addedToTasker(TaskThread t);
    public TaskThread getDefaultTasker();
    public TaskThread getTasker();
    public void removedFromTasker();
    public void setDefaultTasker(TaskThread tasker);
    public void startTasking();
    public void stopTasking();
    public abstract void task();
}
```

> **CLASS HIERARCHY:**
>
> Object→Tasking

Class quicktime.app.time.TaskThread

This class is a collection of `Taskable` objects that periodically have their `task()` method called. Each time an instance of this class is created, a new thread is spawned when the `start()` method of the `TaskThread` object is called. The thread is stopped when the stop method is called. `Taskable` objects can be added or removed from `TaskThread` objects at the application's discretion.

When the thread is running, it calls its `Taskable` member's `task()` method. When it has completed a single iteration of its members, it will sleep for the specified `sleepTime` and then go through the process again until the thread is stopped.

A `TaskThread` object must be explicitly started. Simply adding a `Taskable` object to the collection is not sufficient to start the thread. However, once all of the `Taskable` objects are removed from the collection, the thread will stop. To ensure that the process of adding a `Taskable` object to a `TaskThread` will also have the thread started, you use the `addAndStart()` method.

If a member's `task()` method throws an exception, it is unceremoniously removed from the `TaskThread` collection. No notification is given of such an occurrence.

The getSleepTime() method specifies the time that the thread will sleep between each task call, while setSleepTime() specifies the sleepTime for the thread. If the sleepTime is set to zero, the thread will only yield (but not sleep); otherwise, it sleeps for the given time. start() creates a thread and will start it running, calling a task on each of the items you have added to the TaskThread object. stop() will destroy the thread and end the periodic calling of task objects. You can restart this object later by calling start(). The sleepTime will be persistent across start() and stop() calls, as will the task objects themselves.

```
public class TaskThread extends Object implements Runnable, Collection {
//Constructors
    public TaskThread(String tName);
    public TaskThread(String tName, int sleepTime);

//Static Methods
    public static final void killAllThreads();

//Instance Methods
    public void addAndStart(Taskable t);
    public boolean addMember(Object member);
    public int getPriority();
    public int getSleepTime();
    public boolean hasMember(Object object);
    public boolean isAlive();
    public boolean isAppropriate(Object object);
    public boolean isEmpty();
    public Enumeration members();
    public void removeAll();
    public void removeMember(Object member);
    public void resume();
    public void run();
    public void setPriority(int newPriority);
    public void setSleepTime(int newTime);
    public int size();
    public void start();
    public void stop();
    public void suspend();
    public String toString();
//protected
    protected void finalize();
}
```

CLASS HIERARCHY:

Object→TaskThread

Interface quicktime.app.time.Ticklish

The Ticklish interface is primarily implemented by objects attached to a Timer. The Timer is generally provided with a target object that implements the Ticklish interface.

If the Timer has a target, then when the time is reached, the target will be tickled. The time value given to the the tickle() method when it is invoked is expressed in the scale of this interface. If a time state of the Timer is changed—through the time jumping from one time to another, a rate change from positive to negative, or vice versa—the timer will call the timeChanged() method with the new time, also expressed in the scale of the Ticklish.scale value.

This works in a very similar way to the relationship between the java.lang.Thread object and the java.lang.Runnable interface. However, the Ticklish interface can be used anywhere an object wants to be notified of a time and a rate with which to invoke an action.

The timeChanged() method is invoked by the timer when a time condition of its time base has changed. The Timer invokes the tickle() method when the invocation constraints of the Timer are reached.

```
public interface Ticklish {
//Static Fields
    public static final int kScale;

//Instance Methods
    public abstract boolean tickle(float er, int time);
    public abstract void timeChanged(int newTime);
}
```

Interface quicktime.app.time.Timeable

This interface defines a protocol for dealing with time lines. The Timer, QTPlayer, and MoviePlayer objects all have a TimeBase as the foundation upon which their sense of time is driven. This interface provides a way to access this TimeBase and to set and get its current rate.

In QuickTime, an object with a TimeBase also has the requirement of being tasked. That is, there exist tasks that these objects must perform on a regular basis as their time values change. Think of a movie that is playing: The new frames of the movie must be drawn as time changes. This drawing is one of the tasks of the movie object.

The `Timeable` interface extends the `Taskable` interface to express this relationship. The time values of a time base change regardless—time marches on inexorably. If you need an object to perform tasks as time changes, then you need to give these objects processing time. This is what the `task()` method does for `Timeable` objects.

The `getTimeBase()` method returns the current time base that provides the time foundation of this object. `setRate()` sets the `Timeable` playback rate. Typically, a rate of zero means that the player is stopped; a positive value that the player is playing forwards; a negative value that the time values are decreasing.

See also `Taskable`, `Timer`, `QTPlayer`, `MoviePlayer`, `TimeBase`.

```
public interface Timeable {
//Instance Methods
    public abstract float getRate();
    public abstract TimeBase getTimeBase();
    public abstract void setRate(float rate);

}
```

Class quicktime.app.time.Timer

This class provides timing services for either a subclass or a target object that implements the `Ticklish` interface. The `Timer` invokes the `tickle()` method based on the rate that it is ticking and the scale and period of the timer itself. For instance:

- 10 scale, 1 period => the `tickle()` method is invoked 10 times a second at a rate of 1

- 1 scale, 1 period => the `tickle()` method is invoked 1 time a second at a rate of 1

- 1 scale, 2 period => the `tickle()` method is invoked every 2 seconds at a rate of 1

- 3 scale, 2 period => the `tickle()` method is invoked 3 times every 2 seconds at a rate of 1

The `Timer` uses a QuickTime `TimeBase` object as its time base. The timer's `TimeBase` can be slaved to or be a master of any other `TimeBase`. If this relationship is established, the actual rate of the `TimeBase` (its effective rate) will depend upon the rate of the `TimeBase` and the rates of all of its master time bases.

Whenever the condition of the time base's time line changes, the `Timer` notifies the `Ticklish` target through invoking the `timeChanged()` method with the new time. The conditions under which this method is invoked occur when the time jumps, or the rate changes from positive to negative, or vice versa. Whenever the `tickle()` method is invoked, the effective rate of the timer's `TimeBase` is passed on as is the invocation time of the `tickle()` method. In both cases, this time value is specified in terms of the `Ticklish.scale` value. If the timer is ticking (i.e., its effective rate is not equal to zero), then the change that invokes the `timeChanged` notification will also invoke the `tickle()` method with the same time value of the `timeChanged` call, and a consequent tickle will occur from that time.

If the `tickle()` method returns `true`, the `Timer` will tickle again when the specified scale and period has elapsed. If the `tickle()` method returns `false`, the `Timer` will not tickle again until the timer is reactivated.

The `Timer` is not interrupt-driven, so it does not guarantee that the `tickle()` method will be called by the specified interval. This is affected by two factors. One is latencies in Java threads or other activity in the runtime that does not allow the return of the timer's thread. The other is the amount of time that the `tickle()` method takes to execute. In these cases (i.e., the next tickle is late), it will be called at the earliest possible time. For example, if you have a tickle interval of 100 milliseconds and the previous tickle took 150 milliseconds to execute, then the next tickle will be given at the earliest possible return. A consequent tickle to that will be in the interval specified or as soon as possible if the consequent tickle takes longer than the specified time.

See also `TimeBase`, `Ticklish`, `Timeable`, `TaskAllMovies`.

```
public class Timer extends Object
                        implements Timeable, StdQTConstants, Errors, QDConstants {
//Constructors
    public Timer(int scale, int period);
    public Timer(int scale, int period, Ticklish target);
    public Timer(int scale, int period, Ticklish target, Movie mov);

//Instance Methods
    public int getPeriod();
    public float getRate();
    public int getScale();
    public Ticklish getTicklish();
    public final TimeBase getTimeBase();
    public boolean isActive();
    public boolean isTickling();
    public synchronized void rescheduleTickle(int scale, int period);
    public synchronized void setActive(boolean flag);
```

```
    public void setRate(float rate);
    public void setTickling(boolean flag);
    public String toString();
//protected
    protected boolean tickle(float er, int time);
    protected void timeChanged(int newTime);
}
```

CLASS HIERARCHY:

Object→Timer

27

The quicktime.io Package

The `quicktime.io` package contains a relatively small number of classes and deals with file input/output. The classes in this package represent the access you need for accessing QuickTime files. Note that any exceptions that occur because of I/O-related abilities will be `QTIOExceptions`.

The `IOConstants` class represents all of the constants related to file I/O in the QuickTime interface. These constants are listed on the CD-ROM at the back of this book.

An object of the `AliasHandle` class represents a file, that is, an alias (or pointer) to the real file on the user's hard disk. It may be a minimal alias or an alias that will attempt to be resolved when used.

An object of the `OpenFile` class represents a file that is open for reading or writing. An object of the `OpenMovieFile` class represents a movie file that is open for purposes of reading or writing. The `QTFile` class represents a file for a QuickTime file.

Figure 27.1 shows the class hierarchy for this package.

FIGURE 27.1 *The* quicktime.io *package*

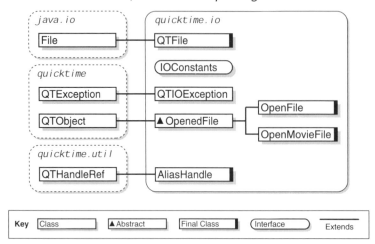

Class quicktime.io.AliasHandle

An alias handle represents a file, that is, an alias (or pointer) to the real file on the user's hard disk. It may be a minimal alias or an alias that will attempt to be resolved when used.

Use the fromQTFile() method to create an alias record that describes the specified target, whether that target is an alias file or a data file. If a security manager is present, you must have read and write permissions to both the incoming file and the resolved resultant file if the initial file was an alias file.

The fromDataRef() method converts an aliasDataRef type DataRef into an AliasHandle. This does not copy the alias DataRef, so any changes that are made to the alias will effect the DataRef as well.

The resolve() method will take an alias and resolve it, returning the full path name of the resolved file.

```
public final class AliasHandle extends QTHandleRef
                        implements Errors, StdQTConstants, QuickTimeLib {
//Static Methods
    public static AliasHandle fromDataRef(DataRef dr);

//Instance Methods
    public boolean isMinimal();
```

```
    public QTFile resolve();
}
```

CLASS HIERARCHY:

Object→QTObject→QTHandleRef→AliasHandle

Interface quicktime.io.IOConstants

This class represents all of the I/O constants in the QuickTime interface. All constants—except for constants that start with an acronym, such as MPEG—start with a lower-case letter. These constants are listed on the CD-ROM at the back of this book.

Class quicktime.io.OpenFile

An object of this class represents a file that is open for reading or writing. Note that only the file's data fork is opened.

```
public final class OpenFile extends OpenedFile {
//Static Methods
    public static OpenFile asRead(QTFile f);
    public static OpenFile asWrite(QTFile f);
}
```

Object→QTObject→OpenedFile→OpenFile

Class quicktime.io.OpenedFile

This class represents an OpenedFile object. Subclasses define the type of file open procedures that are used.

The close() method closes an open stream and the associated movie file.

```
public abstract class OpenedFile extends QTObject implements Errors, QuickTimeLib {
//Instance Methods
    public final void close();
    public final QTFile getFile();
}
```

CLASS HIERARCHY:

Object→QTObject→OpenedFile

Class quicktime.io.OpenMovieFile

An object of this class represents a movie file that is open for reading or writing.

```
public final class OpenMovieFile extends OpenedFile {
//Static Methods
    public static OpenMovieFile asRead(QTFile f);
    public static OpenMovieFile asWrite(QTFile f);
}
```

> **CLASS HIERARCHY:**
>
> Object→QTObject→OpenedFile→OpenMovieFile

Class quicktime.io.QTFile

This class represents a file for a QuickTime movie. For using QTFile with the QuickTime API, the file object must meet two criteria:

- Its complete path must be specified.

- It must be a "real" file—that is, a QTFile cannot be used with the QuickTime API if the file is contained within a zip or jar archive.

```
public final class QTFile extends File
                    implements StdQTConstants, IOConstants, Errors, QuickTimeLib {
//Static Fields
    public static final int kDeletePermission;
    public static final int kReadPermission;
    public static final int[] kStandardQTFileTypes;
    public static final int kWritePermission;

//Constructors
    public QTFile(String pathName);
    public QTFile(File file);

//Static Methods
    public static void checkSecurity(String fileName, int permission);
    public static QTFile fromGraphicsImporter(GraphicsImporter g);
    public static GraphicsImporterInfo fromGraphicsImporter(GraphicsImporter g,
                            QTFile inDefaultSpec, String prompt);
    public static QTFile fromSequenceGrabber(SequenceGrabber s);
    public static QTFile resolveAlias(AliasHandle alias);
    public static QTFile standardGetFilePreview(int[] fileTypes);

//Instance Methods
    public void convertToMovieFile(QTFile outputFile, int fCreator, int inFlags);
    public void convertToMovieFile(QTFile outputFile, int fCreator, int inFlags,
```

```
                                   MovieImporter mic);
    public void convertToMovieFile(QTFile outputFile, int fCreator, int flags,
                                   MovieImporter mic, MovieProgress mp);
    public void createMovieFile(int fCreator, int flags);
    public void createShortcutMovieFile(int creator, int scriptTag,
                                   int createMovieFileFlags, DataRef targetDataRef);
    public boolean delete();
    public final byte[] getFSSpec(boolean fileExists, int permissions);
    public AliasHandle newAlias(boolean minimal);
    public QTFile resolveAlias(boolean resolveAliasChains);
}
```

CLASS HIERARCHY:

Object→File→QTFile

Class quicktime.io.QTIOException

This is a general catch-all class used to signal errors that occur from QuickTime calls that arise due to some file I/O errors.

```
public class QTIOException extends QTException {
//Constructors
    public QTIOException(String fName);
    public QTIOException(int val, String fName);

//Static Methods
    public static void checkError(int err, String fName);

//Instance Methods
    public String getFilePath();
}
```

CLASS HIERARCHY:

Object→Throwable→Exception→QTException→QTIOException

28

The quicktime.qd Package

The `quicktime.qd` package contains a relatively large number of classes that represent the QuickDraw data structures required for the rest of the QuickTime API. These calls are found in Apple's Universal Header files. You do not use QuickDraw to do any drawing in Java; instead, you would use the drawing services that Java provides. However, the QuickTime API expects data structures that belong to QuickDraw, such as `CGrafPort`, `GWorld`, `Rect`, and `Point`. In the Java API, these classes become predominantly read-only. The `quicktime.qd.QDConstants` class represents all of the required constants in the QuickDraw interface.

Different parts of the QuickDraw API use different types of objects that possess a similar functionality. To simplify the usage of these, these similar C structures have been unified into single Java classes:

- QDGraphics
  - ❑ onscreen CGrafPort
  - ❑ offscreen GWorld
- QDColor
  - ❑ RGBColor
  - ❑ ARGBColor
  - ❑ TQ3RGBColor
  - ❑ TQ3ARGBColor
- QDRect
  - ❑ Rect
  - ❑ FixedRect

- QDPoint
  - ❑ Point
  - ❑ T2DPoint

Regions are used throughout QuickTime as masks or clips and represent a capability to control the presentation of graphic content. Figure 28.1 shows the class hierarchy for this package.

FIGURE 28.1 *The* quicktime.qd *package*

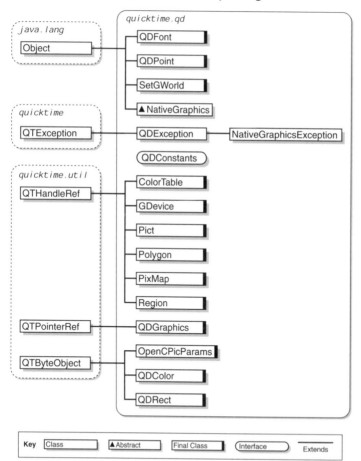

Class quicktime.qd.ColorTable

When creating a `PixMap` for a particular graphics device, QuickDraw creates a `ColorTable` that defines the best colors available for the pixel image on that graphics device. Movies and images designed to display with a select palette of colors will also contain a color table that can be used when viewing them on 8-bit devices/monitors. See also `PixMap`.

```
public final class ColorTable extends QTHandleRef implements QuickTimeLib {
//Static Fields
    public static final int kNativeSize;

//Static Methods
    public static ColorTable fromCompressionDialog(ImageCompressionDialog d);
    public static ColorTable fromImageDescription(ImageDescription id);
    public static ColorTable fromMovie(Movie m);
    public static ColorTable fromPixMap(PixMap pm);

//Instance Methods
    public int getCtSeed();
    public int getCtSize();
    public String toString();
}
```

CLASS HIERARCHY:

Object→QTObject→QTHandleRef→ColorTable

Class quicktime.qd.GDevice

This class returns information about the specific display characteristics of a video card and monitor subsystem.

```
public final class GDevice extends QTHandleRef implements QuickTimeLib, StdQTConstants {
//Static Methods
    public static GDevice fromSequenceGrabber(SequenceGrabber sg);
    public static GDevice get();
    public static GDevice getList();
    public static GDevice getMain();
    public static GDevice getMax(QDRect globalRect);

//Instance Methods
    public QDRect getBounds();
    public GDevice getNext();
    public PixMap getPixMap();
    public void init(int qdRefNum, int mode);
    public void set();
```

```
    public void setAttribute(int attribute, boolean value);
    public boolean testAttribute(int attribute);
}
```

CLASS HIERARCHY:

Object→QTObject→QTHandleRef→GDevice

Class quicktime.qd.NativeGraphics

You use this class to obtain a `QDGraphics` object from a `java.awt.Canvas`.

The `getContext()` method is called with a `Canvas` to return the platform-specific implementation of the `NativeGraphics` class. This object, in turn, is able to return the `QDGraphics` that represent QuickTime's native graphics structure. See `NativeGraphics-Exception` for requirements on use of the `getContext()` call.

`getLocation()` returns the actual x,y location of the `QDGraphics` in the native graphic's coordinate space.

```
public abstract class NativeGraphics extends Object {
//Static Methods
    public static final NativeGraphics getContext(Canvas canv);

//Instance Methods
    public abstract QDGraphics getGWorld();
    public final Point getLocation();
    public void lock();
    public void unlock();
}
```

CLASS HIERARCHY:

Object→NativeGraphics

Class quicktime.qd.NativeGraphicsException

Java's main AWT components contain a native implementation represented by a set of `jawa.awt` peer interfaces.

When initialized, an AWT component has created its peer and thus the platform-specific native graphics structures have been created. Peers are created in the `addNotify()` method of the `awt.component` class. Some of the other calls (such as `Component.Show`) will create the peer for you if your code hasn't explicitly done this. If you request a `NativeGraphics` context from an AWT component that has yet to create its peer, there is no `NativeGraphics` context in existence, and an exception of this type is thrown if trying to get the `QDGraphics` from a `java.awt.Canvas`.

```
public class NativeGraphicsException extends QDException {
//Constructors
    public NativeGraphicsException(String message);
}
```

CLASS HIERARCHY:

Object→Throwable→Exception→QTException→QDException→
NativeGraphicsException

Class quicktime.qd.OpenCPicParams

This class provides information about a picture image relating to the source rectangle and the horizontal and vertical resolution of the image. Its methods offer access to the structure's fields.

```
public final class OpenCPicParams extends QTByteObject implements Cloneable {
//Static Fields
    public static final int kNativeSize;

//Constructors
    public OpenCPicParams(QDRect srcRect, float hRes, float vRes);
    public OpenCPicParams(QDRect srcRect);

//Instance Methods
    public Object clone();
    public float getHRes();
    public QDRect getSrcRect();
    public float getVRes();
    public String toString();
}
```

CLASS HIERARCHY:

Object→QTByteObject→OpenCPicParams

Class quicktime.qd.Pict

This class represents sequences of drawing commands while providing a common medium for sharing image data.

Pict thumbnail methods create an 80-by-80 pixel picture from the source, which can be a movie, QDGraphics, and so on. Use Pict.open() to begin defining a picture, collecting all of your subsequent drawing commands into this record. The returned Pict must be closed before any other methods can be applied to it.

compress() allows your application to compress a single-frame image stored as a picture and places the result in another picture. The toEncodedImage() method returns a version of the Pict as an EncodedImage object. This references the same data as is held within the Pict, which is locked and must be kept locked for the duration of the lifetime of the EncodedImage object.

```
public final class Pict extends QTHandleRef implements QuickTimeLib, Cloneable, Errors {
//Static Methods
    public static Pict fromFile(File file);
    public static Pict fromGraphicsImporter(GraphicsImporter gi);
    public static Pict fromImageCompressionDialog(ImageCompressionDialog icd, Pict src);
    public static Pict fromMovie(Movie m);
    public static Pict fromMovie(Movie m, int time);
    public static Pict fromSequenceGrabber(SequenceGrabber sg, QDRect bounds,
                        int offscreenDepth, int grabPictFlags);
    public static Pict fromTrack(Track t, int time);
    public static Pict open(QDGraphics port, OpenCPicParams params);
    public static Pict thumbnailFromQDGraphics(QDGraphics qd, QDRect src,
                        int colorDepth);

//Instance Methods
    public void close();
    public Pict compress(int quality, int cType);
    public void draw(QDGraphics cg, QDRect frameRect);
    public void drawTrimmed(QDGraphics cg, QDRect frameRect, Region trimMask,
                    int doDither);
    public Pict fCompress(int colorDepth, int quality, int doDither, int compressAgain,
                    int cType, int codec);
    public QDRect getPictFrame();
    public boolean isOpen();
    public Pict makeThumbnail(int colorDepth);
    public RawEncodedImage toEncodedImage();
    public String toString();
    public void writeToFile(File file);
}
```

CLASS HIERARCHY:

Object→QTObject→QTHandleRef→Pict

Class quicktime.qd.PixMap

A pixel map contains information about the dimensions and contents of a pixel image, as well as information on the image's storage format, depth, resolution, and color usage.

When creating a `PixMap` for a particular graphics device, QuickDraw creates a `ColorTable` that defines the best colors available for the pixel image on that particular graphics device.

Using `getBounds()`, you get the boundary rectangle, which links the local coordinate system of a graphics port to QuickDraw's global coordinate system and defines the area of the global bit image that this `PixMap` occupies.

For performance reasons, a `PixMap` may contain extra bytes at the end of a "row" of pixels. The method `getRowBytes()` can help to determine what this value is. You can use this value to help walk through the raw pixel data in a consistent manner.

```
public final class PixMap extends QTHandleRef implements QuickTimeLib, QDConstants {
//Static Fields
    public static final int kNativeSize;

//Static Methods
    public static PixMap fromGDevice(GDevice g);
    public static PixMap fromQDGraphics(QDGraphics g);

//Instance Methods
    public QDRect getBounds();
    public ColorTable getColorTable();
    public RawEncodedImage getPixelData();
    public int getPixelFormat();
    public int getPixelSize();
    public int getRowBytes();
    public boolean isOffscreen();
    public String toString();
}
```

   CLASS HIERARCHY:
   Object→QTObject→QTHandleRef→PixMap

Class quicktime.qd.Polygon

This class represents an arbitrary area or set of areas on the drawing coordinate plane. Methods are implemented for a corresponding QuickDraw structure used by QuickTime.

```
public final class Polygon extends QTHandleRef
                          implements QuickTimeLib, Cloneable, StdQTConstants {
//Constructors
    public Polygon(QDGraphics g);

//Instance Methods
    public Object clone();
    public void close();
    public Polygon copy();
    public QDRect getBounds();
    public QDRect getPolyBBox();
    public int getSize();
    public void offset(int dh, int dv);
    public String toString();
}
```

CLASS HIERARCHY:

Object→QTObject→QTHandleRef→Polygon

Class quicktime.qd.QDColor

This class represents color as 16-bit values for each component and alpha channel. These objects are read-only; thus, color values cannot be changed. The static color variables are the same as the java.awt.Color colors but in 16-bit format. The default format for the class (i.e., the bytes that are returned by getBytes) is RGBColor.

```
public final class QDColor extends QTByteObject implements QuickTimeLib, Cloneable {
//Static Fields
    public static final QDColor black;
    public static final QDColor blue;
    public static final QDColor brown;
    public static final QDColor cyan;
    public static final QDColor darkGray;
    public static final QDColor gray;
    public static final QDColor green;
    public static final int kIsARGBColor;
    public static final int kIsRGBColor;
    public static final int kIsTQ3ColorARGB;
    public static final int kIsTQ3ColorRGB;
    public static final int kMaximumValue;
    public static final QDColor lightGray;
    public static final QDColor magenta;
    public static final QDColor orange;
    public static final QDColor pink;
    public static final QDColor red;
    public static final QDColor white;
    public static final QDColor yellow;
```

```
//Constructors
    public QDColor();
    public QDColor(int red, int green, int blue);
    public QDColor(int red, int green, int blue, int alpha);
    public QDColor(float red, float green, float blue);
    public QDColor(float red, float green, float blue, float alpha);
    public QDColor(Color color);

//Static Methods
    public static int convert16to8(int value);
    public static int convert8to16(int value);
    public static QDColor fromARGBColor(int argb);
    public static QDColor fromArray(byte[] colorBytes, int flag);
    public static final EndianDescriptor getEndianDescriptorARGBColor();
    public static final EndianDescriptor getEndianDescriptorRGBColor();
    public static final EndianDescriptor getEndianDescriptorTQ3Color();
    public static final EndianDescriptor getEndianDescriptorTQ3ColorARGB();

//Instance Methods
    public Object clone();
    public int getARGB();
    public byte[] getARGBColor();
    public int getAlpha();
    public float getAlphaF();
    public int getBlue();
    public float getBlueF();
    public int getGreen();
    public float getGreenF();
    public int getRGB();
    public byte[] getRGBColor();
    public int getRed();
    public float getRedF();
    public byte[] getTQ3ColorARGB();
    public byte[] getTQ3ColorRGB();
    public Color toColor();
    public String toString();
}
```

CLASS HIERARCHY:

Object→QTByteObject→QDColor

Interface quicktime.qd.QDConstants

This class represents all of the constants in the QuickDraw interface. Note that all constants start with a lower-case letter, except for those beginning with an acronym such as MPEG. A full listing of these constants is provided on the CD-ROM at the back of this book.

Class quicktime.qd.QDException

QDExceptions are thrown when the error is due to an exceptional situation in the graphics environment. checkError() will throw an exception if the incoming err argument is a non-zero value.

```
public class QDException extends QTException {
//Constructors
    public QDException(String str);
    public QDException(int val);

//Static Methods
    public static void checkError(int err);
}
```

CLASS HIERARCHY:

Object→Throwable→Exception→QTException→QDException

Class quicktime.qd.QDFont

This class provides basic services for translating font information from Java fonts to the font information that QuickTime requires.

getFontName() gets the name of a font family that has a specified family ID number, whereas getFNum() gets the font family ID for a specified font family name.

```
public final class QDFont extends Object implements QuickTimeLib {
//Constructors
    public QDFont();

//Static Methods
    public static final int getFNum(String theName);
    public static final String getFontName(int familyID);
}
```

CLASS HIERARCHY:

Object→QDFont

Class quicktime.qd.QDGraphics

In QuickTime's API, a color graphics port defines a complete drawing environment that determines where and how color graphics operations take place.

The public constructors create the offscreen (GWorld) version. The onscreen version can be obtained only by going through the `NativeGraphics getContext()` method. The `from.` . . calls do not create a `QDGraphics` object but return the `QDGraphics` that the supplied object is currently drawing into.

```
public final class QDGraphics extends QTPointerRef
                             implements QuickTimeLib, QDConstants {
//Static Fields
    public static final int kDefaultPixelFormat;
    public static final int kNativeSize;
    public static QDGraphics scratch;
    public static QDGraphics validScratch;

//Constructors
    public QDGraphics(ImageCompressionDialog d, QDRect rp, int flags);
    public QDGraphics(ImageDescription id, int flags);
    public QDGraphics(QDRect bounds);
    public QDGraphics(int pixelFormat, QDRect bounds);
    public QDGraphics(int pixelFormat, QDRect bounds, int flags);
    public QDGraphics(int pixelFormat, QDRect bounds, ColorTable cTable,
                   GDevice aGDevice, int flags);

//Static Methods
    public static QDGraphics fromCSequence(CSequence c);
    public static QDGraphics fromDSequenceImage(DSequence d);
    public static QDGraphics fromDSequenceScreen(DSequence d);
    public static QDGraphics fromGraphicsImporter(GraphicsImporter gi);
    public static QDGraphics fromMovie(Movie m);
    public static QDGraphics fromMovieController(MovieController mc);
    public static QDGraphics fromNativeGraphics(WinNativeGraphics ng);
    public static QDGraphics fromNativeGraphics(MacNativeGraphics ng);
    public static QDGraphics fromSequenceGrabber(SequenceGrabber sg);
    public static int getPixelSize(int pixelFormat);
    public static QDGraphics getPort();

//Instance Methods
    public void clipRect(QDRect r);
    public void clipRect();
    public void eraseArc(QDRect area, int startAngle, int arcAngle);
    public void eraseOval(QDRect area);
    public void erasePoly(Polygon poly);
    public void eraseRect(QDRect area);
    public void eraseRgn(Region area);
    public void eraseRoundRect(QDRect area, int ovalWidth, int ovalHeight);
    public void frameArc(QDRect area, int startAngle, int arcAngle);
    public void frameOval(QDRect area);
    public void framePoly(Polygon poly);
    public void frameRect(QDRect area);
    public void frameRgn(Region area);
    public void frameRoundRect(QDRect area, int ovalWidth, int ovalHeight);
```

```
    public QDColor getBackColor();
    public QDRect getBounds();
    public QDColor getCPixel(int h, int v);
    public Region getClip();
    public QDColor getForeColor();
    public PixMap getPixMap();
    public QDRect getPortRect();
    public Region getVisClipRgn();
    public void invertArc(QDRect area, int startAngle, int arcAngle);
    public void invertOval(QDRect area);
    public void invertPoly(Polygon poly);
    public void invertRoundRect(QDRect area, int ovalWidth, int ovalHeight);
    public boolean isOffscreen();
    public void line(int h, int v);
    public void lineTo(int h, int v);
    public Pict makeThumbnail(QDRect src, int colorDepth);
    public void move(int h, int v);
    public void moveTo(int h, int v);
    public void paintArc(QDRect area, int startAngle, int arcAngle);
    public void paintOval(QDRect area);
    public void paintPoly(Polygon poly);
    public void paintRect(QDRect area);
    public void paintRgn(Region area);
    public void paintRoundRect(QDRect area, int ovalWidth, int ovalHeight);
    public void penNormal();
    public void penSize(int width, int height);
    public void setBackColor(QDColor bColor);
    public void setCPixel(int h, int v, QDColor cPix);
    public void setClip(Region rgn);
    public void setForeColor(QDColor fColor);
    public String toString();
}
```

CLASS HIERARCHY:

Object→QTObject→QTPointerRef→QDGraphics

Class quicktime.qd.QDPoint

This class is used to represent a point in two-dimensional space. It can be used to represent integral values, or points that lie within fractional grids.

```
public final class QDPoint extends Object implements PrimitivesLib, Cloneable {
//Static Fields
    public static final int kIsFixedPoint;
    public static final int kIsQ3Point2D;
    public static final int kIsQTVRFloatPoint;

//Constructors
```

```
    public QDPoint(int x, int y);
    public QDPoint(float x, float y);
    public QDPoint(Point origin);

//Static Methods
    public static QDPoint fromArray(byte[] ptBytes, int ptType);
    public static final EndianDescriptor getEndianDescriptorFixedPoint();
    public static final EndianDescriptor getEndianDescriptorQTVRFloatPoint();
    public static final EndianDescriptor getEndianDescriptorTQ3Point2D();

//Instance Methods
    public Object clone();
    public QDPoint copy();
    public boolean equals(Object obj);
    public byte[] getFixedPoint();
    public int getPoint();
    public byte[] getQ3Point2D();
    public byte[] getQTVRFloatPoint();
    public int getX();
    public float getXF();
    public int getY();
    public float getYF();
    public void move(int x, int y);
    public void move(float x, float y);
    public void setX(int x);
    public void setX(float x);
    public void setY(int y);
    public void setY(float y);
    public Point toPoint();
    public String toString();
    public void translate(int deltaX, int deltaY);
    public void translate(float deltaX, float deltaY);
}
```

CLASS HIERARCHY:
Object→QDPoint

Class quicktime.qd.QDRect

This class corresponds to the Rect and FixedRect data structures and represents a rectangle of x and y location and width and height size.

```
public final class QDRect extends QTByteObject implements PrimitivesLib, Cloneable {
//Static Fields
    public static final int kIsFixedRect;
    public static final int kIsRect;

//Constructors
```

```
    public QDRect();
    public QDRect(int x, int y, int width, int height);
    public QDRect(float x, float y, float width, float height);
    public QDRect(int width, int height);
    public QDRect(float width, float height);
    public QDRect(Point origin, Dimension size);
    public QDRect(Point origin);
    public QDRect(Dimension size);
    public QDRect(Rectangle rect);
```

//Static Methods
```
    public static QDRect fromArray(byte[] rectBytes, int flag);
    public static final EndianDescriptor getEndianDescriptorFixedRect();
    public static final EndianDescriptor getEndianDescriptorRect();
```

//Instance Methods
```
    public void add(Point pt);
    public void add(int newX, int newY);
    public void add(float newX, float newY);
    public Object clone();
    public QDRect copy();
    public boolean equals(Object obj);
    public byte[] getFixedRect();
    public int getHeight();
    public float getHeightF();
    public byte[] getRect();
    public int getWidth();
    public float getWidthF();
    public int getX();
    public float getXF();
    public int getY();
    public float getYF();
    public void grow(float h, float v);
    public void grow(int h, int v);
    public int hashCode();
    public boolean inside(float x, float y);
    public boolean inside(int x, int y);
    public QDRect intersection(QDRect r);
    public boolean intersects(QDRect r);
    public boolean isDifferentOrigin(QDRect rect);
    public boolean isDifferentSize(QDRect rect);
    public boolean isEmpty();
    public void move(int x, int y);
    public void move(float x, float y);
    public void reshape(int x, int y, int width, int height);
    public void reshape(float x, float y, float width, float height);
    public void resize(int width, int height);
    public void resize(float width, float height);
    public void setHeight(int height);
    public void setHeight(float height);
    public void setWidth(float width);
    public void setWidth(int width);
```

```
    public void setX(float x);
    public void setX(int x);
    public void setY(float y);
    public void setY(int y);
    public Rectangle toRectangle();
    public String toString();
    public void translate(float deltaX, float deltaY);
    public void translate(int deltaX, int deltaY);
    public QDRect union(QDRect r);
}
```

CLASS HIERARCHY:

Object→QTByteObject→QDRect

Class quicktime.qd.Region

This class represents an arbitrary area or set of areas contiguous or otherwise on the drawing coordinate plane. Use fromMovieDisplayBounds() to determine a movie's display boundary region. The display boundary region encloses all of a movie's enabled tracks after the track matrix, track clip, movie matrix, and movie clip have been applied to all of the movie's tracks. This region is in the display coordinate system of the movie's graphics world.

```
public final class Region extends QTHandleRef
                    implements QuickTimeLib, Cloneable, StdQTConstants {
//Constructors
    public Region();
    public Region(QDRect r);
    public Region(PixMap pMap);

//Static Methods
    public static Region fromGraphicsImporter(GraphicsImporter gi);
    public static Region fromMovieBounds(Movie m);
    public static Region fromMovieClip(Movie m);
    public static Region fromMovieControllerBadge(MovieController mc, Region movieRgn,
                            boolean returnBadgeRgn);
    public static Region fromMovieControllerBounds(MovieController mc);
    public static Region fromMovieControllerClip(MovieController mc);
    public static Region fromMovieControllerWindow(MovieController mc,
                            QDGraphics window);
    public static Region fromMovieDisplayBounds(Movie m);
    public static Region fromMovieDisplayClip(Movie m);
    public static Region fromMovieSegment(Movie m, int time, int duration);
    public static Region fromTrackBounds(Track t);
    public static Region fromTrackClip(Track t);
    public static Region fromTrackDisplay(Track t);
    public static Region fromTrackMovieBounds(Track t);
```

```
    public static Region fromTrackSegment(Track t, int time, int duration);
    public static Region fromVideoChannel(VisualChannel vc);

//Instance Methods
    public Object clone();
    public Region copy();
    public Region diff(Region regionB);
    public boolean empty();
    public boolean equalRgn(Region rgn);
    public QDRect getBounds();
    public QDRect getRgnBBox();
    public int getSize();
    public void inset(int dh, int dv);
    public void map(QDRect srcRect, QDRect dstRect);
    public void offset(int dh, int dv);
    public boolean pointIn(QDPoint pt);
    public void rect(QDRect r);
    public boolean rectIn(QDRect srcRect);
    public Region sect(QDRect r);
    public Region sect(Region regionB);
    public void setEmpty();
    public void setRect(int x, int y, Dimension dim);
    public String toString();
    public Region union(Region regionB);
    public Region union(QDRect rect);
    public Region xor(Region regionB);
}
```

CLASS HIERARCHY:

Object→QTObject→QTHandleRef→Region

Class quicktime.qd.SetGWorld

This class is used to make the incoming QDGraphics the current QDGraphics for drawing. Note that QuickDraw uses a global, current graphics context when drawing. Using the SetGWorld() constructor will save the previously current graphics context and then make the incoming QDGraphics the current context. The incoming QDGraphics may *not* be null.

reset() is called after you have set the context to a specific QDGraphics to reset it to the previous one.

```
public final class SetGWorld extends Object implements Errors, QuickTimeLib {
//Constructors
    public SetGWorld(QDGraphics cg);
    public SetGWorld(QDGraphics cg, GDevice gdh);
```

```
//Instance Methods
    public final void reset();
}
```

CLASS HIERARCHY:

Object→SetGWorld

29

The quicktime.qd3d Package

The `quicktime.qd3d` packages contain classes that represent the QuickDraw 3D data structures required for the rest of the QuickTime API—primarily in the creation of tween tracks in a movie to control the presentation of QD3D models over time.

This package contains only two classes: the `QD3DConstants` interface, which represents all of the constants in the QuickDraw 3D interface, and `QD3DException`, a general catch-all class used to signal errors that occur from QD3D calls. Figure 29.1 shows the class hierarchy for this package.

FIGURE 29.1   *The* `quicktime.qd3d` *package*

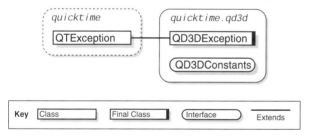

Interface quicktime.qd3d.QD3DConstants

This class represents all of the constants in the QuickDraw 3D interface.

A full listing of these constants is provided on the CD-ROM disc at the back of this book.

Class quicktime.qd3d.QD3DException

This is a general catch-all class used to signal errors that occur from QuickTime calls in the QD3D package.

The QD3DException() constructor creates an exception with a message that could contain information to be displayed to the user.

```
public class QD3DException extends QTException {
//Constructors
    public QD3DException(String str);
    public QD3DException(int val);

//Static Methods
    public static void checkError(int err);
}
```

CLASS HIERARCHY:

Object→Throwable→Exception→QTException→QD3DException

30

The quicktime. qd3d.camera Package

The quicktime.qd3d.camera package contains a set of classes that provide information for a camera's angle and position. In addition, these classes include the camera's placement location, its range, and its viewport plane. Figure 30.1 shows the class hierarchy for this package.

FIGURE 30.1 *The* quicktime.qd3dcamera *package*

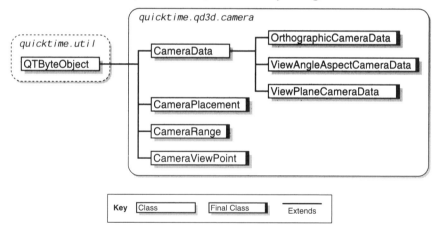

Class quicktime.qd3d.camera.CameraData

This class contains information for the camera angle and position. It includes the camera's placement location, the camera's range, and the camera's viewport plane.

The `CameraData()` constructor creates a `CameraData` object containing no data.

```
public class CameraData extends QTByteObject implements Cloneable {
//Static Fields
    public static final int kNativeSize;

//Constructors
    public CameraData();
    public CameraData(CameraPlacement placement, CameraRange range,
                      CameraViewPort viewPort);

//Static Methods
    public static final EndianDescriptor getEndianDescriptor();

//Instance Methods
    public Object clone();
    public final CameraPlacement getPlacement();
    public final CameraRange getRange();
    public final CameraViewPort getViewPort();
    public final void setPlacement(CameraPlacement placement);
    public final void setRange(CameraRange range);
    public final void setViewPort(CameraViewPort viewPort);
    public String toString();
}
```

CLASS HIERARCHY:CLASS HIERARCHY:

Object→QTByteObject→CameraData

Class quicktime.qd3d.camera.CameraPlacement

This class contains information for the camera's range. It includes the location point of the camera, the camera's point of interest, and the camera's up vector positioning.

```
public final class CameraPlacement extends QTByteObject {
//Static Fields
    public static final int kNativeSize;

//Constructors
    public CameraPlacement();
    public CameraPlacement(Point3D cameraLocation, Point3D pointOfInterest,
                           Vector3D upVector);

//Static Methods
    public static final EndianDescriptor getEndianDescriptor();

//Instance Methods
    public Object clone();
    public Point3D getCameraLocation();
```

```
    public Point3D getPointOfInterest();
    public Vector3D getUpVector();
    public void setCameraLocation(Point3D cameraLocation);
    public void setPointOfInterest(Point3D pointOfInterest);
    public void setUpVector(Vector3D upVector);
    public String toString();
}
```

CLASS HIERARCHY:CLASS HIERARCHY:

Object→QTByteObject→CameraPlacement

Class quicktime.qd3d.camera.CameraRange

This class contains information for the camera's range. It includes the distance to the nearest projection plane (hither plane) and the distance to the farthest projection plane (yon plane).

```
public final class CameraRange extends QTByteObject implements Cloneable {
//Static Fields
    public static final int kNativeSize;

//Constructors
    public CameraRange();
    public CameraRange(float hither, float yon);

//Static Methods
    public static final EndianDescriptor getEndianDescriptor();

//Instance Methods
    public Object clone();
    public float getHither();
    public float getYon();
    public void setHither(float hither);
    public void setYon(float yon);
}
```

CLASS HIERARCHY:

Object→QTByteObject→CameraRange

Class quicktime.qd3d.camera.CameraViewPort

This class contains information for the camera's viewport. Origin is (–1, 1) and corresponds to the upper left-hand corner; width and height maximum is (2.0, 2.0), corresponding to the lower right-hand corner of the window. The viewport specifies a part of the view plane that gets displayed on the window that is to be drawn. Normally, it is set with an origin of (–1.0, 1.0) and a width and height of both 2.0, specifying that the entire window is to be drawn. If, for example, an exposure event of the window exposed the right half of the window, you would set the origin to (0, 1) and the width and height to (1.0) and (2.0), respectively.

```
public final class CameraViewPort extends QTByteObject implements Cloneable {
//Static Fields
    public static final int kNativeSize;

//Constructors
    public CameraViewPort();
    public CameraViewPort(QDPoint origin, float width, float height);

//Static Methods
    public static final EndianDescriptor getEndianDescriptor();

//Instance Methods
    public Object clone();
    public float getHeight();
    public QDPoint getOrigin();
    public float getWidth();
    public void setHeight(float height);
    public void setOrigin(QDPoint origin);
    public void setWidth(float width);
    public String toString();
}
```

CLASS HIERARCHY:

Object→QTByteObject→CameraViewPort

Class quicktime.qd3d.camera.OrthographicCameraData

This class contains information for the camera angle and position. The lens character-istics are set with the dimensions of a rectangular viewPort in the frame of the camera.

```
public final class OrthographicCameraData extends CameraData {
//Static Fields
    public static final int kNativeSize;

//Constructors
    public OrthographicCameraData();
    public OrthographicCameraData(CameraData cameraData, float left, float top,
                                  float right, float bottom);

//Instance Methods
    public Object clone();
```

```
    public float getBottom();
    public float getLeft();
    public float getRight();
    public float getTop();
    public void setBottom(float bottom);
    public void setLeft(float left);
    public void setRight(float right);
    public void setTop(float top);
}
```

CLASS HIERARCHY:

Object→QTByteObject→CameraData→OrthographicCameraData

Class quicktime.qd3d.camera.ViewAngleAspectCameraData

A view angle aspect camera is a perspective camera specified in terms of the minimum view angle and the aspect ratio of X to Y.

```
public final class ViewAngleAspectCameraData extends CameraData {
//Static Fields
    public static final int kNativeSize;

//Constructors
    public ViewAngleAspectCameraData();
    public ViewAngleAspectCameraData(CameraData cameraData, float fov,
                            float aspectRatio);

//Instance Methods
    public Object clone();
    public float getFov();
    public void setAspectRatio(float aspectRatio);
    public float setAspectRatio();
    public void setFov(float fov);
}
```

CLASS HIERARCHY:

Object→QTByteObject→CameraData→ViewAngleAspectCameraData

Class quicktime.qd3d.camera.ViewPlaneCameraData

This class is a perspective camera specified in terms of an arbitrary view plane. This is most useful when setting the camera to look at a particular object. The `mViewPlane` is set to the distance from the camera to the object. The `halfWidth` is set to half the width of the cross section of the object, and the `halfHeight` equal to the `halfWidth` divided by the aspect ratio of the viewPort. This is the only perspective camera with specifications for off-axis viewing, which is desirable for scrolling.

```
public final class ViewPlaneCameraData extends CameraData {
//Static Fields
    public static final int kNativeSize;

//Constructors
    public ViewPlaneCameraData();
    public ViewPlaneCameraData(CameraData cameraData, float viewPlane,
                    float halfWidthAtViewPlane, float halfHeightAtViewPlane,
                    float centerXOnViewPlane, float centerYOnViewPlane);

//Instance Methods
    public Object clone();
    public float getCenterX();
    public float getCenterY();
    public float getHalfHeight();
    public float getHalfWidth();
    public float getViewPlane();
    public void setCenterX(float centerXOnViewPlane);
    public void setCenterY(float centerYOnViewPlane);
    public void setHalfHeight(float halfHeightAtViewPlane);
    public void setHalfWidth(float halfWidthAtViewPlane);
    public void setViewPlane(float viewPlane);
}
```

CLASS HIERARCHY:

Object→QTByteObject→CameraData→ViewPlaneCameraData

The quicktime. qd3d.math Package

Th `quicktime.qd3d.math` package contains information for both a 3 × 3 and 4 × 4 float matrix, as well as information for a three-dimensional point and three-dimensional vector. Figure 31.1 shows the class hierarchy for this package.

FIGURE 31.1 *The* `quicktime.qd3d.math` *package*

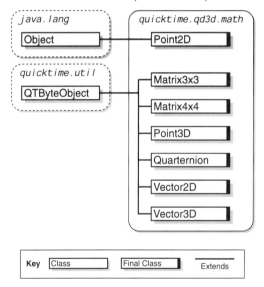

Class quicktime.qd3d.math.Matrix3x3

This class contains information for a 3 x 3 float matrix.

The get and set calls provide access to the row and column of the matrix. Thus, getat01 accesses the 0th row and the 1st column.

```
public final class Matrix3x3 extends QTByteObject
                        implements QuickTimeLib, QuickDraw3DLib, Cloneable {
//Static Fields
    public static final int kNativeSize;

//Constructors
    public Matrix3x3();
    public Matrix3x3(float[][] table);

//Static Methods
    public static final EndianDescriptor getEndianDescriptor();

//Instance Methods
    public Matrix3x3 adjoint();
    public Object clone();
    public Matrix3x3 copy();
    public float determinant();
    public float getAt00();
    public float getAt01();
    public float getAt02();
    public float getAt10();
    public float getAt11();
    public float getAt12();
    public float getAt20();
    public float getAt21();
    public float getAt22();
    public Matrix3x3 invert();
    public Matrix3x3 multiply(Matrix3x3 matrixB);
    public void setAt00(float val);
    public void setAt01(float val);
    public void setAt02(float val);
    public void setAt10(float val);
    public void setAt11(float val);
    public void setAt12(float val);
    public void setAt20(float val);
    public void setAt21(float val);
    public void setAt22(float val);
    public void setIdentity();
    public void setRotateAboutPoint(QDPoint origin, float angle);
    public void setScale(float xScale, float yScale);
    public void setTranslate(float xTrans, float yTrans);
    public Matrix3x3 transpose();
}
```

CLASS HIERARCHY:

Object→QTByteObject→Matrix3×3

Class quicktime.qd3d.math.Matrix4×4

This class contains information for a 4 × 4 float matrix. This has the same get and set calls as the Matrix3x3 class.

```
public final class Matrix4x4 extends QTByteObject
                        implements QuickTimeLib, QuickDraw3DLib, Cloneable {
//Static Fields
    public static final int kNativeSize;

//Constructors
    public Matrix4x4();
    public Matrix4x4(float[][] table);

//Static Methods
    public static final EndianDescriptor getEndianDescriptor();

//Instance Methods
    public Object clone();
    public Matrix4x4 copy();
    public float determinant();
    public float getAt00();
    public float getAt01();
    public float getAt02();
    public float getAt03();
    public float getAt10();
    public float getAt11();
    public float getAt12();
    public float getAt13();
    public float getAt20();
    public float getAt21();
    public float getAt22();
    public float getAt23();
    public float getAt30();
    public float getAt31();
    public float getAt32();
    public float getAt33();
    public Matrix4x4 invert();
    public Matrix4x4 multiply(Matrix4x4 matrixB);
    public void setAt00(float val);
    public void setAt01(float val);
    public void setAt02(float val);
    public void setAt03(float val);
    public void setAt10(float val);
    public void setAt11(float val);
    public void setAt12(float val);
    public void setAt13(float val);
    public void setAt20(float val);
    public void setAt21(float val);
    public void setAt22(float val);
    public void setAt23(float val);
```

```
public void setAt30(float val);
public void setAt31(float val);
public void setAt32(float val);
public void setAt33(float val);
public void setIdentity();
public void setQuaternion(Quaternion quaternion);
public void setRotateAboutAxis(Point3D origin, Vector3D orientation, float angle);
public void setRotateAboutPoint(Point3D origin, float xAngle, float yAngle,
                    float zAngle);
public void setRotateVectorToVector(Vector3D v1, Vector3D v2);
public void setRotateX(float angle);
public void setRotateXYZ(float xAngle, float yAngle, float zAngle);
public void setRotateY(float angle);
public void setRotateZ(float angle);
public void setScale(float xScale, float yScale, float zScale);
public void setTranslate(float xTrans, float yTrans, float zTrans);
public Matrix4x4 transpose();
}
```

CLASS HIERARCHY:
Object→QTByteObject→Matrix4x4

Class quicktime.qd3d.math.Point2D

This class contains static calls—the implementation is found in the QDPoint class.

The rRatio() method returns the two-dimensional point that lies on the line segment between the points p1 and p2 and that is at a distance from the first point determined by the ratio r1/(r1 + r2).

See also QDPoint.

```
public final class Point2D extends Object implements QuickTimeLib, QuickDraw3DLib {
//Static Methods
    public static QDPoint add(QDPoint point2D, Vector2D v);
    public static float distance(QDPoint p1, QDPoint p2);
    public static float distanceSquared(QDPoint p1, QDPoint p2);
    public static QDPoint rRatio(QDPoint p1, QDPoint p2, float r1, float r2);
    public static QDPoint subtract(QDPoint point2D, Vector2D v);
    public static Vector2D subtract(QDPoint p1, QDPoint p2);
}
```

CLASS HIERARCHY:
Object→Point2D

Class quicktime.qd3d.math.Point3D

This class contains information for a three-dimensional point. The rRatio() method returns the three-dimensional point that lies on the line segment between the points p1 and p2 and that is at a distance from the first point determined by the ratio r1/(r1 + r2).

The cross() method returns the cross product of the two vectors determined by subtracting point2 from this and point3 from this.

The transformQuaternion() method returns a three-dimensional point that is the result of transforming the vector specified by the vector parameter using the quaternion specified by the quaternion parameter.

```
public final class Point3D extends QTByteObject
                    implements QuickTimeLib, QuickDraw3DLib, Cloneable {
//Static Fields
    public static final int kNativeSize;

//Constructors
    public Point3D();
    public Point3D(float x, float y, float z);

//Static Methods
    public static final EndianDescriptor getEndianDescriptor();

//Instance Methods
    public Point3D add(Vector3D vector3D);
    public Object clone();
    public Vector3D cross(Point3D point2, Point3D point3);
    public float distance(Point3D p2);
    public float distanceSquared(Point3D p2);
    public float getX();
    public float getY();
    public float getZ();
    public Point3D rRatio(Point3D p2, float r1, float r2);
    public void setX(float x);
    public void setY(float y);
    public void setZ(float z);
    public Point3D subtract(Vector3D vector3D);
    public Vector3D subtract(Point3D p2);
    public String toString();
    public Point3D transformQuaternion(Quaternion quaternion);
}
```

CLASS HIERARCHY:

Object→QTByteObject→Point3D

Class quicktime.qd3d.math.Quaternion

This class is a quadruple of floating-point numbers that obeys the laws of quaternion arithmetic. A quaternion transform will rotate and twist an object according to the mathematical properties of quaternions.

```
public final class Quaternion extends QTByteObject
                              implements QuickTimeLib, QuickDraw3DLib, Cloneable {
//Static Fields
    public static final int kNativeSize;

//Constructors
    public Quaternion();
    public Quaternion(float w, float x, float y, float z);

//Static Methods
    public static final EndianDescriptor getEndianDescriptor();

//Instance Methods
    public Object clone();
    public Quaternion copy();
    public float dot(Quaternion q2);
    public float getW();
    public float getX();
    public float getY();
    public float getZ();
    public Quaternion interpolateFast(Quaternion q2, float t);
    public Quaternion interpolateLinear(Quaternion q2, float t);
    public Quaternion invert();
    public boolean isIdentity();
    public Quaternion matchReflection(Quaternion q2);
    public Quaternion multiply(Quaternion q2);
    public Quaternion normalize();
    public void setIdentity();
    public void setMatrix(Matrix4x4 matrix);
    public void setRotateAboutAxis(Vector3D axis, float angle);
    public void setRotateVectorToVector(Vector3D v1, Vector3D v2);
    public void setRotateX(float angle);
    public void setRotateXYZ(float xAngle, float yAngle, float zAngle);
    public void setRotateY(float angle);
    public void setRotateZ(float angle);
    public void setW(float w);
    public void setX(float x);
    public void setY(float y);
    public void setZ(float z);
}
```

CLASS HIERARCHY:

Object→QTByteObject→Quaternion

Class quicktime.qd3d.math.Vector2D

This class contains information for two-dimensional vectors.

```
public final class Vector2D extends QTByteObject
                        implements QuickTimeLib, QuickDraw3DLib, Cloneable {
//Static Fields
    public static final int kNativeSize;

//Constructors
    public Vector2D();
    public Vector2D(float x, float y);

//Static Methods
    public static final EndianDescriptor getEndianDescriptor();

//Instance Methods
    public Vector2D add(Vector2D v2);
    public Object clone();
    public float cross(Vector2D v2);
    public float dot(Vector2D v2);
    public float getX();
    public float getY();
    public float length();
    public Vector2D normalize();
    public Vector2D scale(float scalar);
    public void setX(float x);
    public void setY(float y);
    public Vector2D subtract(Vector2D v2);
}
```

CLASS HIERARCHY:

Object→QTByteObject→Vector2D

Class quicktime.qd3d.math.Vector3D

This class contains information for three-dimensional vectors.

```
public final class Vector3D extends QTByteObject
                        implements QuickTimeLib, QuickDraw3DLib, Cloneable {
//Static Fields
    public static final int kNativeSize;

//Constructors
    public Vector3D();
    public Vector3D(float x, float y, float z);

//Static Methods
```

```
    public static final EndianDescriptor getEndianDescriptor();

//Instance Methods
    public Vector3D add(Vector3D v2);
    public Object clone();
    public Vector3D cross(Vector3D v2);
    public float dot(Vector2D v2);
    public float getX();
    public float getY();
    public float getZ();
    public float length();
    public Vector3D normalize();
    public Vector3D scale(float scalar);
    public void setX(float x);
    public void setY(float y);
    public void setZ(float z);
    public Vector3D subtract(Vector3D v2);
    public String toString();
    public Vector3D transformQuaternion(Quaternion quaternion);
}
```

CLASS HIERARCHY:

Object→QTByteObject→Vector3D

32

The quicktime. qd3d.transform Package

The `quicktime.qd3d.transform` package, which contains one class, provides information for three-dimensional rotations—that is, rotations around x, y, and z axes. Figure 32.1 shows the class hierarchy for this package.

FIGURE 32.1 *The* `quicktime.qd3dtransform` *package*

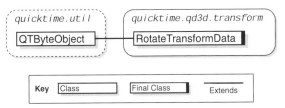

Class quicktime.qd3d.transform.RotateTransformData

This class contains information for three-dimensional rotations.

```
public final class RotateTransformData extends QTByteObject implements Cloneable {
//Static Fields
    public static final int kNativeSize;

//Constructors
    public RotateTransformData();
    public RotateTransformData(int axis, float radians);

//Static Methods
    public static final EndianDescriptor getEndianDescriptor();
```

```
//Instance Methods
    public Object clone();
    public int getAxis();
    public float getRadian();
    public void setAxis(int axis);
    public void setRadian(float radians);
    public String toString();
}
```

CLASS HIERARCHY:

Object →QTByteObject→RotateTransformData

33

The quicktime. sound Package

The quicktime.sound package contains a relatively small number of classes and deals with recording and playing back sound. These classes present a limited subset of the QuickTime Sound Manager API and are derived from Apple's Universal Header files. While some basic sound recording services are provided in this package, for more demanding sound input and output you should use the sequence grabber components and movie playback services.

The SoundConstants interface represents all of the constants in the Sound Manager interface. The Sound class is useful in providing general routines for recording sound. Figure 33.1 shows the class hierarchy for this package.

FIGURE 33.1 *The* quicktime.sound *package*

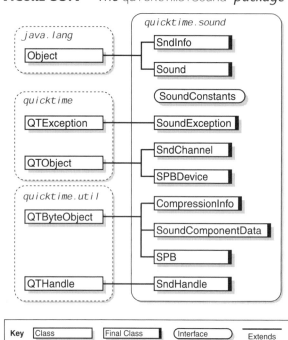

Class quicktime.sound.CompressionInfo

This class contains information about the compression format of sound data.

```
public final class CompressionInfo extends QTByteObject implements SoundLib {
//Static Fields
    public static final int kNativeSize;

//Constructors
    public CompressionInfo();

//Static Methods
    public static CompressionInfo get(int compressionID, int format, int numChannels,
                                      int sampleSize);

//Instance Methods
    public int getBytesPerFrame();
    public int getBytesPerPacket();
    public int getBytesPerSample();
    public int getCompressionID();
```

```
    public int getFormat();
    public int getRecordSize();
    public int getSamplesPerPacket();
    public void setBytesPerFrame(int bytesPerFrame);
    public void setBytesPerPacket(int bytesPerPacket);
    public void setBytesPerSample(int bytesPerSample);
    public void setCompressionID(int compressionID);
    public void setFormat(int format);
    public void setRecordSize(int recordSize);
    public void setSamplesPerPacket(int samplesPerPacket);
    public String toString();
}
```

CLASS HIERARCHY:

Object→QTByteObject→CompressionInfo

Class quicktime.sound.SndChannel

Sound channels are used to play back sound. With the setQuietNow() method, a flag controls whether a sound channel is silent when it is disposed of, which can be some indeterminate time of the Java GarbageCollector or after any sound currently playing is finished. The default setting is to allow the sound to finish playing; the flag is set to false. If you wish to explicitly stop a sound, then you should do so.

The play() method plays a sound asynchronously from memory.

```
public final class SndChannel extends QTObject implements Errors, QuickTimeLib {
//Constructors
    public SndChannel(int synth, int init);

//Instance Methods
    public final boolean isQuietNow();
    public final void play(SndHandle sndHdl);
    public final void setQuietNow(boolean flag);
}
```

CLASS HIERARCHY:

Object→QTObject→SndChannel

Class quicktime.sound.SndHandle

This class contains a sound data header that describes the format and characteristics of the sound data buffer, which follows the header.

You can use the setupHeader() method to construct a sound resource containing sampled sound that can be passed to the play sound methods.

The getSoundHeaderOffset() method returns the number of bytes from the beginning of the sound resource specified by the sndHandle to the sound header that is contained within.

The getSoundData() method returns a reference to the sound data that is contained within the SndHandle. The SndHandle will be locked by this call and should remain locked for the life of the returned data object.

The appendSoundData() method appends the sound buffer to the end of this handle. This is required before the SndHandle can be used for recording or playing sound. If a preexisting buffer has been appended, this will be removed and replaced with the incoming buffer. This copies the incoming buffer.

You use the parseSndHeader() method to retrieve information about a SndHandle.

```
public final class SndHandle extends QTHandle
                            implements Errors, QuickTimeLib, SoundLib {
//Constructors
    public SndHandle(int size, boolean clear);
    public SndHandle(int numChannels, float sampleRate, int sampleSize,
                    int compressionType, int baseNote);

//Instance Methods
    public void appendSoundBuffer(int bufferSize);
    public void appendSoundData(QTPointerRef buffer);
    public QTPointerRef getSoundData();
    public final int getSoundHeaderOffset();
    public final SndInfo parseSndHeader();
    public int setupHeader(int numChannels, float sampleRate, int sampleSize,
                    int compressionType, int baseNote, int numBytes);
}
```

CLASS HIERARCHY:
Object→QTObject→QTHandleRef→QTHandle→SndHandle

Class quicktime.sound.SndInfo

This class is used to represent information about sound data that is stored in memory (in SndHandle).

```
public final class SndInfo extends Object implements SoundLib, InterfaceLib {
//Static Methods
```

```
    public static SndInfo parseAIFFHeader(OpenFile file);

//Instance Fields
    public int dataOffset;
    public int numFrames;
    public SoundComponentData sndData;
}
```

CLASS HIERARCHY:

Object→SndInfo

Class quicktime.sound.Sound

This class provides the play() method to play a sound from data stored in memory.

```
public final class Sound extends Object implements Errors, QuickTimeLib {
//Constructors
    public Sound();

//Static Methods
    public static final void play(SndHandle sndHdl);
}
```

CLASS HIERARCHY:

Object→Sound

Class quicktime.sound.SoundComponentData

The getSampleCount() returns the number of samples in the buffer pointed to by the buffer field. For compressed sounds, this field indicates the number of compressed samples in the sound, not the size of the buffer.

```
public final class SoundComponentData extends QTByteObject {
//Static Fields
    public static final int kNativeSize;

//Constructors
    public SoundComponentData();

//Instance Methods
    public final QTPointer getBuffer();
    public final int getFlags();
    public final int getFormat();
    public final int getNumChannels();
    public final int getSampleCount();
```

```
    public final float getSampleRate();
    public final int getSampleSize();
    public final void setBuffer(QTPointer buffer);
    public final void setFlags(int flags);
    public final void setFormat(int format);
    public final void setNumChannels(int chans);
    public final void setSampleCount(int sampleCount);
    public final void setSampleRate(float sampleRate);
    public final void setSampleSize(int sampleSize);
    public String toString();
}
```

CLASS HIERARCHY:

Object→QTByteObject→SoundComponentData

Interface quicktime.sound.SoundConstants

This class represents all of the constants in the Sound Manager interface. Note that all constants, except for those that start with an acronym such as MPEG, start with a lower-case letter. A listing of these constants is provided on the CD-ROM at the back of this book.

Class quicktime.sound.SoundException

This is a general catch-all class used to signal errors that occur from QuickTime calls in the quicktime.sound package.

The checkError() method throws an exception if the incoming err argument is a nonzero value.

```
public final class SoundException extends QTException {
//Constructors
    public SoundException(String str);
    public SoundException(int val);

//Static Methods
    public static void checkError(int err);
}
```

CLASS HIERARCHY:

Object→Throwable→Exception→QTException→SoundException

Class quicktime.sound.SPB

This class is used in conjunction with an SPBDevice to record sound. It contains fields that describe how much sound the device should record and a buffer in memory where the recorded sound data is stored.

The record() method records audio data into memory either synchronously or asynchronously. The sound is recorded into the specified buffer. If it is recorded synchronously, then the error code will be checked and an exception thrown if required. If recorded asynchronously, then the application will need to check for errors after the recording has completed with the getError() method. After recording, the buffer contains the recorded bytes; the count, how many bytes were recorded; and the milliseconds, how many milliseconds of sound were recorded.

stopRecording() ends a recording from a sound input device. If you call the checkError() instance method, you get an abortErr exception, which indicates that the recording was stopped by calling this method.

isRecording() returns the status of the recording. While the input device is recording, this call returns true. When a recording terminates without an error, this call returns false. When an error occurs during recording or the recording has been terminated by a call to the stopRecording() method, this call throws an abortErr exception.

```
public final class SPB extends QTByteObject implements QuickTimeLib {
//Static Fields
    public static final int kNativeSize;

//Constructors
    public SPB(SPBDevice device, int count, int milliseconds, QTPointerRef buffer);

//Instance Methods
    public QTPointerRef getBuffer();
    public int getBufferLength();
    public int getCount();
    public SPBDevice getDevice();
    public short getError();
    public int getMilliseconds();
    public boolean isRecording();
    public short meterLevel();
    public void pauseRecording();
    public void record(boolean flag);
    public void resumeRecording();
    public void setBuffer(QTPointerRef buffer);
    public void setCount(int count);
```

```
    public void setMilliseconds(int msecs);
    public void stopRecording();
}
```

CLASS HIERARCHY:

Object→QTByteObject→SPB

Class quicktime.sound.SPBDevice

This class represents an input device from which sound can be recorded and allows your application to control the settings of this input device. You can construct a SPBDevice directly or make one from an existing SndChannel.

```
public final class SPBDevice extends QTObject implements SoundConstants, QuickTimeLib {
//Constructors
    public SPBDevice(String deviceName, int permission);

//Static Methods
    public static SPBDevice fromSoundChannel(SGSoundChannel sc);

//Instance Methods
    public int bytesToMilliseconds(int bytes);
    public boolean getAutomaticGainControl();
    public int getChannelAvailable();
    public int[] getCompressionAvailable();
    public int getCompressionType();
    public float getInputGain();
    public int getInputSource();
    public String[] getInputSourceNames();
    public int getLevelMeterLevel();
    public boolean getLevelMeterOnOff();
    public int getNumberChannels();
    public int getPlayThruOnOff();
    public float getSampleRate();
    public float[] getSampleRateAvailable();
    public int getSampleSize();
    public int[] getSampleSizeAvailable();
    public float getStereoInputGainLeft();
    public float getStereoInputGainRight();
    public boolean hasOptionsDialog();
    public int millisecondsToBytes(int msecs);
    public void setAutomaticGainControl(boolean flag);
    public void setCompressionType(int compType);
    public void setInputGain(float gain);
    public void setInputSource(int source);
    public void setLevelMeterOnOff(boolean flag);
    public void setNumberChannels(int channels);
    public void setPlayThruOnOff(int volume);
```

```
public void setSampleRate(float rate);
public void setSampleSize(int sampleSize);
public void setStereoInputGain(float leftChannel, float rightChannel);
public void showOptionsDialog();
}
```

CLASS HIERARCHY:

Object→QTObject→SPBDevice

34

The quicktime.std Package

The original QuickTime header files are a collection of eight files that describe the standard QuickTime API. As such, nearly all of the functions defined in these files are to be found in classes in the `quicktime.std` group of packages.

The standard header files are

- `Components.h`. All calls from this file are in the `quicktime.std.comp` package.

- `ImageCompression.h` and `ImageCodec.h`. All calls from these files are in the `quicktime.std.image` package.

- `MediaHandlers.h`. All calls from this file are in the `quicktime.std.movies.media` package.

- `Movies.h`. This file has been separated into a number of packages to present a finer degree of definition and functional grouping.

  - Sprite animation calls are in the `quicktime.std.anim` package.

  - `CallBack` and `TimeBase` calls are in the `quicktime.std.clocks` package.

  - File I/O calls are in the `quicktime.io` package.

  - All media-related calls are in the `quicktime.std.movies.media` package.

  - The remaining (movies, movie controller, track, atom container) calls are in the `quicktime.std.movies` package.

- `QuickTimeComponents.h`. This file has been separated into a number of packages to present a finer degree of definition and functional grouping.

- ❑ The clocks component is found in the `quicktime.std.clocks` package.

- ❑ Sequence grabber component calls are found in the `quicktime.std.sg` package.

- ❑ The remaining components are found in the `quicktime.std.qtcomponents` package.

- ■ `QuickTimeMusic.h`. All calls from this file are in the `quicktime.std.music` package.

The `quicktime.std` package contains only one interface and one exception. The `quicktime.std.StdQTConstants` interface represents all of the constants in the QuickTime interface. Figure 34.1 shows the class hierarchy for this package.

FIGURE 34.1 *The* `quicktime.std` *package*

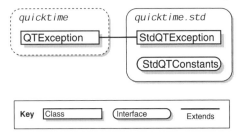

Interface quicktime.std.StdQTConstants

This class represents all of the constants in these standard QuickTime interfaces. All constants, except for those that start with an acronym such as MPEG, start with a lower-case letter. The full listing is contained on the CD-ROM at the back of this book.

Class quicktime.std.StdQTException

This is a general catch-all class that is used to signal errors that occur from QuickTime calls.

```
public class StdQTException extends QTException {
//Constructors
```

```
    public StdQTException(String str);
    public StdQTException(int val);

//Static Methods
    public static void checkError(int err);
}
```

CLASS HIERARCHY:

Object→Throwable→Exception→QTException→StdQTException

35

The quicktime. std.anim Package

The `quicktime.std.anim` package contains classes that provide support for animation. QuickTime can be used as a real-time rendering system for animation, distinct from a data format—the movie. Thus, you can create a graphics space (sprite world) within which characters (sprites) can be manipulated.

The package contains only two classes: `Sprite` and `SpriteWorld`. Both classes implement the corresponding data structures of the QuickTime Movie Toolbox. You can use `SpriteWorld` to make animations. Figure 35.1 shows the class hierarchy for this package.

FIGURE 35.1 *The* `quicktime.std.anim` *package*

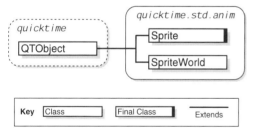

Class quicktime.std.anim.Sprite

This class implements the corresponding data structure of the Movie Toolbox.

getSpriteWorld() returns the sprite world that this sprite belongs to. The invalidate() method invalidates the portion of the sprite's sprite world occupied by the sprite.

The getMatrix() and setMatrix() methods get and set the matrix property of this sprite.

remove() removes the sprite from the SpriteWorld that it is contained in and destroys its internal structures. The Sprite is not usable after this call. If you have any other Java objects that refer to this sprite, they will also be unusable, so you should use this call with care.

```
public final class Sprite extends QTObject
                          implements StdQTConstants, Errors, QuickTimeLib {
//Constructors
    public Sprite(SpriteWorld itsSpriteWorld, ImageDescription idh,
            EncodedImage imageData, Matrix matrix, boolean visible, int layer);

//Instance Methods
    public GraphicsMode getGraphicsMode();
    public RawEncodedImage getImageData();
    public int getImageDataSize();
    public ImageDescription getImageDescription();
    public int getLayer();
    public Matrix getMatrix();
    public SpriteWorld getSpriteWorld();
    public boolean getVisible();
    public boolean hitTest(int flags, QDPoint loc);
    public void invalidate();
    public void remove();
    public void setGraphicsMode(GraphicsMode gMode);
    public void setImageData(EncodedImage data);
    public void setImageDataSize(int size);
    public void setImageDescription(ImageDescription idh);
    public void setLayer(int layer);
    public void setMatrix(Matrix matrix);
    public void setVisible(boolean visible);
}
```

CLASS HIERARCHY:
Object→QTObject→Sprite

Class quicktime.std.anim.SpriteWorld

This class implements the corresponding data structure in the Movie Toolbox, as specified in the QuickTime API. You can use SpriteWorld objects to make animations. A SpriteWorld handles the common tasks of invalidating appropriate areas as sprite properties change, the composition of sprites and their background on an off-screen buffer, and the blitting of the result to the destination QDGraphics provided in the constructor.

setBounds() sets the bounds of the SpriteWorld by scaling its matrix. getBounds() returns the current bounds of the SpriteWorld.

idle() allows the sprite world to update and redraw its invalid portions.

Use hitTest() to determine if a sprite exists at the specified location.

```
public class SpriteWorld extends QTObject implements QDConstants, QuickTimeLib {
//Constructors
    public SpriteWorld(QDGraphics port, QDGraphics spriteLayer, QDColor backgroundColor,
                    QDGraphics background);

//Instance Methods
    public final QDRect getBounds();
    public final Matrix getMatrix();
    public final Sprite hitTest(int flags, QDPoint loc);
    public final int idle(int flagsIn);
    public final void invalidate(QDRect invalidArea);
    public final void setBounds(QDRect bounds);
    public final void setClip(Region clipRgn);
    public final void setFlags(int flags, int flagsMask);
    public final void setGraphicsMode(GraphicsMode gMode);
    public final void setMatrix(Matrix matrix);
}
```

CLASS HIERARCHY:
Object→QTObject→SpriteWorld

36

The quicktime. std.clocks Package

The `quicktime.std.clocks` package contains a number of useful classes that provide timing services. These classes include support for the creation of hierarchical dependencies between time bases, a callback mechanism for user-scheduling of events or notification, and the capability of instantiating the system clocks that provide the timing services. Classes in this package implement methods for their corresponding QuickTime component.

The `Clock` class offers two basic services: generating time information and scheduling time-based callback events. Its methods offer access to a component's structure and its fields. A `Clock` is a pure source of time: It doesn't stop ticking.

A QuickTime `TimeBase` provides an application with an abstract and powerful way of dealing with time. Unlike a clock, which doesn't stop ticking and has values that are always defined, a `TimeBase` allows your application to view and control time on its own terms in whatever resolution (to the resolution of the clock source) you require. For instance, a `TimeBase` allows the setting of start and stop times and allows looping the time value between these times. The current time values can be set to an arbitrary value. The rate at which the time values of a `TimeBase` change can be set: A rate of zero meaning that the time value doesn't change; 1 that it changes in a forward motion at the normal rate (a second == a second); 2 that the time value changes twice as fast as normal. Rates can also be set to negative values, in which case the time value decreases at the specified rate.

QuickTime `TimeBase` objects also allow for the construction of hierarchies of time. When a `TimeBase` is slaved to another, its effective rate is the multiplication of its rate with the rate of its parent—for example, master == 2, slave == 4→effective rate == 8. The depth of a timing hierarchy is at the application's discretion.

QTCallBack is one of the most important classes in that it provides users with a defined operation of some time condition of a clock's time base. The TimeBase class defines the QuickTime time coordinate system. Note that the class that subclasses a particular callback type must define the execute() method. This is the method that will be called when the callback is invoked.

The TimeRecord class allows a full description of a QuickTime time specification structure and contains a time value scaled to a time base coordinate system. Figure 36.1 shows the class hierarchy for this package.

FIGURE 36.1 *The* quicktime.std.clocks *package*

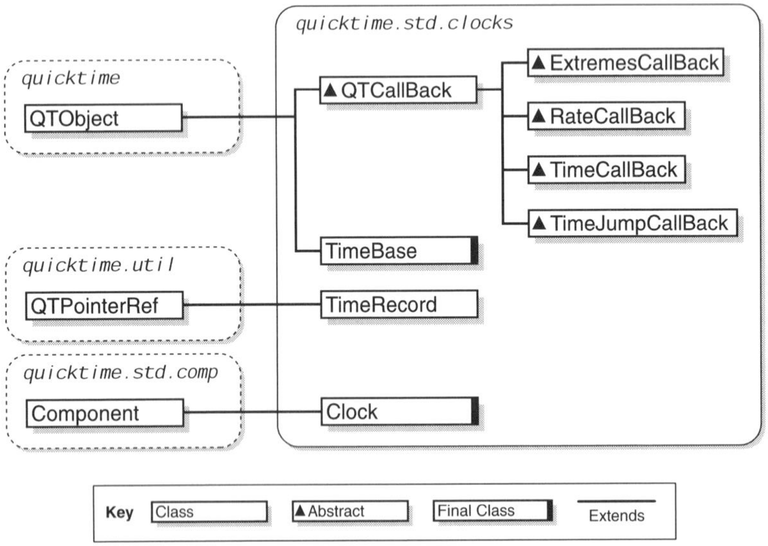

Class quicktime.std.clocks.Clock

This class implements methods for a corresponding QuickTime component. Clock components offer two basic services: They generate time information and schedule time-based callback events. Its methods offer access to a component's structure and its fields. The clock component deals directly with some hardware that provides a source of time. QuickTime provides access to several clocks (sound clock, system tick, and so on) through setting the subtype of the component to the type of clock. The user generally interacts with a TimeBase, and if creating a TimeBase directly, the application must ultimately provide a clock component as the source of time for a TimeBase.

The clock() method opens the specified component, 'clok' with the given sub-Type.

```
public final class Clock extends Component implements StdQTConstants, QuickTimeLib {
//Constructors
    public Clock(int subType);

//Instance Methods
    public TimeRecord getTime();
}
```

CLASS HIERARCHY:

Object→QTObject→ComponentIdentifier→Component→Clock

Class quicktime.std.clocks.ExtremesCallBack

This class provides scheduled operations at the start or stop times of the QTCallBack time base.

callMeWhen() specifies the time when the callback should be called. The application should set flags to specify certain scheduling information as triggerAtStart or triggerAtStop.

The class that subclasses a particular callback type must define the execute() method. This is the method that will be called when the callback is invoked. The application subclasses this class and defines the execute() method to perform tasks at the start and stop times of the TimeBase (i.e., its extremes).

```
public abstract class ExtremesCallBack extends QTCallBack implements StdQTConstants {
//Constructors
    public ExtremesCallBack(TimeBase tb, int flags);

//Instance Fields
    public int flags;

//Instance Methods
    public final void callMeWhen();
    public String toString();
}
```

CLASS HIERARCHY:
Object→QTObject→QTCallBack→ExtremesCallBack

Class quicktime.std.clocks.QTCallBack

This class provides users with a defined operation at some time condition of a clock's time base. Its methods offer access to a QuickTime structure and its fields.

There is a very important issue that must be understood by application developers when using these or any of the callback capabilities of QuickTime in a Java environment. QuickTime native calls are dispatched through a single gateway/lock and run to their completion.

A callback from QuickTime into Java is invoked through the Java application calling a native QuickTime function. In the case of the QTCallBack, the callback is invoked through a direct or indirect call of the QuickTime MoviesTask function.

When the MoviesTask function invokes a callback and calls into Java, this occurs in the same thread of execution. Any other native QuickTime calls originating from another thread are queued until the MoviesTask call is completed (including any callbacks that do not spawn their own threads). There exists a potential thread deadlock issue that can arise with the use of callbacks due to this underlying *modus operandus* that an application developer may cause and must deal with. This is not a bug, but is a feature of the current implementation.

For example: Thread 1 calls MoviesTask (Movie.task or Movie.taskAll), which invokes a callback on say a QTDrawer object, which has a synchronized redraw call. The callback's action is to redraw this QTDrawer object (which will make a native call to QuickTime to draw).

In Thread 2, AWT issues a paint call that goes through to the QTDrawer synchronized redraw call. This redraw call goes through to a native QuickTime call, which halts waiting for the currently executing MoviesTask call to complete in Thread 1.

However, we have a deadlock: Thread 1 is unable to complete and halts at the QTDrawer redraw call because Thread 2 already has the synchronization lock for the QTDrawer object.

However, Thread 2 is unable to continue because Thread 1 has the native QuickTime lock. One alternative is to have the callback that redraws the QTDrawer spawn another thread and redraw the QTDrawer in this spawn thread. Once the thread is spawned, the callback can then complete, and in the above scenario, Thread 1 can finish the MoviesTask, Thread 2 would then be able to continue, and the QTDrawer would redraw itself.

Many of the callback methods in QuickTime are required to execute in place, in that QuickTime requires a result code in order to proceed. These callbacks should provide meaningful feedback when their execute() method returns. The subclasses of the QTCallBack, however, can execute asynchronously; QuickTime does not require a result code in order to proceed. This is also true of any of the execute() methods with no return value.

The callMeWhen() method registers the callback. It uses the state of the subclass to set the parameters that control the callback's activation. The class that subclasses a particular callback type must define the execute() method. This is the method called when the callback is invoked.

```
public abstract class QTCallBack extends QTObject implements QuickTimeLib {
//Instance Methods
    public abstract void callMeWhen();
    public final void cancel();
    public abstract void execute();
    public final TimeBase getTimeBase();
    public final int getType();
}
```

CLASS HIERARCHY:

Object→QTObject→QTCallBack

Class quicktime.std.clocks.RateCallBack

This class provides scheduled operations with changes in a TimeBase ticking rate.

```
public abstract class RateCallBack extends QTCallBack implements StdQTConstants {
//Constructors
    public RateCallBack(TimeBase tb, float rate, int flags);

//Instance Fields
    public int flags;
    public float rate;

//Instance Methods
    public final void callMeWhen();
    public String toString();
```

}

CLASS HIERARCHY:

Object→QTObject→QTCallBack→RateCallBack

Class quicktime.std.clocks.TimeBase

This class defines a QuickTime `TimeBase` time coordinate system. It may be used for general timing purposes, and it provides the time line for a movie.

The `getTime()` method allows your application to obtain the current time value from a time base in its preferred time scale. It returns the time value that contains the current time from the specified time base in the specified time scale.

```
public final class TimeBase extends QTObject implements QuickTimeLib {
//Constructors
    public TimeBase();

//Static Methods
    public static TimeBase fromICMFrameTime(ICMFrameTime ft);
    public static TimeBase fromMovie(Movie m);
    public static TimeBase fromQTCallBack(QTCallBack cb);
    public static TimeBase fromSequenceGrabber(SequenceGrabber sg);
    public static TimeBase fromTimeRecord(TimeRecord tr);
    public static TimeBase fromTunePlayer(TunePlayer tp);

//Instance Methods
    public float getEffectiveRate();
    public int getFlags();
    public Clock getMasterClock();
    public TimeBase getMasterTimeBase();
    public float getRate();
    public int getStartTime();
    public int getStartTime(int scale);
    public int getStatus(TimeRecord unpinnedTime);
    public int getStopTime(int scale);
    public int getStopTime();
    public TimeRecord getTRStartTime(int scale);
    public TimeRecord getTRStartTime();
    public TimeRecord getTRStopTime(int scale);
    public TimeRecord getTRStopTime();
    public TimeRecord getTRTime(int scale);
    public TimeRecord getTRTime();
    public int getTime(int scale);
    public int getTime();
    public void setFlags(int timeBaseFlags);
    public void setMasterClock(Clock clockMeister, TimeRecord slaveZero);
    public void setMasterTimeBase(TimeBase master, TimeRecord slaveZero);
```

```
    public void setRate(float rate);
    public void setStartTime(TimeRecord tr);
    public void setStopTime(TimeRecord tr);
    public void setTime(TimeRecord tr);
    public void setValue(int time, int scale);
    public void setZero(TimeRecord zero);
    public String toString();
}
```

CLASS HIERARCHY:

Object→QTObject→TimeBase

Class quicktime.std.clocks.TimeCallBack

This class provides scheduled operations at specified time values.

```
public abstract class TimeCallBack extends QTCallBack implements StdQTConstants {
//Constructors
    public TimeCallBack(TimeBase tb, int scale, int value, int flags);

//Instance Fields
    public int flags;
    public int scale;
    public int value;

//Instance Methods
    public final void callMeWhen();
    public String toString();
}
```

CLASS HIERARCHY:

Object→QTObject→QTCallBack→TimeCallBack

Class quicktime.std.clocks.TimeJumpCallBack

This class provides scheduled operations when the time value of the TimeBase abruptly changes.

```
public abstract class TimeJumpCallBack extends QTCallBack {
//Constructors
    public TimeJumpCallBack(TimeBase tb);

//Instance Methods
    public final void callMeWhen();
}
```

CLASS HIERARCHY:

Object→QTObject→QTCallBack→TimeJumpCallBack

Class quicktime.std.clocks.TimeRecord

This class encapsulates the QuickTime time specification structure. It contains a time value, which is scaled to the time base coordinate system.

The `TimeRecord()` constructor is an empty record. It has no value for the `TimeBase` field. The `TimeRecord()` constructor takes no parameters. The structure is typically filled out by passing it an argument to various QuickTime for Java method calls.

`getValue()` returns the value of the time value in the current state. `getScale()` returns the current value of the time scale.

```
public class TimeRecord extends QTPointerRef implements QuickTimeLib {
//Constructors
    public TimeRecord();

//Instance Methods
    public final void addTime(TimeRecord source);
    public final void convertTime(TimeBase newBase);
    public final void convertTimeScale(int newScale);
    public final int getScale();
    public final TimeBase getTimeBase();
    public final long getValue();
    public final void setScale(int scale);
    public final void setValue(long value);
    public final void subtractTime(TimeRecord source);
    public String toString();
}
```

CLASS HIERARCHY:

Object→QTObject→QTPointerRef→TimeRecord

37

The quicktime. std.comp Package

Because QuickTime is a component-based architecture, much of its funtionality is provided through the creation and implementation of a particular component's API. The `quicktime.std.comp` package contains classes that provide basic support for this component architecture. These classes are `Component`, `ComponentDescription`, and `Component-Identifier`.

The classes in this package provide the basic capability of opening and closing components and obtaining information about particular components and what components are currently available. Figure 37.1 shows the class hierarchy for this package.

FIGURE 37.1 *The* `quicktime.std.comp` *package*

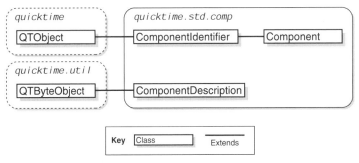

Class quicktime.std.comp.Component

This class represents an open `ComponentInstance`. Subclasses define specific `Component-Instance` types.

```
public class Component extends ComponentIdentifier implements QuickTimeLib, Errors {
//Constructors
    public Component(ComponentIdentifier comp);
    public Component(int type, int subType);

//Instance Methods
    public final int count();
}
```

CLASS HIERARCHY:

Object→QTObject→ComponentIdentifier→Component

Class quicktime.std.comp.ComponentDescription

This class describes component features. A value of zero indicates a nonspecific value and can also be used as a wildcard in searches.

The `ComponentDescription()` constructor creates a default `ComponentDescription` with all zero values.

```
public class ComponentDescription extends QTByteObject implements QuickTimeLib {
//Constructors
    public ComponentDescription();
    public ComponentDescription(int type);
    public ComponentDescription(int type, int subType, int manu, int flag, int mask);

//Instance Methods
    public Object clone();
    public int count();
    public int getFlags();
    public int getManufacturer();
    public int getMask();
    public int getSubType();
    public int getType();
    public void setFlags(int flag);
    public void setManufacturer(int manufacturer);
    public void setMask(int mask);
    public void setSubType(int subType);
    public void setType(int type);
    public String toString();
}
```

CLASS HIERARCHY:

Object→QTByteObject→ComponentDescription

Class quicktime.std.comp.ComponentIdentifier

This class represents a ComponentIdentifier. Use the find() method to determine the next component as specified. It returns null if it can't find a component that matches the specifications. getInfo() returns all of the registration information for a component. The toString() method prints the Component Info.

```
public class ComponentIdentifier extends QTObject implements QuickTimeLib {
//Static Methods
    public static final ComponentIdentifier find(ComponentIdentifier comp,
                                        ComponentDescription desc);
    public static final ComponentIdentifier find(ComponentDescription desc);

//Instance Methods
    public final ComponentDescription getInfo();
    public String toString();
}
```

CLASS HIERARCHY:

Object→QTObject→ComponentIdentifier

38

The quicktime. std.image Package

The `quicktime.std.image` package contains a large number of classes for using the drawing and image importing services of QuickTime.

Some of these classes utilize the Image Compression Manager and provide control for the compression and decompression of both single images and sequences of images. The package also contains the `Matrix` class, which (like the `Region` class in the `quicktime.qd` package) is used generally throughout QuickTime to transform the rendering of 2D images. The `CSequence` class defines methods used for compressing a sequence of images. `DSequence` defines methods used for decompressing a sequence of images.

The `CodecComponent` class enables you to choose the first, fastest, or most accurate compressor or decompressor of the specified type, as well as the compressor that produces the smallest resulting data. The `CodecName` class defines a compressor name structure, and its methods return the compressor type, `CodecComponent`, and name of the compressor component. `DataRateParams` is a class that provides instance methods that allow you to communicate information to compressors that can constrain compressed data to a specific data rate.

The `GraphicsImporter` class is perhaps the most important class in this package, as it defines a large number of methods for importing still images. The class allows you both to display and manipulate various types of image data, regardless of file format or compression.

The `QTImage` class is useful in that it provides static methods and constants for compressing and decompressing QuickTime images. You use an instance of this class to associate an `ImageDescription` object with the encoded image data that it describes.

QuickTime generally separates the actual media data from information that describes the format of this data. In the case of images, this separation is apparent in the `EncodedImage` classes and the `ImageDescription`. The `EncodedImage` classes in the `quicktime.util` package contain raw data—for example, raw pixel values. An `ImageDescription` describes to QuickTime how this data should be interpreted, that is, its format dimensions, etc. Figure 38.1 shows the class hierarchy for this package.

FIGURE 38.1 *The* `quicktime.std.image` *package*

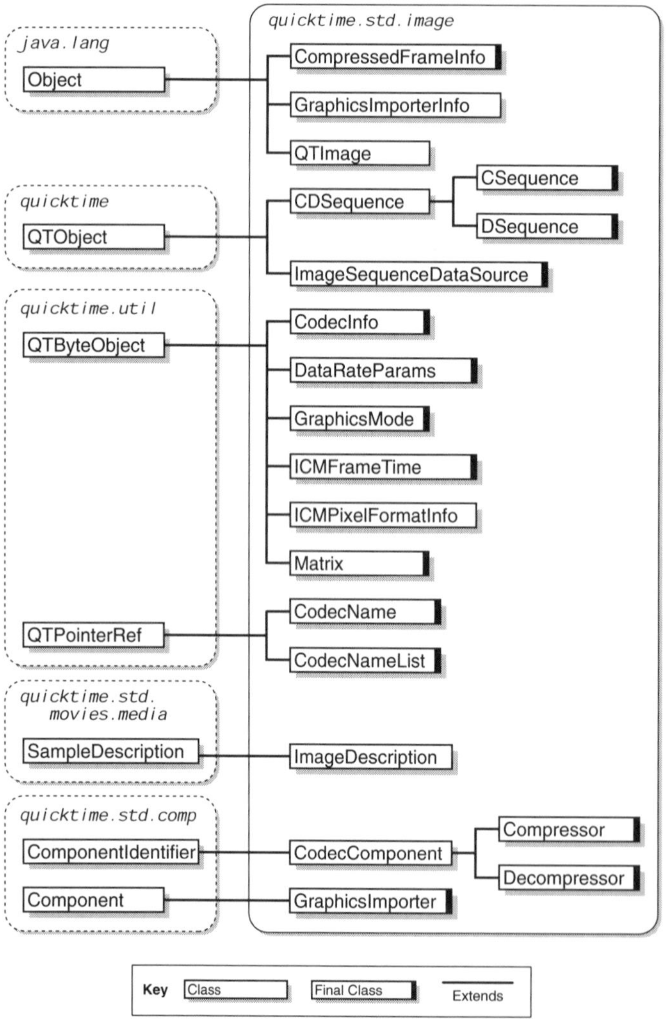

Class quicktime.std.image.CDSequence

This class defines methods that are used during compression and decompression of image sequences.

See also CSequence **and** DSequence.

```
public class CDSequence extends QTObject implements QuickTimeLib {
//Instance Methods
    public boolean busy();
    public final boolean equivalentImageDescription(ImageDescription newDesc);
    public final ImageDescription getDescription();
    public final void setTimeBase(TimeBase base);
}
```

CLASS HIERARCHY:

Object→QTObject→CDSequence

Class quicktime.std.image.CodecComponent

This class enables you to choose the first, fastest, or most accurate compressor or decompressor for a specific task, as well as the compressor that produces the smallest resulting data. The single static method, fromSpatialSettings(), returns the default codec in the dialog box.

```
public class CodecComponent extends ComponentIdentifier implements QuickTimeLib {
//Static Fields
    public static final CodecComponent anyCodec;
    public static final CodecComponent bestCompressionCodec;
    public static final CodecComponent bestFidelityCodec;
    public static final CodecComponent bestSpeedCodec;

//Static Methods
    public static CodecComponent fromSpatialSettings(SpatialSettings ss);
}
```

CLASS HIERARCHY:

Object→QTObject→ComponentIdentifier→CodecComponent

Class quicktime.std.image.CodecInfo

This class corresponds to the compressor information structure, which describes the capabilities of compressors. The various get() methods in this class return information about the compression and decompression capabilities of the component.

```
public final class CodecInfo extends QTByteObject implements QuickTimeLib, Cloneable {
//Static Fields
    public static final int kNativeSize;

//Constructors
    public CodecInfo(int cType, CodecComponent codec);

//Static Methods
    public static int codecVersion();

//Instance Methods
    public Object clone();
    public int getCompressFlags();
    public int getCompressionAccuracy();
    public int getCompressionLevel();
    public int getCompressionSpeed();
    public int getDecompressFlags();
    public int getDecompressionAccuracy();
    public int getDecompressionSpeed();
    public int getFormatFlags();
    public short getMinimumHeight();
    public short getMinimumWidth();
    public short getRevisionLevel();
    public String getTypeName();
    public int getVendor();
    public short getVersion();
    public String toString();
}
```

> **CLASS HIERARCHY:**
>
> Object→QTByteObject→CodecInfo

Class quicktime.std.image.CodecName

This class defines a compressor name structure, and its methods return the compressor type, CodecComponent, and name of the compressor component.

```
public final class CodecName extends QTPointerRef {
//Static Fields
    public static final int kNativeSize;
```

```
//Instance Methods
    public int getCType();
    public CodecComponent getCodecComponent();
    public StringHandle getName();
    public String getTypeName();
    public String toString();
}
```

CLASS HIERARCHY:

Object→QTObject→QTPointerRef→CodecName

Class quicktime.std.image.CodecNameList

This class corresponds to CodecNameSpecListPtr data structure, which contains a list of compressor name structures, as specified in the QuickTime C API.

```
public final class CodecNameList extends QTPointerRef implements QuickTimeLib {
//Static Fields
    public static final int kNativeSize;

//Constructors
    public CodecNameList(int show);

//Instance Methods
    public int getCount();
    public CodecName getNth(int n);
}
```

CLASS HIERARCHY:

Object→QTObject→QTPointerRef→CodecNameList

Class quicktime.std.image.CompressedFrameInfo

This class contains information about a compressed frame. The CSequence.compress-Frame() method returns one of these objects.

```
public final class CompressedFrameInfo extends Object {
//Instance Methods
    public int getDataSize();
    public int getSimilarity();
    public String toString();
}
```

CLASS HIERARCHY:

Object→CompressedFrameInfo

Class quicktime.std.image.Compressor

This class defines a single static method, findCodec(), that determines which of the installed compressors has been chosen to handle requests from a compressor identifier. The cType parameter specifies the type of compressor sought (for example, JPEG, Sorenson, Cinepak, etc.), while the specCodec parameter contains a special qualifier—for example, bestSpeed.

```
public final class Compressor extends CodecComponent implements QuickTimeLib {
//Static Methods
    public static Compressor findCodec(int cType, CodecComponent specCodec);
}
```

CLASS HIERARCHY:

Object→QTObject→ComponentIdentifier→CodecComponent→Compressor

Class quicktime.std.image.CSequence

This class defines methods for compressing a sequence of images. You use the CSequence() constructor to create an instance of this class, which signals the beginning of the process of compressing a sequence of frames. The Image Compression Manager will choose the color depth and may allocate a previous image buffer.

You call one of the compressFrame() methods to compress one of a sequence of frames. The size of the compressed data and the similarity value are returned in the CompressedFrameInfo object. getMaxCompressionSize() allows you to determine the maximum size an image will be after compression for a given compression sequence. The size returned is in the number of bytes that the encoded image will require. Use the setQuality() method to adjust the spatial or temporal quality for the current sequence.

See also CDSequence and DSequence.

```
public final class CSequence extends CDSequence implements QuickTimeLib, Errors {
//Constructors
    public CSequence(QDGraphics src, QDRect srcRect, int cType, CodecComponent codec,
                int spatialQuality, int temporalQuality, int keyFrameRate, int flags);
    public CSequence(QDGraphics src, QDRect srcRect, int colorDepth, int cType,
```

```
                CodecComponent codec, int spatialQuality, int temporalQuality,
                int keyFrameRate, ColorTable clut, int flags);

//Instance Methods
    public CompressedFrameInfo compressFrame(QDGraphics src, QDRect srcRect, int flags,
                                ByteEncodedImage data);
    public CompressedFrameInfo compressFrame(QDGraphics src, QDRect srcRect, int flags,
                                RawEncodedImage data);
    public CompressedFrameInfo compressFrame(QDGraphics src, QDRect srcRect, int flags,
                                EncodedImage data);
    public CompressedFrameInfo compressFrame(QDGraphics src, QDRect srcRect, int flags,
                                IntEncodedImage data);
    public DataRateParams getDataRateParams();
    public int getFrameNumber();
    public int getKeyFrameRate();
    public int getMaxCompressionSize(QDGraphics src);
    public QDGraphics prevBuffer();
    public void setDataRateParams(DataRateParams params);
    public void setFrameNumber(int frameNumber);
    public void setKeyFrameRate(int keyFrameRate);
    public void setPreferredPacketSize(int preferredPacketSize);
    public void setPrev(QDGraphics prev, QDRect prevRect);
    public void setQuality(int spatialQuality, int temporalQuality);
}
```

CLASS HIERARCHY:

Object→QTObject→CDSequence→CSequence

Class quicktime.std.image.DataRateParams

This class provides instance methods that allow you to communicate information to
compressors and constrain compressed data to a specific data rate.

```
public final class DataRateParams extends QTByteObject implements Cloneable {
//Static Fields
    public static final int kNativeSize;

//Constructors
    public DataRateParams();
    public DataRateParams(int dataRate, int dataOverrun, int frameDuration,
                    int keyFrameRate, int minSpatialQuality, int minTemporalQuality);

//Instance Methods
    public Object clone();
    public int getDataOverrun();
    public int getDataRate();
    public int getFrameDuration();
    public int getKeyFrameRate();
```

```
    public int getMinSpatialQuality();
    public int getMinTemporalQuality();
    public void setDataOverrun(int dataOverrun);
    public void setDataRate(int dataRate);
    public void setFrameDuration(int frameDuration);
    public void setKeyFrameRate(int keyFrameRate);
    public void setMinSpatialQuality(int minSpatialQuality);
    public void setMinTemporalQuality(int minTemporalQuality);
}
```

CLASS HIERARCHY:

Object→QTByteObject→DataRateParams

Class quicktime.std.image.Decompressor

This class encapsulates the decompressor component type, as specified in the QuickTime API. Refer to the QuickTime documentation for specific information on this codec component.

The findCodec() method determines which of the installed decompressors has been chosen to handle requests from one of the special compressor identifiers. The parameter cType specifies the type of decompressor sought (for example, JPEG or GIF), while the specCodec parameter contains a special qualifier (for example, bestSpeed).

```
public final class Decompressor extends CodecComponent implements QuickTimeLib {
//Static Methods
    public static Decompressor findCodec(int cType, CodecComponent specCodec);
}
```

CLASS HIERARCHY:

Object→QTObject→ComponentIdentifier→CodecComponent→Decompressor

Class quicktime.std.image.DSequence

This class defines methods used for decompressing a sequence of images. If you need to decompress image data explicitly, you can use this class.

One of the DSequence() constructors allows you to pass a compressed sample so the codec can perform preflighting before the first decompressFrame call. You call the decompressFrame() method to decompress one of a sequence of images, supplying image data that is to be decompressed. Use the decompressFrameWhen() method in this class to queue a frame for decompression and specify the time at which decompression will begin.

The various methods of decompressFrame() allow for better runtime performance if the compiler can determine the type of the image data object. decompressFrameS() is a faster and more efficient version of the decompressFrame() call and should be used.

The presentation of the image (its graphics mode, matrix, and clipping) can be set for a sequence by using the appropriate method.

See also CDSequence and CSequence.

```
public final class DSequence extends CDSequence implements QDConstants, StdQTConstants,
Errors {
//Constructors
    public DSequence(ImageDescription desc, QDGraphics port, QDRect srcRect,
                    Matrix matrix, Region mask, int flags, int accuracy,
                    CodecComponent codec);
    public DSequence(ImageDescription desc, EncodedImage data, QDGraphics port,
                    QDRect srcRect, Matrix matrix, Region mask, int flags,
                    int accuracy, CodecComponent codec);

//Instance Methods
    public int decompressFrame(EncodedImage data, int inFlags);
    public int decompressFrame(ByteEncodedImage data, int inFlags);
    public int decompressFrame(IntEncodedImage data, int inFlags);
    public int decompressFrame(RawEncodedImage data, int inFlags);
    public int decompressFrameS(EncodedImage data, int inFlags);
    public int decompressFrameS(ByteEncodedImage data, int inFlags);
    public int decompressFrameS(IntEncodedImage data, int inFlags);
    public int decompressFrameS(RawEncodedImage data, int inFlags);
    public int decompressFrameWhen(ByteEncodedImage data, int inFlags,
                    ICMFrameTime frameTime);
    public int decompressFrameWhen(IntEncodedImage data, int inFlags,
                    ICMFrameTime frameTime);
    public int decompressFrameWhen(RawEncodedImage data, int inFlags,
                    ICMFrameTime frameTime);
    public int decompressFrameWhen(EncodedImage data, int inFlags,
                    ICMFrameTime frameTime);
    public void flush();
    public QDGraphics getImageBuffer();
    public QDGraphics getScreenBuffer();
    public boolean hitTestData(EncodedImage data, QDPoint where, int hitFlags);
    public void invalidate(Region invalRgn);
    public boolean ptInData(EncodedImage data, QDPoint where);
    public void setAccuracy(int accuracy);
    public void setGraphicsMode(GraphicsMode mode);
    public void setMask(Region mask);
    public void setMatrix(Matrix matrix);
```

```
    public void setMatte(PixMap matte, QDRect matteRect);
    public void setSrcRect(QDRect srcRect);
    public void setTransferMode(int mode, QDColor opColor);
    public void shieldCursor();
}
```

CLASS HIERARCHY:

Object→QTObject→CDSequence→DSequence

Class quicktime.std.image.GraphicsImporter

This class defines a large number of methods for managing still images. The class allows you to display and manipulate various types of image data, regardless of file format or compression. The QTIF (QuickTime image file format, `'qtif'`) accepts GIF, JPEG, PICT, Photoshop, and sgi.rgb files. This class implements methods for a corresponding QuickTime `ComponentInstance` structure, the GraphicsImportComponent.

The `GraphicsImporter()` constructor determines and opens the graphics import component to use for the given `subType` or file, which describes the format of the image data. The various `get()` instance methods in this class return the file, type of data reference, and data handle that the graphics reside in, as well as the data size, offset, and image description information. The `GraphicsImporter` expects that the format of the image data is from a file. For instance, images in the PICT format have a slightly different layout when stored in memory rather than stored in a file.

You call the `setGWorld()` method to give the `GraphicsImporter` the `QDGraphics` object it should use to do its drawing. The `getGWorld()` method returns the current destination graphics port.

This class also defines methods for returning a list of MIME types and for saving images in other file formats. Use the `doExportImageFileDialog()` method to present a dialog box that lets the user save an image in a different file format.

```
public final class GraphicsImporter extends Component
                            implements QuickTimeLib, StdQTConstants, Errors {
//Constructors
    public GraphicsImporter(int subType);
    public GraphicsImporter(QTFile file);
    public GraphicsImporter(QTFile file, int flags);
    public GraphicsImporter(DataRef dataRef);
    public GraphicsImporter(DataRef dataRef, int flags);
```

```
//Instance Methods
    public final GraphicsImporterInfo doExportImageFileDialog(QTFile inDefaultSpec,
                                                    String prompt);
    public final int doesDrawAllPixels();
    public final void draw();
    public void exportImageFile(int fileType, int fileCreator, QTFile theFile,
                          int scriptTag);
    public final QTHandle getAliasedDataReference();
    public final int getAliasedDataType();
    public Pict getAsPicture();
    public final QDRect getBoundsRect();
    public final Region getClip();
    public final QTFile getDataFile();
    public final QTHandle getDataHandle();
    public final int getDataOffset();
    public final int getDataReferenceType();
    public final int getDataSize();
    public final AtomContainer getExportImageTypeList();
    public final AtomContainer getExportSettingsAsAtomContainer();
    public final QDGraphics getGWorld();
    public final GraphicsMode getGraphicsMode();
    public final ImageDescription getImageDescription();
    public AtomContainer getMIMETypeList();
    public final Matrix getMatrix();
    public UserData getMetaData(GraphicsImporter gi);
    public final QDRect getNaturalBounds();
    public final int getQuality();
    public final QDRect getSourceRect();
    public final void readData(EncodedImage data, int dataOffset, int dataSize);
    public final void saveAsPicture(QTFile file, int scriptTag);
    public final void saveAsQuickTimeImageFile(QTFile file, int scriptTag);
    public final void setBoundsRect(QDRect bounds);
    public final void setClip(Region clipRgn);
    public final void setDataFile(QTFile fileIn);
    public final void setDataHandle(QTHandleRef dataRef);
    public final void setDataReference(DataRef dataRef);
    public final void setExportSettingsFromAtomContainer(AtomContainer qtAtomContainer);
    public final void setGWorld(QDGraphics port, GDevice gdh);
    public final void setGraphicsMode(GraphicsMode graphicsMode);
    public final void setMatrix(Matrix matrix);
    public final void setQuality(int quality);
    public final void setSourceRect(QDRect srcRect);
    public final boolean validate();
}
```

CLASS HIERARCHY:

Object→QTObject→ComponentIdentifier→Component→GraphicsImporter

Class quicktime.std.image.GraphicsImporterInfo

This class contains information about the file information after an export dialog has been shown.

```
public class GraphicsImporterInfo extends Object {
//Constructors
    public GraphicsImporterInfo(int outExportedType, QTFile outExportedSpec,
                                short outScriptTag);

//Instance Fields
    public QTFile mOutExportedSpec;
    public int mOutExportedType;
    public short mOutScriptTag;
}
```

> **CLASS HIERARCHY:**
>
> Object→GraphicsImporterInfo

Class quicktime.std.image.GraphicsMode

This class defines methods that implement graphics transfer operations. It is widely used in many of the QuickTime objects that draw image data.

```
public final class GraphicsMode extends QTByteObject
                                implements Cloneable, QDConstants, StdQTConstants {
//Static Fields
    public static final int kNativeSize;

//Constructors
    public GraphicsMode();
    public GraphicsMode(int gMode, QDColor opColor);

//Instance Methods
    public Object clone();
    public QDColor getColor();
    public int getGraphicsMode();
    public boolean isGraphicsModeOpaque();
    public void setColor(QDColor newColor);
    public void setGraphicsMode(int mode);
    public String toString();
}
```

> **CLASS HIERARCHY:**
>
> Object→QTByteObject→GraphicsMode

Class quicktime.std.image.ICMFrameTime

This class contains a frame's time information, including the time at which the frame should be displayed, its duration, and the playback rate.

```
public final class ICMFrameTime extends QTByteObject
                            implements Cloneable, StdQTConstants {
//Static Fields
    public static final int kNativeSize;

//Constructors
    public ICMFrameTime();

//Instance Methods
    public Object clone();
    public TimeBase getBase();
    public int getDuration();
    public int getFlags();
    public int getFrameNumber();
    public float getRate();
    public int getScale();
    public long getValue();
    public int getVirtualDuration();
    public long getVirtualStartTime();
    public void setBase(TimeBase base);
    public void setDuration(int duration);
    public void setFlags(int flags);
    public void setFrameNumber(int frameNumber);
    public void setRate(float rate);
    public void setScale(int scale);
    public void setValue(long value);
    public void setVirtualDuration(int duration);
    public void setVirtualStartTime(long time);
    public String toString();
}
```

CLASS HIERARCHY:

Object→QTByteObject→ICMFrameTime

Class quicktime.std.image.ICMPixelFormatInfo

This class defines methods for obtaining pixel size, information, and format based on a particular pixel format.

```
public class ICMPixelFormatInfo extends QTByteObject implements QuickTimeLib {
//Static Methods
    public static ICMPixelFormatInfo getPixelFormatInfo(int pixelFormat);
```

```
    public static boolean isValidPixelFormat(int pixelFormat);
    public static ICMPixelFormatInfo setPixelFormatInfo(int pixelFormat);

//Instance Methods
    public int getFormatFlags();
    public String toString();
}
```

CLASS HIERARCHY:

Object→QTByteObject→ICMPixelFormatInfo

Class quicktime.std.image.ImageDescription

This class is used to describe to QuickTime the format of the image data that a drawable object presents. The image data is passed in as an EncodedImage object but has no formatting information encapsulated within it. The ImageDescription describes the format and characteristics of the image data. For instance, an ImageDescription describes the encoding of the image data (JPEG, GIF, and so on), its original width and height (in pixels), and how many frames of images the encoded data holds.

```
public class ImageDescription extends SampleDescription
                              implements QuickTimeLib, StdQTConstants {
//Static Fields
    public static final int kNativeSize;

//Constructors
    public ImageDescription(int format);
    public ImageDescription(PixMap pixmap);

//Static Methods
    public static ImageDescription fromGraphicsImporter(GraphicsImporter gi);
    public static QTImage fromImageCompressionDialog(ImageCompressionDialog icd,
                                        QDGraphics src, QDRect srcRect);
    public static ImageDescription fromSprite(Sprite s);
    public static EndianDescriptor getEndianDescriptor();
    public static ImageDescription getJavaDefaultPixelDescription(int width,
                                                    int height);

//Instance Methods
    public Object clone();
    public QDRect getBounds();
    public ColorTable getCTable();
    public int getCType();
    public int getClutID();
    public int getDataSize();
    public int getDepth();
    public int getExtension(int idType, int index);
```

```
    public int getFrameCount();
    public float getHRes();
    public int getHeight();
    public int getIdSize();
    public String getName();
    public int getRevisionLevel();
    public int getSpatialQuality();
    public int getTemporalQuality();
    public float getVRes();
    public int getVendor();
    public int getVersion();
    public int getWidth();
    public QDGraphics newGWorld(int flags);
    public void setCTable(ColorTable cTable);
    public void setCType(int cType);
    public void setClutID(int clutID);
    public void setDataSize(int dataSize);
    public void setDepth(int depth);
    public void setFrameCount(int frameCount);
    public void setHRes(float hRes);
    public void setHeight(int height);
    public void setName(String name);
    public void setRevisionLevel(int revision);
    public void setSpatialQuality(int spatialQuality);
    public void setTemporalQuality(int temporalQuality);
    public void setVRes(float vRes);
    public void setVendor(int vendor);
    public void setVersion(int version);
    public void setWidth(int width);
    public String toString();
}
```

CLASS HIERARCHY:

Object→QTObject→QTHandleRef→SampleDescription→ImageDescription

Class quicktime.std.image.ImageSequenceDataSource

QuickTime 2.1 introduced support for an arbitrary number of sources of data for an image sequence. This functionality forms the basis for dynamically modifying parameters to a decompressor. It also allows for codecs to act as special effects components, providing filtering and transition type effects. A client can attach an arbitrary number of additional inputs to the codec. It is up to the particular codec to determine whether to use each input and how to interpret the input. For example, an 8-bit gray image could be interpreted as a blend mask or as a replacement for one of the RGB data planes.

```
public final class ImageSequenceDataSource extends QTObject
                                    implements QuickTimeLib, Errors {
//Constructors
    public ImageSequenceDataSource(CDSequence seq, int sourceType,
                        int sourceInputNumber);
    public ImageSequenceDataSource(CDSequence seq, int sourceType,
                        int sourceInputNumber, QTHandleRef dataDescription);

//Instance Methods
    public void changedSourceData();
    public void dispose();
    public void setSourceData(EncodedImage data);
}
```

CLASS HIERARCHY:

Object→QTObject→ImageSequenceDataSource

Class quicktime.std.image.Matrix

This class is used to transform and map points from one coordinate space into another coordinate space. It is used extensively by QuickTime drawing objects to manipulate and transform the rendering of image data in a two-dimensional plane. It contains state for changing the location, scaling, rotation, skewing, and the perspective of an image.

```
public final class Matrix extends QTByteObject
                    implements QuickTimeLib, Cloneable, Errors {
//Static Fields
    public static final int kNativeSize;

//Constructors
    public Matrix();
    public Matrix(float[][] table);
    public Matrix(QDPoint[] source, QDPoint[] dest);

//Instance Methods
    public Object clone();
    public void concat(Matrix b);
    public Matrix copy();
    public boolean equals(Matrix m);
    public float getB();
    public float getC();
    public float getSx();
    public float getSy();
    public float getTx();
    public float getTy();
    public short getType();
```

```
public float getU();
public float getV();
public float getW();
public boolean inverse(Matrix mr);
public boolean isIdentity();
public void map(QDRect fromRect, QDRect toRect);
public void rect(QDRect srcRect, QDRect dstRect);
public void rotate(float degrees, float aboutX, float aboutY);
public void scale(float scaleX, float scaleY, float aboutX, float aboutY);
public void setB(float b);
public void setC(float c);
public void setIdentity();
public void setSx(float sx);
public void setSy(float sy);
public void setTx(float tx);
public void setTy(float ty);
public void setU(float u);
public void setV(float v);
public void setW(float w);
public void skew(float skewX, float skewY, float aboutX, float aboutY);
public String toString();
public void transformDPoints(QDPoint[] dpt);
public void transformDPoints(QDPoint dpt);
public boolean transformDRect(QDRect r, QDPoint[] points);
public boolean transformDRect(QDRect r);
public void transformPoints(QDPoint[] pt);
public void transformPoints(QDPoint pt);
public boolean transformRect(QDRect r, QDPoint[] points);
public boolean transformRect(QDRect r);
public void transformRgn(Region r);
public void translate(float deltaH, float deltaV);
}
```

CLASS HIERARCHY:

Object→QTByteObject→Matrix

Class quicktime.std.image.QTImage

This class provides static methods and constants for compressing and decompressing QuickTime images. Use an instance of this class to associate an ImageDescription object with the encoded image data that the description describes.

The QTImage() constructor associates an image description with the image data described by the description. compress() compresses a single frame image stored as a pixel map. The size of the compressed image can be obtained from the ImageDescription object that is returned.

```
public class QTImage extends Object implements QuickTimeLib, Errors {
//Constructors
    public QTImage(ImageDescription id, EncodedImage im);

//Static Methods
    public static final ImageDescription compress(QDGraphics src, QDRect srcRect,
                         int quality, int cType, EncodedImage data);
    public static final ImageDescription convert(ImageDescription srcDD,
                         EncodedImage srcData, int colorDepth, ColorTable clut,
                         int accuracy, int quality, int cType,
                         CodecComponent codec, EncodedImage dstData);
    public static final void decompress(EncodedImage data, ImageDescription desc,
                         QDGraphics dst, QDRect srcRect, QDRect dstRect,
                         int mode, Region mask);
    public static final void decompress(EncodedImage data, ImageDescription desc,
                         QDGraphics dst, QDRect dstRect, int mode);
    public static final ImageDescription fCompress(QDGraphics src, QDRect srcRect,
                         int colorDepth, int quality, int cType, CodecComponent c,
                         ColorTable clut, int flags, EncodedImage data);
    public static final void fDecompress(EncodedImage data, ImageDescription desc,
                         QDGraphics dst, QDRect srcRect, Matrix matrix, int mode,
                         Region mask, PixMap matte, QDRect matteRect, int accuracy,
                         CodecComponent codec);
    public static final int getCompressedSize(ImageDescription desc, EncodedImage data);
    public static final int getCompressionTime(QDGraphics src, QDRect srcRect,
                         int colorDepth, int cType, CodecComponent c,
                         int spatialQuality, int temporalQuality);
    public static final int getMaxCompressionSize(QDGraphics src, QDRect srcRect,
                         int colorDepth, int quality, int cType, CodecComponent c);
    public static final float getSimilarity(QDGraphics src, QDRect srcRect,
                         ImageDescription desc, EncodedImage data);
    public static final void trim(ImageDescription desc, EncodedImage inData,
                         EncodedImage outData, QDRect trimRect);

//Instance Methods
    public ImageDescription getDescription();
    public EncodedImage getImage();
}
```

CLASS HIERARCHY:

Object→QTImage

39

The quicktime. std.movies Package

The `quicktime.std.movies` package is one of the most useful in the QuickTime for Java API. It contains classes that represent QuickTime atoms, atom containers, movies, movie controllers, and tracks—all essential for creating and manipulating QuickTime movies.

A movie containing one or more tracks is the primary way that data is organized and managed in QuickTime. A `Movie` object can be created from a file or from memory and can be saved to a file. This file can be local or remote (HTTP or RTSP). The `MovieController` provides the standard way that QuickTime movies are controlled. `AtomContainer` is the standard data structure used to store and retrieve data in QuickTime.

The `Atom` class represents the `QTAtom` object. In a QuickTime movie resource, the basic data unit is the atom, which contains size and type information, along with its data. `AtomContainer` is a class that corresponds to a QuickTime atom container. It contains a large number of useful methods for manipulating its contents.

Movies contain tracks and a time line. The Movie Toolbox API gives your application control over the display of a movie's visual media (if it has any) and the time characteristics of its media, allowing for different rates of playback and time-based behavior. If the movie has audio data, its overall volume can also be controlled.

The `MovieController` class is an important class in this package. It contains many methods for getting and setting the various features of a QuickTime movie. The `MovieController` object allows you to play and control different types of movies with a standard user interface.

Finally, Track is a class that contains methods for the control of the media that a track presents. A QuickTime movie may contain several tracks; each track refers to a specific media type that contains references to the media data. These may be stored, for example, as images or sound on hard disks, floppy disks, compact discs, or other devices. Figure 39.1 shows the class hierarchy for this package.

FIGURE 39.1 *The* quicktime.std.movies *package*

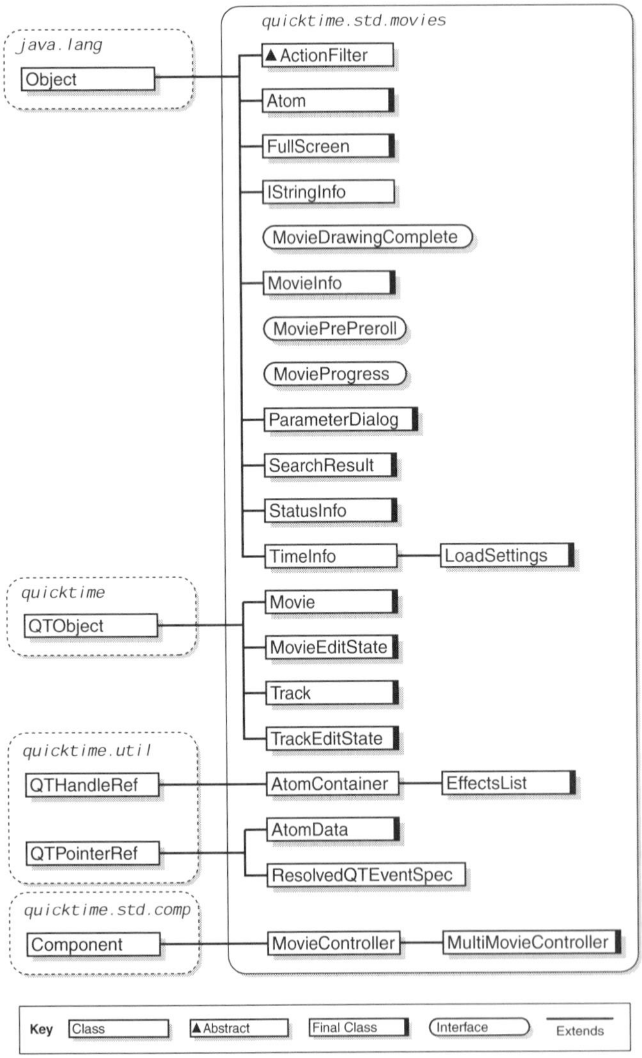

Class quicktime.std.movies.ActionFilter

This class is used by action filters on the `MovieController`. Your application should subclass this class, overriding the methods that it is interested in. Actions associated with methods not overridden will return `false`, indicating to the Movie Toolbox that it should handle the action.

See also `QTCallBack`.

```
public abstract class ActionFilter extends Object {
//Instance Methods
    public boolean execute(MovieController mc, int action);
    public boolean execute(MovieController mc, int action, float value);
    public boolean execute(MovieController mc, int action, float[] value);
    public boolean execute(MovieController mc, int action, boolean[] value);
    public boolean execute(MovieController mc, int action, int[] value);
    public boolean execute(MovieController mc, int action, boolean value);
    public boolean execute(MovieController mc, QDRect rect);
    public boolean execute(MovieController mc, int action, int value);
    public boolean execute(MovieController mc, int action, TimeRecord tr);
    public boolean execute(MovieController mc, int action, ResolvedQTEventSpec es);
    public boolean execute(MovieController mc, int action, AtomContainer container,
                           Atom atom);
    public boolean execute(MovieController mc, int action, StringHandle string);
    public boolean execute(MovieController mc, int action, QDPoint point);
}
```

CLASS HIERARCHY:

Object→ActionFilter

Class quicktime.std.movies.Atom

This class represents the `QTAtom` object. In a QuickTime movie resource, the basic data unit is the atom, which contains size and type information, along with its data.

This class uses the `Atom()` constructor to construct an `Atom` object out of the constant value that defines the atom type. You use the `getAtom()` method to return the current value of the atom.

```
public final class Atom extends Object implements StdQTConstants {
//Static Fields
    public static final Atom kParentIsContainer;

//Constructors
    public Atom(int atom);
```

```
//Instance Methods
    public int getAtom();
}
```

CLASS HIERARCHY:

Object→Atom

Class quicktime.std.movies.AtomContainer

AtomContainer objects are the primary container of data in QuickTime movies. They are containers that are essentially trees of arbitrary depth and width and their internal structure is self-describing. The data stored in leaf atoms of this container are also described by the use of constants to signify the type of the data.

```
public class AtomContainer extends QTHandleRef implements QuickTimeLib, QuickTimeVRLib {
//Constructors
    public AtomContainer();

//Static Methods
    public static AtomContainer fromCompressionDialog(CompressionDialog cd);
    public static AtomContainer fromGraphicsImporterExportImage(GraphicsImporter gi);
    public static AtomContainer fromGraphicsImporterExportSettings(GraphicsImporter gi);
    public static AtomContainer fromGraphicsImporterMIME(GraphicsImporter gi);
    public static AtomContainer fromMediaInput(Media m);
    public static AtomContainer fromMediaProperty(Media m);
    public static AtomContainer fromMovieExporter(MovieExporter me);
    public static AtomContainer fromMovieImporterMIME(MovieImporter mi);
    public static AtomContainer fromMovieImporterSettings(MovieImporter mi);
    public static AtomContainer fromQTHandle(QTHandleRef handle);
    public static AtomContainer fromQTVRInstanceNode(QTVRInstance ins, int nodeID);
    public static AtomContainer fromQTVRInstanceWorld(QTVRInstance ins);
    public static AtomContainer fromThreeDMediaHandlerObject(ThreeDMediaHandler tdm);
    public static AtomContainer fromThreeDMediaHandlerRenderer(ThreeDMediaHandler tdm);

//Instance Methods
    public AtomContainer copyAtom(Atom atom);
    public QTHandle copyAtomDataToHandle(Atom atom);
    public int copyAtomDataToPtr(Atom atom, boolean sizeOrLessOK, QTPointer data);
    public int countChildrenOfType(Atom parentAtom, int childType);
    public Atom findChildByID_Atom(Atom parentAtom, int atomType, int id);
    public int findChildByID_index(Atom parentAtom, int atomType, int id);
    public Atom findChildByIndex_Atom(Atom parentAtom, int atomType, int index);
    public int findChildByIndex_id(Atom parentAtom, int atomType, int index);
    public AtomData getAtomData(Atom atom);
    public int getAtomID(Atom atom);
    public int getAtomType(Atom atom);
    public int getNextChildType(Atom parentAtom, int currentChildType);
    public void iTextAddString(Atom parentAtom, int theRegionCode, String theString);
```

```
    public IStringInfo iTextGetString(Atom parentAtom, int requestedRegion);
    public void iTextRemoveString(Atom parentAtom, int theRegionCode, int flags);
    public Atom insertChild(Atom parentAtom, int atomType, int id, int index);
    public Atom insertChild(Atom parentAtom, int atomType, int id, int index,
                 int intValue);
    public Atom insertChild(Atom parentAtom, int atomType, int id, int index,
                 short shortValue);
    public Atom insertChild(Atom parentAtom, int atomType, int id, int index,
                 QTByteObject data);
    public Atom insertChild(Atom parentAtom, int atomType, int id, int index,
                 QTPointerRef data);
    public Atom insertChild(Atom parentAtom, int atomType, int id, int index,
                 QTHandleRef data);
    public Atom insertChild(Atom parentAtom, int atomType, int id, int index,
                 StringHandle data);
    public void insertChildren(Atom parentAtom, AtomContainer childrenContainer);
    public Atom nextChildAnyType(Atom parentAtom, Atom currentChild);
    public void removeAtom(Atom atom);
    public void removeChildren(Atom atom);
    public void replaceAtom(Atom targetAtom, AtomContainer replacementContainer,
                 Atom replacementAtom);
    public void setAtomData(Atom atom, int data);
    public void setAtomData(Atom atom, short data);
    public void setAtomData(Atom atom, QTByteObject data);
    public void setAtomData(Atom atom, QTHandleRef data);
    public void setAtomData(Atom atom, QTPointerRef data);
    public void setAtomData(Atom atom, StringHandle data);
    public void setAtomID(Atom atom, int newID);
    public void swapAtoms(Atom atom1, Atom atom2);
}
```

CLASS HIERARCHY:

Object→QTObject→QTHandleRef→AtomContainer

Class quicktime.std.movies.AtomData

This class is a read-only structure used to read the values stored in an atom of an
AtomContainer. To store or alter these values, you should use the appropriate methods
in the AtomContainer class.

```
public final class AtomData extends QTPointerRef {
//Instance Methods
    public byte getByte(int offset);
    public byte[] getBytes(int offset, int length);
    public String getCString(int offset);
    public double getDouble(int offset);
    public float getFloat(int offset);
    public int getInt(int offset);
```

```
    public long getLong(int offset);
    public String getPString(int offset);
    public short getShort(int offset);
}
```

CLASS HIERARCHY:

Object→QTObject→QTPointerRef→AtomData

Class quicktime.std.movies.EffectsList

This class consists of a single constructor. It creates an `AtomContainer` that contains the necessary information for displaying a list of effects

The `EffectsList()` constructor creates an effects list from the supplied parameters.

```
public final class EffectsList extends AtomContainer implements QuickTimeLib {
//Constructors
    public EffectsList(int minSources, int maxSources, int getOptions);
}
```

CLASS HIERARCHY:

Object→QTObject→QTHandleRef→AtomContainer→EffectsList

Class quicktime.std.movies.FullScreen

This class implements the behavior for converting a screen to full-screen mode and back to normal mode. Unlike the C API, the QuickTime for Java implementation of the `FullScreen` calls does *not* allow QuickTime to create the window for you. The QuickTime for Java API allows you to put the specified screen into full-screen mode, and then a Java window can be used to fill the screen and allow the full capabilities of Java to use the entire screen.

See also `quicktime.app.display`, `FullScreenFrame`.

```
public final class FullScreen extends Object implements QuickTimeLib, StdQTConstants {
//Constructors
    public FullScreen();

//Instance Methods
    public Dimension begin(int flags);
    public Dimension begin(GDevice gd, int desiredWidth, int desiredHeight, int flags);
    public void end();
    public Dimension getMainScreenSize();
```

```
    public Dimension getScreenSize(GDevice gd);
    public Dimension preflightSize(GDevice gd, int width, int height);
}
```

CLASS HIERARCHY:

Object→FullScreen

Class quicktime.std.movies.IStringInfo

This class is used to return string information from AtomContainer objects.

```
public final class IStringInfo extends Object {
//Instance Fields
    public int region;
    public String string;
}
```

CLASS HIERARCHY:

Object→IStringInfo

Class quicktime.std.movies.LoadSettings

This class provides the load settings information for a track that is part of a movie.

```
public final class LoadSettings extends TimeInfo {
//Constructors
    public LoadSettings(int preloadTime, int preloadDuration, int preloadFlags,
                        int defaultHints);

//Instance Fields
    public int defaultHints;
    public int preloadFlags;
}
```

CLASS HIERARCHY:

Object→TimeInfo→LoadSettings

Class quicktime.std.movies.Movie

This class contains a large number of methods and is the most important class in this package. In QuickTime, a set of time-based data is referred to as a movie. You can control and display any time-based data by using the methods in this class.

Note that movie objects can be made from various sources that contain existing QuickTime movie data, such as memory, files, URLs, and so on. To make a movie from an existing movie source, you use the from. . . class methods. If you wish to create a new movie yourself, you use the movie constructor methods.

```
public final class Movie extends QTObject
                        implements QuickTimeLib, QuickTimeVRLib, StdQTConstants,
                        IOConstants, Errors {
//Constructors
    public Movie();
    public Movie(int flags);

//Static Methods
    public static Movie createMovieFile(QTFile pathName, int fCreator, int flags);
    public static Movie fromDataFork(OpenFile fileIn, int fileOffset, int flags,
                        MovieInfo info);
    public static Movie fromDataRef(DataRef defaultDataRef, int flags);
    public static Movie fromFile(OpenMovieFile fileIn);
    public static Movie fromFile(OpenMovieFile fileIn, int flags, MovieInfo info);
    public static Movie fromHandle(QTHandle hand);
    public static Movie fromHandle(QTHandle hand, int flags, MovieInfo info);
    public static Movie fromScrap(int newMovieFlags);
    public static Movie fromSequenceGrabber(SequenceGrabber sg);
    public static void taskAll(int maxMilliSecToUse);

//Instance Methods
    public void abortPrePreroll(int err);
    public Track addEmptyTrack(Track srcTrack, DataRef dataRef);
    public int addResource(OpenMovieFile fileOut, int resID, String resourceName);
    public void addSelection(Movie srcMovie);
    public Track addTrack(float width, float height, float trackVolume);
    public void clearChanged();
    public void clearSelection();
    public int convertToFile(Track onlyTrack, QTFile outputFile, int fileType,
                        int creator, int scriptTag, int flags, MovieExporter userComp);
    public int convertToFile(Track onlyTrack, QTFile outputFile, int fileType,
                        int creator, int scriptTag);
    public int convertToFile(QTFile outputFile, int fileType, int creator,
                        int scriptTag);
    public int convertToFile(QTFile outputFile, int fileType, int creator,
                        int scriptTag, int flags);
    public Movie copySelection();
    public void copySettings(Movie dstMovie);
    public Movie cutSelection();
    public void deleteSegment(int startTime, int duration);
    public int flatten(int movieFlattenFlags, QTFile fileOut, int creator,
                        int scriptTag, int createQTFileFlags, int resID, String resName);
    public Movie flattenData(int movieFlattenFlags, QTHandle handle);
    public Movie flattenData(int movieFlattenFlags, QTFile fileOut, int creator,
                        int scriptTag, int createQTFileFlags);
```

```
public boolean getActive();
public TimeInfo getActiveSegment();
public QDRect getBounds();
public Region getBoundsRgn();
public QDRect getBox();
public Region getClipRgn();
public ColorTable getColorTable();
public int getCreationTime();
public int getDataSize(int startTime, int duration);
public DataRef getDefaultDataRef();
public Region getDisplayBoundsRgn();
public Region getDisplayClipRgn();
public int getDuration();
public QDGraphics getGWorld();
public Track getIndTrack(int index);
public Track getIndTrackType(int index, int trackType, int flags);
public Matrix getMatrix();
public int getModificationTime();
public QDRect getNaturalBoundsRect();
public TimeInfo getNextInterestingTime(int interestingTimeFlags, int[] mediaTypes,
                                       int time, float rate);
public Track getNextTrackForCompositing(Track theTrack);
public Pict getPict(int time);
public QDRect getPosterBox();
public Pict getPosterPict();
public int getPosterTime();
public float getPreferredRate();
public float getPreferredVolume();
public Track getPrevTrackForCompositing(Track theTrack);
public boolean getPreviewMode();
public TimeInfo getPreviewTime();
public Track getQTVRTrack(int index);
public float getRate();
public Region getSegmentDisplayBoundsRgn(int time, int duration);
public TimeInfo getSelection();
public StatusInfo getStatus();
public TimeRecord getTRTime();
public int getTime();
public TimeBase getTimeBase();
public int getTimeScale();
public Track getTrack(int trackID);
public int getTrackCount();
public UserData getUserData();
public float getVolume();
public void goToBeginning();
public void goToEnd();
public boolean hasChanged();
public void insertEmptySegment(int dstIn, int dstDuration);
public void insertSegment(Movie dstMovie, int srcIn, int srcDuration, int dstIn);
public void invalidateRegion(Region invalidRgn);
public boolean isDone();
public void loadIntoRam(int time, int duration, int flags);
```

```
public final int maxLoadedTimeInMovie();
public final boolean needsTimeTable();
public MovieEditState newEditState();
public Track newTrack(float width, float height, float trackVolume);
public void pasteHandle(QTHandle handle, int handleType, int flags,
                       MovieImporter userComp);
public void pasteSelection(Movie srcMovie);
public void playPreview();
public boolean pointInMovie(QDPoint pt);
public void prePreroll(int time, float rate, MoviePrePreroll proc);
public void prePreroll(int time, float rate);
public void preroll(int time, float rate);
public void putIntoDataFork(OpenMovieFile fileOut, int offset, int maxSize);
public void putIntoHandle(QTHandle intoThisHandle);
public QTHandle putIntoTypedHandle(Track targetTrack, int handleType, int start,
                       int dur, int flags, MovieExporter userComp);
public void putOnScrap(int movieScrapFlags);
public void removeDrawingCompleteProc();
public void removeResource(OpenMovieFile fileOut, int resID);
public void removeTrack(Track track);
public void scaleSegment(int startTime, int oldDuration, int newDuration);
public SearchResult searchText(QTPointer text, int searchFlags, int searchTime,
                       int searchOffset);
public SearchResult searchText(QTPointer text, int searchFlags, Track searchTrack,
                       int searchTime, int searchOffset);
public void selectAlternates();
public void setActive(boolean active);
public void setActiveSegment(TimeInfo activeSegmentTimeInfo);
public void setAutoTrackAlternatesEnabled(boolean enable);
public void setBounds(QDRect boxRect);
public void setBox(QDRect boxRect);
public void setClipRgn(Region theClip);
public void setColorTable(ColorTable ctab);
public void setDefaultDataRef(DataRef newRef);
public void setDisplayClipRgn(Region theClip);
public void setDrawingCompleteProc(int flags, MovieDrawingComplete proc);
public void setGWorld(QDGraphics port, GDevice gdh);
public void setLanguage(int language);
public void setMasterClock(Clock clockMeister, TimeRecord slaveZero);
public void setMasterTimeBase(TimeBase tb, TimeRecord slaveZero);
public void setMatrix(Matrix matrix);
public void setPlayHints(int flags, int flagsMask);
public void setPosterBox(QDRect boxRect);
public void setPosterTime(int posterTime);
public void setPreferredRate(float rate);
public void setPreferredVolume(float volume);
public void setPreviewMode(boolean usePreview);
public void setPreviewTime(TimeInfo previewTimeInfo);
public void setPreviewTime(int previewTime, int previewDuration);
public void setProgressProc();
public void setProgressProc(MovieProgress mp);
public void setRate(float rate);
```

```
    public void setSelection(int selectionTime, int selectionDuration);
    public void setSelection(TimeInfo selectionTimeInfo);
    public void setTime(TimeRecord newtime);
    public void setTimeScale(int timeScale);
    public void setTimeValue(int newtime);
    public void setVolume(float volume);
    public void showInformation();
    public void showPoster();
    public void start();
    public void stop();
    public void task(int maxMilliSecToUse);
    public String toString();
    public void update();
    public void updateResource(OpenMovieFile fileOut, int resID, String resourceName);
    public void useEditState(MovieEditState anEditState);
}
```

CLASS HIERARCHY:

Object→QTObject→Movie

Class quicktime.std.movies.MovieController

This class contains a large number of methods for controlling the various characteristics of the presentation of a QuickTime movie.

The MovieController object allows you to play and control movies of different types (for example, normal, VR pan, and VR object) with a standard API. You obtain this identifier from the Component Manager's OpenComponent or OpenDefaultComponent function, or from the NewMovieController function. These are described in Chapter 2 of *Inside Macintosh: QuickTime Components*.

```
public class MovieController extends Component
                            implements QuickTimeLib, StdQTConstants, Errors {
//Constructors
    public MovieController(Movie itsMovie);
    public MovieController(Movie itsMovie, int someFlags);
    public MovieController(int subType, Movie theMovie, QDGraphics window,
                   QDPoint location);

//Instance Methods
    public final void activate();
    public final void activate(QDGraphics window, boolean activate);
    public final void badgeClick(boolean flag);
    public final void clear();
    public final boolean click(QDPoint where, int modifiers);
    public final boolean clickAndHoldPoint(QDPoint point);
    public final void controllerSizeChanged();
```

```
public final Movie copy();
public final Movie cut();
public final void deactivate();
public final void draw();
public final Region drawBadge(Region movieRgn, boolean returnBadgeRgn);
public final void enableEditing(boolean enabled);
public final void forceTimeTableUpdate();
public final QDRect getBounds();
public final Region getBoundsRgn();
public final Region getClip();
public final int getControllerInfo();
public final int getCurrentTime();
public final boolean getCursorSettingEnabled();
public final boolean getDragEnabled();
public final int getFlags();
public final boolean getKeysEnabled();
public final boolean getLoopIsPalindrome();
public final boolean getLooping();
public final Movie getMovie();
public final boolean getPlayEveryFrame();
public final float getPlayRate();
public final boolean getPlaySelection();
public final QDGraphics getPort();
public final Dimension getRequiredSize();
public final TimeRecord getSelectionBegin();
public final TimeRecord getSelectionDuration();
public final int getTimeScale();
public final QDRect getTimeSliderRect();
public final boolean getUseBadge();
public final boolean getVisible();
public final float getVolume();
public final Region getWindowRgn(QDGraphics window);
public final void goToTime(TimeRecord time);
public final void idle();
public final boolean inController(QDPoint thePt);
public final void invalidate(QDGraphics window, Region invalidRgn);
public final boolean isAttached();
public final boolean isEditingEnabled();
public final boolean key(int key, int modifiers);
public final void linkToURL(URL url);
public final void movieChanged();
public final void movieEdited();
public final void paste(Movie srcMovie);
public final void paste();
public final void play(float rate);
public final void position(QDRect movieRect, QDRect controllerRect, int someFlags);
public final void position(QDRect movieRect, int someFlags);
public final void prerollAndPlay(float rate);
public final void removeActionFilter();
public void removeMovie();
public final void resume();
public final void setActionFilter(ActionFilter filter, boolean doIdle);
```

```
public final void setActionFilter(ActionFilter filter);
public final void setAttached(boolean attached);
public final void setBounds(QDRect newBoundsRect);
public final void setClip(Region theClip);
public final void setColorTable(ColorTable newCTable);
public final void setControllerKeysEnabled(boolean enabled);
public final void setCursorSettingEnabled(boolean enabled);
public final void setDragEnabled(boolean enabled);
public final void setDuration(int duration);
public final void setFlags(int flags);
public final void setGrowBoxBounds(QDRect limits);
public final void setKeysEnabled(boolean enabled);
public final void setLoopIsPalindrome(boolean looping);
public final void setLooping(boolean looping);
public void setMovie(Movie aMovie, QDGraphics movieWindow, QDPoint location);
public final void setMovieClip(Region theClip);
public final void setPlayEveryFrame(boolean play);
public final void setPlaySelection(boolean play);
public final void setPort(QDGraphics grafPtr);
public final void setSelectionBegin(TimeRecord time);
public final void setSelectionDuration(TimeRecord time);
public final void setUseBadge(boolean useBadge);
public final void setVisible(boolean visible);
public final void setVolume(float newVolume);
public final void step(int numberOfSteps);
public final void suspend();
public final void undo();
}
```

CLASS HIERARCHY:

Object→QTObject→ComponentIdentifier→Component→MovieController

Class quicktime.std.movies.MovieDrawingComplete

An object that implements this interface can be installed in a given movie and notified by the Movie Toolbox whenever drawing is completed.

```
public interface MovieDrawingComplete {
//Instance Methods
    public abstract int execute(Movie m);
}
```

Class quicktime.std.movies.MovieEditState

This class contains information about an edit state of a movie. This state can be retrieved by an application and later restored if a consequent edit was undesired.

```
public final class MovieEditState extends QTObject {
}
```

CLASS HIERARCHY:

Object→QTObject→MovieEditState

Class quicktime.std.movies.MovieInfo

This class holds various information returned by the Movie Toolbox when a movie object is created. If you are interested in this information, you pass an empty object into the `from. . .` methods of the movie object and upon completion, the fields of the `MovieInfo` object will contain sought-after information.

The `MovieInfo()` constructor allows you to create an empty `MovieInfo` object.

```
public final class MovieInfo extends Object {
//Constructors
    public MovieInfo();

//Instance Fields
    public boolean dataRefWasChanged;
    public int resID;
    public String resourceName;
}
```

CLASS HIERARCHY:

Object→MovieInfo

Class quicktime.std.movies.MoviePrePreroll

An object that implements this interface can be notified by the Movie Toolbox whenever the pre-preroll of a movie is completed.

```
public interface MoviePrePreroll {
//Instance Methods
    public abstract void execute(Movie m, int err);
}
```

Class quicktime.std.movies.MovieProgress

This interface can be implemented to allow you to attach a progress handler to each movie. The handler will be called whenever a lengthy operation is under way.

```
public interface MovieProgress {
//Instance Methods
    public abstract int execute(Movie theMovie, int message, int whatOperation,
                          float percentDone);
}
```

Class quicktime.std.movies.MultiMovieController

This class allows for multiple movies to be associated with a single controller. You need to appropriately manage the resources consumed by multiple movies.

The getIndMovie() method allows you to get the movie at a specified index among the associated movies of a controller. The movieChanged() method lets you inform a movie controller component that your application has used the Movie Toolbox to change the characteristics of its associated movie.

The removeAMovie() method allows you to remove the specified movie from the controller.

```
public final class MultiMovieController extends MovieController implements QuickTimeLib
{
//Constructors
    public MultiMovieController(Movie itsMovie);
    public MultiMovieController(Movie itsMovie, int someFlags);
    public MultiMovieController(int subType, Movie theMovie, QDGraphics window,
                          QDPoint location);

//Instance Methods
    public final void addMovie(Movie aMovie, QDGraphics movieWindow, QDPoint location);
    public final Movie getIndMovie(int index);
    public final void movieChanged(Movie changedMovie);
    public final void removeAMovie(Movie movie);
    public final void removeAllMovies();
    public final void removeMovie();
    public final void setMovie(Movie aMovie, QDGraphics movieWindow, QDPoint location);
}
```

CLASS HIERARCHY:

Object→QTObject→ComponentIdentifier→Component→MovieController→ MultiMovieController

Class quicktime.std.movies.ParameterDialog

This class creates an `AtomContainer` object that contains the necessary information for displaying a list of effects.

It only contains one method, `showParameterDialog()`, which shows the choose effects dialog with the specified parameters.

```
public final class ParameterDialog extends Object implements QuickTimeLib, StdQTConstants, Errors {
//Static Methods
    public static AtomContainer showParameterDialog(AtomContainer effectList,
                                                    int dialogOptions);
}
```

CLASS HIERARCHY:

Object→ParameterDialog

Class quicktime.std.movies.ResolvedQTEventSpec

This class is returned from `ActionFilter` objects that deal with wired sprite actions.

See also `ExecuteQTEventAction`.

```
public class ResolvedQTEventSpec extends QTPointerRef {
//Static Fields
    public static final int kNativeSize;

//Instance Methods
    public Atom getAtom();
    public AtomContainer getContainer();
    public Track getTargetTrack();
}
```

CLASS HIERARCHY:

Object→QTObject→QTPointerRef→ResolvedQTEventSpec

Class quicktime.std.movies.SearchResult

This class represents the results returned from searching for text within a movie.

The various `get()` methods return the found track, the found offset, and the found time.

```
public final class SearchResult extends Object {
//Instance Methods
    public Track getFoundTrack();
    public int getOffset();
    public int getTime();
}
```

CLASS HIERARCHY:

Object→SearchResult

Class quicktime.std.movies.StatusInfo

This class represents the results returned from querying the status of a movie.

The getProblemTrack() method returns the found problem track.

```
public final class StatusInfo extends Object {
//Instance Methods
    public int getErr();
    public Track getProblemTrack();
}
```

CLASS HIERARCHY:

Object→StatusInfo

Class quicktime.std.movies.TimeInfo

This class encapsulates time and the duration information returned by the Movie Toolbox. TimeInfo objects are also passed to various methods to specify the point at which some action should occur.

Use the TimeInfo() constructor to create a TimeInfo object.

```
public class TimeInfo extends Object {
//Constructors
    public TimeInfo(int time, int duration);

//Instance Fields
    public int duration;
    public int time;
}
```

CLASS HIERARCHY:

Object→TimeInfo

Class quicktime.std.movies.Track

A QuickTime movie may contain several tracks, and each track refers to a single media type that contains references to the media data. This data may be stored, for example, as images or sound on hard disks, floppy disks, compact discs, or other devices. You specify the track for an operation and obtain a track identifier.

You get Track objects through the addTrack() or getTrack() methods on a movie object.

```
public final class Track extends QTObject
                    implements QuickTimeLib, Errors, StdQTConstants {
//Static Methods
    public static Track fromMedia(Media m);
    public static MovieImportInfo fromMovieImporterDataRef(MovieImporter mi,
                    DataRef dataRef, Movie theMovie, Track targetTrack, int atTime,
                    int inFlags)
    public static MovieImportInfo fromMovieImporterFile(MovieImporter mi, QTFile fileIn,
                    Movie theMovie, Track targetTrack, int atTime, int inFlags);
    public static MovieImportInfo fromMovieImporterHandle(MovieImporter mi,
                    QTHandleRef dataRef, Movie theMovie, Track targetTrack,
                    int atTime, int inFlags);

//Instance Methods
    public int addReference(Track refTrack, int refType);
    public void copySettings(Track dstTrack);
    public void deleteReference(int refType, int index);
    public void deleteSegment(int startTime, int duration);
    public Track getAlternate();
    public Region getBoundsRgn();
    public Region getClipRgn();
    public int getCreationTime();
    public int getDataSize(int startTime, int duration);
    public Dimension getDimensions();
    public Region getDisplayBoundsRgn();
    public Matrix getDisplayMatrix();
    public int getDuration();
    public float getEditRate(int atTime);
    public boolean getEnabled();
    public int getID();
    public int getLayer();
    public LoadSettings getLoadSettings();
    public Matrix getMatrix();
    public int getModificationTime();
    public Movie getMovie();
    public Region getMovieBoundsRgn();
    public TimeInfo getNextInterestingTime(int interestingTimeFlags, int time,
                                    float rate);
    public int getNextReferenceType(int refType);
```

```
public int getOffset();
public Pict getPict(int time);
public Track getReference(int refType, int index);
public int getReferenceCount(int refType);
public Region getSegmentDisplayBoundsRgn(int time, int duration);
public QTHandle getSoundLocalizationSettings();
public int getStatus();
public int getUsage();
public UserData getUserData();
public float getVolume();
public void insertEmptySegment(int dstIn, int dstDuration);
public void insertMedia(int trackStart, int mediaTime, int mediaDuration,
                 float mediaRate);
public void insertSegment(Track dstTrack, int srcIn, int srcDuration, int dstIn);
public MovieImporter isScrapMovie();
public void loadIntoRam(int time, int duration, int flags);
public TrackEditState newEditState();
public boolean pointInMovie(QDPoint pt);
public void removeMedia();
public void scaleSegment(int startTime, int oldDuration, int newDuration);
public void setAlternate(Track alternateT);
public void setClipRgn(Region theClip);
public void setDimensions(Dimension d);
public void setEnabled(boolean enabled);
public void setGWorld(QDGraphics port, GDevice gdh);
public void setLayer(int layer);
public void setLoadSettings(LoadSettings settings);
public void setMatrix(Matrix matrix);
public void setOffset(int movieOffsetTime);
public void setReference(Track refTrack, int refType, int index);
public void setSoundLocalizationSettings(QTHandle newSettings);
public void setUsage(int usage);
public void setVolume(float volume);
public String toString();
public int trackTimeToMediaTime(int value);
public void useEditState(TrackEditState state);
}
```

CLASS HIERARCHY:

Object→QTObject→Track

Class quicktime.std.movies.TrackEditState

This class implements the corresponding data structure of the Movie Toolbox. The Movie Toolbox provides functions that allow you to capture and restore the edit state of a track. As with the functions that manipulate a movie's edit state, you can manage a track's edit states in order to implement an undo capability for track editing. For example, you can capture a track's edit state before performing an editing operation, such as a cut, and later restore the old state. This structure specifies the track edit state for an operation. Your application obtains a track edit state identifier when you create the edit state by calling the NewTrackEditState function (described in Chapter 2 of *Inside Macintosh: QuickTime*).

```
public final class TrackEditState extends QTObject {
}
```

CLASS HIERARCHY:

Object→QTObject→TrackEditState

The `quicktime.std.movies.media` package contains a large number of classes for handling the various types that QuickTime supports, as well as supporting custom media types.

One of the most useful classes in this package is the `DataRef` class. This class implements the data reference structure of the Movie Toolbox as specified in the QuickTime API. It contains constructors that create a `DataRef` object that represents an `AliasHandle`, a `QTFile`, or a URL.

Another useful class is `GenericMedia`, which provides a base from which to construct media classes that represent media types unknown to the standard QuickTime distribution. The subclasses define public constructors that call their corollary superclass constructors but internally pass on the media type.

The `Media` class contains a large number of methods for dealing with media generally. The data references of a track constitute the track's media. Each track has a single media data structure. You create a new media object for a track by constructing one from the provided media subclasses. You get an existing media object from a track through the `Media.getTrackMedia` call.

The `AudioMediaHandler` interface defines methods for getting and setting the balance of media with an audio component.

`SampleReference` forms a general base class for information that can be constructed or gleaned about media samples and references. `UserData` is a class that specifies the user data list for an operation. Figure 40.1 shows the class hierarchy for this package.

FIGURE 40.1 *The* quicktime.std.movies.media *package*

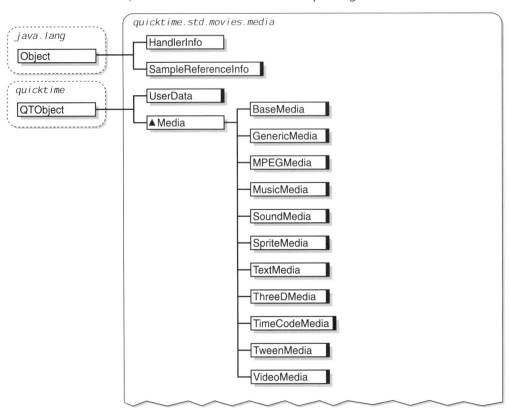

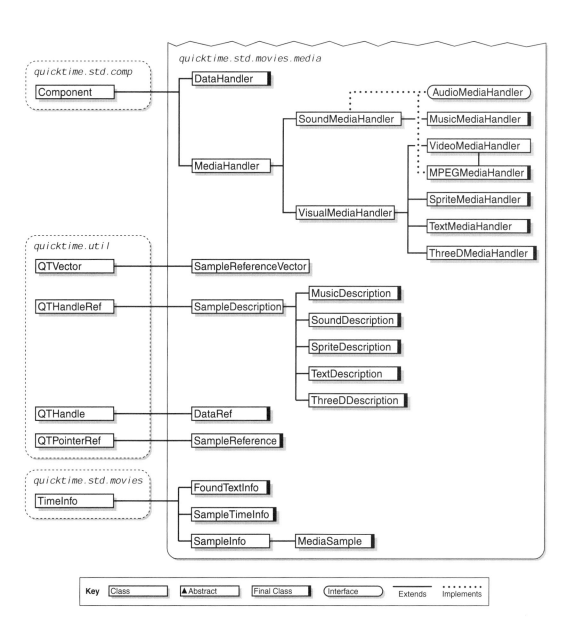

Interface quicktime.std.movies.media.AudioMediaHandler

This interface defines only two methods for getting and setting the balance of audio media. The getBalance() method returns the balance of audio media, with a range from −1.0 (Left) to 0 (Center) to 1.0 (Right).

```
public interface AudioMediaHandler {
//Instance Methods
    public abstract float getBalance();
    public abstract void setBalance(float balance);
}
```

Class quicktime.std.movies.media.BaseMedia

This class represents base media in QuickTime.

Both BaseMedia() constructors create a media structure for the specified Track object.

```
public final class BaseMedia extends Media {
//Constructors
    public BaseMedia(Track itsTrack, int timeScale, DataRef dataRef);
    public BaseMedia(Track itsTrack, int timeScale);
}
```

CLASS HIERARCHY:

Object→QTObject→Media→BaseMedia

Class quicktime.std.movies.media.DataHandler

Data references in QuickTime must have some object that knows "intrinsically" how to retrieve the data from this source, and this is the function of a DataHandler. QuickTime provides DataHandler objects for data that exists as files on both local and remote locations.

```
public final class DataHandler extends Component implements QuickTimeLib, Errors {
//Constructors
    public DataHandler(DataRef dataRef, int flags);
}
```

CLASS HIERARCHY:

Object→QTObject→ComponentIdentifier→Component→DataHandler

Class quicktime.std.movies.media.DataRef

This class implements the data reference structure of the Movie Toolbox specified in the QuickTime API. It contains constructors that create a DataRef that represents an AliasHandle, a QTFile, or a URL.

A DataRef describes where the particular data resides (for example, in a file or in memory), and the corresponding data handler is responsible for reading and writing data to the data referenced.

fromMedia() returns a copy of a specified data reference. fromMovie() allows you to get the default data reference for the movie. Use fromSequenceGrabber() to determine the data reference currently assigned to a sequence grabber component.

```
public final class DataRef extends QTHandle
                           implements StdQTConstants, QuickTimeLib {
//Constructors
    public DataRef(String url);
    public DataRef(QTFile f);
    public DataRef(AliasHandle a);
    public DataRef(QTHandleRef handle);
    public DataRef(QTHandleRef handle, int hintFlag, String hintString);

//Static Methods
    public static DataRef fromMedia(Media m, int index);
    public static DataRef fromMovie(Movie m);
    public static DataRef fromSequenceGrabber(SequenceGrabber sg);

//Instance Methods
    public int getAttributes();
    public int getType();
    public String getUniversalResourceLocator();
}
```

CLASS HIERARCHY:

Object→QTObject→QTHandleRef→QTHandle→DataRef

Class quicktime.std.movies.media.FoundTextInfo

This class contains information returned from searching text in a track's media.

The FoundTextInfo() constructor creates a FoundTextInfo object from the information returned after a search.

```
public final class FoundTextInfo extends TimeInfo {
```

```
//Constructors
    public FoundTextInfo(int foundTime, int foundDuration, int offset);

//Instance Fields
    public int offset;
}
```

CLASS HIERARCHY:

Object→TimeInfo→FoundTextInfo

Class quicktime.std.movies.media.GenericMedia

This class provides a base from which to construct media classes that represent media types unknown to the standard QuickTime distribution. The subclasses define public constructors that call their corollary superclass constructors but internally pass on the media type. By definition, the media type is encapsulated by the particular subclass and does not need to be provided by the program itself.

The newFromType() and getTrackMedia() calls in the Media class will return an appropriate object of a type that corresponds with the mediaType. Your application must make this association known to the Media class. You do this by calling the addMediaType() method with the mediaType and full class name of the associated class. This new class must have a java.lang.Integer constructor that is called by the aforementioned media calls. If a media type is encountered within a QuickTime movie that is unknown at runtime, it will return an instance of GenericMedia. This has no defined public calls (except the getMediaType() call) but enables general calls that can be performed on any media type from its superclass.

The getMediaType() method returns the type of media that this Media object represents.

```
public class GenericMedia extends Media {
//Instance Methods
    public final int getMediaType();
}
```

CLASS HIERARCHY:

Object→QTObject→Media→GenericMedia

Class quicktime.std.movies.media.HandlerInfo

This class contains general information for `Media` and `DataHandler` components on the type of information they handle and the manufacturer's name and ID.

```
public class HandlerInfo extends Object {
//Constructors
    public HandlerInfo(int subType, String name, int manufacturerID);

//Instance Fields
    public int manufacturerID;
    public String name;
    public int subType;
}
```

> **CLASS HIERARCHY:**
> Object→HandlerInfo

Class quicktime.std.movies.media.Media

The data references of a track constitute the track's media. Each track has a single media data structure. You create a new media object for a track by constructing one of the provided media subclasses. You obtain an existing media object from a track through the `Media.getTrackMedia` call.

This class contains a large number of methods. The `newFromType()` static method creates a new media structure for the specified `Track` object. The type of media object created is determined by the `mediaType` argument. If a media class that corresponds to the specified media type is not found, an instance of `GenericMedia` is returned. The `getTrackMedia()` static method returns an existing media object from the `Track`.

The `get()` and `set()` instance methods in this class are particularly useful, allowing you to, among other things, determine a media's data handler, retrieve a sample description from a media, assign a data handler to a media, and obtain a reference to a media handler component.

```
public abstract class Media extends QTObject
                        implements QuickTimeLib, StdQTConstants, Errors {
//Static Methods
    public static Media fromTrack(Track theTrack);
    public static Media getTrackMedia(Track theTrack);
    public static Media newFromType(int mediaType, Track track, int timeScale,
                        DataRef dataRef);
```

```
//Instance Methods
    public final int addDataRef(DataRef dataReference);
    public final int addSample(QTHandleRef data, int dataOffset, int dataSize,
                          int durationPerSample, SampleDescription sampleDesc,
                          int numberOfSamples, int sampleFlags);
    public final int addSampleReference(int dataOffset, int dataSize,
                          int durationPerSample, SampleDescription sampleDesc,
                          int numberOfSamples, int sampleFlags);
    public final int addSampleReference(SampleDescription sampleDescription,
                          int numOfSamples, SampleReferenceVector sampleRefs);
    public final void beginEdits();
    public final void endEdits();
    public final int getCreationTime();
    public final DataHandler getDataHandler(int index);
    public final HandlerInfo getDataHandlerDescription(int index);
    public final DataRef getDataRef(int index);
    public final int getDataRefCount();
    public final int getDataSize(int startTime, int duration);
    public final int getDuration();
    public MediaHandler getHandler();
    public final HandlerInfo getHandlerDescription();
    public final AtomContainer getInputMap();
    public final int getLanguage();
    public final int getModificationTime();
    public final TimeInfo getNextInterestingTime(int interestingTimeFlags,
                                        int time, float rate);
    public final int getPlayHints(int flags, int flagsMask);
    public final int getPreferredChunkSize();
    public final AtomContainer getPropertyAtom();
    public final int getQuality();
    public final MediaSample getSample(int maxSizeToGrow, int time,
                                  int maxNumberOfSamples);
    public final int getSampleCount();
    public SampleDescription getSampleDescription(int index);
    public final int getSampleDescriptionCount();
    public final SampleInfo getSampleReference(int time, int maxNumberOfSamples);
    public final SampleReferenceInfo getSampleReferences(int time,
                                            int maxNumberOfSamples);
    public final int getShadowSync(int frameDiffSampleNum);
    public final int getSyncSampleCount();
    public final int getTimeScale();
    public final Track getTrack();
    public final UserData getUserData();
    public final void loadIntoRam(int time, int duration, int flags);
    public final TimeInfo sampleNumToMediaTime(int logicalSampleNum);
    public final void setDataHandler(int index, DataHandler dH);
    public final void setDataRef(int index, DataRef dataReference);
    public final void setDataRefAttributes(int index, int dataRefAttributes);
    public final void setDefaultDataRefIndex(int index);
    public final void setHandler(MediaHandler mH);
    public final void setInputMap(AtomContainer inputMap);
    public final void setLanguage(int language);
```

```
    public final void setPlayHints(int flags, int flagsMask);
    public final void setPreferredChunkSize(int maxChunkSize);
    public final void setPropertyAtom(AtomContainer propertyAtom);
    public final void setQuality(int quality);
    public final void setSampleDescription(int index, SampleDescription descH);
    public final void setShadowSync(int frameDiffSampleNum, int syncSampleNum);
    public final void setTimeScale(int timeScale);
    public final SampleTimeInfo timeToSampleNum(int time);
}
```

CLASS HIERARCHY:

Object→QTObject→Media

Class quicktime.std.movies.media.MediaSample

This class contains media information and data. The fields from the SampleInfo superclass describe how the raw data in the handle is to be interpreted.

```
public final class MediaSample extends SampleInfo {
//Instance Fields
    public QTHandle data;
}
```

CLASS HIERARCHY:

Object→TimeInfo→SampleInfo→MediaSample

Class quicktime.std.movies.media.MPEGMedia

This class represents MPEG media in QuickTime. MPEGMedia contains both visual and audio data.

The MPEGMedia() constructor creates an MPEGMedia object for the specified Track object.

```
public final class MPEGMedia extends Media implements StdQTConstants {
//Constructors
    public MPEGMedia(Track itsTrack, int timeScale, DataRef dataRef);
    public MPEGMedia(Track itsTrack, int timeScale);
}
```

CLASS HIERARCHY:

Object→QTObject→Media→MPEGMedia

Class quicktime.std.movies.media.MPEGMediaHandler

This class defines only two methods. The `getBalance()` method returns the balance of a sound media, with a range from –1.0 (Left) to 0 (Equal) to 1.0 (Right). The `setBalance()` method sets the balance of a sound media with a range from –1.0 (Left) to 0 (Equal) to 1.0 (Right).

```
public class MPEGMediaHandler extends VideoMediaHandler
                            implements QuickTimeLib, AudioMediaHandler {
//Instance Methods
    public final float getBalance();
    public final void setBalance(float balance);
}
```

CLASS HIERARCHY:

Object→QTObject→ComponentIdentifier→Component→MediaHandler→Visual MediaHandler→VideoMediaHandler→MPEGMediaHandler

Class quicktime.std.movies.media.MusicDescription

`MusicDescriptions` are used when adding and retrieving music media samples to and from music tracks.

```
public final class MusicDescription extends SampleDescription
                        implements InterfaceLib, PrimitivesLib, StdQTConstants {
//Constructors
    public MusicDescription();

//Static Methods
    public static EndianDescriptor getEndianDescriptor();

//Instance Methods
    public Object clone();
    public int getMusicFlags();
    public MusicData getTuneHeader();
    public void setMusicFlags(int flags);
    public void setTuneHeader(MusicData mh);
}
```

CLASS HIERARCHY:

Object→QTObject→QTHandleRef→SampleDescription→MusicDescription

Class quicktime.std.movies.media.MusicMedia

This class represents music media in QuickTime.

The MusicMedia() constructor creates a media structure for the specified Track object. getMusicDescription() allows you to retrieve a sample description from a media and returns the handler that is the appropriate class for this particular media. getMusicHandler() allows you to obtain a reference to a media handler component and returns the description that is the appropriate class for this particular media.

```
public final class MusicMedia extends Media implements StdQTConstants {
//Constructors
    public MusicMedia(Track itsTrack, int timeScale, DataRef dataRef);
    public MusicMedia(Track itsTrack, int timeScale);

//Instance Methods
    public MusicDescription getMusicDescription(int index);
    public MusicMediaHandler getMusicHandler();
}
```

CLASS HIERARCHY:

Object→QTObject→Media→MusicMedia

Class quicktime.std.movies.media.MusicMediaHandler

The getIndexedTunePlayer() method returns the TunePlayer object responsible for rendering the music data contained within a particular music track. If the movie or this media is edited in any way, the returned TunePlayer becomes invalid and must be retrieved again.

```
public final class MusicMediaHandler extends SoundMediaHandler {
//Instance Methods
    public TunePlayer getIndexedTunePlayer(int index);
}
```

CLASS HIERARCHY:

Object→QTObject→ComponentIdentifier→Component→MediaHandler→Sound MediaHandler→MusicMediaHandler

Class quicktime.std.movies.media.SampleDescription

This class is a generic superclass that describes media data and contains fields that are common to all media data in QuickTime movies.

```
public class SampleDescription extends QTHandleRef implements QuickTimeLib, Cloneable {
//Static Fields
    public static final int kNativeSize;

//Constructors
    public SampleDescription(int format);

//Static Methods
    public static SampleDescription fromMovieImporter(MovieImporter mi);
    public static EndianDescriptor getEndianDescriptor();

//Instance Methods
    public Object clone();
    public int getDataFormat();
    public int getDataRefIndex();
    public int getSize();
    public void setDataFormat(int format);
    public void setDataRefIndex(int index);
    public void setSize(int size);
}
```

> ### CLASS HIERARCHY:
> Object→QTObject→QTHandleRef→SampleDescription

Class quicktime.std.movies.media.SampleInfo

This class contains information about a sample that is part of some media.

```
public class SampleInfo extends TimeInfo {
//Instance Fields
    public SampleDescription description;
    public int descriptionIndex;
    public int flags;
    public int numberOfSamples;
    public int offset;
    public int size;
}
```

> ### CLASS HIERARCHY:

Object→TimeInfo→SampleInfo

Class quicktime.std.movies.media.SampleReference

This class forms a general base class for information that can be constructed or gleaned about media samples and references.

```
public final class SampleReference extends QTPointerRef {
//Static Fields
    public static final int kNativeSize;

//Constructors
    public SampleReference();
    public SampleReference(int dataOffset, int dataSize, int durationPerSample,
                    int numberOfSamples, int sampleFlags);

//Instance Methods
    public int getDataOffset();
    public int getDataSize();
    public int getDurationPerSample();
    public int getFlags();
    public int getNumberOfSamples();
    public void setDataOffset(int dataOffset);
    public void setDataSize(int dataSize);
    public void setDurationPerSample(int durationPerSample);
    public void setFlags(int sampleFlags);
    public void setNumberOfSamples(int numberOfSamples);
}
```

CLASS HIERARCHY:

Object→QTObject→QTPointerRef→SampleReference

Class quicktime.std.movies.media.SampleReferenceInfo

This class contains information about media samples references.

```
public final class SampleReferenceInfo extends Object {
//Instance Fields
    public int descriptionIndex;
    public SampleDescription sampleDescription;
    public SampleReferenceVector sampleRefs;
    public int sampleTime;
}
```

CLASS HIERARCHY:

Object→SampleReferenceInfo

Class quicktime.std.movies.media.SampleReferenceVector

This class represents a `SampleReferenceVector` that is an array of `SampleReference` objects.

The `get()` method gets a `SampleReference` at specified position. `insert()` inserts a `SampleReference` into the vector at specified position.

```
public class SampleReferenceVector extends QTVector {
//Constructors
    public SampleReferenceVector(int numberOfElements);

//Instance Methods
    public SampleReference get(int pos);
    public void insert(SampleReference el, int pos);
}
```

CLASS HIERARCHY:

Object→QTObject→QTPointerRef→QTVector→SampleReferenceVector

Class quicktime.std.movies.media.SampleTimeInfo

This class encapsulates a media sample's timing information and specifies which media sample the time settings relate to.

```
public final class SampleTimeInfo extends TimeInfo {
//Constructors
    public SampleTimeInfo(int time, int duration, int sampleNum);

//Instance Fields
    public int sampleNum;
}
```

CLASS HIERARCHY:

Object→TimeInfo→SampleTimeInfo

Class quicktime.std.movies.media.SoundDescription

`SoundDescription` objects are used when adding and retrieving media samples to and from sound tracks and contain specific information about sound media.

```
public final class SoundDescription extends SampleDescription implements QuickTimeLib {
//Static Fields
```

```
    public static final int kNativeSize;

//Constructors
    public SoundDescription(int format);

//Static Methods
    public static EndianDescriptor getEndianDescriptor();

//Instance Methods
    public void addExtension(QTHandleRef extension, int idType);
    public Object clone();
    public int getCompressionID();
    public QTHandle getExtension(int idType);
    public int getNumChannels();
    public int getPacketSize();
    public int getRevLevel();
    public float getSampleRate();
    public int getSampleRateRounded();
    public int getSampleSize();
    public int getVendor();
    public int getVersion();
    public void removeExtension(int idType);
    public void setCompressionID(int compressionID);
    public void setNumChannels(int numChannels);
    public void setPacketSize(int packetSize);
    public void setRevLevel(int revLevel);
    public void setSampleRate(float sampleRate);
    public void setSampleSize(int sampleSize);
    public void setVendor(int vendor);
    public void setVersion(int version);
    public String toString();
}
```

CLASS HIERARCHY:

Object→QTObject→QTHandleRef→SampleDescription→SoundDescription

Class quicktime.std.movies.media.SoundMedia

This class represents sound media in a QuickTime movie.

```
public final class SoundMedia extends Media implements StdQTConstants {
//Constructors
    public SoundMedia(Track itsTrack, int timeScale, DataRef dataRef);
    public SoundMedia(Track itsTrack, int timeScale);

//Instance Methods
    public SoundDescription getSoundDescription(int index);
    public SoundMediaHandler getSoundHandler();
}
```

CLASS HIERARCHY:

Object→QTObject→Media→SoundMedia

Classquicktime.std.movies.media.SoundMediaHandler

This class represents the `MediaHandler` that deals with sound media in a QuickTime movie. It allows the application to both get and set the balance of sound in a stereo field for any given sound track.

```
public class SoundMediaHandler extends MediaHandler
                            implements QuickTimeLib, AudioMediaHandler {
//Instance Methods
    public final float getBalance();
    public final void setBalance(float balance);
}
```

CLASS HIERARCHY:

Object→QTObject→ComponentIdentifier→Component→MediaHandler→ SoundMediaHandler

Class quicktime.std.movies.media.SpriteDescription

This class maps the `SpriteDescription` record of the Movie Toolbox. `SpriteDescription` objects are used when adding and retrieving media samples to and from sprite tracks.

```
public final class SpriteDescription extends SampleDescription
                                    implements StdQTConstants {
//Static Fields
    public static final int kNativeSize;

//Constructors
    public SpriteDescription();

//Static Methods
    public static EndianDescriptor getEndianDescriptor();

//Instance Methods
    public Object clone();
    public int getDecompressorType();
    public int getSampleFlags();
    public int getVersion();
    public void setDecompressorType(int dt);
    public void setSampleFlags(int sf);
    public void setVersion(int version);
```

}

> **CLASS HIERARCHY:**
>
> Object→QTObject→QTHandleRef→SampleDescription→SpriteDescription

Class quicktime.std.movies.media.SpriteMedia

This class represents sprite media in QuickTime.

```
public final class SpriteMedia extends Media implements StdQTConstants {
//Constructors
    public SpriteMedia(Track itsTrack, int timeScale, DataRef dataRef);
    public SpriteMedia(Track itsTrack, int timeScale);

//Instance Methods
    public SpriteDescription getSoundDescription(int index);
    public SpriteMediaHandler getSpriteHandler();
}
```

> **CLASS HIERARCHY:**
>
> Object→QTObject→Media→SpriteMedia

Class quicktime.std.movies.media.SpriteMediaHandler

This class allows the application to interact with sprites that are stored in a `SpriteMedia` object in a QuickTime movie.

```
public final class SpriteMediaHandler extends VisualMediaHandler
                                implements QuickTimeLib, StdQTConstants {
//Instance Methods
    public int countImages();
    public int countSprites();
    public float getActionVariable(int variableID);
    public int getDisplayedSampleNumber();
    public GraphicsMode getGraphicsMode(int spriteID);
    public int getImageIndex(int spriteID);
    public String getImageName(int imageIndex);
    public ImageDescription getIndImageDescription(int imageIndex);
    public int getLayer(int spriteID);
    public Matrix getMatrix(int spriteID);
    public int getSpriteImageGroupID(int imageIndex);
    public QDPoint getSpriteImageRegistrationPoint(int imageIndex);
    public String getSpriteName(int spriteID);
    public boolean getVisible(int spriteID);
    public int hitTestAllSprites(int flags, QDPoint loc);
```

```
    public boolean hitTestOneSprite(int spriteID, int flags, QDPoint loc);
    public void setActionVariable(int variableID, float value);
    public void setGraphicsMode(int spriteID, GraphicsMode gMode);
    public void setImageIndex(int spriteID, int index);
    public void setLayer(int spriteID, int layer);
    public void setMatrix(int spriteID, Matrix matrix);
    public void setVisible(int spriteID, boolean visible);
    public short spriteIDtoIndex(int spriteID);
    public int spriteIndexToID(int spriteIndex);
}
```

CLASS HIERARCHY:

Object→QTObject→ComponentIdentifier→Component→MediaHandler→
VisualMediaHandler→SpriteMediaHandler

Class quicktime.std.movies.media.TextDescription

This class maps the TextDescription record of the Movie Toolbox. TextDescription objects are used when adding and retrieving media samples to and from text tracks.

```
public final class TextDescription extends SampleDescription implements StdQTConstants {
//Static Fields
    public static final int kNativeSize;

//Constructors
    public TextDescription();

//Static Methods
    public static EndianDescriptor getEndianDescriptor();

//Instance Methods
    public Object clone();
    public QDColor getBackgroundColor();
    public QDRect getDefaultTextBox();
    public int getDisplayFlags();
    public int getTextJustification();
    public void setBackgroundColor(QDColor bgColor);
    public void setDefaultTextBox(QDRect textBox);
    public void setDisplayFlags(int flags);
    public void setTextJustification(int just);
}
```

CLASS HIERARCHY:

Object→QTObject→QTHandleRef→SampleDescription→TextDescription

Class quicktime.std.movies.media.TextMedia

This class represents text media in QuickTime.

```
public final class TextMedia extends Media implements StdQTConstants {
//Constructors
    public TextMedia(Track itsTrack, int timeScale, DataRef dataRef);
    public TextMedia(Track itsTrack, int timeScale);

//Instance Methods
    public TextDescription getTextDescription(int index);
    public TextMediaHandler getTextHandler();
}
```

CLASS HIERARCHY:

Object→QTObject→Media→TextMedia

Class quicktime.std.movies.media.TextMediaHandler

This class provides services for an application to interact with text media in a QuickTime movie.

```
public final class TextMediaHandler extends VisualMediaHandler
                            implements QuickTimeLib, StdQTConstants {
//Instance Methods
    public int addTextSample(QTPointerRef text, int fontNumber, int fontSize,
                    int textFace, QDColor textColor, QDColor backColor,
                    int textJustification, QDRect textBox, int displayFlags,
                    int scrollDelay, int hiliteStart, int hiliteEnd,
                    QDColor rgbHiliteColor, int duration);
    public FoundTextInfo findNextText(QTPointerRef text, int findFlags, int startTime);
    public void hiliteTextSample(int sampleTime, int hiliteStart, int hiliteEnd,
                    QDColor hiliteColor);
    public void setDropShadowOffset(QDPoint offset);
    public void setDropShadowTranslucency(int translucency);
}
```

CLASS HIERARCHY:

Object→QTObject→ComponentIdentifier→Component→MediaHandler→
VisualMediaHandler→TextMediaHandler

Class quicktime.std.movies.media.ThreeDDescription

This class maps the `ThreeDDescription` record of the Movie Toolbox. `ThreeDDescription` records are used when adding and retrieving media samples to and from 3D tracks.

```
public final class ThreeDDescription extends SampleDescription {
//Constructors
    public ThreeDDescription(int format);

//Static Methods
    public static EndianDescriptor getEndianDescriptor();

//Instance Methods
    public Object clone();
    public int getRendererType();
    public int getVersion();
    public void setRendererType(int rendererType);
    public void setVersion(int version);
}
```

> ### CLASS HIERARCHY:
> Object→QTObject→QTHandleRef→SampleDescription→ThreeDDescription

Class quicktime.std.movies.media.ThreeDMedia

This class represents ThreeD media in QuickTime.

```
public final class ThreeDMedia extends Media implements StdQTConstants {
//Constructors
    public ThreeDMedia(Track itsTrack, int timeScale, DataRef dataRef);
    public ThreeDMedia(Track itsTrack, int timeScale);

//Instance Methods
    public ThreeDDescription getThreeDDescription(int index);
    public ThreeDMediaHandler getThreeDHandler();
}
```

> ### CLASS HIERARCHY:
> Object→QTObject→Media→ThreeDMedia

Class quicktime.std.movies.media.ThreeDMediaHandler

This class enables an application to interact with ThreeD models that are stored in a ThreeD media object in a QuickTime movie.

```
public class ThreeDMediaHandler extends VisualMediaHandler {
//Instance Methods
    public AtomContainer getNamedObjectList();
    public AtomContainer getRendererList();
}
```

> **CLASS HIERARCHY:**
> Object→QTObject→ComponentIdentifier→Component→MediaHandler→
> VisualMediaHandler→ThreeDMediaHandler

Class quicktime.std.movies.media.TimeCodeMedia

This class represents time code media in QuickTime.

```
public final class TimeCodeMedia extends Media implements StdQTConstants {
//Constructors
    public TimeCodeMedia(Track itsTrack, int timeScale, DataRef dataRef);
    public TimeCodeMedia(Track itsTrack, int timeScale);

//Instance Methods
    public TimeCodeDescription getTimeCodeDescription(int index);
    public TimeCoder getTimeCodeHandler();
}
```

> **CLASS HIERARCHY:**
> Object→QTObject→Media→TimeCodeMedia

Class quicktime.std.movies.media.TweenMedia

This class represents base media in QuickTime.

```
public final class TweenMedia extends Media implements StdQTConstants {
//Constructors
    public TweenMedia(Track itsTrack, int timeScale, DataRef dataRef);
    public TweenMedia(Track itsTrack, int timeScale);
}
```

CLASS HIERARCHY:

Object→QTObject→Media→TweenMedia

Class quicktime.std.movies.media.UserData

This structure specifies the user data list for an operation. You obtain a user data list identifier by calling the GetMovieUserData, GetTrackUserData, or GetMediaUserData functions (described in Chapter 2 of *Inside Macintosh: QuickTime*).

```
public final class UserData extends QTObject implements QuickTimeLib {
//Constructors
    public UserData();
    public UserData(QTHandle handle);

//Static Methods
    public static UserData fromMedia(Media m);
    public static UserData fromMovie(Movie m);
    public static UserData fromSGChannel(SGChannel chan);
    public static UserData fromSequenceGrabber(SequenceGrabber sg);
    public static UserData fromTrack(Track t);

//Instance Methods
    public void addData(QTHandle data, int udType);
    public void addText(QTHandle data, int udType, int index, short itlRegionTag);
    public short countType(int udType);
    public QTHandle getData(int udType, int index);
    public QTPointer getDataItem(int dataSize, int udType, int index);
    public int getNextType(int udType);
    public QTHandle getText(int udType, int index, short itlRegionTag);
    public QTHandle putIntoHandle();
    public void removeData(int udType, int index);
    public void removeText(int udType, int index, short itlRegionTag);
    public void setDataItem(QTPointer data, int udType, int index);
}
```

CLASS HIERARCHY:

Object→QTObject→UserData

Class quicktime.std.movies.media.VideoMedia

This class represents video media in QuickTime.

```
public final class VideoMedia extends Media implements StdQTConstants {
//Constructors
    public VideoMedia(Track itsTrack, int timeScale, DataRef dataRef);
```

```
   public VideoMedia(Track itsTrack, int timeScale);

//Instance Methods
   public ImageDescription getImageDescription(int index);
   public VideoMediaHandler getVideoHandler();
}
```

CLASS HIERARCHY:

Object→QTObject→Media→VideoMedia

Class quicktime.std.movies.media.VideoMediaHandler

This class provides methods that allow you to set the transfer and graphics modes, as well as the blend color, of the video media handler.

```
public class VideoMediaHandler extends VisualMediaHandler implements QuickTimeLib {
//Instance Methods
   public float getStatistics();
   public void resetStatistics();
}
```

CLASS HIERARCHY:

Object→QTObject→ComponentIdentifier→Component→MediaHandler→
VisualMediaHandler→VideoMediaHandler

Class quicktime.std.movies.media.VisualMediaHandler

This class is a base class that represents characteristics that are common to all media types in a QuickTime movie that have a visual aspect. It provides the capability to both get and set the GraphicsMode that is applied to the rendering process of visual media.

```
public class VisualMediaHandler extends MediaHandler implements QuickTimeLib {
//Instance Methods
   public final GraphicsMode getGraphicsMode();
   public final boolean getTrackOpaque();
   public final void setGraphicsMode(GraphicsMode graphicsMode);
}
```

CLASS HIERARCHY:

Object→QTObject→ComponentIdentifier→Component→MediaHandler→
VisualMediaHandler

41

The quicktime. std.music Package

The `quicktime.std.music` package contains a large collection of classes for utilizing QuickTime Music Architecture (QTMA).

Many of the classes correspond to the functionality specified in the QuickTime Music Architecture API's. You can use this architecture to capture and generate music (MIDI) events in real time, customize and create instruments, and eventually provide your own algorithmic synthesis engines. This package currently has a full implementation of the note allocator component and basic support for the music components and tune player component. This provides you with the ability to interact with MIDI hardware connections.

A `NoteChannel` object uses a `NoteRequest` object to initialize a channel to the required instrument. A `NoteChannel` also requires an instance of the `NoteAllocator` when created. Once created, the `NoteChannel` is used to play notes and exercise control over those notes. The `NoteChannel` can be used to send new MIDI data to the MIDI outputs of the channel's note allocator.

The `ToneDescription` class provides the information needed to produce a specific musical sound.

Figure 41.1 shows the class hierarchy for this package. See Chapter 10, "Playing Music with QuickTime," for more information on using this class.

FIGURE 41.1 *The* quicktime.std.music *package*

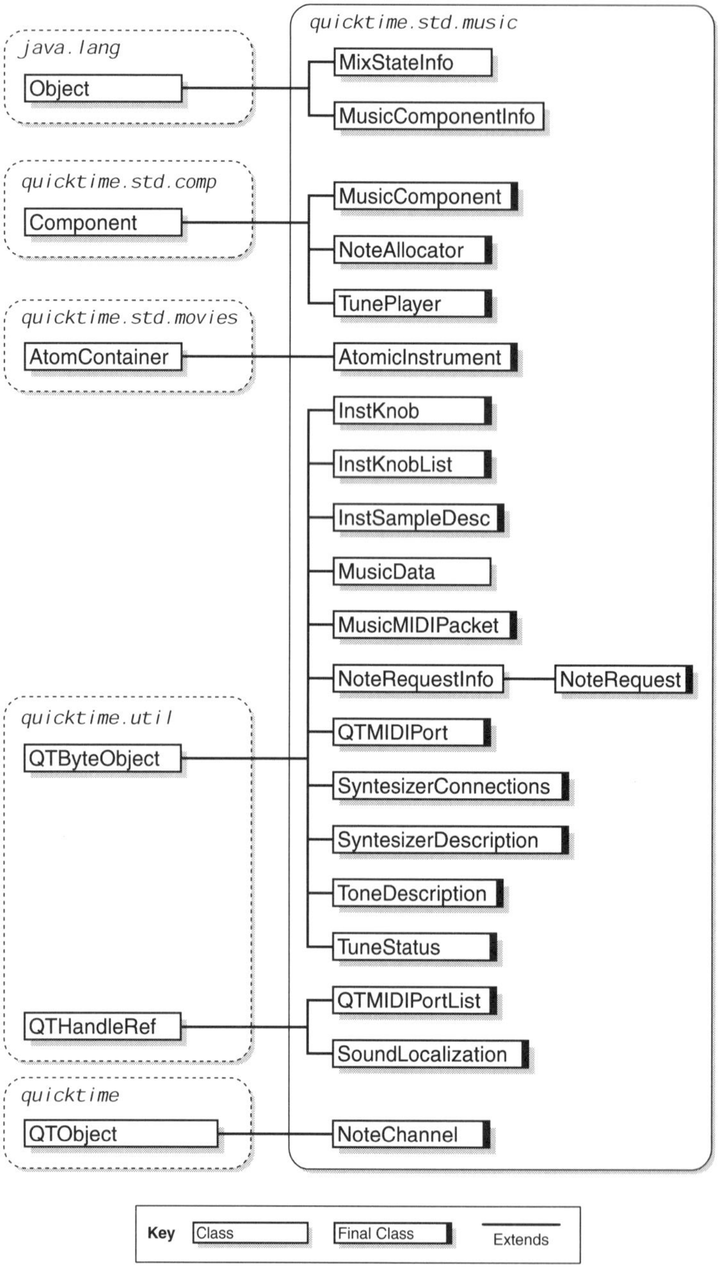

Class quicktime.std.music.AtomicInstrument

This class corresponds to the `AtomicInstrument` type and its accompanying calls, as specified in the QuickTime API.

The `newNoteChannel()` method makes a new note channel for an atomic instrument. The `pickEditInstrument()` method presents a user interface for modifying the `AtomicInstrument`.

```
public final class AtomicInstrument extends AtomContainer
                                              implements QuickTimeLib {
//Constructors
    public AtomicInstrument();

//Instance Methods
    public NoteChannel newNoteChannel(int flags);
    public NoteChannel newNoteChannel(NoteAllocator na, int flags);
    public void pickEditInstrument(NoteAllocator na, String prompt, int flags);
}
```

CLASS HIERARCHY:

Object→QTObject→QTHandleRef→AtomContainer→AtomicInstrument

Class quicktime.std.music.InstKnob

This class contains information about state of a knob.

```
public final class InstKnob extends QTByteObject {
//Constructors
    public InstKnob();

//Instance Methods
    public int getNumber();
    public int getValue();
    public void setNumber(int number);
    public void setValue(int value);
}
```

CLASS HIERARCHY:

Object→QTByteObject→InstKnob

Class quicktime.std.music.InstKnobList

This class contains a list of knobs.

```
public final class InstKnobList extends QTByteObject {
//Constructors
    public InstKnobList();
    public InstKnobList(int knobFlags, InstKnob[] knobs);

//Instance Methods
    public InstKnob getKnob(int index);
    public int getKnobCount();
    public int getKnobFlags();
    public void setKnob(int index, InstKnob knob);
    public void setKnobFlags(int knobFlags);
}
```

CLASS HIERARCHY:

Object→QTByteObject→InstKnobList

Class quicktime.std.music.InstSampleDesc

This class contains information about the mix state of a specified part.

```
public final class InstSampleDesc extends QTByteObject {
//Static Fields
    public static final int kNativeSize;

//Constructors
    public InstSampleDesc();

//Instance Methods
    public int getDataFormat();
    public int getLoopEnd();
    public int getLoopStart();
    public int getLoopType();
    public int getNumChannels();
    public int getNumSamples();
    public int getOffset();
    public int getPitchHigh();
    public int getPitchLow();
    public int getPitchNormal();
    public int getSampleDataID();
    public float getSampleRate();
    public int getSampleRateRaw();
    public int getSampleSize();
    public void setDataFormat(int dataFormat);
    public void setLoopEnd(int loopEnd);
```

```
    public void setLoopStart(int loopStart);
    public void setLoopType(int loopType);
    public void setNumChannels(int numChannels);
    public void setNumSamples(int numSamples);
    public void setOffset(int offset);
    public void setPitchHigh(int pitchHigh);
    public void setPitchLow(int pitchLow);
    public void setPitchNormal(int pitchNormal);
    public void setSampleDataID(int sampleDataID);
    public void setSampleRate(float sampleRate);
    public void setSampleRateRaw(int sampleRate);
    public void setSampleSize(int sampleSize);
    public String toString();
}
```

CLASS HIERARCHY:

Object→QTByteObject→InstSampleDesc

Class quicktime.std.music.MixStateInfo

This class contains information about the mix state of a specified part of a TunePlayer.

```
public class MixStateInfo extends Object {
//Instance Fields
    public float balance;
    public int flags;
    public int partNumber;
    public float volume;

//Instance Methods
    public String toString();
}
```

CLASS HIERARCHY:

Object→MixStateInfo

Class quicktime.std.music.MusicComponent

This class corresponds to a music component.

```
public final class MusicComponent extends Component
                              implements QuickTimeLib, StdQTConstants {
//Constructors
    public MusicComponent();
    public MusicComponent(int subType);
```

```
//Instance Methods
    public SynthesizerDescription getDescription();
}
```

CLASS HIERARCHY:

Object→QTObject→ComponentIdentifier→Component→MusicComponent

Class quicktime.std.music.MusicComponentInfo

This class contains information about a MusicComponent object.

```
public class MusicComponentInfo extends Object {
//Constructors
    public MusicComponentInfo();

//Instance Fields
    public SynthesizerConnections connections;
    public MusicComponent mc;
    public String name;
    public int synthType;

//Instance Methods
    public String toString();
}
```

CLASS HIERARCHY:

Object→MusicComponentInfo

Class quicktime.std.music.MusicData

MusicHData objects contain general information for a music track that the TunePlayer uses when it instantiates NoteChannel objects for the parts contained in the music media.

The MusicData() constructor creates a MusicData object of the specified number of bytes.

```
public class MusicData extends QTHandle implements StdQTConstants {
//Static Fields
    public static final int kNoteRequestHeaderEventLength;

//Constructors
    public MusicData(int size);

//Static Methods
    public static int controlController(int x);
```

```
    public static int controlValue(int x);
    public static int eventType(int x);
    public static int generalLength(int x);
    public static int generalSubtype_Footer(int x);
    public static int markerSubtype(int x);
    public static int markerValue(int x);
    public static int noteDuration(int x);
    public static int notePitch(int x);
    public static int noteVelocity(int x);
    public static int part(int x);
    public static int restDuration(int x);
    public static int stuffControlEvent(int part, int control, int value);
    public static int stuffGeneralEvent_Footer(int subType, int length);
    public static int stuffGeneralEvent_Header(int part, int length);
    public static int stuffMarkerEvent(int markerType, int markerValue);
    public static int stuffNoteEvent(int part, int pitch, int velocity, int duration);
    public static int stuffRestEvent(int duration);
    public static long stuffXControlEvent(int part, int control, int value);
    public static long stuffXKnobEvent(int part, int knob, int value);
    public static long stuffXNoteEvent(int part, int pitch, int volume, int duration);
    public static int xControlController(long x);
    public static int xControlValue(long x);
    public static int xKnobID(long x);
    public static int xKnobValue(long x);
    public static int xNoteDuration(long x);
    public static int xNotePitch(long x);
    public static int xNoteVelocity(long x);
    public static int xPart(long x);

//Instance Methods
    public AtomicInstrument getAtomicInstrument(int offset);
    public int getMusicEvent(int offset);
    public NoteRequest getNoteRequest(int offset);
    public long getXMusicEvent(int offset);
    public void setAtomicInstrument(int offset, int partNumber, AtomicInstrument ai);
    public void setMusicEvent(int offset, int musicData);
    public void setNoteRequest(int offset, int partNumber, NoteRequest nr);
    public void setSize(int newSize);
    public void setXMusicEvent(int offset, long musicData);
}
```

CLASS HIERARCHY:

Object→QTObject→QTHandleRef→QTHandle→MusicData

Class quicktime.std.music.MusicMIDIPacket

This class describes the MIDI data passed by NoteChannel calls.

```
public final class MusicMIDIPacket extends QTByteObject implements Cloneable {
```

```
//Static Fields
    public static final int kNativeSize;

//Constructors
    public MusicMIDIPacket();
    public MusicMIDIPacket(byte[] midiData);

//Instance Methods
    public Object clone();
    public byte[] getMIDIData();
    public int getReserved();
    public void setDataByte(int index, int val);
    public void setMIDIData(byte[] mData[]);
    public String toString();
}
```

CLASS HIERARCHY:

Object→QTByteObject→MusicMIDIPacket

Class quicktime.std.music.NoteAllocator

This class corresponds to the NoteAllocator component type, with the ability to inter-act with MIDI hardware connections.

```
public final class NoteAllocator extends Component
                              implements QuickTimeLib, StdQTConstants {
//Constructors
    public NoteAllocator();
    public NoteAllocator(int subType);

//Static Methods
    public static NoteAllocator getDefault();

//Instance Methods
    public void copyrightDialog(Pict p, String author, String copyright,
                            String other, String title);
    public SynthesizerConnections getDefaultMIDIInput();
    public NoteChannel getIndNoteChannel(int index);
    public QTMIDIPortList getMIDIInPorts();
    public QTMIDIPortList getMIDIOutPorts();
    public MusicComponentInfo getRegisteredMusicDevice(int index);
    public void loseDefaultMIDIInput();
    public int numMusicComponents();
    public int numNoteChannels();
    public void pickArrangement(String prompt, Track track, String songName);
    public void registerMusicDevice(int synthType, String name,
                            SynthesizerConnections connections);
    public void saveMusicConfiguration();
```

```
    public void setDefaultMIDIInput(SynthesizerConnections sc);
    public void task();
    public void unregisterMusicDevice(int index);
}
```

CLASS HIERARCHY:

Object→QTObject→ComponentIdentifier→Component→NoteAllocator

Class quicktime.std.music.NoteChannel

A NoteChannel uses a NoteRequest to initialize a channel to the required instrument. A NoteChannel also requires an instance of the NoteAllocator component when created. Once created, the NoteChannel is used to play notes and exercise control over those notes.

Notes can be specified in a resolution of 128 steps per semitone, with the 128 note semitones relating to MIDI note values. Middle C is equal to 60.

The NoteChannel can also be used to send new MIDI data to the MIDI outputs of the channel's note allocator.

```
public final class NoteChannel extends QTObject implements QuickTimeLib {
//Static Fields
    public static final float kMicroControllerResolution;
    public static final float kMicrotonalResolution;

//Constructors
    public NoteChannel(int gmNumber, int poly);
    public NoteChannel(NoteRequest nr);
    public NoteChannel(NoteAllocator na, NoteRequest nr);
    public NoteChannel(NoteAllocator na, int gmNumber);

//Instance Methods
    public final int findTone(ToneDescription td);
    public final float getController(int controllerNumber);
    public final int getIndexInfo();
    public final int getKnob(int knobNumber);
    public final NoteAllocator getNoteAllocator();
    public final NoteRequest getNoteRequest();
    public final int getPartInfo();
    public final void pickEditInstrument(String prompt, int flags);
    public final void playNote(float pitch, int velocity);
    public final void playNoteCents(int noteNumber, int cents, int velocity);
    public final void playNoteRaw(int pitch, int velocity);
    public final void preroll();
    public final void reset();
    public final void sendMIDI(MusicMIDIPacket mp);
    public final void setAtomicInstrument(AtomicInstrument instrument, int flags);
```

```
    public final void setBalance(int balance);
    public final void setController(int controllerNumber, float controllerValue);
    public final void setControllerRaw(int controllerNumber, int controllerValue);
    public final void setInstrumentNumber(int instrumentNumber);
    public final void setKnob(int knobNumber, int knobValue);
    public final void setSoundLocalization(SoundLocalization slData);
    public final void setVolume(float volume);
    public final void unroll();
}
```

CLASS HIERARCHY:

Object→QTObject→NoteChannel

Class quicktime.std.music.NoteRequest

This class provides all the information required to initialize a NoteChannel. It specifies settings for a QuickTime software synthesizer's instrument that the note channel uses to play notes.

```
public final class NoteRequest extends NoteRequestInfo implements Cloneable {
//Static Fields
    public static final int kNativeSize;

//Constructors
    public NoteRequest();
    public NoteRequest(ToneDescription td);
    public NoteRequest(ToneDescription td, int poly);
    public NoteRequest(int gmNumber, int poly);

//Instance Methods
    public Object clone();
    public ToneDescription getToneDescription();
    public void setToneDescription(ToneDescription desc);
    public String toString();
}
```

CLASS HIERARCHY:

Object→QTByteObject→NoteRequestInfo→NoteRequest

Class quicktime.std.music.NoteRequestInfo

This class provides all the information required to initialize a NoteChannel. The constructors for a NoteRequest will correctly fill in the default values for the typical-Polyphony field (1.0), and flags will be set to zero.

```
public class NoteRequestInfo extends QTByteObject implements Cloneable {
//Static Fields
    public static final int kNativeSize;

//Constructors
    public NoteRequestInfo();
    public NoteRequestInfo(int poly);

//Instance Methods
    public Object clone();
    public final int getFlags();
    public final int getPolyphony();
    public final float getTypicalPolyphony();
    public final void setFlags(int flags);
    public final void setPolyphony(int poly);
    public final void setTypicalPolyphony(float poly);
    public String toString();
}
```

CLASS HIERARCHY:

Object→QTByteObject→NoteRequestInfo

Class quicktime.std.music.QTMIDIPort

This class provides information about the MIDI port used by the QuickTime synthesizer.

```
public final class QTMIDIPort extends SynthesizerConnections {
//Static Fields
    public static final int kNativeSize;

//Instance Methods
    public Object clone();
    public String getPortName();
    public void setPortName(String name);
}
```

CLASS HIERARCHY:

Object→QTByteObject→SynthesizerConnections→QTMIDIPort

Class quicktime.std.music.QTMIDIPortList

This class provides a list of MIDI ports used by the QuickTime synthesizer.

```
public final class QTMIDIPortList extends QTHandleRef
```

```
                             implements Cloneable, StdQTConstants {
//Instance Methods
    public Object clone();
    public int getLength();
    public QTMIDIPort getPort(int index);
    public String toString();
}
```

CLASS HIERARCHY:

Object→QTObject→QTHandleRef→QTMIDIPortList

Class quicktime.std.music.SoundLocalization

This class contains data that locates a sound in pseudo three-dimensional space.

The SoundLocalization() constructor creates an empty sound localization.

```
public final class SoundLocalization extends QTHandleRef {
//Constructors
    public SoundLocalization();
}
```

CLASS HIERARCHY:

Object→QTObject→QTHandleRef→SoundLocalization

Class quicktime.std.music.SynthesizerConnections

This class defines methods for connecting the synthesizer to the computer.

```
public class SynthesizerConnections extends QTByteObject implements Cloneable {
//Static Fields
    public static final int kNativeSize;

//Constructors
    public SynthesizerConnections();

//Instance Methods
    public Object clone();
    public final int getClientID();
    public final int getFlags();
    public final int getInputID();
    public final int getMIDIChannel();
    public final int getOutputID();
    public final int getUniqueID();
    public final void setClientID(int id);
    public final void setFlags(int flag);
```

```
    public final void setInputID(int id);
    public final void setMIDIChannel(int channel);
    public final void setOutputID(int id);
    public final void setUniqueID(int id);
    public String toString();
}
```

CLASS HIERARCHY:

Object→QTByteObject→SynthesizerConnections

Class quicktime.std.music.SynthesizerDescription

This class describes the configuration settings of the QuickTime Software Synthesizer.

```
public final class SynthesizerDescription extends QTByteObject implements Cloneable {
//Instance Methods
    public Object clone();
    public boolean controllerAvailable(int controllerNum);
    public int getChannelMask();
    public int getDrumChannelMask();
    public int getDrumCount();
    public int getDrumPartCount();
    public int getFlags();
    public int getInstrumentCount();
    public int getLatency();
    public int getModifiableDrumCount();
    public int getModifiableInstrumentCount();
    public String getName();
    public int getOutputCount();
    public int getPartCount();
    public int getSynthesizerType();
    public int getVoiceCount();
    public boolean gmDrumAvailable(int gmDrumNum);
    public boolean gmInstrumentAvailable(int gmInstNum);
    public String toString();
}
```

CLASS HIERARCHY:

Object→QTByteObject→SynthesizerDescription

Class quicktime.std.music.ToneDescription

This class provides the information that describes a particular instrument. It can be used with both the QuickTime Software Synthesizer and MIDI hardware instruments.

```
public final class ToneDescription extends QTByteObject
                                    implements QuickTimeLib, Cloneable {
//Static Fields
    public static final int kNativeSize;

//Constructors
    public ToneDescription();
    public ToneDescription(int gmNumber);
    public ToneDescription(NoteAllocator na, int gmNumber);

//Instance Methods
    public Object clone();
    public final int getGMNumber();
    public final String getInstrumentName();
    public final int getInstrumentNumber();
    public final String getSynthesizerName();
    public final int getSynthesizerType();
    public final void pickInstrument(NoteAllocator na, String prompt, int flags);
    public final void setGMNumber(int gmNumber);
    public final void setInstrumentName(String name);
    public final void setInstrumentNumber(int num);
    public final void setSynthesizerName(String name);
    public final void setSynthesizerType(int type);
    public final void stuff(NoteAllocator na, int gmNumber);
    public String toString();
}
```

CLASS HIERARCHY:

Object→QTByteObject→ToneDescription

Class quicktime.std.music.TunePlayer

This class corresponds to the tune player component type, as specified in the QuickTime Music Architecture API.

```
public final class TunePlayer extends Component
                              implements QuickTimeLib, StdQTConstants, Errors {
//Constructors
    public TunePlayer();

//Static Methods
    public static TunePlayer fromMusicMediaHandler(MusicMediaHandler mh, int index);

//Instance Methods
    public NoteChannel getIndexedNoteChannel(int index);
    public NoteAllocator getNoteAllocator();
    public int getNumberOfNoteChannels();
    public MixStateInfo getPartMix(int partNumber);
```

```
    public TuneStatus getStatus();
    public TimeBase getTimeBase();
    public int getTimeScale();
    public float getVolume();
    public void instant(TuneStatus tune, int tunePosition);
    public void preroll();
    public void queue(MusicData tune, float tuneRate, int tuneStartPosition,
                      int tuneStopPosition, int queueFlags);
    public void setBalance(int balance);
    public void setHeader(MusicData header);
    public void setHeaderWithSize(MusicData header, int size);
    public void setNoteChannels(NoteChannel[] noteChannelList);
    public void setPartMix(int partNumber, float volume, float balance, int mixFlags);
    public void setPartTranspose(int part, float transpose, int velocityShift);
    public void setSofter(boolean softer);
    public void setSoundLocalization(SoundLocalization data);
    public void setTimeScale(int scale);
    public void setVolume(float volume);
    public void stop();
    public void task();
    public void unroll();
}
```

CLASS HIERARCHY:

Object→QTObject→ComponentIdentifier→Component→TunePlayer

Class quicktime.std.music.TuneStatus

This class presents information on the currently playing tune and corresponds to the function TuneGetStatus() in the QuickTime API.

```
public final class TuneStatus extends QTByteObject {
//Instance Methods
    public int getQueueCount();
    public int getQueueSpots();
    public int getQueueTime();
    public int getTime();
    public int getTunePosition();
}
```

CLASS HIERARCHY:

Object→QTByteObject→TuneStatus

42

The quicktime.
std.qtcomponents
Package

The `quicktime.std.qtcomponents` package provides a set of classes that lets you access level-low compression and decompression QuickTime components. The `Movie-Exporter` class defines methods for exporting movie data and other data conversion operations. Similarly, the `MovieImporter` class assists in importing movie data and other data conversion operations. Figure 42.1 shows the class hierarchy for this package.

This package also provides support for the Time Code, Data Compression, and Compression Dialogs of QuickTime.

FIGURE 42.1 *The* `quicktime.std.qtcomponents` *package*

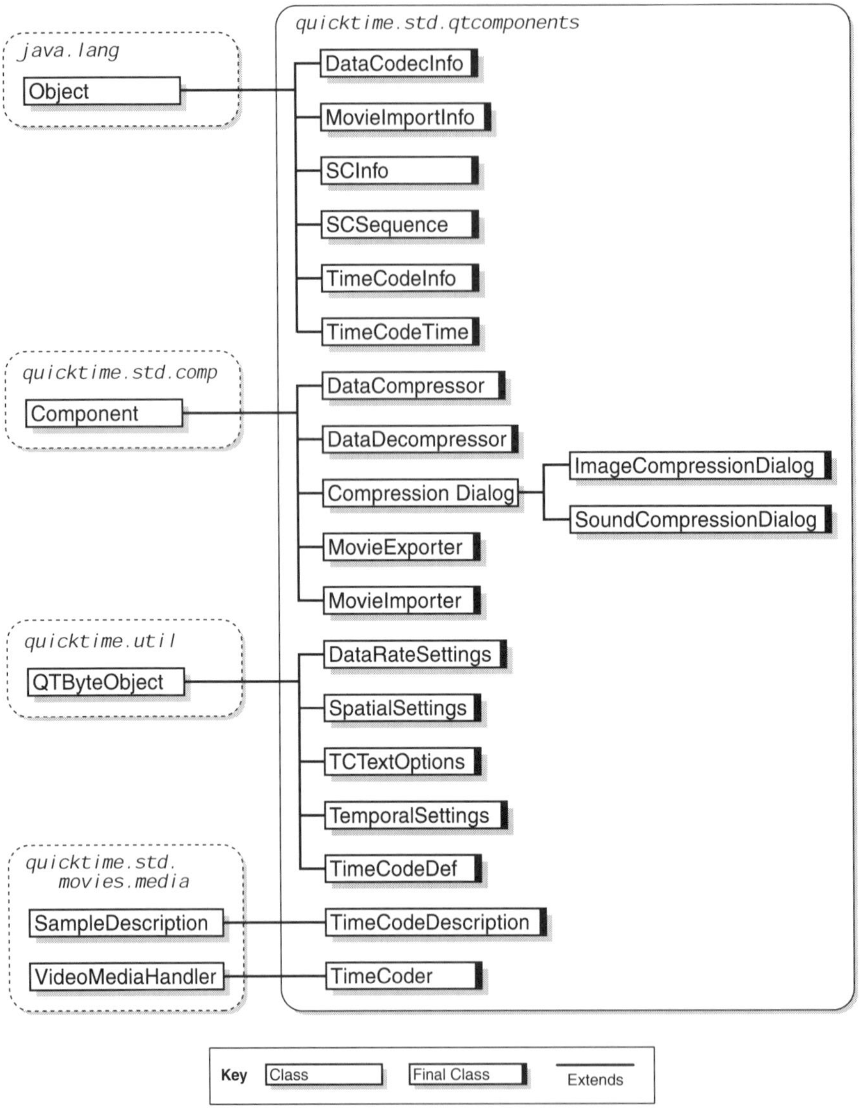

Class quicktime.std.qtcomponents.CompressionDialog

This class represents the standard compression dialog.

```
public class CompressionDialog extends Component
                               implements QuickTimeLib, StdQTConstants {
//Instance Methods
    public int getInfoPreferences();
    public QTHandleRef getInfoState();
    public AtomContainer getSettings();
    public void requestSettings();
    public void setInfoPreferences(int flags);
    public void setInfoState(QTHandleRef settings);
    public void setInfoState(AtomContainer settings);
}
```

CLASS HIERARCHY:

Object→QTObject→ComponentIdentifier→Component→CompressionDialog

Class quicktime.std.qtcomponents.DataCodecCompressor

This class enables applications to compress arbitrary amounts of data.

```
public class DataCodecCompressor extends Component implements QuickTimeLib {
//Constructors
    public DataCodecCompressor(int subType);
    public DataCodecCompressor(ComponentIdentifier comp);

//Instance Methods
    public DataCodecInfo compress(QTPointerRef srcData, QTPointerRef dstData);
    public int getCompressBufferSize(int srcSize);
}
```

CLASS HIERARCHY:

Object→QTObject→ComponentIdentifier→Component→DataCodecCompressor

Class quicktime.std.qtcomponents.DataCodecDecompressor

This class enables applications to decompress arbitrary amounts of data.

```
public class DataCodecDecompressor extends Component implements QuickTimeLib {
//Constructors
    public DataCodecDecompressor(int subType);
    public DataCodecDecompressor(ComponentIdentifier comp);
```

```
//Instance Methods
    public void decompress(QTPointerRef srcData, QTPointerRef dstData);
}
```

CLASS HIERARCHY:

Object→QTObject→ComponentIdentifier→Component→
DataCodecDecompressor

Class quicktime.std.qtcomponents.DataCodecInfo

This class is used to return information from a compress call of the DataCodecCompressor class.

```
public class DataCodecInfo extends Object {
//Instance Fields
    public int actualDstSize;
    public int decompressSlop;
}
```

CLASS HIERARCHY:

Object→DataCodecInfo

Class quicktime.std.qtcomponents.DataRateSettings

This class is used to both get and set properties related to data rates in the Image-CompressionDialog that is shown to the user.

```
public final class DataRateSettings extends QTByteObject {
//Static Fields
    public static final int kNativeSize;

//Constructors
    public DataRateSettings(int dataRate, int frameDuration, int minSpatialQuality,
                    int minTemporalQuality);

//Instance Methods
    public int getDataRate();
    public int getFrameDuration();
    public int getMinSpatialQuality();
    public int getMinTemporalQuality();
    public void setDataRate(int dataRate);
    public void setFrameDuration(int frameDuration);
    public void setMinSpatialQuality(int minSpatialQuality);
    public void setMinTemporalQuality(int minTemporalQuality);
}
```

CLASS HIERARCHY:

Object→QTByteObject→DataRateSettings

Class quicktime.std.qtcomponents.ImageCompressionDialog

This class represents the standard compression dialog for images.

```
public final class ImageCompressionDialog extends CompressionDialog
                                          implements QuickTimeLib {
//Constructors
    public ImageCompressionDialog();

//Instance Methods
    public QTImage compressImage(QDGraphics src, QDRect srcRect);
    public Pict compressPicture(Pict src);
    public void compressPictureFile(OpenFile src, OpenFile dest);
    public SCSequence compressSequenceBegin(QDGraphics src, QDRect srcRect);
    public void defaultPictFileSettings(OpenFile src, boolean motion);
    public void defaultPictSettings(Pict src, boolean motion);
    public void defaultPixMapSettings(PixMap src, boolean motion);
    public int getCompressFlags();
    public ColorTable getInfoColorTable();
    public DataRateSettings getInfoDataRateSettings();
    public SpatialSettings getInfoSpatialSettings();
    public TemporalSettings getInfoTemporalSettings();
    public QDGraphics newGWorld(QDRect rp, int flags);
    public void requestImageSettings();
    public void requestSequenceSettings();
    public void setCompressFlags(int flags);
    public void setInfoColorTable(ColorTable ctab);
    public void setInfoDataRateSettings(DataRateSettings settings);
    public void setInfoSpatialSettings(SpatialSettings settings);
    public void setInfoTemporalSettings(TemporalSettings settings);
    public void setTestImagePict(Pict testPict, QDRect testRect, int testFlags);
    public void setTestImagePictFile(OpenFile testPict, QDRect testRect, int testFlags);
    public void setTestImagePixMap(PixMap testPixMap, QDRect testRect, int testFlags);
}
```

CLASS HIERARCHY:

Object→QTObject→ComponentIdentifier→Component→CompressionDialog→
ImageCompressionDialog

Class quicktime.std.qtcomponents.MovieExporter

This class assists in exporting movie data and data conversion operations. The Movie-
Exporter implements methods for a corresponding QuickTime ComponentInstance
structure: MovieExportComponent.

```
public final class MovieExporter extends Component
                                  implements QuickTimeLib, StdQTConstants {
//Constructors
    public MovieExporter(int subType);
    public MovieExporter(ComponentIdentifier comp);

//Instance Methods
    public boolean doUserDialog(Movie theMovie, Track onlyThisTrack, int startTime,
                        int duration);
    public int getAuxiliaryData(QTHandle dataH);
    public int getCreatorType();
    public final int getExportFileNameExtension();
    public AtomContainer getExportSettingsFromAtomContainer();
    public final String getExportShortFileTypeString();
    public final int getExportSourceMediaType();
    public void setExportSettingsFromAtomContainer(AtomContainer settings);
    public void setProgressProc(MovieProgress mp);
    public void setSampleDescription(SampleDescription desc, int mediaType);
    public void toDataRef(DataRef dataRef, Movie theMovie, Track onlyThisTrack,
                        int startTime, int duration);
    public void toFile(QTFile theFile, Movie theMovie, Track onlyThisTrack,
                        int startTime, int duration);
    public QTHandle toHandle(Movie theMovie, Track onlyThisTrack, int startTime,
                        int duration);
    public boolean validate(Movie theMovie, Track onlyThisTrack);
}
```

CLASS HIERARCHY:

Object→QTObject→ComponentIdentifier→Component→MovieExporter

Class quicktime.std.qtcomponents.MovieImporter

This class assists in importing movie data and data conversion operations. The Movie-
Importer implements methods for a corresponding QuickTime ComponentInstance
structure: MovieImportComponent.

```
public final class MovieImporter extends Component
                                  implements QuickTimeLib, StdQTConstants {
//Constructors
    public MovieImporter();
```

```
    public MovieImporter(int subType);
    public MovieImporter(ComponentIdentifier comp);
    public MovieImporter(DataRef dataRef, int flags);
    public MovieImporter(DataRef dataRef, int flags, String fileExt);

//Static Methods
    public static MovieImporter fromTrack(Track t);

//Instance Methods
    public boolean doUserDialog(QTFile fileIn);
    public boolean doUserDialog(QTHandleRef theData);
    public MovieImportInfo fromDataRef(DataRef dataRef, Movie theMovie,
                            Track targetTrack, int atTime, int inFlags);
    public MovieImportInfo fromFile(QTFile fileIn, Movie theMovie, Track targetTrack,
                            int atTime, int inFlags);
    public MovieImportInfo fromHandle(QTHandleRef dataRef, Movie theMovie,
                            Track targetTrack, int atTime, int inFlags);
    public int getAuxiliaryDataType();
    public int getFileType();
    public AtomContainer getImportSettingsFromAtomContainer();
    public AtomContainer getMIMETypeList();
    public int getMediaType();
    public SampleDescription getSampleDescription();
    public void setAuxiliaryData(QTHandleRef data, int handleType);
    public void setChunkSize(int chunkSize);
    public void setDimensions(float width, float height);
    public void setDuration(int duration);
    public void setFromScrap(boolean fromScrap);
    public void setImportSettingsFromAtomContainer(AtomContainer settings);
    public void setMediaFile(AliasHandle alias);
    public void setOffsetAndLimit(int offset, int limit);
    public void setProgressProc(MovieProgress mp);
    public void setSampleDescription(SampleDescription desc, int mediaType);
    public void setSampleDuration(int duration, int scale);
    public boolean validate(QTHandleRef theData);
    public boolean validate(QTFile fileIn);
}
```

CLASS HIERARCHY:

Object→QTObject→ComponentIdentifier→Component→MovieImporter

Class quicktime.std.qtcomponents.MovieImportInfo

This class contains information for the movie import component. The results are returned from querying a movie import component using a movie, a data reference, and time values.

```
public final class MovieImportInfo extends Object {
```

```
//Constructors
    public MovieImportInfo(Track t, int timeVal, int f);

//Instance Methods
    public int getDuration();
    public int getFlags();
    public Track track();
}
```

CLASS HIERARCHY:

Object→MovieImportInfo

Class quicktime.std.qtcomponents.SCInfo

This class contains information about the compression of a single frame from a SCSequence.

```
public final class SCInfo extends Object {
//Constructors
    public SCInfo(QTHandleRef imageData, int dataSize, short nSyncFlag);

//Instance Fields
    public int dataSize;
    public QTHandleRef imageData;
    public short notSyncFlag;
}
```

CLASS HIERARCHY:

Object→SCInfo

Class quicktime.std.qtcomponents.SCSequence

The SCSequence is returned from the ImageCompressionDialog that allows the user to configure preferences for compressing video. The application can then use this sequence to compress the video frames as required.

```
public final class SCSequence extends Object implements QuickTimeLib {
//Instance Methods
    public SCInfo compressFrame(QDGraphics src, QDRect srcRect);
    public ImageDescription getDescription();
    public ImageCompressionDialog getDialog();
}
```

CLASS HIERARCHY:

Object→SCSequence

Class quicktime.std.qtcomponents.SoundCompressionDialog

This class represents the standard compression dialog for sound.

```
public final class SoundCompressionDialog extends CompressionDialog
                                          implements QuickTimeLib {
//Constructors
    public SoundCompressionDialog();

//Instance Methods
    public int getInfoChannelCount();
    public int getInfoCompression();
    public int[] getInfoCompressionList();
    public float getInfoSampleRate();
    public int getInfoSampleSize();
    public void setInfoChannelCount(int n);
    public void setInfoCompression(int compType);
    public void setInfoCompressionList(int[] compTypes);
    public void setInfoSampleRate(float rate);
    public void setInfoSampleSize(int size);
}
```

CLASS HIERARCHY:

Object→QTObject→ComponentIdentifier→Component→CompressionDialog→
SoundCompressionDialog

Class quicktime.std.qtcomponents.SpatialSettings

This class contains spatial settings and is used to interact with the ImageCompression-
Dialog.

```
public final class SpatialSettings extends QTByteObject {
//Static Fields
    public static final int kNativeSize;

//Constructors
    public SpatialSettings(int codecType, CodecComponent codec, int depth,
                   int spatialQuality);

//Instance Methods
    public CodecComponent getCodec();
    public int getCodecType();
```

```
    public int getDepth();
    public int getSpatialQuality();
    public void setCodec(CodecComponent codec);
    public void setCodecType(int codecType);
    public void setDepth(int depth);
    public void setSpatialQuality(int spatialQuality);
}
```

CLASS HIERARCHY:

Object→QTByteObject→SpatialSettings

Class quicktime.std.qtcomponents.TCTextOptions

This class is used to both get and set the display characteristics of the text that is used to display time code.

```
public final class TCTextOptions extends QTByteObject {
//Constructors
    public TCTextOptions();

//Instance Methods
    public QDColor getBackColor();
    public QDColor getForeColor();
    public int getTXFace();
    public int getTXFont();
    public int getTXSize();
    public void setBackColor(QDColor backColor);
    public void setForeColor(QDColor foreColor);
    public void setTXFace(int txFace);
    public void setTXFont(int txFont);
    public void setTXSize(int txSize);
}
```

CLASS HIERARCHY:

Object→QTByteObject→TCTextOptions

Class quicktime.std.qtcomponents.TemporalSettings

This class is used to get and set the temporal properties of the image compression configured by the user in the ImageCompressionDialog.

```
public final class TemporalSettings extends QTByteObject {
//Static Fields
    public static final int kNativeSize;
```

```
//Constructors
    public TemporalSettings(int temporalQuality, float frameRate, int keyFrameRate);

//Instance Methods
    public float getFrameRate();
    public int getKeyFrameRate();
    public int getTemporalQuality();
    public void setFrameRate(float frameRate);
    public void setKeyFrameRate(int keyFrameRate);
    public void setTemporalQuality(int temporalQuality);
}
```

CLASS HIERARCHY:

Object→QTByteObject→TemporalSettings

Class quicktime.std.qtcomponents.TimeCodeDef

This class contains timecode formatting information.

```
public final class TimeCodeDef extends QTByteObject
                            implements PrimitivesLib, Cloneable, StdQTConstants {
//Static Fields
    public static final int kNativeSize;

//Constructors
    public TimeCodeDef();

//Instance Methods
    public Object clone();
    public int getFlags();
    public int getFrameDuration();
    public int getFramesPerSecond();
    public int getTimeScale();
    public void setFlags(int flags);
    public void setFrameDuration(int frameDuration);
    public void setFramesPerSecond(int fps);
    public void setTimeScale(int timeScale);
    public String toString();
}
```

CLASS HIERARCHY:

Object→QTByteObject→TimeCodeDef

Class quicktime.std.qtcomponents.TimeCodeDescription

This class encapsulates the `TimeCodeDescription` record of the Movie Toolbox. `Time-CodeDescription` objects are used when adding and getting media samples to/from timecode tracks.

```
public final class TimeCodeDescription extends SampleDescription
                                  implements PrimitivesLib, StdQTConstants {
//Static Fields
    public static final int kNativeSize;

//Constructors
    public TimeCodeDescription();

//Static Methods
    public static EndianDescriptor getEndianDescriptor();

//Instance Methods
    public Object clone();
    public TimeCodeDef getTimeCodeDef();
    public void setTimeCodeDef(TimeCodeDef tcd);
    public String toString();
}
```

CLASS HIERARCHY:

Object→QTObject→QTHandleRef→SampleDescription→TimeCodeDescription

Class quicktime.std.qtcomponents.TimeCodeInfo

This class represents timecode as frame count or as HH:MM:SS:FF. If frame count is used in construction, then `TimeCodeTime` time will be null. If `TimeCodeTime` time is used in construction, then frame count will be 0.

```
public final class TimeCodeInfo extends Object {
//Constructors
    public TimeCodeInfo();
    public TimeCodeInfo(int frameNumber, TimeCodeDef definition, TimeCodeTime time,
                    QTHandleRef userData);
    public TimeCodeInfo(int frameNumber, TimeCodeDef definition, int counter,
                    QTHandleRef userData);

//Instance Fields
    public int counter;
    public TimeCodeDef definition;
    public int frameNumber;
    public TimeCodeTime time;
```

```
    public QTHandleRef userData;
```

```
//Instance Methods
    public String toString();
}
```

CLASS HIERARCHY:

Object→TimeCodeInfo

Class quicktime.std.qtcomponents.TimeCoder

This class is the `MediaHandler` for time code media. It enables an application to get and set the display properties of the time code.

```
public final class TimeCoder extends VisualMediaHandler
                            implements QuickTimeLib, StdQTConstants {
//Static Methods
    public static TimeCoder fromMedia(TimeCodeMedia m);

//Instance Methods
    public TimeCodeInfo getAtTime(int mediaTime);
    public TimeCodeInfo getCurrent();
    public TCTextOptions getDisplayOptions();
    public int getFlags();
    public QTHandle getSourceRef(TimeCodeDescription tcd);
    public void setDisplayOptions(TCTextOptions textOptions);
    public void setFlags(int flags, int flagsMask);
    public void setSourceRef(TimeCodeDescription tcd, QTHandleRef sref);
    public String timeCodeToString(TimeCodeDef tcdef, TimeCodeTime tct);
    public String timeCodeToString(TimeCodeDef tcdef, int counter);
    public int toFrameNumber(TimeCodeTime tcrec, TimeCodeDef tcdef);
    public TimeCodeTime toTimeCode(int frameNumber, TimeCodeDef tcdef);
}
```

CLASS HIERARCHY:

Object→QTObject→ComponentIdentifier→Component→MediaHandler→
VisualMediaHandler→TimeCoder

Class quicktime.std.qtcomponents.TimeCodeTime

This class represents time as HH:MM:SS:FF. No range checking is done on values set, and no frame rate is known. It is purely an information class.

```
public final class TimeCodeTime extends QTByteObject implements Cloneable {
```

```
//Constructors
    public TimeCodeTime(int hh, int mm, int ss, int ff);
    public TimeCodeTime();
    public TimeCodeTime(int counter);

//Instance Methods
    public Object clone();
    public int getFrames();
    public int getHours();
    public int getMinutes();
    public int getSeconds();
    public void setFrames(int ff);
    public void setHours(int hh);
    public void setMinutes(int mm);
    public void setSeconds(int ss);
    public int toCounter();
    public String toString();
}
```

CLASS HIERARCHY:

Object→QTByteObject→TimeCodeTime

43

The quicktime. std.sg Package

The `quicktime.std.sg` package contains many classes that define methods for capturing sound and video to a QuickTime movie from an external source. Notably, `SequenceGrabber` provides methods for capturing audio and video media to a movie.

The `SGSoundChannel` class provides methods for capturing sound to a movie, while `SGTextChannel` provides methods for capturing text tracks into a movie. The `AudioChannel` class defines methods for capturing sound-based media in a movie. You use the `SGChannel` class for capturing sound or video into a movie. `SGMusicChannel` provides methods for capturing MIDI data.

`SGOutput` defines methods for capturing to multiple files. By capturing to multiple files, you can improve the performance and flexibility of captures and enable larger total captures. Figure 43.1 shows the class hierarchy for this package.

FIGURE 43.1 *The* quicktime.std.sg *package*

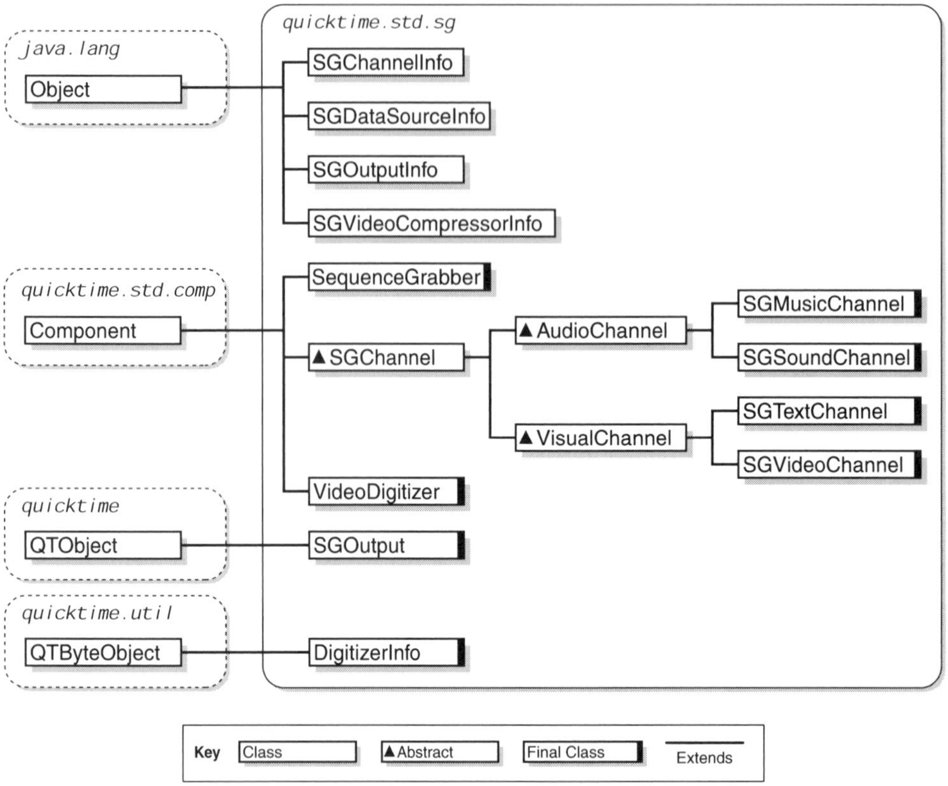

Class quicktime.std.sg.AudioChannel

This class defines methods for capturing audio to a movie. It enables importing sound into a movie. The SGChannel implements methods for a corresponding QuickTime ComponentInstance structure.

The getVolume() and setVolume() methods of this class allow you to determine and set a channel's volume setting.

```
public abstract class AudioChannel extends SGChannel
                                implements QuickTimeLib, StdQTConstants {
//Instance Methods
    public float getVolume();
    public void setVolume(float volume);
}
```

CLASS HIERARCHY:

Object→QTObject→ComponentIdentifier→Component→SGChannel→
AudioChannel

Class quicktime.std.sg.DigitizerInfo

This class encapsulates the capabilities of digitizing hardware.

```
public final class DigitizerInfo extends QTByteObject
                            implements QuickTimeLib, Cloneable {
//Static Fields
    public static final int kNativeSize;

//Instance Methods
    public Object clone();
    public int getInputCapabilityFlags();
    public short getMinDestHeight();
    public short getMinDestWidth();
    public int getOutputCapabilityFlags();
    public short getblendLevels();
    public short getmaxDestHeight();
    public short getmaxDestWidth();
    public String toString();
}
```

CLASS HIERARCHY:

Object→QTByteObject –> DigitizerInfo

Class quicktime.std.sg.SequenceGrabber

This class provides methods for capturing audio and video media to a movie. It implements methods for a corresponding QuickTime `ComponentInstance` structure, as specified in the QuickTime API.

```
public final class SequenceGrabber extends Component
                            implements QuickTimeLib, StdQTConstants, Errors {
//Constructors
    public SequenceGrabber();
    public SequenceGrabber(int subType);
    public SequenceGrabber(int type, int subType);

//Instance Methods
    public void disposeChannel(SGChannel c);
    public void disposeOutput(SGOutput c);
    public QTFile getDataOutputFile();
```

```
    public int getDataOutputFlags();
    public DataRef getDataRef();
    public int getDataRefFlags();
    public QDGraphics getGWorld();
    public GDevice getGWorldDevice();
    public SGChannel getIndChannel(int index);
    public int getIndChannelType(int index);
    public int getMaximumRecordTime();
    public Movie getMovie();
    public int getPause();
    public UserData getSettings();
    public int getStorageSpaceRemaining();
    public TimeBase getTimeBase();
    public int getTimeRemaining();
    public Pict grabPict(QDRect bounds, int offscreenDepth, int grabPictFlags);
    public void idle();
    public boolean isPreviewMode();
    public boolean isRecordMode();
    public void pause(int pause);
    public void prepare(boolean prepareForPreview, boolean prepareForRecord);
    public void release();
    public void setDataOutput(QTFile movieFile, int whereFlags);
    public void setDataRef(DataRef dataRef, int whereFlags);
    public void setGWorld(QDGraphics port, GDevice gdh);
    public void setMaximumRecordTime(int ticks);
    public void setSettings(UserData ud);
    public void startPreview();
    public void startRecord();
    public void stop();
    public void update(Region updateRgn);
    public void writeExtendedMovieData(SGChannel c, int p, int len, long offset,
                                SGOutput sgOut);
}
```

CLASS HIERARCHY:

Object→QTObject→ComponentIdentifier→Component→SequenceGrabber

Class quicktime.std.sg.SGChannel

This class provides methods for capturing audio or video media to a movie.

```
public abstract class SGChannel extends Component
                                implements QuickTimeLib, StdQTConstants, Errors {
//Instance Methods
    public SGDataSourceInfo getDataSourceName();
    public int getPlayFlags();
    public SequenceGrabber getSequenceGrabber();
    public UserData getSettings();
    public int getUsage();
```

```
    public void setDataSourceName(String name, int scriptTag);
    public void setPlayFlags(int playFlags);
    public void setSettings(UserData ud);
    public void setUsage(int usage);
    public void settingsDialog(int flags, Component[] panelList);
    public void settingsDialog();
}
```

CLASS HIERARCHY:

Object→QTObject→ComponentIdentifier→Component→SGChannel

Class quicktime.std.sg.SGChannelInfo

This class contains information about the reference information of a media sample.

```
public class SGChannelInfo extends Object {
//Instance Fields
    public int mCompressionType;
    public int mNumChannels;
    public int mSampleSize;
}
```

CLASS HIERARCHY:

Object→SGChannelInfo

Class quicktime.std.sg.SGDataSourceInfo

This class contains information on an SGChannel data source.

```
public class SGDataSourceInfo extends Object {
//Instance Fields
    public String mName;
    public int mScriptTag;
}
```

CLASS HIERARCHY:

Object→SGDataSourceInfo

Class quicktime.std.sg.SGMusicChannel

This class provides methods for capturing MIDI data, assigning or getting the instrument that is used by this MIDI data.

The `SGMusicChannel()` constructor creates a sequence grabber music channel and assigns a channel component to the channel.

```
public final class SGMusicChannel extends AudioChannel
                          implements QuickTimeLib, StdQTConstants {
//Constructors
    public SGMusicChannel(SequenceGrabber owner);

//Instance Methods
    public ToneDescription getInstrument();
    public void setInstrument(ToneDescription td);
}
```

CLASS HIERARCHY:

Object→QTObject→ComponentIdentifier→Component→SGChannel→
AudioChannel→SGMusicChannel

Class quicktime.std.sg.SGOutput

This class defines methods for capturing to multiple files. By capturing to multiple files, you can improve the performance and flexibility of captures and enable larger total captures.

```
public final class SGOutput extends QTObject
                       implements QuickTimeLib, StdQTConstants, Errors {
//Instance Methods
    public SGOutputInfo getDataReference();
    public int getDataStorageSpaceRemaining();
    public long getMaximumOffset();
    public int getNextOutput();
    public void setChannel(SGChannel c);
    public void setMaximumOffset(long maxOffset);
    public void setNextOutput(SGOutput nextOutput);
    public void setOutputFlags(int whereFlags);
}
```

CLASS HIERARCHY:
Object→QTObject→SGOutput

Class quicktime.std.sg.SGOutputInfo

This class contains information about the data reference associated with the specified sequence grabber output.

```
public class SGOutputInfo extends Object {
//Instance Fields
    public int mDataRef;
    public int mDataRefType;
}
```

CLASS HIERARCHY:

Object→SGOutputInfo

Class quicktime.std.sg.SGSoundChannel

This class provides methods for capturing sound to a movie.

```
public final class SGSoundChannel extends AudioChannel
                             implements QuickTimeLib, StdQTConstants {
//Constructors
    public SGSoundChannel(SequenceGrabber owner);

//Instance Methods
    public SPBDevice getInputDriver();
    public int getRecordChunkSize();
    public SGChannelInfo getSoundInputParameters();
    public float getSoundInputRate();
    public void setInputDriver(String driverName);
    public void setRecordChunkSize(int seconds);
    public void setSoundInputParameters(int sampleSize, int numChannels,
                                   int compressionType);
    public void setSoundInputRate(float rate);
}
```

CLASS HIERARCHY:

Object→QTObject→ComponentIdentifier→Component→SGChannel→
AudioChannel→SGSoundChannel

Class quicktime.std.sg.SGTextChannel

This class provides methods for importing text into a movie.

The SGTextChannel() constructor creates a sequence grabber channel text and assigns a channel component to the channel.

```
public final class SGTextChannel extends VisualChannel
                             implements QuickTimeLib, StdQTConstants {
//Constructors
    public SGTextChannel(SequenceGrabber owner);
```

```
//Instance Methods
    public int getReturnToSpaceValue();
    public void setBackColor(QDColor theColor);
    public void setFontName(String fontName);
    public void setFontSize(int fontSize);
    public void setForeColor(QDColor theColor);
    public void setJustification(int just);
    public void setReturnToSpaceValue(int rettospace);
}
```

CLASS HIERARCHY:

Object→QTObject→ComponentIdentifier→Component→SGChannel→
VisualChannel→SGTextChannel

Class quicktime.std.sg.SGVideoChannel

This class provides methods for capturing video to a movie.

```
public final class SGVideoChannel extends VisualChannel
                            implements QuickTimeLib, StdQTConstants {
//Constructors
    public SGVideoChannel(SequenceGrabber owner);

//Instance Methods
    public void digitizerChanged();
    public SGVideoCompressorInfo getCompressor();
    public int getCompressorType();
    public VideoDigitizer getDigitizerComponent();
    public QDRect getSrcVideoBounds();
    public QDRect getVideoRect();
    public void setCompressor(int depth, int compressor, int spatialQuality,
                            int temporalQuality, int keyFrameRate);
    public void setCompressorType(int compressorType);
    public void setDigitizerComponent(VideoDigitizer vdig);
    public void setVideoRect(QDRect r);
}
```

CLASS HIERARCHY:

Object→QTObject→ComponentIdentifier→Component→SGChannel→
VisualChannel→SGVideoChannel

Class quicktime.std.sg.SGVideoCompressorInfo

This class contains information about the reference information of a media sample.

```
public class SGVideoCompressorInfo extends Object {
//Instance Fields
    public int mCompressor;
    public int mDepth;
    public int mKeyFrameRate;
    public int mSpatialQuality;
    public int mTemporalQuality;
}
```

CLASS HIERARCHY:

Object→SGVideoCompressorInfo

Class quicktime.std.sg.SGVideoChannel

This abstract class provides methods to get and set a video channel's display boundary rectangle and clipping regions, as well as a channel's display transformation matrix.

```
public final class SGVideoChannel extends VisualChannel
                             implements QuickTimeLib, StdQTConstants {
//Constructors
    public SGVideoChannel(SequenceGrabber owner);

//Instance Methods
    public void digitizerChanged();
    public SGVideoCompressorInfo getCompressor();
    public int getCompressorType();
    public VideoDigitizer getDigitizerComponent();
    public QDRect getSrcVideoBounds();
    public QDRect getVideoRect();
    public void setCompressor(int depth, int compressor, int spatialQuality,
                             int temporalQuality, int keyFrameRate);
    public void setCompressorType(int compressorType);
    public void setDigitizerComponent(VideoDigitizer vdig);
    public void setVideoRect(QDRect r);
}
```

CLASS HIERARCHY:

Object→QTObject→ComponentIdentifier→Component→SGChannel→
VisualChannel→SGVideoChannel

Class quicktime.std.sg.SGVideoCompressorInfo

This class contains information about the reference information of a media sample.

```
public class SGVideoCompressorInfo extends Object {
//Instance Fields
    public int mCompressor;
    public int mDepth;
    public int mKeyFrameRate;
    public int mSpatialQuality;
    public int mTemporalQuality;
}
```

CLASS HIERARCHY:

Object→SGVideoCompressorInfo

Class quicktime.std.sg.VideoDigitizer

This is the component (generally supplied by the manufacturer of video capture cards) that provides an interface for the application to handle some of the characteristics that are applied in the process of digitizing the incoming video source.

```
public final class VideoDigitizer extends Component
                                implements QuickTimeLib, StdQTConstants {
//Constructors
    public VideoDigitizer();
    public VideoDigitizer(int subType);

//Instance Methods
    public void clearClipRgn(Region clipRegion);
    public boolean getClipState();
    public DigitizerInfo getDigitizerInfo();
    public int getInput();
    public int getNumberOfInputs();
    public void setClipRgn(Region clipRegion);
    public void setClipState(boolean clipEnable);
    public void setInput(int input);
}
```

CLASS HIERARCHY:

Object→QTObject→ComponentIdentifier→Component→VideoDigitizer

Class quicktime.std.sg.VisualChannel

This class encapsulates the top-level capabilities common to all visual components.

```
public abstract class VisualChannel extends SGChannel
                                implements QuickTimeLib, StdQTConstants {
```

```
//Instance Methods
    public QDRect getBounds();
    public Region getClip();
    public Matrix getMatrix();
    public void setBounds(QDRect bounds);
    public void setClip(Region theClip);
    public void setMatrix(Matrix m);
}
```

CLASS HIERARCHY:

Object→QTObject→ComponentIdentifier→Component→SGChannel→
VisualChannel

44

The quicktime. util Package

The `quicktime.util` package defines a number of useful classes and interfaces for allocating memory that is then used by other QuickTime classes. It also contains classes and interfaces for storing and encoding image data.

The `EncodedImage` interface lets you specify a particular format for storing encoded image data. Images can be kept in a format appropriate for a particular usage. This interface can only be implemented by classes that are part of the QuickTime for Java library; applications are not able to extend this interface.

The `ByteEncodedImage` class provides methods for encoded image data as an array of bytes. `IntEncodedImage` provides methods for encoded image data as an array of integers. `RawEncodedImage` is a native pointer to a block of memory.

The `QTByteObject` class provides a representation of the native data structure as a byte array.

The `QTHandleRef` class is notable as a "smart" handle, in that it can be either a reference to a handle that is not disposable, or it can be an "independent" handle that is automatically disposed on finalization. The same applies to the `QTPointerRef` class.

Finally, the `QTUtils` class provides a set of routines to convert between types that QuickTime calls expect and the basic Java classes and types. Some of the structures in QuickTime are kept in their native big endian format. This class contains a large number of static methods for converting bytes and byte arrays to and from big endian format. Figure 44.1 shows the class hierarchy for this package.

FIGURE 44.1 *The* `quicktime.util` *package*

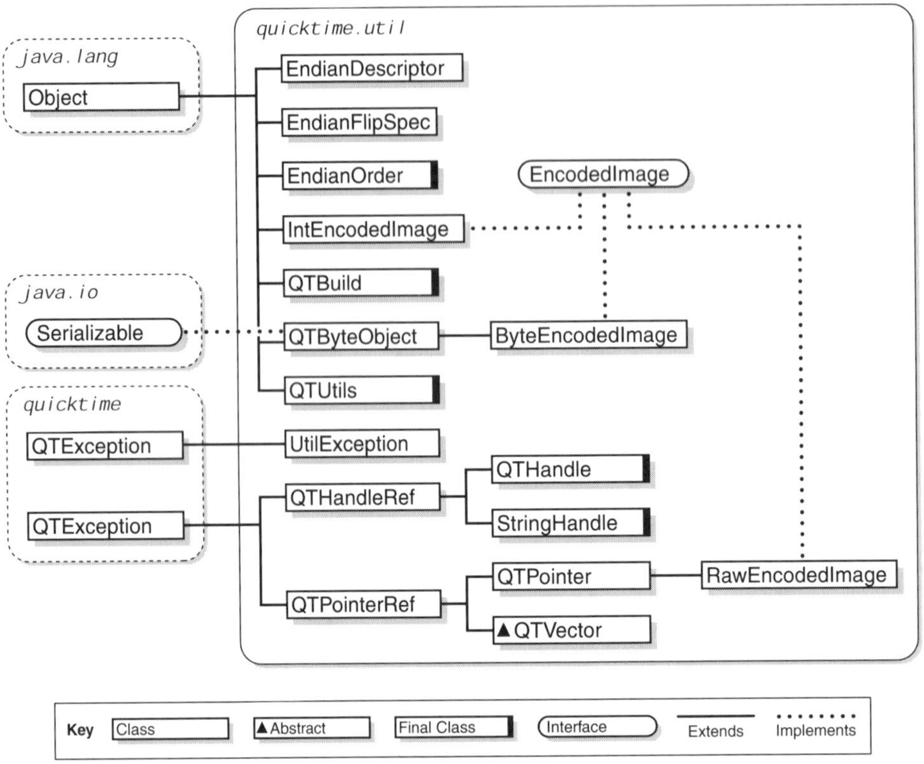

Class quicktime.util.ByteEncodedImage

This class provides methods for representing image data to QuickTime that is encoded as an array of bytes.

The `getBytes()` method (from `QTByteObject`) returns the actual byte array that contains the data. If this data is pixel data, then your application can operate directly on the data to change the colors of pixels.

```
public class ByteEncodedImage extends QTByteObject implements EncodedImage, Cloneable {
//Constructors
    public ByteEncodedImage(RawEncodedImage ptr);
    public ByteEncodedImage(int size);
    public ByteEncodedImage(int size, int rowBytes);
```

```
//Static Methods
    public static ByteEncodedImage fromByteArray(byte[] ar, int rowBytes);
    public static ByteEncodedImage fromByteArray(byte[] ar);

//Instance Methods
    public Object clone();
    public byte getByte(int offset);
    public int getInt(int offset);
    public int getRowBytes();
    public short getShort(int offset);
}
```

CLASS HIERARCHY:

Object→QTByteObject→ByteEncodedImage

Interface quicktime.util.EncodedImage

Objects that implement the EncodedImage interface specify a particular format for storing encoded image data. This allows images to be kept in a format appropriate for a particular usage but simplifies the APIs that use encoded image data. This interface can only be implemented by classes that are a part of the QuickTime for Java library; applications are not able to extend or apply usage of this interface. Applications can use the image encoding options that are provided.

The EncodedImage interface contains no information about the encoding format of the image. The particular encoding format of the image data is described by the encoded image's accompanying ImageDescription object. The ImageDescription contains all of the metadata required to completely describe the format and characteristics of the encoded image data.

If you are examining pixel values directly, bear in mind that you may need to deal with the endian issue—pixel values need to be in the native endian format. Also, if the ImageDescription describes a format other than raw pixels, the get() methods are probably not very useful, as you won't be looking at pixel values.

The value kRowBytesUnknown is returned by an EncodedImage class from the getRowBytes() method if the encoded image does not know how many bytes per row, or the data does not contain any extra byte data beyond the image encoding. The getRowBytes() method returns either kRowBytesUnknown or the number of bytes per row that the encoded image data is comprised of. This number will at least be as big as width*pixelSize and may be larger.

The getSize() method returns the size in bytes of the EncodedImage data. The getByte() method returns the byte at the specified offset. The offset is specified in bytes into the encoded image object.

See also ImageDescription, ByteEncodedImage, IntEncodedImage, and RawEncodedImage.

```
public interface EncodedImage {
//Static Fields
    public static final int kRowBytesUnknown;

//Instance Methods
    public abstract byte getByte(int offset);
    public abstract int getInt(int offset);
    public abstract int getRowBytes();
    public abstract short getShort(int offset);
    public abstract int getSize();
}
```

Class quicktime.util.EndianDescriptor

This class is used to describe the flipping requirements of a particular data structure. It has three modes, which are determined by the format flag provided in the constructor:

- kFlipSpecifiedFields is used when describing an object where either only some of the data should be flipped or the fields are different sizes and thus should be flipped according to their size. Only when a descriptor is in this state can a profile of the endian requirements be built up using the EndianFlipSpec class.

- The data is consistent for the entire size of the object, in which case the format describes the size of the flipping that should be applied.

- The data should *not* be flipped at all.

Your application can build EndianDescriptor objects for any custom data structures that require endian flipping for consistency between platforms with different endian orders and data files (like the QuickTime movie file) that generally require data to have a particular endian format.

The EndianDescriptor objects are used with the QTUtils.endianFlip calls or the platform-sensitive EndianOrder.flip methods.

The `getFormatFlag()` method returns the format of the `EndianDescriptor` object, which determines the behavior of the descriptor when used with the endian flip methods.

```
public class EndianDescriptor extends Object {
//Static Fields
    public static final EndianDescriptor flipAll16;
    public static final EndianDescriptor flipAll32;
    public static final EndianDescriptor flipAll64;
    public static final int kFlipAllFields16;
    public static final int kFlipAllFields32;
    public static final int kFlipAllFields64;
    public static final int kFlipNoFields;
    public static final int kFlipSpecifiedFields;

//Constructors
    public EndianDescriptor(int formatFlag);

//Instance Methods
    public void addFlipSpec(EndianFlipSpec spec);
    public Enumeration flipSpecs();
    public EndianFlipSpec getFlipSpec(int offset);
    public int getFormatFlag();
    public void removeFlipSpec(EndianFlipSpec member);
    public String toString();
}
```

CLASS HIERARCHY:

Object→EndianDescriptor

Class quicktime.util.EndianFlipSpec

This class is used to describe the fields of a data structure that should have its endian order flipped. The class is used to describe a particular part of a data structure that should be flipped around a consistent size—for example, flip 3 16 bit values from 2 bytes into object n.

The class is used when an `EndianDescriptor` is created that describes the endian flipping requirements of a particular data structure. An `EndianDescriptor` can be built that contains a collection of `EndianFlipSpec` objects that completely describe the endian flipping characteristics of the data. An `EndianFlipSpec` is an individual specification for contiguous fields that have the same flipping characteristics.

See also `EndianDescriptor`.

```
public class EndianFlipSpec extends Object {
```

```
//Static Fields
    public static final int kFlip16BitValue;
    public static final int kFlip32BitValue;
    public static final int kFlip64BitValue;

//Constructors
    public EndianFlipSpec(int offset, int sizeFlag, int num);

//Instance Methods
    public boolean equals(Object o);
    public int getNumberOfFlips();
    public int getOffset();
    public int getSizeFlag();
    public String toString();
}
```

CLASS HIERARCHY:

Object→EndianFlipSpec

Class quicktime.util.EndianOrder

The endian methods in this class are context sensitive in that the big-endian methods only flip if the current platform is little endian, and the little-endian methods only flip if the current platform is big endian.

The names of the methods are provided as a means of documenting the usage of the method itself. To operate as specified, they rely upon the application correctly providing the expected endian-ordered number to the method. Thus, the `flipNativeToBigEndian()` and `flipBigEndianToNative()` methods will both flip when executed on a little-endian architecture, but the methods are unable to determine if the argument is actually (in this case) in native little-endian order or big-endian order. The application itself must ensure that the provided argument is correct for these methods to return their expected result.

```
public final class EndianOrder extends Object {
//Static Methods
    public static void flipBigEndianToNative(Object src, int srcOffset,
                                    EndianDescriptor ed);
    public static void flipBigEndianToNative(Object src, int srcOffset, Object dest,
                                    int destOffset, EndianDescriptor ed);
    public static short flipBigEndianToNative16(short s);
    public static int flipBigEndianToNative32(int i);
    public static long flipBigEndianToNative64(long l);
    public static void flipLittleEndianToNative(Object src, int srcOffset,
                                    EndianDescriptor ed);
```

```
    public static void flipLittleEndianToNative(Object src, int srcOffset, Object dest,
                                  int destOffset, EndianDescriptor ed);
    public static short flipLittleEndianToNative16(short s);
    public static int flipLittleEndianToNative32(int i);
    public static long flipLittleEndianToNative64(long l);
    public static void flipNativeToBigEndian(Object src, int srcOffset,
                                  EndianDescriptor ed);
    public static void flipNativeToBigEndian(Object src, int srcOffset, Object dest,
                                  int destOffset, EndianDescriptor ed);
    public static short flipNativeToBigEndian16(short s);
    public static int flipNativeToBigEndian32(int i);
    public static long flipNativeToBigEndian64(long l);
    public static void flipNativeToLittleEndian(Object src, int srcOffset, Object dest,
                                  int destOffset, EndianDescriptor ed);
    public static void flipNativeToLittleEndian(Object src, int srcOffset,
                                  EndianDescriptor ed);
    public static short flipNativeToLittleEndian16(short s);
    public static int flipNativeToLittleEndian32(int i);
    public static long flipNativeToLittleEndian64(long l);
    public static boolean isNativeBigEndian();
    public static boolean isNativeLittleEndian();
}
```

CLASS HIERARCHY:

Object→EndianOrder

Class quicktime.util.IntEncodedImage

This class provides methods for encoding image data as an array of integers.

getInts() returns the actual data. If this data is pixel data, then your application can operate directly on the data to manipulate the pixels.

fromIntArray() makes a ByteEncodedImage from an array of ints. It will not copy the int array but creates a proxy for the same ints. It will set the row bytes as specified.

```
public class IntEncodedImage extends Object
                          implements PrimitivesLib, EncodedImage, Cloneable {
//Constructors
    public IntEncodedImage(RawEncodedImage ptr);
    public IntEncodedImage(int numOfInts);
    public IntEncodedImage(int numOfInts, int rowBytes);

//Static Methods
    public static IntEncodedImage fromIntArray(int[] ar, int rowBytes);
    public static IntEncodedImage fromIntArray(int[] ar);

//Instance Methods
```

```
    public Object clone();
    public boolean equals(Object obj);
    public byte getByte(int offset);
    public int getInt(int offset);
    public int[] getInts();
    public int getRowBytes();
    public short getShort(int offset);
    public int getSize();
    public String toString();
}
```

CLASS HIERARCHY:

Object→IntEncodedImage

Class quicktime.util.QTBuild

This class contains build information for the QuickTime for Java library.

The info() method returns an info string about the current version and build of QuickTime for Java.

Typically, a build identified as, for example, 1.0.0.b2 specifies a major version of 1, a 0 minor revision, a 0 qualifying version, a b as the build stage (i.e., alpha, beta, or gm), and the number of the build itself—in this case, build 2.

```
public final class QTBuild extends Object {
//Static Fields
    public static final int build;
    public static final String buildStage;
    public static final int qualifyingSubVersion;
    public static final int subVersion;
    public static final int version;

//Static Methods
    public static String info();
}
```

CLASS HIERARCHY:

Object→QTBuild

Class quicktime.util.QTByteObject

This class represents a native data structure as a byte array. It is analogous to the struct type declarations found in a C program.

`fromArray()` return a QTByteObject, which becomes a proxy for the specified byte array. It does not copy the byte array but references it.

`getBytes()` returns the actual byte array that the native structure is stored in. Subclasses generally provide accessor methods to the different fields of their structure.

```
public class QTByteObject extends Object
                              implements Serializable, PrimitivesLib, Errors {
//Static Methods
    public static QTByteObject fromArray(byte[] ar);

//Instance Methods
    public boolean equals(Object obj);
    public final byte[] getBytes();
    public int getSize();
    public String toString();
}
```

CLASS HIERARCHY:

Object→QTByteObject

Class quicktime.util.QTHandle

This class implements a handle that is used in calls to QuickTime.

```
public class QTHandle extends QTHandleRef implements QuickTimeLib, StdQTConstants {
//Constructors
    public QTHandle();
    public QTHandle(int size, boolean clear);
    public QTHandle(byte[] byteArray);
    public QTHandle(QTPointerRef ptr, int offset, int size);
    public QTHandle(QTHandleRef firstHandle, QTHandleRef secondHandle);

//Static Methods
    public static QTHandle fromEncodedImage(EncodedImage image);
    public static QTHandle fromGraphicsImporterAlias(GraphicsImporter gi);
    public static QTHandle fromGraphicsImporterData(GraphicsImporter gi);
    public static QTHandle fromSoundDescription(SoundDescription sd, int idType);
    public static TimeCodeInfo fromTimeCoderCurrent(TimeCoder tc);
    public static QTHandle fromTimeCoderSource(TimeCoder tc, TimeCodeDescription tcd);
    public static TimeCodeInfo fromTimeCoderTime(TimeCoder tc, int mediaTime);
    public static QTHandle fromTrack(Track t);
    public static void reserveMemory(int size);

//Instance Methods
    public Object clone();
    public void concatenate(QTHandleRef hand);
    public void setSize(int size);
```

}

CLASS HIERARCHY:
Object→QTObject→QTHandleRef→QTHandle

Class quicktime.util.QTHandleRef

A QTHandleRef is a "smart" handle in that it can be either a reference to a handle, which is not disposable, or it can be an "independent" handle automatically disposed on finalization. Thus, the subclasses of this class are safe and will dispose of their memory usage in the normal course of the garbage collector's operation.

The default setting is for the handle to be disposable. Subclasses must use the QTHandleRef(int, Object) constructor to create a nondisposable reference. For nondisposable handles, there are two situations to look out for:

- Upon finalization the handle should *not* be disposed of—it belongs to a parent struct.

- The parent object from which the handle is obtained should not be allowed to go away while the reference object is alive.

In both situations, you must maintain a reference to the parent or owner object. When defining a clone operation, subclasses should define it as

```
public Object clone() { return new QTHandleSubclass
(makeAndCopyHandle (), null); }
```

```
public class QTHandleRef extends QTObject
                                    implements QuickTimeLib, Errors, StdQTConstants {
//Static Methods
    public static QTHandleRef fromCompressionDialogState(CompressionDialog cd);
    public static SCInfo fromSCSequence(SCSequence sc, QDGraphics src, QDRect srcRect);

//Instance Methods
    public final void copyFromArray(int handleOffset, long[] srcArray, int srcOffset,
                            int length);
    public final void copyFromArray(int handleOffset, double[] srcArray, int srcOffset,
                            int length);
    public final void copyFromArray(int handleOffset, byte[] srcArray, int srcOffset,
                            int length);
    public final void copyFromArray(int handleOffset, short[] srcArray, int srcOffset,
                            int length);
    public final void copyFromArray(int handleOffset, char[] srcArray, int srcOffset,
                            int length);
```

```
public final void copyFromArray(int handleOffset, int[] srcArray, int srcOffset,
                                int length);
public final void copyFromArray(int handleOffset, float[] srcArray, int srcOffset,
                                int length);
public final void copyToArray(int handleOffset, double[] destArray, int destOffset,
                              int length);
public final void copyToArray(int handleOffset, byte[] destArray, int destOffset,
                              int length);
public final void copyToArray(int handleOffset, short[] destArray, int destOffset,
                              int length);
public final void copyToArray(int handleOffset, char[] destArray, int destOffset,
                              int length);
public final void copyToArray(int handleOffset, int[] destArray, int destOffset,
                              int length);
public final void copyToArray(int handleOffset, float[] destArray, int destOffset,
                              int length);
public final void copyToArray(int handleOffset, long[] destArray, int destOffset,
                              int length);
public byte[] getBytes();
public int getSize();
public boolean inMemory();
public final boolean isLocked();
public final void lock();
public void lockHigh();
public final void moveHigh();
public QTPointerRef toQTPointer();
public QTPointerRef toQTPointer(int offset, int size);
public String toString();
public final void unlock();
}
```

CLASS HIERARCHY:

Object→QTObject→QTHandleRef

Class quicktime.util.QTPointer

This class implements a pointer that is used in calls to QuickTime.

Use QTPointer() to construct a pointer from the concatenation of the two supplied pointers. The first pointer will appear first in the concatentated result.

fromSCData() returns the QTPointer buffer. The fromEncodedImage() returns EncodedImage data as a QTPointer. This will copy the data if the source is an int or byte encoded image but will return the same object if it is a RawEncodedImage.

Use concatenate() to concatenate the supplied pointer to this pointer. This operation will fail if unable to resize the pointer.

```
public class QTPointer extends QTPointerRef implements QuickTimeLib, Cloneable {
//Constructors
    public QTPointer(int size, boolean clear);
    public QTPointer(byte[] byteArray);
    public QTPointer(QTHandleRef hdl, int offset, int size);
    public QTPointer(QTPointerRef firstPtr, QTPointerRef secondPtr);

//Static Methods
    public static QTPointer fromEncodedImage(EncodedImage image);
    public static QTPointer fromSCData(SoundComponentData scd);

//Instance Methods
    public Object clone();
    public void concatenate(QTPointerRef ptr);
    public void setSize(int newSize);
}
```

CLASS HIERARCHY:
Object→QTObject→QTPointerRef→QTPointer

Class quicktime.util.QTPointerRef

A QTPointerRef is a "smart" pointer in that it can be either a reference to a pointer that is not disposable or it can be an "independent" pointer that is automatically disposed on finalization.

The default setting is for the pointer to be disposable—you must use the QTPointerRef(int, int, Object) constructor to create a nondisposable reference For nondisposable pointers, there are two situations to look out for:

- Upon finalization the pointer should *not* be disposed of—it belongs to a parent struct.

- The parent object from which the pointer is obtained should not be allowed to go away while the reference object is alive.

In both situations, you must maintain a reference to the parent or owner object.

```
public class QTPointerRef extends QTObject implements QuickTimeLib, Errors {
//Instance Methods
    public final void copyFromArray(int ptrOffset, long[] srcArray, int srcOffset,
                                    int length);
    public final void copyFromArray(int ptrOffset, double[] srcArray, int srcOffset,
                                    int length);
    public final void copyFromArray(int ptrOffset, byte[] srcArray, int srcOffset,
                                    int length);
```

```
public final void copyFromArray(int ptrOffset, short[] srcArray, int srcOffset,
                                int length);
public final void copyFromArray(int ptrOffset, char[] srcArray, int srcOffset,
                                int length);
public final void copyFromArray(int ptrOffset, int[] srcArray, int srcOffset,
                                int length);
public final void copyFromArray(int ptrOffset, float[] srcArray, int srcOffset,
                                int length);
public final void copyToArray(int ptrOffset, long[] destArray, int destOffset,
                                int length);
public final void copyToArray(int ptrOffset, double[] destArray, int destOffset,
                                int length);
public final void copyToArray(int ptrOffset, byte[] destArray, int destOffset
                                int length);
public final void copyToArray(int ptrOffset, short[] destArray, int destOffset,
                                int length);
public final void copyToArray(int ptrOffset, char[] destArray, int destOffset,
                                int length);
public final void copyToArray(int ptrOffset, int[] destArray, int destOffset,
                                int length);
public final void copyToArray(int ptrOffset, float[] destArray, int destOffset,
                                int length);
public byte[] getBytes();
public int getSize();
public String toString();
}
```

CLASS HIERARCHY:

Object→QTObject→QTPointerRef

Class quicktime.util.QTUtils

This class provides a set of routines to convert between types that QuickTime calls expect and the basic Java classes and types. Some of the structures in QuickTime are kept in their native big-endian format. QuickTime structures with big-endian formats include:

-    ToneDescription
-    NoteRequest

These conversions are generally performed for you where they are required in the get() and set() methods of the classes concerned.

The Fixed and Fract types are not supported in QuickTime for Java; rather, Java floats are used. The float values are converted to Fix and Fract types by the methods themselves.

This class also provides methods for converting endian values. On Windows, Java keeps ints, shorts, and floats in little-endian format. The QuickTime movie generally requires its data to be in big-endian format. Most of these conversions are handled by QuickTime itself, so in most cases your application does not need to do these conversions. The QuickTime documentation itself describes the situations when an application must convert the endian layout. The endian calls provided here will only do the endian flipping when running on Windows; on a big-endian architecture (like the Mac OS/PowerPC) these method do nothing.

Thus, they can be used safely by your application, and at runtime the methods themselves decide if they need to perform their flipping.

```
public final class QTUtils extends Object implements QuickTimeLib, Errors {
//Static Methods
    public static String CString2String(byte[] str, int offset);
    public static float Fix2X(int fix);
    public static float Fract2X(int fract);
    public static String PString2String(byte[] pString, int offset);
    public static float ShortFix2X(short fix);
    public static byte[] String2CString(String str);
    public static byte[] String2PString(String str, int len);
    public static int UByte2Int(byte b);
    public static float UFix2X(int fix);
    public static long UInt2Long(int i);
    public static int UShort2Int(short s);
    public static int X2Fix(float x);
    public static int X2Fract(float x);
    public static short X2ShortFix(float x);
    public static int X2UFix(float x);
    public static void checkFreeMemory();
    public static int convertEventModifier(int javaEvtMod);
    public static int convertKeyValue(int javaKeyValue);
    public static void endianFlip(Object src, int srcOffset, Object dest,
                       int destOffset, EndianDescriptor ed);
    public static void endianFlip(Object src, int srcOffset, EndianDescriptor ed);
    public static short endianFlip16(short s);
    public static int endianFlip32(int i);
    public static long endianFlip64(long l);
    public static String fromOSType(int osType);
    public static void reclaimMemory();
    public static final int toOSType(String str);
    public static final int toOSType(char a, char b, char c, char d);
}
```

CLASS HIERARCHY:

Object→QTUtils

Class quicktime.util.QTVector

This abstract class represents a vector of uniform-sized objects into a handle. It is used when adding a collection of sample references to a media class.

```
public abstract class QTVector extends QTPointerRef implements QuickTimeLib {
//Instance Methods
    public Enumeration elements();
    public int getSize();
    public boolean isEmpty();
    public void remove(int pos);
    public void removeAll();
    public int size();
}
```

> **CLASS HIERARCHY:**
>
> Object→QTObject→QTPointerRef→QTVector

Class quicktime.util.RawEncodedImage

This class keeps the encoded image data as a pointer to some block of memory (sometimes referred to as the base address in the case of PixMap pixel data). The application can set the values within this structure; however, this should only be done when the application has a thorough knowledge of the format of the data. Generally, this will only be done when the data is raw pixel data. In this case, allowance for the difference between the width (from the description) and the row bytes must be taken into account.

```
public final class RawEncodedImage extends QTPointer
                        implements QuickTimeLib, EncodedImage, StdQTConstants {
//Constructors
    public RawEncodedImage(byte[] bytes);
    public RawEncodedImage(int[] ints);
    public RawEncodedImage(int[] ints, int rowBytes);
    public RawEncodedImage(int size, boolean clear);
    public RawEncodedImage(int size, boolean clear, int rowBytes);

//Static Methods
    public static RawEncodedImage fromPixMap(PixMap pm);
    public static RawEncodedImage fromQTHandle(QTHandleRef hdl);
    public static RawEncodedImage fromQTPointer(QTPointerRef ptr);
    public static RawEncodedImage fromSprite(Sprite s);

//Instance Methods
    public Object clone();
```

```
    public byte getByte(int offset);
    public int getInt(int offset);
    public int getRowBytes();
    public short getShort(int offset);
    public void setByte(int offset, byte value);
    public void setInt(int offset, int value);
    public void setInts(int offset, int[] value);
    public void setShort(int offset, short value);
}
```

CLASS HIERARCHY:

Object→QTObject→QTPointerRef→QTPointer→RawEncodedImage

Class quicktime.util.StringHandle

This class is used to store 7-bit ASCII value strings.

```
public class StringHandle extends QTHandleRef implements QuickTimeLib, Errors {
//Static Fields
    public static final int kCStringFormat;
    public static final int kPStringFormat;

//Constructors
    public StringHandle(String str, int format);

//Static Methods
    public static StringHandle fromCodecName(CodecName cn);

//Instance Methods
    public void fromJavaString(String str);
    public int getFormat();
    public int getStringLength();
    public String toJavaString();
    public String toString();
}
```

CLASS HIERARCHY:

Object→QTObject→QTHandleRef→StringHandle

Class quicktime.util.UtilException

This is a general catch-all class used to signal errors that occur from QuickTime utility calls.

```
public class UtilException extends QTException {
```

```
//Constructors
    public UtilException(String str);
    public UtilException(int val);

//Static Methods
    public static void checkError(int err);
}
```

CLASS HIERARCHY:

Object→Throwable→Exception→QTException→UtilException

45

The quicktime.vr Package

The `quicktime.vr` package contains a number of interfaces and several classes, providing limited support for QuickTime VR. Future releases of QuickTime for Java hold the promise of more extensive support.

The `QTVRConstants` interface contains a large number of constants. The constants defined by this interface specify various hot spot and atom types. Other constants let you set flags to control elements of the QTVR control bar.

You use the `QTVRInstance` class for making QuickTime VR calls. This class defines a large number of useful methods for pan and tilt operations, as well as for obtaining node information and triggering hotspots in a QuickTime VR movie. Figure 45.1 shows the class hierarchy for this package.

FIGURE 45.1   *The* `quicktime.vr` *package*

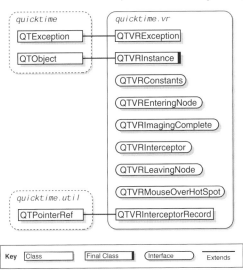

Interface quicktime.vr.QTVRConstants

This class contains a large number of constants. A complete listing is provided on the CD-ROM at the back of this book.

Interface quicktime.vr.QTVREnteringNode

This interface is defined by an application to receive and process interactions with a VR movie's nodes

See also QTVRInstance.

```
public interface QTVREnteringNode {
//Instance Methods
    public abstract int execute(QTVRInstance vr, int nodeID);
}
```

Class quicktime.vr.QTVRException

This is a general catch-all class used to signal errors that occur from QuickTime VR calls.

The checkError() method will throw an exception if the incoming err argument is a nonzero value.

```
public class QTVRException extends QTException {
//Constructors
    public QTVRException(String str);
    public QTVRException(int val);

//Static Methods
    public static void checkError(int err);
}
```

CLASS HIERARCHY:

Object→Throwable –> Exception→QTException→QTVRException

Interface quicktime.vr.QTVRImagingComplete

This interface is defined by an application to receive callbacks when a QTVRInstance has finished rendering in an offscreen QDGraphics and is ready to be blitted to the screen.

See also QTVRInstance.

```
public interface QTVRImagingComplete {
//Instance Methods
    public abstract int execute(QTVRInstance inst, QDGraphics qd);
}
```

Class quicktime.vr.QTVRInstance

This class is used for making QuickTime VR calls. There are a number of useful methods for defining the behavior and functionality of a QuickTime VR movie.

Use triggerHotSpot() to trigger a hot spot. Usually, you need only specify the QTVRInstance and the hot spot ID. You can pass zero for the nodeInfo and selectedAtom parameters.

The getNodeInfo() method is helpful in getting the node information atom container and describing a node and all the hot spots. You can use the ptToPanAngle() method to get the pan angle of a point.

```
public final class QTVRInstance extends QTObject
                               implements QuickTimeLib, QuickTimeVRLib {
//Constructors
    public QTVRInstance(Track qtvrTrack, MovieController mc);

//Instance Methods
    public void callInterceptedProc(QTVRInterceptRecord qtvrMsg);
    public float columnToPan(int column);
    public void enableHotSpot(int enableFlag, int hotSpotValue, boolean enable);
    public int getAngularUnits();
    public float getConstraints_max(int kind);
    public float getConstraints_min(int kind);
    public int getCurrentNodeID();
    public float getFieldOfView();
    public int getHotSpotType(int hotSpotID);
    public int getImagingProperty(int imagingMode, int imagingProperty);
    public AtomContainer getNodeInfo(int nodeID);
    public int getNodeType(int nodeID);
    public float getPanAngle();
    public float getTiltAngle();
```

```
    public AtomContainer getVRWorld();
    public QDPoint getViewCenter();
    public void goToNodeID(int nodeID);
    public void installInterceptProc(int selector, QTVRInterceptor interceptProc,
                                     int flags);
    public void nudge(int direction);
    public int panToColumn(float panAngle);
    public float ptToPanAngle(QDPoint pt);
    public float ptToTiltAngle(QDPoint pt);
    public void removeEnteringNodeProc();
    public void removeLeavingNodeProc();
    public void removeMouseOverHotSpotProc();
    public void removePrescreenImagingCompleteProc();
    public float rowToTilt(int row);
    public void setAngularUnits(int units);
    public void setConstraints(int kind, float minValue, float maxValue);
    public void setEnteringNodeProc(QTVREnteringNode enteringNodeProc, int flags);
    public void setFieldOfView(float fieldOfView);
    public void setImagingProperty(int imagingMode, int imagingProperty,
                                   int propertyValue);
    public void setLeavingNodeProc(QTVRLeavingNode leavingNodeProc, int flags);
    public void setMouseOverHotSpotProc(QTVRMouseOverHotSpot mouseOverHotSpotProc,
                                        int flags);
    public void setPanAngle(float panAngle);
    public void setPrescreenImagingCompleteProc(QTVRImagingComplete imageCompleteProc,
                                                int flags);
    public void setTiltAngle(float tiltAngle);
    public void setViewCenter(QDPoint viewCenter);
    public void showDefaultView();
    public int tiltToRow(float tiltAngle);
    public void triggerHotSpot(int hotSpotID, AtomContainer nodeInfo,
                               Atom selectedAtom);
    public void update(int imagingMode);
    public float wrapAndConstrain(int kind, float value);
}
```

CLASS HIERARCHY:

Object→QTObject→QTVRInstance

Interface quicktime.vr.QTVRInterceptor

This interface is defined by an application to receive and process interactions with a VR movie's nodes.

See also QTVRInstance.

```
public interface QTVRInterceptor {
```

```
//Instance Methods
    public abstract boolean execute(QTVRInstance vr, QTVRInterceptRecord qtvrMsg);
}
```

Class quicktime.vr.QTVRInterceptRecord

The QTVRInterceptRecord is passed to the QTVRInterceptor execute() method by
QuickTime. The application can look at the about-to-occur change in the VR movie
through the parameters of this record and can, in turn, call the intercepted method itself with any particular changes it wants to make, passing the QTVRInterceptor record
to this method.

getSelector() returns the selector that will in turn describe the parameters that
this record will contain. This is a read-only field.

getAngle() returns the pan or tilt angle, depending on the selector.
getFieldOfView() returns the field of view for the kQTVRSetFieldOfViewSelector.
setFieldOfView() sets the field of view for the kQTVRSetFieldOfViewSelector.
getHotSpotID() gets the hot spot ID.

```
public class QTVRInterceptRecord extends QTPointerRef
                                implements PrimitivesLib, QTVRConstants {
//Instance Methods
    public float getAngle();
    public float getFieldOfView();
    public int getHotSpotID();
    public int getHotSpotType();
    public final int getParamCount();
    public final int getSelector();
    public QDPoint getViewCenter();
    public void setAngle(float angle);
    public void setFieldOfView(float fieldOfView);
    public void setHotSpotID(int hotSpotID);
    public void setHotSpotType(int hotSpotType);
    public void setViewCenter(QDPoint viewCenter);
    public String toString();
}
```

CLASS HIERARCHY:
Object→QTObject→QTPointerRef→QTVRInterceptRecord

Interface quicktime.vr.QTVRLeavingNode

This interface is defined by an application to receive and process interactions with a VR movie's nodes.

See also QTVRInstance.

```
public interface QTVRLeavingNode {
//Instance Methods
    public abstract int execute(QTVRInstance vr, int fromNodeID, int toNodeID,
                            boolean[] cancel);
}
```

Interface quicktime.vr.QTVRMouseOverHotSpot

This interface is defined by an application to receive notification of mouse over events when the mouse is over a hot-spot in a VR movie.

See also QTVRInstance.

```
public interface QTVRMouseOverHotSpot {
//Instance Methods
    public abstract int execute(QTVRInstance vr, int hotSpotID, int flags);
}
```

Appendix A:
Nomenclature

METHODS

In naming methods and classes, the QuickTime for Java API observes these guidelines:

Methods with `addedTo()` or `removedFrom()` names are generally not called by the application itself but are called by a class that has a requirement to notify another class of some condition or state being acquired. For instance, when a client is set in the `QTCanvas`, the canvas calls the client's `addedTo()` method; when removed, the canvas calls the client's `removedFrom()` method.

`get()` and `set()` methods are for setting/getting a property or state of a class as in normal Java usage.

CLASSES

COLLECTIONS

All objects within the `quicktime.app` framework that are collections implement the `quicktime.app.spaces.Collection` interface. This interface defines the standard way of adding and removing members and obtaining other general information about the state of a collection.

DYNAMICCOLLECTION

This is a collection where the members that are added use a Protocol object to perform the isAppropriate test. The Protocol allows you to tighten the requirements of membership for a collection and ensures that only objects of a desired class are admitted.

SEQUENCE

A Sequence is an ordered Collection. Though it has no interface, the use of the term *Sequence* (for example, ImageDataSequence) denotes a collection that is ordered.

SEQUENCER

A Sequencer is an iterator with the capability to loop through a sequence. quicktime.app.spaces.Sequencer is an abstract class that defines this looping and current frame capability.

ImageSequencer is also an iterator. In sprite animations, a single data source can be used (ImageDataSequence), and multiple sequencers are created to provide different sprites with their particular images. There is also a SequencerAction that can be subclassed to provide sequencer style actions over other Sequences/Sequencer pairs an application may define.

PRESENTERS

A Presenter is some object that "draws" image data. In QuickTime, for image data to draw, you provide the raw image data and an ImageDescription that describes the data to QuickTime's imaging engine. Presenters can also have graphics modes applied to them—for instance, transparency and alpha blending.

Presenters are objects within the `quicktime.app` framework that are able to draw data in this format. `quicktime.app.image.ImagePresenter` is the simplest example of this. Presenters are "expensive" objects, in that they have image data loaded into memory as against the `GraphicsImporterDrawer` object that uses the `GraphicsImporter` and reads the image data from its data reference, typically a file, each time it draws.

The `quicktime.app.anim.TwoDSprite` class is a specialized kind of `Presenter` that presents its image data in the context of QuickTime's sprite world. As such it also embodies state about the layer within which the sprite world it has been placed and whether it is currently visible. The `TwoDSprite` is used as the `Presenter` for members of the `SWCompositor` display space.

SPACES AND CONTROLLERS

The spaces package includes a `Space` interface and a collection of `Controller` interfaces.

Space

This is an interface that provides the standard API that all spaces should support. A `Space` is a `DynamicCollection` of members. A `Space` has a timer that represents the fundamental time base for a `Space`. A `Space` also has controllers that are attached to it and provide differing mechanisms for controlling its members. `Space` itself and the `SimpleSpace` implementation provided in QuickTime for Java have no requirement to work in a display or presentation space: The `SimpleSpace` class can be used in a model space as well as the implementations provided in the presentation space.

Controllers

A `Controller` is an object that exerts some control over members of a `Space`. The `Controller` interface defines a minimal requirement for all `Controller` objects—that is, they are notified whenever they are added or removed from a `Space`. No particular functionality or modus operandi of a controller is assumed. Several Controller interfaces are provided. The requirements of adding these types of controllers to a Space are dealt with in the SimpleSpace implementation.

TickleList

The TickleList represents a list of objects that are Ticklish objects. A Space maintains a list of TicklishController objects that are tickled whenever the Space is tickled itself by its Timer.

Glossary

abstract class   A class that contains one or more abstract methods and therefore can never be instantiated. Abstract classes are defined so that other classes can extend them and make them concrete by implementing the abstract methods.

abstract method   A method that has no implementation.

Abstract Window Toolkit (AWT)   A collection of graphical user interface (GUI) components that were implemented using native-platform versions of the components. These components provide that subset of functionality that is common to all native platforms. Largely supplanted by the Project Swing component set. See also Swing Set.

action   One of many integer constants used by QuickTime movie controller components in the `MCDoAction` function. Applications that include action filters may receive any of these actions.

active movie segment   A portion of a QuickTime movie that is to be used for playback. By default, the active segment is set to the entire movie. You can change the active segment of a movie by using the Movie Toolbox.

active source rectangle   The portion of the maximum source rectangle that contains active video that can be digitized by a video digitizer component.

actual parameter list   The arguments specified in a particular method call.

alpha channel   The upper bits of a display pixel, which control the blending of colors of video and graphical image data.

alpha value   A value that indicates the opacity of a pixel.

alternate track   A movie track that contains alternate data for another track. The Movie Toolbox chooses one track to be used when the movie is played. The choice may be based on such considerations as image quality or localization.

anti-aliasing   The process of sampling a signal at more than twice its natural frequency to ensure that aliasing artifacts do not occur.

API   (Application   Programming Interface)   The set of function calls, data structures, and other programming elements by which a structure of code (such as a system-level toolbox) can be accessed by other code (such as an application program).

applet   In the Java runtime environment, an executable program that must run within a larger host application.

applet tag   Text in an HTML document that describes an embedded applet. This text is bounded by the <APPLET> and </APPLET> delimiters.

argument   A data item specified in a method call. An argument can be a literal value, a variable, or an expression.

atom   The basic unit of data in a movie resource, sprite, or other QuickTime data structure. There are a number of different atom types, including movie atoms, track atoms, and media atoms. There are two varieties of atoms: chunk atoms, which you access through code offsets, and QT atoms, which you access through QuickTime calls. Either kind can be a container atom, which contains other atoms, or a leaf atom, which does not contain any other atoms.

background color   The color of the background behind a sprite or other image.

badge   A visual element in a movie's display that distinguishes a movie from a static image. The movie controller component supplied by Apple supports badges.

base media handler component   A component that handles most of the duties that must be performed by all media handlers. See also derived media handler component.

big endian   An addressing mode in which the address for a field points to its most significant byte.

bit depth   The number of bits used to encode the color of each pixel in a graphics buffer.

black level   The degree of blackness in an image. This is a common setting on a video digitizer. The highest setting will produce an all-black image, whereas the lowest setting will yield very little, if any, black, even with black objects in the scene. Black level is an important digitization setting, since it can be adjusted so that there is little or no noise in an image.

blend matte   A pixel map that defines the blending of video and digital data for a video digitizer component. The value of each pixel in the pixel map governs the relative intensity of the video data for the corresponding pixel in the result image.

button   A region of a wired sprite or movie that sends a message to your software if the user touches it.

callback event A scheduled invocation of a Movie Toolbox callback function. Applications establish the criteria that determine when the callback function is to be invoked. When those criteria are met, the Movie Toolbox invokes the callback function.

callback function An application-defined function that is invoked at a specified time or based on specified criteria. These callback functions are data-loading functions, data-unloading functions, completion functions, and progress functions. See also callback event.

change-based data Data forms, such as video and sound, in which change is an essential part of the information content.

channel component See sequence grabber channel component.

child atom An atom contained within a parent atom.

chunk atom An atom whose header contains only type and size information. You access chunk atoms by means of code offsets. Compare QT atom.

class In the Java programming language, a type that defines the implementation of a particular kind of object. A class definition defines instance and class variables and methods, as well as specifying the interfaces the class imple-

ments and the immediate superclass of the class. If the superclass is not explicitly specified, the superclass will implicitly be `Object`.

class method A method that is invoked without reference to a particular object. Class methods affect the class as a whole, not a particular instance of the class. Also called a static method.

classpath A classpath is an environmental variable that tells the Java virtual machine and Java technology-based applications (for example, the tools located in the JDK1.1.X\bin directory) where to find the class libraries, including user-defined class libraries.

class variable A data item associated with a particular class as a whole, not with particular instances of the class. Class variables are defined in class definitions. Also called a static field.

client In the client/server model of communications, the client is a process that remotely accesses resources of a compute server, such as compute power and large memory capacity.

clipped movie boundary region The region that is clipped by the Movie Toolbox. This region combines the union of all track movie boundary regions for a movie, which is the movie's movie boundary region, with the movie's movie clipping region, which defines the portion of the movie boundary region that is to be used.

clipping The process of defining the boundaries of a graphics area.

clock component A component that supplies basic time information to its clients.

codec A compression/decompression component.

color conversion A stage in video digitizing that makes the colors in the image compatible with the destination display.

component A software entity, managed by the QuickTime Component Manager, that provides a defined set of services to its clients. Examples include clock components, movie controller components, and image compressor components.

component description record A data structure containing information about a component, such as its type and subtype.

component instance A channel of communication between a component and its client.

Component Manager A part of QuickTime that lets other software build, install, and manage components.

component subtype An element in the classification hierarchy used by the Component Manager to define the services provided by a component. Within a component type, the component subtype provides additional information about the component. For example, image compressor components all have the same component type value; the component subtype value indicates the compression algorithm implemented by the component.

component type An element in the classification hierarchy used by the Component Manager to define the services provided by a component. The component type value indicates the type of services provided by the component. For example, all image compressor components have a component type value of `'imco'`. See also component subtype.

compositing The process of superimposing one image on another to create a single image.

compressor component A general term used to refer to both image compressor components and image decompressor components.

connection A channel of communication between a component and its client. A component instance is used to identify the connection.

constructor A pseudo-method that creates an object. In the Java programming language, constructors are instance methods with the same name as their class. Constructors are invoked using the new keyword.

container atom A QuickTime atom that contains other atoms, possibly including other container atoms. Examples of container atoms are track atoms and edit atoms. Compare leaf atom.

control settings In QuickTime VR, instructions that tell the VR controller what to do when it reaches a viewing constraint.

creator On the Mac OS, a 4-byte character string that identifies the application that created a file.

creator signature In the Macintosh file system, a 4-character code that identifies the application program to which a file belongs.

current selection A portion of a QuickTime movie that has been selected for a cut, copy, or paste operation.

data dependency An aspect of image compression in which compression ratios are highly dependent on the image content. Using an algorithm with a high degree of data dependency, an image of a crowd at a football game (which contains a lot of detail) may produce a very small compression ratio, whereas an image of a blue sky (which consists mostly of constant colors and intensities) may produce a very high compression ratio.

data fork In a Macintosh file, the section that corresponds to a DOS/Windows file.

data handler A component software that is responsible for reading and writing a media's data. The data handler provides data input and output services, such as storage and retrieval, to the media's media handler.

data reference A reference to a media's data.

declaration A statement that establishes an identifier and associates attributes with it, without necessarily reserving its storage (for data) or providing the implementation (for methods).

definition A declaration that reserves storage (for data) or provides implementation (for methods). See also declaration.

deprecation Refers to a class, interface, constructor, method, or field that is no longer recommended and may cease to exist in a future version.

derived from Class X is "derived from" class Y if class X extends class Y.

derived media handler component A component that allows the Movie Toolbox to access the data in a media. Derived media handler components isolate the Movie Toolbox from the details of how or where a particular media is stored. These components are referred to as *derived* components because they rely on the services of a common base media handler component, which is supplied by Apple. See also base media handler component.

desktop sprite A sprite that lives in a sprite world and can act anywhere on the user's desktop. Desktop sprites are animated by the Sprite Toolbox.

detached controller A movie controller component that is separate from its associated movie.

digitizer rectangle The portion of the active source rectangle that you want to capture and convert with a video digitizer component.

display coordinate system The Quick-Draw graphics world, which can be used to display QuickTime movies, as opposed to the movie's time coordinate system, which defines the basic time unit for each of the movie's tracks.

dithering A technique used to improve picture quality when you are attempting to display an image that exists at a higher bit-depth representation on a lower bit-depth device. For example,

you might want to dither a 24-bits-per-pixel image for display on an 8-bit screen.

dropframe A synchronizing technique that skips timecodes to keep them current with video frames.

duration A time interval. Durations are time values that are interpreted as spans of time, rather than as points in time.

edit list A data structure that arranges a media into a time sequence.

edit state Information defining the current state of a movie or track with respect to an edit session. The Movie Toolbox uses edit states to support its undo facilities.

effect description A data structure that specifies which component will be used to implement an effect in a movie and how the component will be configured.

effect track A modifier track that applies an effect (such as a wipe or dissolve) to a movie.

encapsulation The localization of knowledge within a module. Because objects encapsulate data and implementation, the user of an object can view the object as a black box that provides services. Instance variables and methods can be added, deleted, or changed, but as long as the services provided by the object remain the same, code that uses the object can continue to use it without being rewritten. See also instance variable, instance method.

exception   An event during program execution that prevents the program from continuing normally; generally, an error. The Java programming language supports exceptions with the `try`, `catch`, and `throw` keywords. See also exception handler.

exception handler   A block of code that reacts to a specific type of exception. If the exception is for an error that the program can recover from, the program can resume executing after the exception handler has executed.

executable content   An application that runs from within an HTML file. See also applet.

extends   Class X extends class Y to add functionality, either by adding fields or methods to class Y or by overriding methods of class Y. An interface extends another interface by adding methods. Class X is said to be a subclass of class Y.

field   A data member of a class in Java. Unless specified otherwise, a field is not static.

file fork   A section of a Macintosh file. See data fork, resource fork.

file preview   A **thumbnail picture** from a movie that is displayed in the Open File dialog box.

file system specification   On the Macintosh platform, a data structure that defines a file's location and name.

flattening   The process of copying all of the original data referred to by reference in QuickTime tracks into a QuickTime movie file. Flattening is used to bring in all of the data that may be referred to from multiple files after QuickTime editing is complete. It makes a QuickTime movie stand-alone—that is, it can be played on any system without requiring any additional QuickTime movie files or tracks, even if the original file referenced hundreds of files. The flattening operation is essential if QuickTime movies are to be used with CD-ROM discs.

formal parameter list   The parameters specified in the definition of a particular method. See also actual parameter list.

frame   A user interface window in the Java virtual machine. Frames usually contain a title bar and often correspond to a user-visible window. Frames are analogous to a window record on the Mac OS.

frame animation   In QuickTime VR, the technique of playing all the frames of the current view.

frame differencing A form of temporal compression that involves examining redundancies between adjacent frames in a moving image sequence. Frame differencing can improve compression ratios considerably for a video sequence.

frame rate The rate at which a movie is displayed—that is, the number of frames per second that are actually being displayed. In QuickTime the frame rate at which a movie was recorded may be different from the frame rate at which it is displayed.

garbage collection The automatic detection and freeing of memory that is no longer in use. The Java runtime system performs garbage collection so that programmers never explicitly free objects.

general event In the QuickTime Music Architecture, an event that specifies a synthesizer to be used by subsequent events.

General MIDI component A component built into QuickTime that plays music on any general MIDI device.

graphics exporter component A QuickTime component that lets you store still images in various formats.

graphics importer component A QuickTime component that opens and displays still images.

graphics mode In sprite programming, the property of a sprite that determines how it blends with its background.

graphics world A device-independent environment for preparing images before displaying them on the screen. A graphics world (often called a GWorld) combines a graphics port and a device record, which together completely determine the graphics environment in which QuickTime does its drawing.

GSM The digital cellular telephony system defined by the European Union; in this context, the audio compression algorithm used by GSM phones, giving 10:1 compression.

H.261 A video compression scheme defined by the ITU, originally for use in video telephony and related systems; particularly suited to operation at moderately low rates (e.g., ISDN).

H.263 A video compression scheme defined by the ITU, originally for use in video telephony and related systems; particularly suited to operation at very low rates (e.g. over a modem).

hierarchy A classification of relationships in which each item except the top one (known as the root) is a specialized form of the item above it. Each item can have one or more items below it in the hierarchy. In the Java class hierarchy, the root is the `Object` class.

hint track A track in a QuickTime movie containing precomputed additional information about a media stream in the same QuickTime movie.

hot spot A place in a virtual reality scene where the software recognizes cursor actions.

HTTP streaming The process of sending a movie file over the Internet, using HTTP transport, so that it starts playing before the entire file has arrived. Compare real-time streaming.

identifier The name of an item in a program written in the Java programming language.

image In sprite programming, one of a sprite's properties.

Image Compression Manager (ICM) A QuickTime component that lets other code compress and decompress images and movies.

image compressor component A component that provides image-compression services. Image compressor components have a component type of `'imco'`.

image data The data that determines a sprite's appearance.

image decompressor component A **component** that provides image-decompression services. Image decompressor components have a component type value of `'imdc'`.

image description Information about a compressed image or sequence, including its uncompressed size and resolution, the type of compression used, and so on.

immersive imaging See virtual reality.

inheritance The concept of classes automatically containing the variables and methods defined in their supertypes.

input map A data structure that describes where to find information about tracks that are targets of a modifier track.

instance An object of a particular class. In programs written in the Java programming language, an instance of a class is created using the `new` operator followed by the class name.

instance method Any method that is invoked with respect to an instance of a class. Also called simply a method. See also class method.

instance variable Any item of data that is associated with a particular object. Each instance of a class has its own copy of the instance variables defined in the class. Also called a field. See also class variable.

interface   In the Java programming environment, a group of methods that can be implemented by several classes, regardless of where the classes are in the class hierarchy.

ISO   Acronym for the International Standards Organization. ISO establishes standards for multimedia data formatting and transmission, such as JPEG and MPEG.

JAR file format   JAR (Java Archive) is a platform-independent file format that aggregates many files into one. Multiple applets and their requisite components (class files, images, sounds and other resource files) can be bundled in a JAR file and subsequently downloaded to a browser in a single HTTP transaction. It also supports file compression and digital signatures.

JAR file A file in the JAE file format. JAR files have a .jar extension.

Java   An object-oriented programming language developed by Sun Microsystems that is widely used to write cross-platform programs that can be transmitted over a network and run on a variety of platforms. The QuickTime API is implemented in Java as a set of classes and methods.

Java Runtime Environment (JRE)   A subset of the Java(™) Development Kit for end-users and developers who want to redistribute the runtime environment alone. The Java runtime environment consists of the Java virtual machine, the Java core classes, and supporting files.

Java runtime session   An instantiation of the Java runtime environment (that is, an instantiation of the Java virtual machine and associated software).

Joint Photographic Experts Group (JPEG)   Refers to an international standard for compressing still images. This standard supplies the algorithm for image compression. The version of JPEG supplied with QuickTime complies with the baseline ISO standard bitstream, version 9R9. This algorithm is best suited for use with natural images.

JPEG   See Joint Photographic Experts Group.

key color   A color in a destination image that is replaced with video data by a video digitizer component. Key colors represent one technique for selectively displaying video on a computer display. Other techniques include the use of alpha channels and blend mattes.

key frame   A sample in a sequence of temporally compressed samples that does not rely on other samples in the sequence for any of its information.

Key frames are placed into temporally compressed sequences at a frequency that is determined by the key frame rate. Typically, the term *key frame* is used with respect to temporally compressed sequences of image data. See also sync sample.

key frame rate The frequency with which key frames are placed into temporally compressed data sequences.

knob In the QuickTime Music Architecture, software that controls a defined characteristic of the process used to generate musical notes, such as their attack and decay times.

knob event In the QuickTime Music Architecture, an event that modifies a specific knob for specific parts.

layer A mechanism for prioritizing the tracks in a movie or the overlapping of sprites. When it plays a movie, the Movie Toolbox displays the movie's tracks according to their layer—tracks with lower layer numbers are displayed in front; tracks with higher layer numbers are displayed over those tracks in back.

leaf atom A QuickTime atom that contains no other atoms. A leaf atom, however, may contain a table. An example of a leaf atom is an edit list atom. The edit list atom contains the edit list table. Compare container atom.

link In QuickTime VR, a software action that carries the viewer from one node to another.

link hot spot In QuickTime VR, a hot spot that executes a link.

lossless compression A compression scheme that preserves all of the original data.

lossy compression A compression scheme that does not preserve the data precisely; some data is lost, and it cannot be recovered after the compression. Most lossy schemes try to compress the data as much as possible, without decreasing the image quality in a noticeable way.

marker event In the QuickTime Music Architecture, an event that specifies the beat or tempo of a series of notes, or the end of a series of events.

mask region A 1-bit-deep region that defines how an image is to be displayed in the destination coordinate system. For example, during decompression, the Image Compression Manager displays only those pixels in the source image that correspond to bits in the mask region that are set to 1. Mask regions must be defined in the destination coordinate system.

matrix See transformation matrix.

matte A defined region of a movie display that can be clipped and filled. See blend matte, track matte.

maximum source rectangle A rectangle representing the maximum source area that a video digitizer component can grab. This rectangle usually encompasses both the vertical and horizontal blanking areas.

MBone A set of interconnected routers on the public internet that are enabled to handle IP multicast (Multicast Backbone).

media A Movie Toolbox data structure that contains information that describes the data for a track in a movie. Note that a media does not contain its data; rather, a media contains a reference to its data, which may be stored on disk, CD-ROM disc, or any other mass storage device. Also called a media structure.

media handler A piece of software that is responsible for mapping from the movie's time coordinate system to the media's time coordinate system. The media handler also interprets the media's data.

media information Control information about a media's data that is stored in the media structure by the appropriate media handler.

media sample A single chunk of data in a media.

MIDI Acronym for Musical Instrument Digital Interface, a standard format for sending instructions to a musical synthesizer.

MIDI component A component built into QuickTime that controls a MIDI synthesizer connected to the computer through a single MIDI channel.

modifier track A track in a movie that modifies the data or presentation of other tracks. For example, a tween track is a modifier track.

movie A structure of time-based data that is managed by the Movie Toolbox. A QuickTime movie may contain sound, video, animation, and user-defined media such as laboratory results, financial data, or a combination of any of these types of time-based data. A QuickTime movie contains one or more tracks; each track represents a single data stream in the movie.

movie boundary region A region that describes the area occupied by a movie in the movie coordinate system before the movie has been clipped by the movie clipping region. A movie's boundary region is built up from the track movie boundary regions for each of the movie's tracks.

movie clipping region The clipping region of a movie in the movie's coordinate system. The Movie Toolbox applies the movie's clipping region to the movie boundary region to obtain a clipped movie boundary region. Only that portion of the movie that lies in the clipped movie boundary region is then transformed into an image in the display coordinate system.

movie controller component A component that manages movie controllers, which present a user interface for playing and editing movies.

movie data exchange component A component that allows applications to move various types of data into and out of a QuickTime movie. The two types of data exchange components, which provide data conversion services to and from standard QuickTime movie data formats, are the movie import component and the movie export component.

movie data export component A component that converts QuickTime movie data into other formats.

movie data import component A component that converts other data formats into QuickTime movie data format.

movie display boundary region A region that describes the display area occupied by a movie in the display coordinate system, before the movie has been clipped by the movie display clipping region.

movie display clipping region The clipping region of a movie in the display coordinate system. Only that portion of the movie that lies in the clipping region is visible to the user. The Movie Toolbox applies the movie's display clipping region to the movie display boundary region to obtain the visible image.

movie file A QuickTime file that stores all information about the movie in a Macintosh resource and stores all the associated data for the movie separately. The resource is stored in the resource fork and the data in the data fork. Most QuickTime movies are stored in files with double forks.

Movie Player An application, furnished with the QuickTime system software, that plays QuickTime movies.

movie preview A short dynamic representation of a QuickTime movie. Movie previews typically last no more than 3 to 5 seconds, and they should give the user some idea of what the movie contains. You define a movie preview by specifying its start time, its duration, and its tracks.

movie resource One of several data structures that provide the medium of exchange for movie data between applications on the Mac OS and other operating systems.

movie sprite A sprite that lives in a sprite track and acts in a movie.

MPEG-4 An ISO standard that is based on the QuickTime file format and that supports video and audio streaming.

multicast A stream delivery technique whereby each packet can be delivered to multiple recipients who form a group. Recipients must join the group, and routers only forward multicast packets to members of the group. More efficient than either broadcast (which always goes to every recipient on every net) and unicast, when a separate packet must be sent to every recipient.

music control panel A dialog box that lets users select a music synthesizer.

music media handler Part of the QuickTime Music Architecture that processes data in the music tracks of QuickTime movies.

National Television System Committee (NTSC) Refers to the color-encoding method adopted by the committee in 1953. This standard was the first monochrome-compatible, simultaneous

color transmission system used for public broadcasting. This method is used widely in the United States.

node In QuickTime VR, a position in a scene from which an object or panorama can be viewed.

note allocator The part of the QuickTime Music Architecture that plays individual musical notes.

note event In the QuickTime Music Architecture, an event that specifies the pitch, velocity, and duration of a note.

NTSC See National Television System Committee.

object image array In QuickTime VR, a two-dimensional array that stores images of an object from various angles.

Object Metafile In QuickDraw 3D, a file format for storing information about 3D models.

object node In QuickTime VR, a position for viewing an object from the outside.

object view In QuickTime VR, a description of the angle and other characteristics for viewing an object node.

offscreen bit depth A sprite property that specifies a preferred bit depth for its offscreen buffer.

PAL See Phase Alternation Line.

palindrome looping Running a movie in a circular fashion from beginning to end and end to beginning, alternating forward and backward. Looping must also be enabled in order for palindrome looping to take effect.

panorama A structure of QuickTime VR data that forms a virtual-world environment within which the user can navigate.

panorama view In QuickTime VR, a part of a panorama seen from a particular angle.

panoramic node In QuickTime VR, a position from which a surrounding panorama is viewed.

parent atom An atom that contains other atoms, called child atoms.

partial panorama In QuickTime VR, a panorama that runs less than 360 degrees.

Phase Alternation Line (PAL) A color-encoding system used widely in Europe, Japan, and Australia in which one of the subcarrier phases derived from the color burst is inverted in phase from one line to the next. This technique minimizes hue errors that may result during color video transmission. Sometimes called *Phase Alternating Line*.

poster A frame shot from a movie, used to represent its content to the user.

preferred rate The default playback rate for a QuickTime movie.

preferred volume The default sound volume for a QuickTime movie.

preroll A technique for improving movie playback performance. When prerolling a movie, the Movie Toolbox informs the movie's media handlers that the movie is about to be played. The media handlers can then load the appropriate movie data. In this manner, the movie can play smoothly from the start.

preview A short, potentially dynamic, visual representation of the contents of a file. The Standard File Package can use previews in file dialog boxes to give the user a visual cue about a file's contents. See also file preview.

preview component A component used by the Movie Toolbox's standard file preview functions to display and create visual previews for files. Previews usually consist of a single image, but they may contain many kinds of data, including sound. In QuickTime, the Movie Toolbox is the primary client of preview components. Rarely, if ever, do applications call preview components directly.

property Information about a sprite that describes its location or appearance. One sprite property is its image, the original bitmapped graphic of the sprite.

QT atom An atom that you create and access by means of QuickTime calls. Compare chunk atom.

QuickTime Music Architecture (QTMA) The part of QuickTime that allows for the creation and manipulation of music tracks in movies.

QuickDraw The original Mac OS two-dimensional drawing software, used by QuickTime.

QuickDraw 3D A cross-platform code library that other code can use to create, configure, and render three-dimensional graphical models. QuickTime can import and handle the data objects that it creates.

QuickTime A set of Macintosh system extensions or a Windows dynamic-link library that other code can use to create and manipulate time-based data.

QuickTime for Java A set of Java classes and methods that implements the QuickTime API.

QuickTime Music Synthesizer A software music synthesizer, built into QuickTime, that plays sounds through the computer's audio hardware.

QuickTime VR A QuickTime media type that lets users interactively explore and examine photorealistic three-dimensional virtual worlds. QuickTime VR data structures are also called panoramas and object movies.

rate A value that specifies the pace at which time passes for a time base. A time base's rate is multiplied by the time scale to obtain the number of time units that pass per second. For example, consider a time base that operates in a time coordinate system that has a time scale of 60. If that time base has a rate of 1, 60 time units are processed per second. If the rate is set to 1/2, 30 time units pass per second. If the rate is 2, 120 time units pass per second.

recording The process of saving captured data into a QuickTime movie.

resizing The process of applying a transformation matrix to a digitized image to enlarge, shrink, or distort it.

resource In Macintosh programming, an entity in a file or in memory that may contain executable code or a description of a user interface item. Resources are loaded as needed by the Resource Manager and are identified by their type and ID number.

resource fork In a Macintosh file, the section that contains resources.

rest event In the QuickTime Music Architecture, an event that specifies the time interval between notes.

RTCP Real-Time Control Protocol. A back-channel used with RTP to provide low-level status of the connection, timing synchronization, and other control.

RTP Real-Time Transport Protocol. An IETF protocol defining packetization and handling of real-time media such as audio and video. Based on UDP.

RTSP Real-Time Streaming Protocol. A protocol currently in draft at the IETF, used to control a streaming server.

sample A single element of a sequence of time-ordered data.

sample format The format of data samples in a track, such as a sprite track.

scene In QuickTime VR, a collection of nodes that creates a virtual reality effect.

SECAM (Systeme Electronique Couleur avec Memoire) Sequential Color With Memory; refers to a color-encoding system in which the red and blue color-difference information is transmitted on alternate lines, requiring a one-line memory in order to decode green information.

sequence A series of images that may be compressed as a sequence. To do this, the images must share an image description structure. In other words, each image or frame in the sequence must have the same compressor type, pixel depth, color lookup table, and boundary dimensions.

sequence grabber channel component A component that manipulates captured data for sequence grabber components.

sequence grabber component A component that allows applications to obtain digitized data from sources that are external to a computer. For example, you can use a sequence grabber component to record video data from a video digitizer component. Your application can then request that the sequence grabber store the captured video data in a QuickTime movie. In this manner you can acquire movie data from various sources that can augment the movie data you create by other means, such as computer animation. You can also use sequence grabber components to obtain and display data from external sources, without saving the captured data in a movie.

sequence grabber panel component A component that allows sequence grabber components to obtain configuration information from the user for a particular sequence grabber channel component. An application never calls a sequence grabber panel component directly; application developers use panel components only by calling the sequence grabber component.

SMPTE Acronym for Society of Motion Picture and Television Engineers, an organization that sets video and movie technical standards.

Sound Input Manager A part of the QuickTime built-in software that lets a computer record sounds from a microphone or other audio input device.

Sound Manager A part of the QuickTime built-in software that plays sounds through the computer's audio hardware and also provides tools to manipulate sounds at the system level.

spatial compression Image compression that is performed within the context of a single frame. This compression technique takes advantage of redundancy in the image to reduce the amount of data required to accurately represent the image. Compare temporal compression.

sprite An animated image that is managed by QuickTime. A sprite is defined once and is then animated by commands that change its position or appearance. See desktop sprite, movie sprite, wired sprite.

sprite matrix A property of a sprite that describes its location and scaling within a sprite world.

sprite media handler Part of QuickTime that lets other code install sprites in a sprite track and manipulate them.

sprite toolbox Part of the QuickTime software that provides calls that other software can use to animate desktop sprites.

sprite track A movie track populated by movie sprites.

sprite world A graphics environment populated by desktop sprites.

standard image-compression dialog component A component that provides a consistent user interface for selecting parameters that govern compression of an image or image sequence and then manages the compression operation.

standard parameters A dialog box that lets users select and configure video effects.

standard sound A dialog box that lets users select and configure a sound compressor.

streaming Delivery of video or audio data over a network in real time, to support applications such as videophone and video conferencing. See MPEG-4.

s-video A video format in which color and brightness information are encoded as separate signals. The s-video format is component video, as opposed to composite video, which is the NTSC standard.

Swing Set The code name for a collection of graphical user interface (GUI) components that runs uniformly on any native platform that supports the Java virtual machine. Because they are written entirely in the Java programming language, these components may provide functionality above and beyond that provided by native-platform equivalents.

sync sample A sample that does not rely on preceding frames for its content.

synthetic music Music created by software commands.

temporal compression Image compression that is performed between frames in a sequence. This compression technique takes advantage of redundancy between adjacent frames in a sequence to reduce the amount of data that is required to accurately represent each frame in the sequence. Sequences that have been temporally compressed typically contain key frames at regular intervals. Compare spatial compression.

text channel component A variety of QuickTime sequence grabber channel component that uses the services of a text digitizer to import text into a movie.

text descriptor A QuickTime data structure that stores text formatting commands.

text digitizer component A QuickTime component that obtains text from an external source, such as a file.

text display A data structure that stores the text descriptors for styled text.

3D Movie Maker An application that helps you work with QuickDraw 3D.

3D object A graphic on the computer screen that realistically represents a three-dimensional figure.

3D Viewer A utility that displays models made with QuickDraw 3D and lets you manipulate them.

thread The basic unit of program execution. A process can have several threads running concurrently, each performing a different job, such as waiting for events or performing a time-consuming job that the program doesn't need to complete before going on. When a thread has finished its job, the thread is suspended or destroyed.

thumbnail picture A picture that can be created from an existing image that is stored as a pixel map, a picture, or a picture file. A thumbnail picture is useful for creating small representative images of a source image and in previews for files that contain image data.

tile In **QuickTime VR,** the equivalent of movie frames that together make up a panorama.

time base A set of values that define the time basis for an entity, such as a QuickTime movie. A time base consists of a time coordinate system (that is, a time scale and a duration) along with a rate value. The rate value specifies the speed with which time passes for the time base.

time-based data Data that changes or interacts with the user along a time dimension. QuickTime is designed to handle time-based data.

timecode media handler A component that interprets the data in a timecode track.

timecode track A movie track that stores external timing information, such as SMPTE timecodes.

time coordinate system A set of values that defines the context for a time base. A time coordinate system consists of a time scale and a duration. Together, these values define the coordinate system in which a time value or a time base has meaning.

time scale The number of time units that pass per second in a time coordinate system. A time coordinate system that measures time in sixtieths of a second, for example, has a time scale of 60.

time stamp A data structure that describes a text sample's starting time and duration in a movie.

time unit The basic unit of measure for time in a time coordinate system. The value of the time unit for a time coordinate system is represented by the formula (1/time scale) seconds. A time coordinate system that has a time scale of 60 measures time in terms of sixtieths of a second.

time value A value that specifies a number of time units in a time coordinate system. A time value may contain information about a point in time or about a duration.

track A Movie Toolbox data structure that represents a single data stream in a QuickTime movie. A movie may contain one or more tracks. Each track is independent of other tracks in the movie and represents its own data stream. Each track has a corresponding media, which describes the data for the track.

track boundary region A region that describes the area occupied by a track in the track's coordinate system. The Movie Toolbox obtains this region by applying the track clipping region and the track matte to the visual image contained in the track rectangle.

track clipping region The clipping region of a track in the track's coordinate system. The Movie Toolbox applies the track's clipping region and the track matte to the image contained in the track rectangle to obtain the track boundary region. Only that portion of the track that lies in the track boundary region is then transformed into an image in the movie coordinate system.

track matte A pixel map that defines the blending of track visual data. The value of each pixel in the pixel map governs the relative intensity of the track data for the corresponding pixel in the result image. The Movie Toolbox applies the track matte, along with the track clipping region, to the image contained in the track rectangle to obtain the track boundary region.

track movie boundary region A region that describes the area occupied by a track in the movie coordinate system, before the movie has been clipped by the movie clipping region. The movie boundary region is built up from the track movie boundary regions for each of the movie's tracks.

track reference Code that defines the relations between tracks, such as the synchronization of a text track to a karaoke audio track.

transcoder A component that translates data from one compressed form to another without having to decompress it in between.

transformation matrix A 3-by-3 matrix that defines how to map points from one coordinate space into another coordinate space.

tune player The part of the QTMA that plays sequences of musical notes.

tween component A component that performs a specific kind of tweening, such as path-to-matrix rotation.

tweening A process interpolating new data between given values in conformance to an algorithm.

tween media handler A component that selects the appropriate tween component to perform tweening.

tween track A track that modifies the display of other tracks by tweening.

UDP (Used Datagram Protocol) An unreliable delivery mechanism; packets are sent, and delivered to the higher-level software with no attempt to track or resend lost packets.

unicast A stream delivery technique whereby packets are sent to a unique destination. Compare multicast.

user data Auxiliary data that your application can store in a QuickTime movie, track, or media structure. The user data is stored in a user data list; items in the list are referred to as user data items. Examples of user data include a copyright, date of creation, name of a movie's director, and special hardware and software requirements.

user data item A single element in a user data list, such as a modification date or copyright notice.

user data list The collection of user data for a QuickTime movie, track, or media. Each element in the user data list is called a user data item.

vectors In QuickTime, mathematical descriptions of images that are more compact than bitmaps. The description language is based on Apple Computer's QuickDraw GX technology.

vertical blanking rectangle A rectangle that defines a portion of the input video signal that is devoted to vertical blanking. This rectangle occupies lines 10 through 19 of the input signal. Broadcast video sources may use this portion of the input signal for closed captioning, teletext, and other nonvideo information. Note that the blanking rectangle cannot be contained in the maximum source rectangle.

video bottleneck Places in sequence grabbing code where the grabber will call a client code's callback function.

video digitizer component A component that provides an interface for obtaining digitized video from an analog video source. The typical client of a video digitizer component is a sequence grabber component, which uses the services of video digitizer components to create a very simple interface for making and previewing movies. Video digitizer components can also operate independently, placing live video into a window.

viewing constraints In QuickTime VR, special limits on viewing a node (such as hiding part of it during a game), which are imposed by application software.

viewing limits In QuickTime VR, the limits of pan and tilt angle from which a node can be viewed.

virtual machine (VM) An abstract specification for a computing device that can be implemented in different ways, in software or hardware. You compile to the instruction set of a virtual machine much like you would compile to the instruction set of a microprocessor. The Java virtual machine consists of a byte-code instruction set, a set of registers, a stack, a garbage-collected heap, and an area for storing methods.

virtual reality The effect achieved by QuickTime VR, where users appear to be manipulating real objects or environments.

visible In sprite programming, the property of a sprite that determines whether or not it is visible.

white level   The degree of whiteness in an image. It is a common video digitizer setting.

window record   A Mac OS data structure that contains a graphics port and information about a window.

window registration   In Windows code, the process of associating a window (designated by a HWND handle) with QuickTime.

wired sprite   A variety of sprite that acts like a button, telling other software when the user has clicked its image or passed the cursor over it.

wrapper   An object that encapsulates and delegates to another object to alter its interface or behavior in some way.

Bibliography

QUICKTIME PROGRAMMING

This book is the second in the QuickTime Developer Series published by Morgan Kaufmann. The first book, which supplements much of the information in **QuickTime for Java**, provides a valuable introduction to QuickTime programming:

- *Discovering QuickTime,* **by George Towner** (Morgan Kaufmann): an introductory guide for programmers who want to use QuickTime. It includes a full description of the QuickTime API and its component architecture, and comes with a companion CD-ROM that includes many useful working examples, code snippets, and QuickTime movies.

  The third book in this series (scheduled for publication Fall 1999) is

- *QuickTime for the Web,* **by Steven Gulie** (Morgan Kaufmann): the official guide to QuickTime for Web authors and CD-ROM designers. It includes practical advice and many examples on its CD–ROM.

THE QUICKTIME SDK AND WEBSITE

The complete set of technical resources for QuickTime programming is provided on the QuickTime SDK. This SDK is available from Apple Computer. Check the QuickTime website at http://www.apple.com/ quicktime for more information.

The complete QuickTime technical documentation suite consists of 12 books, totaling more than 7,000 pages. You can get Adobe Acrobat files of these books, which you can print yourself, from the QuickTime SDK or from the QuickTime online PDF site at

`http://developer.apple.com/techpubs/quicktime/qtdevdocs/pdfdocs.htm`

To view the documentation in HTML, go to

`http://developer.apple.com/techpubs/quicktime/qtdevdocs/RM/frameset.htm`

JAVA PROGRAMMING

The following are a sampling of useful Java books in the field. No list can be quite complete, as new Java books are being published every day.

Abstract Data Types in Java, by Michael S. Jenkins (McGraw-Hill)

Core Java, by Gary Cornell and Cay S. Horstmann (SunSoft Press)

Data Structures and Algorithms in Java, by Michael T. Goodrich and Roberto Tamassia (John *Wiley)*

Data Structures and Problem Solving Using Java, by Mark Allen Weiss (Addison-Wesley)

Java Algorithms, by Scott Robert Ladd (McGraw-Hill)

The Java Handbook: The Authoritative Guide to the Java Revolution, by Patrick Naughton (Osborne McGraw-Hill)

Java in a Nutshell, by David Flanagan (O'Reilly & Associates)

Java Programming Language Handbook, by David H. Friedel, Jr., and Anthony Potts (Coriolis Group Books)

The Java Application Programming Interface Volumes I & II, by James Gosling and Frank Yellin (SunSoft Press/Prentice Hall).

Java Foundation Classes, by Matthew T. Nelson (McGraw-Hill)

The Java Virtual Machine Specification, by Tim Lindholm and Frank Yellin (Addison-Wesley)

JFC: Java Foundation Classes, by Daniel I. Joshi and Pavel A. Vorobiev (IDG Books)

Just Java, by Peter van der Linden (SunSoft Press/Prentice Hall)

Programming with JFC, by Scott R. Weiner and Stephen Asbury (John Wiley)

Thinking in Java, by Bruce Eckel (Prentice Hall)

Up to Speed with Swing: User Interfaces with Java Foundation Classes, by Steven Gutz (Manning)

Index

Apple Computer, Inc.
Software License Agreement

English—Apple Computer, Inc. Software License

Français—Apple Computer, Inc. Contrat de Licence Logiciel

Español—Licencia de Software de Apple Computer, Inc.

Deutsch—Apple Computer, Inc. -Software-Lizenzvertrag

Italiano—Apple Computer, Inc. Licenza Software

Svensk—Apple Computer, Inc. Licensavtal

Nederlands—Apple Computer, Inc. Software-licentie

日本語—アップルコンピュータ・インクソフトウェア使用許諾契約

If for any reason a court of competent jurisdiction finds any provision, or portion thereof, to be unenforceable, the remainder of this License shall continue in full force and effect.

9. Complete Agreement. This License constitutes the entire agreement between the parties with respect to the use of the Apple Software and supersedes all prior or contemporaneous understandings regarding such subject matter. No amendment to or modification of this License will be binding unless in writing and signed by Apple.

APPLE COMPUTER, INC.
INTERNATIONAL SALES SUBSIDIARY LIST

COUNTRY	SUBSIDIARY
Austria	Apple Computer Gesellschaft m.b.H.
Brazil	Apple Computer Brasil Ltda.
Canada	Apple Canada Inc.
France	Apple Computer France S.A.R.L.
Germany	Apple Computer GmbH
Hong Kong	Apple Computer International Ltd
India	Apple Computer International Pte. Ltd.
Ireland	Apple Computer (UK) Limited
Italy	Apple Computer S.p.A.
Japan	Apple Japan, Inc.
Mexico	Apple Computer Mexico, S.A. de C.V.
Netherlands, Belgium	Apple Computer Benelux B.V.
Singapore	Apple Computer South Asia Pte Ltd
South Africa	Apple Computer (Proprietary) Limited
Spain	Apple Computer Espana, S.A.
Sweden, Norway, Denmark	Apple Computer AB
Switzerland	Apple Computer AG (SA) (Ltd.)
Taiwan	Apple Computer Asia, Inc.
United Kingdom	Apple Computer (UK) Limited

EA0054

partir du Logiciel Apple ou transmettre le Logiciel Apple par un réseau ou vers un autre ordinateur. La présente Licence sera résiliée immédiatement et de plein droit, sans notification préalable de la part d'Apple, si vous ne vous conformez pas à l'une quelconque de ses dispositions. Apple pourra également résilier la présente Licence dans le cas où une nouvelle version du Mac OS serait incompatible avec le Logiciel Apple.

3. Garantie des Supports (le cas échéant). Apple garantit les supports sur lesquels le Logiciel Apple est enregistré contre tout vice de matière et de main d'oeuvre, sous condition d'une utilisation normale, pendant une période de quatre-vingt-dix (90) jours à compter de la date d'achat initiale. Votre seul recours, au titre du présent article se limite, et ceci au choix d'Apple, soit au remboursement du prix du produit contenant le Logiciel Apple, soit au remplacement du Logiciel Apple, lorsqu'il est retourné à Apple ou à un représentant autorisé d'Apple avec une copie de la facture. CETTE LIMITATION DE GARANTIE ET TOUTES GARANTIES IMPLICITES CONCERNANT LE SUPPORT Y COMPRIS LES GARANTIES IMPLICITES DE QUALITE MARCHANDE ET D'ADEQUATION A UN USAGE PARTICULIER SONT LIMITEES À UNE DUREE DE QUATRE-VINGT-DIX (90) JOURS À COMPTER DE LA DATE D'ACHAT INITIALE. CERTAINES LEGISLATIONS NE PERMETTENT PAS DE LIMITER LA DUREE D'UNE GARANTIE IMPLICITE, IL EST DONC POSSIBLE QUE LA LIMITATION MENTIONNEE CI-DESSUS NE S'APPLIQUE PAS A VOUS. CETTE LIMITATION DE GARANTIE TELLE QU'EXPRIMEE CI-DESSUS EST EXCLUSIVE DE TOUTE AUTRE GARANTIE QUELLE QUE SOIT SA FORME, ORALE, ECRITE, EXPRESSE OU TACITE. APPLE EXCLUT EXPRESSEMENT L'APPLICATION DE TOUTE AUTRE GARANTIE. CETTE GARANTIE VOUS DONNE DES DROITS SPECIFIQUES. VOUS POUVEZ EGALEMENT AVOIR D'AUTRES DROITS QUI VARIENT SELON LES LEGISLATIONS.

La disposition qui suit n'est applicable que pour la France : l'application de la présente garantie ne pourra vous priver de vos droits à la garantie légale (en cas de défauts ou de vices cachés).

4. Exclusion de Garantie sur le Logiciel Apple. Certains des Logiciels Apple peuvent être identifiés comme des versions du Logiciel Apple de type alpha, bêta, développement, pré-version, non-testées ou partiellement testées. De tels Logiciels Apple peuvent contenir des dysfonctionnements qui sont susceptibles de provoquer des erreurs et des pertes de données et peuvent se révéler incomplets ou contenir des inexactitudes. Vous reconnaissez et admettez expressément que l'utilisation du Logiciel Apple est à vos risques et périls. Le Logiciel Apple est fourni "TEL QUEL" sans garantie d'aucune sorte, et Apple et le(s) concédant(s) d'Apple (aux fins des dispositions des paragraphes 4 et 5, l'expression "Apple" désigne collectivement Apple et le(s) concédant(s) d'Apple) EXCLUENT EXPRESSEMENT TOUTE GARANTIE, EXPLICITE OU IMPLICITE, Y COMPRIS DE FACON NON LIMITATIVE LES GARANTIES IMPLICITES DE QUALITE MARCHANDE ET D'ADEQUATION A UN USAGE PARTICULIER ET TOUTE GARANTIE DE NON-CONTREFACON. APPLE NE GARANTIT PAS QUE LES FONCTIONS CONTENUES DANS LE LOGICIEL APPLE CORRESPONDRONT A VOS BESOINS OU QUE LE FONCTIONNEMENT DU LOGICIEL APPLE SERA ININTERROMPU, EXEMPT D'ERREUR OU QUE TOUT DEFAUT DU LOGICIEL APPLE SERA CORRIGE. DE PLUS, APPLE NE GARANTIT PAS NI NE FAIT AUCUNE DECLARATION CONCERNANT L'UTILISATION OU LES RESULTATS DE L'UTILISATION DU LOGICIEL APPLE OU DE LA DOCUMENTATION Y AFFERENT EN CE QUI CONCERNE LEUR EXACTITUDE, FIABILITE OU AUTREMENT. AUCUNE INFORMATION OU AUCUN CONSEIL, COMMUNIQUES VERBALEMENT OU PAR ECRIT PAR APPLE OU PAR UN DE SES REPRESENTANTS AUTORISES NE POURRA CREER UNE GARANTIE OU AUGMENTER DE QUELQUE MANIERE QUE CE SOIT L'ETENDUE DE LA PRESENTE GARANTIE. SI LE LOGICIEL APPLE S'AVERAIT DEFECTUEUX, VOUS ASSUMERIEZ SEUL (ET NON PAS APPLE NI UN REPRESENTANT AUTORISE D'APPLE) LE COUT TOTAL DE TOUT ENTRETIEN, REPARATION OU MODIFICATION NECESSAIRE. CERTAINES LEGISLATIONS NE PERMETTENT PAS L'EXCLUSION DE GARANTIES IMPLICITES, IL EST DONC POSSIBLE QUE L'EXCLUSION MENTIONNEE CI-DESSUS NE S'APPLIQUE PAS A VOUS.

La disposition suivante n'est applicable que pour la France : les présentes ne pourraient vous priver de vos droits à la garantie légale (en cas de défauts ou de vices cachés), dans la mesure où elle trouverait à s'appliquer.

5. Limitation de Responsabilité. EN AUCUN CAS, Y COMPRIS LA NEGLIGENCE, APPLE NE SERA RESPONSABLE DE QUELQUES DOMMAGES INDIRECTS, SPECIAUX OU ACCESSOIRES RESULTANT OU RELATIF À LA PRESENTE LICENCE. CERTAINES JURIDICTIONS NE PERMETTENT PAS LA LIMITATION OU L'EXCLUSION DE RESPONSABILITE POUR DOMMAGES INDIRECTS OU ACCESSOIRES, IL EST DONC POSSIBLE QUE L'EXCLUSION OU LA LIMITATION MENTIONNEE CI-DESSUS NE S'APPLIQUE PAS A VOUS. La seule responsabilité d'Apple envers vous au titre de tout dommage n'excédera en aucun cas la somme de deux cent cinquante francs (250FF).

6. Engagement Relatif aux Exportations. Vous ne pouvez pas utiliser ou autrement exporter ou réexporter le Logiciel Apple sauf autorisation par les lois des Etats-Unis et les lois du pays dans lequel vous avez obtenu le Logiciel Apple. En particulier mais sans limitation, le Logiciel Apple ne peut être exporté ou réexporté (i) dans tout pays soumis à embargo des Etats-Unis (ou à tout résident ou ressortissant de ce pays) ou (ii) à toute personne figurant sur la liste "Specially Designated Nationals" du Ministère des Finances des Etats-Unis ou sur le classement "Table of Denial Orders" du Ministère du Commerce des Etats-Unis. En utilisant le Logiciel Apple, vous déclarez et garantissez que vous n'êtes pas situé, sous le contrôle de, ou ressortissant ou résident d'un pays spécifié ci-dessus ou inscrit sur les listes mentionnées ci-dessus.

7. Gouvernement des Etats-Unis. Si le Logiciel Apple est fourni au Gouvernement des Etats-Unis, le Logiciel Apple est classé "restricted computer software" tel que ce terme est défini dans la clause 52.227-19 du FAR. Les droits du Gouvernement des Etats-Unis sur le Logiciel Apple sont définis pas la clause 52.227-19 du FAR.

8. Loi Applicable et Divisibilité du Contrat. Si une filiale Apple est présente dans le pays où vous avez acquis la licence du Logiciel Apple, la présente Licence sera régie par la loi du pays dans lequel la filiale est installée. Dans le cas contraire, la présente Licence sera régie par les lois des Etats-Unis et de l'Etat de Californie. Si pour une quelconque raison, un tribunal ayant juridiction juge qu'une disposition de la présente Licence est inapplicable, en totalité ou en partie, les autres dispositions de la présente Licence resteront entièrement applicables.

9. Entente Complète. Cette Licence constitue l'intégralité de l'accord entre les parties concernant l'utilisation du Logiciel Apple et remplace toutes les propositions ou accords antérieurs ou actuels, écrits ou verbaux, à ce sujet. Aucune modification de cette Licence n'aura quelque effet à moins d'être stipulée par écrit et signée par un représentant dûment autorisé d'Apple.

APPLE COMUTER, INC.
LISTE DES FILIALES

Pays	Filiales
Canada	Apple Canada Inc.
Afrique du Sud	Apple Computer (Proprietary) Limited
Royaume Uni	Apple Computer (UK) Limited
Suède, Norvège, Danemark, Finlande	Apple Computer AB
Suisse	Apple Computer AG (SA) (Ltd.)
Taiwan	Apple Computer Asia, Inc.
Pays Bas, Belgique	Apple Computer Benelux B.V.
Brésil	Apple Computer Brasil Ltda.
Espagne	Apple Computer Espana, S.A.
France	Apple Computer France S.A.R.L.
Autriche	Apple Computer Gesellschaft m.b.H.
Allemagne	Apple Computer GmbH
Hong Kong	Apple Computer International Ltd
Irlande	Apple Computer (UK) Limited
Mexique	Apple Computer Mexico, S.A. de C.V.
Italie	Apple Computer S.p.A.
Singapour	Apple Computer South Asia Pte Ltd
Japon	Apple Japan, Inc.

ESPAÑOL
Licencia de Software de Apple Computer, Inc.

ROGAMOS LEA DETENIDAMENTE EL PRESENTE CONTRATO DE LICENCIA DE SOFTWARE (EN ADELANTE DENOMINADO "LICENCIA") ANTES DE UTILIZAR EL SOFTWARE. EN EL SUPUESTO DE QUE UTILICE EL SOFTWARE, ELLO SE INTERPRETARÁ COMO UN HECHO INEQUÍVOCO DE SU ACEPTACIÓN A LOS TÉRMINOS Y CONDICIONES DE ESTA LICENCIA. SI VD. NO ACEPTA LOS TÉRMINOS Y CONDICIONES DE ESTA LICENCIA, NO UTILICE EL SOFWARE Y (EN SU CASO) DEVUELVA EL SOFTWARE AL ESTABLECIMIENTO DONDE LO ADQUIRIÓ PARA SU REEMBOLSO.

1. Licencia. Apple Computer Inc. ("Apple") le concede una licencia (sin que ello suponga su venta) para el uso del software, herramientas, utilidades, documentación y cualquier material complementario objeto de esta Licencia, ya sea en disco, en disco compacto, en memoria de lectura de ordenador o en cualquier otro soporte o de cualquier otra forma (el "Software Apple"). El Software Apple contenido en este paquete y cualesquiera copias, modificaciones y distribuciones que la presente Licencia le autorice a realizar están sujetos a esta Licencia.

2. Usos Permitidos y Restricciones. Esta Licencia le permite utilizar el Software Apple para (i) probar el Software Apple y (ii) desarrollar aplicaciones de software. Vd. puede hacer tantas copias del Software Apple como razonablemente sean necesarias para utilizar el Software según lo expresamente permitido por esta Licencia. Igualmente, Vd. puede distribuir estas copias a sus empleados siempre y cuando el trabajo de estos empleados requiera que utilicen el Software y, siempre y cuando, se cumplan los límites permitidos por la presente Licencia. Con sujeción a lo previsto en los términos complementarios de esta Licencia contenidos en la carpeta informática de Licencia ("Licensing Info Folder") que forma parte integrante de la presente Licencia y del Software Apple, el Software Apple podrá ser usado, copiado, modificado para poder desarrollar aplicaciones del software, así como incorporarlo o decompilarlo en combinación con sus propios programas, y distribuirlo (siempre en forma codificada) únicamente junto con todos sus propios programas y, siempre y cuando en todo caso se reproduzca en cada copia los derechos de Apple y cualquier otra leyenda en relación a los derechos de Apple que estuviesen en la copia original del Software Apple. Vd. puede también distribuir este Software Apple siempre que celebre con los terceros que lo reciban o utilicen un contrato que al menos proteja el Software Apple en los mismos términos que la presente Licencia. Salvo lo expresamente permitido por esta Licencia o por el derecho aplicable, no podrá Vd. descompilar, cambiar la ingeniería, desensamblar, modificar, alquilar, arrendar, prestar, distribuir, sublicenciar o crear trabajos derivados o basados en el Software de Apple o transmitir el Software Apple a terceros a través de una red o de un ordenador. Sus derechos bajo esta Licencia dejarán de estar en vigor de forma automática y sin necesidad de notificación de Apple en el supuesto de que Vd. incumpla cualesquiera término(s) de esta Licencia. Además, Apple se reserva el derecho de resolver la presente Licencia en el supuesto de comercializar una nueva versión del Mac Os que sea incompatible con el Software Apple.

3. Garantía Limitada sobre los Soportes. Apple garantiza que los soportes en los cuales está grabado el Software Apple carecen de defectos sobre materiales y mano de obra en circunstancias normales de uso y durante un plazo de noventa (90) días desde el momento de la adquisición inicial al por menor. Su único derecho bajo este apartado será, a opción de Apple, el reembolso del precio de compra del producto que contenía el Software Apple o la sustitución del Software Apple. ESTA GARANTÍA LIMITADA Y CUALESQUIERA GARANTÍAS IMPLÍCITAS Y/O CONDICIONES RELATIVAS A LOS SOPORTES, INCLUYENDO GARANTÍAS IMPLÍCITAS Y/O CONDICIONES DE COMERCIABILIDAD O CALIDAD SATISFACTORIA E IDONEIDAD PARA UN FIN DETERMINADO ESTÁN LIMITADAS A LA DURACIÓN DE NOVENTA (90) DÍAS DESDE LA FECHA DE ADQUISICIÓN AL POR MENOR. ALGUNAS

LEGISLACIONES NO PERMITEN LAS LIMITACIONES RESPECTO A LA DURACIÓN DE LAS GARANTÍAS IMPLÍCITAS, POR LO CUAL EN DICHO CASO ESTA LIMITACIÓN PODRÍA NO SER DE APLICACIÓN A VD. LA GARANTÍA LIMITADA PREVISTA EN ESTE APARTADO ES EXCLUSIVA Y SUSTITUYE A CUALESQUIERA OTRAS, SEAN VERBALES O ESCRITAS, EXPRESAS O IMPLÍCITAS. APPLE EXCLUYE EXPRESAMENTE TODAS LAS OTRAS GARANTÍAS. ESTA GARANTÍA LIMITADA LE CONFIERE DERECHOS ESPECÍFICOS. VD. PUEDE TAMBIÉN TENER OTROS DERECHOS EN FUNCIÓN DEL DERECHO IMPERATIVO APLICABLE.

4. Exclusión de Garantía en relación con el Software Apple. Algunos de los Software Apple pueden ser versiones designadas como alfa, beta, desarrollo, prototipo, sin probar o no probados completamente. Este Software Apple puede contener errores que causaren fallos o pérdida de información y pueden ser incompletos o contener inexactitudes. Vd. reconoce y acepta expresamente que el uso del Software Apple se realiza a su exclusivo riesgo. El Software Apple se suministra TAL Y COMO SE PRESENTA, sin garantía de ninguna clase y Apple y/o su(s) Licenciador(es) (a los efectos de las estipulaciones 4 y 5, Apple y el/los Licenciador(es) de Apple se denominarán de forma conjunta como "Apple") EXCLUYEN EXPRESAMENTE TODAS LAS GARANTÍAS EXPRESAS O IMPLÍCITAS, INCLUYENDO, CON CARÁCTER MERAMENTE ENUNCIATIVO Y NO LIMITATIVO, LAS GARANTÍAS DE COMERCIABILIDAD O CALIDAD SATISFACTORIA E IDONEIDAD PARA UN FIN DETERMINADO. APPLE NO GARANTIZA QUE LAS FUNCIONES CONTENIDAS EN EL SOFTWARE APPLE SATISFAGAN SUS NECESIDADES NI QUE EL SOFTWARE APPLE FUNCIONE ININTERRUMPIDAMENTE O SIN ERRORES O QUE LOS DEFECTOS DEL SOFTWARE APPLE SERÁN CORREGIDOS. ASIMISMO, APPLE NO GARANTIZA NI FORMULA DECLARACIÓN ALGUNA RELATIVA A LA UTILIZACIÓN O A LOS RESULTADOS DE LA UTILIZACIÓN DEL SOFTWARE APPLE O DE LA DOCUMENTACIÓN EN CUANTO A LA INEXISTENCIA DE ERRORES, EXACTITUD, FIABILIDAD U OTROS. NINGUNA INFORMACIÓN O ASESORAMIENTO ESCRITO O VERBAL FACILITADOS POR APPLE O POR UN REPRESENTANTE AUTORIZADO DE APPLE CONSTITUIRÁN GARANTÍA ALGUNA Y NO AUMENTARÁN EN MODO ALGUNO EL ÁMBITO DE LA PRESENTE GARANTÍA. EN EL SUPUESTO DE QUE EL SOFTWARE APPLE RESULTARA SER DEFECTUOSO, VD. (Y NO APPLE NI UN REPRESENTANTE AUTORIZADO DE APPLE) ASUMIRÁ EL COSTE ÍNTEGRO DE TODOS LOS SERVICIOS, REPARACIONES Y CORRECCIONES NECESARIOS. LOS HONORARIOS DE LA PRESENTE LICENCIA YA INCLUYEN ESTA DISTRIBUCIÓN DE RIESGOS. HABIDA CUENTA DE QUE LA NORMATIVA IMPERATIVA DE ALGUNOS PAÍSES NO PERMITE LA EXCLUSIÓN DE GARANTÍAS IMPLÍCITAS, LA ANTERIOR EXCLUSIÓN PUEDE NO SERLE APLICABLE.

5. Límite de responsabilidad. APPLE NO SERÁ RESPONSABLE EN NINGÚN CASO, INCLUYENDO POR NEGLIGENCIA, DEL LUCRO CESANTE O DAÑO EMERGENTE, DIRECTO O INDIRECTO, QUE PUDIERA DERIVARSE O ESTAR RELACIONADO CON LA PRESENTE LICENCIA, ELLO AUNQUE APPLE O REPRESENTANTE AUTORIZADO POR APPLE YA HAYAN AVISADO DE LA EXISENCIA DEL POSIBLE DAÑO. ALGUNOS PAÍSES NO PERMITEN LA LIMITACIÓN DEL LUCRO CESANTE O DAÑO EMERGENTE, DIRECTO O INDIRECTO, POR LO CUAL ESTA LIMITACIÓN PUEDE NO SERLE APLICABLE A VD. La responsabilidad total de Apple frente a Vd. por daños y perjuicios no excederá, en ningún caso, de la cantidad de cincuenta dólares de EE.UU. (50 dólares).

6. Restricciones a la exportación. Vd. no podrá utilizar o, de otra forma, exportar o reexportar, el Software Apple, salvo en la forma permitida por la legislación de los Estados Unidos y del país en el cual se obtuvo el Software Apple. En particular, pero sin estar limitado a ello, el Software Apple no podrá ser exportado o reexportado (i) a ningún país que haya sido objeto de embargo por parte de los EE.UU. (o a ningún nacional o residente en ese país), (ii) a nadie que figure en la lista de Ciudadanos Especialmente Designados del Departamento del Tesoro de EE.UU. o en la Tabla de Órdenes de Denegación del Departamento de Comercio de EE.UU. La utilización por su parte del Software Apple se considerará un hecho inequívoco de su manifestación y garantía de no estar situado, no estar bajo control y no ser nacional de ninguno de tales países y de que no figura en ninguna de tales listas.

7. La Administración como usuario final. Si el Software Apple es suministrado al Gobierno de los Estados Unidos, el Software Apple se calificará como "software informático restringido", tal como se define en la cláusula 52.227-19 del FAR. Los derechos de la Administración de los Estados Unidos respecto del Software Apple serán los definidos en la cláusula 52.227-19 del FAR.

8. Ley aplicable e independencia de las estipulaciones. En el supuesto de existir una filial de Apple en el país en el cual fue obtenida la Licencia de Software Apple, esta licencia se regirá por el derecho de dicho país. En caso contrario, la presente Licencia se regirá por las leyes de los Estados Unidos y del Estado de California. Si por cualquier razón un tribunal competente declarara no exigible o ineficaz cualquier disposición de la presente Licencia o parte de la misma, el resto de la presente Licencia conservará plena vigencia y efecto.

9. Contrato Íntegro. La presente Licencia constituye el acuerdo completo entre las partes respecto a la utilización del Software Apple y sustituye todos los acuerdos anteriores o contemporáneos relativos a su objeto. La presente Licencia únicamente podrá ser modificada mediante acuerdo escrito firmado por Apple.

APPLE COMPUTER, INC.
LISTA DE FILIALES A NIVEL INTERNACIONAL DEDICADAS A LA VENTA

PAÍS	FILIAL
Austria	Apple Computer Gesellschaft m.b.H.
Brasil	Apple Computer Brasil Ltda.
Canadá	Apple Canada Inc.
Francia	Apple Computer France S.A.R.L.
Alemania	Apple Computer Gmb H
Hong Kong	Apple Computer International Ltd.
India	Apple Computer International Pte. Ltd.
Irlanda	Apple Computer (UK) Limited
Italia	Apple Computer S.p.a.
Japón	Apple Japan, Inc
México	Apple Computer Mexico, S.A. de C.V.

Holanda, Bélgica	Apple Computer Benelux, B.V.
Singapur	Apple Computer South Asia Pte Ltd
Sudafrica	Apple Computer (Proprietary) Limited
España	Apple Computer España, S.A.
Suecia, Noruega, Dinamarca	Apple Computer AB
Suiza	Apple Computer AG (SA) (Ltd.)
Taiwan	Apple Computer Asia, Inc.
Reino Unido	Apple Computer (UK) Limited

DEUTSCH
Apple Computer, Inc. -Software-Lizenzvertrag

BITTE LESEN SIE DIESEN LIZENZVERTRAG SORGFÄLTIG DURCH, BEVOR SIE DIE SOFTWARE BENUTZEN. WENN SIE DIE SOFTWARE BENUTZEN, ERKLÄREN SIE DAMIT IHR EINVERSTÄNDNIS MIT DEN BESTIMMUNGEN DES FOLGENDEN LIZENZVERTRAGES. EINER GESONDERTEN MITTEILUNG AN APPLE ODER IHREN HÄNDLER BEDARF ES NICHT. WENN SIE MIT DEM LIZENZVERTRAG NICHT EINVERSTANDEN SIND, BENUTZEN SIE DIE SOFTWARE NICHT UND — SOFERN ANWENDBAR — GEBEN SIE DIE SOFTWARE DORT ZURÜCK, WO SIE SIE ERWORBEN HABEN.

1. Lizenz. Die Apple Computer, Inc., Cupertino, California, USA, ("Apple"), erteilt Ihnen hiermit das Recht zur Benutzung der beigefügten Software, Software – Werkzeuge und Dienstprogrammen, einschließlich der beigefügten Dokumentation und sonstiger Materialien (im folgenden "Apple-Software"), unabhängig davon, ob diese auf einer Diskette, einem ROM oder einem anderen Datenträger gespeichert ist. Alle sonstigen Rechte an der Apple-Software bleiben vorbehalten. Auch alle Kopien und Bearbeitungen sowie der Vertrieb der Apple-Software unterliegen dieser Vereinbarung.

2. Nutzung und Beschränkungen. Apple erteilt Ihnen hiermit das Recht zur Installation und Benutzung der Apple-Software auf der Festplatte eines Computers. Sie sind berechtigt, die Apple-Software zu benutzen, um (a) die Apple-Software zu testen und (b) Anwendungs- Programme zu entwickeln. Sie sind berechtigt, Kopien der Apple Software im nach diesem Lizenzvertrag notwendigen Umfang zu erstellen und an ihre Mitarbeiter zu verteilen, sofern diese die Apple Software zur Erfüllung ihrer dienstlichen Aufgaben benötigen und sofern die Einhaltung der Bestimmungne dieses Lizenzvertrages sichergestellt ist. Zum Zwecke der Entwicklung von Anwendungs – Software sind Sie berechtigt, die Apple Software zu benutzen, zu kopieren, nach Maßgabe der in der Apple Software im Ordner Licensing Info enthaltenen Bedingungen zu modifizieren, in Ihre eigenen Programme einzufügen oder in Kombination mit Ihren Programmen zu kompilieren sowie in maschinenlesbarer Form nur mit Ihren eigenen Programmen zu vertreiben, vorausgesetzt, daß Sie gleichzeitig als Teil Ihrer eigenen Programme auf jeder Kopie den Apple-Urheberrechtshinweis und alle anderen Schutzrechtshinweise, die auf dem Original der Apple-Software enthalten sind, reproduzieren. Sie verpflichten sich ferner, sofern Sie die so entwickelte Anwendungssoftware vertreiben, mit dem Endbenutzer einen rechtsgültigen Lizenzvertrag zu schließen, der sämtliche Rechte von Apple an der Apple Software nach Maßgabe der Bestimmungen dieses Lizenzvertrages in vollem Umfang berücksichtigt. Alle sonstigen Rechte an der Apple-Software bleiben vorbehalten. Sie verpflichten sich, es zu unterlassen, die Apple-Software zu dekompilieren, zurückzuentwickeln, zu disassemblieren oder in sonstiger Weise in eine für Personen wahrnehmbare Form zu bringen, zu modifizieren, zu adaptieren, zu übersetzen, von der Apple-Software ganz oder teilweise abgeleitete Werke zu erstellen, die Apple-Software über ein Netzwerk von einem Computer auf einen anderen zu übertragen oder diese zu verkaufen oder Dritten auf sonstige Weise unentgeltlich oder gegen Bezahlung zum Gebrauch zu überlassen, soweit dies nicht nach diesem Vertrag oder zwingenden gesetzlichen Vorschriften ausdrücklich gestattet ist. Sollten Sie diese Einschränkungen nicht beachten, sind Sie nicht mehr berechtigt, die Apple-Software zu benutzen, auch wenn der Apple diesen Vertrag noch nicht gekündigt haben sollte. Darüber hinaus behält sich Apple das Recht vor, diesen Lizenzvertrag zu kündigen, wenn eine neue Version von MacOS freigegeben wird, die mit der Apple Software nicht kompatibel ist.

3. Gewährleistung. Fehler in der Apple-Software können nicht ausgeschlossen werden; dies gilt insbesondere für solche Versionen der Apple-Software, die als Alpha-, Beta-, Development-, Pre-Release-, ungetestete oder nicht vollständig getestete Versionen der Apple-Software bezeichnet sind. Apple übernimmt eine Gewährleistung nur im Rahmen der gesetzlichen Vorschriften. Es gilt eine Verjährungsfrist von sechs Monaten ab Lieferung der Apple-Software. Die Gewährleistung erfolgt ausschließlich nach Wahl des Lizenzgebers durch Nachbesserung oder Ersatzlieferung. Bleiben Nachbesserung und/oder Ersatzlieferung erfolglos, können Sie nach Ihrer Wahl Herabsetzung der Lizenzgebühr oder die Rückgängigmachung des Vertrages verlangen. Für Apple-Software, die geändert, erweitert oder beschädigt wurde, wird keine Gewähr übernommen, es sei denn, daß die Änderung, Erweiterung oder Beschädigung für den Mangel nicht ursächlich war.

4. Schadenersatz. Eine vertragliche oder außervertragliche Schadensersatzpflicht seitens des Lizenzgebers sowie seiner Angestellten und Beauftragten besteht nur, sofern der Schaden auf grobe Fahrlässigkeit oder Vorsatz zurückzuführen ist. Eine weitergehende zwingende gesetzliche Haftung bleibt unberührt. Die Haftung des Lizenzgebers ist auf die Vermögensnachteile begrenzt, die er bei Abschluß des Vertrages als mögliche Folge der Vertragsverletzung hätte voraussehen müssen, es sei denn, daß der Schaden auf grobe Fahrlässigkeit eines Organs oder eines leitenden Angestellten des Lizenzgebers oder auf Vorsatz zurückzuführen ist. Für den Verlust von Daten wird keinesfalls gehaftet, es sei denn, daß dieser Verlust durch regelmäßige - im kaufmännischen Geschäftsverkehr tägliche - Sicherung der Daten in maschinenlesbarer Form nicht hätte vermieden werden können. Ferner wird keinesfalls für Schäden gehaftet, die durch sonstige Fehlleistungen der Apple-Software entstanden sind und die durch regelmäßige, zeitnahe Überprüfungen der bearbeiteten Vorgänge hätte vermieden werden können. Soweit Schadensersatzansprüche nicht nach den gesetzlichen Vorschriften früher verjähren, verjähren sie - mit Ausnahme von Ansprüchen aus unerlaubter Handlung und nach dem Produkthaftungsgesetz - spätestens mit dem Ablauf von zwei Jahren ab Erbringung der mangelhaften Leistung.

5. Export. Sie stehen dafür ein, daß die Apple-Software nur unter Beachtung aller anwendbaren Exportbestimmungen des Landes, in dem Sie die Apple-Software erhalten haben, und der Vereinigten Staaten von Amerika ausgeführt wird. Insbesondere darf die Apple-Software nicht (i) in ein Land exportiert oder reexportiert werden, über das die Vereinigten Staaten ein Embargo verhängt haben, oder einem Staatsangehörigen oder Bewohner eines solchen Landes überlassen werden oder (ii) einer Person überlassen werden, die auf der Liste der Specially Designated Nationals des U.S. Treasury Department oder dem Table of Denial Orders des U.S. Department of Commerce verzeichnet sind. Indem Sie die Apple-Software benutzen, erklären Sie, daß Sie weder in einem dieser Länder wohnhaft sind noch seiner Kontrolle unterliegen noch ein Staatsangehöriger oder Bewohner eines dieser Länder sind noch auf einer der vorstehend erwähnten Listen genannt werden.

6. US-Behörden. Wenn die Apple-Software für Behörden der Vereinigten Staaten von Amerika erworben wird, gilt sie als "restricted computer software" nach Maßgabe der Bestimmung Nr. 52.227-19 der FAR. Die Rechte der Behörden der Vereinigten Staaten von Amerika an der Apple - Software werden in der Bestimmung Nr. 52.227-19 der FAR geregelt.

7. Anwendbares Recht und Teilnichtigkeit. Dieser Lizenzvertrag unterliegt deutschem Recht. Die Unwirksamkeit einzelner Bestimmungen berührt die Wirksamkeit des Vertrages im übrigen nicht.

8. Vollständigkeit. Dieser Lizenzvertrag enthält die gesamte Vereinbarung zwischen den Parteien in Bezug auf die Lizenz und tritt an die Stelle aller diesbezüglichen früheren mündlichen oder schriftlichen Vereinbarungen. Änderungen und Ergänzungen dieses Vertrages sind schriftlich niederzulegen.

APPLE COMPUTER, INC.
LISTE DER INTERNATIONALEN TOCHTERGESELLSCHAFTEN

LAND	TOCHTERGESELLSCHAFT
Österreich	Apple Computer Gesellschaft m.b.H.
Brasilien	Apple Computer Brasil Ltda.
Kanada	Apple Canada Inc.
Frankreich	Apple Computer France S.A.R.L.
Deutschland	Apple Computer GmbH
HongKong	Apple Computer International Ltd.
Indien	Apple Computer International Pte. Ltd.
Irland	Apple Computer (UK) Limited
Italien	Apple Computer S.p.A.
Japan	Apple Japan Inc.
Mexiko	Apple Computer Mexico, S.A. de C.V.
Niederlande, Belgien	Apple Computer Benelux B.V.
Singapur	Apple Computer South Asia Pte. Ltd.
Südafrika	Apple Computer (Proprietary) Ltd.
Spanien	Apple Computer Espana, S.A.
Schweden, Norwegen, Dänemark	Apple Computer AB
Schweiz	Apple Computer AG (SA) (Ltd.)
Taiwan	Apple Computer Asia, Inc.
England	Apple Computer (UK) Limited

ITALIANO
Apple Computer, Inc. Licenza Software

SI PREGA DI LEGGERE QUESTA LICENZA CON LA MASSIMA ATTENZIONE PRIMA DI FARE USO DEL SOFTWARE. L'USO DEL SOFTWARE SI CONFIGURA COME ACCETTAZIONE DA PARTE VOSTRA DELLE CONDIZIONI E DEI TERMINI DI QUESTA LICENZA. QUALORA NON SIATE D'ACCORDO CON DETTE CONDIZIONE E DETTI TERMINI, VORRETE RESTITUIRE PRONTAMENTE IL SOFTWARE DOVE LO AVETE ACQUISTATO ED IL PREZZO VERSATO VI SARA' RESTITUITO.

1. Licenza. Il Software, gli strumenti, le utilità, la documentazione e tutti i fonts relativi a questa Licenza sia su disco, su compact disc o a memoria di sola lettura o in altro supporto, la relativa documentazione e altri materiali (collettivamente il "Software Apple") Vi vengono dati in licenza, e non venduti, da Apple Computer Inc. ("Apple"). Il Software Apple che si trova in questo pacchetto e le eventuali copie, modificazioni e distribuzioni autorizzate dalla presente Licenza sono soggetti a questa Licenza.

2. Usi consentiti e restrizioni. Questa Licenza Vi consente di usare il Software Apple per (i) testare il Software Apple e (ii) sviluppare applicazioni software. Vi é consentito di effettuare il numero di copie del Software Apple che siano ragionevolmente necessarie a farne uso nei modi consentiti dalla presente Licenza e distribuire dette copie ai Vostri dipendenti i quali, per ragioni di ufficio, debbano fare uso del Software semprechè detto uso sia limitato agli usi consentiti dalla presente Licenza. Al fine di sviluppare applicazioni software Vi è consentito di usare, copiare, modificare (subordinatamente alle restrizioni descritte nel folder Licensing Info che è parte integrante del Software Apple), incorporare e compilare unitamente ai Vostri programmi e distribuire (solo in forma di codice oggetto) esclusivamente con i Vostri programmi il Software Apple descritto nel folder Licensing Info sul supporto purché riproduciate su ciascuna copia tutti i dati relativi al copyright Apple contenuti nell'originale ed ogni altra informazione sulla proprietà industriale e distribuiate detto Software Apple in forza di un valido contratto altrettanto protettivo dei diritti di Apple nel Software quanto lo é questa Licenza. Salvo quanto consentito dalla legge applicabile e dalla presente Licenza, non Vi é consentito di decompilare, disassemblare, assemblare a riverso, modificare, dare in locazione, in leasing, dare in prestito, sublicenziare, distribuire o ricavare entità derivate dal Software Apple, in tutto o in parte, o trasmettere detto Software in rete o da un computer ad un altro. I Vostri diritti in forza di questa Licenza cesseranno automaticamente, senza onere di comunicazione da parte di Apple, qualora vi sia inadempimento da parte Vostra delle condizioni indicate nella Licenza stessa. Apple si riserva inoltre il diritto di risolvere la presente licenza qualora venga prodotta una nuova versione di Mac™ OS che sia incompatibile con il Software Apple.

3. Garanzia limitata dei Media. Apple garantisce che i supporti sui quali il Software Apple é stato registrato sono immuni da difetti di materiali e manodopera, in condizioni normali d'uso, per un periodo di novanta (90) giorni dalla data di acquisto originario al dettaglio. L'unica garanzia in forza del presente paragrafo potrà essere, a scelta di Apple, il rimborso del prezzo di acquisto o la sostituzione del Software Apple. LA PRESENTE GARANZIA E QUALSIASI ALTRA GARANZIA IMPLICITA RIGUARDANTE I SUPPORTI, IVI INCLUSA QUELLA RIGUARDANTE LA COMMERCIABILITà E L'IDONEITà A SCOPI PARTICOLARI é LIMITATA IN DURATA A NOVANTA (90) GIORNI DALLA DATA DELL'ACQUISTO ORIGINARIO AL DETTAGLIO. Gli esoneri di responsabilità che precedono avranno efficacia nella misura massima consentita dalle norme in vigore. LA PRESENTE GARANZIA LIMITATA E' ESCLUSIVA E SOSTITUISCE OGNI ALTRA SCRITTA OD ORALE, ESPRESSA O IMPLICITA. APPLE ESPRESSAMENTE DISCONOSCE OGNI ALTRA GARANZIA. Dette norme possono altresì contemplare altri vostri diritti oltre a quelli espressamente citati.

4. Esonero dalla garanzia del Software Apple. Parte del Software Apple potrà essere designato come alpha, beta, sviluppo, pre-release, non testato o potranno essere versioni non pienamente testate del Software Apple. Detto Software Apple potrebbe contenere errori che potrebbero causare errori o perdite di dati e potrebbe essere incompleto o contenere inaccuratezze. Voi espressamente accettate che l'uso del Software Apple avviene a Vostro esclusivo rischio. Il Software Apple viene fornito nello Stato in cui si trova e senza garanzia di sorta da parte di Apple. Sia Apple, sia il licenziante di Apple, ai fini di cui ai Par. 4 e 5, collettivamente denominati "Apple", si esonerano espressamente da ogni garanzia, espressa o implicita, ivi inclusa, ma senza limitazioni, la garanzia implicita di commerciabilità ed idoneità del prodotto a soddisfare scopi particolari. Apple non garantisce che le funzioni contenute nel Software Apple siano idonee a soddisfare le Vostre esigenze né garantisce un'operazione ininterrotta o immune da difetti né che i difetti riscontrati nel Software APPLE vengano corretti. Apple non garantisce altresì né dà affidamento alcuno relativamente all'uso o ai risultati derivanti dall'uso del Software Apple, né sotto il profilo della loro correttezza, accuratezza, affidabilità o sotto altri profili. Le eventuali informazioni orali o scritte o le eventuali consulenze da parte di esponenti o incaricati o di rappresentanti di Apple non possono in ogni caso configurarsi come affidamenti o garanzie o comunque inficiare questo esonero di garanzia. Nel caso di difettosità del Software Apple, saranno a vostro esclusivo carico tutti i costi e le spese per gli interventi, correzioni e ripristini che dovessero occorrere. IL PREZZO DELLA LICENZA PER IL SOFTWARE APPLE RIFLETTE L'ALLOCAZIONE DI RISCHI COME SOPRA. L'esonero di garanzia qui contemplato é da interpretarsi secondo quanto previsto dalla legge applicabile ed é pertanto da ritenersi inefficace nella parte che dovesse risultare incompatibile con le prescrizioni inderogabili della legge applicabile.

5. Limiti di responsabilità. IN OGNI CASO Apple é espressamente sollevata da ogni responsabilità, anche nell'eventualità di sua colpa, per qualsiasi danno, diretto o indiretto, di ogni genere e specie derivante O COLLEGATO all'uso del Software Apple, anche NELL'EVENTUALITà' in cui apple sia stata avvertita della POSSIBILITà del verificarsi del danno stesso. I limiti di responsabilità contemplati in questo paragrafo possono essere diversamente regolati dalle norme in vigore nel Vostro ordinamento giuridico. In nessun caso il limite di responsabilità nei Vostri confronti a carico di Apple per il complesso di danni, delle perdite o per ogni altra causa, potrà superare l'importo di USA $ 50.

6. Impegno all'osservanza delle norme relative all'esportazione. Varrà la presente quale Vostro impegno a non esportare il Software Apple se ciò non è espressamente consentito dalle norme degli Stati Uniti d'America e dalle leggi del paese in cui il Software Apple é stato ottenuto. In particolare, ma senza limitazioni, il Software Apple non potrà essere esportato o riesportato (i) in nessun Paese che si trovi sotto embargo statunitense né a residenti di detti Paesi o (ii) a chicchessia compreso nell'elenco dell'U.S. Treasury Department denominato Specially Designated Nationals o dell'U.S. Department of Commerce's Table denominato Denial Orders. Usando il Software Apple, Voi date espressamente atto e garantite di non essere cittadino o residente, anche solo di fatto, di un Paese compreso negli elenchi sopra citati, ovvero sotto il controllo di uno di detti Paesi.

7. Utilizzatori Finali Enti Governativi. Nel caso in cui il Software Apple venga fornito al Governo degli Stati Uniti d'America, il Software Apple viene classificato come "Software riservato" in base alla definizione di cui alla Clausola 52.227-19 del FAR. I diritti del Governo sul Software Apple sono quelli di cui alla Clausola 52.227-19 del FAR.

8. Legge regolatrice ed eventuale nullità di una o più clausole. Qualora nel Paese in cui avete acquistato il Software Apple vi sia una consociata Apple, in tale eventualità la legge del luogo dove si trova detta consociata regolerà questa Licenza. In caso diverso questa Licenza sarà regolata ed interpretata secondo le leggi degli Stati Uniti d'America ed particolare e dello Stato della California. Se per qualsiasi ragione il giudice competente dovesse ritenere inefficace uno o più clausole o parti di clausole di questa Licenza, le altre clausole o parti di clausole rimarranno efficaci.

9. Interezza dell'Accordo. Questa Licenza costituisce l'intero accordo tra le parti relativamente all'uso del Software Apple e supera ed assorbe ogni eventuale precedente o contemporanea intesa o proposta riguardante quanto in oggetto. Le eventuali modifiche o integrazioni di questa Licenza dovranno essere effettuate, per essere efficaci, in forma scritta e dovranno essere sottoscritte da Apple.

APPLE COMPUTER INC.
LISTA DELLE CONSOCIATE LOCALI A LIVELLO INTERNAZIONALE

PAESE	CONSOCIATA
Austria	Apple Computer Gesellschaft mbH
Brasile	Apple Computer Brasil Ltda.
Canada	Apple Canada Inc.
Francia	Apple Computer France S.A.R.L.
Germania	Apple Computer GmbH
Hong Kong	Apple Computer International Ltd.
India	Apple Computer International Pte. Ltd.
Irlanda	Apple Computer (UK) Limited

Italia	Apple Computer S.r.l.
Giappone	Apple Japan, Inc.
Messico	Apple Computer Mexico, S.A. de C.V.
Olanda, Belgio	Apple Computer Benelux B.V.
Singapore	Apple Computer South Asia Pte Ltd
Sud Africa	Apple Computer (Proprietary) Limited
Spagna	Apple Computer Espana, S.A.
Svezia, Norvegia, Danimarca	Apple Computer AB
Svizzera	Apple Computer AG (SA) (Ltd.)
Taiwan	Apple Computer Asia, Inc.
Regno Unito	Apple Computer (UK) Limited

SVENSK
Apple Computer, Inc. Licensavtal

LÄS DETTA LICENSAVTAL ("LICENSAVTAL") NOGGRANT INNAN DU ANVÄNDER PROGRAMPRODUKTEN. GENOM ATT ANVÄNDA PROGRAMPRODUKTEN SAMTYCKER DU TILL OCH BLIR AUTOMATISKT BUNDEN AV VILLKOREN I DETTA LICENSAVTAL. OM DU INTE SAMTYCKER TILL DESSA VILLKOR, SKALL DU INTE ANVÄNDA PROGRAMPRODUKTEN OCH (OM TILLÄMPLIGT) ÅTERLÄMNA PROGRAMPRODUKTEN TILL FÖRSÄLJNINGSSTÄLLET, VAREFTER DINA PENGAR KOMMER ATT ÅTERBETALAS.

1. Licens. Programprodukten, verktygen, hjälpmedlen, dokumentationen och typsnitten som levereras med detta Licensavtal, på diskett, CD, ROM eller på annat medium, tillämplig dokumentation och annat material (nedan gemensamt kallat "Apple Programprodukten"), licensieras till Dig av Apple Computer Inc.(nedan "Apple"). Både den Apple Programprodukt som finns i förpackningen och eventuella kopior, modifieringar och distribution som Du har rätt att göra enligt detta Licensavtal regleras av detta Licensavtal.

2. Tillåten användning och restriktioner. Detta Licensavtal ger Dig rätt att använda Apple Programprodukten för (i) test av Apple Programprodukten, och (ii) utveckling av tillämpningar. Du får göra så många kopior av Apple Programprodukten som är rimligt för att kunna använda Apple Programprodukten på det sätt som tillåts enligt detta Licensavtal, och distribuera dessa kopior till de av Dina anställda vars arbetsuppgifter kräver att de skall kunna använda Apple Programprodukten, under förutsättning att sådan användning ligger inom ramen för vad som är tillåtet enligt detta Licensavtal. För att utveckla tillämpningar får Du använda, kopiera, förändra (under förutsättning att sådan förändring inte står i strid med de restriktioner som anges i Licensierings Informations mappen i Apple Programprodukten), införliva med och sammanställa med Dina egna tillämpningar och distribuera (endast i objektkodsform), dock endast tillsammans med Dina egna tillämpningar, den Apple Programprodukt som beskrivs i Licensierings Informations mappen på mediet, under förutsättning att Du på varje kopia återge alla upplysningar om upphovsrätt som finns på originalet av Apple Programprodukten, och distribuerar sådan kopia av Apple Programprodukten tillsammans med ett giltigt licensavtal som skyddar Apples rättigheter till Apple Programprodukten i minst lika hög grad som detta Licensavtal. Du får inte, på annat sätt än som uttryckligen tillåts av detta Licensavtal, dekompilera, dekonstruera, bryta ner, förändra, hyra ut, leasa, låna ut, underlicensiera, distribuera, skapa härledda produkter helt eller delvis baserade på Apple Programprodukten eller överföra Apple Programprodukten från en dator till en annan via ett nätverk. Dina rättigheter enligt detta licensavtal kommer automatiskt, utan varsel från Apple, att upphöra om Du bryter mot bestämmelserna i detta Licensavtal. Apple förbehåller sig vidare rätten att säga upp detta Licensavtal om en ny version av MacOs™, vilken inte är kompatibel med Apple Programprodukten, lanseras.

3. Begränsad garanti för medium (om tillämpligt). Apple garanterar att det medium på vilket Apple Programprodukten är lagrat vid normal användning är fritt från defekter i material och utförande under en period av nittio (90) dagar från det första slutanvändarinköpet. Apples enda skyldighet i enlighet med denna garanti skall vara att, efter eget skön, antingen återbetala köpeskillingen för produkten som innehöll Apple Programprodukten eller att leverera en ny Apple Programprodukt. ALLA EGENSKAPER ELLER GARANTIER SOM UNDERFÖRSTÅTT KAN ANSES TILLFÖRSÄKRADE MEDIA INKLUSIVE EGENSKAPEN ATT VARA FUNKTIONELLT OCH ÄNDAMÅLSENLIGT, BEGRÄNSAS HÄRMED I TIDEN TILL EN PERIOD AV NITTIO (90) DAGAR FRÅN LEVERANS. DENNA GARANTI SKALL INTE TOLKAS SOM EN INSKRÄNKNING AV DE RÄTTIGHETER SOM KAN TILLKOMMA DIG ENLIGT TVINGANDE TILLÄMPLIG LAGSTIFTNING. APPLE FRISKRIVER SIG HÄRIGENOM UTTRYCKLIGEN FRÅN ALLT ÖVRIGT ANSVAR FÖR APPLE PROGRAMPRODUKTEN.

4. Ingen garanti för Apple Programprodukten. Vissa Apple Programprodukter kan vara angivna som sk alpha- eller beta-versioner, utvecklingsversioner, icke testade-versioner eller inte helt testade versioner av Apple Programprodukten. Dessa Apple Programprodukter kan innehålla brister som kan förorsaka felaktigheter eller resultera i att data förloras, de kan även vara ofullständiga eller innehålla felaktigheter. Du förklarar Dig uttryckligen medveten om detta förhållande och att all användningen av Apple Programprodukten sker på Din egen risk. Apple Programprodukten tillhandahålles i befintligt skick och utan några som helst garantier. Apple och Apples Licensgivare (i denna punkt 4 och punkt 5 kollektivt benämnda "Apple") FRISKRIVER SIG HÄRIGENOM FRÅN ALLA, SÅVÄL UTTRYCKLIGA SOM UNDERFÖRSTÅDDA, GARANTIER, SÅLEDES OCKSÅ UNDERFÖRSTÅDDA GARANTIER AVSEENDE KVALITET, FUNKTIONALITET OCH ÄNDAMÅLSENLIGHET FÖR VISST SPECIFIKT SYFTE, SAMT PROGRAMPRODUKTENS EVENTUELLA INTRÅNG I ANNANS IMMATERIELLA RÄTTIGHETER. APPLE KAN EJ HELLER GARANTERA ATT PROGRAMPRODUKTEN UPPFYLLER DINA FÖRVÄNTNINGAR, ÄR FELFRI ELLER KAN ANVÄNDAS UTAN AVBROTT ELLER ATT FEL OCH BRISTER I PROGRAMPRODUKTEN KOMMER ATT ÅTGÄRDAS. APPLE GER INGA GARANTIER VAD GÄLLER ANVÄNDNING ELLER RESULTATET AV ANVÄNDNINGEN AV PROGRAMPRODUKTEN OCH DOKUMENTATIONEN, DESS PÅLITLIGHET, NOGGRANNHET, ELLER ÖVRIGA EGENSKAPER. DENNA BEGRÄNSADE GARANTI KAN EJ UTÖKAS GENOM MUNTLIGA ELLER SKRIFTLIGA UTSAGOR FRÅN VARE SIG APPLE ELLER APPLES REPRESENTANTER. OM PROGRAMPRODUKTEN SKULLE VARA FELAKTIG ELLER BRISTFÄLLIG FRISKRIVER SIG APPLE FRÅN ALLA KOSTNADER FÖR SERVICE, REPARATION ELLER ANNAT AVHJÄLPANDE. VID ÅSÄTTANDE AV LICENSAVGIFTEN FÖR PROGRAMPRODUKTEN HAR HÄNSYN TAGITS TILL DENNA RISKALLOKERING. I HÄNDELSE AV ATT DENNA BESTÄMMELSE STRIDER MOT TVINGANDE LAG ÄR BESTÄMMELSEN I DENNA DEL EJ TILLÄMPLIG.

5. Ansvarsbegränsning. APPLE ÄR INTE, OBEROENDE AV VÅLLANDE, ANSVARIG FÖR SKADA, VARKEN DIREKT ELLER INDIREKT SÅDAN, VILKEN ORSAKATS AV ELLER ÄR RELATERAD TILL DENNA LICENS. I HÄNDELSE AV ATT DENNA BESTÄMMELSE STRIDER MOT TVINGANDE LAG ÄR BESTÄMMELSEN I DENNA DEL EJ TILLÄMPLIG. I inget fall skall Apples totala skadeståndsansvar, oberoende av vållande, överstiga ett belopp motsvarande US$ 50.

6. Försäkran avseende export. Försäkran avseende export. Du har inte rätt att exportera eller vidareexportera Apple Programprodukten förutom på sådant sätt som är i enlighet med gällande exportlagstiftning i USA och gällande lagstiftning i det land där Apple Programprodukten förvärvades. I synnerhet (dock inte begränsat till) gäller att Apple Programprodukten inte får exporteras eller vidareexporteras till i) något av de länder som lyder under USAs embargo (eller till en medborgare eller innevånare i sådant land), eller ii) någon som anges på US Treasury Departments lista över sk Specially Designated Nationals eller US Department of Commerces sk Table of Denial Orders. Genom att använda Apple Programprodukten försäkrar Du att Du inte bor i, lyder under, är medborgare eller bosatt i något sådant land eller finns upptagen på någon av de ovan angivna listorna.

7. Amerikanska statliga slutanvändare. Om Apple Programprodukten distribueras till amerikansk statlig myndighet är Apple Programprodukten klassificerad som " restricted computer software" som denna term definieras i punkt 52.227-19 av FAR. Den amerikanska myndighetens rättigheter till programprodukten kommer i detta fall att regleras av punkt 52.227-19 av FAR.

8. Gällande lag och genomförbarhet. Om det finns ett dotterbolag till Apple i det land där licensrättigheterna till denna Apple Programprodukt förvärvades, skall detta lands lag tillämpas på denna licens. I annat fall skall USAs och delstaten Kaliforniens lagstiftning tillämpas. För den händelse att något villkor i detta licensavtal av domstol eller administrativ myndighet inte bedöms giltigt eller verkställbart, skall övriga delar av avtalet ändock gälla fullt ut och tolkas på sådant sätt som skulle gällt om den exkluderade delen av avtalet gällde.

9. Fullständigt avtal. Detta licensavtal innehåller allt som avtalats mellan parterna med avseende på användningen av Apple Programprodukten och ersätter samtliga tidigare skriftliga eller muntliga avtal, utfästelser eller överenskommelser parterna emellan. Ändring i detta licensavtal kan endast ske genom särskild upprättad och av behörig representant för Apple undertecknad handling.

APPLE COMPUTER, INC.
INTERNATIONELLA DOTTERBOLAG

LAND	DOTTERBOLAG
Kanada	Apple Canada Inc.
Sydafrika	Apple Computer (Proprietary) Limited
England	Apple Computer (UK) Limited
Sverige, Norge, Danmark, Finland	Apple Computer AB
Schweitz	Apple Computer AG (SA) (Ltd.)
Taiwan	Apple Computer Asia, Inc.
Holland och Belgien	Apple Computer Benelux B.V.
Brasilien	Apple Computer Brasil Ltda.
Spanien	Apple Computer Espana, S.A.
Frankrike	Apple Computer France S.A.R.L.
Österrike	Apple Computer Gesellschaft m.b.H.
Tyskland	Apple Computer GmbH
Hong Kong	Apple Computer International Ltd
Irland	Apple Computer (UK) Limited
Mexico	Apple Computer Mexico, S.A. de C.V.
Italien	Apple Computer S.p.A.
Singapore	Apple Computer South Asia Pte Ltd
Japan	Apple Japan, Inc.
Indien	Apple Computer International Pte. Ltd.

NEDERLANDS
Apple Computer, Inc. Software-licentie

LEES DEZE SOFTWARE-LICENTIE-OVEREENKOMST ("LICENTIE") AANDACHTIG DOOR VOOR U DE PROGRAMMATUUR GEBRUIKT. DOOR DE PROGRAMMATUUR TE GEBRUIKEN VERKLAART U ZICH AKKOORD MET DE VOORWAARDEN VAN DEZE LICENTIE. INDIEN U HET NIET EENS BENT MET DE VOORWAARDEN VAN DEZE LICENTIE, DIENT U DE ONGEBRUIKTE PROGRAMMATUUR TE RETOURNEREN AAN DE PLAATS WAAR U DEZE HEBT AANGESCHAFT. DE DOOR U BETAALDE PRIJS ZAL IN DAT GEVAL WORDEN TERUGBETAALD.

1. Licentie. De programmatuur, tools, hulpprogramma's, documentatie en lettertypen bij deze Licentie, hetzij op schijf, op compact disc, in "read only"-geheugen of op enig ander medium (de "Apple programmatuur"), worden aan u in licentie gegeven, en niet verkocht, door Apple Computer, Inc. ("Apple").

Deze Licentie is van toepassing op de Apple programmatuur in dit pakket en op eventuele kopieën, gewijzigde versies of te distribueren versies die u krachtens deze licentie maakt.

2. Toegestaan gebruik en beperkingen. Krachtens deze licentie is het u toegestaan de Apple programmatuur te gebruiken ten einde (i) de Apple programmatuur te testen en (ii) applicatiesoftware te ontwikkelen. Het is u toegestaan zoveel kopieën van de Apple programmatuur te maken als redelijkerwijs noodzakelijk is om de programmatuur te kunnen gebruiken zoals beoogd in deze Licentie, en deze ter beschikking te stellen aan werknemers wier taak het gebruik van deze programmatuur vereist, op voorwaarde dat dit gebruik niet strijdig is met de voorwaarden van deze Licentie. Ten einde applicatiesoftware te ontwikkelen is het u toegestaan de Apple programmatuur zoals beschreven in de Licensing Info-informatie op het medium waarop de programmatuur is geleverd, te gebruiken, te kopiëren, te wijzigen (mits wordt voldaan aan de beperkingen die worden vermeld in de Licensing Info-informatie), te integreren in een te compileren in combinatie met uw eigen programma's, en deze, uitsluitend met eigen programma's (en uitsluitend in de vorm van objectcode) te distribueren, op voorwaarde dat u op elke kopie de volledige auteursrechtvermelding en alle andere mededelingen betreffende het eigendomsrecht welke op het origineel van de Apple programmatuur vermeld zijn, overneemt, en u de Apple programmatuur distribueert voorzien van een geldige overeenkomst die voorziet in minimaal dezelfde bescherming van de rechten van Apple met betrekking tot de Apple programmatuur als deze Licentie. Behalve voor zover uitdrukkelijk toegestaan krachtens deze Licentie is het u niet toegestaan de Apple programmatuur te decompileren, aan ontwerp te herleiden, te ontmantelen, aan te passen, te (doen) verhuren, in gebruik te (doen) geven, in sublicentie te geven, te distribueren, geheel of gedeeltelijk van de Apple programmatuur afgeleide werken te creëren of de Apple programmatuur te verspreiden via een netwerk of over te dragen van de ene naar de andere computer. Uw rechten ingevolge deze Licentie vervallen automatisch zonder voorafgaande kennisgeving van Apple indien u een van de voorwaarden van deze Licentie niet nakomt. Daarnaast behoudt Apple zich het recht voor deze Licentie te beëindigen indien een nieuwe versie van het Mac OS wordt geïntroduceerd die niet compatibel is met de Apple programmatuur.

3. Beperkte garantie op media. Apple garandeert dat de media welke de Apple programmatuur bevatten bij normaal gebruik gedurende een periode van negentig (90) dagen na de oorspronkelijke datum van aankoop in de detailhandel, vrij zijn van materiaal- en fabrikagefouten. U kunt krachtens deze paragraaf uitsluitend aanspraak maken, naar keuze van Apple, op terugbetaling van de aankoopprijs of op vervanging van de Apple programmatuur. DEZE BEPERKTE GARANTIE EN ELKE IMPLICIETE GARANTIE OP DE MEDIA, INCLUSIEF DE IMPLICIETE GARANTIE VAN VERHANDELBAARHEID EN GESCHIKTHEID VOOR EEN BEPAALD DOEL, IS BEPERKT TOT EEN PERIODE VAN NEGENTIG (90) DAGEN NA DE OORSPRONKELIJKE DATUM VAN AANKOOP IN DE DETAILHANDEL. IN BEPAALDE RECHTSGEBIEDEN IS BEPERKING VAN DE DUUR VAN EEN IMPLICIETE GARANTIE NIET TOEGESTAAN, WAARDOOR DE BOVENSTAANDE UITSLUITING VOOR U MOGELIJK NIET VAN TOEPASSING IS. DE HIER BESCHREVEN BEPERKTE GARANTIE IS EXCLUSIEF EN KOMT IN DE PLAATS VAN ALLE ANDERE GARANTIES, HETZIJ MONDELING OF SCHRIFTELIJK, HETZIJ EXPLICIET OF IMPLICIET. APPLE SLUIT UITDRUKKELIJK ALLE ANDERE GARANTIES UIT. DEZE BEPERKTE GARANTIE GEEFT U SPECIFIEKE JURIDISCHE RECHTEN. BOVENDIEN KUNNEN AFHANKELIJK VAN HET RECHTSGEBIED ANDERE RECHTEN GELDEN.

4. Beperking van garantie. Bepaalde Apple programmatuur kan zijn aangeduid als alfa-, bèta-, pre-release-, ontwikkel-, niet geteste of gedeeltelijk geteste versie van de Apple programmatuur. Dergelijke Apple programmatuur kan fouten bevatten die kunnen resulteren in storingen of het verlies van gegevens, en kan incompleet zijn of onjuistheden bevatten. U erkent en aanvaardt uitdrukkelijk dat gebruik van de Apple programmatuur uitsluitend voor uw eigen risico is. De Apple programmatuur wordt "IN DE STAAT WAARIN DEZE OP HET MOMENT VAN AANKOOP VERKEERT" (op "as is"-basis) en zonder enige garantie geleverd en Apple en Apple's Licentiegever(s) (voor het doel van paragraaf 4 en 5 hierna gezamenlijk te noemen "Apple") SLUITEN HIERBIJ UITDRUKKELIJK ALLE GARANTIES UIT, EXPLICIET OF IMPLICIET, DAARONDER BEGREPEN DOCH NIET BEPERKT TOT ALLE DENKBARE GARANTIES VAN VERHANDELBAARHEID EN GESCHIKTHEID VOOR EEN BEPAALD DOEL. APPLE GARANDEERT NIET DAT DE FUNCTIES WELKE IN DE APPLE PROGRAMMATUUR ZIJN VERVAT AAN UW EISEN ZULLEN VOLDOEN OF DAT MET DE APPLE PROGRAMMATUUR ONONDERBROKEN OF FOUTLOOS ZAL KUNNEN WORDEN GEWERKT OF DAT GEBREKEN IN DE APPLE PROGRAMMATUUR GECORRIGEERD ZULLEN WORDEN. VERDER VERLEENT APPLE GEEN GARANTIES BETREFFENDE HET GEBRUIK OF DE RESULTATEN VAN HET GEBRUIK VAN DE APPLE PROGRAMMATUUR TERZAKE VAN CORRECTHEID, NAUWKEURIGHEID, BETROUWBAARHEID OF ANDERSZINS. GEEN ENKELE MONDELINGE OF SCHRIFTELIJKE INFORMATIE OF KENNISGEVING VAN DE ZIJDE VAN APPLE OF EEN DOOR APPLE GEAUTORISEERDE VERTEGENWOORDIGER KAN EEN GARANTIE INHOUDEN OF DE OMVANG VAN DEZE GARANTIE UITBREIDEN. MOCHT DE APPLE PROGRAMMATUUR GEBREKEN VERTONEN, DAN KOMEN ALLE KOSTEN VAN ALLE NOODZAKELIJKE REVISIE, HERSTEL OF CORRECTIE VOOR UW REKENING (EN NIET VOOR DIE VAN APPLE OF EEN DOOR APPLE GEAUTORISEERDE VERTEGENWOORDIGER). DE LICENTIEVERGOEDING VOOR DE APPLE PROGRAMMATUUR WEERSPIEGELT DEZE OVERDRACHT VAN RISICO. IN BEPAALDE RECHTSGEBIEDEN IS UITSLUITING VAN IMPLICIETE GARANTIES NIET TOEGESTAAN, WAARDOOR DE BOVENSTAANDE UITSLUITING VOOR U MOGELIJK NIET VAN TOEPASSING IS.

5. Beperking van aansprakelijkheid. ONDER GEEN ENKELE OMSTANDIGHEID, WAARONDER BEGREPEN ONACHTZAAMHEID, ZAL APPLE AANSPRAKELIJK ZIJN VOOR SECUNDAIRE, SPECIALE OF GEVOLGSCHADE VOORTVLOEIEND UIT HET GEBRUIK OF DE ONMOGELIJKHEID GEBRUIK TE MAKEN VAN DE APPLE PROGRAMMATUUR, ZELFS INDIEN APPLE OF EEN DOOR APPLE GEAUTORISEERDE VERTEGENWOORDIGER VAN DE MOGELIJKHEID VAN DERGELIJKE SCHADE OP DE HOOGTE IS GESTELD. IN BEPAALDE RECHTSGEBIEDEN IS BEPERKING VAN OF UITSLUITING VAN AANSPRAKELIJKHEID VOOR SECUNDAIRE OF GEVOLGSCHADE NIET TOEGESTAAN, WAARDOOR DEZE BEPERKING VOOR U MOGELIJK NIET VAN TOEPASSING IS. In geen geval zal Apple's totale aansprakelijkheid voor alle schade, verliezen en juridische procedures (hetzij voortvloeiend uit een contractuele relatie, onrechtmatige daad - waaronder begrepen onachtzaamheid - of anderszins) ooit meer bedragen dan $50 (vijftig Amerikaanse dollar).

6. Bepaling betreffende de Amerikaanse exportwetten. Het is u niet toegestaan de Apple programmatuur te gebruiken of anderszins te exporteren of te herexporteren behalve voor zover toegestaan krachtens de wetten van de Verenigde Staten en van het rechtsgebied waarin u de Apple programmatuur hebt verkregen. In het bijzonder, maar zonder beperking, is het u niet toegestaan de Apple programmatuur te exporteren of te herexporteren (i) naar (een staatsburger of ingezetene van) een land waarvoor door de Verenigde Staten een embargo is ingesteld of (ii) enige persoon die voorkomt op de door het U.S. Treasury Department samengestelde lijst van "Specially Designated Nationals" of op de door het U.S. Department of Commerce samengestelde "Table of Denial Orders". Door de Apple programmatuur te gebruiken, verklaart u dat u zich niet bevindt in, onder controle staat van staatsburger of ingezetene bent van een dergelijk land of op een van de bovengenoemde lijsten voorkomt.

7. Eindgebruikers binnen de Amerikaanse overheid. Indien de Apple programmatuur wordt geleverd aan de Amerikaanse overheid, wordt de Apple programmatuur aangemerkt als "restricted computer software" zoals omschreven in paragraaf 52.227-19 van de FAR. De rechten van de Amerikaanse overheid met betrekking tot de Apple programmatuur zullen zijn als omschreven in paragraaf 52.227-19 van de FAR.

8. Toepasselijk recht en deelbaarheid. Indien in het land waar de Apple programmatuur-licentie is aangeschaft, een lokale dochteronderneming van Apple aanwezig is, zal deze licentie onderworpen zijn aan het lokale recht. Indien geen lokale dochteronderneming aanwezig is, zal deze licentie onderworpen zijn aan de wetten van de Verenigde Staten en de staat Californië. In het geval dat enige bepaling van deze overeenkomst of een gedeelte daarvan door een bevoegde rechter nietig geacht zal worden, zullen de overige bepalingen van deze licentie onverkort van kracht blijven.

9. Volledige overeenkomst. Deze licentie vormt de volledige overeenkomst tussen partijen met betrekking tot het gebruik van de Apple programmatuur en gaat uit boven alle voorgaande of gelijktijdige overeenkomsten betreffende dit onderwerp. Aanpassingen of wijzigingen van deze Licentie zijn slechts geldig voorzover deze zijn opgesteld in schriftelijke vorm en zijn ondertekend door Apple.

APPLE COMPUTER, INC.
INTERNATIONALE DOCHERONDERNEMINGEN

LAND	DOCHTERONDERNEMING
Brazilië	Apple Computer Brasil Ltda.
Canada	Apple Canada, Inc.
Duitsland	Apple Computer GmbH
Frankrijk	Apple Computer France S.A.R.L.
Hongkong	Apple Computer International Ltd.
Ierland	Apple Computer (UK) Limited
India	Apple Computer International Pte. Ltd.
Italië	Apple Computer S.p.A.
Japan	Apple Japan, Inc.
Mexico	Apple Computer Mexico, S.A. de C.V.
Nederland, België	Apple Computer Benelux B.V.
Oostenrijk	Apple Computer Gesellschaft m.b.H.
Singapore	Apple Computer South Asia Pte. Ltd.
Spanje	Apple Computer Espana, S.A.
Taiwan	Apple Computer Asia, Inc.
Verenigd Koninkrijk	Apple Computer (UK) Limited
Zuid-Afrika	Apple Computer (Proprietary) Limited
Zweden, Noorwegen, Denemarken	Apple Computer AB
Zwitserland	Apple Computer AG (SA) (Ltd.)

日本語
アップルコンピュータ・インクソフトウェア使用許諾契約

　本ソフトウェアを御使用になる前に本使用許諾契約をよくお読みください。本ソフトウェアを使用されることにより、本使用許諾契約の各条項に拘束されることに同意したことになります。本使用許諾契約の条項に同意されない場合には、本ソフトウェアを御使用にはならず、購入された場所にご返却下さい（適用ある場合）。そうすれば代金は返却されます。

1. 使用許諾　ディスク、コンパクトディスク、読み出し専用メモリー、その他の記録媒体又は他の一切のフォーム上の、本使用許諾契約書が添付されているソフトウェア、ツール、ユーティリティー、書類及びすべてのフォント、関連する書類及びその他のマテリアル（以下「アップルソフトウェア」という）は、アップルコンピュータ・インク（以下「アップル社」という）がお客様に使用許諾するものです。お客様は、アップルソフトウェアが記録されている媒体自体の所有権を有しますが、アップルソフトウェアに対する権利はアップル社及び/又はアップル社への許諾者に留保されます。本使用許諾契約は、本パッケージ中のアップルソフトウェア及び本使用許諾契約に基づく複製物、修正及び販売に適用されるものとします。

2. 使用方法及びその制限　本使用許諾契約により、お客様は、アップルソフトウェアを(i)アップルソフトウェアをテストするため及び(ii)アプリケーションソフトウェアを開発するために、使用することができます。お客様は、本許諾契約書による許諾に基づきソフトウェアを使用するために合理的に必要な限度の部数につきアップルソフトウェアの複製物を作成することができ、かかる複製物を、お客様の従業員に対して、業務上ソフトウェアを利用する必要のある従業員の方に限定してこれを配付することができます。但し、かかる従業員の方は、本許諾契約書により許諾された限りにおいてのみこれを使用することができます。アプリケーションソフトウェアの開発のため、お客様は、媒体の「ライセンス情報」フォルダーに記載されたアップルソフトウェアを使用、複製、変更し（但し、アップルソフトウェアの一部である「ライセンス情報」フォルダーに記載された制限に服します）、お客様自身のプログラムに組み込み若しくはお客様自身のプログラムと共にコンパイルし、お客様自身のプログラムと共にする場合に限り販売（但し、オブジェクトコード形式に限ります）することができます。但し、アップルソフトウェアのオリジナルに表示されているアップル社の著作権表示及びその他一切の権利表示を付することを要し、本許諾契約書と少なくとも同程度にアップルソフトエアに対するアップルの権利を保護する有効な契約に基づいて販売することを要します。本使用許諾契約により明確に許可される場合を除き、お客様は、アップルソフトウェア又はその一部を、逆コンパイルし、リバースエンジニアし、逆アッセンブルし、修正し、賃貸し、リースし、貸与し、再使用許諾し、頒布し、二次的著作物を創作してはならず、かつ、

アップルソフトウェアをネットワークを通じて、またはあるコンピューターから別のコンピューターへ送ってはなりません。お客様が本使用許諾契約の一条項にでも違反した場合、本使用許諾契約に基づくお客様の権利は、アップル社からの通知なく、自動的に終了するものとします。さらにアップル社は、アップルソフトウェアと互換性のないニューバージョンのマックOSがリリースされた場合、本使用許諾契約を終了させる権利を保有します。

3. 媒体についての限定保証　アップル社は、通常の使用下において、最初の購入日より90日間、アップルソフトウェアが記録されている媒体に材質上及び製造上の瑕疵がないことを保証します。本条に基づくお客様に対するアップル社の唯一の保証実行方法は、アップル社の選択により、アップルソフトウェアを含む製品の代金の返還またはアップルソフトウェアの交換に限定されるものとし、お客様は、当該交換を受けるためには、アップルソフトウェアにその領収書をそえてアップル社又はアップル社の権限ある代表者に返却する必要があります。商品適格性および特定目的への適合性に関する黙示的保証を含む媒体に対する本限定的保証および一切の黙示的保証は、最初の購入日より90日間に限定されます。黙示的保証の継続期間に対する限定が許されない地域では、当該期間限定がお客様に適用されないことがあります。本書中に規定された限定的保証は唯一の保証であり、口頭または文書によるか、明示もしくは黙示によるとを問わず、他の一切の保証に代わるものです。アップル社は、他の一切の保証の責任を負いません。本限定的保証は、媒体についてお客様に対し特別の法的権利を賦与するものであり、お客様はその地域により認められるその他の権利も行使できます。

4. アップルソフトウェアに関する保証の放棄　アップルソフトウェアは、アルファバージョン、ベータバージョン、開発バージョン、未リリースバージョン、未テストバージョン、または十分にテストが行われていないバージョンのアップルソフトウェアが指定されることがあります。かかるアップルソフトウェアには、故障やデータ損失の原因となりうるエラーが含まれていることがあり、不完全であったり正確性に欠けることがあります。お客様は、アップルソフトウェアの使用に係わる全ての危険はお客様が負担することを明示的に確認し、同意するものとします。アップルソフトウェアは、一切の保証を伴わない「現状渡し」で提供されるものとし、アップル社及びアップル社に対する使用許諾者（第4条及び第5条において、アップル社及びアップル社に対する使用許諾者を総称して「アップル社」といいます）は、商品適格又は満足できる品質、特定目的への適合性及び第三者の権利の不侵害性に関する黙示的保証及び／又は条件等を含む一切の明示的及び黙示的保証及び／又は条件の責任を明示的に放棄します。アップル社は、アップルソフトウェアに含まれた機能がお客様の要求を満足させるものであること、アップルソフトウェアが支障なく若しくは誤作動なく作動すること、アップルソフトウェアの瑕疵が修正されること、のいずれも保証いたしません。また、アップル社は、アップルソフトウェアの使用、又はその使用の結果に係る的確性、正確性若しくは信頼性等に関し、何らの保証若しくは表明もいたしません。アップル社又はアップル社の権限ある代表者の口頭又は書面によるいかなる情報又は助言も、新たな保証をおこなうものではなく又はその他いかなる意味においても本保証の範囲を拡大するものではありません。アップルソフトウェアに瑕疵が発見された場合、お客様（アップル社又はアップル社の権限ある代表者ではなく）が、すべてのサービス、修理又は修正に要する一切の費用を負担するものとします。アップルソフトウェアの使用許諾料には、この危険分担が反映されています。黙示的保証の免責を認めていない地域においては、上記の保証免責規定はお客様に適用されない場合もあります。

5. 責任の限定　過失を含むいかなる場合であっても、アップル社は、アップルソフトウェアの使用または使用不能に起因する若しくは関連する付随的、特別、間接又は結果損害について一切の責任を負いません。たとえアップル社又はアップル社の権限ある代表者がかかる損害発生の可能性につき助言されていたとしても同様とします。付随的又は結果損害に対する責任の限定を認めていない地域においては、この当該限定がお客様に適用されない場合もあります。いかなる場合も、お客様の一切の損害、損失、訴訟原因（契約上、過失を含む不法行為その他何であるかを問わない）に対するアップル社の賠償責任額は、５０米ドルを上限とします。

6. 輸出規制法に関する保証　お客様は、アメリカ合衆国の法律及びアップルソフトウェアを購入した国の法律により認められている場合を除き、アップルソフトウェアを使用せず、輸出または再輸出しないことに同意するものとします。特に、アップルソフトウェアは、(i) アメリカ合衆国の通商禁止国（またはその国民もしくは居住者）または(ii) アメリカ合衆国財務省の特別指定国リストもしくはアメリカ合衆国商務省の拒否命令表上に記載される一切の者に輸出または再輸出されてはならないものとします。アップルソフトウェアを使用することにより、お客様は、上記国家に居住を定めておらず、上記国家の支配に服しておらず、かつ上記国家の国民もしくは居住者ではないこと、及び上記リストに該当するものではないことを表明し、かつ保証するものとします。

7. エンドユーザーがアメリカ合衆国政府である場合　アップルソフトウェアがアメリカ合衆国政府機関に対して提供される場合、アップルソフトウェアは、FAR第52.227-19条に定める「制限されたコンピュータソフトウェア」に分類されます。アメリカ合衆国政府のアップルソフトウェアに対する権利は、FAR第52.227-19条に定めるとおりです。

8. 準拠法及び契約の分離性　お客様がアップルソフトウェア使用権を許諾された国にアップルの子会社が存在する場合、当該子会社が所在する地域の法律を本使用許諾契約の準拠法とします。その他の場合、アメリカ合衆国及びカリフォルニア州の法律が適用されるものとします。何らかの理由により、管轄権を有する裁判所が本使用許諾契約のいずれかの条項又はその一部について執行力がないと判断した場合であっても、本使用許諾契約の他の条項は依然として完全な効力を有するものとします。

9. 完全な合意　本使用許諾契約は、アップルソフトウェアの使用について、お客様とアップル社の取り決めのすべてを記載するものであり、本件に関する、従前または同時期になされる一切の合意に優先して適用されるものです。本使用許諾契約の改訂又は変更は、アップル社が署名した文書による場合を除き効力を一切生じません。

アップルコンピュータ・インク
海外販売子会社リスト

国	子会社
オーストリア	Apple Computer Gesellschaft m.b.H.
ブラジル	Apple Computer Brasil Ltda.
カナダ	Apple Canada Inc.
フランス	Apple Computer France S.A.R.L.
ドイツ	Apple Computer GmbH
香港	Apple Computer International Ltd.
インド	Apple Computer International Pte. Ltd.
アイルランド	Apple Computer (UK) Limited
イタリア	Apple Computer S.p.A.
日本	アップルコンピュータ株式会社
メキシコ	Apple Computer Mexico, S.A. de C.V.
オランダ、ベルギー	Apple Computer Benelux B.V.
シンガポール	Apple Computer South Asia Pte Ltd.
南アフリカ	Apple Computer (Proprietary) Limited
スペイン	Apple Computer Espana, S.A.
スエーデン、ノルウェー、デンマーク	Apple Computer AB
スイス	Apple Computer AG (SA) (Ltd.)
台湾	Apple Computer Asia, Inc.
イギリス	Apple Computer (UK) Limited